McKENNA BROTHERS
Clearly Leading th...

The Choice is yours...
LED

- No E-Prom changes
- Non Multiplexing
- Ultra violet resistant LED's
- High contrast
- Automatic intensity control

Smartblind

- Intelligent sensors
- Enclosed glass fronted case
- Easy access to roller blind
- Update by smart card
- Will operate in conjunction with LED & Flip-Dot

Printed

- Unbeatable clarity
- Manual or Electronic
- Any colour, Any logo
- Choice of text
- McKennaglo non fade yellow

Dot-Matrix

- LED illumination
- Toughend front glass
- Aluminium case
- High contrast

Quality, Service & Flexibility, Just ask our customers

Printers of Destination Indicators & Route Numbers, Suppliers of LED, Dot-Matrix & Electronic Roller Blind Destination Signs, Passenger Information Systems, Legal Lettering & All Types of Self-Adhesive Vehicle Markings.

McKenna House, Jubilee Road, Middleton, Manchester, M24 2LX
Telephone 0161 655 3244 Fax 0161 655 3059
Email vincent@mckennabrothers.co.uk   www.mckennabrothers.co.uk

KONI
BUS TRUCK & TRAILER
YOU'LL GO THE DISTANCE

More safety and comfort?
Rely on KONI Bus dampers

KONI is the leading manufacturer of high quality shock absorbers for buses and coaches. When it comes to safety, road holding and comfort KONI dampers are the reliable solution.

ROADLINK INTERNATIONAL®

Strawberry Lane, Willenhall, West Midlands, WV13 3RL
Sales Tel: +44 (0)1902 636206 Sales Fax: +44 (0)1902 631515
e-mail: sales@roadlink-international.co.uk
Web Site: www.roadlink-international.co.uk

Roadlink International Ltd is the exclusive UK and Ireland concessionaire for KONI truck, trailer and bus shock absorbers.

THE LITTLE RED BOOK 2005

ROAD PASSENGER TRANSPORT DIRECTORY

for
the British Isles

Editor: Tony Pattison

Riverdene Business Park, Molesey Road, Hersham, Surrey KT12 4RG
Tel: 01932 266600 Fax: 01932 266601

contents

List of Abbreviations	4
Index to Advertisers	4
Foreword	6
Section 1: Trade Directory	7
Section 2: Tendering Authorities	53
Traffic Commissioners, Department for Transport	58
Section 3: Organisations and Societies	59
Section 4: British Isles Operators	70
Section 5: Index (Trade)	223
Index (British Isles Operators)	228

List of Abbreviations

Acct = Accountant
Admin = Administrative
Asst = Assistant
Ch = Chief
Chmn = Chairman
Co = Company
Comm Man = Commercial Manager
Cont = Controller
Dep = Deputy
Dir = Director
Eng = Engineer
Exec = Executive
Fin = Financial
Gen Man = General Manager
Insp = Inspector
Jnt = Joint
Man = Manager
Man Dir = Managing Director
Mktg = Marketing
Off = Officer
Op = Operating
Ops = Operations
Plan = Planning
Pres = President
Prin = Principal
Prop = Proprietor(s)
Ptnrs = Partner(s)
Reg Off = Registered Office
sd = single-deck bus
Sec = Secretary
Supt = Superintendent
Svce = service
Traf Man = Traffic Manager
Traf Supt = Traffic Superintendent
Tran Man = Transport Manager

First published 2004

ISBN 0 7110 3028 6

All rights reserved. No part of this book may be reproduced or transmitted in any form or by any means, electronic or mechanical, including photocopying, recording or by any information storage and retrieval system, without permission from the Publisher in writing.

© Ian Allan Publishing Ltd 2004

Published by Ian Allan Publishing; an imprint of Ian Allan Publishing Ltd, Riverdene Business Park, Hersham, Surrey KT12 4RG; and printed by Ian Allan Printing Ltd, Riverdene Business Park, Hersham, Surrey KT12 4RG.

Code: 0409

LITTLE RED BOOK: For information regarding a free listing contact: The Editor, Little Red Book, c/o Ian Allan Publishing Ltd, Riverdene Business Park, Hersham, Surrey KT12 4RG

Index to Advertisers

Airconco	15
Scan Coin	19
Ian Allan Publishing Ltd	27, 39, 51, 187
BRT Bearings Ltd	5
Crewe Engines	24
Cummins-Allison Ltd	18
Furtex	35
Grasshopper Inn	123
McKenna Brothers Ltd	Front endpaper
Midland Counties Publications	52
Norbury Blinds	21
Partline	Back cover
PSV Glass	Front cover, 2, 42
PSV Products	16
Roadlink International Ltd	Opposite title page
Harold L. Smith	40
Transport Benevolent Fund	Bookmark
Triscan	28
Van Hool (UK) Ltd	9
VIP Group	Front endpaper

LITTLE RED BOOK: For information regarding advertising contact: David Lane, Little Red Book Advertising, Ian Allan Publishing Ltd, Foundry Road, Stamford, Lincolnshire PE9 2PP
Tel: 01780 484632   Fax: 01780 763388.

BRT BEARINGS
BALL ROLLER AND TRANSMISSION BEARINGS LIMITED

Quality Products for the Bus & Coach Operator

SPECIALIST STOCKIST OF
Bearings · Universal Joints
Drive Belts · Speedi Sleeves
Oil Seals · Couplings

A comprehensive parts range in excess of 1,000 line items suitable for

BUS - COACH - MINI BUS - MIDI BUS

AEC	FORD	MCW	SETRA
BEDFORD	IVECO	NEOPLAN	TOYOTA
BOVA	IVECO-FORD	OPTARE	VAN HOOL
BRISTOL	LEYLAND	RENAULT	VOLKSWAGEN
DAF	LEYLAND-DAF	RENAULT-DODGE	VOLVO
DAIMLER	MARSHALL	SCANIA	
DENNIS	MERCEDES	SEDDON	

Years of experience enable us to quickly identify parts, in many instances by application or OE part number.
For parts procurement and identification
- Please contact your local branch -

ABERDEEN
Tel 01224 772000 Fax 01224 773777

HANWORTH
Tel 0208 898 8561 Fax 0208 894 2430

REDDITCH
Tel 01527 510808 Fax 01527 510402

ASHFORD
Tel 01233 611797 Fax 01233 611882

HOVE
Tel 01273 410000 Fax 01273 430435

SCUNTHORPE
Tel 01724 860113 Fax 01724 271108

BELFAST
Tel 02890 642901 Fax 02890 491898

ILFORD
Tel 0208 553 4117 Fax 0208 553 4951

SOUTHAMPTON
Tel 02380 230456 Fax 02380 230567

BRISTOL
Tel 01179 820101 Fax 01179 828258

INVERNESS
Tel 01463 225956 Fax 01463 225969

WICKFORD
Tel 01268 762555 Fax 01268 763222

CHORLEY
Tel 01257 264266 Fax 01257 274698

LINCOLN
Tel 01522 526263 Fax 01522 524967

WISBECH
Tel 01945 461168 Fax 01945 464523

CUMBERNAULD
Tel 01236 728131 Fax 01236 736504

POOLE
Tel 01202 697631 Fax 01202 603320

EDINBURGH
Tel 01313 353330 Fax 01313 353334

PORTSMOUTH
Tel 02392 669641 Fax 02392 663995

GREAT YARMOUTH
Tel 01493 656834 Fax 01493 442913

READING
Tel 01189 575011 Fax 01189 503449

Head Office - Algores Way, Wisbech, Cambs, PE13 2TQ
Tel. 01945 464097 - Fax. 01945 464523 - email brt.sales@brt-bearings.com - www.brt-bearings.com
Emergency & Out of Hours - Telephone Your Local Branch, Your Call Will Be Diverted

PREMIER

Foreword

New for 2005 is the enlargement of the coach parking to include Coach Interchange and Parking Facilities and a new section, Tree Guards.

It is always difficult to keep up with current operators but this year we have concentrated on Herefordshire, Shropshire and Wales.

We are very grateful to all who returned their entries - we know it is isn't easy to find the time to do chores like this. This year we were able to update about 40 per cent of entries through replies received - thank you to all who replied. Many of the other entries were updated from our own sources.

If there is no change to your entry there is no need to re-write it all — just say something like 'as for last year' but please say who you are. We have had forms returned complete but with no indication as to who they are from.

For the next edition there will be the continuing challenge of sorting out the problem of entries for which there has been no reply for a number of years and for which it has been impracticable to gain information from other sources. I have increased the input from other experts in the bus industry so that more accuracy can be attained. Some pruning has been carried out in this edition and will be taken forward for the next.

Tony Pattison, Editor

Acknowledgements

I would like to thank Ian Barlex, Stephen Morris and Chris Bushell for their major help in updating and correcting many entries throughout the whole book.

I would also like to thank Graham Sharp who has visited operators, updating Herefordshire, Shropshire and much of the Wales section.

I am very grateful to Alan Butcher for all his help and advice with layout and production, and also to Laurie Bowles for much support with both the entries and the mailing list.

Thanks, too, must go to our many advertisers who support the Little Red Book. Please use them and say you saw the advert in the LRB. Steve Skinner, Advertising Manager, has worked hard to bring all the adverts in.

I would also like to thank Mary Webb and Colin Oggelsby for their substantial input to the current edition and Ann Pattison for compiling the index. I would also like to say thanks to Mark Jamieson for his help.

How *LRB* entries are compiled

As usual, every operator, manufacturer, supplier and other organisation featured in *LRB 2004* received an invitation to correct their entry for this edition free of charge.

Not all operators responded, which means that some existing, unchanged entries are repeated. This is done reluctantly, and we are aware that there must be some entries for companies that are no longer in business; unless we are told of these, perhaps by neighbouring operators, it is impossible to follow up every non-response, although we do try to correct as much information as possible from whatever sources we can obtain. We have used an asterisk to signify those companies that have responded this time.

By the same token, new entrants to the bus and coach market should not wait for *LRB* to make contact. If you are in the bus or coach business, and would like to appear (free of charge) in the next *LRB*, please write to the Editor of *LRB* at Ian Allan Publishing Ltd, Riverdene Business Park, Molesey Road, Hersham, Surrey KT12 4RG, requesting to receive a form for the next edition.

LRB is used by a substantial number of bus and coach operators, as well as by national and local government, trade organisations, tendering authorities, group travel organisers, hotels and leisure attractions.

section 1

Trade Directory

Vehicle suppliers and dealers	**8**
A-Z listing of suppliers and manufacturers	**15**
Bus & Coach industry service providers	**43**

VEHICLE SUPPLIERS & DEALERS
Full-size bus and coach chassis and integrals

ALEXANDER DENNIS
Dennis Way, Guildford GU1 1AF
Tel: 01483 571271
Range: chassis for rear-engined low-floor midibus, rear-engined low-floor single-deck bus, mid-engined coach, rear-engined coach, rear-engined low-floor double-deck bus, two- or three-axle.

ALEXANDER DENNIS
91 Glasgow Road, Falkirk FK1 4JB
Tel: 01324 621672
Fax: 01324 630811
Range: Enviro rear-engined low-floor single-deck bus

AYATS
UK Supplier: **AYATS (GB) LTD**
Meadow Drive, Earith, Cambridge PE28 3SA
Tel: 01487 843333
Fax: 01487 843285
E-mail: david@sunfunholidays.co.uk
Web site: www.carroceriasayats.es
Ireland supplier: **BARTONS TRANSPORT**
Straffan Road, Maynooth, Co Kildare
Tel: 00 353 1 628 6026
Fax: 00 353 1 628 6722
E-mail: info@bartons-transport.ie
Models: Rear-engined integral coach range - up to 15m

BMC UK LTD
BMC House, Three Spires, Ibstock Road, Coventry CV8 6JR
Tel: 024 7636 3003
Fax: 024 7636 5835
E-mail: enquiries@bmcukltd.com
Website: www.bmcukltd.com
Models: integral front-engined schoolbus, integral front-engined midicoach, inegral rear-engined 11m low-floor single-deck bus

BOVA
UK Suppliers: **MOSELEY (PCV) LTD**
Elmsall Way, Dale Lane, South Elmsall, Pontefract WF9 2XS
Tel: 01977 609000
Fax: 01977 609900
E-mail: enquiries@moseleycoachsales.co.uk
Website: www.moseleycoachsales.co.uk
MOSELEY IN THE SOUTH LTD
Summerfield Avenue, Chelston Business Park, Wellington TA21 9JF
Tel: 01823 653000
Fax: 01823 663502
E-mail: enquiries@moseleysouth.co.uk
Models: Futura (rear-engined integral coach).

*IRISBUS (UK) LTD
Iveco House, Station Road, Watford WD17 1SR
Tel: 01923 259660
Fax: 01923 259623
E-mail: info@irisbus.co.uk
Web site: www.irisbus.co.uk
Uk Supplier: ***UK COACH & BUS**
Carlton House, Euroway Estate, Hellaby, Rotherham S66 8QL
Tel: 01709 705570
Fax: 01709 705569
Web site: www.uk-cb.com
Models: midibus, low-floor midibus, minibuses, guided bus system, low-floor rear-engined single-deck bus, rear-engined single-deck coach.

MAN
UK Supplier: ***Mentor Coach & Bus Ltd**
Carlton House, Euroway Industrial Estate, Hellaby, Rotherham S66 8QL
Tel: 01709 705570
Fax: 01709 705569
E-mail: sales@mentorplc.com
Web site: www.mentorplc.com
Ireland supplier: **BRIAN NOONE**
Straffan Road, Maynooth, Co Kildare
Tel: 00 353 1 628 6311
Fax: 00 353 1 628 5404
Web site: www.briannooneltd.ie
Models: single-deck low-floor bus, rear-engined coach

MERCEDES-BENZ
UK Supplier: **EvoBus (UK) Ltd**, Cross Point Business Park, Ashcroft Way, Coventry CV2 2TU
Tel: 024 7662 6000
Fax: 024 7662 6043
Website: www.evobus.com, www.mercedes-benz.com
Models: rear-engine coach, rear-engine integral low-floor single-deck bus, rear-engine integral low-floor single-deck articulated bus

NEOPLAN
UK Supplier: ***Mentor Coach & Bus Ltd**
Cartlon House, Euroway Industrial Estate, Hellaby, Rotherham S66 8QL
Tel: 01709 705570
Fax: 01709 705569
E-mail: sales@mentorplc.com
Web site: www.mentorplc.com
Models: single-deck and double-deck rear-engine integral coaches

OPTARE GROUP LTD
Manston Lane, Leeds LS15 8SU
Tel: 0113 264 5182
Fax: 0113 260 6635
Web site: www.optare.com
Models: low-floor minibus, rear-engined integral low-floor single-deck midibus, rear-engined integral low-floor single-deck bus.

SCANIA
Scania Bus & Coach (UK) Ltd, Claylands Avenue, Worksop S81 7DJ
Tel: 01909 500822
Fax: 01909 500165
Web site: www.scania.co.uk
E-mail: buscoachinfo@scania.com
Range: rear-engined low-floor single-deck and double-deck bus chassis, integral low-floor single-deck bus, rear-engined coach.

SETRA
UK Supplier: **EvoBus (UK) Ltd**, Ashcroft Way, Cross Point Business Park, Ashcroft Way, Coventry CV2 2TU
Tel: 024 7662 6000
Fax: 024 7662 6020
Website: www.evobus.com, www.setra.de
Models: rear-engined integral coaches

*VAN HOOL
Bernard Van Hoolstraat 58, B-2500 Lier-Koningshooikt, Belgium
Tel: 00 32 3 420 20 20
Fax: 00 32 3 482 33 60
E-mail: info@vanhool.be
Website: www.vanhool.be
Models: integral coaches

VDL BUS INTERNATIONAL
UK Supplier: ARRIVA BUS AND COACH LTD
Lodge Garage, Whitehall Road West, Gomersal BD19 4BJ
Tel: 01274 681144
Fax: 01274 651198
Web site: www.arriva.co.uk, www.vdlbus.nl
E-mail: busandcoachsales@arriva.co.uk
Models: rear-engined low-floor single-deck bus, rear-engined low-floor double-deck bus, rear-engined coach, rear-engined three-axle single- or double-deck coach.

VOLVO BUS LTD
Wedgnock Lane, Warwick CV34 5YA
Tel: 01926 401777
Fax: 01926 407407
Website: www.volvobuses.volvo.co.uk, www.volvo.com
Models: rear-engined low-floor single-deck bus, rear-engined low-floor articulated single-deck bus, mid-engined coach, rear-engined coach, rear-engined low-floor double-deck bus.

Light Rail

ALSTOM TRANSPORT SA
Worldwide headquarters: 48 rue Albert Dhalenne, F-93482 Saint-Ouen Cedex, France
Tel: 00 33 1 41 66 90 00
Fax: 00 33 1 41 66 96 66
Web site: www.transport.alstom.com
Models: rail vehicles including light rail vehicles, traction equipment, infrastructure and maintenance services.

BOMBARDIER TRANSPORTATION
Management Office: 1101 Parent Street, Saint-Bruno, Quebec J3V 6E6, Canada
Tel: 00 1 450 441 20 20
Fax: 00 1 450 441 15 15
Web site: www.transportation.bombardier.com
BOMBARDIER TRANSPORTATION METROS
Litchurch Lane, Derby DE24 8AD
Tel: 01332 344666
Fax: 01332 266271
Models: light rail vehicles, trams, guided or unguided bi-mode rubber tyred electric vehicle.

*MINITRAM SYSTEMS LTD
12 Waterloo Park Estate, Bidford on Avon B50 4JH
Tel: 01789 490707
Fax: 01789 490592
E-mail: enquiries@tdi.uk.com
Website: www.minitram.com
Models: Rubber tyre-guided/unguided/rail 7.8m vehicle

*PARRY PEOPLE MOVERS LTD
Overend Road, Cradley Heath, Dudley B64 7DD
Tel: 01384 569553
Fax: 01384 637753
E-mail: jpmparry@aol.com
Website: www.parrypeoplemovers.com
Models: Small light rail vehicles and trams

Van Hool NV - Bus and Trailer Manufacturers
Bernard Van Hoolstraat 58 - 2500 Lier / Koningshooikt - Belgium
Tel.: +32-3-420 20 20 - Fax: +32-3-482 30 68
Site: www.vanhool.be

Bodybuilders (large vehicles)

ALEXANDER DENNIS
91 Glasgow Road, Falkirk FK1 4JB
Tel: 01324 621672
Fax: 01324 630811
Range: double-deck low-floor bus, single-deck low-floor bus, single-deck low-floor midibus.

SALVADOR CAETANO (UK) LTD
Mill Lane, Heather, Coalville LE67 2QA
Tel: 01530 263333
Fax: 01530 263379
E-mail: enquiries@caetano.co.uk

SC COACHBUILDERS LTD
Hambledon Road, Waterlooville PO7 7UA
Tel: 023 9225 8211
Fax: 023 9225 5611
E-mail: sccaetano.co.uk
Web site: www.caetano.co.uk
Models: single-deck coach, single-deck low-floor midibus.

*EAST LANCASHIRE COACHBUILDERS LTD (ELC)
Lower Philips Road, Whitebirk Industrial Estate, Blackburn BB1 5UD
Tel: 01254 504150
Fax: 01254 504181
E-mail: john.horn@elcb.co.uk
Web site: www.elcb.co.uk
Models: double-deck low-floor bus, single-deck low floor bus, single-deck low-floor midibus

JONCKHEERE
Importer: **Volvo Coach Sales (Loughborough) Ltd**, Brisco Avenue, Loughborough LE11 5HP
Tel: 01509 217777
Fax: 01509 260978
Models: single-deck coach

*MCV BUS & COACH LTD
Sterling Place, Elean Business Park, Sutton, Cambridge CB6 2QE
Tel: 01353 773000
Fax: 01353 773001
E-mail: enquiries@mcvbus.com

MOSELEY (PCV) LTD
Elmsall Way, Dale Lane, South Elmsall, Pontefract WF9 2XS
Tel: 01977 609000
Fax: 01977 609900
E-mail: enquiries@moseleycoachsales.co.uk
Web site: www.moseleycoachsales.co.uk

NEOPLAN
UK Supplier: ***Mentor Coach & Bus Ltd**
Carlton House, Euroway Industrial Estate, Hellaby, Rotherham S66 8QL
Tel: 01709 705570
Fax: 01709 705569
E-mail: sales@mentorplc.com
Web site: www.mentorplc.com
Models: single-deck coach, also integral coach.

NOGE
UK Supplier: ***Mentor Coach & Bus Ltd**
Cartlon House, Euroway Industrial Estate, Hellaby, Rotherham S66 8QL
Tel: 01709 705570
Fax: 01709 705569
E-mail: sales@mentorplc.com
Web site: www.mentorplc.com
Ireland supplier: **BRIAN NOONE**
Straffan Road, Maynooth, Co Kildare
Tel: 00 353 1 628 6311
Fax: 00 353 1 628 5404
Models: two-axle and three-axle integral coach bodies.

OPTARE LTD
Manston Lane, Leeds LS15 8SU
Tel: 0113 264 5182
Fax: 0113 260 6635
Web site: www.optare.com
Models: double-deck and single-deck buses, also integral

PLAXTON LTD
Eastfield, Scarborough YO11 3BY
Tel: 01723 581500
Fax: 01723 5813238
Range: coaches; midicoach and midibus bodies.

*VAN HOOL
Bernard Van Hoolstraat 58, B-2500 Lier-Koningshooikt, Belgium
Tel: 00 32 3 420 20 20
Fax: 00 32 3 482 33 60
E-mail: info@vanhool.be
Web site: www.vanhool.be
Models: coach bodies

*WRIGHTBUS LTD
Galgorm, Ballymena BT42 1PY
Tel: 028 2564 1212
Fax: 028 2564 9703
E-mail: info@wright-bus.com
Web site: www.wright-bus.com
Models: double-deck low-floor bus, single-deck low-floor articulated bus, single-deck low-floor bus, single-deck low-entry coach, single-deck low-floor midibus.

Chassis and integral vehicles (small vehicles - under 9m)

ALEXANDER DENNIS
Dennis Way, Guildford GU1 1AF
Tel: 01483 571271
Range: rear-engined low-floor midibus

FORD MOTOR COMPANY
Ford Motor Co Ltd, Eagle Way, Brentwood CM13 3BW
Tel: 0845 7111 888
Web site: www.fordvans.co.uk/peoplemovers
Models: Transit, complete minibus or chassis-cowl.

*IRISBUS (UK) LTD
Iveco House, Station Road, Watford WD17 1SR
Tel: 01923 259660
Fax: 01923 259623
E-mail: info@irisbus.co.uk
Web site: www.irisbus.co.uk
UK Supplier: ***UK COACH & BUS**
Cartlon House, Euroway Estate, Hellaby, Rotherham S66 8QL
Tel: 01709 705570
Fax: 01709 705569
Web site: www.uk-cb.com

JOHN BRADSHAW LTD
New Lane, Stibbington, Peterborough PE8 6LW
Tel: 01780 781801
Web site: www.john-bradshaw.co.uk
Models: Electric minibus/taxi

KVC MANUFACTURING LTD
Comagh Business Park, Kilbeggan, Co Westmeath, Ireland
Tel: 00 353 506 32699
Fax: 00 353 506 32691
Web site: www.kvc.ie
E-mail: info@kvc.ie

LDV LTD
Bromford House, Drews Lane, Birmingham B8 2QG
Tel: 0121 322 2000
Fax: 0121 327 4487
Web site: www.ldv.co.uk
Models: Complete minibus or chassis-cowl.

LEYLAND PRODUCT DEVELOPMENTS LTD
Aston Way, Leyland, Preston PR26 7TZ
Tel: 01772 435834
Web site: www.lpdl.co.uk
Models: CNG, LPG and electric low-floor minibus conversions

MERCEDES-BENZ
UK Supplier: **EvoBus (UK) Ltd**, Ashcroft Way, Cross Point Business Park, Ashcroft Way, Coventry CV2 2TU
Tel: 024 7662 6000
Fax: 024 7662 6034
Web site: www.evobus.com
Models: Complete low-floor minibus or chassis cowl

*MINITRAM SYSTEMS LTD
12 Waterloo Park Estate, Bidford on Avon B50 4JH
Tel: 01789 490707
Fax: 01789 490592
E-mail: enquiries@tdi.uk.com
Web site: www.minitram.com
Models: Rubber tyre-guided/unguided/rail 7.8m vehicle

OPTARE LTD
Manston Lane, Leeds LS15 8SU
Tel: 0113 264 5182
Fax: 0113 260 6635
Web site: www.optare.com
Models: front-engined integral low-floor minibus, rear-engined integral low-floor midibus.

RENAULT UK LTD
Rivers Office Park, Denham Way, Maple Cross, Rickmansworth WD3 9YS
Tel: 0800 521088
Web site: www.renault.co.uk
Models: Complete minibus or chassis-cowl; electric vehicle.

PIAGGIO LTD
1 Boundary Row, London SE1 8HP
Tel: 020 7401 4300
E-mail: piaggio@piaggio.co.uk
Web site: www.piaggio.com
Models: 6-seat minibus, diesel/petrol/electric

TOYOTA (GB) PLC
Great Burgh, Burgh Heath, Epsom KT18 5UX
Tel: 01737 363633
Mobile: 07785 238798
E-mail: steve.prime@tgb.toyota.co.uk
Web site: www.toyota.com
UK suppliers:
A&D Coach Sales
Tel: 01884 860767
Holloway Commercials
Tel: 01902 636661
Salvador Caetano
Tel: 01530 26333
Models: Optimo midicoach, chassis cowl

VAUXHALL MOTORS LTD
PO Box 777, Luton LU2 0ST
Tel: 020 7439 0303
Fax: 020 7439 0202
Web site: www.vauxhall.co.uk
Models: Complete minibus or chassis-cowl.

*VOLKSWAGEN COMMERCIAL VEHICLES
Yeomans Drive, Blakelands, Milton Keynes MK14 5AN
Tel: 0800 71731
Web site: www.volkswagen-vans.co.uk
Models: Complete minibus or chassis-cowl.

Bodybuilder (small vehicles)

ADVANCED VEHICLE BUILDERS
Upper Mantle Close, Clay Cross S45 9NU
Tel: 01246 250022
Fax: 01246 250016
E-mail: info@minibus.co.uk

BMC UK LTD
BMC House, Three Spires, Ibstock Road, Coventry CV8 6JR
Tel: 024 7636 3003
Fax: 024 7636 5835
E-mail: enquiries@bmcukltd.com
Web site: www.bmcukltd.com
Models: integral front-engined schoolbus, integral front-engined midicoach, iintegral rear-engined 11m low-floor single-deck bus

COACH DIRECT
The Coach House, 22 South Street, Rochford SS4 1BQ
Tel: 0870 550 2069
Web site: www.coachdirect.co.uk

CONCEPT COACHCRAFT
Far Cromwell Road, Bredbury, Stockport SK6 2SE
Tel: 0161 406 9322
Fax: 0161 406 9588
E-mail: sales@conceptcoachcraft.com
Web site: www.conceptcoachcraft.com

CREST COACH CONVERSIONS
Unit 5, Holmeroyd Road, Bentley Moor Lane, Carcroft, Doncaster DN6 7AP
Tel: 01302 723723
Fax: 01302 724724
E-mail: info@crestcoachconversions.co.uk
Web site: www.crestcoachconversions.co.uk

CROWN COACHBUILDERS LTD
32 Flemington Industrial Park, Flemington, Motherwell ML1 1SN
Tel: 01698 276087
Fax: 01698 276144
E-mail: davidgreer@hotmail.com
Web site: www.crowncoachbuilders.co.uk

CRYSTALS CONVERSIONS
127 Dartford Road, Dartford DA1 3EN
Tel: 01322 228538
Fax: 01322 288344

ESKER BUS & COACH SALES LTD
Comagh Business Park, Kilbeggan, Co Westmeath, Ireland
Tel: 00 353 506 33070
Fax: 00 353 506 33070
E-mail: info@eskerbusandcoach.com
Web site: www.eskerbusandcoach.com

EURO COACH BUILDERS LTD
Deerybeg Industrial Estate, Gweedore, Co Donegal, Ireland
Tel: 00 353 75 31528
Fax: 00 353 75 31930
Web site: www.eurocoachbuilders.ie

*EXCEL CONVERSIONS LTD
Unit 5, Century Close, Kirk Sandall Industrial Estate, Doncaster DN3 1TR
Tel: 01302 888811
Fax: 01302 888900
E-mail: sales@excelconversions.co.uk
Web site: www.excelconversions.co.uk

FRANK GUY LTD
Bridge Street, Clay Cross S45 9NG.
Tel: 01246 862980
Fax: 01246 250277
E-mail: sales@ frank-guy.co.uk
Web site: www.frank-guy.co.uk

GM COACHWORK LTD
Teign Valley, Trusham, Newton Abbot TQ13 0NX
Tel: 01626 853050
Fax: 01626 853083
Web site: www.gmcoachwork.co.uk

JAYCAS MINIBUS SALES
11 John Street, Bamber Bridge, Preston PR5 6TJ
Tel/Fax: 01772 321491
E-mail: john@minibusjaycas.co.uk

JUBILEE AUTOMOTIVE GROUP
Woden Road South, Wednesbury WS10 0NQ
Tel: 0121 502 2252
Fax: 0121 502 2258
E-mail: sales@jubileeauto.co.uk

LEICESTER CARRIAGE BUILDERS
Marlow Road, Leicester LE3 2BQ
Tel: 0116 282 4270
Fax: 0116 263 0554
E-mail: johnson@midlandsco-op.com
Web site: www.leicestercarriagebuilders.co.uk

*MCV BUS & COACH LTD
Sterling Place, Elean Business Park, Sutton, Cambridge CB6 2QE
Tel: 01353 773000
Fax: 01353 773001
E-mail: enquiries@mcvbus.com

*MELLOR COACHCRAFT
Miall Street, Rochdale OL11 1HY
Tel: 01706 860610
Fax: 01706 860402
Web site: www.woodhall-nicholson.co.uk

*MINIBUS OPTIONS LTD
Bingswood Industrial Estate, Whaley Bridge SK23 7LY
Tel: 01663 735355
Fax: 01663 735352
E-mail: info@minibusoptions.co.uk
Web site: www.minibusoptions.co.uk

OLYMPUS COACHCRAFT LTD
7 Temperance Street, Manchester M12 6DX
Tel/Fax: 0161 273 4259
E-mail: geoffolympus@aol.com
Web site: www.olympuscoaches.co.uk

OPTARE LTD
Manston Lane, Leeds, LS15 8SU
Tel: 0113 264 5182
Fax: 0113 260 6635
Web site: www.optare.com

PLAXTON
Eastfield, Scarborough YO11 3BY
Tel: 01723 581500
Fax: 01723 5813238

PVS MANUFACTURING LTD
8 Ardboe Business Park, Kilmascally Road, Ardboe, Dungannon, Co Tyrone BT71 5BP
Tel: 028 8673 6969
Fax: 028 8673 7178
E-mail: mail@pvsltd.com
Web site: www.conversionspecialists.com

ROHILL BODIES LTD
Mitchell Close, West Portway Industrial Estate, Andover SP10 3TJ
Tel: 01264 353437
Fax: 01264 333764
Web site: www.rohill-uk.com

STANFORD COACH WORKS
Mobility House, Stanhope Industrial Park, Wharf Road, Stanford-le-Hope SS15 0EH
Tel: 01375 676088
Fax: 01375 677999
Range: mini- and midibuses, mini- and midicoaches

JOHN STEWART & CO (WISHAW) LTD
Smith Avenue, Garrion Business Park, Wishaw ML2 0RY
Tel: 01698 373483
Fax: 01698 357185

WHITACRES COACHBUILDERS
Clough Street, Hanley, Stoke-on-Trent ST1 4BA
Tel: 01782 281365
Fax: 01782 283505
E-mail: sales@whitacres.co.uk
Models: minibus bodywork

Dealers

AD COACH SALES
Newbridge Coach Depot, Witheridge EX16 8PY
Tel: 01884 860787
Fax: 01884 860711
E-mail: ggoodwin@adcoachsales.co.uk
Web site: www.adcoachsales.co.uk

AJP COMMERCIALS
305-317 Wednesbury Road, Walsall WS2 9QJ
Tel: 01922 639652
Fax: 01922 611700

ARRIVA BUS AND COACH LTD
Lodge Garage, Whitehall Road West, Gomersal BD19 4BJ
Tel: 01274 681144
Fax: 01274 651198
Web site: www.arriva.co.uk
E-mail: busandcoachsales@arriva.co.uk

AVONDALE INTERNATIONAL LTD
451 Clifton Drive North, Lytham St Annes FY8 2PS
Tel: 01253 727211
Fax: 01253 714210

B.A.S.E. LTD
Crosse Hall Street, Chorley PR6 0QQ
Tel: 01257 247999, 0771 504 2415
E-mail: ian@holmeswood.com
Web site: www.holmeswood.uk.com

BLYTHSWOOD MOTORS LTD
1175 Argyle Street, Glasgow G3 8TQ
Tel: 0141 221 3165
Fax: 0141 221 3172
E-mail: blythswoodmotors@aol.com
Web site: www.blythswoodmotors.co.uk

BN - BRIAN NOONE
Straffan Road, Maynooth, Co Kildare, Ireland
Tel: 00 353 1 628 6311
Web site: www.briannooneltd.ie

*BOB VALE COACH SALES
Kingshill House, Spurlands End Road, Great Kingshill, High Wycombe HP15 6PE
Tel: 01494 716996
Fax: 01494 716331
E-mail: bobvalecoachsales@web-hq.com

*BRISTOL BUS & COACH SALES
6/7 Freestone Road, St Philips, Bristol BS2 0QN
Tel: 0117 971 0251
Fax: 0117 972 3121
E-mail: andrew.munden@bristolbusandcoach.co.uk
Web site: www.bristolbusandcoach.co.uk

*BRITISH BUS SALES
c/o Mike Nash, PO Box 534, Dorking RH5 5XB
Tel: 07836 656692
Fax: 01306 628001
E-mail: nashionalbus1@btconnect.com
Web site: www.britishbussales.co.uk

SALVADOR CAETANO (UK) LTD
Mill Lane, Heather, Coalville LE67 2QA
Tel: 01530 263333
Fax: 01530 263379
E-mail: enquiries@caetano.co.uk
Web site: www.caetano.co.uk
Models: single-deck coach, single-deck low-floor midibus

COOPERS COACH SALES
Aldred Road, Killamarsh, Sheffield
Tel: 01670 824900
Fax: 01302 724724

CREST COACH CONVERSIONS
Unit 5, Holmeroyd Road, Bentley Moor Lane, Carcroft, Doncaster DN6 7BH
Tel: 01302 723723
Fax: 01302 724724

CRYSTALS MIDICOACH SALES
127 Dartford Road, Dartford DA1 3EN
Tel: 01322 228538
Fax: 01322 288344

*DAWSONRENTALS BUS AND COACH LTD
Delaware Drive, Tongwell, Milton Keynes MK15 8JH
Tel: 01908 218111
Fax: 01908 610156
E-mail: info@dawsongroup.co.uk
Web site: www.dawsongroup.co.uk

ENSIGN BUS CO LTD
Juliette Way, Purfleet Industrial Park, Purfleet RM15 4YA
Tel: 01708 865656
Fax: 01708 864340
E-mail: sales@ensignbus.com
Web site: www.ensignbus.com

ERRINGTONS OF EVINGTON LTD
Glenrise Garage, London Road (A6), Oadby LE2 4RG
Tel: 0116 259 2131
Fax: 0116 259 2313

EVOBUS (UK) LTD
Ashcroft Way, Cross Point Business Park, Ashcroft Way, Coventry CV2 2TU
Tel: 024 7662 6000
Fax: 024 7662 6020
Web site: www.evobus.com

DAVID FISHWICK VEHICLE SALES
North Valley, Colne BB8 0RF
Tel: 01282 615138/867772

FLEETMASTER BUS & COACH LTD
Regent House, Silverwood, Snow Hill, Copthorne RH10 3ED
Tel: 01342 859058
Fax: 01342 859059
E-mail: fleet.master@btinternet.com
Web site: www.fleetmaster.co.uk

FURROWS COMMERCIAL VEHICLES
Kemberton Road, Halesfield, Telford TF7 4QS
Tel: 01952 684433

GM COACHWORK LTD
Teign Valley, Trusham, Newton Abbot TQ13 0NX
Tel: 01626 853050
Fax: 01626 853083
Web site: www.gmcoachwork.co.uk
E-mail: david.vadght@gmcoachwork.co.uk

THOMAS HARDIE - WIGAN
Lockett Road, Ashton-in-Makerfield WN4 8DE
Tel: 01942 505124
Fax: 01942 505119

IAN GORDON COMMERCIALS
Schawkark Garage, Stair Ayr KA5 5JA
Tel: 01292 591764

HOLLOWAY COMMERCIALS
60 Walsall Road, Willenhall WV13 2EF
Tel: 01902 636661
Fax: 01902 609476
E-mail: sales@hollowaycommercials.co.uk
Web site: www.hollowaycommercials.co.uk

B & D HOLT LTD
Cuthbert Street, Bolton BL3 3SD
Tel: 01204 650999
Fax: 01204 665300
E-mail: bevholt@bdholt.co.uk
Web site: www.bdholt.co.uk

IRISH COMMERCIALS (SALES)
Naas, Co Kildare, Ireland

LEINSTER VEHICLE DISTRIBUTORS
Leinster Vehicle Distributors Ltd, Urlingford, Co Kilkenny, Ireland
Tel: 00 353 56 31189
Mobile: 00 353 86 256 3607
E-mail: sales@lvd.ie
Web site: www.lvd.ie

LHE FINANCE LTD
21 Headlands Business Park, Salisbury Road, Ringwood BH24 3PB
Tel: 01425 474070
Fax: 01425 474090
E-mail: sales@lhefinance.co.uk
Web site: www.lhefinance.co.uk

LONDON BUS EXPORT
PO Box 12, Chepstow NP6 7NQ
Tel: 01291 689741
Fax: 01291 681361
E-mail: lonbusco@globalnet.co.uk
Web site: www.london.bus.co.uk

LOUGHSHORE AUTOS LTD
26 Killycanavan Road, Ardboe, Dungannon, Co Tyrone BT71 5BP
Tel: 028 8673 7325
Fax: 028 8673 5882
E-mail: michael@loughshoreautosltd.com
Web site: www.loughshoreautosltd.com

MAJORLINE ENGINEERING LTD
Baybridge Industrial Units, Baybridge Lane, Owslebury, Winchester SO21 1JN
Tel: 01962 777077
Fax: 01962 777661, 777667
E-mail: majorline@compuserve.com

MASS SPECIAL ENGINEERING LTD
Anston, Sheffield S25 4SD
Tel: 01909 550480
Fax: 01909 550486

*MENTOR COACH & BUS LTD
Cartlon House, Euroway Industrial Estate, Hellaby, Rotherham S66 8QL
Tel: 01709 705570
Fax: 01709 705569
E-mail: sales@mentorplc.com
Web site: www.mentorplc.com

MID WEST BUS & COACH SALES LTD
The Coach Centre, Golden Valley, Staverton, Cheltenham GL51 0TE
Tel: 01452 859111
Fax: 01452 859222
Web site: www.bussales.co.uk

*MISTRAL GROUP (UK) PLC
PO Box 130, Knutsford WA16 6AG
Tel: 0870 241 5786
Fax: 0870 241 5784
E-mail: sales@mistral-group.com
Web site: www.mistral-group.com

MOSELEY (PCV) LTD
Elmsall Way, Dale Lane, South Elmsall WF9 2XS
Tel: 01977 609000
Fax: 01977 609900
E-mail: enquiries@moseleycoachsales.co.uk
Web site: www.moseleycoachsales.co.uk

MOSELEY IN THE SOUTH LTD
Summerfield Avenue, Chelston Business Park, Wellington TA21 9JF
Tel: 01823 653000
Fax: 01823 663502
E-mail: enquiries@moseleysouth.co.uk

MIKE NASH
See British Bus Sales (above)

NORTH EAST BUS BREAKERS & SALES
Morrison Industrial Estate, Annfield Plain, Stanley DH9 9AW
Tel: 01207 280353
Fax: 01207 281490
Web site: www.nebussales.co.uk

W. NORTHS (PV) LTD
Moor Lane Trading Estate, Sherburn in Elmet LS25 6ET
Tel: 01977 682415
Fax: 01977 681119

OPTARE COACH SALES
Denby Way, Hellaby, Rotherham S66 8HR
Tel: 01709 535100
Fax: 01709 535102
Web site: www.optare.com

OPTARE ROTHERHAM
Denby Way, Hellaby, Rotherham S66 8HR
Tel: 01709 535100
Fax: 01709 535102
Web site: www.optare.com

OWENS OF OSWESTRY BMC
Unit 3, Foxen Monor Industrial Park, Four Crosses, Llanymynech
Tel: 01691 831313
E-mail: sales@owens-bmc.co.uk

PLAXTON COACH SALES
Crossroads, Anston, Sheffield S25 4ES
Tel: 01909 551166
Fax: 01909 567994

HOUSTON RAMM
Roeacre House, Fir Street, Heywood OL10 1NW
Tel: 01706 691411
Fax: 01706 627584
Web site: www.houstonramm.co.uk
E-mail: sales@houstonramm.co.uk

REGAL COACH SALES LTD
Old Mill Park, Kirkintilloch G66 1SP
Tel: 0141 776 3268

SCANIA BUS & COACH (UK) LTD
Claylands Avenue, Worksop S81 7DJ
Tel: 01909 500822
Fax: 01909 500165
Web site: www.scania.co.uk

SOMERBUS
Paulton, Bristol BS39 7YR
Web site: www.somerbus.co.uk
E-mail: somerbus@tinyworld.co.uk
Tel/Fax: 01761 415456

SOUTHDOWN PSV LTD
Unit 3, Silverwood, Snow Hill, Copthorne RH10 3EN
Tel: 01342 715222
Fax: 01342 719617
E-mail: southdownpsv@btinternet.com
Web site: www.southdownpsv.co.uk

STAFFORDSHIRE BUS CENTRE
Unit 2, Moorfields Industrial Estate, Cotes Heath ST21 6QY
Tel: 01782 791774, 07803 222552
E-mail: sales@staffordbuscentre.com
Web site: www.staffordbuscentre.com

STEPHENSONS OF ESSEX
Riverside Industrial Estate, South Street, Rochford SS4 1BS
Tel: 01702 541511

STOKE TRUCK & BUS CENTRE
Bute Street, Fenton, Stoke-on-Trent ST4 3PS
Tel: 01782 598310
Fax: 01782 598674
Web site: www.bmcstoke.co.uk

TAYLORS COACH SALES
102 Beck Road, Isleham, Ely CB7 5QP
Tel (mobile): 07850 241848
Tel: 01638 780010

TOYOTA (GB) PLC
Great Burgh, Burgh Heath, Epsom KT18 5UX
Tel: 01737 363633
Fax: 01737 367713
E-mail: steve.prime@tgb.toyota.co.uk
Web site: www.toyota.com
UK suppliers:
A&D Coach Sales
Tel: 01884 860767
Holloway Commercials
Tel: 01902 636661
Salvador Caetano
Tel: 01530 263333

*TRAMONTANA COACH DISTRIBUTORS
Chapelknowe Road, Carfin, Motherwell ML1 5LE
Tel: 01698 861790
Fax: 01698 860778
E-mail: wdt@tranta90.freeserve.co.uk

*UK COACH & BUS
Carlton House, Euroway Estate, Hellaby, Rotherham S66 8QL
Tel: 01709 705570
Fax: 01709 705569
Web site: www.uk-cb.com

VENTURA
Unit 39, Hobbs Industrial Estate, Newchapel, Lingfield RH7 6HN
Tel: 01342 835206
Fax: 01342 835813
E-mail: info@venturasales.co.uk

VOLVO TRUCK & BUS LTD
Wedgnock Lane, Warwick CV34 5YA
Tel: 01926 401777
Fax: 01926 407407
Web site: www.volvobuses.com, www.volvo.com

VOLVO COACH CENTRE
Brisco Avenue, off Belton Road West, Loughborough LE11 5HP
Tel: 01509 217777
Fax: 01509 260978
Web site: www.volvo.com, www.volvobuses.volvo.co.uk

WACTON COACH SALES & SERVICES
Linton Trading Estate, Bromyard HR7 4QL
Tel: 01885 482782
Fax: 01885 482127

WEALDEN PSV LTD
The Bus Garage, 64 Whetsted Road, Five Oak Green, Tonbridge TN12 6RT
Tel: 01892 833830
Fax: 01892 836977

WESTERN COMMERCIAL
Bridge Street, Newbridge, nr Edinburgh EH28 8SH
Tel: 0131 333 2001

ALAN WHITE COACH SALES
135 Nutwell Lane, Doncaster DN3 3JR
Tel: 01302 833203
Fax: 01302 831756
E-mail: sales@alanwhitecoachsales.com
Web site: www.alanwhitecoachsales.com

TREVOR WIGLEY
Baulder Bridge Road, Carlton, Barnsley S71 3HJ
Tel: 01226 723147

A-Z Listing of Bus, Coach & Tram Suppliers

Air Conditioning / Ventilation

AIRCONCO
Tel: 01706 361966
Fax: 01706 627275
Web site: www.airconco.net

AMA LTD
Unit 17, Springmill Industrial Estate, Avening Road, Nailsworth GL6 0BH
Tel: 01453 832884
Fax: 01453 832040
E-mail: ama@ftech.co.uk

***BROXWOOD VEHICLE SPECIALISTS**
Unit 2 Parkside Garage, Old Stafford Road, Slade Heath, Wolverhampton WV10 7PH
Tel: 01902 798770
Fax: 01902 798564
E-mail: sharon@broxwood.net

***CARRIER SUTRAK**
Unit 6, I O Centre, Barn Way, Lodge Farm Industrial Estate, Northampton NN5 7UW
Tel: 01604 581468
Fax: 01604 758132
E-mail: kim.neale@carrier.utc.com

***CLAYTON HEATERS LTD**
Hunter Terrace, Fletchworth Gate, Burnsall Road, Coventry CV5 6SP
Tel: 024 7669 1916
Fax: 024 7669 1969
E-mail: admin@claytoncc.co.uk

***COLDCARE**
Unit 10, Langley Wharf, Railway Terrace, Kings Langley WD4 8JE
Tel: 01923 261177
Fax: 01923 264058
E-mail: sales@coldcare-refrigeration.co.uk
Web site: www.coldcare-refrigeration.co.uk

CONCEPT COACHCRAFT
Far Cromwell Road, Bredbury, Stockport SK6 2SE
Tel: 0161 406 9322
Fax: 0161 406 9588
E-mail: sales@conceptcoachcraft.com
Web site: www.conceptcoachcraft.com

***CONSERVE (UK) LTD**
Suite 7, Logistics House, Kingsthorpe Road, Northampton NN2 6LJ
Tel: 01604 710055
Fax: 01604 710065
E-mail: information@conserveuk.co.uk
Web site: www.conserveuk.co.uk

CREST COACH CONVERSIONS
Unit 5, Holmeroyd Road, Bentley Moor Lane, Carcroft, Doncaster DN6 7BH
Tel: 01302 723723
Fax: 01302 724724

***EBERSPACHER (UK) LTD**
Headlands Business Park, Salisbury Road, Ringwood BH24 3PB
Tel: 01425 480151
Fax: 01425 480152
E-mail: enquiries@eberspacher.com
Web site: www.eberspacher.com

HISPACOLD
See: Clayton Heaters above
Web Site: www.hispacold.es

JAYCAS MINIBUS SALES
11 John Street, Bamber Bridge, Preston PR5 6TJ
Tel/Fax: 01772 321491
E-mail: john@minibusjaycas.co.uk

***M A C LTD**
Unit 8, Oldends Lane Industrial Estate, Oldends Lane, Stonehouse GL10 3RQ
Tel: 01453 828781
Fax: 01453 828167
E-mail: sales@macai.uk.com
Web site: www.macair.uk.com

***NEALINE WINDSCREEN WIPER PRODUCTS**
Unit 1, The Sidings Industrial Estate, Birdingbury Road, Marton CV23 9RX
Tel: 01926 633256
Fax: 01926 632600

PACET MANUFACTURING LTD
Wyebridge House, Cores End Road, Bourne End SL8 5HH
Tel: 01628 526754
Fax: 01628 810080
E-mail: sales@pacet.co.uk
Web site: www.pacet.co.uk

PARTLINE LTD
Dockfield Road, Shipley BD17 7AZ
Tel: 01274 531531
Fax: 01274 531088
E-mail: sales@partline.co.uk
Web site: www.partline.co.uk

SCANIA
Scania Bus & Coach (UK) Ltd, Claylands Avenue, Worksop S81 7DJ.
Tel: 01909 500822.
Fax: 01909 500165.

SUTRAK
See Carrier Sütrak, above.

UWE VERKEN AB (UK branch)
Meadow Works, Walton Summit Industrial Estate, Bamber Bridge, Preston PR5 8AL
Tel: 0700 289 3893
Fax: 0700 289 3329
E-mail: uwe.uk@btinternet.com

WEBASTO PRODUCT UK LTD
Webasto House, White Rose Way, Doncaster Carr DN4 5JH
Tel: 01302 322232
Fax: 01302 322231
E-mail: info@webasto.co.uk
Web site: www.webasto.co.uk

Audio/Video Systems

***AFTERMARKET COACH SUPPLIES (UK) LTD**
6a Riley Road, Telford Way Industrial Estate, Kettering NN16 8NN
Tel: 01536 416979
Fax: 01539 415709
Web site: www.acsuk.freeuk.com

***AUTOSOUND LTD**
4 Lister Street, Bradford BD11 2DE
Tel: 01274 688930
Fax: 01274 651318
Web site: www.autosound.ltd.uk
E-mail: sales@autosound.ltd.uk

***AVT SYSTEMS**
Unit 3/4, Tything Road East, Arden Forest Trading Estate, Alcester B49 6ES
Tel: 01789 400357
Fax: 01789 400359
E-mail: info@avtsystems.co.uk
Web site: www.avtsystems.co.uk

***BROXWOOD VEHICLE SPECIALISTS**
Unit 2 Parkside Garage, Old Stafford Road, Slade Heath, Wolverhampton WV10 7PH
Tel: 01902 798770
Fax: 01902 798564
E-mail: sharon@broxwood.net

CYBERLYNE COMMUNICATIONS LTD
Unit 5, Hatfield Way, South Church Industrial Estate, Bishop Auckland DL14 6XB
Tel: 01388 773761
Fax: 01388 773778
E-mail: david@cyberlynecommunications.co.uk
Web site: www.cyberlynecommunications.co.uk

EXPRESS COACH REPAIRS LTD
Outgang Lane, Pickering YO18 7EL
Tel: 01751 475215.

Coach & Bus Air Conditioning

Approved Service Centre for:
Carrier
SUTRAK
Transport Air Conditioning, Heating and Ventilation

Servicing and repairs on all makes of a/c systems in the North West

Airconco LIMITED
Parts supplied for Sutrak systems
www.airconco.net

Tel: 01706 361966   Fax: 01706 627275

Trade Directory

FCAV & CO
Brooklyn House, Coleford Road, Bream
GL15 6EU
Tel: 01594 564552
Fax: 01594 564556
E-mail: sales@coachaudiovisual.co.uk
Web site: www.coachaudiovisual.co.uk

JAYCAS MINIBUS SALES
11 John Street, Bamber Bridge, Preston
PR5 6TJ
Tel/Fax: 01772 321491
E-mail: john@minibusjaycas.co.uk

MENTOR
Mentor Coach & Bus Ltd, Carlton House,
Euroway Industrial Estate, Hellaby,
Rotherham S66 8QL
Tel: 01709 700600
Fax: 01709 700007
E-mail: sales@mentorplc.com
Web site: www.mentorplc.com
24 hour Neopart assistance:
07801 027702
24 hour Neoservice support:
07801 027701

PSV PRODUCTS
PO Box 166, Warrington WA4 5FG
Tel: 01925 210220.
Fax: 01925 601534
E-mail: daly@merseymail.com
Web site: www.psvproducts.com

VERIFEYE (UK) LTD
1 Cortry Close, Poole BH12 4BQ
Tel: 01202 732266
Fax: 01202 730022
E-mail: verifeye@v21mail.co.uk
Web site: www.verifeye.com

Badges – Drivers/Conductors

ABBOT BROWN
Barnfleet Works, Fleet Street, Beaminster
DT8 3EJ
Tel: 01308 862404
Fax: 01308 863402
E-mail: sales@abbotbrown.co.uk

*FIRST CHOICE NAMEPLATES, LABELS & SIGNS
Lynden 2c, Russell Avenue, Balderton,
Newark NG24 3BT
Tel: 01636 678035
Fax: 01636 707066
E-mail: firstchoice@handbag.com

MARK TERRILL PSV BADGES
5 De Grey Close, Lewes BN7 2JR
Tel: 01273 474816
Fax: 01273 474816
Mobile: 07770 666159

TRANSPORTATION MANAGEMENT SOLUTIONS
PO Box 15174, Glasgow, G3 6WB
Tel: 0141 332 4733
Fax: 0141 354 0076
E-mail: tramsol@aol.com

Batteries

THOMAS HARDIE – WIGAN
Lockett Road, Ashton-in-Makerfield, Wigan,
WN4 8DE.
Tel: 01942 505124
Fax: 01942 505119

LEXCEL POWER SYSTEMS PLC
35 Manor Road, Henley on Thames,
RG9 1LU.
Tel: 01491 874414
E-mail: sales@lexcelpower.com
Web site: www.lexcelpower.com
Advanced battery systems for electric traction and automotive application.

MASS SPECIAL ENGINEERING LTD
Anston, Sheffield, S25 4SD.
Tel: 01909 550480
Fax: 01909 550486

MENTOR
Mentor Coach & Bus Ltd, Carlton House,
Euroway Industrial Estate, Hellaby,
Rotherham S66 8QL
Tel: 01709 700600
Fax: 01709 700007
E-mail: sales@mentorplc.com
Web site: www.mentorplc.com
24 hour Neopart assistance:
07801 027702
24 hour Neoservice support:
07801 027701

MULTIPART PSV
Pilling Lane, Chorley PR7 3EL.
Tel: 01257 225577
Fax: 01257 225575
E-mail: info@multipart.com
Web site: www.multipart.co.uk

PARTLINE LTD
Dockfield Road, Shipley BD17 7AZ
Tel: 01274 531531
Fax: 01274 531088
E-mail: sales@partline.co.uk
Web site: www.partline.co.uk

VARTA AUTOMOTIVE BATTERIES LTD
Broadwater Park, North Orbital Road,
Denham, Uxbridge UB9 5AG
Tel: 01895 838999
Fax: 01895 838981
Web site: www.varta.co.uk

Body Repairs and Refurbishing

AD COACH SALES
Newbridge Coach Depot, Witheridge EX16 8PY
Tel: 01884 860787
Fax: 01884 860711
E-mail: ggoodwin@adcoachsales.co.uk
Web site: www.adcoachsales.co.uk

AVS STEPS LTD
Alders Farmhouse, Alders Lane, Whixall
SY13 2BR
Tel: 01948 880010
Fax: 01948 880020
Web site: www.avssteps.co.uk

Trade Directory

BLACKPOOL COACH SERVICES
Moss Hey Garage, Chapel Road, Blackpool FY4 5HU.
Tel/Fax: 01253 698686

*BROXWOOD VEHICLE SPECIALISTS
Unit 2 Parkside Garage, Old Stafford Road, Slade Heath, Wolverhampton WV10 7PH
Tel: 01902 798770
Fax: 01902 798564
E-mail: sharon@broxwood.net

BULWARK BUS & COACH ENGINEERING LTD
Gate 3, Bulwark Industrial Estate, Chepstow NP16 5QZ
Tel: 01291 622326.
Fax: 01291 622726.

CARLYLE BUS & COACH LTD
Carlyle Business Park, Great Bridge Street, Swan Village, West Bromwich B70 0X4
Tel: 0121 524 1200
Fax: 0121 524 1201

CREST COACH CONVERSIONS
Unit 5, Holmeroyd Road, Bentley Moor Lane, Carcroft, Doncaster DN6 7BH
Tel: 01302 723723
Fax: 01302 724724

CROWN COACHBUILDERS LTD
32 Flemington Industrial Park, Flemington, Motherwell ML1 1SN
Tel: 01698 276087
Fax: 01698 276144
E-mail: davidgreer@hotmail.com
Web site: www.crowncoachbuilders.co.uk

DRURY & DRURY
Unit 6. Cobbs Wood Industrial Estate, Brunswick Road, Ashford TN23 1EH
Tel: 01303 610555.
Fax: 01303 610666.
E-mail: martinstrange@channelcommercials.co.uk

*EAST LANCASHIRE COACHBUILDERS LTD (ELC)
Lower Philips Road, Whitebirk Industrial Estate, Blackburn BB1 5UD
Tel: 01254 504150
Fax: 01254 504181
E-mail: john.horn@elcb.co.uk
Web site: www.elcb.co.uk

EXPRESS COACH REPAIRS LTD
Outgang Lane, Pickering YO18 7EL.
Tel: 01751 475215.

GHE
Unit 30, Fort Industrial Park, Fort Parkway, Castle Bromwich, Birmingham, B35 7AR..
Tel: 0121 747 4400.
Fax: 0121 747 4977.

HANTS & DORSET TRIM LTD
Canada Road, West Wellow SO51 6DE.
Tel: 023 8033 4335

THOMAS HARDIE – WIGAN
Lockett Road, Ashton-in-Makerfield, Wigan, WN4 8DE.
Tel: 01942 505124.
Fax: 01942 505119

*HATTS COACHWORKS
Foxham, Chippenham SN15 2AY
Tel: 01249 740444
Fax: 01249 740447

*INVERTEC LTD
Whelford Road, Fairford GL7 4DT
Tel: 01285 713550
Fax: 01285 713548
Mobile: 07802 793828
E-mail: ian@invertec.co.uk
Web site: www.invertec.co.uk

KENT COACHWORKS
Lower Road, Northfleet DA11 9BB.
Tel: 01474 330320.
Fax: 01474 330321
Web site: www.londoncoaches.com.

*THE LAWTON MOTOR BODY BUILDING CO LTD
Knutsford Road, Church Lawton ST7 3DN
Tel: 01270 882056
Fax: 01270 883014
E-mail: info@lawtonmotorbody.co.uk
Web site: www.lawtonmotorbody.co.uk

*MARTYN INDUSTRIALS LTD
5 Brunel Way, Durranhill Industrial Esate, Harraby, Carlisle CA4 8JZ
Tel: 01228 544000
Fax: 01228 544001
E-mail: enquiries@martyn-industrials.co.uk
Web site: www.martyn-industrials.co.uk

MASS SPECIAL ENGINEERING LTD
Anston, Sheffield, S25 4SD.
Tel: 01909 550480.
Fax: 01909 550486.

*MCV BUS & COACH LTD
Sterling Place, Elean Business Park, Sutton CB6 2QE
Tel: 01353 773000
Fax: 01353 773001
E-mail: enquiries@mcvbus.com

MOSELEY (PCV) LTD
Elmsall Way, Dale Lane, South Elmsall WF9 2XS
Tel: 01977 609000
Fax: 01977 609900

MENTOR
Mentor Coach & Bus Ltd, Carlton House, Euroway Industrial Estate, Hellaby, Rotherham S66 8QL
Tel: 01709 700600
Fax: 01709 700007
E-mail: sales@mentorplc.com
Web site: www.mentorplc.com
24 hour Neopart assistance: 07801 027702
24 hour Neoservice support: 07801 027701

MULTIPART PSV
Pilling Lane, Chorley PR7 3EL
Tel: 01257 225577
Fax: 01257 225575
E-mail: info@multipart.com
Web site: www.multipart.co.uk

NU-TRACK LTD
Steeple Industrial Estate, Antrim BT41 1AB.
Tel: 028 9446 9550
E-mail: enquiries@nu-track.co.uk
Web site: www.nu-track.co.uk

OLYMPUS COACHCRAFT LTD
7 Temperance Street, Manchester M12 6HR
Tel/Fax: 0161 273 4259
E-mail: geofolympus@aol.com
Web site: www.olympuscoaches.co.uk

PLAXTON PARTS & SERVICE
101 Kelburn Street, Barrhead G78 1LD
Tel: 0141 880 8008
Fax: 0141 881 4306
Also at: Widbury Hill, Ware SG12 7AS.
Tel: 01920 465943
Fax: 01920 485671
Ryton Road, Anston, Sheffield S25 4ES
Tel: 01909 551155
Fax: 01909 562263

*TRAMONTANA COACH DISTRIBUTORS
Chapelknowe Road, Carfin, Motherwell ML1 5LE
Tel: 01698 861790
Fax: 01698 860778
E-mail: wdt@tramta90.freeserve.co.uk

TRUCKALIGN
Truck Align Co Ltd, Vip Trading Estate, Anchor & Hope Lane, Charlton, London SE7 7RY
Tel: 020 8858 3781
Fax: 020 8858 3781

VOLVO COACH CENTRE
Brisco Avenue, off Belton Road West, Loughborough LE11 5HP
Tel: 01509 217777
Fax: 01509 260978

Brakes and Brake Linings

ARVIN MERITOR
Unit 21, Suttons Park Avenue, Reading RG6 1LA.
Tel: 0118 935 9126
Fax: 0118 935 9138
E-mail: james.randall@arvinmeritor.com
Web site: www.arvinmeritor.com

ASHLEY BANKS LTD
5 King Street Estate, Langtoft, Peterborough PE6 9NF
Tel: 01778 560651
Fax: 01778 560721
E-mail: user@ashleybanks.fsnet.co.uk

AUTOMOTIVE PRODUCTS GROUP LTD – AP BORG & BECK / AP LOCKHEED
Tachbrook Road. Leamington Spa CV31 3ER.
Tel: 01926 470000.
Fax: 01926 472000.

BBA FRICTION LTD
PO Box 18, Hunsworth Lane, Cleckheaton BD19 3UJ.
Tel: 01274 854000.
Fax: 01274 854001.

*BROXWOOD VEHICLE SPECIALISTS
Unit 2 Parkside Garage, Old Stafford Road, Slade Heath, Wolverhampton WV10 7PH
Tel: 01902 798770
Fax: 01902 798564
E-mail: sharon@broxwood.net

ERENTEK
Malt Kiln Lane, Waddington, Lincoln LN5 9RT.
Tel: 01522 720065.
Fax: 01522 729155.

IMEXPART LTD
Links 31, Willowbridge Way, Whitwood,
Castleford WF10 5NP
Tel: 0845 6050404
Fax: 01977 513412
E-mail: parts@imexpart.com
Web site: www.imexpart.com

IMPERIAL ENGINEERING
Delamare Road, Cheshunt EN8 9UD
Tel: 01992 634255
Fax: 01992 630506
E-mail: sales@imperialengineering.co.uk
Web site: www.imperialengineering.co.uk

KELLETT (UK) LTD
8 Stevenson Way, Sheffield S9 3WZ.
Tel: 0114 261 1122.
Fax: 0114 261 1199.
E-mail: sales@kellett.co.uk

KNORR-BREMSE SYSTEMS FOR COMMERCIAL VEHICLES LTD
Douglas Road, Kingswood, Bristol BS15 8NL.
Tel: 0117 984 6100.
Fax: 0117 984 6101.
Web site: www.knorr-bremse.com

MAJORLINE ENGINEERING LTD
Baybridge Industrial Units, Baybridge Lane, Owslebury, Winchester SO21 1JN.
Tel: 01962 777077.
Fax: 01962 777661, 777667
E-mail: majorline@compuserve.com

MULTIPART PSV
Pilling Lane, Chorley PR7 3EL.
Tel: 01257 225577.
Fax: 01257 225575.
E-mail: info@multipart.com
Web site: www.multipart.co.uk

*PARTLINE LTD
Dockfield Road, Shipley BD17 7AZ
Tel: 01274 531531
Fax: 01274 531088
E-mail: sales@partline.co.uk
Web site: www.partline.co.uk

ROADLINK INTERNATIONAL LTD
Strawberry Lane, Willenhall WV13 3RL.
Tel: 01902 606210
Fax: 01902 606604
E-mail: sales@roadlink-international.co.uk
Web site: www.roadlink-international.co.uk

*SERGEANT (P&P) (B&A) LTD
PO Box 11, New Hall Lane, Hoylake CH47 4DH
Tel: 0151 632 5903
Fax: 0151 632 5908
E-mail: enq@sergeant.co.uk
Web site: www.sergeant.co.uk

UNITEC PARTS & SERVICE LTD
Manston Lane, Leeds LS15 8SU
Tel: 0113 264 5182
Fax: 0113 260 2294
Web site: www.optare.com

WABCO AUTOMOTIVE UK
Texas Street, Leeds LS27 0HQ
Tel: 0113 251 2510
Fax: 0113 251 2844

Cash Handling Equipment

*CUMMINS-ALLISON LTD
Unit B13, Holly Farm Business Park, Honiley, Kenilworth CV8 1NP
Tel: 01926 484644
Fax: 01926 484626
E-mail: sales@cummins-allison.co.uk
Web site: www.cumminsallison.co.uk

*ETM SOFTWARE SERVICES
9 Dorset Avenue, Ferndown BH22 8HJ
Tel: 01202 246710
Fax: 01202 687537
E-mail: info@etmss.com
Web site: www.etmss.com

JOHN GROVES TICKET SYSTEMS
Unit 5, Rennie Business Units, Factory Place, Saltcoats KA21 5LZ
Tel: 01294 471133
Fax: 01294 471166
Web site: www.cambist.se

MARK TERRILL TICKET MACHINERY
5 De Grey Close, Lewes BN7 2JR.
Tel: 01273 474816.
Fax: 01273 474816.
Mobile: 07770 666159.

transport counts on it

The Jetsort range of coin counter/sorters are Euro ready

High speed, high volume coin processing

Counts & sorts up to 9 denominations at 6000 mixed coins a minute

Optional dual bag and coin discrimination
Integrates with industry standard software

We also provide a range of note counters and mixed note scanners

0800 0186484
www.cumminsallison.co.uk

SCAN COIN

Cash depositing
for improved customer service

Automated
operation completes the transaction quickly and eliminates the need for pre-sorting of coins

Integrated software systems
to interface with industry standard management information systems

CASH HANDLING SOLUTIONS
SCAN COIN Ltd
Dutch House, 110 Broadway, Salford Quays, Salford M50 2UW
Tel: 0161 873 0500   Fax: 0161 873 0501

e-mail: sales@scancoin.co.uk   www.scancoin.co.uk

Trade Directory

SCAN COIN LTD
Dutch House, 110 Broadway, Salford Quays, Salford M5 2UW
Tel: 0161 873 0500
Fax: 0161 873 0501
E-mail: sales@scancoin.co.uk
Web site: www.scancoin.co.uk

*THOMAS AUTOMATICS
Bishop Meadow Road, Loughborough LE11 5RE
Tel: 0700 4 THOMAS (846627)
Fax: 01509 266836
E-mail: sales@thomasa.co.uk
Web site: www.thomasa.co.uk

*TRANSPORT TICKET SERVICES
Yew Tree Cottage, Newcastle, Monmouth NP25 5NT
Tel/Fax: 01600 750650
E-mail: tts@waitrose.com

Chassis Lubricating Systems

MULTIPART PSV
Pilling Lane, Chorley PR7 3EL
Tel: 01257 225577
Fax: 01257 225575
E-mail: info@multipart.com
Web site: www.multipart.co.uk

Clutches

ASHLEY BANKS LTD
5 King Street Estate, Langtoft, Peterborough PE6 9NF
Tel: 01778 560651
Fax: 01778 560721
E-mail: user@ashleybanks.fsnet.co.uk

AUTOMOTIVE PRODUCTS GROUP LTD – AP BORG & BECK / AP LOCKHEED
Tachbrook Road, Leamington Spa CV31 3ER.
Tel: 01926 470000.
Fax: 01926 472000.

BBA FRICTION LTD
PO Box 18, Hunsworth Lane, Cleckheaton BD19 3UJ.
Tel: 01274 854000.
Fax: 01274 854001.

BORG & BECK
See Automotive Products, above.

*BROXWOOD VEHICLE SPECIALISTS
Unit 2 Parkside Garage, Old Stafford Road, Slade Heath, Wolverhampton WV10 7PH
Tel: 01902 798770
Fax: 01902 798564
E-mail: sharon@broxwood.net

BUSS BIZZ
Goughs Transport Depot, Morestead, Winchester SO21 1JD.
Tel: 01962 715555/66.
Fax: 01962 714868.

*COACH-AID
Unit 2, Brindley Close, Tollgate Industrial Estate, Stafford ST16 3SU
Tel: 01785 222666
E-mail: workshop@coach-aid.com

EATON LTD
Truck Components Marketing – PO Box 11, Worsley Road North, Worsley M28 5GJ.
Tel: 01204 797219.
Fax: 01204 797204.

IMEXPART LTD
Links 31, Willowbridge Way, Whitwood, Castleford WF10 5NP
Tel: 0845 605 0404
Fax: 01977 513412
E-mail: parts@imexpart.com
Web site: www.imexpart.com

KELLETT (UK) LTD
8 Stevenson Way, Sheffield S9 3WZ.
Tel: 0114 261 1122.
Fax: 0114 261 1199.
E-mail: sales@kellett.co.uk

MAJORLINE ENGINEERING LTD
Baybridge Industrial Units, Baybridge Lane, Owslebury, Winchester SO21 1JN.
Tel: 01962 777077.
Fax: 01962 777661, 777667
E-mail: majorline@compuserve.com

MENTOR
Mentor Coach & Bus Ltd, Carlton House, Euroway Industrial Estate, Hellaby, Rotherham S66 8QL
Tel: 01709 700600
Fax: 01709 700007
E-mail: sales@mentorplc.com
Web site: www.mentorplc.com
24 hour Neopart assistance: 07801 027702
24 hour Neoservice support: 07801 027701

MULTIPART PSV
Pilling Lane, Chorley PR7 3EL.
Tel: 01257 225577.
Fax: 01257 225575.
E-mail: info@multipart.com
Web site: www.multipart.co.uk

*PARTLINE LTD
Dockfield Road, Shipley BD17 7AZ
Tel: 01274 531531
Fax: 01274 531088
E-mail: sales@partline.co.uk
Web site: www.partline.co.uk

*SERGEANT (P&P) (B&A) LTD
PO Box 11, New Hall Lane, Hoylake CH47 4DH
Tel: 0151 632 5903
Fax: 0151 632 5908
E-mail: enq@sergeant.co.uk
Web site: www.sergeant.co.uk

SHAWSON SUPPLY LTD
12 Station Road, Saintfield BT24 7DU.
Tel: 028 9751 0994
Fax: 028 9751 0816
E-mail: shawson@btinternet.com

UNITEC PARTS & SERVICE LTD
Manston Lane, Leeds LS15 8SU
Tel: 0113 264 5182
Fax: 0113 260 2294
Web site: www.optare.com

Cooling Systems

CLAYTON HEATERS LTD
Fletchworth Gate, Burnsall Road, Coventry CV5 6SP.
Tel: 024 7669 1916.
Fax: 024 7669 1969.

DBG PRODUCTS (UK) LTD
Haven Road, The Hythe, Colchester CO2 8HT.
Tel: 01206 791751.
Fax: 01206 791991.

MAJORLINE ENGINEERING LTD
Baybridge Industrial Units, Baybridge Lane, Owslebury, Winchester SO21 1JN.
Tel: 01962 777077.
Fax: 01962 777661, 777667
E-mail: majorline@compuserve.com

*PARTLINE LTD
Dockfield Road, Shipley BD17 7AZ
Tel: 01274 531531
Fax: 01274 531088
E-mail: sales@partline.co.uk
Web site: www.partline.co.uk

MULTIPART PSV
Pilling Lane, Chorley PR7 3EL.
Tel: 01257 225577
Fax: 01257 225575
E-mail: info@multipart.com
Web site: www.multipart.co.uk

SILFLEX LTD
Unit E4, Coed Cae Lane Industrial Estate, Pontyclun CF72 9HG
Tel: 01443 238464
Fax: 01443 237781

Destination Indicator Equipment

BRIGHT-TECH DEVELOPMENTS LTD
Fleets Point House, Willis Way, Poole BH15 3SS
Tel: 01202 679627
Fax: 01202 684519
E-mail: sales@bright-tech.co.uk
Web site: www.bright-tech.co.uk

CARLYLE BUS & COACH LTD
Carlyle Business Park, Great Bridge Street, Swan Village, West Bromwich B70 0XA
Tel: 0121 524 1200
Fax: 0121 524 1201

HANOVER DISPLAYS LTD
Unit 24, Cliffe Industrial Estate, Lewes BN8 6JL
Tel: 01273 477528
Fax: 01273 407766
E-mail: nrobertson@hanoverdisplays.com
Web site: www.hanoverdisplays.com

INDICATORS INTERNATIONAL LTD
41 Aughrim Road, Magherafelt BT45 6JX.
Tel: 028 7963 2591.
Fax: 028 7963 3927.
E-mail: sales@indicators-int.com
Web site: www.indicators-int.com

Trade Directory

*INVERTEC LTD
Whelford Road, Fairford GL7 4DT
Tel: 01285 713550
Fax: 01285 713548
Mobile: 07802 793828
E-mail: ian@invertec.co.uk
Web site: www.invertec.co.uk

*McKENNA BROTHERS LTD
McKenna House, Jubilee Road, Middleton, Manchester M24 2LX
Tel: 0161 655 3244
Fax: 0161 655 3059
E-mail: vincent@mckennabrothers.co.uk
Web site: www.mckennabrothers.co.uk

MULTIPART PSV
Pilling Lane, Chorley PR7 3EL.
Tel: 01257 225577.
Fax: 01257 225575.
E-mail: info@multipart.com
Web site: www.multipart.co.uk

*NORBURY BLINDS LTD
41-45 Hanley Street, Newtown, Birmingham B19 3SP
Tel: 0121 359 4311
Fax: 0121 359 6388
Web site: www.norbury-blinds.com
E-mail: norburyblinds@talk21.com

*PERCY LANE PRODUCTS LTD
Lichfield Road, Tamworth B79 7TL
Tel: 01827 63821
Fax: 01827 310159
E-mail: sales@percy-lane.co.uk
Web site: www.percy-lane.co.uk

*TOP GEARS DESTINATIONS
46 Fulwoodhall Lane, Fulwood, Preston PR1 8DD
Tel/Fax: 01772 700536
Web site: www.pitlane-2000.com

VULTRON INTERNATIONAL LTD
City Park Industrial Estate, Gelderd Road, Leeds LS12 6DR
Tel: 0113 263 0323
Fax: 0113 279 4127
Web site: www.vultron.co.uk
E-mail: sales@vultron.co.uk

WEBASTO PRODUCT UK LTD
Webasto House, White Rose Way, Doncaster Carr DN4 5JH
Tel: 01302 322232
Fax: 01302 322231
E-mail: info@webastouk.com
Web site: www.webastouk.com

Door Operating Gear

AIR DOOR SERVICES
The Pavilions, Holly Lane Industrial Estate, Atherstone CV9 2QZ
Tel: 01827 11660
Fax: 01827 713577
E-mail: airdoorservices@aol.com

CARLYLE BUS & COACH LTD
Carlyle Business Park, Great Bridge Street, Swan Village, West Bromwich B70 0XA
Tel: 0121 524 1200
Fax: 0121 524 1201

DEANS POWERED DOORS
PO Box 8, Borwick Drive, Grovehill, Beverley HU17 0HQ
Tel: 01482 868111
Fax: 01482 881890
E-mail: info@deans-doors.com

KELLETT (UK) LTD
8 Stevenson Way, Sheffield S9 3WZ.
Tel: 0114 261 1122.
Fax: 0114 261 1199.
E-mail: sales@kellett.co.uk

KNORR-BREMSE SYSTEMS FOR COMMERCIAL VEHICLES LTD
Douglas Road, Kingswood, Bristol BS15 8NL.
Tel: 0117 984 6100.
Fax: 0117 984 6101.
Web site: www.knorr-bremse.com

MULTIPART PSV
Pilling Lane, Chorley PR7 3EL.
Tel: 01257 225577.
Fax: 01257 225575.
E-mail: info@multipart.com
Web site: www.multipart.co.uk

MET UK LIMITED
PO Box 205, Southam CV47 0ZL
Tel: 01926 813938
Fax: 01926 814898
E-mail: met.uk@btinternet.com

*NEALINE WINDSCREEN WIPER PRODUCTS
Unit 1, The Sidings Industrial Estate, Birdingbury Road, Marton CV23 9RX
Tel: 01926 633256
Fax: 01926 632600

NORBURY BLINDS LTD

DESTINATION Blinds
NUMERAL Blinds

any **SIZE** COLOUR or QUANTITY

LEGAL LETTERING VEHICLE SIGNS

DESTINATION BLINDS

Owners of T. Norbury & Co. Ltd., now trading as Norbury Blinds Ltd.

We have years of experience in the manufacture and printing of Destination and Route Numeral Blinds, offering a friendly and professional service to the Bus and Train industry.

We print destination blinds for both automatic and manual mechanisms in this country and abroad in many colours.

Our workforce is committed to providing a competitive quality product.

So when you need Destination Blinds come to the experts - **"NORBURYS"**

**FOR IMMEDIATE ATTENTION
RING: 0121 359 4311
FAX US ON: 0121 359 6388**

**NORBURY BLINDS LTD
41-45 Hanley Street, Newtown
Birmingham B19 3SP**
www.norbury-blinds.com
email: info@norbury-blinds.com

Advice on colours, letters, styles, sizes etc
Ring: 0121 359 4311
Fax: 0121 359 6388

DIGITAL GRAPHIC DESIGN SERVICE

"WE CARE WHERE YOU'RE GOING"

NEXT BUS LTD
Vincents Road, Bumpers Farm Industrial Estate, Chippenham SN14 6QA
Tel: 01249 462462
Fax: 01249 448844
E-mail: sales@next-bus.co.uk
Web site: www.next-bus.co.uk

*PARTLINE LTD
Dockfield Road, Shipley BD17 7AZ
Tel: 01274 531531
Fax: 01274 531088
E-mail: sales@partline.co.uk
Web site: www.partline.co.uk

PETERS DOOR SYSTEMS LTD
Bradbury Drive, Springwood Industrial Estate, Braintree CM7 2ET
Tel: 01376 555277
Fax: 01376 555292
E-mail: petersdoors@petersdoors.co.uk

VAPOR-STONE UK LTD
2nd Avenue, Centrum 100, Burton-on-Trent DE14 3WF
Tel: 01283 743300
Fax: 01283 743333
Web site: www.wabtec.com

WABCO AUTOMOTIVE UK LTD
Texas Street, Morley LS27 0HQ.
Tel: 0113-251 2510
Fax: 0113-251 2844

Drinks Dispensing Equipment

*AVT SYSTEMS
Unit 3/4, Tything Road East, Arden Forest Trading Estate, Alcester B49 6ES
Tel: 01789 400357
Fax: 01789 400359
E-mail: info@avtsystems.co.uk
Web site: www.avtsystems.co.uk

BRADTECH LTD
Unit 3, Ladford Covert, Seighford, Stafford ST18 9QD
Tel: 01785 282800
Fax: 01785 282558
E-mail: sales@bradtech.ltd.uk

*DRINKMASTER LTD
Plymouth Road, Liskeard PL14 3PG
Tel: 01579 342082
Fax: 01579 342591
E-mail: info@drinkmaster.co.uk
Web site: www.drinkmaster.co.uk

ELSAN LTD
Bellbrook Park, Uckfield TN22 1QF
Tel: 01825 748200
Fax: 01825 761212
E-mail: sales@elsan.co.uk

SHADES TECHNICS
Marshgate Drive, Hertford SG13 7AJ
Tel: 01992 501683
Fax: 01992 501669
E-mail: sales@shades-technics.com
Web site: www.shades-technics.com

Driving Axles and Gears

ALBION AUTOMOTIVE LTD
South Street, Scotstoun, Glasgow G14 0DT.
Tel: 0141 434 2400.
Fax: 0141 959 6362
E-mail: sales@albion_auto.co.uk
Web site: www.albion_auto.co.uk

ARVIN MERITOR
Unit 21, Suttons Park Avenue, Reading RG6 1LA.
Tel: 0118 935 9126
Fax: 0118 935 9138
E-mail: james.randall@arvinmeritor.com
Web site: www.arvinmeritor.com

ASHLEY BANKS LTD
5 King Street Estate, Langtoft, Peterborough PE6 9NF
Tel: 01778 560651
Fax: 01778 560721
E-mail: user@ashleybanks.fsnet.co.uk

BUSS BIZZ
Goughs Transport Depot, Morestead, Winchester SO21 1JD.
Tel: 01962 715555/66.
Fax: 01962 714868.

EATON LTD
Truck Components Marketing – PO Box 11, Worsley Road North, Worsley M28 5GJ
Tel: 01204 797219.
Fax: 01204 797204.

GKN AXLES LTD
(Kirkstall Division) – Abbey Road, Kirkstal LS5 3NF.
Tel: 0113 258 4611.

*HL SMITH TRANSMISSIONS LTD
Enterprise Business Park, Cross Road, Albrighton, Wolverhampton WV7 3BJ
Tel: 01902 373011
Fax: 01902 373608
E-mail: sales@hlsmith.co.uk
Web site: www.hlsmith.co.uk

IMPERIAL ENGINEERING
Delamare Road, Cheshunt EN8 9UD
Tel: 01992 634255
Fax: 01992 530506
E-mail: sales@imperialengineering.co.uk
Web site: www.imperialengineering.co.uk

LH GROUP (SERVICES) LTD
Graycar Business Park, Barton Turns, Barton Under Needwood DE13 8EN.
Tel: 01283 713615.
Fax: 01283 713551.
E-mail: l/h/llords@classic.msn.com

MAJORLINE ENGINEERING LTD
Baybridge Industrial Units, Baybridge Lane, Owslebury, Winchester SO21 1JN.
Tel: 01962 777077.
Fax: 01962 777661, 777667
E-mail: majorline@compuserve.com

MULTIPART PSV
Pilling Lane, Chorley PR7 3EL.
Tel: 01257 225577.
Fax: 01257 225575.
E-mail: info@multipart.com
Web site: www.multipart.co.uk

NEXT BUS LTD
Vincents Road, Bumpers Farm Industrial Estate, Chippenham SN14 6QA
Tel: 01249 462462
Fax: 01249 448844
E-mail: sales@next-bus.co.uk
Web sitel: www.next-bus.co.uk

*PARTLINE LTD
Dockfield Road, Shipley BD17 7AZ
Tel: 01274 531531
Fax: 01274 531088
E-mail: sales@partline.co.uk
Web site: www.partline.co.uk

POWERTRAIN PRODUCTS LTD
Stringes Close, Willenhall WV13 1LE
Tel: 01902 366000
Fax: 01902 366504

UNITEC PARTS & SERVICE LTD
Manston Lane, Leeds LS15 8SU
Tel: 0113 264 5182
Fax: 0113 260 2294
Web site: www.optare.com

*VOR TRANSMISSIONS LTD
Little London House, St Anne's Road, Little London, Willenhall WV13 1DT
Tel: 0800 018 4141
Fax: 01902 603868
E-mail: vor@globalnet.co.uk
Web site: www.vor.co.uk

Electrical Equipment

*AFTERMARKET COACH SUPPLIES (UK) LTD
6a Riley Road, Telford Way Industrial Estate, Kettering NN16 8NN
Tel: 01536 416979
Fax: 01539 415709
Web site: www.acsuk.freeuk.com

*AVT SYSTEMS
Unit 3/4, Tything Road East, Arden Forest Trading Estate, Alcester B49 6ES
Tel: 01789 400357
Fax: 01789 400359
E-mail: info@avtsystems.co.uk
Web site: www.avtsystems.co.uk

*BRITAX PMG LTD
Bressingby Industrial Estate, Bridlington YO16 4SJ
Tel: 01262 670161
Fax: 01262 605666
E-mail: info@britax-pmg.com
Web site: www.britax-pmg.com

CARLYLE BUS & COACH LTD
Carlyle Business Park, Great Bridge Street, Swan Village, West Bromwich B70 0XA
Tel: 0121 524 1200
Fax: 0121 524 1201

*ETM SOFTWARE SERVICES
9 Dorset Avenue, Ferndown BH22 8HJ
Tel: 01202 246710
Fax: 01202 687537
E-mail: info@etmss.com
Web site: www.etmss.com

IMEXPART LTD
Links 31, Willowbridge Way, Whitwood, Castleford WF10 5NP
Tel: 0845 6050404
Fax: 01977 513412
E-mail: parts@imexpart.com
Web site: www.imexpart.com

Trade Directory

*INVERTEC LTD
Whelford Road, Fairford GL7 4DT
Tel: 01285 713550
Fax: 01285 713548
Mobile: 07802 793828
E-mail: ian@invertec.co.uk
Web site: www.invertec.co.uk

*THE LAWTON MOTOR BODY BUILDING CO LTD
Knutsford Road, Church Lawton ST7 3DN
Tel: 01270 882056
Fax: 01270 883014
E-mail: info@lawtonmotorbody.co.uk
Web site: www.lawtonmotorbody.co.uk

LEXCEL POWER SYSTEMS PLC
35 Manor Road, Henley on Thames RG9 1LU.
Tel: 01491 874414.
E-mail: sales@lexcelpower.com
Web site: lexcelpower.com

MAJORLINE ENGINEERING LTD
Baybridge Industrial Units, Baybridge Lane, Owslebury, Winchester SO21 1JN.
Tel: 01962 777077.
Fax: 01962 777661, 777667
E-mail: majorline@compuserve.com

MULTIPART PSV
Pilling Lane, Chorley PR7 3EL.
Tel: 01257 225577.
Fax: 01257 225575.
E-mail: info@multipart.com
Web site: www.multipart.co.uk

*NEALINE WINDSCREEN WIPER PRODUCTS
Unit 1, The Sidings Industrial Estate, Birdingbury Road, Marton CV23 9RX
Tel: 01926 633256
Fax: 01926 632600

PACEL ELECTRONICS
Fleets Point House, Willis Way, Poole BH15 3SS
Tel: 01202 676616
Fax: 01202 681357
E-mail: sales@pacel.co.uk
Web site: www.pacel.co.uk

*PARTLINE LTD
Dockfield Road, Shipley BD17 7AZ
Tel: 01274 531531
Fax: 01274 531088
E-mail: sales@partline.co.uk
Web site: www.partline.co.uk

Electronic Control

ACTIA UK LTD
Unit 81, Mochdre Industrial Estate, Newtown SY16 4LE
Tel: 01686 621067
Fax: 01686 621068
E-mail: mail@actia.co.uk
Web site: www.actia.co.uk

*AVT SYSTEMS
Unit 3/4, Tything Road East, Arden Forest Trading Estate, Alcester B49 6ES
Tel: 01789 400357
Fax: 01789 400359
E-mail: info@avtsystems.co.uk
Web site: www.avtsystems.co.uk

*HILTECH DEVELOPMENTS LTD
22 Larbre Crescent, Whickham, Newcastle upon Tyne NE16 5YG.
Tel: 0191 488 6258.
Fax: 0191 488 9158.
E-mail: executive@hiltechdevelopments.com
Web site: www.hiltechdevelopments.com

KNORR-BREMSE SYSTEMS FOR COMMERCIAL VEHICLES LTD
Douglas Road, Kingswood, Bristol BS15 8NL.
Tel: 0117 984 6100.
Fax: 0117 984 6101.
Web site: www.knorr-bremse.com

*PARTLINE LTD
Dockfield Road, Shipley BD17 7AZ
Tel: 01274 531531
Fax: 01274 531088
E-mail: sales@partline.co.uk
Web site: www.partline.co.uk

VDO KIENZLE UK LTD
36 Gravelly Industrial Park, Birmingham B24 8TA.
Tel: 0121 326 1234.
Fax: 0121 326 1299.

WABCO AUTOMOTIVE UK
Texas Street, Morley LS27 0HQ.
Tel: 0113 251 2510.
Fax: 0113 251 2844.

Emission Control Devices

*EMINOX LTD
North Warren Road, Gainsborough DN21 2TU
Tel: 01427 810088
Fax: 01427 810061
E-mail: post@eminox.com
Web site: www.eminox.com

MULTIPART PSV
Pilling Lane, Chorley PR7 3EL.
Tel: 01257 225577.
Fax: 01257 225575.
E-mail: info@multipart.com
Web site: www.multipart.co.uk

*PARTLINE LTD
Dockfield Road, Shipley BD17 7AZ
Tel: 01274 531531
Fax: 01274 531088
E-mail: sales@partline.co.uk
Web site: www.partline.co.uk

Engineering

ARRIVA BUS AND COACH LTD
Lodge Garage, Whitehall Road West, Gomersal, Cleckheaton BD19 4BJ.
Tel: 01274 681144
Fax: 01274 651198
Web site: www.arriva.co.uk
E-mail: busandcoachsales@arriva.co.uk

*BROXWOOD VEHICLE SPECIALISTS
Unit 2 Parkside Garage, Old Stafford Road, Slade Heath, Wolverhampton WV10 7PH
Tel: 01902 798770
Fax: 01902 798534
E-mail: sharon@broxwood.net

BUSS BIZZ
Goughs Transport Depot, Morestead, Winchester SO21 1JD.
Tel: 01962 715555/66.
Fax: 01962 714838.

*COACH-AID
Unit 2, Brindley Close, Tollgate Industrial Estate, Stafford ST16 3SU
Tel: 01785 222666
E-mail: workshop@coach-aid.com

DIRECT PARTS LTD
Unit 1, Churnet Court, Churnetside Business Park, Harrison Way, Cheddleton ST13 7EF.
Tel: 01538 361777.
Fax: 01538 369100
E-mail: sales@direct-group.co.uk
Web site: www.direct-group.co.uk

FTA VEHICLE INSPECTION SERVICE
Hermes House, St John's Road, Tunbridge Wells TN4 9UZ.
Tel: 01892 526171
Fax: 01892 534939
E-mail: enquiries@fta.co.uk
Web site: www.fta.co.uk

THOMAS HARDIE – WIGAN
Lockett Road, Ashton-in-Makerfield, Wigan WN4 8DE.
Tel: 01942 505124.
Fax: 01942 505119.

*HART BROTHERS (ENGINEERING) LTD
Soho Works, Soho Street, Oldham OL2 6BP
Tel: 0161 737 6791

*HILTECH DEVELOPMENTS LTD
22 Larbre Crescent, Whickham, Newcastle upon Tyne NE16 5YG.
Tel: 0191 488 6258.
Fax: 0191 488 9158.
E-mail: executive@hiltechdevelopments.com
Web site: www.hitechdevelopments.com

IMPERIAL ENGINEERING
Delamare Road, Cheshunt EN8 9UD
Tel: 01992 634255
Fax: 01992 530506
E-mail: sales@imperialengineering.co.uk
Web site: www.imperialengineering.co.uk

JBF SERVICES LTD
Southedge Works, Hipperholme, Halifax HX3 8EF
Tel: 01422 202840
Fax: 01422 206070
E-mail: jbfservices@aol.com

MENTOR
Mentor Coach & Bus Ltd, Carlton House, Euroway Industrial Estate, Hellaby, Rotherham S66 8QL
Tel: 01709 700600
Fax: 01709 700007
E-mail: sales@mentorplc.com
Web site: www.mentorplc.com
24 hour Neopart assistance: 07801 027702
24 hour Neoservice support: 07801 027701

Trade Directory

*PARRY PEOPLE MOVERS LTD
Overend Road, Cradley Heath, Dudley B64 7DD
Tel: 01384 569553
Fax: 01384 637753
E-mail: jpmparry@aol.com
Web site: www.parrypeoplemovers.com

MAJORLINE ENGINEERING LTD
Baybridge Industrial Units, Baybridge Lane, Owslebury, Winchester SO21 1JN.
Tel: 01962 777077.
Fax: 01962 777661, 777667
E-mail: majorline@compuserve.com

*MCE LTD
Firbank Way, Leighton Buzzard LU7 4YP
Tel: 01525 375301
Fax: 01525 850967
Web site: www.mce-ltd.com

MASS SPECIAL ENGINEERING LTD
Anston, Sheffield S25 4SD
Tel: 01909 550480.
Fax: 01909 550486.

NEXT BUS LTD
Vincents Road, Bumpers Farm Industrial Estate, Chippenham SN14 6QA
Tel: 01249 462462
Fax: 01249 448844
E-mail: sales@next-bus.co.uk
Web sitel: www.next-bus.co.uk

*PARTLINE LTD
Dockfield Road, Shipley BD17 7AZ
Tel: 01274 531531
Fax: 01274 531088
E-mail: sales@partline.co.uk
Web site: www.partline.co.uk

POWERTRAIN PRODUCTS LTD
Stringes Close, Willenhall WV13 1LE
Tel: 01902 366000
Fax: 01902 366504

*PSS-STEERING & HYDRAULICS DIVISION
Folgate Road, North Walsham NR28 0AJ
Tel: 01692 406017
Fax: 01692 406957
E-mail: sales@pss.co.uk
Web site: www.pss.co.uk

QES
Quality Engine Services
Tel: 01270 253323
Fax: 01270 253324
Web site: www.qualityengineservices.co.uk

*SOUTHDOWN PSV LTD
Unit 3/7, Silverwood, Snow Hill, Copthorne RH10 3EN
Tel: 01342 715222
Fax: 01342 719617
E-mail: southdownpsv@btinternet.com
Web site: www.southdownpsv.co.uk

*TRANSPORT DESIGN INTERNATIONAL
12 Waterloo Road Estate, Bidford on Avon B50 4JH
Tel: 01789 490370
Fax: 01789 490592
E-mail:enquiries@tdi.uk.com
Web site: www.tdi.uk.com

TRUCKALIGN
Truck Align Co Ltd, Vip Trading Estate, Anchor & Hope Lane, Charlton, London SE7 7RY
Tel: 020 8858 3781
Fax: 020 8858 5663

UNITEC PARTS & SERVICE LTD
Manston Lane, Leeds LS15 8SU
Tel: 0113 264 5182
Fax: 0113 260 2294
Web site: www.optare.com

Engines

BUSS BIZZ
Goughs Transport Depot, Morestead, Winchester SO21 1JD.
Tel: 01962 715555/66.
Fax: 01962 714868.

*CRAIG TILSEY & SON LTD
Moorfields Industrial Estate, Cotes Heath, Stoke-on-Trent ST21 6QY
Tel: 01782 791524
Fax: 01782 791316

CREWE ENGINES
Warmingham Road, Crewe CW1 4PQ
Tel: 01270 526333
Fax: 01270 526433
E-mail: jim@creweengines.co.uk
Web site: www.creweengines.co.uk

The UK's No.1 for Mercedes-Benz Engines

Join the UK's major bus & coach groups and choose Crewe Engines for Mercedes-Benz engines. From fast delivery of an exchange engine to collection of your vehicle and fitting of the engine, we have the expertise and resources to provide great service at very competitive prices.

also.. MAN, Cummins, IVECO, VOLVO, DAF

01270 526333
sales@creweengines.co.uk
Warmingham Road, Crewe, Cheshire, England, CW1 4PQ
web site www.creweengines.co.uk

ENGINES
- UK's No.1 for Mercedes-Benz
- Also Iveco, Cummins, DAF, MAN, etc
- Petrol & diesel, 4 cylinder to V12
- Fast, friendly & efficient

ENGINE PARTS
- Cylinder heads, crankshafts, con-rods, etc
- Pistons, bearings, gaskets, camshafts, etc
- Oil pumps, water pumps, filters, etc

Crewe Engines

*CUMMINS UK
Rutherford Drive, Park Farm South, Wellingborough NN8 6AN
Tel: 01933 334200
Fax: 01933 334198
Web site: www.cummins-uk.com

DAF COMPONENTS LTD
Eastern Bypass, Thame OX9 3FB
Tel: 01844 261111
Fax: 01844 217111
Web site: www.daftrucks.com.

DAYCO – TRANSPORT & TRADE DISTRIBUTION LTD
Davis House, Lodge Causeway Trading Estate, Fishponds, Bristol BS16 3JB.
Tel: 0117 965 9999.
Fax: 0117 965 4724.

DIESEL POWER ENGINEERING
Goughs Transport Depot, Morestead, Winchester SO21 1JD.
Tel/Fax: 01962 711314.

ERF MEDWAY LTD
Sir Thomas Longley Road, Medway City Estate, Rochester ME2 4QW.
Tel: 01634 711144.
Fax: 01634 711188.

FUMOTO ENGINEERING OF EUROPE
24 Charles II Street, London SW1Y 4QU
Tel: 020 7976 1840
Fax: 020 7976 1850
E-mail: fumoto@tankcontainers.co.uk

*HART BROTHERS (ENGINEERING) LTD
Soho Works, Soho Street, Oldham OL2 6BP
Tel: 0161 737 6791

IVECO
Iveco Ford Truck Ltd, Iveco Ford House, Station Road, Watford WD1 1SR.
Tel: 01923 246400.
Fax: 01923 240574.

LH GROUP (SERVICES) LTD
Graycar Business Park, Barton Turns, Barton Under Needwood DE13 8EN.
Tel: 01283 713615.
Fax: 01283 713551.
E-mail: l/h/llords@classic.msn.com

MAJORLINE ENGINEERING LTD
Baybridge Industrial Units, Baybridge Lane, Owslebury, Winchester SO21 1JN.
Tel: 01962 777077.
Fax: 01962 777661, 777667
E-mail: majorline@compuserve.com

MAN TRUCK & BUS UK LTD
Frankland Road, Blagrove, Swindon SN5 8YU.
Tel: 01793 448000.
Fax: 01793 448262.

MULTIPART PSV
Pilling Lane, Chorley PR7 3EL.
Tel: 01257 225577.
Fax: 01257 225575.
E-mail: info@multipart.com
Web site: www.multipart.co.uk

NEXT BUS LTD
Vincents Road, Bumpers Farm Industrial Estate, Chippenham SN14 6QA
Tel: 01249 462462
Fax: 01249 448844
E-mail: sales@next-bus.co.uk
Web sitel: www.next-bus.co.uk

*PARTLINE LTD
Dockfield Road, Shipley BD17 7AZ
Tel: 01274 531531
Fax: 01274 531088
E-mail: sales@partline.co.uk
Web site: www.partline.co.uk

PERKINS GROUP LTD
Peterborough PE1 5NA.
Tel: 01733 567474.
Fax: 01733 582240.
Web site: www.perkins.com

SHAWSON SUPPLY LTD
12 Station Road, Saintfield BT24 7DU.
Tel: 028 9751 0994.
Fax: 028 9751 0816.
E-mail: shawson@btinternet.com

UNITEC PARTS & SERVICE LTD
Manston Lane, Leeds LS15 8SU
Tel: 0113 264 5182
Fax: 0113 260 2294
Web site: www.optare.com

WEALDSTONE ENGINEERING
Sanders Lodge Industrial Estate, Rushden NN10 6AZ.
Tel: 01933 316622.
Fax: 01933 358742.
Web site: www.wealdstone.co.uk

Engine Oil Drain Valves

FUMOTO ENGINEERING OF EUROPE
24 Charles II Street, London SW1Y 4QU
Tel: 020 7976 1840
Fax: 020 7976 1850
E-mail: info@tankcontainers.co.uk

MULTIPART PSV
Pilling Lane, Chorley PR7 3EL.
Tel: 01257 225577.
Fax: 01257 225575.
E-mail: info@multipart.com
Web site: www.multipart.co.uk

*PARTLINE LTD
Dockfield Road, Shipley BD17 7AZ
Tel: 01274 531531
Fax: 01274 531088
E-mail: sales@partline.co.uk
Web site: www.partline.co.uk

Exhaust Systems

ARVIN MERITOR
Unit 21, Suttons Park Avenue, Reading RG6 1LA.
Tel: 0118 935 9126
Fax: 0118 935 9138
E-mail: james.randall@arvinmeritor.com
Web site: www.arvinmeritor.com

ASHLEY BANKS LTD
5 King Street Estate, Langtoft, Peterborough PE6 9NF
Tel: 01778 560651
Fax: 01778 560721
E-mail: user@ashleybanks.fsnet.co.uk

*BROXWOOD VEHICLE SPECIALISTS
Unit 2 Parkside Garage, Old Stafford Road, Slade Heath, Wolverhampton WV10 7PH
Tel: 01902 798770
Fax: 01902 798564
E-mail: sharon@broxwood.net

BUSS BIZZ
Goughs Transport Depot, Morestead, Winchester SO21 1JD.
Tel: 01962 715555/66.
Fax: 01962 714868.

CARLYLE BUS & COACH LTD
Carlyle Business Park, Great Bridge Street, Swan Village, West Bromwich B70 0XA
Tel: 0121 524 1200
Fax: 0121 524 1201

COMMERCIAL EXHAUSTS LTD
Unit 1, Bank Quay Trading Estate, Warrington WA1 1PJ
Tel: 01925 632397
Fax: 01925 418039
E-mail: sales@commercialexhaustsltd.co.uk
Web site: www.commercialexhaustsltd.co.uk

CRESCENT FACILITIES LTD
72 Willow Crescent, Chapeltown, Sheffield S35 1QS
Tel: 07718 742466
Fax: 0114 245 1050
E-mail: cfl.chris@btinternet.com

DINEX EXHAUSTS LTD
14 Chesford Garage, Woolston, Warrington WA1 4RE
Tel: 01925 849849
Fax: 01925 849850
E-mail: enquiries@dinex.co.uk
Web site: www.dinex.dk

*EMINOX LTD
North Warren Road, Gainsborough DN21 2TU
Tel: 01427 810088
Fax: 01427 810061
E-mail: post@eminox.com
Web site: www.eminox.com

IMEXPART LTD
Links 31, Willowbridge Way, Whitwood, Castleford WF10 5NP
Tel: 0845 6050404
Fax: 01977 513412
E-mail: parts@imexpart.com
Web site: www.imexpart.com

MAJORLINE ENGINEERING LTD
Baybridge Industrial Units, Baybridge Lane, Owslebury, Winchester SO21 1JN.
Tel: 01962 777077.
Fax: 01962 777661, 777667
E-mail: majorline@compuserve.com

*PARTLINE LTD
Dockfield Road, Shipley BD17 7AZ
Tel: 01274 531531
Fax: 01274 531088
E-mail: sales@partline.co.uk
Web site: www.partline.co.uk

Fans and Drive Belts

CARLYLE BUS & COACH LTD
Carlyle Business Park, Great Bridge Street, Swan Village, West Bromwich B70 0XA
Tel: 0121 524 1200
Fax: 0121 524 1201

IMEXPART LTD
Links 31, Willowbridge Way, Whitwood,
Castleford WF10 5NP
Tel: 0845 6050404
Fax: 01977 513412
E-mail: parts@imexpart.com
Web site: www.imexpart.com

IMPERIAL ENGINEERING
Delamare Road, Cheshunt EN8 9UD
Tel: 01992 634255
Fax: 01992 630506
E-mail: sales@imperialengineering.co.uk
Web site: www.imperialengineering.co.uk

MAJORLINE ENGINEERING LTD
Baybridge Industrial Units, Baybridge Lane,
Owslebury, Winchester SO21 1JN.
Tel: 01962 777077.
Fax: 01962 777661, 777667
E-mail: majorline@compuserve.com

MULTIPART PSV
Pilling Lane, Chorley PR7 3EL.
Tel: 01257 225577.
Fax: 01257 225575.
E-mail: info@multipart.com
Web site: www.multipart.co.uk

*PARTLINE LTD
Dockfield Road, Shipley BD17 7AZ
Tel: 01274 531531
Fax: 01274 531088
E-mail: sales@partline.co.uk
Web site: www.partline.co.uk

PIONEER WESTON
Smithfold Lane, Worsley, Manchester
M28 0GP.
Tel: 0161 703 2000
Fax: 0161 703 2025
E-mail: pioneer.weston@wyko.co.uk

*SERGEANT (P&P) (B&A) LTD
PO Box 11, New Hall Lane, Hoylake CH47 4DH
Tel: 0151 632 5903
Fax: 0151 632 5908
E-mail: enq@sergeant.co.uk
Web site: www.sergeant.co.uk

Fare Boxes

CUBIC TRANSPORTATION SYSTEMS LTD
AFC House, Honeycrock Lane, Salfords,
Redhill RH1 5LA
Tel: 01737 782200
Fax: 01737 789759
Web site: www.cubic.com

*ETM SOFTWARE SERVICES
9 Dorset Avenue, Ferndown BH22 8HJ
Tel: 01202 246710
Fax: 01202 687537
E-mail: info@etmss.com
Web site: www.etmss.com

JOHN GROVES TICKET SYSTEMS
Unit 5, Rennie Business Units, Factory
Place, Saltcoats KA21 5LZ
Tel: 01294 471133
Fax: 01294 471166
Web site: www.cambist.se

MARK TERRILL TICKET MACHINERY
5 De Grey Close, Lewes BN7 2JR.
Tel/Fax: 01273 474816.
Mobile: 07770 666159.

Fire Extinguishers

ASHLEY BANKS LTD
5 King Street Estate, Langtoft, Peterborough
PE6 9NF
Tel: 01778 560651
Fax: 01778 560721
E-mail: user@ashleybanks.fsnet.co.uk

*BROXWOOD VEHICLE SPECIALISTS
Unit 2 Parkside Garage, Old Stafford Road,
Slade Heath, Wolverhampton WV10 7PH
Tel: 01902 798770
Fax: 01902 798564
E-mail: sharon@broxwood.net

CARLYLE BUS & COACH LTD
Carlyle Business Park, Great Bridge Street,
Swan Village, West Bromwich B70 0XA
Tel: 0121 524 1200
Fax: 0121 524 1201

FIREMASTER EXTINGUISHER LTD
Firex House, 174-176 Hither Green Lane,
London SE13 6QB
Tel: 020 8852 8585
Fax: 020 8297 8020
E-mail: info@firemaster.co.uk
Web site: www.firemaster.co.uk

*HAPPICH V & I COMPONENTS LTD
Unit 30/31, Fort Industrial Park, Fort
Parkway, Castle Bromwich, Birmingham,
B35 7AR.
Tel: 0121 747 4400
Fax: 0121 747 4977
E-mail: sales@happich.co.uk
Web site: www.happich.co.uk

KELLETT (UK) LTD
8 Stevenson Way, Sheffield S9 3WZ.
Tel: 0114 261 1122.
Fax: 0114 261 1199.
E-mail: sales@kellett.co.uk

*THE LAWTON MOTOR BODY BUILDING CO LTD
Knutsford Road, Church Lawton ST7 3DN
Tel: 01270 882056
Fax: 01270 883014
E-mail: info@lawtonmotorbody.co.uk
Web site: www.lawtonmotorbody.co.uk

MENTOR
Mentor Coach & Bus Ltd, Carlton House,
Euroway Industrial Estate, Hellaby,
Rotherham S66 8QL
Tel: 01709 700600
Fax: 01709 700007
E-mail: sales@mentorplc.com
Web site: www.mentorplc.com
24 hour Neopart assistance:
07801 027702
24 hour Neoservice support:
07801 027701

MULTIPART PSV
Pilling Lane, Chorley PR7 3EL.
Tel: 01257 225577.
Fax: 01257 225575.
E-mail: info@multipart.com
Web site: www.multipart.co.uk

NU-TRACK LTD
Steeple Industrial Estate, Antrim BT41 1AB.
Tel: 028 9446 9550
E-mail: enquiries@nu-track.co.uk
Web site: www.nu-track.co.uk

PARTLINE LTD
Dockfield Road, Shipley BD17 7AZ
Tel: 01274 531531
Fax: 01274 531088
E-mail: sales@partline.co.uk
Web site: www.partline.co.uk

PSV PRODUCTS
PO Box 166, Warrington WA4 5FG
Tel: 01925 210220.
Fax: 01925 601534
E-mail: daly@merseymail.com
Web site: www.psvproducts.com

First Aid Equipment

ASHLEY BANKS LTD
5 King Street Estate, Langtoft, Peterborough
PE6 9NF
Tel: 01778 560651
Fax: 01778 560721
E-mail: user@ashleybanks.fsnet.co.uk

*BROXWOOD VEHICLE SPECIALISTS
Unit 2 Parkside Garage, Old Stafford Road,
Slade Heath, Wolverhampton WV10 7PH
Tel: 01902 798770
Fax: 01902 798564
E-mail: sharon@broxwood.net

CARLYLE BUS & COACH LTD
Carlyle Business Park, Great Bridge Street,
Swan Village, West Bromwich B70 0XA
Tel: 0121 524 1200
Fax: 0121 524 1201

FIREMASTER EXTINGUISHER LTD
Firex House, 174-176 Hither Green Lane,
London SE13 6QB
Tel: 020 8852 8585
Fax: 020 8297 8020
E-mail: info@firemaster.co.uk
Web site: www.firemaster.co.uk

*HAPPICH V & I COMPONENTS LTD
Unit 30/31, Fort Industrial Park, Fort
Parkway, Castle Bromwich B35 7AR.
Tel: 0121 747 4400
Fax: 0121 747 4977
E-mail: sales@happich.co.uk
Web site: www.happich.co.uk

*THE LAWTON MOTOR BODY BUILDING CO LTD
Knutsford Road, Church Lawton, Stoke-on-Trent ST7 3DN
Tel: 01270 882056
Fax: 01270 883014
E-mail: info@lawtonmotorbody.co.uk
Web site: www.lawtonmotorbody.co.uk

MULTIPART PSV
Pilling Lane, Chorley PR7 3EL.
Tel: 01257 225577.
Fax: 01257 225575.
E-mail: info@multipart.com
Web site: www.multipart.co.uk

NU-TRACK LTD
Steeple Industrial Estate, Antrim BT41 1AB.
Tel: 028 9446 9550
E-mail: enquiries@nu-track.co.uk
Web site: www.nu-track.co.uk

Trade Directory

PARTLINE LTD
Dockfield Road, Shipley BD17 7AZ
Tel: 01274 531531
Fax: 01274 531088
E-mail: sales@partline.co.uk
Web site: www.partline.co.uk

PSV PRODUCTS
PO Box 166, Warrington WA4 5FG
Tel: 01925 210220.
Fax: 01925 601534
E-mail: daly@merseymail.com
Web site: www.psvproducts.com

Floor Covering

ALTRO TRANSFLOOR
Works Road, Letchworth SG6 1NW
Tel: 01462 489263
Fax: 01462 475263
E-mail: lkni@altro.co.uk
Web site: www.altrotransfloor.com

*AUTOMATE WHEEL COVERS LTD
California Mills, Oxford Road, Gomersal, Cleckheaton BD19 4HQ
Tel: 01274 862700
Fax: 01274 851989
E-mail: sales@wheelcovers.co.uk
Web site: www.euroliners.com

*AUTOMOTIVE TEXTILE INDUSTRIES
Unit 126, Springfield Business Park, Grantham NG31 7BG
Tel: 01476 593050
Fax: 01476 593607
E-mail: sales@autotex.com
Web site: www.autotex.u-net.com

CARLYLE BUS & COACH LTD
Carlyle Business Park, Great Bridge Street, Swan Village, West Bromwich B70 0XA
Tel: 0121 524 1200
Fax: 0121 524 1201

COACH CARPETS
Unit 12, Hamilton Street, Blackburn BB2 4AJ.
Tel: 01254 53549.
Fax: 01254 261873.

CONCEPT COACHCRAFT
Far Cromwell Road, Bredbury, Stockport SK6 2SE
Tel: 0161 406 9322
Fax: 0161 406 9588
E-mail: sales@conceptcoachcraft.com
Web site: www.conceptcoachcraft.com

CRESCENT FACILITIES LTD
72 Willow Crescent, Chapeltown, Sheffield S35 1QS
Tel: 0771 874 2466
Fax: 0114 245 1050
E-mail: cfl.chris@btinternet.com

FIRTH FURNISHINGS LTD
PO Box 22, Flush Mills, Heckmondwike WF16 0EP.
Tel: 01924 406141.
Fax: 01924 401128.

*THE LAWTON MOTOR BODY BUILDING CO LTD
Knutsford Road, Church Lawton, Stoke-on-Trent ST7 3DN
Tel: 01270 882056
Fax: 01270 883014
E-mail: info@lawtonmotorbody.co.uk
Web site: www.lawtonmotorbody.co.uk

*MARTYN INDUSTRIALS LTD
5 Brunel Way, Durranhill Industrial Esate, Harraby, Carlisle CA4 8JZ
Tel: 01228 544000
Fax: 01228 544001
E-mail: enquiries@martyn-industrials.co.uk
Web site: www.martyn-industrials.co.uk

MULTIPART PSV
Pilling Lane, Chorley PR7 3EL.
Tel: 01257 225577.
Fax: 01257 225575.
E-mail: info@multipart.com
Web site: www.multipart.co.uk

NU-TRACK LTD
Steeple Industrial Estate, Antrim BT41 1AB.
Tel: 028 9446 9550
E-mail: enquiries@nu-track.co.uk
Web site: www.nu-track.co.uk

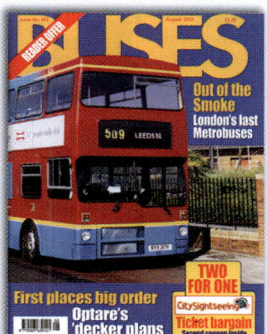

Buses is Britain's leading monthly which gives great coverage of the bus industry by those who really know. This readable and entertaining magazine carries features on most areas of interest, giving an authoritative distillation of the month's most important news and looking in detail at vehicle operation, technical developments, ticketing, publicity, old vehicle preservation and the latest books, models and features, all of which are accompanied by stunning colour photography. If buses are your business, this magazine is for you.
£3.25 monthly

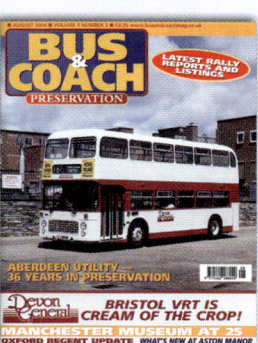

Bus & Coach Preservation magazine gives the best possible all-round coverage of all that's happening in the world of old buses today. This lively monthly provides a round-up of news and views of vehicle restoration, details of old buses and coaches that need to be saved for posterity, news of museums, groups and individual preservationists and coverage of events. High quality features and photography present a window on the preserved bus and coach world for enthusiasts and vehicle owners alike.
£3.25 monthly

Call the Subs Hotline anytime on: 01932 266622

Trade Directory

TIFLEX LTD (Treadmaster)
Tiflex House, Liskeard PL14 4NB
Tel: 01579 320808.
Fax: 01579 320802.
Web site: www.tiflex.co.uk

Fuel and Lubricants

CENTAUR FUEL MANAGEMENT LTD
Clifton Technology Park, Wynne Avenue, Clifton M27 8FF
Tel: 0161 793 6323
Fax: 0161 794 8031

INTERLUBE SYSTEMS LTD
St Modwen Road, Plymouth PL6 8LH
Tel: 01752 676000
Fax: 01752 676001
E-mail: info@interlubesystems.com
Web site: www.interlubesystems.com

MULTIPART PSV
Pilling Lane, Chorley PR7 3EL.
Tel: 01257 225577.
Fax: 01257 225575.
E-mail: info@multipart.com
Web site: www.multipart.co.uk

Fuel Management Systems

TRISCAN FUELLING SOLUTIONS
Harwood Street, Blackburn BB1 3BD
Tel: 01254 686048
Fax: 01254 686002
E-mail: info@triscansystems.com
Web site: www.triscansystems.com

Garage Equipment

*ATLANTIS INTERNATIONAL LTD
Unit 2, 18 Weldon Road, Loughborough LE11 5RA
Tel: 01509 233770
Fax: 01509 210542
E-mail: sales@atlantisint.co.uk
Web site: www.atlantisint.co.uk

TERENCE BARKER TANKS
Tel: 01376 330661
E-mail: terencebarkertanks.co.uk
Web site: www.terencebarkertanks.co.uk

FUMOTO ENGINEERING OF EUROPE
24 Charles II Street, London SW1Y 4QU
Tel: 020 7976 1840
Fax: 020 7976 1850
E-mail: fumoto@tankcontainers.co.uk

IMPERIAL ENGINEERING
Delamare Road, Cheshunt EN8 9UD
Tel: 01992 634255
Fax: 01992 630506
E-mail: sales@imperialengineering.co.uk
Web site: www.imperialengineering.co.uk

PHIL STOCKFORD GARAGE EQUIPMENT
7 Badger Way, North Cheshire Trading Estate, Prenton CH43 3HQ
Tel: 0151 609 1007
Fax: 0151 609 1008

VARLEY & GULLIVER LTD
Alfred Street, Sparkbrook, Birmingham B12 8JR.
Tel: 0121 773 2441.
Fax: 0121 766 6875.

MAJORLIFT HYDRAULIC EQUIPMENT LTD
Arnold's Field Industrial Estate, Wickwar GL12 8JD
Tel: 01454 299299
Fax: 01454 294003
Web site: www.majorlift.com
E-mail: info@majorlift.com

SOMERS VEHICLE LIFTS
15 Forge Trading Estate, Mucklow Hill, Halesowen B62 8TR
Tel: 0121 582 2700
Fax: 0121 585 2725
E-mail: sales@somers-vl.co.uk
Web site: www.somersvehiclelifts.co.uk

Secure and control your fuel, whatever the size of your fleet with a Triscan Fuel Management System:
- Control access to your fuel stocks
- Detect theft or leakage from storage tanks
- Highlight vehicles using more fuel than they should

For more details on how we can help with your fuel management, call us on 01254 686048.

Triscan, Harwood Street, Blackburn, Lancashire BB1 3BD Tel: 01254 686048
Fax: 01254 686002 Email:info@vbitriscan.com
www.vbilimited.com

STERTIL UK LTD
Unit A, Brackmills Business Park, Caswell Road, Northampton NN4 7PW
Tel: 01604 677384
Fax: 01604 765181
E-mail: info@stertil.com
Web site: www.stertil.com

V L TEST SYSTEMS LTD
3-4 Middle Slade, Buckingham Industrial Park, Buckingham MK18 1WA
Tel: 01280 822488
Fax: 01280 822489
E-mail: sales@vltestuk.com
Web site: www.vltest.com

Gearboxes

ALLISON TRANSMISSION
Allison House, 36 Duncan Close, Moulton Park, Northampton NN3 6WL
Tel: 01604 495496

DAVID BROWN VEHICLE TRANSMISSIONS LTD
Park Gear Works, Lockwood, Huddersfield HD4 5DD.
Tel: 01484 422180.
Fax: 01484 435292.

*BROXWOOD VEHICLE SPECIALISTS
Unit 2 Parkside Garage, Old Stafford Road, Slade Heath, Wolverhampton WV10 7PH
Tel: 01902 798770
Fax: 01902 798564
E-mail: sharon@broxwood.net

BUSS BIZZ
Goughs Transport Depot, Morestead, Winchester SO21 1JD.
Tel: 01962 715555/66.
Fax: 01962 714868.

EATON LTD
Truck Components Marketing, PO Box 11, Worsley Road North, Worsley M28 5GJ
Tel: 01204 797219.
Fax: 01204 797204.

GARDNER PARTS LTD
Barton Hall, Hardy Street, Eccles M30 7WA.
Tel: 0161 278 9200
Fax: 0161 787 7549.

*HL SMITH TRANSMISSIONS LTD
Enterprise Business Park, Cross Road, Albrighton, Wolverhampton WV7 3BJ
Tel: 01902 373011
Fax: 01902 373608
E-mail: sales@hlsmith.co.uk
Web site: www.hlsmith.co.uk

LH GROUP (SERVICES) LTD
Graycar Business Park, Barton Turns, Barton Under Needwood DE13 8EN.
Tel: 01283 713615.
Fax: 01283 713551.
E-mail: l/h/llords@classic.msn.com

MAJORLINE ENGINEERING LTD
Baybridge Industrial Units, Baybridge Lane, Owslebury, Winchester SO21 1JN.
Tel: 01962 777077
Fax: 01962 777661, 777667
E-mail: majorline@compuserve.com

MULTIPART PSV
Pilling Lane, Chorley PR7 3EL.
Tel: 01257 225577.
Fax: 01257 225575.
E-mail: info@multipart.com
Web site: www.multipart.co.uk

NEXT BUS LTD
Vincents Road, Bumpers Farm Industrial Estate, Chippenham SN14 6QA
Tel: 01249 462462
Fax: 01249 448844
E-mail: sales@next-bus.co.uk
Web site: www.next-bus.co.uk

PARTLINE LTD
Dockfield Road, Shipley BD17 7AZ
Tel: 01274 531531
Fax: 01274 531088
E-mail: sales@partline.co.uk
Web site: www.partline.co.uk

POWERTRAIN PRODUCTS LTD
Stringes Close, Willenhall WV13 1LE
Tel: 01902 366000
Fax: 01902 366504

QUEENSBRIDGE (PSV) LTD
Milner Way, Ossett HD7 2FB.
Tel: 01924 281871.
Fax: 01924 281807.

SHAWSON SUPPLY LTD
12 Station Road, Saintfield BT24 7DU.
Tel: 028 9751 0994.
Fax: 028 9751 0816.
E-mail: shawson@btinternet.com

*VOITH TURBO LTD
6 Beddington Farm Road, Croydon CR0 4XB
Tel: 020 8667 0333
Fax: 020 8667 0403
E-mail:turbo.uk@voith.com
Web site: www.voith.co.uk

*VOR TRANSMISSIONS LTD
Little London House, St Anne's Road, Little London, Willenhall WV13 1DT
Tel: 08000 184141
Fax: 01902 603868
E-mail: vor@globalnet.co.uk
Web site: www.vor.co.uk

*ZF GREAT BRITAIN LTD
Abbeyfield Road, Lenton, Nottingham NG7 2SX
Tel: 0115 986 9211
Fax: 0115 986 9261
E-mail: info@zf-group.co.uk
Web site: www.zf-group.co.uk

Hand Driers (Coach Mounted)

BRADTECH LTD
Unit 3, Ladford Covert, Seighford, Stafford ST18 9QD
Tel: 01785 282800
Fax: 01785 282558
E-mail: sales@bradtech.ltd.uk

SHADES TECHNICS
Marshgate Drive, Hertford SG13 7AJ
Tel: 01992 501683
Fax: 01992 501669
E-mail: sales@shades-technics.com
Web site: www.shades-technics.com

Handrails

*ABACUS TUBULAR PRODUCTS LTD
Abacus House, Highlode Industrial Estate, Ramsey PE26 2RB
Tel: 01487 710700
Fax: 01487 710626
E-mail: info@abacus-tp.com
Web site: www.abacus-tp.com

CARLYLE BUS & COACH LTD
Carlyle Business Park, Great Bridge Street, Swan Village, West Bromwich B70 0XA
Tel: 0121 524 1200
Fax: 0121 524 1201

CROWN COACHBUILDERS LTD
32 Flemington Industrial Park, Flemington, Motherwell ML1 1SN.
Tel: 01698 276037.
Fax: 01698 276144.
E-mail: davidgreer@hotmail.com
Web site: www.crowncoachbuilders.co.uk

DEANS POWERED DOORS
PO Box 8, Borwick Drive, Grovehill, Beverley HU17 0HQ
Tel: 01482 868111
Fax: 01482 881890
E-mail: info@deans-doors.com

*GABRIEL & CO LTD
Abro Works, 10 Hay Hall Road. Tyseley, Birmingham B11 2AU
Tel: 0121 248 3333
Fax: 0121 248 3330/3331
Web site: www.gabrielco.com

*HAPPICH V & I COMPONENTS LTD
Unit 30/31, Fort Industrial Park, Fort Parkway, Castle Bromwich B35 7AR.
Tel: 0121 747 4400
Fax: 0121 747 4377
E-mail: sales@happich.co.uk
Web site: www.happich.co.uk

IMH BIRMINGHAM LTD
286 Upper Balsall Heath Road, Birmingham B12 9DR.
Tel: 0121 440 4808.
Fax: 0121 440 6520.
E-mail: Sales@imhLTD.com
Web site: www.imhLTD.com

JBF SERVICES LTD
Southedge Works, Hipperholme, Halifax HX3 8EF
Tel: 01422 202840
Fax: 01422 206070
E-mail: jbfservices@aol.com

*THE LAWTON MOTOR BODY BUILDING CO LTD
Knutsford Road, Church Lawton ST7 3DN
Tel: 01270 882056
Fax: 01270 883014
E-mail: info@lawtonmotorbody.co.uk
Web site: www.lawtonmotorbody.co.uk

Headrest Covers and Curtains

*DUOFLEX LTD
Trimingham House, 2 Shires Road, Buckingham Road Industrial Estate, Brackley NN13 7EZ
Tel: 01280 701366
Fax: 01280 704799
E-mail: sales@duoflex.co.uk
Web site: www.duoflex.co.uk

ORVEC INTERNATIONAL LTD
Malmo Road, Hull HU7 0YF.
Tel: 01482 879146
Fax: 01482 878989.
E-mail: service@orvec.co.uk
Web site: www.orvec.co.uk

Heating and Ventilating Systems

AMA LTD
Unit 17, Springmill Industrial Estate, Avening Road, Nailsworth GL6 0BH.
Tel: 01453 832884.
Fax: 01453 832040.
E-mail: ama@ftech.co.uk

CARLYLE BUS & COACH LTD
Carlyle Business Park, Great Bridge Street, Swan Village, West Bromwich B70 0XA
Tel: 0121 524 1200
Fax: 0121 524 1201

*CARRIER SUTRAK
Unit 6, I O Centre, Barn Way, Lodge Farm Industrial Estate, Northampton NN5 7UW
Tel: 01604 581468
Fax: 01604 758132
E-mail: kim.neale@carrier.utc.com

CLAYTON HEATERS LTD
Fletchworth Gate, Burnsall Road, Coventry CV5 6SP.
Tel: 024 7669 1916.
Fax: 024 7669 1969.

*CONSERVE (UK) LTD
Suite 7, Logistics House, Kingsthorpe Road, Northampton NN2 6LJ
Tel: 01604 710055
Fax: 01604 710065
E-mail: information@conserveuk.co.uk
Web site: www.conserveuk.co.uk

*EBERSPACHER (UK) LTD
Headlands Business Park, Salisbury Road, Ringwood BH24 3PB
Tel: 01425 480151
Fax: 01425 480152
E-mail: enquiries@eberspacher.com
Web site: www.eberspacher.com

*HAPPICH V & I COMPONENTS LTD
Unit 30/31, Fort Industrial Park, Fort Parkway, Castle Bromwich B35 7AR.
Tel: 0121 747 4400
Fax: 0121 747 4977
E-mail: sales@happich.co.uk
Web site: www.happich.co.uk

KARIVE LIMITED
PO Box 205, Southam CV47 0ZL
Tel: 01926 813938
Fax: 01926 814898
E-mail: karive.uk@btinternet.com

*NEALINE WINDSCREEN WIPER PRODUCTS
Unit 1, The Sidings Industrial Estate, Birdingbury Road, Marton CV23 9RX
Tel: 01926 633256
Fax: 01926 632600

SUTRAK
See Carrier Sütrak, above.

UWE VERKEN AB (UK branch)
Meadow Works, Walton Summit Industrial Estate, Bamber Bridge, Preston, PR5 8AL.
Tel: 07002 893893.
Fax: 07002 893329.
E-mail: uwe.uk@btinternet.com

WEBASTO PRODUCT UK LTD
Webasto House, White Rose Way, Doncaster Carr DN4 5JH
Tel: 01302 322232
Fax: 01302 322231
E-mail: info@webastouk.com
Web site: www.webastouk.com

Hub Odometers

KELLETT (UK) LTD
8 Stevenson Way, Sheffield S9 3WZ.
Tel: 0114 261 1122.
Fax: 0114 261 1199.
E-mail: sales@kellett.co.uk

MULTIPART PSV
Pilling Lane, Chorley PR7 3EL.
Tel: 01257 225577.
Fax: 01257 225575.
E-mail: info@multipart.com
Web site: www.multipart.co.uk

*PARTLINE LTD
Dockfield Road, Shipley BD17 7AZ
Tel: 01274 531531
Fax: 01274 531088
E-mail: sales@partline.co.uk
Web site: www.partline.co.uk

PIONEER WESTON
Smithfold Lane, Worsley, Manchester M28 0GP.
Tel: 0161 703 2000.
Fax: 0161 703 2025
E-mail: pioneer.weston@wyko.co.uk

ROADLINK INTERNATIONAL LTD
Strawberry Lane, Willenhall WV13 3RL.
Tel: 01902 606210
Fax: 01902 606604
E-mail: sales@roadlink-international.co.uk
Web site: www.roadlink-international.co.uk

WALLMINSTER LTD
24 Charles II St, London SW1Y 4QU
Tel: 020 7976 1840
Fax: 020 7976 1850
E-mail: info@tankcontainers.co.uk

In-Coach Catering Equipment

BRADTECH LTD
Unit 3, Ladford Covert, Seighford, Stafford ST18 9QD
Tel: 01785 282800
Fax: 01785 282558
E-mail: sales@bradtech.ltd.uk

EXPRESS COACH REPAIRS LTD
Outgang Lane, Pickering YO18 7EL.
Tel: 01751 475215.

*THE LAWTON MOTOR BODY BUILDING CO LTD
Knutsford Road, Church Lawton ST7 3DN
Tel: 01270 882056
Fax: 01270 883014
E-mail: info@lawtonmotorbody.co.uk
Web site: www.lawtonmotorbody.co.uk

PSV PRODUCTS
PO Box 166, Warrington WA4 5FG
Tel: 01925 210220.
Fax: 01925 601534
E-mail: daly@merseymail.com
Web site: www.psvproducts.com

SHADES TECHNICS
Marshgate Drive, Hertford SG13 7AJ
Tel: 01992 501683
Fax: 01992 501669
E-mail: sales@shades-technics.com
Web site: www.shades-technics.com

Labels, Nameplates and Decals

*ADGROUP - ADBUS
Ad House, East Parade, Harrogate HG1 5LT.
Tel: 01423 526253
Fax: 01423 502522
E-mail: info@adbus.co.uk
Web site: www.adbus.co.uk

BEST IMPRESSIONS
15 Starfield Road, London W12 9SN
Tel: 020 8740 6993
Fax: 020 8740 9134
E-mail: talk2us@best-impressions.co.uk

*FIRST CHOICE NAMEPLATES, LABELS & SIGNS
Lynden 2c, Russell Avenue, Balderton, Newark NG24 3BT
Tel: 01636 678035
Fax: 01636 707066
E-mail: firstchoice@handbag.com

*THE LAWTON MOTOR BODY BUILDING CO LTD
Knutsford Road, Church Lawton ST7 3DN
Tel: 01270 882056
Fax: 01270 883014
E-mail: info@lawtonmotorbody.co.uk
Web site: www.lawtonmotorbody.co.uk

*NORBURY BLINDS LTD
41-45 Hanley Street, Newtown, Birmingham B19 3SP
Tel: 0121 359 4311
Fax: 0121 359 6388
Web site: www.norbury-blinds.com
E-mail: norburyblinds@talk21.com

Lifts/Ramps (Passenger)

*BROXWOOD VEHICLE SPECIALISTS
Unit 2 Parkside Garage, Old Stafford Road, Slade Heath, Wolverhampton WV10 7PH
Tel: 01902 798770
Fax: 01902 798564
E-mail: sharon@broxwood.net

CROWN COACHBUILDERS LTD
32 Flemington Industrial Park, Flemington, Motherwell ML1 1SN.
Tel: 01698 276087
Fax: 01698 276144
E-mail: davidgreer@hotmail.com
Web site: www.crowncoachbuilders.co.uk

*THE LAWTON MOTOR BODY BUILDING CO LTD
Knutsford Road, Church Lawton ST7 3DN
Tel: 01270 882056
Fax: 01270 883014
E-mail: info@lawtonmotorbody.co.uk
Web site: www.lawtonmotorbody.co.uk

PASSENGER LIFT SERVICES LTD
Unit 10, Crystal Drive, Sandwell Business Park, Smethwick B66 1QG.
Tel: 0121 552 0600.
Fax: 0121 552 0200.

*PERCY LANE PRODUCTS LTD
Lichfield Road, Tamworth B79 7TL
Tel: 01827 63821
Fax: 01827 310159
E-mail: sales@percy-lane.co.uk
Web site: www.percy-lane.co.uk

RATCLIFF TAIL LIFTS LTD
Bessemer Road, Welwyn Garden City AL7 1ET
Tel: 01707 325571
Fax: 01707 327752
Web site: www.ratcliff.co.uk

RICON UK LIMITED
Littlemoss Business Park, Littlemoss Road, Droylsden, Manchester M43 7EF
Tel: 0161 301 6000
Fax: 0161 301 6050
E-mail: info@riconuk.com
Web site: www.riconuk.com

TRUCKALIGN
Truck Align Co Ltd, Vip Trading Estate, Anchor & Hope Lane, Charlton, London SE7 7RY
Tel: 020 8858 3781
Fax: 020 8858 5663

UNWIN SAFETY SYSTEMS
Willow House, Artillery Road, Lufton Trading Estate, Yeovil BA22 8RP
Tel: 01935 410920
Fax: 01935 410921
Web site: www.unwin-safety.com

Lighting / lighting design

ATLAS LIGHTING COMPONENTS
3 King George Close, Eastern Avenue, West Romford RM7 7PP.
Tel: 01708 776375
Fax: 01708 776376

*BRITAX PMG LTD
Bressingby Industrial Estate, Bridlington YO16 4SJ
Tel: 01262 670161
Fax: 01262 605666
E-mail: info@britax-pmg.com
Web site: www.britax-pmg.com

CARLYLE BUS & COACH LTD
Carlyle Business Park, Great Bridge Street, Swan Village, West Bromwich B70 0XA
Tel: 0121 524 1200
Fax: 0121 524 1201

CSM LIGHTING
Suite 1b, Cobb House, Oyster Lane, Byfleet KT14 7DU
Tel: 01932 349661
Fax: 01932 349991
Web site: www.csmauto.com

*HAPPICH V & I COMPONENTS LTD
Unit 30/31, Fort Industrial Park, Fort Parkway, Castle Bromwich B35 7AR.
Tel: 0121 747 4400
Fax: 0121 747 4977
E-mail: sales@happich.co.uk
Web site: www.happich.co.uk

IMEXPART LTD
Links 31, Willowbridge Way, Whitwood, Castleford WF10 5NP
Tel: 0845 6050404
Fax: 01977 513412
E-mail: parts@imexpart.com
Web site: www.imexpart.com

*INVERTEC LTD
Whelford Road, Fairford GL7 4DT
Tel: 01285 713550
Fax: 01285 713548
Mobile: 07802 793828
E-mail: ian@invertec.co.uk
Web site: www.invertec.co.uk

KELLETT (UK) LTD
8 Stevenson Way, Sheffield S9 3WZ.
Tel: 0114 261 1122.
Fax: 0114 261 1199.
E-mail: sales@kellett.co.uk

*THE LAWTON MOTOR BODY BUILDING CO LTD
Knutsford Road, Church Lawton ST7 3DN
Tel: 01270 882056
Fax: 01270 883014
E-mail: info@lawtonmotorbody.co.uk
Web site: www.lawtonmotorbody.co.uk

MULTIPART PSV
Pilling Lane, Chorley PR7 3EL.
Tel: 01257 225577.
Fax: 01257 225575.
E-mail: info@multipart.com
Web site: www.multipart.co.uk

*PARTLINE LTD
Dockfield Road, Shipley BD17 7AZ
Tel: 01274 531531
Fax: 01274 531088
E-mail: sales@partline.co.uk
Web site: www.partline.co.uk

Oil Management Systems

INTERLUBE SYSTEMS LTD
St Modwen Road, Plymouth PL6 8LH
Tel: 01752 676000
Fax: 01752 676001
E-mail: info@interlubesystems.com
Web site: www.interlubesystems.com

STERTIL UK LTD
Unit A, Brackmills Business Park, Caswell Road, Northampton NN4 7PW
Tel: 01604 677334
Fax: 01604 765181
E-mail: info@stertil.com
Web site: www.stertil.com

Painting and Signwriting

*ADGROUP - ADBUS
Ad House, East Parade, Harrogate HG1 5LT.
Tel: 01423 526253
Fax: 01423 502522
E-mail: info@adbus.co.uk
Web site: www.adbus.co.uk

BLACKPOOL COACH SERVICES
Moss Hey Garage, Chapel Road, Blackpool FY4 5HU.
Tel/Fax: 01253 698686

*BROXWOOD VEHICLE SPECIALISTS
Unit 2 Parkside Garage, Old Stafford Road, Slade Heath, Wolverhampton WV10 7PH
Tel: 01902 798770
Fax: 01902 798564
E-mail: sharon@broxwood.net

BULWARK BUS & COACH ENGINEERING LTD
Gate 3, Bulwark Industrial Estate, Chepstow NP16 5QZ
Tel: 01291 622326.
Fax: 01291 622726.

DRURY & DRURY
Unit 6, Cobbs Wood Industrial Estate, Brunswick Road Ashford TN23 1EH.
Tel: 01303 610535.
Fax: 01303 610666.
E-mail: martinstrange@channelcommercials.co.uk

EXPRESS COACH REPAIRS LTD
Outgang Lane, Pickering YO18 7EL.
Tel: 01751 475215.

HANTS & DORSET TRIM LTD
Canada Road, West Wellow SO51 6DE.
Tel: 023 8033 4335

*HATTS COACHWORKS
Foxham, Chippenham SN15 2AY
Tel: 01249 740444
Fax: 01249 740447

*THE LAWTON MOTOR BODY BUILDING CO LTD
Knutsford Road, Church Lawton ST7 3DN
Tel: 01270 882056
Fax: 01270 883014
E-mail: info@lawtonmotorbody.co.uk
Web site: www.lawtonmotorbody.co.uk

*NORBURY BLINDS LTD
41-45 Hanley Street, Newtown, Birmingham B19 3SP
Tel: 0121 359 4311
Fax: 0121 359 6388
Web site: www.norbury-blinds.com
E-mail: norburyblinds@talk21.com

NU-TRACK LTD
Steeple Industrial Estate, Antrim BT41 1AB
Tel: 028 9446 9550
E-mail: enquiries@nu-track.co.uk
Web site: www.nu-track.co.uk

TRUCKALIGN
Truck Align Co Ltd, Vip Trading Estate, Anchor & Hope Lane, Charlton, London SE7 7RY
Tel: 020 8858 3781
Fax: 020 8858 5663

VOLVO COACH CENTRE
Brisco Avenue, off Belton Road West, Loughborough LE11 5HP.
Tel: 01509 217777.
Fax: 01509 260978.

Parts Suppliers

AIR DOOR SERVICES
Unit D, The Pavillions, Holly Lane Industrial Estate, Atherstone CV9 2QZ.
Tel: 01827 711660.
Fax: 01827 713577.
Web site: www.airdoorservices.co.uk

ARRIVA BUS AND COACH LTD
Lodge Garage, Whitehall Road West, Gomersal BD19 4BJ.
Tel: 01274 681144
Fax: 01274 651198
Web site: www.arriva.co.uk
E-mail: busandcoachsales@arriva.co.uk

ASHLEY BANKS LTD
5 King Street Estate, Langtoft, Peterborough PE6 9NF
Tel: 01778 560651
Fax: 01778 560721
E-mail: user@ashleybanks.fsnet.co.uk

*ATLANTIS INTERNATIONAL LTD
Unit 2, 18 Weldon Road, Loughborough LE11 5RA
Tel: 01509 233770
Fax: 01509 210542
E-mail: sales@atlantisint.com
Web site: www.atlantisint.com

M BARNWELL SERVICES LTD
Reginald Road, Smethwick B67 5AS
Tel: 0121 420 0700
Fax: 0121 420 3080
E-mail: sales@barnwell.co.uk

BRT BEARINGS LTD
Algores Way, Wisbech PE13 2TQ
Tel: 01945 464097
Fax: 01945 464523
Web site: www.brt-bearings.com
Email: brt.sales@brt-bearings.com

*BROXWOOD VEHICLE SPECIALISTS
Unit 2 Parkside Garage, Old Stafford Road, Slade Heath, Wolverhampton WV10 7PH
Tel: 01902 798770
Fax: 01902 798564
E-mail: sharon@broxwood.net

BUSS BIZZ
Goughs Transport Depot, Morestead, Winchester SO21 1JD.
Tel: 01962 715555/66.
Fax: 01962 714868.

CARLYLE BUS & COACH LTD
Carlyle Business Park, Great Bridge Street, Swan Village, West Bromwich B70 0XA
Tel: 0121 524 1200
Fax: 0121 524 1201

*CONSERVE (UK) LTD
Suite 7, Logistics House, 1 Horsley Road, Kingsthorpe Road, Northampton NN2 6LJ
Tel: 01604 710055
Fax: 01604 710065
E-mail: information@conserveuk.co.uk
Web site: www.conserveuk.co.uk

CRESCENT FACILITIES LTD
72 Willow Crescent, Chapeltown, Sheffield S35 1QS
Tel: 07718 742466
Fax: 0114 245 1050
E-mail: cfl.chris@btinternet.com

CREST COACH CONVERSIONS
Unit 5, Holmeroyd Road, Bentley Moor Lane, Carcroft, Doncaster DN6 7BH
Tel: 01302 723723
Fax: 01302 724724

CREWE ENGINES
Warmingham Road, Crewe CW1 4PQ
Tel: 01270 526333
Fax: 01270 526433
E-mail: jim@creweengines.co.uk
Web site: www.creweengines.co.uk

*CUMMINS UK
Rutherford Drive, Park Farm South, Wellingborough NN8 6AN
Tel: 01933 334200
Fax: 01933 334198
Web site: www.cummins-uk.com

DIRECT PARTS LTD
Unit 1, Churnet Court, Churnetside Business Park, Harrison Way, Cheddleton ST13 7EF.
Tel: 01538 361777.
Fax: 01538 369100
E-mail: sales@direct-group.co.uk
Web site: www.direct-group.co.uk

ERENTEK
Malt Kiln Lane, Waddington, Lincoln LN5 9RT.
Tel: 01522 720065.
Fax: 01522 729155.

FLIGHTS COACH TRAVEL LTD
Beacon House, Long Acre, Birmingham B7 5JJ
Tel: 0121 322 2222.
Fax: 0121 322 2224.
E-mail: sales@motorcoach.co.uk

GARDNER PARTS LTD
Barton Hall, Hardy Street, Eccles, Manchester M30 7WA.
Tel: 0161 278 9200
Fax: 0161 787 7549.

GREIG OF HEREFORD LTD
Blackfriars Street, Hereford HR4 9HS.
Tel: 01432 352352.
Fax: 01432 358776.

*HAPPICH V & I COMPONENTS LTD
Unit 30/31, Fort Industrial Park, Fort Parkway, Castle Bromwich B35 7AR.
Tel: 0121 747 4400
Fax: 0121 747 4977
E-mail: sales@happich.co.uk
Web site: www.happich.co.uk

THOMAS HARDIE – WIGAN
Lockett Road, Ashton-in-Makerfield WN4 8DE
Tel: 01942 505124.
Fax: 01942 505119.

*HART BROTHERS (ENGINEERING) LTD
Soho Works, Soho Street, Oldham OL2 6BP
Tel: 0161 737 6791

IMEXPART LTD
Links 31, Willowbridge Way, Whitwood, Castleford WF10 5NP
Tel: 0845 6050404
Fax: 01977 513412
E-mail: parts@imexpart.com
Web site: www.imexpart.com

IMPERIAL ENGINEERING
Delamare Road, Cheshunt EN8 9UD
Tel: 01992 634255
Fax: 01992 630506
E-mail: sales@imperialengineering.co.uk
Web site: www.imperialengineering.co.uk

KELLETT (UK) LTD
8 Stevenson Way, Sheffield S9 3WZ
Tel: 0114 261 1122.
Fax: 0114 261 1199.
E-mail: sales@kellett.co.uk

KNORR-BREMSE SYSTEMS FOR COMMERCIAL VEHICLES LTD
Douglas Road, Kingswood, Bristol BS15 8NL.
Tel: 0117 984 6100
Fax: 0117 984 6101.
Web site: www.knorr-bremse.com

*THE LAWTON MOTOR BODY BUILDING CO LTD
Knutsford Road, Church Lawton ST7 3DN
Tel: 01270 882056
Fax: 01270 883014
E-mail: info@lawtonmotorbody.co.uk
Web site: www.lawtonmotorbody.co.uk

MAJORLINE ENGINEERING LTD
Baybridge Industrial Units, Baybridge Lane, Owslebury, Winchester SO21 1JN.
Tel: 01962 777077.
Fax: 01962 777661, 777667
E-mail: majorline@compuserve.com

MOCAP LIMITED
Hortonwood 35, Telford TF1 7YW
Tel: 01952 670247
Fax: 01952 670241
Web site: www.mocap.co.uk
E-mail: sales@mocap.com

MULTIPART PSV
Pilling Lane, Chorley PR7 3EL.
Tel: 01257 225577.
Fax: 01257 225575.
E-mail: info@multipart.com
Web site: www.multipart.co.uk

NEXT BUS LTD
Vincents Road, Bumpers Farm Industrial Estate, Chippenham SN14 6QA
Tel: 01249 462462
Fax: 01249 448844
E-mail: sales@next-bus.co.uk
Web site: www.next-bus.co.uk

*NORBURY BLINDS LTD
41-45 Hanley Street, Newtown, Birmingham B19 3SP
Tel: 0121 359 4311
Fax: 0121 359 6388
Web site: www.norbury-blinds.com
E-mail: norburyblinds@talk21.com

*PARTLINE LTD
Dockfield Road, Shipley BD17 7AZ
Tel: 01274 531531
Fax: 01274 531088
E-mail: sales@partline.co.uk
Web site: www.partline.co.uk

PIONEER WESTON
Smithfold Lane, Worsley, Manchester M28 0GP.
Tel: 0161 703 2000.
Fax: 0161 703 2025
E-mail: pioneer.weston@wyko.co.uk

POWERTRAIN PRODUCTS LTD
Stringes Close, Willenhall WV13 1LE
Tel: 01902 366000
Fax: 01902 366504

PSS-STEERING & HYDRAULICS DIVISION
Folgate Road, North Walsham NR28 0AJ.
Tel: 01692 406017.
Fax: 01692 406957.
E-mail: sales@pss.co.uk
Web site: www.pss.co.uk

SHAWSON SUPPLY LTD
12 Station Road, Saintfield BT24 7DU.
Tel: 028 9751 0994.
Fax: 028 9751 0816.
E-mail: shawson@btinternet.com

*TRAMONTANA COACH DISTRIBUTORS
Chapelknowe Road, Carfin, Motherwell ML1 5LE
Tel: 01698 861790
Fax: 01698 860778
E-mail: wdt@tranta90.freeserve.co.uk

UNITEC PARTS & SERVICE LTD
Manston Lane, Leeds LS15 8SU
Tel: 0113 264 5182
Fax: 0113 260 2294
Web site: www.optare.com

VOLVO COACH CENTRE
Brisco Avenue, off Belton Road West, Loughborough LE11 5HP.
Tel: 01509 217777.
Fax: 01509 260978.

WABCO AUTOMOTIVE UK LTD
Texas Street, Morley, Leeds LS27 0HQ.
Tel: 0113 251 2510.
Fax: 0113 251 2844.

WACTON COACH SALES & SERVICES
Linton Trading Estate, Bromyard HR7 4QL.
Tel: 01885 482782.
Fax: 01885 482127

Passenger Information Systems

HANOVER DISPLAYS LTD
Unit 24, Cliffe Industrial Estate, Lewes BN8 6JL
Tel: 01273 477528
Fax: 01273 407766
E-mail: hanover@hanoverdisplays.com
Web site: www.hanoverdisplays.com

SSL SIMULATION SYSTEMS LTD
Unit 12, Market Industrial Estate, Yatton BS49 4RF
Tel: 01934 838803
Fax: 01934 876202
E-mail: ssl@simulation-systems.co.uk
Web site: www.simulation-systems.co.uk

VULTRON INTERNATIONAL LTD
City Park Industrial Estate, Gelderd Road, Leeds LS12 6DR
Tel: 0113 263 0323
Fax: 0113 279 4127
Web site: www.vultron.co.uk
E-mail: sales@vultron.co.uk

Pneumatic Valves/Cylinders

PNEUMAX LTD
8 Venture Industrial Park, Fareham Road, Gosport PO13 0BA.
Tel: 01329 823999.
Fax: 01329 822345.
E-mail: sales@pneumax.co.uk
Web site: www.pneumax.co.uk

Repairs/Refurbishment — See Body Repairs, above

Retarders and Speed Control Systems

BUSS BIZZ
Goughs Transport Depot, Morestead, Winchester SO21 1JD.
Tel: 01962 715555/66.
Fax: 01962 714868.

CHASSIS DEVELOPMENTS LTD
Grovebury Road, Leighton Buzzard LU7 8SL.
Tel: 01525 374151.
Fax: 01525 370127.

LH GROUP (SERVICES) LTD
Graycar Business Park, Barton Turns, Barton Under Needwood DE13 8EN.
Tel: 01283 713615.
Fax: 01283 713551.
E-mail: l/h/llords@classic.msn.com

MULTIPART PSV
Pilling Lane, Chorley PR7 3EL.
Tel: 01257 225577.
Fax: 01257 225575.
E-mail: info@multipart.com
Web site: www.multipart.co.uk

*SERGEANT (P&P) (B&A) LTD
PO Box 11, New Hall Lane, Hoylake CH47 4DH
Tel: 0151 632 5903
Fax: 0151 632 5908
E-mail: enq@sergeant.co.uk
Web site: www.sergeant.co.uk

TELMA RETARDER LTD
25 Clarke Road, Mount Farm, Milton Keynes MK1 1LG
Tel: 01908 642822
Fax: 01908 641348
E-mail: telma@telma.co.uk
Web site: www.telma.co.uk

*VOITH TURBO LTD
6 Beddington Farm Road, Croydon CR0 4XB
Tel: 020 8667 0333
Fax: 020 8667 0403
E-mail: turbo.uk@voith.com
Web site: www.voith.co.uk

WABCO AUTOMOTIVE UK LTD
Texas Street, Morley LS27 0HQ.
Tel: 0113 251 2510.
Fax: 0113 251 2844

*ZF GREAT BRITAIN LTD
Abbeyfield Road, Lenton, Nottingham NG7 2SX
Tel: 0115 986 9211
Fax: 0115 986 9261
E-mail: info@zf-group.co.uk
Web site: www.zf-group.co.uk

Reversing Safety Systems

*AUTOSOUND LTD
4 Lister Street, Bradford BD11 2DE
Tel: 01274 688990
Fax: 01274 651318
Web site: www.autosound.ltd.uk
E-mail: sales@autosound.ltd.uk

*AVT SYSTEMS
Unit 3/4, Tything Road East, Arden Forest Trading Estate, Alcester B49 6ES
Tel: 01789 400357
Fax: 01789 400359
E-mail: info@avtsystems.co.uk
Web site: www.avtsystems.co.uk

BRIGADE ELECTRONICS plc
Brigade House, The Mills, Station Road,
Brigade Street, South Darenth DA4 9BD
Tel: 0870 774 1500
Fax: 0870 774 1502
E-mail: sales@brigade-electronics.co.uk
Web site: www.brigade-electronics.co.uk,
www.bbs-tek.com

CARLYLE BUS & COACH LTD
Carlyle Business Park, Great Bridge Street,
Swan Village, West Bromwich B70 0XA
Tel: 0121 524 1200
Fax: 0121 524 1201

CLAN TOOLS & PLANT LTD
3 Greenhill Avenue, Giffnock, Glasgow
G46 6QX.
Tel: 0141 638 8040.
Fax: 0141 638 8881.

CYBERLYNE COMMUNICATIONS LTD
Unit 5, Hatfield Way, South Church Industrial
Esate, Bishop Auckland DL14 6XB
Tel: 01388 773761
Fax: 01388 773778
E-mail:
david@cyberlynecommunications.co.uk
Web site:
www.cyberlynecommunications.co.uk

KELLETT (UK) LTD
8 Stevenson Way, Sheffield S9 3WZ.
Tel: 0114 261 1122.
Fax: 0114 261 1199.
E-mail: sales@kellett.co.uk

*****PARTLINE LTD**
Dockfield Road, Shipley BD17 7AZ
Tel: 01274 531531
Fax: 01274 531088
E-mail: sales@partline.co.uk
Web site: www.partline.co.uk

Roller Blinds – Passenger & Driver

*****HAPPICH V & I COMPONENTS LTD**
Unit 30/31, Fort Industrial Park,
Parkway, Castle Bromwich B35 7AR.
Tel: 0121 747 4400
Fax: 0121 747 4977
E-mail: sales@happich.co.uk
Web site: www.happich.co.uk

*****THE LAWTON MOTOR BODY BUILDING CO LTD**
Knutsford Road, Church Lawton ST7 3DN
Tel: 01270 882056
Fax: 01270 883014
E-mail: info@lawtonmotorbody.co.uk
Web site: www.lawtonmotorbody.co.uk

*****MTB EQUIPMENT LTD**
Sixth Avenue, Deeside Industrial Estate,
Welsh Road, Deeside CH5 2LR
Tel: 0870 870 1282
Fax: 01244 289818
E-mail: info@mtb-equipment.com
Web site: www.mtb-equipment.com

WIDNEY UK LTD
Plume Street, Aston, Birmingham B6 7SA
Tel: 0121 327 5500
Fax: 0121 328 2466
E-mail: richard@widney.co.uk

Roof-Lining Fabrics

*****AUTOMATE WHEEL COVERS LTD**
California Mills, Oxford Road, Gomersal,
Cleckheaton BD19 4HQ
Tel: 01274 862700
Fax: 01274 851989
E-mail: sales@wheelcovers.co.uk
Web site: www.euroliners.com

*****AUTOMOTIVE TEXTILE INDUSTRIES**
Unit 126, Springfield Business Park,
Grantham NG31 7BG
Tel: 01476 593050
Fax: 01476 593607
E-mail: sales@autotex.com
Web site: www.autotex.u-net.com

*****HAPPICH V & I COMPONENTS LTD**
Unit 30/31, Fort Industrial Park, Fort
Parkway, Castle Bromwich B35 7AR.
Tel: 0121 747 4400
Fax: 0121 747 4977
E-mail: sales@happich.co.uk
Web site: www.happich.co.uk

Seat Belts

*****ABACUS TUBULAR PRODUCTS LTD**
Abacus House, Highlode Industrial Estate,
Ramsey PE26 2RB
Tel: 01487 710700
Fax: 01487 710626
E-mail: info@abacus-tp.com
Web site: www.abacus-tp.com

*****BROXWOOD VEHICLE SPECIALISTS**
Unit 2 Parkside Garage, Old Stafford Road,
Slade Heath, Wolverhampton WV10 7PH
Tel: 01902 798770
Fax: 01902 798564
E-mail: sharon@broxwood.net

CARLYLE BUS & COACH LTD
Carlyle Business Park, Great Bridge Street,
Swan Village, West Bromwich B70 0XA
Tel: 0121 524 1200
Fax: 0121 524 1201

CONCEPT COACHCRAFT
Far Cromwell Road, Bredbury, Stockport
SK6 2SE
Tel: 0161 406 9322
Fax: 0161 406 9588
E-mail: sales@conceptcoachcraft.com
Web site: www.conceptcoachcraft.com

ELITE SEATBELT SPECIALIST LTD
Unit 6, Adswood Road Industrial Estate,
Stockport SK3 8LF.
Tel: 0161 480 0617.
Fax: 0161 480 3099.
E-mail: elite.seatbelts@btinternet.com
Web site: www.seatbelts.co.uk
Mobile: 0467 486 700 (0161 976 1280 after hours).

*****MTB EQUIPMENT LTD**
Sixth Avenue, Deeside Industrial Estate,
Welsh Road, Deeside CH5 2LR
Tel: 0870 870 1282
Fax: 01244 289818
E-mail: info@mtb-equipment.com
Web site: www.mtb-equipment.com

MULTIPART PSV
Pilling Lane, Chorley PR7 3EL.
Tel: 01257 225577.
Fax: 01257 225575.
E-mail: info@multipart.com
Web site: www.multipart.co.uk

NU-TRACK LTD
Steeple Industrial Estate, Antrim BT41 1AB
Tel: 028 9446 9550
E-mail: enquiries@nu-track.co.uk
Web site: www.nu-track.co.uk

*****PARTLINE LTD**
Dockfield Road, Shipley BD17 7AZ
Tel: 01274 531531
Fax: 01274 531088
E-mail: sales@partline.co.uk
Web site: www.partline.co.uk

Q'STRAINT
175 John Wilson Business Park, Whitstable
CT5 3RB
Tel: 01227 773035
Fax: 01227 770035
E-mail: info@qstraint.co.uk
Web site: www.qstraint.com

SAFETEX LTD
Unit 16/17, Bookham Industrial Park,
Church Road, Bookham KT23 3EV
Tel: 01372 451272
Fax: 01372 451282
E-mail: sales@safetex.com
Web site: www.safetex.com

SECURON (AMERSHAM) LTD
Winchmore Hill, Amersham HP7 0NZ.
Tel: 01494 434455.
Fax: 01494 726499.
E-mail: securon@securon.co.uk
Web site: www.securon.co.uk

*****TRAMONTANA COACH DISTRIBUTORS**
Chapelknowe Road, Carfin, Motherwell ML1 5LE
Tel: 01698 861790
Fax: 01698 860778
E-mail: wdt@tranta90.freeserve.co.uk

UNWIN SAFETY SYSTEMS
Willow House, Artillery Road, Lufton Trading
Estate, Yeovil BA22 8RP
Tel: 01935 410920
Fax: 01935 410921
Web site: www.unwin-safety.com

Seats, Seat Cushions & Seat Frames

*****ABACUS TUBULAR PRODUCTS LTD**
Abacus House, Highlode Industrial Estate,
Ramsey PE26 2RB
Tel: 01487 710700
Fax: 01487 710626
E-mail: info@abacus-tp.com
Web site: www.abacus-tp.com

ARDEE COACH TRIM LTD
Artnalivery, Ardee, Co Louth, Ireland
Tel: 00 353 41 685 3599
Web site: www.ardeecoachtrim.com

Furtex

www.Furtex.co.uk

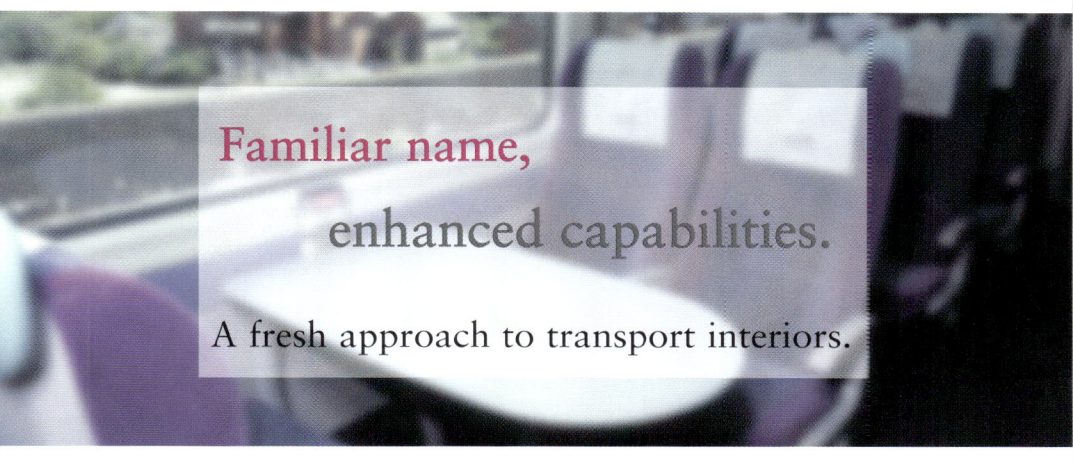

INTERFACE TEXTILES IN MOTION

Familiar name, enhanced capabilities.

A fresh approach to transport interiors.

InterfaceFabrics

www.InterfaceFabrics.com

BLACKPOOL TRIM SHOPS LTD
Brun Grove, Blackpool FY1 6PG.
Tel: 01253 766762
Fax: 01253 798443
E-mail: sales@blackpooltrimshops.co.uk
Web site: www.blackpooltrimshops.co.uk

CARLYLE BUS & COACH LTD
Carlyle Business Park, Great Bridge Street, Swan Village, West Bromwich B70 0XA
Tel: 0121 524 1200
Fax: 0121 524 1201

COGENT PASSENGER SEATING LTD
Unit 12, Prydwen Road, Swansea West Industrial Estate, Swansea SA5 4HN
Tel: 01792 585444
Fax: 01792 588191
Web site: www.cogent.demon.co.uk
E-mail: seats@cogent.demon.co.uk

CONCEPT COACHCRAFT
Far Cromwell Road, Bredbury, Stockport SK6 2SE
Tel: 0161 406 9322
Fax: 0161 406 9588
E-mail: sales@conceptcoachcraft.com
Web site: www.conceptcoachcraft.com

*DUOFLEX LTD
Trimingham House, 2 Shires Road, Buckingham Road Industrial Estate, Brackley NN13 7EZ
Tel: 01280 701366
Fax: 01280 704799
E-mail: sales@duoflex.co.uk
Web site: www.duoflex.co.uk

*HAPPICH V & I COMPONENTS LTD
Unit 30/31, Fort Industrial Park, Fort Parkway, Castle Bromwich B35 7AR.
Tel: 0121 747 4400
Fax: 0121 747 4977
E-mail: sales@happich.co.uk
Web site: www.happich.co.uk

IMH BIRMINGHAM LTD
286 Upper Balsall Heath Road, Birmingham B12 9DR
Tel: 0121 440 4808.
Fax: 0121 440 6520

JAYCAS MINIBUS SALES
11 John Street, Bamber Bridge, Preston PR5 6TJ
Tel/Fax: 01772 321491
E-mail: john@minibusjaycas.co.uk

JBF SERVICES LTD
Southedge Works, Hipperholme, Halifax HX3 8EF
Tel: 01422 202840
Fax: 01422 206070
E-mail: jbfservices@aol.com

KAB SEATING LTD
Round Spinney, Northampton NN3 8RS
Tel: 01604 790500
Fax: 01604 790155

KUSTOMBILT
See RICHARDS & SHAW TRIM, below

*THE LAWTON MOTOR BODY BUILDING CO LTD
Knutsford Road, Church Lawton ST7 3DN
Tel: 01270 882056
Fax: 01270 883014
E-mail: info@lawtonmotorbody.co.uk
Web site: www.lawtonmotorbody.co.uk

LUNAR SEATING LTD
Unit 3, Packhorse Place, Watling Street, Kensworth LU6 3QU
Tel: 01582 841535
Fax: 01582 841749
E-mail: sue@lunar-seating.co.uk

MAJORLINE ENGINEERING LTD
Baybridge Industrial Units, Baybridge Lane, Owslebury, Winchester SO21 1JN.
Tel: 01962 777077.
Fax: 01962 777561, 777667
E-mail: majorline@compuserve.com

*MARTYN INDUSTRIALS LTD
5 Brunel Way, Curranhill Industrial Esate, Harraby, Carlisle CA4 8JZ
Tel: 01228 544000
Fax: 01228 544001
E-mail: enquiries@martyn-industrials.co.uk
Web site: www.martyn-industrials.co.uk

*MTB EQUIPMENT LTD
Sixth Avenue, Deeside Industrial Estate, Welsh Road, Deeside CH5 2LR
Tel: 0870 870 1282
Fax: 01244 289818
E-mail: info@mtb-equipment.com
Web site: www.mtb-equipment.com

METRONET (REW) LTD
130 Bollo Lane, London W3 8BZ.
Tel: 020 7918 6666.
Fax: 020 7918 6599.
E-mail: fraser@r-e-w.co.uk
Web site: www.r-e-w.co.uk

NU-TRACK LTD
Steeple Industrial Estate, Antrim BT41 1AB
Tel: 028 9446 9550
E-mail: enquiries@nu-track.co.uk
Web site: www.nu-track.co.uk

RICHARDS & SHAW TRIM LTD (KUSTOMBILT)
Nomex House, Powke Lane, Cradley Heath B64 5PX.
Tel: 01384 633800.
Fax: 01384 410791
Web site: www.richards-shaw.demon.co.uk

TUBE PRODUCTS LTD
PO Box 13, Oldbury, Warley B69 4PF.
Tel: 0121 552 1511.
Fax: 0121 544 6026.

WOODBRIDGE FOAM UK LTD
Caxton Road, Elms Industrial Estate, Bedford MK41 0EJ.
Tel: 01234 211333.
Fax: 01234 272047

Shock Absorbers/Suspension

ASHLEY BANKS LTD
5 King Street Estate, Langtoft, Peterborough PE6 9NF
Tel: 01778 560651
Fax: 01778 560721
E-mail: user@ashleybanks.fsnet.co.uk

*BROXWOOD VEHICLE SPECIALISTS
Unit 2 Parkside Garage, Old Stafford Road, Slade Heath, Wolverhampton WV10 7PH
Tel: 01902 798770
Fax: 01902 798564
E-mail: sharon@broxwood.net

CARLYLE BUS & COACH LTD
Carlyle Business Park, Great Bridge Street, Swan Village, West Bromwich B70 0XA
Tel: 0121 524 1200
Fax: 0121 524 1201

CRESCENT FACILITIES LTD
72 Willow Crescent, Chapeltown, Sheffield S35 1QS
Tel: 0771 874 2466
Fax: 0114 245 1050
E-mail: cfl.chris@btinternet.com

DIRECT PARTS LTD
Unit 1, Churnet Court, Churnetside Business Park, Harrison Way, Cheddleton ST13 7EF.
Tel: 01538 361777.
Fax: 01538 369100
E-mail: sales@direct-group.co.uk
Web site: www.direct-group.co.uk

*HART BROTHERS (ENGINEERING) LTD
Soho Works, Soho Street, Oldham OL2 6BP
Tel: 0161 737 6791

IMEXPART LTD
Links 31, Willowbridge Way, Whitwood, Castleford WF10 5NP
Tel: 0845 605 0404
Fax: 01977 513412
E-mail: parts@imexpart.com
Web site: www.imexpart.com

IMPERIAL ENGINEERING
Delamare Road, Cheshunt EN8 9UD
Tel: 01992 634255
Fax: 01992 630506
E-mail: sales@imperialengineering.co.uk
Web site: www.imperialengineering.co.uk

KELLETT (UK) LTD
8 Stevenson Way, Sheffield S9 3WZ.
Tel: 0114 261 1122.
Fax: 0114 261 1199.
E-mail: sales@kellett.co.uk

MAJORLINE ENGINEERING LTD
Baybridge Industrial Units, Baybridge Lane, Owslebury, Winchester SO21 1JN.
Tel: 01962 777077.
Fax: 01962 777661, 777667
E-mail: majorline@compuserve.com

MULTIPART PSV
Pilling Lane, Chorley PR7 3EL.
Tel: 01257 225577.
Fax: 01257 225575.
E-mail: info@multipart.com
Web site: www.multipart.co.uk

NEXT BUS LTD
Vincents Road, Bumpers Farm Industrial Estate, Chippenham SN14 6QA
Tel: 01249 462462
Fax: 01249 448844
E-mail: sales@next-bus.co.uk
Web sitel: www.next-bus.co.uk

*PARTLINE LTD
Dockfield Road, Shipley BD17 7AZ
Tel: 01274 531531
Fax: 01274 531088
E-mail: sales@partline.co.uk
Web site: www.partline.co.uk

ROADLINK INTERNATIONAL LTD
Strawberry Lane, Willenhall WV13 3RL.
Tel: 01902 606210
Fax: 01902 606604
E-mail: sales@roadlink-international.co.uk
Web site: www.roadlink-international.co.uk

SHAWSON SUPPLY LTD
12 Station Road, Saintfield BT24 7DU.
Tel: 028 9751 0994.
Fax: 028 9751 0816.
E-mail: shawson@btinternet.com

TRUCKALIGN
Truck Align Co Ltd, Vip Trading Estate, Anchor & Hope Lane, Charlton, London SE7 7RY
Tel: 020 8858 3781
Fax: 020 8858 5663

Steering

*BROXWOOD VEHICLE SPECIALISTS
Unit 2 Parkside Garage, Old Stafford Road, Slade Heath, Wolverhampton WV10 7PH
Tel: 01902 798770
Fax: 01902 798564
E-mail: sharon@broxwood.net

CRESCENT FACILITIES LTD
72 Willow Crescent, Chapeltown, Sheffield S35 1QS
Tel: 0771 874 2466
Fax: 0114 245 1050
E-mail: cfl.chris@btinternet.com

DIRECT PARTS LTD
Unit 1, Churnet Court, Churnetside Business Park, Harrison Way, Cheddleton ST13 7EF.
Tel: 01538 361777.
Fax: 01538 369100
E-mail: sales@direct-group.co.uk
Web site: www.direct-group.co.uk

*HL SMITH TRANSMISSIONS LTD
Enterprise Business Park, Cross Road, Albrighton, Wolverhampton WV7 3BJ
Tel: 01902 373011
Fax: 01902 373608
E-mail: sales@hlsmith.co.uk
Web site: www.hlsmith.co.uk

IMEXPART LTD
Links 31, Willowbridge Way, Whitwood, Castleford WF10 5NP
Tel: 0845 6050404
Fax: 01977 513412
E-mail: parts@imexpart.com
Web site: www.imexpart.com

IMPERIAL ENGINEERING
Delamare Road, Cheshunt EN8 9UD
Tel: 01992 634255
Fax: 01992 630506
E-mail: sales@imperialengineering.co.uk
Web site: www.imperialengineering.co.uk

MAJORLINE ENGINEERING LTD
Baybridge Industrial Units, Baybridge Lane, Owslebury, Winchester SO21 1JN.
Tel: 01962 777077.
Fax: 01962 777661, 777667
E-mail: majorline@compuserve.com

MULTIPART PSV
Pilling Lane, Chorley PR7 3EL.
Tel: 01257 225577.
Fax: 01257 225575.
E-mail: info@multipart.com
Web site: www.multipart.co.uk

NEXT BUS LTD
Vincents Road, Bumpers Farm Industrial Estate, Chippenham SN14 6QA
Tel: 01249 462462
Fax: 01249 448844
E-mail: sales@next-bus.co.uk
Web sitel: www.next-bus.co.uk

*PARTLINE LTD
Dockfield Road, Shipley BD17 7AZ
Tel: 01274 531531
Fax: 01274 531088
E-mail: sales@partline.co.uk
Web site: www.partline.co.uk

POWERTRAIN PRODUCTS LTD
Stringes Close, Willenhall WV13 1LE
Tel: 01902 366000
Fax: 01902 366504

PSS-STEERING & HYDRAULICS DIVISION
Folgate Road, North Walsham NR28 0AJ.
Tel: 01692 406017.
Fax: 01692 406957.
E-mail: sales@pss.co.uk
Web site: www.pss.co.uk

SHAWSON SUPPLY LTD
12 Station Road, Saintfield BT24 7DU.
Tel: 028 9751 0994.
Fax: 028 9751 0816.
E-mail: shawson@btinternet.com

*ZF GREAT BRITAIN LTD
Abbeyfield Road, Lenton, Nottingham NG7 2SX
Tel: 0115 986 9211
Fax: 0115 986 9261
E-mail: info@zf-group.co.uk
Web site: www.zf-group.co.uk

Surveillance Systems

*AUTOSOUND LTD
4 Lister Street, Bradford BD11 2DE
Tel: 01274 688990
Fax: 01274 651318
Web site: www.autosound.ltd.uk
E-mail: sales@autosound.ltd.uk

*AVT SYSTEMS
Unit 3/4, Tything Road East, Arden Forest Trading Estate, Alcester B49 6ES
Tel: 01789 400357
Fax: 01789 400359
E-mail: info@avtsystems.co.uk
Web site: www.avtsystems.co.uk

CLAN TOOLS & PLANT LTD
3 Greenhill Avenue, Giffnock, Glasgow G46 6QX.
Tel: 0141 638 8040.
Fax: 0141 638 8881.

CYBERLYNE COMMUNICATIONS LTD
Unit 5, Hatfield Way, South Church Industrial Esate, Bishop Auckland DL14 6XB
Tel: 01388 773761
Fax: 01388 773778
E-mail: david@cyberlynecommunications.co.uk
Web site: www.cyberlynecommunications.co.uk

KELLETT (UK) LTD
8 Stevenson Way, Sheffield S9 3WZ.
Tel: 0114 261 1122.
Fax: 0114 261 1199.
E-mail: sales@kellett.co.uk

KNORR-BREMSE SYSTEMS FOR COMMERCIAL VEHICLES LTD
Douglas Road, Kingswood, Bristol BS15 8NL.
Tel: 0117 984 6100.
Fax: 0117 984 6101.
Web site: www.knorr-bremse.com

LOOK CCTV LTD
Look House, Aldon Road, Poulton-le-Fylde FY6 8JL
Tel: 01253 891222
Fax: 01253 891221
Web site: www.look-cctv.co.uk
E-mail: enquiries@look-cctv.co.uk

MAJORLINE ENGINEERING LTD
Baybridge Industrial Units, Baybridge Lane, Owslebury, Winchester SO21 1JN.
Tel: 01962 777077.
Fax: 01962 777661, 777667
E-mail: majorline@compuserve.com

MULTIPART PSV
Pilling Lane, Chorley PR7 3EL.
Tel: 01257 225577.
Fax: 01257 225575.
E-mail: info@multipart.com
Web site: www.multipart.co.uk

NU-TRACK LTD
Steeple Industrial Estate, Antrim BT41 1AB
Tel: 028 9446 9550
E-mail: enquiries@nu-track.co.uk
Web site: www.nu-track.co.uk

SHAWSON SUPPLY LTD
12 Station Road, Saintfield BT24 7DU.
Tel: 028 9751 0994.
Fax: 028 9751 0816.
E-mail: shawson@btinternet.com

VERIFEYE (UK) LTD
1 Cortry Close, Poole BH12 4BQ
Tel: 01202 732266
Fax: 01202 730022
E-mail: verifeye@v21mail.co.uk
Web site: www.verifeye.com

WABCO AUTOMOTIVE UK LTD
Texas Street, Morley LS27 0HQ.
Tel: 0113 251 2510
Fax: 0113 251 2844

Tachographs

ARRIVA BUS AND COACH LTD
Lodge Garage, Whitehall Road West, Gomersal BD19 4BJ.
Tel: 01274 681144.
Fax: 01274 651198.
Web site: www.arriva.co.uk
E-mail: busandcoachsales@arriva.co.uk

CHASSIS DEVELOPMENTS LTD
Grovebury Road, Leighton Buzzard LU7 8SL.
Tel: 01525 374151.
Fax: 01525 370127.

ERF MEDWAY LTD
Sir Thomas Longley Road, Medway City Estate, Rochester ME2 4QW.
Tel: 01634 711144.
Fax: 01634 711188.

THOMAS HARDIE – WIGAN
Lockett Road, Ashton-in-Makerfield WN4 8DE.
Tel: 01942 505124.
Fax: 01942 505119.

JAYCAS MINIBUS SALES
11 John Street, Bamber Bridge, Preston PR5 6TJ
Tel/Fax: 01772 321491
E-mail: john@minibusjaycas.co.uk

MAJORLINE ENGINEERING LTD
Baybridge Industrial Units, Baybridge Lane, Owslebury, Winchester SO21 1JN.
Tel: 01962 777077.
Fax: 01962 777661, 777667
E-mail: majorline@compuserve.com

MULTIPART PSV
Pilling Lane, Chorley PR7 3EL.
Tel: 01257 225577.
Fax: 01257 225575.
E-mail: info@multipart.com
Web site: www.multipart.co.uk

NEXT BUS LTD
Vincents Road, Bumpers Farm Industrial Estate, Chippenham SN14 6QA
Tel: 01249 462462
Fax: 01249 448844
E-mail: sales@next-bus.co.uk
Web sitel: www.next-bus.co.uk

*PARTLINE LTD
Dockfield Road, Shipley BD17 7AZ
Tel: 01274 531531
Fax: 01274 531088
E-mail: sales@partline.co.uk
Web site: www.partline.co.uk

SIEMENS VDO TRADING LTD
36 Gravelly Industrial Park, Birmingham B24 8TA
Tel: 0121 326 1234
Fax: 0121 326 1299
Web site: www.siemens-datatrack.com

UNITEC PARTS & SERVICE LTD
Manston Lane, Leeds LS15 8SU
Tel: 0113 264 5132
Fax: 0113 260 2294
Web site: www.optare.com

WARD INTERNATIONAL CONSULTING LTD
Funtley Court, 19 Funtley Hill, Fareham PO16 7UY
Tel: 01329 280280
Fax: 01329 221010
E-mail: info@wardint.fsnet.co.uk
Web site: www.wardint.com

Tachograph Calibrators

MAJORLINE ENGINEERING LTD
Baybridge Industrial Units, Baybridge Lane, Owslebury, Winchester SO21 1JN.
Tel: 01962 777077.
Fax: 01962 777661, 777667
E-mail: majorline@compuserve.com

*MCE LTD
Firbank Way, Leighton Buzzard LU7 4YP
Tel: 01525 375301
Fax: 01525 850967
Web site: www.mce-ltd.com

SIEMENS VDO TRADING LTD
36 Gravelly Industrial Park, Birmingham B24 8TA
Tel: 0121 326 1234
Fax: 0121 326 1299
Web site: www.siemens-datatrack.com

VISECT LTD (TACH:TRAK)
PO Box 1478, Pill, Bristol BS20 0DZ.
Tel: 01275 372274.
Fax: 01275 375091.

Tachograph Chart Analysis Service

CHASSIS DEVELOPMENTS LTD
Grovebury Road, Leighton Buzzard LU7 8SL.
Tel: 01525 374151.
Fax: 01525 370127.

SIEMENS VDO TRADING LTD
36 Gravelly Industrial Park, Birmingham B24 8TA
Tel: 0121 326 1234
Fax: 0121 326 1299
Web site: www.siemens-datatrack.com

*TACHOGRAPH BUREAUX LTD
Lodge Farm, Kineton CV35 0JH
Tel/Fax: 01926 641224
E-mail: sales@tachograph-bureaux.co.uk

Tickets, Ticket Machines and Ticket Systems

*ALMEX INFORMATION SYSTEMS
Metric House, Love Lane, Cirencester GL7 1YG
Tel: 01285 651441
Fax: 01285 650633
E-mail: info@almex.co.uk
Web site: www.hoeft-wessel.de

ATOS ORIGIN
4 Triton Square, Regents Place, London NW1 3HG
Tel: 020 7830 4444

BEMROSEBOOTH LTD
Stockholm Road, Sutton Fields Industrial Estate, Hull HU7 0XY
Tel: 01482 826343
Fax: 01482 371386
E-mail: lprecious@bemrosebooth.com
Web site: www.bemrosebooth.com

*BRITANNIA ROLL/TICKETMEDIA
Maple Works, Old Shoreham Road, Hove BN3 7ED
Tel: 01273 726325
Fax: 01273 324936
E-mail: edmund.jackson@ticketmedia.com
Web site: www.ticketmedia.com

CANN PRINT
Block C, Unit 2, Crookedhold Commercial Centre, Mainroad, Crookedholm, Kilmarnock KA3 6JT.
Tel/Fax: 01563 572440.

CUBIC TRANSPORTATION SYSTEMS LTD
AFC House, Honeycrock Lane, Salfords, Redhill RH1 5LA
Tel: 01737 782200
Fax: 01737 789759
Web site: www.cubic.com

DE LA RUE
De La Rue House, Jays Close, Viables, Basingstoke RG22 4BS
Tel: 01256 605000
Fax: 01256 605004
Web site: www.delarue.com

*KEITH EDMONDSON
The Garden House, Tittensor Road, Tittensor, Stoke-on-Trent ST12 9HQ
Tel: 01782 372305
Fax: 01782 351136
E-mail: kedmo.ticket@zoom.co.uk

*ETM SOFTWARE SERVICES
9 Dorset Avenue, Ferndown BH22 8HJ
Tel: 01202 246710
Fax: 01202 687537
E-mail: info@etmss.com
Web site: www.etmss.com

JOHN GROVES TICKET SYSTEMS
Unit 5, Rennie Business Units, Factory Place, Saltcoats KA21 5LZ
Tel: 01294 471133
Fax: 01294 471166
Web site: www.cambist.se

PJ ASSOCIATES
Locks House, Locks Lane, Wantage OX12 9EH.
Tel: 07071 226593.
Fax: 020 7681 2456.
E-mail: peter.r.johnson@compuserve.com
Web site: www.ourworld.compuserve.com/homepages/peter.r.johnson

SCHADES LTD
Brittain Drive, Codnor Gate Business Park, Ripley DE5 3RZ
Tel: 01773 748721
Fax: 01773 745601
Web site: www.schades.com
E-mail: sales@schades.co.uk

STUART MANUFACTURING CO LTD
Craft House, 135 Hayes Lane, Kenley CR8 5JR
Tel: 020 8668 8107
Fax: 020 8668 8277
E-mail: sales@smco.co.uk
Web site: www.smco.co.uk

MARK TERRILL TICKET MACHINERY
5 De Grey Close, Lewes BN7 2JR
Tel: 01273 474816
Fax: 01273 474816
Mobile: 07770 666159

*THOMAS AUTOMATICS
Bishop Meadow Road, Loughborough LE11 5RE.
Tel: 0700 4 THOMAS (846627)
Fax: 01509 266836.
E-mail: sales@thomasa.co.uk
Web site: www.thomasa.co.uk

*TRANSPORT TICKET SERVICES
Yew Tree Cottage, Newcastle, Monmouth NP25 5NT
Tel/Fax: 01600 750650
E-mail: tts@waitrose.com

*WAYFARER TRANSIT SYSTEMS LTD
10 Willis Way, Fleets Industrial Estate, Poole BH15 3SS
Tel: 01202 339339
Fax: 01202 339324
E-mail: sales@wayfarer.co.uk
Web site: www.wayfarer.co.uk

Timetable Display Frames

*ADGROUP - ADBUS
Ad House, East Parade, Harrogate HG1 5LT.
Tel: 01423 526253
Fax: 01423 502522
E-mail: info@adbus.co.uk
Web site: www.adbus.co.uk

*M BISSELL DISPLAY
20 Spring Road, Walsall WS4 1QQ
Tel: 01922 692300
Fax: 01922 693830
E-mail: sales@bisseldisplay.com
Web site: www.bisseldisplay.com

BROADWATER MOULDINGS LTD
Horham, Eye IP21 5JL.
Tel: 01379 384145.
Fax: 01379 384150.

FIRST CHOICE NAMEPLATES
Lynden 2c, Russell Avenue, Balderton, Newark NG24 3BT
Tel: 01636 678035
Fax: 01636 707066
E-mail: firstchoice@handbag.com

Timetable Printing

BEMROSEBOOTH LTD
Stockholm Road, Sutton Fields Industrial Estate, Hull HU7 0XY
Tel: 01482 826343
Fax: 01482 371386
E-mail: lprecious@bemrosebooth.com
Web site: www.bemrosebooth.com

BEST IMPRESSIONS
15 Starfield Road, London W12 9SN
Tel: 020 8740 6993
Fax: 020 8740 9134
E-mail: talk2us@best-impressions.co.uk

FIGUREHEAD DATA SYSTEMS
Felindre, Swansea SA5 7PP.
Tel: 01792 883155.
Fax: 01792 884934.
E-mail: BusTimes@aol.com

IMAGE & PRINT GROUP
Unit 9, Oakbank Industrial Estate, Garscube Road, Glasgow G20 7LU.
Tel: 0141 353 1900.
Fax: 0141 353 8611.
E-mail: alan@imageandprint.co.uk
Web site: www.imageandprint.co.uk

WILTSHIRE (BRISTOL) LTD
First Avenue, Portbury West, Bristol BS20 9WP.
Tel: 01275 375555.
Fax: 01275 375590.

Toilet Equipment

BRADTECH LTD
Unit 3, Ladford Covert, Seighford, Stafford ST18 9QD
Tel: 01785 282800
Fax: 01785 282558
E-mail: sales@bradtech.ltd.uk

CARLYLE BUS & COACH LTD
Carlyle Business Park, Great Bridge Street, Swan Village, West Bromwich B70 0XA
Tel: 0121 524 1200
Fax: 0121 524 1201

ELSAN LTD
Bellbrook Park, Uckfield TN22 1QF
Tel: 01825 748200
Fax: 01825 761212
E-mail: sales@elsan.co.uk

EXPRESS COACH REPAIRS LTD
Outgang Lane, Pickering YO18 7EL.
Tel: 01751 475215.

IA IAN ALLAN BOOKSHOPS

Trade Directory

Choose from our extensive range for the bus enthusiast, from historic to modern subjects:

- Books
- Magazines
- Die-Cast Models
- Videos
- DVDs
- CD-ROMs
- *& much more...*

BIRMINGHAM
47 Stephenson Street, Birmingham. B2 4DH
Tel: 0121 643 2496
Fax: 0121 643 6855

CARDIFF
31 Royal Arcade, Cardiff. CF10 1AE
Tel: 029 2039 0615
Fax: 029 2039 0621

LONDON
45/46 Lower Marsh, Waterloo, London. SE1 7RG
Tel: 020 7401 2100
Fax: 020 7401 2887

MANCHESTER
5 Piccadilly Station Approach, Manchester. M1 2GH
Tel: 0161 237 9840
Fax: 0161 237 9921

visit: www.ianallan.com   *email:* bookshops@ianallanpublishing.co.uk

Trade Directory

***THE LAWTON MOTOR BODY BUILDING CO LTD**
Knutsford Road, Church Lawton ST7 3DN
Tel: 01270 882056
Fax: 01270 883014
E-mail: info@lawtonmotorbody.co.uk
Web site: www.lawtonmotorbody.co.uk

SHADES TECHNICS
Marshgate Drive, Hertford SG13 7AJ
Tel: 01992 501683
Fax: 01992 501669
E-mail: sales@shades-technics.com
Web site: www.shades-technics.com

Tramway & Light Transit Equipment and Services

ACIS
ACIS House, Knaves Beech Business Centre, Loudwater HP10 9QR
Tel: 01628 524900

ALSTOM TRANSPORT SA
Worldwide headquarters: 48 rue Albert Dhalenne, F-93482 Saint-Ouen Cedex, France
Tel: 00 33 1 41 66 90 00
Fax: 00 33 1 41 66 96 66
Web site: www.transport.alstom.com

BALFOUR BEATTY RAIL PLANT LTD
PO Box 5065, Raynesway, Derby DE21 7QZ
Tel: 01332 661491
Fax: 01332 288222
Web site: www.bbrail.com

BRECKNELL WILLIS & CO LTD
PO Box 10, Chard TA20 2DE
Tel: 01460 64941
Fax: 01460 66122
Web site: www.brecknell-willis.co.uk

BRISTOL ELECTRIC RAILBUS LTD
Heron House, Chiswick Mall, London W4 2PR
Tel: 020 8995 3000
Fax: 020 8994 6060
E-mail: james@skinner.demon.co.uk

***HILTECH DEVELOPMENTS LTD**
22 Larbre Crescent, Whickham, Newcastle upon Tyne NE16 5YG
Tel: 0191 488 6258
Fax: 0191 488 9158
E-mail: executive@hiltechdevelopments.com
Web site: www.hiltechdevelopments.com

***PARRY PEOPLE MOVERS LTD**
Overend Road, Cradley Heath, Dudley B64 7DD
Tel: 01384 569553
Fax: 01384 637753
E-mail: jpmparry@aol.com
Web site: www.parrypeoplemovers.com

PRE METRO OPERATIONS
21 Woodglade Croft, Kings Norton, Birmingham B38 8TD
Tel: 0121 243 9926
E-mail: premetro@aol.com

SIEMENS TRAFFIC CONTROLS LTD
Sopers Lane, Poole BH17 7ER
Tel: 01202 782000
Web site: www.siemenstraffic.com

SUSTRACO LTD
Heron House, Chiswick Mall, London W4 2PR
Tel: 020 8995 3000
Fax: 020 8994 6060
Web site: www.ultralightrail.com

Transmission Overhaul

BUSS BIZZ
Goughs Transport Depot, Morestead, Winchester SO21 1JD.
Tel: 01962 715555/66.
Fax: 01962 714868.

GARDNER PARTS LTD
Barton Hall, Hardy Street, Eccles, Manchester M30 7WA.
Tel: 0161 278 9200
Fax: 0161 787 7549.

***HL SMITH TRANSMISSIONS LTD**
Enterprise Business Park, Cross Road, Albrighton, Wolverhampton WV7 3BJ
Tel: 01902 373011
Fax: 01902 373608
E-mail: sales@hlsmith.co.uk
Web site: www.hlsmith.co.uk

LH GROUP (SERVICES) LTD
Graycar Business Park, Barton Turns, Barton Under Needwood DE13 8EN.
Tel: 01283 713615.
Fax: 01283 713551.
E-mail: l/h/llords@classic.msn.com

METRONET (REW) LTD
130 Bollo Lane, London W3 8BZ.
Tel: 020 7918 6666.
Fax: 020 7918 6599.
E-mail: fraser@r-e-w.co.uk
Web site: www.r-e-w.co.uk

MULTIPART PSV
Pilling Lane, Chorley PR7 3EL.
Tel: 01257 225577.
Fax: 01257 225575.
E-mail: info@multipart.com
Web site: www.multipart.co.uk

PARTLINE LTD
Dockfield Road, Shipley BD17 7AZ
Tel: 01274 531531
Fax: 01274 531088
E-mail: sales@partline.co.uk
Web site: www.partline.co.uk

POWERTRAIN PRODUCTS LTD
Stringes Close, Willenhall WV13 1LE
Tel: 01902 366000
Fax: 01902 366504

QUEENSBRIDGE (PSV) LTD
Milner Way, Ossett HD7 2FB.
Tel: 01924 281871.
Fax: 01924 281807.

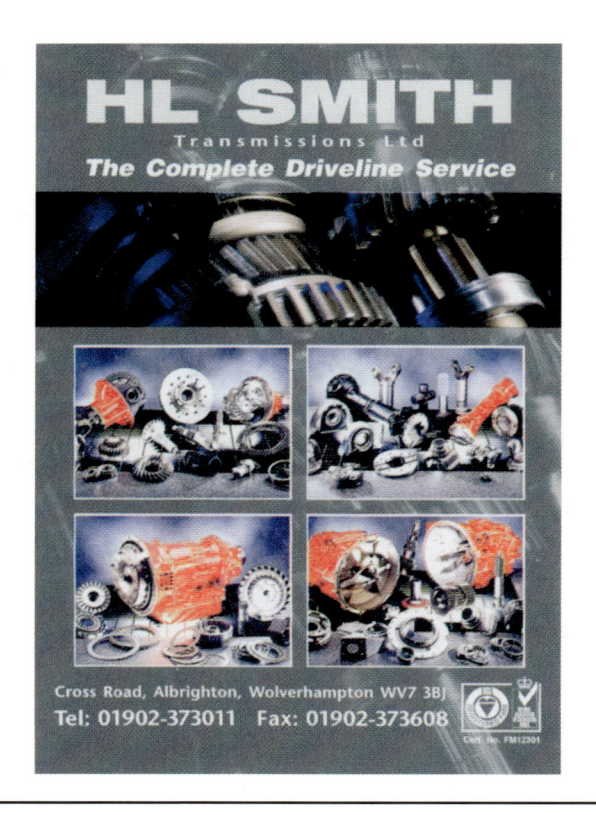

HL SMITH
Transmissions Ltd
The Complete Driveline Service

Cross Road, Albrighton, Wolverhampton WV7 3BJ
Tel: 01902-373011 Fax: 01902-373608

Cert. No. FM12301

UNITEC REPAIR & SERVICE CENTRE
Denby Way, Hellaby, Rotherham S66 8HR
Tel: 01709 535101
Fax: 01709 535103
Web site: www.optare.com

*VOITH TURBO LTD
6 Beddington Farm Road, Croydon CR0 4XB
Tel: 020 8667 0333
Fax: 020 8667 0403
E-mail:turbo.uk@voith.com
Web site: www.voith.co.uk

*VOR TRANSMISSIONS LTD
Little London House, St Anne's Road, Little London, Willenhall WV13 1DT
Tel: 08000 184141
Fax: 01902 603868
E-mail: vor@globalnet.co.uk
Web site: www.vor.co.uk

*ZF GREAT BRITAIN LTD
Abbeyfield Road, Lenton, Nottingham NG7 2SX
Tel: 0115 986 9211
Fax: 0115 986 9261
E-mail: info@zf-group.co.uk
Web site: www.zf-group.co.uk

Tree guards

*GABRIEL & CO LTD
Abro Works, 10 Hay Hall Road. Tyseley, Birmingham B11 2AU
Tel: 0121 248 3333
Fax: 0121 248 3330/3331
Web site: www.gabrielco.com

Tyres

DUNLOP TYRES LTD
TyreFort, 88-98 Wingfoot Way, Birmingham B24 9HY
Tel: 0121 306 6000
Web site: www.dunloptyres.co.uk

SNOWCHAINS EUROPRODUCTS
Borough Green TN15 8DG
Tel: 01732 884408
Web site: www.snowchains.co.uk

Uniforms

ALLEN & DOUGLAS CORPORATE CLOTHING LTD
Compton Park, Wildmere Road, Banbury OX16 3EZ
Tel: 01295 228456
Fax: 01295 278972
E-mail: telesales@aandd.co.uk
Web site: www.aandd.co.uk

*LEISUREWEAR DIRECT LTD
Harpur Hill Industrial Estate, Harpur Hill, Buxton SK17 9JL
Tel: 01298 74737
Fax: 01298 71674
E-mail: jane@leisureweardirect.com
Web site: www.leisureweardirect.com

*IMAGE FIRST CORPORATE CLOTHING LTD
11 Hudswell Road Leeds LS10 1AG
Tel: 0113 243 3855
Fax: 0113 242 1040
E-Mail: reception@image-first.co.uk
Web site: www.image-first.co.uk

TALISMAN
26 North Road, Yate BS37 7DA
Tel: 01454 335155
Fax: 01454 335133
E-mail: sales@talisman.ms.com
Web site: www.talisman.ms.com

Upholstery

*ABACUS TUBULAR PRODUCTS LTD
Abacus House, Highlode Industrial Estate, Ramsey PE26 2RB
Tel: 01487 710700
Fax: 01487 710626
E-mail: info@abacus-tp.com
Web site: www.abacus-tp.com

*AUTOMOTIVE TEXTILE INDUSTRIES
Unit 126, Springfield Business Park, Grantham NG31 7BG
Tel: 01476 593050
Fax: 01476 593607
E-mail: sales@autotex.com
Web site: www.autotex.u-net.com

BLACKPOOL TRIM SHOPS LTD
Brun Grove, Blackpool FY1 6PG.
Tel: 01253 766762
Fax: 01253 798443
E-mail: sales@blackpooltrimshops.co.uk
Web site: www.blackpooltrimshops.co.uk

BRIDGE OF WEIR LEATHER CO LTD
Clydesdale Works, Bridge of Weir PA11 3LF.
Tel: 01505 612132.
Fax: 01505 614964.

*DUOFLEX LTD
Trimingham House, 2 Shires Road, Buckingham Road Industrial Estate, Brackley NN13 7EZ
Tel: 01280 701366
Fax: 01280 704799
E-mail: sales@duoflex.co.uk
Web site: www.duoflex.co.uk

EXPRESS COACH REPAIRS LTD
Outgang Lane, Pickering YO18 7EL.
Tel: 01751 475215.

FIRTH FURNISHINGS LTD
PO Box 22, Flush Mills, Heckmondwike WF16 0EP.
Tel: 01924 406141.
Fax: 01924 401128.

JOHN HOLDSWORTH & CO LTD
Shaw Lodge Mills, Halifax HX3 9ET
Tel: 01422 433000
Fax: 01422 433300
E-mail: info@holdsworth.co.uk
Web site: www.holdsworth.co.uk

INTERFACE FURTEX LTD
Hopton Mills, Mirfield WF1 8HE
Tel: 01924 490591
Fax: 01924 495605
E-mail: james.newton@ev.interfaceinc.com
Web site: www.furtex.co.uk

*THE LAWTON MOTOR BODY BUILDING CO LTD
Knutsford Road. Church Lawton ST7 3DN
Tel: 01270 882056
Fax: 01270 883014
E-mail: info@lawtonmotorbody.co.uk
Web site: www.lawtonmotorbody.co.uk

LISTER FURNISHINGS
Manningham Mills, Heaton, Bradford BD9 4SH.
Tel: 01274 42222.
Fax: 01274 547120.

*MARTYN INDUSTRIALS LTD
5 Brunel Way, Durranhill Industrial Estate, Harraby, Carlisle CA4 8JZ
Tel: 01228 544000
Fax: 01228 544001
E-mail: enquiries@martyn-industrials.co.uk
Web site: www.martyn-industrials.co.uk

METRONET REW LTD
130 Bollo Lane, London W3 8BZ.
Tel: 020 7918 6666.
Fax: 020 7918 6599.
E-mail: fraser@r-e-w.co.uk
Web site: www.r-e-w.co.uk

WIDNEY UK LTD
Plume Street, Aston, Birmingham B6 7SA.
Tel: 0121 327 8500.
Fax: 0121 328 2466.
E-mail: richard@widney.co.uk

Vacuum systems

SMART CENTRAL COACH SYSTEMS
1 Eastholme Court, Belmont, Hereford HR2 7UH
Tel: 01432 276380
Fax: 01432 351800
Web site: www.smartcoachsystems.co.uk
E-mail: info@smartcoachsystems.co.uk

Vehicle Washing & Washers

*ATLANTIS INTERNATIONAL LTD
Unit 2, 18 Welcon Road, Loughborough LE11 5RA
Tel: 01509 233770
Fax: 01509 210542
E-mail: sales@atlantisint.co.uk
Web site: www.atlantisint.co.uk

MONOWASH (BRUSH REPLACEMENT SERVICE)
8 Contessa Close, Farnborough BR6 7ER.
Tel: 01689 860061.
Fax: 01689 861469.

NATIONWIDE CLEANING SYSTEMS LTD
54 Sussex Avenue, Gawsworth, Macclesfield SK11 7UT
Tel: 01625 615983
Web Site: www.nationwide-cleaning.com

SMITH BROS & WEBB
Britannia House, Arden Forest Industrial Estate, Alcester B49 6EX
Tel: 01789 400096
Fax: 01789 400231
E-mail: jbp@vehicle-washing-systems.co.uk
Web site: www.vehicle-washing-systems.co.uk

Trade Directory

*WINDOW CLEAN SERVICES
309 Cow Gate, Edinburgh EH1 1HA
Tel: 0131 556 5720.
Fax: 0131 558 7377

Wheeltrims and Covers

*AUTOMATE WHEEL COVERS LTD
California Mills, Oxford Road, Gomersal, Cleckheaton BD19 4HQ
Tel: 01274 862700
Fax: 01274 851989
E-mail: sales@wheelcovers.co.uk
Web site: www.euroliners.com

CARLYLE BUS & COACH LTD
Carlyle Business Park, Great Bridge Street, Swan Village, West Bromwich B70 0XA
Tel: 0121 524 1200
Fax: 0121 524 1201

HATCHER COMPONENTS LTD
Broadwater Road, Framlingham IP13 9LL.
Tel: 01728 723675.
Fax: 01728 724475.

J. HIPWELL & SON
427 Warwick Road, Greet, Birmingham B20 1JE.
Tel: 0121 706 7175.
Fax: 0121 706 0502.

Windows, Windscreens and Wiper Motors

AUTOGLASS COACH & BUS SERVICES
PO Box 343, Goldington Road, Bedford MK40 3BX.
Tel: 01234 279572.
Fax: 01234 279460.
Central control: Tel: 0800 222777.
Tel: 01234 279559.

*BRITAX PMG LTD
Bressingby Industrial Estate, Bridlington YO16 4SJ
Tel: 01262 670161
Fax: 01262 605666
E-mail: info@britax-pmg.com
Web site: www.britax-pmg.com

*BROXWOOD VEHICLE SPECIALISTS
Unit 2 Parkside Garage, Old Stafford Road, Slade Heath, Wolverhampton WV10 7PH
Tel: 01902 798770
Fax: 01902 798564
E-mail: sharon@broxwood.net

CARLYLE BUS & COACH LTD
Carlyle Business Park, Great Bridge Street, Swan Village, West Bromwich B70 0XA
Tel: 0121 524 1200
Fax: 0121 524 1201

DUDLEYS SCREENWIPERS
Hepworth House, Brook Street, Redditch B98 8NF
Tel: 01527 61243
Fax: 01527 66836
Web site: www.b-hepworth.com
E-mail: bhepworth@b-hepworth.com

EXPRESS COACH REPAIRS LTD
Outgang Lane, Pickering YO18 7EL
Tel: 01751 475215.

INDUSTRIAL & COMMERCIAL WINDOW CO LTD
Unit 2, Caldervale Ind Est, Horbury Junction, Wakefield UF4 5ER.
Tel: 01924 260106.
Fax: 01924 260152.

J W GLASS (STEAMY WINDOWS) LTD
Units 6 & 7, Scropton Road, Hatton DE65 5DT
Tel: 01283 520202
Fax: 01283 520022
E-mail: info@jwglass.co.uk
Web site: www.jwglass.co.uk

*THE LAWTON MOTOR BODY BUILDING CO LTD
Knutsford Road, Church Lawton ST7 3DN
Tel: 01270 882056
Fax: 01270 883014
E-mail: info@lawtonmotorbody.co.uk
Web site: www.lawtonmotorbody.co.uk

MULTIPART PSV
Pilling Lane, Chorley PR7 3EL.
Tel: 01257 225577.
Fax: 01257 225575.
E-mail: info@multipart.com
Web site: www.multipart.co.uk

*NEALINE WINDSCREEN WIPER PRODUCTS
Unit 1, The Sidings Industrial Estate, Birdingbury Road, Marton CV23 9RX
Tel: 01926 633256
Fax: 01926 632600

NU-TRACK LTD
Steeple Industrial Estate, Antrim BT41 1AB
Tel: 028 9446 9550
E-mail: enquiries@nu-track.co.uk
Web site: www.nu-track.co.uk

*PARTLINE LTD
Dockfield Road, Shipley BD17 7AZ
Tel: 01274 531531
Fax: 01274 531088
E-mail: sales@partline.co.uk
Web site: www.partline.co.uk

*PERCY LANE PRODUCTS LTD
Lichfield Road, Tamworth B79 7TL
Tel: 01827 63821
Fax: 01827 310159
E-mail: sales@percy-lane.co.uk
Web site: www.percy-lane.co.uk

*PSV GLASS
Hillbottom Road, High Wycombe HP12 4HJ
Tel: 01494 533131
Fax: 01494 462675
E-mail: sales@psvglass.co.uk

*TRAMONTANA COACH DISTRIBUTORS
Chapelknowe Road, Carfin, Motherwell ML1 5LE
Tel: 01698 861790
Fax: 01698 860778
E-mail: wdt@tranta90.freeserve.co.uk

VOLVO COACH CENTRE
Brisco Avenue, off Belton Road West, Loughborough LE11 5HP.
Tel: 01509 217777.
Fax: 01509 260978.

WIDNEY UK LTD
Plume Street, Aston, Birmingham, B6 7SA.
Tel: 0121 327 5500.
Fax: 0121 328 2466.
E-mail: richard@widney.co.uk

Over 12,500 product lines. Nationwide Delivery.

PSV GLASS
BUS · COACH · RAIL
01494 533131

Bus & Coach Industry Service Providers

Accident Investigation

KERNOW ASSOCIATES
18 Tresawla Court, Tolvaddon, Camborne TR14 0HF.
Tel/Fax: 01209 711870.
E-mail: 106472.3264@compuserve.com

Accountancy and Audit

BARRONS CHARTERED ACCOUNTANTS
Monometer House, Rectory Grove, Leigh on Sea SS9 2HN
Tel: 01702 481910
Fax: 01702 481911
E-mail: mail@barrons-bds.com
Web site: www.barrons-bds.com

CHRIS BORLAND & ASSOCIATES LTD
PO Box 1075, Beaminster DT8 3YA
Tel: 01460 72769
Fax: 01460 72769
E-mail: borland_chris@hotmail.com

Advertising Contractors

*ADGROUP - ADBUS
Ad House, East Parade, Harrogate HG1 5LT.
Tel: 01423 526253
Fax: 01423 502522
E-mail: info@adbus.co.uk
Web site: www.adbus.co.uk

DECKER MEDIA LTD
Decker House, Lowater Street, Carlton, Nottingham NG4 1JJ
Tel: 0115 940 2406.
Fax: 0115 940 2407.
E-mail: sales@deckermedia.co.uk,
Web site: www.deckermedia.co.uk

Advisory Services

AD COACH SALES
Newbridge Coach Depot, Witheridge EX16 8PY
Tel: 01884 860787
Fax: 01884 860711
E-mail: ggoodwin@adcoachsales.co.uk
Web site: www.adcoachsales.co.uk

*ADG TRANSPORT CONSULTANTS
Oak Cottage, Royal Oak, Machen CF83 8SN
Tel: 01633 441491
Fax: 01633 440591.
E-mail: a.dgettins@btinternet.com

AKM TECHSERVICES
Unit F2, Scope House, Weston Road, Crewe CW1 6DD
Tel: 01270 250829
E-mail: akmtec@aol.com

AUSTIN ANALYTICS
Crown House, 183 High Street, Bottisham, Cambridge CB5 9BB.
Tel: 07050 686729.
Fax: 07050 686730.
E-mail: ja@analytics.co.uk
Web site: www.analytics.co.uk

CAPOCO DESIGN
Stone Cross House, Chickgrove, Salisbury SP3 6NA
Tel: 01722 716722
Fax: 01722 716226

*COLIN BUCHANAN AND PARTNERS
Newcombe House, 45 Notting Hill Gate, London W11 3PB
Tel: 020 7309 7000
Fax: 020 7309 0906
E-mail: cbp@cbuchanan.co.uk
Web site: www.cbuchanan.co.uk

*ETM SOFTWARE SERVICES
9 Dorset Avenue, Ferndown BH22 8HJ
Tel: 01202 246710
Fax: 01202 687537
E-mail: info@etmss.com
Web site: www.etmss.com

*FCAV & CO
Brooklyn House, Coleford Road, Bream GL15 6EU
Tel: 01594 564552
Fax: 01594 564556
E-mail: sales@coachaudiovisual.co.uk
Web site: www.coachaudiovisual.co.uk

*MINIMISE YOUR RISK
11 Chatsworth Park, Telscombe Cliffs, Brighton BN10 7DZ
Tel: 01273 580189
Fax: 01273 580189
Web site: www.minimiseyourrisk.co.uk
E-mail: minimise1@btclick.com

MVA
MVA House, Victoria Way, Woking GU21 1DD
Tel: 01483 755207
Web site: www.mva-group.com

*MYSTERY TRAVELLERS
Bestchart Ltd, 6A Mims Yard, Down Road, Horndean, Waterlooville PO8 0YP
Tel: 023 9259 7707
Fax: 023 9259 1700
E-mail: info@bestchart.co.uk
Web site: www.bestchart.co.uk

*PASSENGER TRANSPORT CONSULTANCY ASSOCIATES
1-2 Charity Street, Carlton Scroop, Grantham NG32 3AT
Tel/Fax: 01400 251009
E-mail: petertownley@amserve.com

*ROBERTSON TRANSPORT CONSULTING LTD
Field House, Braceby, Sleaford NG34 0SZ
Tel: 01529 497354
E-mail: robertson@rtclincs.co.uk

*STEPHEN C MORRIS
Transport Writing and Editorial, PO Box 119, Shepperton TW17 8UX
Tel: 01932 232574
Fax: 01932 246394
E-mail: buswriter@aol.com

*SALTIRE COMMUNICATIONS
39 Lilyhill Terrace, Edinburgh EH8 7DR
Tel: 0131 652 0205
Fax: 0131 652 0856
E-mail: gavin@classicbus.sol.uk

STATUS
M M U, Chester Street, Manchester M1 5GD
Tel: 0161 247 6242
Fax: 0161 247 6779
Web site: www.status.org.uk
E-mail: a.g.read@mmu.ac.uk

TRANSPORTATION MANAGEMENT SOLUTIONS
PO Box 15174, Glasgow G3 6WB.
Tel: 0141 332 4733.
Fax: 0141 354 0076.
E-mail: tramsol@aol.com

Artwork

*ADGROUP - ADBUS
Ad House, East Parade, Harrogate HG1 5LT.
Tel: 01423 526253
Fax: 01423 502522
E-mail: info@adbus.co.uk
Web site: www.adbus.co.uk

BEST IMPRESSIONS
15 Starfield Road, London W12 9SN
Tel: 020 8740 6993
Fax: 020 8740 9134
E-mail: talk2us@best-impressions.co.uk

*BRITANNIA ROLL/TICKETMEDIA
Maple Works, Old Shoreham Road, Hove BN3 7ED
Tel: 01273 726325
Fax: 01273 324936
E-mail: edmund.jackson@ticketmedia.com
Web site: www.ticketmedia.com

*FWT
Whittington House, 764-768 Holloway Road, London N19 3JQ
Tel: 020 7281 2161
Fax: 020 7281 4117
E-mail: sales@fwt.co.uk
Web site: www.fwt.co.uk

*TONY GREAVES GRAPHICS
19 Perth Mount, Horsforth, Leeds LS18 5SH
Tel/Fax: 0113 258 4795
E-mail: tony@greavesgraphics.fsnet.co.uk

NEERMAN & PARTNERS
c/o 22 Larbre Crescent, Whickham, Newcastle-upon-Tyne NE16 5YG
Tel: 0191 488 6258
Web site: www.neerman.net
E-mail: executive@neerman.net

*NORBURY BLINDS LTD
41-45 Hanley Street, Newtown, Birmingham B19 3SP
Tel: 0121 359 4311
Fax: 0121 359 6388
Web site: www.norbury-blinds.com
E-mail: norburyblinds@talk21.com

*TIME TRAVEL (UK) DESIGN & MARKETING
247 Bradford Road, Pudsey LS28 6QB
Tel: 0113 255 1188
Mobile: 07967 192901
E-mail: enquiries@bums-on-seats.co.uk
Web site: www.bums-on-seats.co.uk

Auctioneers & Valuators

SHIRLAW-CATHCART
212 Elliot Street, Broomielaw, Glasgow G3 8EX
Tel: 0141 248 6939
Fax: 0141 221 1198
Web site: www.shirlaw-cathcart.co.uk
E-mail: auction@shirlaw-cathcart.co.uk

Breakdown and Recovery Services

NB - Operator lists also indicate bus and coach operators able to provide breakdown and recovery services.

AD COACH SALES
Newbridge Coach Depot, Witheridge EX16 8PY
Tel: 01884 860787
Fax: 01884 860711
E-mail: ggoodwin@adcoachsales.co.uk
Web site: www.adcoachsales.co.uk

BUZZLINES
Unit G1, Lympne Industrial Park, Lympne, Hythe CT21 4LR
Tel: 01303 261870 (mobile 07767 475475)
Fax: 01303 230093
E-mail: sales@buzzlines.co.uk
Web site: www.buzzlines.co.uk

***COACH-AID**
Unit 2, Brindley Close, Tollgate Industrial Estate, Stafford ST16 3SU
Tel: 01785 222666
E-mail: workshop@coach-aid.com

DRURY & DRURY
Unit 6, Cobbs Wood Industrial Estate, Brunswick Road, Ashford TN23 1EH.
Tel: 01303 610555.
Fax: 01303 610666.
E-mail: martinstrange@channelcommercials.co.uk

LANTERN RECOVERY SPECIALISTS PLC
Lantern House, 39/41 High Street, Potters Bar EN6 5AJ
Tel: 0870 6090333
Fax: 01707 640650
Web site: www.lrs.uk.com
E-mail: bob@lrs.uk.com

THOMAS HARDIE – WIGAN
Lockett Road, Ashton-in-Makerfield WN4 8DE.
Tel: 01942 505124
Fax: 01942 505119

***MCE LTD**
Firbank Way, Leighton Buzzard LU7 4YP
Tel: 01525 375301
Fax: 01525 850967
Web site: www.mce-ltd.com

MASS SPECIAL ENGINEERING LTD
Anston, Sheffield S25 4SD.
Tel: 01909 550480.
Fax: 01909 550486.

Coach Driver Agency Coach Hire Broker

AVENTA
66B Victoria Road, Horley RH6 7PZ.
Tel: 01293 825001.
Fax: 01293 825002.
E-mail: info@aventa.co.uk
Web site: www.aventa.co.uk

***COACHFINDER LTD**
Park House, 17 Pottinger Street, Ashton under Lyne OL7 0PW
Tel: 0161 612 8867
Web site: www.coachfinder.uk.com

***DRIVER HIRE CANTERBURY**
East Suite, Parsonage Office, Nackington, Canterbury CT4 7AD
Tel: 01227 479529
Fax: 01227 479531
E-mail: canterbury@driver-hire.co.uk

HAYWARD TRAVEL (CARDIFF)
2 Murch Crescent, Dinas Powys CF64 4RF
Tel: 029 2051 5551
Fax: 029 2051 5113
E-mail: haytvl@aol.com

Coach Interchange & Parking Facilities

***T & E DOCHERTY**
40 Bank Street, Irvine KA12 0LP
Tel: 01294 278440
Web site: www.coach-hires.co.uk

SAMMYS GARAGE
Victoria Coach Station, Arrivals Hall, 3 Eccleston Place, London SW1W 9NF
Tel: 020 7793 7533/7730/8867

***TOP LINE TRAVEL OF YORK LTD**
23 Hospital Fields Road, Fulford Industrial Estate, York YO10 4EW
Tel: 01904 655585
Web site: www.city-sightseeing.com

***VICTORIA COACH STATION LTD**
164 Buckingham Palace Road, London SW1W 9TP
Tel: 020 7824 0000
Fax: 020 7824 0008
Web site: www.tfl.co.uk

Computer Systems/Software

AKM TECHSERVICES
Unit F2, Scope House, Weston Road, Crewe CW1 6DD
Tel: 01270 250829
E-mail: akmtec@aol.com

***AUTOPRO SOFTWARE**
1 Kingsmeadow, Norton Cross, Runcorn WA7 6PB
Tel: 01928 715962
Fax: 01928 714538
E-mail: sales@autoprouk.com
Web site: www.autoprosoftware.com

CYBERLYNE COMMUNICATIONS LTD
Unit 5, Hatfield Way, South Church Industrial Esate, Bishop Auckland DL14 6XB
Tel: 01388 773761
Fax: 01388 773778
E-mail: david@cyberlynecommunications.co.uk
Web site: www.cyberlynecommunications.co.uk

***DISTINCTIVE SYSTEMS LTD**
Amy Johnson Way, York YO30 4XT
Tel: 01904 692269
Fax: 01904 690810
E-mail: sales@distinctive-systems.com
Web site: www.distinctive-systems.com

***ETM SOFTWARE SERVICES**
9 Dorset Avenue, Ferndown BH22 8HJ
Tel: 01202 246710
Fax: 01202 687537
E-mail: info@etmss.com
Web site: www.etmss.com

FIGUREHEAD DATA SYSTEMS
Felindre, Swansea, SA5 7PP.
Tel: 01792 883155.
Fax: 01792 884934.
E-mail: BusTimes@aol.com

GRAMPIAN SOFTWARE LTD
Whitemyres Avenue, Aberdeen AB16 6YY
Tel: 01224 692903
Fax: 01224 693078
E-mail: info@grampian-software.co.uk
Web site: www.grampian-software.co.uk

***HILTECH DEVELOPMENTS LTD**
22 Larbre Crescent, Whickham, Newcastle upon Tyne NE16 5YG.
Tel: 0191 488 6258.
Fax: 0191 488 9158.
E-mail: executive@hiltechdevelopments.com
Web site: www.hiltechdevelopments.com

JOHN GROVES TICKET SYSTEMS
Unit 5, Rennie Business Units, Factory Place, Saltcoats KA21 5LZ
Tel: 01294 471133
Fax: 01294 471166
Web site: www.cambist.se

MCL TRANSPORT CONSULTANTS
PO Box 974, Lewes BN7 1GA
Tel: 01273 486346
Fax: 01273 487446
Web site: www.martlet.uk.com
E-mail: consult@martlett.uk.com

MITEC SYSTEMS
Unit 18, The Business Centre, Eanam Wharf, Blackburn BB1 5BL.
Tel: 01254 679898
Fax: 01254 662590
E-mail: info@mitec-systems.co.uk
Web site: www.mitec-systems.co.uk

ROEVILLE COMPUTER SYSTEMS
Hay Green, Fishlake, Doncaster DN7 5JY
Tel: 01302 841333
Fax: 01302 843966
E-mail: sales@roeville.co.uk
Web site: www.roeville.com

Trade Directory

*TACHOGRAPH BUREAUX LTD
Lodge Farm, Kineton CV35 0JH
Tel/Fax: 01926 641224
E-mail: sales@tachograph-bureaux.co.uk

TAGTRONICS LTD
410 Daisyfield Business Centre, Appleby Street, Blackburn BB1 3BL
Tel: 01254 297732
Fax: 01254 698484
E-mail: info@tagtronics.co.uk
Web site: www.tagtronics.co.uk

TRANMAN SOLUTIONS
Thornbury Office Park, Midland Way, Thornbury BS35 2BS.
Tel: 01454 874000.
Fax: 01454 874001.
E-mail: enquire@tranman.co.uk

TRAVEL INFOSYSTEMS
Tranley House, Tranley Mews, Fleet Road, London NW3 2QW
Tel: 020 7267 7055
Fax: 020 7267 2745
E-mail: sales@travelinfosystems.com
Web site: www.travelinfosystems.com

Consultants

*ADG TRANSPORT CONSULTANTS
Oak Cottage, Royal Oak, Machen CF83 8SN
Tel: 01633 441491
Fax: 01633 440591
E-mail: a.dgettins@btinternet.com

AKM TECHSERVICES
Unit F2, Scope House, Weston Road, Crewe CW1 6DD
Tel: 01270 250829
E-mail: akmtec@aol.com

ATKINS
Television House, Mount Street, Manchester M2 5NT.
Tel: 0161 839 3113.
Fax: 0161 839 3137.
E-mail: peter.kelly@atkinsglobal.com
Web site: www.atkinsglobal.com

AUSTIN ANALYTICS
Crown House, 183 High Street, Bottisham, Cambridge CB5 9BB.
Tel: 07050 686729.
Fax: 07050 686730.
E-mail: ja@analytics.co.uk
Web site: www.analytics.co.uk.

AVENTA
66B Victoria Road, Horley RH6 7DZ.
Tel: 01293 825001.
Fax: 01293 825002.
E-mail: info@aventa.co.uk
Web site: www.aventa.co.uk

BABTIE GROUP LTD
School Green, Shinfield, Reading RG2 9HL.
Tel: 0118 988 1555.
Fax: 0118 988 1653.

IAN BALDRY PUBLIC TRANSPORT SERVICES
43 Cage Lane, Felixstowe IP11 9BJ
Tel: 01394 672344
Fax: 01394 672344
Web site: http://mysite.freeserve.com/ianbaldry
E-mail: ic.baldry@talk21.com

CAREYBROOK LTD
PO Box 205, Southam CV47 0ZL
Tel: 01926 813619
Fax: 01926 814898
E-mail: cb.ltd@btinternet.com

*COLIN BUCHANAN AND PARTNERS
Newcombe House, 45 Notting Hill Gate, London W11 3PB
Tel: 020 7309 7000
Fax: 020 7309 0906
E-mail: cbp@cbuchanan.co.uk
Web site: www.cbuchanan.co.uk

CRESCENT FACILITIES LTD
72 Willow Crescent, Chapeltown, Sheffield S35 1QS
Tel: 07718 742466
Fax: 0114 245 1050
E-mail: cfl.chris@btinternet.com

CRONER.CCH GROUP LTD
145 London Road, Kingston upon Thames KT2 6SR.
Tel: 020 8247 1261.
Fax: 020 8547 2638.
E-mail: info@croner.cch.co.uk

*ELLIS TRANSPORT SERVICES
61 Bodycoats Road, Chandlers Ford SO53 2HA
Tel: 023 8027 0447
Fax: 023 8027 6736
E-mail: info@ellistransportservices.co.uk
Web site: www.ellistransportservices.co.uk

*ETM SOFTWARE SERVICES
9 Dorset Avenue, Ferndown BH22 8HJ
Tel: 01202 246710
Fax: 01202 687537
E-mail: info@etmss.com
Web site: www.etmss.com

*R W FAULKS FCIT
Penthouse J, Ross Court, Putney Hill, London SW15 3NY
Tel: 020 8785 1584

*FCAV & CO
Brooklyn House, Coleford Road, Bream GL15 6EU
Tel: 01594 564552
Fax: 01594 564556
E-mail: sales@coachaudiovisual.co.uk
Web site: www.coachaudiovisual.co.uk

FINANCIAL INSPECTION SERVICES LTD
PO Box 1075, Beaminster DT8 3YA.
Tel: 01460 74337.
Fax: 01460 72154.
E-mail: fininspect@aol.com

*LEONARD GREEN ASSOCIATES
2 Short Clough Close, Reedsholme, Rawtenstall BB4 8PT
Tel: 01706 218539
Fax: 01706 601485
E-mail: lgreen@dsl.pipex.com

*HILTECH DEVELOPMENTS LTD
22 Larbre Crescent, Whickham, Newcastle upon Tyne NE16 5YG.
Tel: 0191 488 6258.
Fax: 0191 488 9158.
E-mail: executive@hiltechdevelopments.com
Web site: www.hiltechdevelopments.com

*ANDY IZATT
10 Briton Court, St Thomas's Road, Spalding PE11 2TS
Tel: 01775 712542
Fax: 01775 712542
E-mail: andy.izatt@btinternet.com
Web site: andy.izatt.btinternet.com

KERNOW ASSOCIATES
18 Tresawla Court, Tolvaddon, Camborne TR14 0HF.
Tel/Fax: 01209 711870.
E-mail: 106472.3264@compuserve.com

*THOMAS KNOWLES
5 Sweetmore Close, Lower Oddington, Moreton-in-Marsh GL56 0XR
Tel: 01451 870932
Fax: 01451 870932
E-mail: twwknowles@hotmail.com

MASS SPECIAL ENGINEERING LTD
Anston, Sheffield S25 4SD.
Tel: 01909 550480.
Fax: 01909 550486.

MAUN INTERNATIONAL
New Cross House, 8-10 Mansfield Road, Sutton in Ashfield NG17 4GR.
Tel: 01623 555621.
Fax: 01623 555671.

MAUNSELL LTD
St James's House, 7 Charlotte Street, Manchester M1 4DZ.
Tel: 0161 236 0766.
Fax: 0161 236 0694.
E-mail: mldmar.maunsell.co.uk
Web site: www.maunsell.co.uk

MCL TRANSPORT CONSULTANTS
PO Box 974, Lewes BN7 1GA
Tel: 01273 486346
Fax: 01273 487446
Web site: www.martlet.uk.com
E-mail: consult@martlett.uk.com

*MINIMISE YOUR RISK
11 Chatsworth Park, Telscombe Cliffs, Brighton BN10 7DZ
Tel: 01273 580189
Fax: 01273 580189
Web site: www.minimiseyourrisk.co.uk
E-mail: minimise1@btclick.com

*STEPHEN C. MORRIS
Transport Writing and Editorial, PO Box 119, Shepperton TW17 8UX
Tel: 01932 232574
Fax: 01932 246394
E-mail: buswriter@aol.com

MOTT MACDONALD
St Anne House Wellesley House, Croydon CR9 2UL
Tel: 020 8774 2000
Fax: 020 8681 5706
E-mail: marketing@mottmac.com
Web site: www.mottmac.com

*MYSTERY TRAVELLERS
Bestchart Ltd, 6A Mims Yard, Down Road, Horndean, Waterlooville PO8 0YP
Tel: 023 9259 7707
Fax: 023 9259 1700
E-mail: info@bestchart.co.uk
Web site: www.bestchart.co.uk

NEERMAN & PARTNERS
c/o 22 Larbre Crescent, Whickham,
Newcastle-upon-Tyne NE16 5YG
Tel: 0191 488 6258
Web site: www.neerman.net
E-mail: executive@neerman.net

*PARRY PEOPLE MOVERS LTD
Overend Road, Cradley Heath, Dudley B64 7DD
Tel: 01384 569553
Fax: 01384 637753
E-mail: jpmparry@aol.com
Web site: www.parrypeoplemovers.com

PJ ASSOCIATES
Locks House, Locks Lane, Wantage OX12 9EH.
Tel: 07071 226593.
Fax: 020 7681 2456.
E-mail: peter.r.johnson@compuserve.com
Web site:
www.ourworld.compuserve.com/homepages/peter.r.johnson

*PASSENGER TRANSPORT CONSULTANCY ASSOCIATES
1-2 Charity Street, Carlton Scroop, Grantham NG32 3AT
Tel/Fax: 01400 251009
E-mail: petertownley@amserve.com

PRE METRO OPERATIONS
21 Woodglade Croft, Kings Norton, Birmingham B38 8TD
Tel: 0121 243 9906
E-mail: premetro@aol.com

*ROBERTSON TRANSPORT CONSULTING LTD
Field House, Braceby, Sleaford NG34 0SZ
Tel: 01529 497354
E-mail: robertson@rtclincs.co.uk

*SALTIRE COMMUNICATIONS
39 Lilyhill Terrace, Edinburgh EH8 7DR
Tel: 0131 652 0205
Fax: 0131 652 0856
E-mail: gavin@classicbus.sol.uk

*TACHOGRAPH BUREAUX LTD
Lodge Farm, Kineton CV35 0JH
Tel/Fax: 01926 641224
E-mail: sales@tachograph-bureaux.co.uk

*TAS PARTNERSHIP LTD
Guildhall House, Guildhall Street, Preston PR1 3NU
Tel: 01772 204988
Fax: 01722 562070
E-mail: info@tas-part.co.uk
Web site: www.tas-part.co.uk

*TIME TRAVEL (UK) DESIGN & MARKETING
247 Bradford Road, Pudsey, Leeds LS28 6QB
Tel: 0113 255 1188
Mobile: 07967 192901
E-mail: enquiries@bums-on-seats.co.uk
Web site: www.bums-on-seats.co.uk

TRANSPORTATION MANAGEMENT SOLUTIONS
PO Box 15174, Glasgow G3 6WB.
Tel: 0141 332 4733.
Fax: 0141 354 0076.
E-mail: tramsol@aol.com

*TRANSPORT DESIGN INTERNATIONAL
12 Waterloo Road Estate, Bidford on Avon B50 4JH
Tel: 01789 490370
Fax: 01789 490592
E-mail:enquiries@tdi.uk.com
Web site: www.tdi.uk.com

WARD INTERNATIONAL CONSULTING LTD
Funtley Court, 19 Funtley Hill, Fareham PO16 7UY
Tel: 01329 280280
Fax: 01329 221010
E-mail: info@wardint.fsnet.co.uk
Web site: www.wardint.com

Cross Sea Carriers

*BRITTANY FERRIES LTD
Group Travel, The Brittany Centre, Wharf Road, Portsmouth PO7 8RU
Tel: 0870 901 2100
Fax: 0870 901 3100
E-mail: grouptravel@brittany-ferries.com

CALEDONIAN MACBRAYNE LTD
Head Office, The Ferry Terminal, Gourock PA19 1QP
Tel: 01475 650100
Web site: www.calmac.co.uk

CIE TOURS INTERNATIONAL
Loveitts Farm, Brinklow CV23 0LG
Tel: 01788 833388
Fax: 01788 833710
E-mail: anne@ciegroups.freeserve.co.uk
Web site: www.cietours.co.uk

CONDOR FERRIES LTD
Condor House, New Harbour Road South, Hamworthy, Poole BH15 4AJ
Tel: 01305 776883
Web site: www.condorferries.co.uk

DFDS TOR LINE LTD
Scandinavia House, Refinery Road, Parkeston CO12 4QG
Tel: 020 1255 242242
Web site: www.dfdsseaways.com
www.dfdstorline.com

EUROTUNNEL SERVICES
PO Box 2000, Folkestone CT18 8XY
Tel: 01303 288660
Web site: www.eurotunnel.com

*FJORD LINE
Royal Quays, North Shields NE29 6EG
Tel: 0191 296 1313
Fax: 0191 296 1540
E-mail: fjordline.uk@fjordline.com
Web site: www.fjordline.com

IRISH FERRIES LTD
Groups Department, Salt Island, Holyhead LL65 1DR
Tel: 01407 764261
Web site: www.irishferries.ie
www.irishferries.com

*ISLE OF MAN STEAM PACKET COMPANY
Imperial Buildings, Douglas IM1 2BY
Tel: 01624 661661
Tel: 01624 645618
E-mail: resesteam-packet.com
Web site: www.steam-packet.com

NORFOLKLINE
Norfolk House, Eastern Dock, Dover CT16 1JA
Tel: 0870 870 1020
Web site: www.norfolkline.com

P&O IRISH SEA LTD
Rosslare Europort, Rosslare, Co Wexford, Ireland
Tel: 00 353 85 57001
Fax: 00 353 83 66422
King George Dock, Hedon Road, Hull HU9 5QA
Tel: 08705 20 20 20
Fax: 01482 706438
Web site: www.poferries.com

P&O FERRIES
Peninsular House, Wharf Road, Portsmouth PO2 8TA
Tel: 0870 08705 20 20 20
Fax: 023 9230 1075
Web site: www.poferries.com

P&O FERRIES
Channel House, Channel View Road, Dover CT17 9TJ
Tel: 08705 980444
Fax: 01304 863884
E-mail: groups@poferries.com
Web site: www.poferries.com

*SEAFRANCE
Whitfield Court, Honeywood Close, Whitfield CT16 3PX
Tel: 08705 711 711
Fax: 01304 828384
E-mail: groups@seafrance.fr
Web site: www.seafrance.com

STENA LINE
Station Approach, Holyhead LL65 1DQ
Web site: www.stenaline.co.uk

SUPERFAST FERRIES
The Terminal Building, Port of Rosyth KY11 2XP
Tel: 0870 234 221
Web site: www.superfast.com

SWANSEA CORK FERRIES LTD
Harbour Office, Kings Dock, Swansea SA1 1SF
Tel: 01792 456116
Fax: 01792 644356
E-mail: scferries@aol.com
Web site: www.swanseacork.ie

*WIGHTLINK FERRIES
70 Broad Street, Portsmouth PO7 2LB
Tel: 023 9285 5242
Fax: 023 9285 5211
E-mail: sales@wightlink.co.uk
Web site: www.wightlink.co.uk

Driver Supply

WEBB'S
St Peters Farm, Middle Drove, Peterborough PE14 8JJ
Tel: 01945 430123
E-mail: webb-s-cant@fsbdial.co.uk

Driver Training

*ADG TRANSPORT CONSULTANTS
Oak Cottage, Royal Oak, Machen CF83 8SN
Tel: 01633 441491
Fax: 01633 440591.
E-mail: a.dgettins@btinternet.com

*INOVAS
1 Glenbervie, Glenbervie Business Park, Larbert, Falkirk FK5 4RB
Tel: 01324 682268
Fax: 01324 682269
Web site: www.inovas.co.uk
E-mail: info@inovas.co.uk

*MINIMISE YOUR RISK
11 Chatsworth Park, Telscombe Cliffs, Brighton BN10 7DZ
Tel: 01273 580189
Fax: 01273 580189
Web site: www.minimiseyourrisk.co.uk
E-mail: minimise1@btclick.com

*OMNIBUS TRAINING LTD
8 Lombard Road, South Wimbledon, London SW19 3TZ
Tel: 020 8543 4499
Fax: 020 8543 0011
E-mail: enquiries@omnibusltd.com

SKILLPLACE TRAINING
Acacia Avenue, Sandfields Estate, Port Talbot SA12 7DW.
Tel: 01639 899849.

TRANSFED
Regency House, 43 High Street, Rickmansworth WD3 1ET.
Tel: 01923 896607.
Fax: 01923 896881

VOSA
Vehicle & Operator Services Agency, Berkeley House, Croydon Street, Bristol BS5 0DA
Tel: 0117 954 3359
Fax: 0117 954 3496
E-mail:commercial@vosa.gsi.gov.uk

Exhibition Organisers

COACH & BUS
PO Box 1359, Leamington Spa CV32 5GT.
Tel: 020 7240 5800.
Fax: 020 7240 5805.
E-mail: info@expom.co.uk
Web site: www.cpt-uk.org

COACH DISPLAYS LTD (UK Coach Rally)
21 The Poynings, Richings Park, Iver SL0 9DS
Tel: 01753 631170
Fax: 01753 655980
E-mail:
uk.rally@coachdisplays.demon.co.uk

EXPOMANAGEMENT LTD
Linden House, 21 Dormer Place, Leamington Spa CV32 5AA.
Tel: 01926 888123.
Fax: 01926 888004.
E-mail: info@expom.co.uk
Web site: www.expocoach.com

MCI EXHIBITIONS LTD
Starley House, Eaton Road, Coventry CV1 2FH.
Tel: 0870 330 7834.
Fax: 0870 076 3292
E-mail: john@motorcycleshow.co.uk
Web site: www.motorcycleshow.co.uk

Finance and Leasing

AD COACH SALES
Newbridge Coach Depot, Witheridge EX16 8PY
Tel: 01884 860787
Fax: 01884 860711
E-mail: ggoodwin@adcoachsales.co.uk
Web site: www.adcoachsales.co.uk

ARRIVA BUS AND COACH LTD
Lodge Garage, Whitehall Road West, Gomersal BD19 4BJ.
Tel: 01274 681144.
Fax: 01274 651198.
Web site: www.arriva.co.uk
E-mail: busandcoachsales@arriva.co.uk

BANK OF SCOTLAND LTD
Tel: 0845 300 4624
Web site:
www.bankofscotland.co.uk/business

*DAWSONRENTALS BUS AND COACH LTD
Delaware Drive, Tongwell, Milton Keynes MK15 8JH
Tel: 01908 218111
Fax: 01908 610156
E-mail: info@dawsongroup.co.uk
Web site: www.dawsongroup.co.uk

*HANSAR FINANCE LTD
Bridgeway House, Mellor Road, Cheadle Hulme SK8 5AU.
Tel: 0161 488 4000
Fax: 0161 488 4567
Web site: www.hansar.co.uk

LHE FINANCE LTD
21 Headlands Business Park, Salisbury Road, Ringwood BH24 3PB
Tel: 01425 474070
Fax: 01425 474090
E-mail: sales@lhefinance.co.uk
Web site: www.lhefinance.co.uk

NORTON FOLGATE FG PLC
50A St Andrew Street, Hertford SG14 1JA.
Tel: 01992 537735
Fax: 01992 537733

*MISTRAL GROUP (UK) PLC
PO Box 130, Knutsford WA16 6AG
Tel: 0870 2415786
Fax: 0870 241 5784
E-mail: sales@mistral-group.com
Web site: www.mistral-group.com

ROADLEASE
Crossroads, Anston, Sheffield S25 7ES.
Tel: 01909 551177.
Fax: 01909 567994.
E-mail: roadlease@kirkbycoachandbus.com
Web site: www.roadlease.com

VOLVO FINANCIAL SERVICES
Wedgnock Lane, Warwick CV34 5YA
Tel: 01926 498888
Fax: 01926 410278

Graphic Design

*ADGROUP - ADBUS
Ad House, East Parade, Harrogate HG1 5LT.
Tel: 01423 526253
Fax: 01423 502522
E-mail: info@adbus.co.uk
Web site: www.adbus.co.uk

BEST IMPRESSIONS
15 Starfield Road, London W12 9SN
Tel: 020 8740 6993
Fax: 020 8740 9134
E-mail: talk2us@best-impressions.co.uk

BLACKPOOL TRIM SHOPS LTD
Brun Grove, Blackpool FY1 6PG
Tel: 01253 766732
Fax: 01253 798443
E-mail: sales@blackpooltrimshops.co.uk
Web site: www.blackpooltrimshops.co.uk

*FWT
Whittington House, 764-768 Holloway Road, London N19 3JC
Tel: 020 7281 2161
Fax: 020 7281 4117
E-mail: sales@fwt.co.uk
Web site: www.fwt.co.uk

IMAGE & PRINT GROUP
Unit 9, Oakbank Industrial Estate, Garscube Road, Glasgow G20 7LU
Tel: 0141 353 1900
Fax: 0141 353 8611

PINDAR PLC
31 Edison Road, Rabans Lane Industrial Estate, Aylesbury HP19 8TE
Tel/fax: 01296 390100
Web site: www.pindarplc.com

Hotels

CALOTELS HOTELS
88 Jordan Avenue, Stretton, Burton-on-Trent DE13 0JD
Tel: 01283 542455
Fax: 01283 542455

CIE TOURS INTERNATIONAL
Loveitts Farm, Brinklow CV23 0LG
Tel: 01788 833358
Fax: 01788 833710
E-mail: anne@ciegroups.freeserve.co.uk
Web site: www.cietours.co.uk

GREATDAYS TRAVEL GROUP
2 Stamford Park Road, Altrincham WA15 9EN
Tel: 0161 928 9966
Fax: 0161 928 1332
E-mail: sales@greatdays.co.uk
Web site: www.greatdays.co.uk

GREATDAYS TRAVEL GROUP
10 Thurloe Place. London SW7 2RZ
Tel: 020 7581 5606
Fax: 020 7225 0068
E-mail: sales@london.greatdays.co.uk
Web site: www.greatdays.co.uk

STAGE HOTEL – LEICESTER
299 Leicester Road, (A5199) Wigston Fields, Leicester LE18 1JW
Tel: 0116 288 6161
Fax: 0116 281 1874

Trade Directory

Insurance

BELMONT INTERNATIONAL LTD
1 The Square, Riverhead, Sevenoaks TN13 2AA.
Tel: 01732 744700.
Fax: 01732 744729.
Web site: www.belmontint.com

R. L. DAVISON & CO LTD
Bury House, 31 Bury Street, London EC3A 5AH.
Tel: 020 7816 9876.
Fax: 020 7816 9880.

*LEONARD GREEN ASSOCIATES
2 Short Clough Close, Reedsholme, Rawtenstall BB4 8PT.
Tel: 01706 218539
Fax: 01706 601485
E-mail: len@lghreen.f9.co.uk

JARDINE TRANSPORTATION RISKS
See Omni Whittington, below

OMNI WHITTINGTONS
Arthur Castle House, 33 Creechurch Lane, London EC3A 5EB.
Tel: 020 7709 9991
Fax: 020 7456 1225.

*TOWERGATE CHAPMAN STEVENS
Towergate House, 22 Wintersells Roaod, Wintersells Business Park, Byfleet KT14 7LF
Tel: 01932 334140
Fax: 01932 351238
E-mail: tcs@towergate.co.uk
Web site: www.towergate.co.uk

VOLVO INSURANCE SERVICES
Wedgnock Lane, Warwick CV34 5YA
Tel: 01926 401777.
Fax: 01926 407407.
Web site: www.volvobuses.volvo.co.uk
www.volvo.com

WILSURE INSURANCE BROKERS
9 Crusader Business Park, Stephenson Road West, Clacton on Sea CO15 4TN.
Tel: 01255 420564.
Fax: 01255 222764.
E-mail: info@wilsure.co.uk
Web site: www.wilsure.co.uk

WRIGHTSURE GROUP
799 London Road, West Thurrock RM20 3LH.
Tel: 01708 865553.
Fax: 01708 865100.
E-mail: info@wrightsure.com
Web site: www.wrightsure.com

Legal and Operations Advisers

*ELLIS TRANSPORT SERVICES
61 Bodycoats Road, Chandlers Ford SO53 2HA
Tel: 023 8027 0447
Fax: 023 8027 6736
E-mail: info@ellistransportservices.co.uk
Web site: www.ellistransportservices.co.uk

FREIGHT TRANSPORT ASSOCIATION
Hermes House, St John's Road, Tunbridge Wells TN4 9UZ.
Tel: 01892 526171.

KERNOW ASSOCIATES
18 Tresawla Court, Tolvaddon, Camborne TR14 0HF.
Tel/Fax: 01209 711870.
E-mail: 106472.3264@compuserve.com

*MINIMISE YOUR RISK
11 Chatsworth Park, Telscombe Cliffs, Brighton BN10 7DZ
Tel: 01273 580189
Fax: 01273 580189
Web site: www.minimiseyourrisk.co.uk
E-mail: minimise1@btclick.com

WARD INTERNATIONAL CONSULTING LTD
Funtley Court, 19 Funtley Hill, Fareham PO16 7UY
Tel: 01329 280280
Fax: 01329 221010
E-mail: info@wardint.fsnet.co.uk
Web site: www.wardint.com

WEDLAKE SAINT
14 John Street, London WC1N 2EB.
Tel: 020 7405 9446.
Fax: 020 7242 9877.

Life Insurance and Pensions

BELMONT INTERNATIONAL LTD
1 The Square, Riverhead, Sevenoaks TN13 2AA.
Tel: 01732 744700.
Fax: 01732 744729.
Web site: www.belmontint.com

WILSURE INSURANCE BROKERS
9 Crusader Business Park, Stephenson Road West, Clacton on Sea CO15 4TN.
Tel: 01255 420564.
Fax: 01255 222764.
E-mail: info@wilsure.co.uk
Web site: www.wilsure.co.uk

Livery Design

*ADGROUP - ADBUS
Ad House, East Parade, Harrogate HG1 5LT.
Tel: 01423 526253
Fax: 01423 502522
E-mail: info@adbus.co.uk
Web site: www.adbus.co.uk

BEST IMPRESSIONS
15 Starfield Road, London W12 9SN
Tel: 020 8740 6993
Fax: 020 8740 9134
E-mail: talk2us@best-impressions.co.uk

DRURY & DRURY
Unit 6, Cobbs Wood Industrial Estate, Brunswick Road, Ashford TN23 1EH.
Tel: 01303 610555.
Fax: 01303 610666.
E-mail: martinstrange@channelcommercials.co.uk

*TONY GREAVES GRAPHICS
19 Perth Mount, Horsforth, Leeds LS18 5SH
Tel/Fax: 0113 258 4795
E-mail: tony@greavesgraphics.fsnet.co.uk

*HATTS COACHWORKS
Foxham, Chippenham SN15 2AY
Tel: 01249 740444
Fax: 01249 740447

NEERMAN & PARTNERS
c/o 22 Larbre Crescent, Whickham, Newcastle-upon-Tyne NE16 5YG
Tel: 0191 488 6258
Web site: www.neerman.net
E-mail: executive@neerman.net

*NORBURY BLINDS LTD
41-45 Hanley Street, Newtown, Birmingham B19 3SP
Tel: 0121 359 4311
Fax: 0121 359 6388
Web site: www.norbury-blinds.com
E-mail: norburyblinds@talk21.com

*TIME TRAVEL (UK) DESIGN & MARKETING
247 Bradford Road, Pudsey, Leeds LS28 6QB
Tel: 0113 255 1188
Mobile: 07967 192901
E-mail: enquiries@bums-on-seats.co.uk
Web site: www.bums-on-seats.co.uk

Maps for the Bus Industry

BEST IMPRESSIONS
15 Starfield Road, London W12 9SN
Tel: 020 8740 6993
Fax: 020 8740 9134
E-mail: talk2us@best-impressions.co.uk

FIGUREHEAD DATA SYSTEMS
Felindre, Swansea SA5 7PP
Tel: 01792 883155.
Fax: 01792 884934.
E-mail: BusTimes@aol.com

*FWT
Whittington House, 764-768 Holloway Road, London N19 3JQ
Tel: 020 7281 2161
Fax: 020 7281 4117
E-mail: sales@fwt.co.uk
Web site: www.fwt.co.uk

*TONY GREAVES GRAPHICS
19 Perth Mount, Horsforth, Leeds LS18 5SH
Tel/Fax: 0113 258 4795
E-mail: tony@greavesgraphics.fsnet.co.uk

IMAGE & PRINT GROUP
Unit 9, Oakbank Industrial Estate, Garscube Road, Glasgow G20 7LU.
Tel: 0141 353 1900.
Fax: 0141 353 8611.
E-mail: alan@imageandprint.co.uk
Web site: www.imageandprint.co.uk

*TIME TRAVEL (UK) DESIGN & MARKETING
247 Bradford Road, Pudsey, Leeds LS28 6QB
Tel: 0113 255 1188
Mobile: 07967 192901
E-mail: enquiries@bums-on-seats.co.uk
Web site: www.bums-on-seats.co.uk

Mechanical Investigation

KERNOW ASSOCIATES
18 Tresawla Court, Tolvaddon, Camborne TR14 0HF.
Tel/Fax: 01209 711870.
E-mail: 106472.3264@compuserve.com

On-Bus Advertising

*ADGROUP - ADBUS
Ad House, East Parade, Harrogate HG1 5LT.
Tel: 01423 526253
Fax: 01423 502522
E-mail: info@adbus.co.uk
Web site: www.adbus.co.uk

BEST IMPRESSIONS
15 Starfield Road, London W12 9SN
Tel: 020 8740 6993
Fax: 020 8740 9134
E-mail: talk2us@best-impressions.co.uk

*BRITANNIA ROLL/TICKETMEDIA
Maple Works, Old Shoreham Road, Hove BN3 7ED
Tel: 01273 726325
Fax: 01273 324936
E-mail: edmund.jackson@ticketmedia.com
Web site: www.ticketmedia.com

DECKER MEDIA LTD
Decker House, Lowater Street, Carlton, Nottingham NG4 1JJ
Tel: 0115 940 2406
Fax: 0115 940 2407
E-mail: sales@deckermedia.co.uk
Web site: www.deckermedia.co.uk

*FCAV & CO
Brooklyn House, Coleford Road, Bream GL15 6EU
Tel: 01594 564552
Fax: 01594 564556
E-mail: sales@coachaudiovisual.co.uk
Web site: www.coachaudiovisual.co.uk

*TONY GREAVES GRAPHICS
19 Perth Mount, Horsforth, Leeds LS18 5SH
Tel/Fax: 0113 258 4795
E-mail: tony@greavesgraphics.fsnet.co.uk

*TIME TRAVEL (UK) DESIGN & MARKETING
247 Bradford Road, Pudsey, Leeds LS28 6QB
Tel: 0113 255 1188
Mobile: 07967 192901
E-mail: enquiries@bums-on-seats.co.uk
Web site: www.bums-on-seats.co.uk

Printing

*ADGROUP - ADBUS
Ad House, East Parade, Harrogate HG1 5LT.
Tel: 01423 526253
Fax: 01423 502522
E-mail: info@adbus.co.uk
Web site: www.adbus.co.uk

*IAN ALLAN PRINTING LTD
Riverdene Business Park, Molesey Road, Hersham KT12 4RG.
Tel: 01932 266600
Fax: 01932 266601
E-mail: jonathan.bingham@ianallanprinting.co.uk
Web site: www.ianallanprinting.co.uk

BEMROSEBOOTH LTD
Stockholm Road, Sutton Fields Industrial Estate, Hull HU7 0XY
Tel: 01482 826343
Fax: 01482 371386
E-mail: lprecious@bemrosebooth.com
Web site: www.bemrosebooth.com

BEST IMPRESSIONS
15 Starfield Road, London W12 9SN
Tel: 020 8740 6993
Fax: 020 8740 9134
E-mail: talk2us@best-impressions.co.uk

THE HENRY BOOTH GROUP
Stockholm Road, Sutton Fields Industrial Estate, Hull HU7 0XY
Tel: 01482 826343.
Fax: 01482 839767.
E-mail: mshanley@henrybooth.co.uk
Web site: www.henrybooth.co.uk

*BRITANNIA ROLL/TICKETMEDIA
Maple Works, Old Shoreham Road, Hove BN3 7ED
Tel: 01273 726325
Fax: 01273 324936
E-mail: edmund.jackson@ticketmedia.com
Web site: www.ticketmedia.com

FIGUREHEAD DATA SYSTEMS
Felindre, Swansea SA5 7PP
Tel: 01792 883155.
Fax: 01792 884934
E-mail: BusTimes@aol.com

*FWT
Whittington House, 764-768 Holloway Road, London N19 3JQ
Tel: 020 7281 2161
Fax: 020 7281 4117
E-mail: sales@fwt.co.uk
Web site: www.fwt.co.uk

*FIRST CHOICE NAMEPLATES, LABELS & SIGNS
Lynden 2c, Russell Avenue, Balderton, Newark NG24 3BT
Tel: 01636 678035
Fax: 01636 707066
E-mail: firstchoice@handbag.com

*TONY GREAVES GRAPHICS
19 Perth Mount, Horsforth, Leeds LS18 5SH
Tel/Fax: 0113 258 4795
E-mail: tony@greavesgraphics.fsnet.co.uk

IMAGE & PRINT GROUP
Unit 9, Oakbank Industrial Estate, Garscube Road, Glasgow G20 7LU
Tel: 0141 353 1900
Fax: 0141 353 8611
E-mail: alan@imageandprint.co.uk
Web site: www.imageandprint.co.uk

*NORBURY BLINDS LTD
41-45 Hanley Street, Newtown, Birmingham B19 3SP
Tel: 0121 359 4311
Fax: 0121 359 6388
Web site: www.norbury-blinds.com
E-mail: norburyblinds@talk21.com

*TIME TRAVEL (UK) DESIGN & MARKETING
247 Bradford Road, Pudsey LS28 6QB
Tel: 0113 255 1188
Mobile: 07967 192901
E-mail: enquiries@bums-on-seats.co.uk
Web site: www.bums-on-seats.co.uk

*TRANSPORT STATIONERY SERVICES
61 Bodycoats Road, Chandlers Ford SO53 2HA
Tel: 07041 471008
Fax: 07041 471009
E-mail: info@transportstationeryservices.co.uk
Web site: www.transportstationeryservices.co.uk

Promotional Material

*ADGROUP - ADBUS
Ad House, East Parade, Harrogate HG1 5LT.
Tel: 01423 526253
Fax: 01423 502522
E-mail: info@adbus.co.uk
Web site: www.adbus.co.uk

BEST IMPRESSIONS
15 Starfield Road, London W12 9SN
Tel: 020 8740 6993
Fax: 020 8740 9134
E-mail: talk2us@best-impressions.co.uk

*BRITANNIA ROLL/TICKETMEDIA
Maple Works, Old Shoreham Road, Hove BN3 7ED
Tel: 01273 726325
Fax: 01273 324936
E-mail: edmund.jackson@ticketmedia.com
Web site: www.ticketmedia.com

FIGUREHEAD DATA SYSTEMS
Felindre, Swansea SA5 7PP.
Tel: 01792 883155.
Fax: 01792 884934.
E-mail: BusTimes@aol.com

*FIRST CHOICE NAMEPLATES, LABELS & SIGNS
Lynden 2c, Russell Avenue, Balderton, Newark NG24 3BT
Tel: 01636 678035
Fax: 01636 707066
E-mail: firstchoice@handbag.com

*FWT
Whittington House, 764-768 Holloway Road, London N19 3JQ
Tel: 020 7281 2161
Fax: 020 7281 4117
E-mail: sales@fwt.co.uk
Web site: www.fwt.co.uk

*TONY GREAVES GRAPHICS
19 Perth Mount, Horsforth, Leeds LS18 5SH
Tel/Fax: 0113 258 4795
E-mail: tony@greavesgraphics.fsnet.co.uk

*NORBURY BLINDS LTD
41-45 Hanley Street, Newtown, Birmingham B19 3SP
Tel: 0121 359 4311
Fax: 0121 359 6388
Web site: www.norbury-blinds.com
E-mail: norburyblinds@talk21.com

*TIME TRAVEL (UK) DESIGN & MARKETING
247 Bradford Road, Pudsey, Leeds LS28 6QB
Tel: 0113 255 1188
Mobile: 07967 192901
E-mail: enquiries@bums-on-seats.co.uk
Web site: www.bums-on-seats.co.uk

Publications, Magazines and Reference Books

*BRITISH BUS PUBLISHING
16 St Margarets Drive, Wellington, Telford TF1 3PH
Tel: 01952 255669
E-mail: bill@britishbuspublishing.co.uk
Web site: www.britishbuspublishing.co.uk

*BUSES
Ian Allan Publishing Ltd
Riverdene Business Park, Molsey Road, Hersham KT12 4RG.
Tel: 01932 266600
Fax: 01932 266601
Web site: www.busesmag.com

*BUS & COACH BUYER
The Publishing Centre, 1 Woolram Wygate, Spalding PE11 1NU
Tel: 01775 711777
Fax: 01775 711777
E-mail: bcbsales@busandcoachbuyer.com

BUS AND COACH PROFESSIONAL
2 Crown Street, Wellington TF1 1LP
Tel: 01952 415334
Fax: 01952 245077.
E-mail: info@ww.busandcoach.com
Web site: www.busandcoach.com

BUS USER
National Federation of Bus Users, PO Box 320, Portsmouth PO5 3SD
Tel: 023 9281 4493
Fax: 023 9285 3080
Web site: www.nfbu.org

COACH & BUS WEEK
Bretton Court, Bretton, Peterborough PE3 8DZ
Tel: 01733 467778
Fax: 01733 467770
E-mail: jacqui.grobler@emap.com
Web site: www.cbwnet.com

CRONER CCH GROUP LTD
145 London Road, Kingston upon Thames KT2 6SR
Tel: 020 8247 1261
Fax: 020 8547 2638
E-mail: info@croner.cch.co.uk

*TONY GREAVES GRAPHICS
19 Perth Mount, Horsforth, Leeds LS18 5SH
Tel/Fax: 0113 258 4795
E-mail: tony@greavesgraphics.fsnet.co.uk

JANES URBAN TRANSPORT SYSTEMS
163 Brighton Road, Coulsdon CR5 2YH
Tel: 020 8700 3700
Web site: www.janes.com/www.juts.janes.com

ROUTE ONE
Expo Publishing, Suite 4, Century House, Towermead Business Park, Fletton, Peterborough PE2 9DY
Tel: 0870 241 8745
Fax: 0870 241 8891
E-mail: mike.morgan@route-one.net
Web site: www.route.one.net

TRANSIT
Landor Publishing, 3rd Floor Quadrant House, 250 Kennington Lane, London SE11 5RD
Tel: 020 7820 0848
Fax: 020 7587 0497

Quality Management Systems

FTA VEHICLE INSPECTION SERVICE
Hermes House, St John's Road, Tunbridge Wells TN4 9UZ.
Tel: 01892 526171
Fax: 01892 534989
E-mail: enquiries@fta.co.uk
Web site: www.fta.co.uk

*MYSTERY TRAVELLERS
Bestchart Ltd, 6A Mims Yard, Down Road, Horndean, Waterlooville PO8 0YP
Tel: 023 9259 7707
Fax: 023 9259 1700
E-mail: info@bestchart.co.uk
Web site: www.bestchart.co.uk

*PASSENGER TRANSPORT CONSULTANCY ASSOCIATES
1-2 Charity Street, Carlton Scroop, Grantham NG32 3AT
Tel/Fax: 01400 251009
E-mail: petertownley@amserve.com

WARD INTERNATIONAL CONSULTING LTD
Funtley Court, 19 Funtley Hill, Fareham PO16 7UY
Tel: 01329 280280
Fax: 01329 221010
E-mail: info@wardint.fsnet.co.uk
Web site: www.wardint.com

Timetable Production

BEMROSEBOOTH LTD
Stockholm Road, Sutton Fields Industrial Estate, Hull HU7 0XY
Tel: 01482 826343
Fax: 01482 371386
E-mail: lprecious@bemrosebooth.com
Web site: www.bemrosebooth.com

BEST IMPRESSIONS
15 Starfield Road, London W12 9SN
Tel: 020 8740 6993
Fax: 020 8740 9134
E-mail: talk2us@best-impressions.co.uk

FIGUREHEAD DATA SYSTEMS
Felindre, Swansea SA5 7PP.
Tel: 01792 883155.
Fax: 01792 884934.
E-mail: BusTimes@aol.com

*FWT
Whittington House, 764-768 Holloway Road, London N19 3JQ
Tel: 020 7281 2161
Fax: 020 7281 4117
E-mail: sales@fwt.co.uk
Web site: www.fwt.co.uk

*TONY GREAVES GRAPHICS
19 Perth Mount, Horsforth, Leeds LS18 5SH
Tel/Fax: 0113 258 4795
E-mail: tony@greavesgraphics.fsnet.co.uk

IMAGE & PRINT GROUP
Unit 9, Oakbank Industrial Estate, Garscube Road, Glasgow G20 7LU.
Tel: 0141 353 1900.
Fax: 0141 353 8611.
E-mail: alan@imageandprint.co.uk
Web site: www.imageandprint.co.uk

SOUTHERN VECTIS PLC
Nelson Road, Newport PO30 1RD.
Tel: 01983 812983.
E-mail: pwhite@southernvectis.com
Web site: www.southernvectis.com

*TIME TRAVEL (UK) DESIGN & MARKETING
247 Bradford Road, Pudsey, Leeds LS28 6QB
Tel: 0113 255 1188
Mobile: 07967 192901
E-mail: enquiries@bums-on-seats.co.uk
Web site: www.bums-on-seats.co.uk

TRAVEL INFOSYSTEMS
Tranley House, Tranley Mews, Fleet Road, London NW3 2QW
Tel: 020 7267 7055
Fax: 020 7267 2745
E-mail: sales@travelinfosystems.com
Web site: www.travelinfosystems.com

Tour Wholesalers

BOTEL LTD
Botel House, 50 Northern Road, Wickersley, Rotherham S66 1EN
Tel: 01709 703535
Fax: 01709 703525
Web site: www.botel.co.uk

*CI COACHLINES
14 Tugby Place, Chelmsford CM1 4XL
Tel: 01245 248669
E-mail: cicoachlines@btopenworld.com

CIE TOURS IINTERNATIONAL
Loveitts Farm, Brinklow CV23 0LG
Tel: 01788 833388
Fax: 01788 833710
E-mail: anne@ciegroups.freeserve.co.uk
Web site: www.cietours.co.uk

FJORD LINE
Royal Quays, North Shields NE29 6EG.
Tel: 0191 296 1313.
Fax: 0191 296 1540.
E-mail: fjordline.uk@fjordline.com
Web site: www.fjordline.com

GREATDAYS TRAVEL GROUP
Travel House, 2 Stamford Park Road, Altrincham WA15 9EN
Tel: 0161 928 9966
Fax: 0161 928 1332
E-mail: sales@greatdays.co.uk
Web site: www.greatdays.co.uk
Sales Dir: Paul Beaumont

GROUPWAYS LEISURE LTD
Overseas House, Broadway Court, The Broadway, Chesham HP5 1EG.
Tel: 01494 792722.
Fax: 01494 792723.
E-mail: sales@groupways.co.uk
Web site: www.groupways.co.uk

*TRAVELPATH 3000
PO Box 32, Grantham NG31 7JA
Tel: 01476 570187
Fax: 01476 572718
E-mail: info@travelpath-uk.com
Web site: www.travelpath3000.com

Training and Marketing Services

*ADG TRANSPORT CONSULTANTS
Oak Cottage, Royal Oak, Machen CF83 8SN
Tel: 01633 441491
Fax: 01633 440591.
E-mail: a.dgettins@btinternet.com

AVENTA
66B Victoria Road, Horley RH6 7DZ.
Tel: 01293 825001.
Fax: 01293 825002.
E-mail: info@aventa.co.uk
Web site: www.aventa.co.uk

*CREATIVE MANAGEMENT DEVELOPEMNT LTD
Okebourne Park, Liden, Swindon SN3 6AJ

Tel: 01793 428401
Fax: 01793 428401
E-mail: jowencmd@aol.com
Web site: www.cmd-training.co.uk

CRONER.CCH GROUP LTD
145 London Road, Kingston upon Thames KT2 6SR.
Tel: 020 8247 1261.
Fax: 020 8547 2638.
E-mail: info@croner.cch.co.uk

ELLIS TRANSPORT SERVICES
61 Bodycoats Road, Chandlers Ford SO53 2HA
Tel: 023 8027 0447
Fax: 023 8027 6736
E-mail: info@ellistransportservices.co.uk

KERNOW ASSOCIATES
18 Tresawla Court, Tolvaddon, Camborne TR14 0HF.
Tel/Fax: 01209 711870.
E-mail: 106472.3264@compuserve.com

*MINIMISE YOUR RISK
11 Chatsworth Park, Telscombe Cliffs, Brighton BN10 7DZ
Tel: 01273 580189
Fax: 01273 580189
Web site: www.minimiseyourrisk.co.uk
E-mail: minimise1@btclick.com

*OMNIBUS TRAINING LTD
8 Lombard Road, South Wimbledon SW19 3TZ
Tel: 020 8543 4499
Fax: 020 8543 0011
E-mail: enquiries@omnibusltd.com

*PASSENGER TRANSPORT CONSULTANCY ASSOCIATES
1-2 Charity Street, Carlton Scroop, Grantham NG32 3AT
Tel/Fax: 01400 251009
E-mail: petertownley@amserve.com

*SALTIRE COMMUNICATIONS
39 Lilyhill Terrace, Edinburgh EH8 7DR
Tel: 0131 652 0205
Fax: 0131 652 0856
E-mail: gavin@classicbus.sol.uk

TRANSFED
Regency House, 43 High Street, Rickmansworth WD3 1ET.
Tel: 01923 896607.
Fax: 01923 896381.

More popular annuals from Ian Allan PUBLISHING

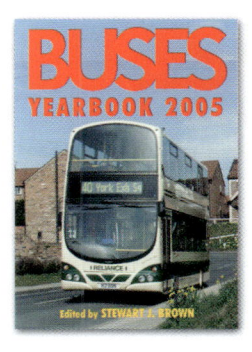

Buses Yearbook 2005
S J Brown
ISBN: 0 7110 2997 0
235mm x 172mm HB
128pp £13.99

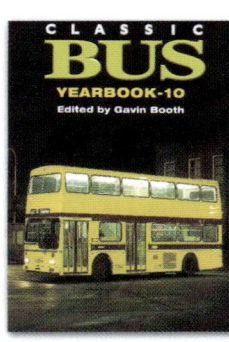

Classic Bus Yearbook 10
G Booth
ISBN: 0 7110 2996 2
235mm x 172mm HB
128pp £14.99

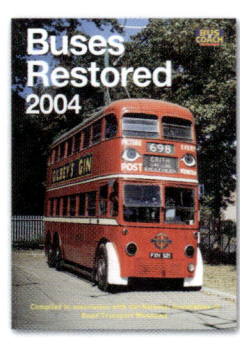

Buses Restored 2004
NARTM
ISBN: 0 7110 3019 7
235mm x 172mm PB
128pp £13.99

ORDER VIA POST, FAX OR E-MAIL TO:

Ian Allan Publishing Mail Order Dept, 4 Watling Drive, Hinckley, Leics LE10 3EY

Tel: 01455 254450
Fax: 01455 233737

e-mail:
midlandbooks@compuserve.com

Online:
www.ianallansuperstore.com

Visit our website on:
www.ianallanpublishing.com

Interested in Transport subjects?

Like a good read?
FREE?
send for our illustrated catalogue

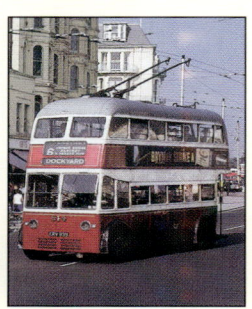

Call 01455 254 470 or write to:

Midland Counties Publications
4 Watling Drive, Hinckley,
Leicestershire LE10 3EY

E-mail midlandbooks@compuserve.com
www.midlandcountiessuperstore.com

section 2
Tendering & Regulatory Authorities

Tendering & Regulatory Authorities etc	
PTAs	54
PTEs	54
Transport Co-ordinating Officers	55
Traffic Commissioners	57
Department for Transport	58

Passenger Transport Authorities

*Greater Manchester PTA:
PO Box 532, Town Hall, Manchester M60 2LA
Tel: 0161 234 3335
Fax: 0161 236 6459
Chmn: Cllr J. R. Jones. **Vice-Chmn**: Cllr G. Harkin.

Merseyside PTA:
24 Hatton Garden, Liverpool L3 2AN
Tel: 0151 227 5181
Fax: 0151 236 2457
Chmn: Cllr Mark Dowd; **Vice-Chmn**: Cllr Hugh G. Lloyd;
Clerk: Steve Maddox; **Gen Man Mersey Tunnels**: John Gillard.
Operates with Merseyside PTE (qv) as Merseytravel.

South Yorkshire PTA:
PO Box 37, Regent Street, Barnsley S70 2PQ.
Tel: 01226 772848.
Web site: www.southyorks.org.uk
Chmn: Cllr J. M. Hoare; **Vice-Chmn**: Cllr M. Edgell;
Clerk/Treasurer: W J Wilkinson.

Strathclyde PTA:
See Strathclyde Passenger Transport

Tyne & Wear PTA:
Civic Centre, Newcastle upon Tyne NE99 2BN.
Tel: 0191 203 3209.
Fax: 0191 203 3180.
Chmn: Cllr T. D. Marshall; **Vice-Chairman & Monitoring Officer**:
E. Holt; **Clerk**: K. G. Lavery; **Deputy Clerk & Treasurer**:
D. Johnson; **Engineer**: J. Millar; **Legal advisor**: V. A. Dodds.

*West Midlands PTA:
Room 120, Centro House, 16 Summer Lane, Birmingham B19 3SD.
Tel: 0121 236 0661
Fax: 0121 233 1841
Web site: www.wmpta.ork.uk
E-mail for Councillors: PTAteam@centro.org.uk
E-mail for Committee Team: PTA team@centro.org.uk
Chair: Cllr R V Worrall **Vice-Chair**: Cllr G S Manku
Clerk: Ms S Manzie **Deputy Clerk/Solicitor**: C Hinde **Treasurer**:
Ms A Ridgewell

*West Yorkshire PTA:
Wellington House, 40-50 Wellington Street, Leeds LS1 2DE.
Tel: 0113 251 7272.
Fax: 0113 251 7373.
Chmn: Cllr M. Lyons; **Vice-Chmn**: Cllr G. Phelps;
Clerkto the Authority: K. T. Preston.

Passenger Transport Executives

*GMPTE

9 Portland Street, Manchester M60 1HX **Tel**: 0161 242 6000
GMPTE is responsible to the Greater Manchester Passenger Transport Authority. The PTE is responsible for contracting socially necessary bus services and supporting the local rail service. It also owns the Metrolink light rail system on behalf of the Authority and is responsible for planning for the future of the Metrolink network.
GMPTE and the Authority are also committed to developing accessible transport, funding Ring and Ride, a fully accessible door to door transport service for people with mobility difficulties.
The PTE administers the concessionary fares scheme, which allows participants (pensioners, children and people with disabilities) either free or reduced rate travel. GMPTE owns and is responsible for the upkeep of bus stations and on-street infrastructure. It also provides information about public transport through telephone information lines, timetables, general publicity and Travelshops.

Director General: C J Mulligan
Director of Monitoring: Tim Tristram
Director of Planning & Communications: Keith Howcroft

Director of Projects & Infrastructure: Michael Renshaw
Director of Organisational Development & Performance: Carlena Higton

Merseyside Passenger Transport Authority and Executive (Merseytravel)

24 Hatton Garden, Liverpool L3 2AN **Tel**: 0151 227 5181
Fax: 0151 236 2457 **Web site**: www.merseytravel.gov.uk
Merseytravel ensures the availability of public transport in Merseyside, including financial support for the Merseyrail rail network and those bus services not provided for by the private sector.
It also promotes public transport by providing bus stations and infrastructure, comprehensive travel tickets and free travel with minimum restrictions for the elderly and those with mobility difficulties.
Merseytravel also owns and operates the Mersey ferries and Mersey tunnels.
Chair to PTA: Cllr M. Dowd. **Vice-Chair to PTA**: Cllr H. Lloyd.
Chief Executive PTA & Director General PTE: Neil Scales.
Clerk to PTA: Steve Maddox. **Director of Resources**: John Wilkinson. **Director of Operations**: Brian Fisher. **Secretary, PTE**: Louise Outram. **Tunnels Manager**: John Gillard.

Nexus (Tyne & Wear PTE)

Nexus House, St James Boulevard, Newcastle upon Tyne NE1 4AX
Tel: 0191 203 3333 **Fax**: 0191 203 3180
Web site: www.nexus.org.uk
Metro: www.tyneandwearmetro.co.uk
Nexus operates within the policies of the Tyne & Wear Passenger Transport Authority. Nexus owns and operates both the Tyne & Wear Metro system - extended in 2002 to South Hylton via Sunderland - and the Shields Ferry (between North Shields and South Shields). Nexus financially supports the rail service between Newcastle and Sunderland; ensures that bus services not operated commercially are provided where there is evidence of social need; operates a demand-responsive transport system, U-call; and organises the provision of special transport for those who can only use ordinary public transport with difficulty if at all. Nexus adminsters the Concessionary Travel scheme and provides comprehensive travel information and sales outlets for countywide season tickets, as well as related administrative support for the scheme.
Director General: M. J. Parker; **Development Director**: B. Garner;
Director of Metro: K Mackay **Non-exec Directors**: I. Stratford (Clerk to the PTA); Paul Woods (Treasurer to the PTA); J. F. Miller (Engineer to the Tyne Tunnel); A. Sarginson; J. V. Anderson. **Secretary**: G. E. Merrylees.
Rolling Stock: 90 light rail cars. **Ferries**: MFs 'Pride of the Tyne' and 'Shieldsman'

South Yorkshire Passenger Transport Executive

PO Box 801, Exchange Street, Sheffield S2 5YT
Tel: 0114 276 7575 **Fax**: 0114 275 9908
Web site: www.sypte.co.uk (also for customer comments)
The Executive is responsible to the South Yorkshire Passenger Transport Authority.

*Strathclyde Passenger Transport (SPT)

Consort House, 12 West George Street, Glasgow G2 1HN
Tel: 0141 332 6811   **Fax**: 0141 332 3076   **Web site**: www.spt.co.uk
SPT is Scotland's only passenger transport authority and executive, investing in rail, bus, Subway and ferry services for 42% of Scotland's population. .
Director General: M. C. Reed, 0141 333 3100; **Director of Operations**: D. Ferguson, 0141 333 3244; **Director of Corporate Affairs**: W. I. Wylie, 0141 333 3179; **Director (Non Executive)**: Aiden O'Donnell; **Chair**: Cllr A Watson; **Vice chairs**: Cllr D McLachlan, Cllr D Selfridge.

Transport for London

Windsor House, 42-50 Victoria Street, London SW1H 0NL
Tel: 020 7941 4000
Web Site: www.tfl.gov.uk
Transport for London (TfL) took over most of the functions of London Transport from July 2000. It is under the control of the Mayor of London and Greater London Authority. TfL assumed control of London Underground Ltd in 2003.
The board comprises:
Ken Livingstone (**Chair, Mayor of London**), **Vice Chair**: Dave Wetzel **Board Members**: David Begg, Bob Crow, Stephen Glaister, Noel Hawerth, Kirsten Hearn, Mike Hodgkinson, Oli Jackson, Susan Kramer, Paul Moore, Murziline Parchment, David Quarmby, Tony West, Brian Heiser, Lynne Sloman
Commissioner of Transport for London: Robert Kiley.
Director of Surface Transport: Peter Hendy.
Director of Road Safety Unit: Chris Lines
Director of Street Management: Peter Hendy
Web Site: www.streetmanagement.org.uk
Director of Integration: Jeroen Weimar

TfL's subsidiary companies:

London Bus Services Ltd (t/a London Buses)
172 Buckingham Palace Road, London SW1W 9TN.
Tel: 020 7222 5600.
Man Dir: Peter Hendy. **Fin Dir:** W. G. Bostock. **Procurement Dir:** vacant. **Ops & Services Dir:** G. Elliott. **Strategy Dir:** R. W. Hallé. **Comm Dir:** vacant.

London Buses Ltd (t/a East Thames Buses)
172 Buckingham Palace Road, London SW1W 9TN.
Tel: 020 7222 5600. **Man Dir:** Alan Barrett

Victoria Coach Station Ltd
164 Buckingham Palace Road, London SW1W 9TP.
Tel: 020 7730 3466. **Fax:** 020 7730 2589. **Man Dir:** W. Hillman.

Transport Trading Ltd
55 Broadway, London SW1H 0BD. **Tel:** 020 7222 5600.

London River Services Ltd
55 Broadway, London SW1H 0BD. **Tel:** 020 7222 5600.
Man Dir: G. Elliott.

London Underground Ltd
55 Broadway, London SW1H 0BD. **Tel:** 020 7222 5600

*West Midlands Passenger Transport Executive (Centro)

16 Summer Lane, Birmingham B19 3SD **Tel: 0121 200 2787**
Fax: 0121 214 7010
The Executive is responsible to the West Midlands Passenger Transport Authority
Director General: Rob Donald
Services Director: Robert Smith
Projects Director: Tom Magrath
Resources Director: Trevor Robinson
Member of Executive/Treasurer to PTA: Angie Rigwell
PTA Committee: Dan Essex, Tina Dewsbery

West Yorkshire Passenger Transport Executive (Metro)

Wellington House, 40-50 Wellington Street, Leeds LS1 2DE
Tel: 0113 251 7272 **Fax:** 0113-251 7333
WYPTE activities are conducted under the corporate name Metro. Metro is financed and supported by the West Yorkshire Passenger Transport Authority.
Director General: Kieran Preston **Dir Corp Sers**: Sheena Pickersgill **Dir Pass Sers**: John Henkel **Dir Projects**: John Carr

Transport Co-ordinating Officers

Under the Transport Act 1978 the non-Metropolitan Counties were given power to co-ordinate public transport facilities in their areas. From 1 April 1996 Welsh Counties and Scottish Regions were replaced by new single-tier authorities. At the same time certain English Counties were replaced by new single-tier authorities. The major role is now to secure socially necessary services which are not provided commercially. The names of most of the responsible officers are set out below.

ENGLAND

*****Bedfordshire** - M S Roxburgh, Transport Policy Adviser, Environmental Strategy, County Hall, Bedford MK42 9AP.
Tel: 01234 228638.
Bracknell Forest Borough Council - R. Cook, Time Square, Bracknell RG12 1JD
Tel: 01344 424642.
Buckinghamshire - R. Slevin, County Passenger Transport Officer, County Hall, Aylesbury HP20 1YZ.
Tel: 01296 383751. **Fax:** 01296 383749.
Cambridgeshire - B. E. Jackson, Head of Passenger Transport, Department of Environment & Transport. Mailbox ET1015, Shire Hall, Castle Hill, Cambridge CB3 0AP.
Tel: 01223 717744. **Fax:** 01223 717789
Cheshire - G. Goddard, County Transport Co-ordinator, Rivacre Business Centre, Mill Lane, Ellesmere Port CH66 3TL.
Tel: 01244 603218. **Fax:** 01244 603200
*****Cornwall** - Stephen Nicholson, Principal Transport Officer, County Hall, Truro TR1 2AY.
Tel: 01872 322000 **Fax:** 01872 323844
E-mail: snicholson@cornwall.gov.uk
*****Cumbria County Council** - Citadel Chambers, Carlisle CA3 8SG.
Tel: 01228 606720 **Fax:** 01228 606755
E-mail: graham.whiteley@cumbriacc.gov.uk
Derbyshire - T. M. Hardy, Public Transport Manager, County Hall, Matlock DE4 3AG.
Tel: 01629 580000. **Fax:** 01629 585740.
*****Devon** - A. T. W. Davies, Head, Transport Co-ordination Service, Environment Directorate, County Hall, Exeter EX2 4QW
Tel: 01392 383244 **Fax:** 01392 382904
E-mail: tim.davies@devon.gov.uk
*****Dorset** - Barry Thirlwall, Passenger Transport Manager, Environmental Services Directorate, County Hall, Dorchester DT1 1XJ
Tel: 01305 224537 **Fax:** 01305 225166
E-mail: bthirlwall@dorset-cc.gov.uk
*****Durham** - Adrian J White, Business Manager Public Transport, Environment Dept, County Hall, Durham DH1 5UQ.
Tel: 0191 383 3435 **Fax:** 0191 383 4096.
*****East Riding of Yorkshire Council** - David Boden, Passenger Services Manager; Chris Mottershaw, Assistant Passenger Services Manager, Passenger Services, Operational Services Department, The Fleet Building, Grovehill Road, Beverley HU17 0JP.
Tel: 01482 395527 **Fax:** 01482 395054
East Sussex - E. Bassford, Group Manager (Passenger Transport), Transport & Environment, East Sussex County Council, County Hall, St Anne's Crescent, Lewes BN7 1UE.
Tel: 01273 482326. **Fax:** 01273 474361.
E-mail: ed.bassford@eastsexcc.gov.uk
Essex - F. Garthwaite, Passenger Transport Co-ordination Manager, Environmental Services Directorate, County Hall, Chelmsford CM1 1QH.
Tel: 01245 492211.
Gloucestershire - D Lucas, Operations & Procurement Manager, Shire Hall, Bearland, Gloucester GL1 2TH.
Tel: 01452 425609. **Fax:** 01452 425343
E-mail: dlucas@gloscc.gov.uk
*****Hampshire** - K Wilcox, Head of Passenger Transport, Hampshire County Council, Environment Department, The Castle, Winchester SO23 8UD.
Tel: 01962 846997 **Fax:** 01962 845855
E-mail: keith.wilcox@hants.gov.uk
Hartlepool Borough Council – Ian Jopling Transport Team Leader, Department of Neighbourhood Services, Bryan Hanson House, Hanson Square, Hartlepool TS24 7BT
Tel: 01429 284140 **Fax:** 01429 860830
E-mail: ian.jopling@hartlepool.gov.uk
Web site: www.hartlepool.gov.uk

Hertfordshire - Entry deleted at request of County Council.
Tel: 01992 588620. **Fax:** 01992 588649.
*****Isle of Wight Council** - A A Morris, Transport Manager, Jubilee Stores, The Quay, Newport PO30 2EH
Tel: 01983 823710. **Fax**: 01983 823707.
*****Kent County Council** - Julia Seaward, Head of Transport, Commercial Services, Kent County Council, Gibson Drive, Kings Hill, West Malling ME19 4QG
Tel: 01622 605091 **Fax**: 01622 605084
E-mail: passenger.transport@kent.gov.uk
Web site: www.kentpublictransport.info
*****Lancashire** - Stuart Wrigley, Head of Transport Policy, PO Box 9, Guild House, Cross Street, Preston PR1 8RD
Tel: 01772 534660. **Fax**: 01772 533833
*****Leicestershire** - Tony Kirk, Group Manager (Public Transport), Department of Highways, Transportation & Waste Management, County Hall, Glenfield, Leicester LE3 8RJ
Tel: 0116 265 6270 **Fax**: 0116 265 7181
E-mail: tkirk@leics.gov.uk
Web site: www.leics.gov.uk
Lincolnshire - A. R. Cross, Head of Transport Services Highways & Planning Directorate, 4th Floor, City Hall, Beaumont Fee, Lincoln LN1 1DN.
Tel: 01522 553132. **Fax:** 01522 568735.
Norfolk - Gordon Hanning, Head of Passenger Transport, Department of Planning & Transportation, County Hall, Martineau Lane, Norwich NR1 2SG.
Tel: 01603 223831. **Fax:** 01603 222144
Northamptonshire - B. Welch, Highways, Northamptonshire County Council, PO Box 221, John Dryden House, 8-10 The Lakes, Northampton NN4 7DE
Tel: 01604 236711 **Fax:** 01604 236393
*****Northumberland** - P J Stoner, Public Transport Officer, Environment Directorate, Northumberland County Council, County Hall, Morpeth NE61 2EF.
Tel: 01670 534238 **Fax**: 01670 533086.
E-mail: pstoner@northumberland.gov.uk
North Yorkshire - R. Owens, Passenger Transport Officer, County Hall, Northallerton DL7 8AH.
Tel: 01609 780780, Ext 2870. **Fax:** 01609 779838.
Nottinghamshire County Council - County Hall, West Bridgford, Nottingham NG2 7QP
Tel: 0115 982 3829 **E-mail**: enquiries@nottscc.gov.uk
Web site: www.nottscc.gov.uk
Oxfordshire - R. Helling, Public Transport Officer, Environmental Services, Speedwell House, Speedwell Street, Oxford OX1 1NE.
Tel: 01865 815859. **Fax:** 01865 815085.
Reading Borough Council – Mrs P. Baxter, Civic Centre, Reading RG1 7TD.
Tel: 0118 939 0813.
Shropshire - K. R. Gallop, Principal Passenger Transport Officer, Environment Department, The Shirehall, Abbey Foregate, Shrewsbury SY2 6ND.
Tel: 01743 253031. **Fax:** 01743 254382.
Slough Borough Council - R. Fraser, PO Box 570, Slough SL1 1FA.
*****Somerset County Council** - County Hall, The Crescent, Taunton TA20 1JS
Tel: 01823 356700 **Fax**: 01823 351356
E-mail: transport@somerset.gov.uk
Web site: www.somerset.gov.uk
Staffordshire - Charles Soutar, Head of Passenger Transport, Development Services Department, Riverway, Stafford ST16 3TJ.
Tel: 01785 276735. **Fax:** 01785 276621.
Suffolk - G. K. Butterwick, Public Transport Manager, Environment & Transport Department, St Edmund House, County Hall, Ipswich IP4 1LZ.
Tel: 01473 583331. **Fax:** 01473 583542. **E-mail:** geoff.butterwick@et-suffolkcc.gov.uk
Surrey - A. Teer, Group Manager Passenger Transport, Room 311, County Hall, Penrhyn Road, Kingston-on-Thames KT1 2DY
Tel: 020 8541 9371. **Fax:** 020 8541 9389.
*****Warwickshire** - K McGovern, Passenger Tranport Operations Manager, Warwickshire County Council, Planning & Transport Dept, PO Box 43, Shire Hall, Warwick CV34 4SX
Tel: 01926 412790 **Fax**: 01926 491665.
West Berkshire Council – J. Sherry, Market Street, Newbury
Tel: 01635 42400.
West Sussex County Council - Mark Miller, Group Manager, Transport Co-ordination, Transport Planning Services, The Grange, Tower Street, Chichester PO19 1RH
Tel: 01243 777811 **Web site:** www.westsussex.gov.uk

*****Wiltshire** - I. White, Passenger Transport Co-ordinator, Environmental Services Dept, County Hall, Trowbridge BA14 8JD.
Tel: 01225 713322. **Fax:** 01225 713565.
*****Royal Borough of Windsor & Maidenhead** – E. Mouser, Yorkstream House, St. Ives Road, Maidenhead SL6 1RF.
Tel: 01628 796732. **Fax:** 01628 796774.
*****Wokingham District Council** - Mr Roland Clausen-Thue, Transport, Environment, Shute End, Wokingham RG40 1WR.
Tel: 0118 974 6468. **Fax:** 0118 974 6486.
Worcestershire - R Wigginton, Director of Environmental Services, County Hall, Spetchley Road, Worcester WR5 2NP. C Pettifer, Passenger & Fleet Transport Manager, PO Box 82, Pershore Lane, Worcester WR4 0AA.
Tel: 01905 768410 **Fax**: 01905 453754

WALES

*****Anglesey** - The Isle of Anglesey County Council, Council Offices, Llangefni LL7 7TW.
Tel: 01248 752300 **Fax**: 01248 724839
E-mail: dwrpl@anglesey.gov.uk **Web site**: www.anglesey.gov.uk
Blaenau Gwent - Blaenau Gwent County Borough Council, Municipal Offices, Civic Centre, Ebbw Vale NP3 6XB
Tel: 01495 350555. **Fax**: 01495 301255
Bridgend - M. Thomas, Director of Environmental & Planning Services, Bridgend County Borough Council, PO Box 4, Civic Offices, Angel Street, Bridgend CF31 1LX.
Tel: 01656 643643. **Fax**: 01656 668126
*****Caerphilly County Borough Council** - Huw Morgan, Principal Passenger Transport Officer, Directorate of the Environment, Council Offices, Pontllanfraith, Blackwood NP12 2YW.
Tel: 01495 235089 **Fax**: 01495 235045 **E-mail**: morgash@caerphilly.gov.uk **Web site**: www.caerphilly.gov.uk
*****Cardiff** - Cardiff County Council, Traffic and Transportation Service, County Hall, Atlantic Wharf, Cardiff CF1 0 4UW.
Cardiganshire - see Ceredigion
Carmarthenshire: Dir. of Economic Development: Gerald Campbell Phillips. Carmarthenshire Council Council, County Hall, Carmarthen SA31 1JP.
Tel: 01267 234567. **Fax:** 01267 230848.
Ceredigion: Cyngor Sir Ceredigion, County Council, County Hall, Market Street, Aberaeron SA46 0AT.
Tel: 01545 572501 **Fax:** 01545 571089
Conwy - Conwy County Borough Council, Bodlondeb, Conwy LL32 8DU.
Tel: 01492 574000, 592114. **Fax:** 01492 592114.
*****Denbighshire** - Denbighshire County Council, Council Offices,Wynnstay Road, Ruthin LL15 1AT.
Tel: 01824 706000 **Fax**: 01824 707446.
Public Transport: M G Rhodes, Passenger Transport Coordinator, Caledfryn, Smithfield Road, Denbigh LL16 3RJ.
Tel: 01824 706879. **Fax**: 01824 706970
*****Flintshire County Council** - Directorate of Transportation, Planning & the Environment, County Hall, Mold CH7 6NG
Tel: 01352 704530 **Fax**: 01352 704540
Web site: www.flintshire.gov.uk
Gwynedd Council - M Cowban, Public Transport Officer, Council Offices, Shirehall 56, Caernarfon LL55 1SH.
Tel: 01286 679541 **Fax**: 01286 673324
E-mail: malcolmwaltercowban@gwynnedd.gov.uk
*****Merthyr Tydfil** - Martin Haworth, Senior Transport Officer, Merthyr Tydfil County Borough Council, Civic Centre, Castle Street, Merthyr Tydfil CF47 8AN
Tel: 01685 726288 **Fax**: 01685 387982
E-mail: martin.howarth@merthyr.gov.uk
*****Monmouthshire** - Monmouthshire County Council, County Hall, Cwmbran NP44 2XH
Tel: 01633 644644 **Fax**: 01633 644701 **E-mail**: transport@monmouthshire.gov.uk
Web site: www.monmouthshire.gov.uk
Neath Port Talbot - Neath Port Talbot County Borough Council, Civic Centre, Port Talbot SA13 1PJ .
Tel: 01639 763333. **Fax**: 01639 763444.
Newport - Dir. of Development/Transport: Brian Adcock. Newport County Borough Council, Civic Centre, Newport NP9 4UR.
Tel: 01633 244491. **Fax**: 01633 244721

Pembrokeshire - Dir. of Transport: John S Heys, Pembrokeshire County Council, Cambria House, PO Box 27, Haverfordwest SA61 1TP.
Tel: 01437 764551. **Fax:** 01437 760703
Powys - Transport Co-ordination Unit, County Hall, Llandrindod Wells LD1 5LG.
Tel: 01597 826642 **Fax:** 01597 826260.
Rhondda Cynon Taff - Rhondda Cynon Taff County Borough Council, The Pavilions, Cambrian Park, Clydach Vale CF40 2XX
Tel 01443 424000. **Fax:** 01443 424027. Public Transport: D M Sherrard, Divisional Director (Transportation & Development Control), Sardis House, Sardis Road, Pontypridd CF37 1DU
Tel: 01443 494700. **Fax:** 01443 494875
City & County of Swansea - Catherine Swain, Team Leader - Passenger Transport, Environment Department, County Hall, Oystermouth Road, Swansea SA1 3SN
Tel: 01792 636079 **Fax:** 01792 652712 **E-mail:** cath.swain@swansea.gov.uk **Web site:** www.swansea.gov.uk
Torfaen - Torfaen County Borough Council, Civic Centre, Pontypool NP4 6YB.
Tel: 01495 762200. **Fax:** 01495 755513.
Vale of Glamorgan Council - Transportation Unit, Dock Offices, Barry Docks, Barry CF63 4RT
Tel: 01446 704687 **Fax** 01446 704891 **E-mail:** cedwards@valeofglamorgan.gov.uk **Web site:** valeofglamorgan.gov.uk
Wrexham - Wrexham County Borough Council, PO Box 1284, Guildhall, Wrexham LL11 1WF.
Tel: 01978 292000. **Fax:** 01978 292106

SCOTLAND

Aberdeen City - The Director, Environment & Infrastructure Services, Aberdeen City Council, St Nicholas House, Broad Street, Aberdeen AB10 1WL
Tel: 01224 523762. **Fax:** 01224 523764.
E-mail: rwaters@roads.aberdeen.net.uk.
Web site: www.aberdeencity.gov.uk
Aberdeenshire - E. Guthrie, Head of Transportation, Aberdeenshire Council, Woodhill House, Westburn Road, Aberdeen AB16 5GB.
Tel: 01224 664580. **Fax:** 01224 662005.
Angus Council - A Anderson, Director, Planning & Transport, Angus Council, St James House, St James Road, Forfar DD8 2ZD
Tel: 01307 461774 **Fax:** 01307 473711
E-mail: millarle@angus.gov.uk
Argyll & Bute Council - Kilmory, Lochgilphead PA31 8RT
Tel: 01546 604360 **Fax:** 01546 604695.
Web site: www.argyll-bute.gov.uk
Clackmannanshire - David Taylor, Public Transport Officer, Clackmannanshire Council, Lime Tree House, Alloa FK10 1EX.
Tel: 01259 452603 **Fax:** 01786 442739
E-mail: dtaylor@clacks.gov.uk **Web site:** www.clacksweb.org.uk
Dundee City - Mark Devine, Transport Officer, Dundee City Council, Planning & Transportation Department, Floor 15, Tayside House, Crichton Street, Dundee DD1 3RB.
Tel: 01382 433831. **Fax:** 01382 433060.
E-mail: mark.devine@dundeecity.gov.uk.
Web site: www.dundeecity.gov.uk
Dumfries & Galloway - D. Kirkpatrick, Passenger Transport Officer, Dumfries & Galloway Council, Militia House, English Street, Dumfries DG1 2HR.
Tel: 01387 260133 **Fax:** 01387 260383
East Ayrshire - East Ayrshire Council, London Road, Kilmarnock KA3 7BU.
East Dunbartonshire - East Dunbartonshire Council, PO Box 4, Civic Way, Kirkintilloch G66 4TJ.
East Lothian - Transport Planning Manager, Department of Planning, East Lothian Council, 25 Court Street, Haddington EH41 3HA.
East Renfrewshire - East Renfrewshire Council, Eastwood Park, Rouken Glen Road, Giffnock G46 6UG.
City of Edinburgh Council - Max Thomson, Public Transport Manager, City Development, 1 Cockburn Street, Edinburgh EH1 1BJ
Tel: 0131 469 3631. **Fax:** 0131 469 3635.
E-mail: max.thomson@edinburgh.gov.uk
Falkirk - Stephen Bloomfield, Public Transport Co-ordinator, Development Services, Falkirk Council, Abbotsfold House, David's Loan, Falkirk FK2 7YZ.
Tel: 01324 504723. **Fax:** 01324 504914.

Fife - Trond Haugen, Transportation Manager - Transportation Services, Fife Council, Fife House, North Street, Glenrothes KY7 5LT.
Tel: 01592 413106. **Fax:** 01592 413061
E-mail: trond.haugen@fife.gov.uk
Highland - Transport Officer, Highland Council, Glenurquhart Road, Inverness IV3 5NX.
Tel: 01463 702612. **Fax:** 01463 702606.
Inverclyde - Inverclyde Council, Municipal Buildings, Greenock PA15 1LY.
Midlothian - Brian Sharkie, Public Transport Manager, Midlothian Council, Fairfield House, 8 Lothian Road, Dalkeith EH22 3ZN.
Tel: 0131 271 3520. **Fax:** 0131 271 3537.
E-mail: brian.sharkie@midlothian.gov.uk
Moray - Peter Findlay, Public Transport Manager, Moray Council, Council Office, Academy Street, Elgin IV30 1LL
Tel: 01343 562541. **Fax:** 01343 545628.
E-mail: peter.findlay@moray.gov.uk
North Ayrshire - North Ayrshire Council, Cunningham House, Irvine KA12 8EE.
North Lanarkshire - North Lanarkshire Council, Po Box 14, Civic Centre, Motherwell ML1 1TW
Tel: 01224 664580. **Fax:** 01224 662005.
Orkney - Orkney Islands Council, Council Offices, School Place, Kirkwall KW15 1NY.
Perth & Kinross - Andrew J Warrington, Public Transport Manager; Planning & Transportation, Pullar House, 35 Kinnoull Street, Perth PH1 5GD.
Tel: 01738 476530. **Fax:** 01738 476510.
E-mail: awarrington@pkc.gov.uk
Renfrewshire - Renfrewshire Council, North Building, Cotton Street, Paisley PA1 1WB.
Scottish Borders - B Young, Transport Policy Manager, Scottish Borders Council, Council Headquarters, Newtown St Boswells, Melrose TD6 0SA.
Tel: 01835 824000 **Fax:** 01835 823008
Shetland Islands - Ian Bruce, Service Manager - Transport Operations, Infrastructure Service Dept. Shetland Islands Council, Grantfield, Lerwick ZE1 0NT.
Tel: 01595 744872. **Fax:** 01595 744869.
E-mail: ian.bruce@sic.shetland.gov.uk
South Ayrshire - South Ayrshire Council, County Buildings, Wellington Square, Ayr KA7 1DR.
South Lanarkshire - South Lanarkshire Council, Council Offices, Almada Street, Hamilton ML3 0AA. **(No Public Transport responsibilities - see Strathclyde in Passenger Transport Executive section)**
Stirling - Stirling Council, Council Headquarters, Viewforth, Stirling FK8 2ET.
Strathclyde -SPT, Consort House, 12 West George Street, Glasgow G2 1HN. (*see main entry*)
West Dunbartonshire - West Dunbartonshire Council, Council Offices, Garshake Road, Dunbarton, G82 3PU.
(No Public Transport responsibilities - see Strathclyde)
Western Isles - Western Isles Council, Council Offices, Balivanich, Benbecula HS7 5LA.
West Lothian - Roy Mitchell, Public Transport Manager, West Lothian Council, County Buildings, Linlithgow EH49 7EZ
Tel: 01506 775282. **Fax:** 01506 775265.
E-mail: roy.mitchell@westlothian.gov.uk .
Web site: www.wlonline.org.uk

Traffic Commissioners

EASTERN TRAFFIC AREA
Terrington House, 13-15 Hills Road, Cambridge CB2 1NP
Tel: 01223 531060 **Fax:** 01223 309681
Traffic Commissioner: Geoffrey Simms
Deputy Traffic Commissioners: D. N. Stevens, R. C. Lockwood, M. J. Guy. **Area covered:** Leicestershire, Lincolnshire, Cambridgeshire, Norfolk, Suffolk, Essex, Bedfordshire, Northamptonshire, Hertfordshire, Buckinghamshire.

NORTH EASTERN TRAFFIC AREA
Hillcrest House, 386 Harehills Lane, Leeds LS9 6NF
Tel: 0113 283 3533. **Fax:** 0113 248 9607
Traffic Commissioner: Tom Macartney
Deputy Traffic Commissioners: M. Hinchcliffe, Mrs B. Bell, Ms L. Perrett, P. J. Mulvenna
Administrative Director: Sharon McNair

Area covered: Northumberland, Tyne & Wear, Co Durham, Yorkshire, Nottinghamshire

*NORTH WESTERN TRAFFIC AREA
Hillcrest House, 386 Harehills Lane, Leeds LS9 6NF
Tel: 0113 283 3533 **Fax:** 0113 248 9607
Traffic Commissioner: Beverley Bell.
Deputy Traffic Commissioners: M Hinchcliffe, T Macartney, Miss L Perrett, P J Mulvenna
Area covered: Cumbria, Lancashire, Greater Manchester, Merseyside, Cheshire, Derbyshire.

SCOTTISH TRAFFIC AREA
J Floor, 3 Lady Lawson Street, Edinburgh EH3 9SE
Tel: 0131 200 4955 **Fax:** 0131 529 8501
Traffic Commissioner: Miss Joan Aitken
Deputy Traffic Commissioner: R. H. McFarlane
Area covered: Scotland

*SOUTH EASTERN & METROPOLITAN TRAFFIC AREA
Ivy House, 3 Ivy Terrace, Eastbourne BN21 4QT.
Tel: 01323 452400. **Fax:** 01323 721057
Traffic Commissioner: Chris Heaps
Deputy Traffic Commissioners: R Lockwood, A R Bourlet
Area covered: Greater London, Kent, Surrey, Sussex.

WELSH TRAFFIC AREA
Cumberland House, 200 Broad Street, Birmingham B15 1TD.
Tel: 0121 608 1090. **Fax:** 0121 608 1001.
Traffic Commissioner: David Dixon.
Deputy Traffic Commissioners: A. R. Bourlet, A. Jenkins, A. L. Maddrell, C. R. Seymour.
Administrative Director: Mrs C. Norris.
Area covered: Wales.

WEST MIDLAND TRAFFIC AREA
Cumberland House, 200 Broad Street, Birmingham B15 1TD.
Tel: 0121 609 6813/03. **Fax:** 0121 608 1001.
Traffic Commissioner: David Dixon.
Deputy Traffic Commissioners: A. R. Bourlet, A. Jenkins, A. L. Maddrell, C. R. Seymour.
Administrative Director: Mrs C. Norris.
Area covered: Shropshire, Staffordshire, West Midlands, Warwickshire, Worcestershire, Herefordshire.

WESTERN TRAFFIC AREA
The Gaunts' House, Denmark Street, Bristol BS1 5DR.
Tel: 0117 975 5000. **Fax:** 0117 975 5055.
Traffic Commissioner: Philip Brown.
Deputy Traffic Commissioners: Brig M. H. Turner, Mrs F. R. Burton, A. L. Maddrell.
Administrative Director: Tim Hughes.
Area covered: Cornwall, Devon, Somerset, Dorset, Hampshire, Wiltshire, Gloucestershire, Oxfordshire, Berkshire.

Government Department responsible for keeping a watch on competition matters under the Competition Act 1998 and the Fair Trading Act 1973.
Address: Fleetbank House, 2-6 Salisbury Square, London EC4Y 8JX.
Tel: 020 7211 8000 **Fax:** 020 7211 8800.

Department for Transport

Eland House, Bressenden Place, London SW1E 5DU
Tel: 020 7944 3000
Web site: www.dft.co.uk

Board:
Permanent Secretary: David Rowlands
Director of Communications: Charles Skinner

Executive Agencies: (includes:)
Driving Standards Agency (DSA)
Driver and Vehicle Licensing Agency (DVLA)
Highways Agency (HA)
Tel: 020 7081 7443
Web Site: www.highways.gov.uk

Vehicle Certification Agency (VCA)
1 Eastgate Office Centre, Eastgate Road, Bristol BS5 6XX
Web site: www.vca.gov.uk
Chief Executive: Paul Markwick
Vehicle and Operator Services Agency (VOSA) (see also Driver Training A-Z Manufacturers section)

Advisory Non-Departmental Bodies: (includes:)
Commission for Integrated Transport
E-mail: cfit@dft.gsi.gov.uk
Disabled Persons Transport Advisory Committee
E-mail: dptac@dft.gsi.gov.uk

Executive Non-departmental Bodies: (includes:)
Health and Safety Commission
Health and Safety Executive
Strategic Rail Authority

Tribunals
Traffic Areas

Public Corporations
Civil Aviation Authority
Transport for London

section 3
Organisations and Societies

British Operators Organisations	*60*
Institutions	*60*
International Associations	*62*
Other Organisations	*62*
First Aid and Sports Associations	*63*
Trade Organisations	*64*
Societies	*64*

British Operators' Organisations

*ASSOCIATION OF LOCAL BUS COMPANY MANAGERS

The Association represents the professional views of the Executive Directors of those bus companies owned by district council and major independent operators on matters specifically affecting locally-owned bus company management and operations.
Secretary: D Cunningham, Halton Borough Transport Ltd, Moor Lane, Widnes WA8 7AF **Tel**: 0151 423 3333.

*COACH OPERATORS FEDERATION

Rose Vista, 261 Stowey Road, Yatton BS49 4QX.
Tel: 01934 832074 **Fax**: 0117 964 2004
President: F. J. Catt.
Secretary: T. P. Jones

*THE COACH TOURISM COUNCIL

Berkeley House, 18 Elmfield Road, Bromley BR1 1LR
Tel: 020 8641 8325 **Fax**: 020 8641 8326
Web site: www.coachtourismcouncil.co.uk
The CTC's mission is to promote tourism and travel by coach.

*CONFEDERATION OF PASSENGER TRANSPORT UK

Imperial House, 15-19 Kingsway, London WC2B 6UN
Tel: 020 7240 3131 **Fax**: 020 7240 6565
E-mail: cpt@cpt-uk.org **Web site**: www.cpt-uk.org
The Confederation of Passenger Transport UK (CPT) is the trade association representing the UK's bus and coach operators and the light rail sector. CPT has wide responsibilities ranging from representation on government working parties (national, local, EU); establishing operating codes of practice; advising on legal, technical and mechanical standards; management of the Bonded Coach Holiday Scheme, a government recognised consumer travel protection scheme and Coachmarque, an industry quality standard; 24-hour Crisis Control service for members; organisation of industry events and the first point of contact for the media on transport and other related issues.

OFFICERS AND COUNCIL
President: S Clayton
Immediate Past President: S Telling
Director General: B Nimick
Manager, Director General's Office: Miss L Tang
Finance Director: W Wright
Communications Director: S Posner
Assistant Director, Public Affairs: S Heard
Communications Executive: Miss K Allen
Press Office: C Nice
Director of Membership: Peter Gomersall
Membership Executive: Mrs K Hudson
Operations Director: S Salmon
Head of Coach Services & Deputy Director of Operations: A Edmonson
Technical Executive: C Copelin
Operations Executive: M James
Fixed Track Executive: Dr D. Walmsley

Director of Government Relations, Scotland:
Mrs M Rodger, 29 Drumsheugh Gardens, Edinburgh EH13 7RN
Tel: 0131 272 2150 **Fax**: 0131 272 2152
Director of Government Relations, Wales:
J. Pockett, 70 Hillside View, Craigwen, Pontypridd CF37 2LG
Tel: 01443 485814 **Fax**: 01443 485816

Regional Secretaries
East Midlands: Andrew Norman, c/o Trent Buses, Mansfield Road, Heanor DE75 7BG **Tel**: 01773 536334 **Fax**: 01773 536333
London & Home Counties: Mrs K Hudson, Imperial House, 15-19 Kingsway, London WC2B 6UN
Tel: 020 7240 3131. **Fax**: 020 7240 6565
Northern: J. Smith, 35 Great North Road, Brunton Park, Newcastle upon Tyne NE3 5LX. **Tel/Fax:** 0191 217 0825
North Western: Leonard Green, 2 Short Clough Close, Reedsholme, Rawtenstall BB4 8PT **Tel**: 01706 218539 **Fax**: 01706 601485
Scotland: Gail Hume, 29 Drumsheugh Gradens, Edinburgh EH13 7RR **Tel**: 0131 272 2150 **Fax**: 0131 272 2152
Wales: E Marsh, Flat 102, The Aspect, 140 Queen Street, Cardiff CF10 2GP **Tel**: 029 2093 0069
West Midlands: G. Sutton, Imperial House, 15-19 Kingsway, London WC2B 6UN. **Tel:** 020 7240 3131 **Fax:** 020 7240 6565
Western: R Anderson, Heather Cottage, Smokey Cross, Haytor, Newton Abbot TQ13 9QU
Tel: 01365 661365 **Fax**: 01752 777931
Yorkshire: G. Peach, Green Acres, 332 Barnsley Road, Flockton WF4 4AT
Tel: 01924 840767 **Fax**: 01924 849685

TRANSFED

PO Box 29085, London WC2B 6TR
Tel: 020 7240 3131 **Fax**: 020 7240 6565
Formerly known as Bus and Coach Training Ltd, Transfed is the national training organisation representing the UK passenger transport industry. It covers training and national occupational standards for the industry.

WEST YORKSHIRE COACH OPERATORS ASSOCIATION

C/O Wallace Arnold Travel Shop, 20 Ivegate, Bradford BD1 1SW. **Tel:** 01274 613315.

Institutions

*THE CHARTERED INSTITUTE OF LOGISTICS & TRANSPORT

Logistics & Transport Centre, Earlstrees Court, Earlstrees Road, Corby NN17 4AX
Tel: 01536 740100 **Fax**: 01536 740101
E-mail: enquiry@ciltuk.org.uk.
Web site: www.ciltuk.org.uk

The Chartered Institute of Logistics and Transport (UK) is the professional body for individuals and organisations involved in all disciplines, modes and aspects of logistics and transport.
  The Institute's 22,000 members have privileged access to a range of benefits and services, which support them,

professionally and personally, throughough their careers and help connect them with world-wide expertise.

For further information and to join please contact Membership Services, Tel: 01536 740104 or visit the CILT(UK) web site: www.ciltuk.org.uk

THE INSTITUTE OF THE MOTOR INDUSTRY

The Institute of the Motor Industry (IMI) is the major professional and awarding body for the motor industry. Established in 1920, the Institute performs the role of promoting and recognising professionalism in the motor industry and has some 25,000 members worldwide. Information is available on a wide variety of qualifications offered by the Institute including NVQs/SVQs, the 600 Series learning programmes and the Certificate of Management offered by the Awarding Body. There are six levels of membership, student, graduate, affiliate, associate, member and fellow.

OFFICERS AND VICE PRESIDENTS
Patron: HRH Prince Michael of Kent KCVO FIMI.
President: Rt Hon Lord Brabazon of Tara FIMI.
Honorary Treasurer: Martin Austin FIMI.
Vice Presidents: Sir T. Chinn CVO FIMI, Sir I. Gibson CBE FIMI, T. Gibson FIMI, P. Johnson FIMI, J. Hughes FIMI, M. Marshall CBE FIMI, I. McAllister CBE FIMI, J. Neill CBE FIMI, Prof G. Rhys OBE FIMI, Sir N. Scheele FIMI, T. Taylor FIMI, V. Thomas CBE FIMI
Representative Vice Presidents:
The Presidents of:
Motor & Allied Trades Benevolent Fund: Mrs Sue Brownson OBE FIMI.
Retail Motor Industry Federation: John Bond-Smith FIMI.
Scottish Motor Trade Association: John Chessor FIMI.
Society of the Irish Motor Industry: Michael Forde.
Society of Motor Manufacturers & Traders: Nick Reilly FIMI.
Vehicle Builders & Repairers Association: Rt Hon Lord Strathcarron FIMI
Members of the Council of Managemt:
Chairman: Edward Ciack FIMI
Chief Executive Offier: Sarah Sillars
Council of Management: M. W. Austin FIMI, G. Braddock FIMI, C. Brass MIMI, E. Clark FIMI, S. Collins MIMI, T. Copley FIMI, S. Collins MIMI, T. Copley FIMI, I Creek FIMI, M. Green FIMI, N. Lindsay FIMI, J. Livingstone FIMI, E. Loft FIMI, F. Maguire FIMI, K. Muddimer FIMI, P. Murphy FIMI, G. Owen FIMI, J.Simpkins FIMI, J. Small FIMI, J Stone MIMI, M. Trainer FIMI.
Company Secretary: Allan Tyrer.

OPERATING BOARD
Chief Executive: Peter Creasey FIMI
Company Secretary and Finance Director: Allan Tyrer
Director, Membership Services: Ian Philpott FIMI
Address: 'Fanshaws', Brickendon, Hertford SG13 8PQ. **Tel:** 01992 511521. **Fax:** 01992 511548. **E-mail:** imi@motor.org.uk **Website:** www.motor.org.uk

*THE INSTITUTE OF TRANSPORT ADMINISTRATION

IOTA House, 7b St Leonards Road, Horsham RH13 6EH
Tel: 01403 242412 **Fax:** 01403 242413
E-mail: director.iota@btclick.com **Web site:** www.iota.org.uk
OFFICERS
President: D. MacCuish
Trustees: Cllr G G Fiegel, J D Bailey, M Braid, I M Marshall
National Chairman: F A Robertson
National Chairman Elect: A Varney
National Vice Chairmen: A Varney, G. Fletcher, M Walker

National Treasurer: J Amos
Finance & General Purposes Chairman: J Amos
Membership/Training Chairman: S G Hegren
External Affairs Chairman: G. Fletcher
Director: P R Carey

CHAIRMEN/HON SECRETARIES OF CENTRES
Bristol – Chairman: E. J. Reece **Secretary:** Miss M. Lane, 137 Hilston Avenue, Penn, Wolverhampton WV4 4SB
Cheshire, Mersey & North Wales –
Chairman: F. A. Robertson **Secretary:** A. Woolfall, 4 Mereworth Drive, Kingsmead, Northwich CW9 8W
Devon/Cornwall – Chairman: I. A. Smith. **Secretary:** Ms J. M. Land, 44 Parkside Road, Westclyst, Pinhoe, Exeter EX1 3TN
East Anglia – Chairman: B. Young. **Secretary:** A. J. Clay, RTT Training Services Ltd, Gippeswyk Hall, Gippeswyk Avenue, Ipswich IP2 9AF
Edinburgh – Chairman: K. G. Welch
Secretary: C. M. McDaid, 46 Bervie Drive, Murieston, Livingston EH54 9HA
Essex – Chairman: A. C. Williams **Secretary:** B. A. Mason, 2 Regency Close, Runwell, Wickford SS11 7BN
Falkirk – Chairman: A. Cormack
Secretary: Mrs M. Struthers, 48 Livingstone Drive, Laurieston-by-Falkirk FK2 9JW
Herts/Bucks & Beds – Chairman: A. L. Bell
Secretary: M. Mullet, 129 Littleworth Road, Downley, High Wycombe HP13 5UZ
Hull – Chairman: S. R. NcNight. **Secretary:** C. Trumper, 5 Well Lane, Main Street, Willerby, Hull
Inverness – Chairman: G. W. Masson
Secretary: Ms J. C. Morrison, 8 Mackenzie Road, Inverness IV2 3DF
Kent – Chairman: W. Wilford **Secretary:** B. W. Freeman, 34 Hunters Way West, Chatham Kent ME5 7HL
Lancashire – Chairman: D. Uttley **Secretary:** W. A. Jefferies, 34 Broadfield Drive, Penwortham, Preston PR1 9DU
Leeds – Chairman: J. M. Walker **Secretary:** D. Russell, 4 Beechfield Drive, Harvest Meadows, Sharlston Common, Wakefield WF4 1EG
Leicester – Chairman: J. D. Bailey. **Secretary:** Mrs A. Coupland, 193 Bardon Road, Coalville, Leicester LE67 4BG
London Central – Chairman: A. Varney **Secretary:** R. A. Ellis, Bridgeview, Hill Road, Borstal, Rochester ME1 3NN
Manchester – Chairman: H. Haworth **Secretary:** J. P. Egan, 45 Sherway Drive, Timperley, Altrincham WA15 7NU
North East – Chairman: D. Holland **Secretary:** T. A. Simpson, 11 Gleneagles Drive, Usworth, Washington NE37 1PL.
Peterborough – Chairman: T. Hill. **Secretary:** C. Brown, 18 Deeping St James Road, Northborough PE6 9BQ.
Sheffield – Chairman: A. Hawcroft **Secretary:** M. Baines, 58 Hollins Spring Ave, Dronfield S18 1RP
Southampton – Chairman: A. Evans **Secretary:** R. Brown, 25 Downscroft Gardens, Hedge End, Southampton SO30 4RR
South Wales – Chairman/Secretary: A. D. Gettins, Oak Cottage, Royal Oak, Machen CF83 8SN
Sussex – Chairman: I Greenlow **Secretary:** Julia Merton
Swindon – Chairman: D. Brooks. **Secretary:** C. Harling, 128 Beech Drive, Pinehurst, Swindon SN2 1JR
West Midlands – Chairman/Secretary: P Hastelow Hamilton Cottage, 66 Duke Street, Cheltenham GL52 6BP

*THE INSTITUTION OF MECHANICAL ENGINEERS

1 Birdcage Walk, London SW1H 9JJ
Tel: 020 7222 7899. **Fax:** 020 7222 4557
Web site: www.imeche.org.uk

Founded in 1847
Chief Executive: Sir Michael Moore KBE LVO
President 2004/5: W Edgar, MSc, ARCST, FREng, CEng, FIMechE
Technical Manager, Transport Industries: David Atton
Incorporates as the Automobile Division the former Institution of Automobile Engineers and as the Railway Division the former Institution of Locomotive Engineers.

*SOCIETY OF OPERATIONS ENGINEERS

22 Greencoat Place, London SW1P 1PR
Tel: 020 7630 1111 **Fax**: 020 7630 6677
E-mail: ian.chisholm@soe.org.uk **Web site**: www.soe.org.uk
The SOE is the umbrella professional body for those working in road transport and plant engineering. The Institute of Road Transport Engineers is a professional sector within the SOE.

TRL LTD (TRANSPORT RESEARCH LABORATORY)

Address: Old Wokingham Road, Crowthorne RG45 6AU.
Tel: 01344 770007 **Fax**: 01344 770880
E-mail: enquiries@trl.co.uk
Web site: www.trl.co.uk

International Associations

INTERNATIONAL ROAD TRANSPORT UNION (IRU)

INTERNATIONAL ROAD TRANSPORT UNION (IRU
Founded in 1948 in Geneva, the IRU is an international association of national road transport federations which has consultative status in the United Nations and the liaison committees with the European Union. One of its three sections is concerned with road passenger transport and the bodies which this represents are set out below.
General Secretariat: IRU, Centre International, 3 Rue de Varemb, B.P.44, 1211 Geneva 20, Switzerland
Tel: 00 41 22 918 2700 **Fax**: 00 41 22 918 2741
E-mail: info@iru.org **Web site**: www.iru.org

UITP, THE INTERNATIONAL ASSOCIATION OF PUBLIC TRANSPORT

President: Wolfgang Meyer (Germany).
Secretary General: Hans Rat
Offices: Rue Sainte Marie 6, B-1080 Bruxelles
Tel: 00 32 2 673 6100 **Fax**: 00 32 2 660 1072
Web site: www.uitp.com **E-mail**: administration@uitp.com

WORLD ROAD ASSOCIATION (PIARC)

Hon Sec/Hon Treas: Room 914, Sunley Tower, Piccadilly Plaza, Manchester M1 4BE **Tel**: 0161 930 5579
E-mail: piarc.bnc@highways.gsi.gov.uk **Web site**: www.piarc.org
The Association is an international body with headquarters in Paris, administered by an elected President and other office bearers. Members are recruited from governments, local authorities, technical and industrial groups and private individuals whose interests are centred on roads and road traffic. The association is maintained by subscriptions from its members. International congresses are held every four years.

OFFICE BEARERS
President: O. Michaud (Switzerland).
International Vice-Presidents: P. Anguitas Salas (Chile), C. Jordan (Australia), K. Ghellab (Morocco).
Secretary General: J F Corte, PIARC, La Grande Arche, Paroi Nord, Niveau 8, 92055 La Defense Cedex, France. **Tel**: 00 33 1 47 96 81 21 **Fax**: 00 33 1 49 00 02 02
The British National Committee's role is to ensure adequate representation of British methods and experience on PIARC's international committees and Congresses, to disseminate the findings of those committees and generally look after British interests. The present officers of this committee are:
Patron: Minister for Transport.
UK President: Sir Richard Mottram KCB.
UK Chairman: W. J. McCoubrey.
Vice-Chairman: S. Clarke.
Hon Treasurer: C. B. Goodwillie.
Hon Secretary/Hon Treasurer: M Neave

Other Organisations

ASSOCIATION OF TRANSPORT CO-ORDINATING OFFICERS (ATCO)

Chairman: D. V. Goodwin (Kent CC)
Immediate Past Chairman: B. Dodds (Lancashire CC)
Vice-Chairman: B. Welch (Northamptonshire CC)
Secretary: T. Dobson (Cheshire CC)
Training Liaison Officer: R. Slevin (Buckinghamshire CC)
Members of Committee representing: **South Eastern Region**: G. Burnett (Surrey CC)
South Western Region: I. White (Wiltshire CC)
Midlands Region: B. Davies (Nottinghamshire CC)
North Eastern Region: C. Brooke-Taylor (SYPTE)
North Western Region: R. Trippe (GMPTE)
Eastern Region: M. Roxburgh (Bedfordshire CC)
Welsh Region: T. Goodman (Powys CC)
Scottish Region: R. Mitchell (West Lothian)

*COACH DRIVERS CLUB OF GB

24-50 South Parade, Yate BS37 4BB
Tel: 01454 273573 **Fax**: 01454 273200
E-mail: cdc-coachmonthly@.btconnect.com
Web site: www.cdc-coachmonthly.co.uk
Membership club for coach drivers, coaching and tourism.

LOCAL GOVERNMENT ASSOCIATION

Local Government House, Smith Square, London SW1P 3HZ. **Tel: 020 7664 3000. Fax: 020 7664 3030. Web Site: www.lga.gov.uk.**
The Local Government was formed by the merger of the Association of County Councils, the Association of District Councils and the Association of Metropolitan Authorities in 1997. The LGA has just under 500 members, including all 238 shire district councils; 36 metropolitan district councils; 34 county councils; 46 new unitary authorities; 33 London authorities; and 22 Welsh authorities. In addition, the LGA represents police authorities, fire authorities and passenger transport authorities. The LGA provides the national voice for local communities in England and Wales; its members represent over 50 million people, employ more than 2 million staff and spend over £65 billion on local services.
Amongst the LGA's policy priorities is integrated transport; local authorities lead the way in encouraging the use of public transport and thereby reducing congestion, ill-health and environmental damage through a programme of partnerships

between local authorities and other agencies.
President: Lord Ousley
Chair: Sir Jeremy Beecham (Labour, Newcastle)
Vice-Chair: Harry Jones CBE (Labour, Newport), Lord Hanningfield (Conservative, Essex).
Deputy Chairs:
Ian Swithenbank CBE (Labour, Northumberland)
Sir David Williams CBE (Liberal Democrat, Richmond)
Gordon Keymer (Conservative, Tandridge).
Milner Whiteman (Independent, Bridgnorth).

Chief Executive: Sir Brian Briscoe
Director of Economic & Environmental Policy: Sarah Wood
Director of Communications & Public Affairs: Phil Swann
Programme Manager, Planning & Transport: Lee Searles

*LONDON TRANSPORT USERS COMMITTEE (LTUC)

6 Middle Street, London EC1A 7JA
Tel: 020 7505 9000 **Fax:** 020 7505 9003
Web site: www.ltuc.org.uk **E-mail:** info@ltuc.org.uk
LTUC is the independent statutory body set up to represent the interests of the users of all transport for which the Greater London Authority and Transport for London is responsible for operating, providing, procuring and licensing. LTUC is also the Rail Passengers Committee for London.
Chairperson: Suzanne May OBE.
Director: Rufus Barnes

*THE NATIONAL FEDERATION OF BUS USERS

PO Box 320, Portsmouth PO5 3SD
Tel: 023 9281 4493 **Fax:** 023 9286 3080.
E-mail: caroline@nfbu.fsnet.co.uk **Website:** www.nfbu.org
The Federation was formed in 1985 to bring together national and local organisations with an interest in bus services and concerned individual bus users to seek to give an effective voice to the consumer. It is actively involved in developing constructive dialogue between the users and providers of bus services. It publishes a quarterly newsletter – *Bus User*.
Chairman: Dr Caroline Cahm.
Vice Chairman: Gavin Booth
Secretary: Mrs Deirdre Parkinson.
Treasurer: Stephen Le Bras
Areas Officer: Joe Lynch
Officer in Wales: Leo Markham, NFBU Wales, 4 Wimmerfield Crescent, Swansea SA2 7BU **E-mail:** wnfbu@aol.com
Bus User **Editor:** Stephen Morris, PO Box 119, Shepperton TW17 8UX **Tel:** 01932 232574 **Fax:** 01932 246394 **E-mail:** buswriter@aol.com

*ROAD OPERATORS' SAFETY COUNCIL (ROSCO)

395 Cowley Road, Oxford OX4 2DJ
Tel: 01865 775552 **Fax:** 01865 711745
E-mail: rosco-oxford@supanet.com
Web site: www.rosco.org.uk
Chairman: Peter Shipp
Secretary: Tony Beetham

THE ROYAL SOCIETY FOR THE PREVENTION OF ACCIDENTS

Edgbaston Park, 353 Bristol Road, Birmingham B5 7ST
Tel: 0121 248 2000. **Fax:** 0121 248 2001.

RoSPA promotes safety at work and in the home, at leisure and in schools, on (or near water) and on the roads, through providing information, publicity, training and consultancy.
The Society works with central and local government, the caring services, the police and public and private sector organisations large and small. Some work is funded by grant and sponsorship, but most relies on the support of the Society's membership.
The Society also produces and supplies a comprehensive selection of publications ranging from reference books to low-cost booklets for mass distribution.
Training Offered: Training courses cover practical skills and management training through to professional qualifications in Health and Safety.

Chief Executive: John Hooper
Head of Road Safety: Kevin Clinton
Director of Public Safety: J. L. Howard

*TRANSPORT 2000

Transport 2000, 1st Floor, The Impact Centre, 12-18 Hoxton Street, London N1 6NG
Tel: 020 7613 0743 **Fax:** 020 7613 5280.
Web site: www.transport2000.org.uk
Transport 2000 is an environmental transport campaign group.
President: Michael Palin
Executive Director: Stephen Joseph

*TRANSPORT BENEVOLENT FUND

87A Leonard Street, London EC2A 4QS
Tel: 0870 0000 172/173 **Fax:** 0870 831 2882
Web site: www.tbf.org.uk
E-mail: help@tbf.co.uk
TBF is a Registered Charity (No 1058032) and was founded in 1923. Membership was formerly restricted to staff associated with London Transport, but is now open to most staff engaged in the public transport industry. Members pay £1 a week and in return are granted, at the discretion of the Trustees, cash help, convalescence, recuperation, a wide range of complementary medical treatments, legal advice, and medical equipment in times of need. Membership starts after 12 weeks' contributions and covers the employee and their partner and dependent children. Subject to age and length of membership, free membership may be awarded on leaving the industry. There are payroll deduction facilities in many companies.
Director: Chris Godbold
Senior Trustee: Ray Jordan (**President**)
Patrons: Sir Wilfrid Newton, CBE (Past Chairman, London Transport), Brian Souter (Stagecoach Group plc), Lew Adams OBE (Strategic Rail Authority), Moir Lockhead (FirstGroup), Bob Davies (Arriva), Peter Hendy and Dave Wetzel (Transport for London), Phil White (National Express), Robert Crow (RMT), Chris Moyes (Go-Ahead Group), Graham Stevenson (T&GWU), Shaun Brady (ASLEF), Gerry Doherty (TSSA).

First Aid and Sports Associations

*COACH & BUS FIRST AID ASSOCIATION

President: J. Mackie, Commercial Director, First Aberdeen; 395 King Street, Aberdeen AB24 5RD
Hon Secretary: D. A. Crew, 11 Chertsey Road, Windlesham GU20 6EN.
Tel: 01276 451977 (**Mobile**) 07721 457735 **E-mail:** crew1@g+internet.com

Membership of the Association is open to all companies in the passenger transport industry for a nominal annual subscription. The Association is purely a non profit making voluntary body administered by an executive committee comprising the elected president, secretary and treasurer plus other members who meet four times per year.

CABFAA is supported by the Confederation of Passenger Transport. As no other representative body exists for the bus and coach industry to exchange views and be kept up to date on First Aid matters and legislation, it is hoped that all companies both large and small will give support to the Association.

Trade Organisations and Associations

BEAMA LTD

The British Electrotechnical & Allied Manufacturers' Association.
Founded 1902. Incorporated 1905.
Objects: By co-operative action to promote the interests of the industrial, electrical and electronic manufacturing industries of Great Britain.
Director-General: A. A. Bullen
Offices: Westminster Tower, 3 Albert Embankment, London SE1 7SL. **Tel:** 020 7793 3000. **Fax:** 020 7793 3003.

FREIGHT TRANSPORT ASSOCIATION VEHICLE INSPECTION SERVICE

The Freight Transport Association represents the interests of over 11,000 companies throughout the UK. FTA carries out over 100,000 vehicle inspections each year including many PSVs. The FTA Vehicle Inspection Service supports operators in maintaining their vehicles in a roadworthy condition - both mechanically and legally.
Further details from Alan Osborne, Head of Vehicle Inspection Services, FTA, Tunbridge Wells (01892 526171).
Publications: *Freight* (monthly journal), FTA Yearbook.
Chief Executive: Richard Turner.
Address: Hermes House, St John's Road, Tunbridge Wells TN4 9UZ.
Tel: 01892 526171. **Web Site:** www.fta.co.uk.

MOTOR INDUSTRY RESEARCH ASSOCIATION (MIRA)

MIRA an independent product engineering and technology centre and offers skills in innovation, problem-solving and consultancy.
Chairman: C. Ennos.
Executive Directors:
Managing Director: J. R. Wood.
Director of Finance & Company Secretary: C. H. Phillipson.
Director of Engineering: G. Townsend.
Director of Research & Business Development:
Dr V. Considine
Registered Office: MIRA Ltd, Watling Street, Nuneaton CV10 0TU
Tel: 024 7635 5000. **Fax:** 024 7635 5355.

*SOCIETY OF MOTOR MANUFACTURERS & TRADERS (SMMT)

Forbes House, Halkin Street, London SW1X 7DS.
Tel: 020 7344 9235 **Fax:** 020 7344 1676
Web site: www.smmt.co.uk
E-mail: buscoachweb@smmt.co.uk
Contact: Bob Davis

STATUS

Manchester Metropolitan University, Chester Street, Manchester
M1 5GD
Tel: 0161 247 6242
Fax: 0161 247 6779
Web site: www.status.org.uk
E-mail: a.g.read@mmu.acc.uk
STATUS provides members, from all areas of the specialist road transport industry, with engineering development and test services, technical legislative consultancy and a range of general technical information.

It is involved on behalf of its members in contributing to consultation documents, influencing transport related legislation and lobbying government departments and agencies.
STATUS is located in Manchester Metropolitan University's John Dalton Building.

The organisation can call on a diverse range of personnel to help deal with more difficult problems. A primary benefit is the availability of telephone consultancy on technical or legislative matters.

STATUS plays a prominent role in representing its members' interests on legislative matters and lobbies government agencies on behalf of members.

A monthly newsletter is publsihed, featuring industry related stories.

TRADE VALUERS INSTITUTE

Office: Monomark House, 27 Old Gloucester Street, London WC1N 3XX
Tel: 020 7242 2474 **Fax:** 01625 423453
E-mail: secretary@tvi.org.uk **Web site:** www.tvi.org.uk

*THE VEHICLE BUILDERS & REPAIRERS ASSOCIATION LTD

President: The Rt Hon Lord Strathcarron.
Director General: R. D. Nicholson.
Journal Editor: Judi Barton
Offices: Belmont House, Gildersome, Leeds LS27 7TW.
Tel: 0113 253 8333. **Fax:** 0113 238 0496.
E-mail: vbra@vbra.co.uk **Web site:** www.vbra.co.uk

Societies

THE ASSOCIATION OF FRIENDS OF THE BRITISH COMMERCIAL VEHICLE MUSEUM TRUST

The Association was formed when The British Commercial Vehicle Museum was opened in 1983. Its aims are to support the full-time staff in matters of publicity, fund raising, maintenance and documentation of exhibits, work in the archives, organising rallies, etc. Facilities for members include a newsletter, meetings, visits to places of interest, free admission to the museum and its archives to undertake

museum work and socialise with colleagues. New members are always welcome and special rates exist for families, students and senior citizens.
Hon Chairman and Secretary: G. Baron
Hon Treasurer: J. P. Potter
Members of the Committee: C. Simister, D. Lewis, P. Sennant, I. Bell.
Museum Manager: A. Buchan
Address: The British Commercial Vehicle Museum, King St, Leyland, Preston PR25 2LE. **Tel:** 01772 451011.

*BIRMINGHAM & MIDLAND MOTOR OMNIBUS TRUST

Birmingham & Midland Museum of Transport, Chapel Lane, Wythall B47 6JX
Web site: www.bammot.org.uk
E-mail: enquiries@bammot.org.uk
The Trust dates back to 1973, taking its present title in 1977, when it became a registered educational charity to establish and develop a regional transport museum.

Two large halls house a broad collection of around 100 buses, coaches, fire engines and battery-electric vehicles from all parts of the Midlands and beyond. Birmingham and the Black Country especially are featured, and the museum has a unique collection of buses and coaches designed, built and operated by Midland Red, a company which pioneered many technical innovations over a 50 year manufacturing period.

A museum archive to record the development of the bus and coach industry in the Midlands is also being established, with collections of photographs, uniforms, tickets, ticket equipment and street furniture.

Members receive the bi-monthly museum journal *Omnibus* containing details of museum developments. The museum is open to the public every weekend between Easter and the end of October. Special event days are held on some Sundays and holiday Mondays when vehicles are on display and historic bus services operate, including a link with Birmingham city centre. Also buses for hire - see Worcestershire in Operators section.

*BRITISH BUS PRESERVATION GROUP

1-4 The Mews, Hatherley Road, Sidcup DA14 4BH
Membership enquiries: 6 Pine Close, Billingshurst RH14 9NL
Tel: 020 8302 7551
Web site: www.bbpg.co.uk
E-mail: enquiries@bbpg.co.uk, john-witt@eurobell.co.uk
The BBPG was formed in 1990 and has been responsible for securing the future of more than 250 historic buses and coaches, many of which were saved at extremely short notice from being broken up. The society has more than 600 members, both individuals and preservation groups. The BBPG caters for all bus enthusiasts, whether or not they own a bus.
Chairman: Glyn Matthews.
General Secretary: Mike Lloyd.
Membership Secretary: John Witt

*BRITISH TROLLEYBUS SOCIETY

Formed as the Reading Transport Society in 1961, the title was changed to the present one in 1971, having acquired a number of trolleybuses for preservation from all over Britain. In 1969 it founded the Trolleybus Museum at Sandtoft, near Doncaster, where its vehicles are housed and regularly operate on mains power from the overhead wiring. West Yorkshire Transport Circle merged into the Society in January 1991. Currently membership stands at about 320. Members receive a monthly journal *Trolleybus* containing news and articles from home and abroad. Additionally members can subscribe to *Bus Fare* and *Wheels*, monthly magazines for motorbus operation in the Thames Valley and West Yorkshire areas respectively. Monthly meetings are also held in Reading, London. and Bradford.
Chairman: M. J. C. Dare, 14 Ilkley Road, Caversham, Reading RG4 7BD.
Secretary: A. J. Barton, 2 Josephine Court, Southcote Road, Reading RG30 2DG.
Treasurer: R. V. Fawcett, 57 Sutcliffe Avenue, Earley RG6 7JN.

*BUSES WORLDWIDE (BWW)

Web site: www.busesworldwide.org
Established in 1982 to associate those particularly interested in bus operation in countries other than their own. Meetings are held, a bi-monthly magazine is published and visits abroad are organised.
Chairman: J. W. Smith
Membership Secretary: S. Guess, 37 Oyster Lane, Byfleet KT14 7HS
News Editor: N. R. Bartlett, 1 Hopping Jacks Lane, Danbury, Chelmsford CM3 4PN.
Features Editor: D. Corke, 8 Priestland Gardens, Berkhamsted HP4 2GT.

*CLASSIC BUS HERITAGE TRUST (INCORPORATING THE ROUTEMASTER HERITAGE TRUST)

The Classic Bus Heritage Trust aims to advance preservation of buses and coaches by fostering the interests of the general public. It is a Registered Charity.
Treasurer & Hon Sec: W. Ackroyd, 1 Hawthorn Road, Send, Surrey GU23 6LH.

*ESSEX BUS ENTHUSIASTS' GROUP

Web site: www.essexbus.org.uk
This group was formed in 1962, under its previous title, Eastern National Enthusiasts' Group. The present title was adopted in 1987 to reflect more fully the activities of the group. A monthly magazine is circulated to all members giving information on all aspects of First Essex Buses, Thamesway, Colchester and Southend and all other operators in Essex. Meetings are arranged on a regular basis whilst tours are also organised. A range of publications and photographs is also available. Membership is open to all over the age of 12.
Membership Secretary: Derek Stebbing, Conifers, Thorpe Road, Weeley, Clacton-on-Sea CO16 9JJ
E-mail: derekstebbing@hotmail.com.

*HISTORIC COMMERCIAL VEHICLE SOCIETY

The Society was founded in 1958 and four years later absorbed the Vintage Passenger Vehicle Society and the London Vintage Taxi Club. Its membership of over 4,000 owns more than 6,000 preserved vehicles. Activities include the organisation of rallies, among them the well known London to Brighton and Trans-Pennine runs. The club caters for all commercial vehicles over 20 years old.
OFFICERS
President: Lord Montagu of Beaulieu
Senior Exec Officer and Vice-President: M. Banfield, Iden Grange, Cranbrook Road, Staplehurst TN12 0ET
Tel: 01580 892929. **Fax:** 01580 893227.
E-mail: hcvs@btinternet.com **Web site**: www.hcvs.co.uk

*LEYLAND NATIONAL GROUP

Website: www.leylandnationalgroup.org
E-mail: timothy.wild@ntlworld.com
Address: 27 Dukeshill Road, Bracknell RG42 2DU
Tel: 01344 640095

The Leyland National Group was formed in 1997. Since then its growth has been rapid and it now has members not just throughout Britain but abroad as well. Although the group does not own vehicles itself, some of its members are bus owners. There are more than 100 Leyland Nationals from a variety of operators, preserved by group members. However, one does not need to own a bus to join the group, as membership is open to anyone with an interest in Leyland Nationals. Members receive a bi-monthly newsletter as well as other benefits. Please contact the Membership Secretary for more information about the group, the benefits of membership and to receive a membership application form.

Chairman: Alan Fairbrother
Secretary: Michael Whiteman, 8 Leyton Way, Andover SP10 2UD
Tel: 01264 337556
E-mail: whiteman@annafields.fsnet.co.uk
Treasurer: Mike Bellinger
Publicity Officer: Paul Barrett.
Membership Sec: Tim Wild, 27 Dukeshill Road, Bracknell RG42 2DU
Tel: 01344 640095
E-mail: timothy.wild@ntlworld.com
Newsletter Editor: Anthony Poulton

LIGHT RAIL TRANSIT ASSOCIATION

PO Box 302, Gloucester GL4 4ZD **Tel/Fax**: 01452 419900
Web site: www.lrta.org
E.mail: office@lrta.org
Founded in 1937 to advocate and encourage interest in light rail and modern tramways.
Chairman: David F Russell

*LINCOLNSHIRE VINTAGE VEHICLE SOCIETY

Road Transport Museum, Whisby Road, North Hykeham LN6 5TR Tel: 01522 500566/689497

The LVVS was founded in 1959 by local businessmen with the aim of forming a road transport museum. Charitable status was obtained some time ago, and with a capital grant from its local district council, it has now completed the first stage of its new museum project. Over 60 vehicles dating from the 1920s to the 1980s can be seen in the new exhibition hall with many more in the workshop. Opening times November–April Sundays 13.00-16.00. May–October Mon-Fri 12.00-16.00, Sun 10.00-16.00.
Chairman: S Milner
Hon Treasurer: J Child
Secretary: Mrs J Jefford

*LONDON OMNIBUS TRACTION SOCIETY (LOTS)

Unit 305N, Westminster Business Square, 1-45 Durham Street London SE11 5JH
Tel: 020 7582 9777 **Web site**: www.lots.org.uk
Formed in 1964, LOTS has some 2,500 members and is the largest bus society in the British Isles.

An Illustrated monthly newsletter is sent to all members. This covers all the current operators in the former London Transport area and includes General and Industry News, Route Developments, and Vehicle News for the former London Transport area. Monthly meetings are held in central London featuring guest speakers, slide and film presentations during the year as well as the annual free bus rides from central London using vehicles of London interest.

Regular LOTS publications include fleet allocations and route working publications as well as the annual popular *London Bus and Tram Fleetbook*. A quarterly 64 page glossy magazine, the *London Bus Magazine (LBM)* has been produced for over 30 years.

Regular sales lists are produced and sent out to all members. An information service is also available to all members to answer those historical queries.

The Autumn Transport Spectacular (ATS) is held in London every Autumn and is one of London's biggest transport sales.

All enquiries should be directed to the above address.

LOW CARBON VEHICLE PARTNERSHIP

17 Queen Anne's Gate, London SW1H 9BU **Tel**: 020 7222 8000
E-mail: secretariat@lowcvp.org.uk **Web site**: www.lowcvp.org.uk

The LowCVP is an action and advisory group providing a forum through which partners can work together towards shared goals and take the lead in the transition to a low-carbon future for road transport in the UK.
Bus Working Group Chmn: John Smith

*THE M & D AND EAST KENT BUS CLUB

42 St Albans Hill, Hemel Hempstead HP3 9NG
Web site: www.mdekbusclub.org.uk **E-mail**: ndk@mdekbusclub.fsnet.co.uk

This club was formed in 1952 with the object of bringing together all those interested in road passenger transport in an area covering Kent and East Sussex. Facilities for members include a monthly news booklet (illustrated), information service, tours, meetings, vehicle photograph sales and vehicle preservation. A series of publications is also produced, including illustrated fleet histories.
Hon Chairman: J. V. Spillett
Hon Editor/Sec: N. D. King
Hon Treasurer: S. J. Champion
Membership Officer: J. A. Fairley
Photographic Officer: R. A. Lewis
Sales Officer: J. M. Poultney
Tours Officer: D. R. Cobb
Management Committee: N. D. King, R. A. Lewis, J. V. Spillett, S. J. Champion, P. J. Evans, J. M. Poultney. Area Organisers in Ashford, Dover, Folkestone, Tunbridge Wells, Hastings, North-East Kent, Maidstone and the Medway Towns.

THE NATIONAL TRAMWAY MUSEUM

Crich, Matlock DE4 5DP.
Tel: 01773 852565. Fax: 01773 852326.

The Society was founded in 1955 to establish and operate a working tramway museum. The Museum is at Crich Tramway Village, near Matlock, in Derbyshire, and owns over 70 English, Irish, Scottish, Welsh and overseas tramcars. Membership carries with it the right to receive a copy of the Society's quarterly journal.
Patron: HRH The Duke of Gloucester GCVO
Vice-Presidents: G. S. Hearse, W. G. S. Hyde, G. B. Claydon, D. J. H. Senior
Chairman: D. F. Russell

Vice-Chairman: C. Heaton
Hon Secretary: I. M. Dougill
Hon Treasurer: A. W. Bond
Operations Superintendent: K. B. Hulme
Property & Engineering Services Manager: J. Miller
Development Maager: M Trembath

*NATIONAL TROLLEYBUS ASSOCIATION

Formed in 1963, and incorporated in 1968 as The Trolleybus Museum Co Ltd. The vehicles and ancillary equipment collected by the NTA since its inception are now owned by the company, which is limited by guarantee and is a registered charity. Members receive *Trolleybus Magazine*, a printed and illustrated bi-monthly journal documenting all aspects of trolleybus operation past and present throughout the world.
Chairman: R. D. Helliar-Symons
Secretary: J. H. Ward
Treasurer: A. Dinkenor
Membership Secretary: vacant
Enquiries: nattbassn@msn.com

THE OMNIBUS SOCIETY

Website: www.omnibussoc.org.
The Omnibus Society was founded in 1929. Today it is a nationwide organisation with a network of provincial branches, offering a comprehensive range of facilities for those interested in the bus and coach industry. The Society has accumulated a wealth of information on public road transport. Members have the opportunity to receive and exchange data on every aspect of the industry including route developments, operational/traffic matters and fleet changes. Each branch has a full programme of activities and publishes its own Branch Bulletin to give local news of route changes, etc. A scheme exists whereby members subscribe to receive bulletins from branches other than that of which they are a member. A programme of indoor meetings is customary during winter, including film shows, invited speakers and discussions. In the summer months visits to manufacturers and tours visiting operators are featured.
OFFICERS
President: Peter Hendy
Vice-Presidents: F P Groves, A W Mills, G Wedlake, T. F. McLachlan, K. W. Swallow, R. G. Westgate.
Chairman: B. Le Jeune.
Secretary: A. J. Francis, 185 Southlands Road, Bromley BR2 9QZ.
Treasurer: H. L. Barker, 31 High Street, Tarporley CW6 0DP.
Editors, Society's Publications: D. Brendan Chandler, Oliver Howarth.
Members of the Council: I. D. Barlex, J. Hart, D. M. Perssons, D. Roy, J Howie and nominations from each branch
Branch Officers:
Midland Branch: C R Warn, 11 The Meadows, Shawbury, Shrewsbury SY4 4HS
South Wales and West Branch: D. J. Bubier, 15 Alianore Road, Caldicot NP26 5DF.
Northern Branch: Philip Battersby, 12 Crescent Lodge, Tile Crescent, Middlesbrough TS5 6SF.
North Western & Yorkshire Branch: P. Wilkinson, 10 Bradley Close, Timperley, Altrincham WA15 6SH.
Scottish Branch: I. Allan, 10 Miller Avenue, Crossford, Dunfermline KY12 8PY.
Essex & South Suffolk Group: J. L. Rugg, 86 Worthing Road, Laindon SS15 6JU.
East Midland Group: A. Oxley, 4 Gordon Close, Attenborough, Nottingham NN4 9UF
Herts & Beds Group: R. C. Barton, 5 Viscount Court, Knights Field, Luton LU2 7LD

London Historical Research Group: L. E. Akehurst, 3 Ivy House, Eastbury Road, Watford WD1 4QH.
Provincial Historical Research Group: R. M. Warwick, 101 Broadway East, Northampton NN3 3PP

THE PSV CIRCLE

30 Bonnersfield Lane, Harrow HA1 2LE.
The Circle is an association of over 2,400 members, interested in various ways in the vehicles used by the passenger transport industry on the roads of the United Kingdom and abroad. Membership is open to all over the age of 16, and in certain exceptional cases to those under this age. News Sheets, comprising nine regional sections, are published each month, together with numerous supplements and fleet histories which fully record information relating to operators, chassis builders and body constructors. There is no entrance fee. Annual subscriptions vary with the number of regional news sheets required, with a minimum for one area and graded additional payments according to members' requirements. Frequent meetings, mainly of a social nature, are held in London and several provincial towns.
HONORARY OFFICERS
Chairman: C. R. Costella
Secretary: W. S. Byers
Treasurer: A. G. Johnson
Managing Editor: C Elkin
The above with another eight members constitute the Committee of Management, and for convenience all mail other than editorial matters is handled at the above address.

*RIBBLE ENTHUSIASTS' CLUB

36 Wales Road, Waterfoot BB4 9SU
Tel: 01706 218176.
Founded in 1954 by the late T. B. Colinge for the study of road transport past and present and in particular Ribble Motor Services and associated companies. Meetings are held and a monthly news sheet produced.
President: A. E. Chapman
Vice Presidents: M. Shires, N. Barrett.
Chairman/Secretary: C. McKernan, 36 Wales Road, Waterfoot BB4 9SU
Records Officer: S. Blake, 23 Fairfield Road, North Shore, Blackpool FY1 2RA
Treasurer: vacant
Sales/Visits Officer: M. J. Yates, 23 Richmond Road, Hindley Green, Wigan WN2 4ND
Editor: R A Harpum, 22 Woodside Road, Ferndown BH22 9LD
Archive/Sales Officer: B. Ashcroft, 11 Regent Road, Walton Le Dale, Preston PR5 4QA.

*ROADS AND ROAD TRANSPORT HISTORY ASSOCIATION

Founded in 1992, the society promotes, encourages and co-ordinates the study of the history of roads and road transport, both passenger and freight. It aims to encourage those interested in a particular aspect of transport to understand their chosen subject in the context of developments in other areas and at other periods. It publishes a newsletter four times a year and holds an annual conference each autumn.

Membership is open to transport societies, museums and individuals. The publication, *Companion to British Road Haulage History*, was produced in 2003.
President: Garry Turvey, CBE
Chairman: Professor John Hibbs, OBE

Hon. Secretary: Gordon Knowles, 7 Squirrels Green, Great Bookham, Leatherhead KT23 3LE

*ROUTEMASTER OPERATORS & OWNERS ASSOCIATION

31 Pooley Avenue, Egham TW20 8AB Tel: 017811 367960
Mobile: 07811 367960 **Web Site**: www.routemaster.org.uk
The Routemaster Operators & Owners Association provides assistance, advice and news for operators, owners and enthusiasts of these vehicles. From the specification of a screw to a complete bus, the Association provides authoritative technical information. Bus rallies and events are organised and other selected events are supported each year. Members receive a quarterly news magazine and discounts on parts and accessories including a maintenance manual, owners handbook technical bulletins, suppliers handbook, badges and transfers, window sealing rubber and many other unique products. Large batches of Routemaster spares have been acquired from the London Buses RM refurbishment programme including original specification mechanical units, electrical items, bodywork spares, windows, tyres and wheels.
President: Colin Curtis OBE
Secretary: Graham Lunn
Press and Publicity: Steven Wood, 97 Fordwich Rise, Hertford SG14 2DI **E-mail**: steven.wood@claranet.co.uk

*THE SAMUEL LEDGARD SOCIETY

C/O 58 Kirklees Drive, Farsley, Pudsey LS28 5TE
Tel: 0113 236 3695 **Fax**: 0113 259 1125
The Samuel Ledgard Society was formed in 1998 at the Rose & Crown Inn, Otley, during the second annual reunion of the devotees of this well-known bus company. Reunions are held twice yearly at Armley during April and Otley on or about October 14. A Christmas dinner is also part of the established calendar of events. The quarterly journal of the Society, *The Chat*, is published in March, June, September and December each year. Founding officers were Barry Rennison, Tony Greaves and Don Bate, all of whom have a wealth of knowledge about the Samuel Ledgard company. Membership is open to all with a subscription of £5 - contact any member of the Committee for details.
Hon President: Samuel Ledgard Mather AMIRTE (Retd)
COMMITTEE
Chairman: Barry Rennison, 58 Kirklees Drive, Farsley, Pudsey LS28 5TE
Vice-Chairman, Magazine Editor & Publicity Officer: Tony Greaves, 19 Perth Mount, Horsforth LS18 5SH
Treasurer & Society Historian: Don Bate, 11 St Margaret's Road, Horsforth LS18 5BD
Secretary & Membership: Margaret Rennison, 58 Kirklees Drive, Farsley, Pudsey LS28 5TE

*SCOTTISH TRAMWAY & TRANSPORT SOCIETY

PO Box 7342, Glasgow G51 4YQ
Founded in 1951 as the Scottish Tramway Museum Society, the Society claims to be 'Scotland's foremost tramway enthusiast organisation', publishing books and videos on tramways and other transport subjects and supporting the National Tramway Museum. Monthly meetings and newsletter.
Hon Chairman: A Murray
Gen Secretary: H. McAulay
E-mail: hughmc@87gv.freeserve.co.uk
Hon Treasurer: A. Ramsay
Members of Committee: F Mitchell, N Bates, G Ewing, W Tuckwell, I Stewart, A Muir, B Longworth, B Quinn

*SHEFFIELD BUS MUSEUM TRUST LTD

Tinsley Tram Sheds, Sheffield Road, Tinsley, Sheffield S9 2FY
Tel: 0114 255 3010
The Sheffield Bus Museum Trust was formed in 1987 with the purpose of co-ordinating the bus preservation movement in Sheffield and to establish a permanent museum. This has been achieved at the former Sheffield Tramways Company's Tinsley Tram Depot. The majority of the Trust's collection is local and extremely varied, ranging from a 1926 Sheffield tramcar to a 1985 Dennis Domino. In recent years the Museum Trust has benefitted from Heritage Fund Lottery grants. The museum is an educational charity and promotes an ever-expanding schools visits programme. The museum is open every Saturday and Sunday afternoon with special theme days from April to December.
Chairman: M W Greenwood
Membership Secretary: Dr. John Willis, 2 Pwll-Y-Waen, Ty'n-Y-Groes, Conwy LL32 8TQ.

*SOUTHDOWN ENTHUSIASTS' CLUB

Web site: www.southdownenthusiastsclub.org.uk
This club was founded in 1954 to bring together people interested in the vehicles, routes and history of Southdown Motor Services Ltd and now includes Stagecoach South (Hastings & District, South Coast Buses, Hampshire Bus, Hants & Surrey, East Kent), Brighton & Hove, Eastbourne Buses and First Hampshire. There is a monthly news publication and winter meetings. Membership is open to persons aged 14 years and over and details may be had from the Hon Secretary.
Hon Chairman: J Allpress, 9 Phoenix Way, Southwick, Brighton BN42 4HQ
Hon Secretary: N Simes, 11 High Cross Fields, Crowborough TN6 2SN
Hon Treasurer: D E Still, 12 Westway Close, Mile Oak, Portslade BN42 2RT
Hon Sales Officer: D Chalkley, 6 Valebridge Drive, Burgess Hill RH15 0RW
Hon News Sheet Editor: P Gainsbury, Park Cottage, Guestling TN35 4LT
Hon Publications Officer: J Smith, 1 Sackville Way, Worthing BN14 8BJ
Committee Member: J Barley, 84 Kipling Avenue, Brighton BN2 6UE.
Hon Photographic Officer: C Churchill, 53 Monks Close, Lancing BN15 9DB

*SWINDON VINTAGE OMNIBUS SOCIETY

10 Fraser Close, Nythe, Swindon SN3 3RP
Tel: 01793 526001
Preserved Daimler Weymann double deck, ex Swindon corporation society vehicle.
Chairman: M. Naughton
Secretary: D. Nicol
Treasurer: D. Mundy

*TRAMWAY & LIGHT RAILWAY SOCIETY

Web site: www.tramways.freeserve.co.uk
Founded in 1938, the Tramway & Light Railway Society caters for those interested in all aspects of tramways. Members receive *Tramfare*, a bi-monthly illustrated magazine. There are regular meetings throughout the country. The Society promotes

tramway modelling, drawings, castings, and technical details are available to modellers. There are also comprehensive library facilities. For fuller details of the Society and of membership please write to the Membership Secretary.

HONORARY OFFICERS
President: P. J. Davis.
Vice-Presidents: Mr E. R. Oakley, G. B. Claydon, C.B
Chairman: J. R. Prentice, 216 Brentwood Road, Romford RM1 2RP.
Secretary: G. R. Tribe, 47 Soulbury Road, Linslade, Leighton Buzzard LU7 7RW.
Membership Secretary: H. J. Leach, 6 The Woodlands, Brightlingsea CO7 0RY.

THE TRANSPORT TICKET SOCIETY

An association of students and collectors of passenger tickets and fare collection methods. Founded in 1946 the TTS now has some 500 members worldwide. An illustrated monthly Journal, and regular distributions of tickets, keep members up to date with both historical and recent developments in ticketing in all modes of transport. The TTS welcomes offers of obsolete tickets for distribution to members. Full details of membership together with a sample Journal will be sent on request to the TTS publicity officer, or visit the TTS website: www.transport-ticket.com.

Publicity Officer: Martin Rickitt, Bromes House, Isle Abbots, Taunton TA3 6RW. **Tel:** 01460 281228 **E-mail:** mrickitt@hotmail.com
Chairman: John Tolson
Membership Secretary: David Randal
General Secretary: Patrick Geall
Treasurer: Graham Wootton.
Managing Editor: David Harman

THE TRANSPORT TRUST

202 Lambeth Road, London SE1 7JW.
Tel: 020 7928 6464. **Fax:** 020 7928 6535. **E-mail:** hq@thetransporttrust.org.uk

The national charity for the preservation and restoration of Britain's transport heritage.

section 4

British Isles Operators

Major Groups	71
English Operators	
Bedfordshire	72
Berkshire (West Berkshire, Bracknell Forest, Reading, Slough, Windsor & Maidenhead, Wokingham)	73
Bristol	75
Buckinghamshire, Milton Keynes	77
Cambridgeshire and Peterborough City	79
Cheshire, Halton and Stockport	81
Cornwall	84
Cumbria	86
Derbyshire	88
Devon	91
Dorset, Bournemouth, Poole	95
Durham	97
East Sussex, Brighton & Hove	100
East Riding of Yorkshire, Kingston upon Hull	102
Essex	103
Gloucestershire	107
Greater Manchester, Bolton, Bury, Oldham, Rochdale, Salford, Tameside, Wigan	109
Hampshire	112
Herefordshire	115
Hertfordshire	116
Isle of Wight	119
Kent	120
Lancashire, Blackburn with Darwen, Blackpool, Wigan,	124
Leicestershire, City of Leicester, Rutland	128
Lincolnshire	130
London	132
Merseyside area (St Helens, Knowsley, Liverpool, Sefton, Wirral)	139
Middlesex	140
Norfolk	143
North Lincolnshire, North East Lincolnshire	145
North Yorkshire, York	146
Northamptonshire	149
Northumberland	150
Nottinghamshire, Nottingham	151
Oxfordshire	154
Shropshire	155
Somerset, Bath & North East Somerset/North Somerset	157
South Yorkshire	160
Staffordshire	163
Suffolk	166
Surrey	168
Tyne & Wear	171
Warwickshire	172
West Midlands	173
West Sussex	178
West Yorkshire, Bradford, Calderdale, Kirklees, Leeds, Wakefield	179
Wiltshire	183
Worcestershire	185
Scottish Operators	
Aberdeen, City of	188
Aberdeenshire	188
Angus	189
Argyll & Bute	189
Borders	190
Clackmannanshire	190
Dumfries & Galloway	190
Dundee, City of	191
East Ayrshire	191
East Lothian	192
East Renfrewshire	192
Edinburgh, City of	192
Falkirk	193
Fife	193
Glasgow, City of	194
Highland	194
Inverclyde	195
Midlothian	195
Moray	196
North Ayrshire	196
North Lanarkshire	196
Orkney	197
Perth & Kinross	197
Renfrewshire	198
Shetland	
South Ayrshire	
South Lanarkshire	
Stirling	
West Dunbartonshire	
West Lothian	
Western Isles	
Welsh Operators	
Anglesey	
Blaenau Gwent	
Bridgend	
Caerphilly	
Cardiff	
Carmarthenshire	
Ceredigion	
Conwy	
Denbighshire	
Flintshire	
Gwynedd	
Merthyr Tydfil	
Monmouthshire	
Neath & Port Talbot	
Newport	
Pembrokeshire	
Powys	
Rhondda, Cynon, Taff	
Swansea	
Torfaen	
Vale of Glamorgan	
Wrexham	
Channel Islands Operators	
Alderney	
Guernsey	
Jersey	
Isles of Man Operators	
Isle of Man	
Isle of Scilly Operators	
Isle of Scilly	
Northern Ireland Operators	
Northern Ireland	
Republic of Ireland Operators	
Republic of Ireland	

Unitary authorities are included within the postal boundaries.

Major Groups

ARRIVA PLC
ADMIRAL WAY, DOXFORD INTERNATIONAL BUSINESS PARK, SUNDERLAND SR3 3XP
Tel: 0191 520 4000 **Fax**: 0191 520 4115
E-mail: enquires@arriva.co.uk
Website: www.arriva.co.uk
Chairman (Non Exec): Sir Richard Broadbent **Mktng Dir, Bus Ops**: Catherine Mason **Chief Executive**: Bob Davies **Man Dir**: Mark Bowd **Man Dir, UK Trains**: Euan Cameron **Man Dir, UK Bus Operations**: Steve Clayton **Development Dir**: Tony Depledge **Finance Director**: Steve Lonsdale **Managing Director - International**: David Martin **Head of Public Relations**: Joanne Granville
DEALERSHIP
ARRIVA BUS & COACH, LODGE GARAGE, WHITEHALL ROAD WEST, GOMERSAL, CLECKHEATON BD19 4BJ.

ARRIVA PASSENGER SERVICES
5 DOMINUS WAY, LEICESTER LE3 2RP
Tel: 0116 240 5500
Fax: 0116 240 5501
Managing Director UK Bus: Steve Clayton **Eng Dir**: Mark Bowd **Mktng Dir**: Catherine Mason

BLAZEFIELD HOLDINGS LTD
PROSPECT PARK, BROUGHTON WAY, STARBECK, HARROGATE HG2 7NY
Tel: 01423 884020
Chmn: Giles Fearnley **Man Dir**: Stuart Wilde **Fin Dir**: Clive R Smith **Com Dir**: David Hurry **Group Tech Dir**: Mike Mullins
Subsidiary companies: Burnley & Pendle, Harrogate & District Travel Ltd, Keighley & District Travel Ltd, Lancashire United, Yorkshire Coastliner Ltd.

*FIRST
395 KING STREET, ABERDEEN AB24 5RP
Tel: 01224 650100
Fax: 01224 650140
Website: www.firstgroup.com
E-mail: contactus@firstgroup.com
Chmn: Martin Gilbert **DepChmn/Ch Exec**: Moir Lockhead **Fin Dir**: Dean Finch **Business Change Dir**: Mike Mitchell **Man Dir, UK Bus**: David Leeder **Ops Dir**: David Kaye **Comm Dir**: Leon Daniels **Senior Independent Non-Exec Dir**: David Dunn **Non Exec Dir**: Jim Forbes
Non-exec Dir: John Sievwright **Non-Exec Employee Dir**: Martyn Williams
Fleet: 9335 - 2893 double-deck bus, 2510 single-deck bus, 109 articulated bus, 256 coach, 2662 midibus, 925 minibus.
Chassis: 44 AEC. 1 Albion. 20 Bluebird. 74 Bristol. 24 DAF. 1 Daimler. 3197 Dennis. 5 Duple. 5 Iveco. 6 LDV. 973 Leyland. 137 MCW. 962 Mercedes. 281 Optare. 720 Scania. 2861 Volvo.
Bodies: 2012 Alexander. 8 Berkhof. 59 Caetano. 7 Carlyle. 21 Duple. 183 East Lancs. 157 ECW. 14 Ikarus. 10 Irizar. 10 Jonckheere. 4 Leicester. 205 Leyland. 558 Marshall. 85 MCW. 9 Mellor. 111 Mercedes. 597 Northern Counties. 379 Optare. 45 Park Royal. 2748 Plaxton. 20 Reeve Burgess. 141 Roe. 2 Transbus. 26 UVG. 15 Van Hool. 2 Wadham Stringer. 760 Wright.
Ops incl: local bus services, tram services, school contracts, excursions & tours, private hire, express, continental tours.
Livery: standard First
Ticket System: Wayfarer

*THE GO-AHEAD GROUP PLC
3RD FLOOR, 41-51 GREY STREET, NEWCASTLE UPON TYNE NE1 6EE
Tel: 0191 232 3123
Fax: 0191 221 0315
Website: www.go-ahead.com
E-mail: admin@go-ahead.com
Non-Exec Chmn: Sir Patrick Brown **Non-Exec Dirs**: Christopher Collins, Rupert Pennant-Rea **Ch Exec**: Chris Moyes **Fin Dir/Co Sec**: Ian Butcher.
Fleet: 2694 - 1312 double-deck bus, 369 single-deck bus, 74 coach, 71 articulated bus, 870 midibus.
Ops incl: local bus services, school contracts, excursions & tours, private hire, express, continental tours.
Livery: local fleet identity
Ticket System: various
Subsidiary companies: Brighton & Hove Bus & Coach Company, City of Oxford Motor Services, Go North East, London General Transport Services, London Central Bus Company, Metrobus, Wilts & Dorset Bus Company, Metro City Taxis, Meteor, Thameslink Rail, Southern, Aviance UK.

NATIONAL EXPRESS GROUP PLC
75 DAVIES STREET, LONDON W1K 5HT
Tel: 020 7529 2000
Fax: 020 7529 2100
Website: www.nationalexpress.com
E-mail: info@natex.co.uk
Chief Executive: Phil White **Chief Executive (National Express Corporation, USA)**: Keith Stock **Man Dir (AirLinks)**: Bill Cahill **Financial Director**: Adam Walker **Ch Ops Officer**: Ray O'Toole **Co Sec**: Tony McDonald **Group Customer Service Dir**: David Bird
Subsidiary companies
Bus and coach: National Express (nationwide express coach network using coaches hired in from local operators under contract). National Express owns Travel West Midlands, Travel Dundee and Travel London.
Rail: Central Trains, Midland Mainline, Silverlink, Gatwick Express, C2C, Maintrain, Wessex Trains, Travel Midland Metro.
Overseas: National Express Corporation (USA) - Bauman, Crabtree-Harmaan, Durham Transportation, Robinson Bus, SSL, ATC, Forsythe & Associates, Intelitran, Multisystems, Stewart International; National Express Australia pty National Bus Company, shareholding in Westbus, Southern Coast Transit; Bronckaers.

SOUTHERN VECTIS PLC
NELSON ROAD, NEWPORT PO30 1RD.
Tel: 01983 522456. Fax: 01983 524961
Website: www.southernvectis.plc.uk
Non-Exec Chmn: Mike Killingley **Non-Exec Dir**: Tony Holmes **Group Man Dir**: Stuart Linn **Group Fin Dir**: Ian Palmer **Exec Dir/Co Sec**: Kate Boyes **Subsidiary companies**: The Southern Vectis Omnibus Co Ltd, Vikki Osborne (IW) Holidays Ltd, Southern Vectis Coaches Ltd., Southern Vectis Commercials Ltd, Musterphantom Ltd (Solent Blue Line).

*STAGECOACH GROUP
10 DUNKELD ROAD, PERTH PH1 5TW
Tel: 01738 442111
Fax: 01738 643648
Web site: www.stagecoachgroup.com
Ch Exec: Brian Souter **Fin Dir**: Martin Griffiths **Man Dir (UK bus)**: Les Warneford **Exec Dir (Rail)**: Graham Eccles **Non-Exec Chmn**: Robert Spiers **Non-Exec Dirs**: Ann Gloag, Ewan Brown, Iain Duffin, Janet Morgan, Russell Walls **Regional Dir South**: B Cox **Co Sec**: Derek Scott
Fleet: 2589 double-deck bus, 1408 single-deck bus, 334 coach, 27 double-deck coach, 35 articulated bus, 1536 midibus, 855 minibus.
Livery: Stagecoach
Ticket system: ERG/Wayfarer
Overseas Division: Coach USA, Stagecoach New Zealand
Rail Division: South West Trains, Island Line, joint venture Virgin Rail Group, Sheffield Supertram (Sheffie d).

TRACTION GROUP LTD
UPPER SHEFFIELD ROAD, BARNSLEY S70 4PP.
Tel: 01226 202555, 202666.
Subsidiary companies: Lincolnshire Road Car Co Ltd, Barnsley & District Traction Co Ltd, W. Gash & Sons Ltd, Strathtay Scottish Omnibuses Ltd, James Meffan & Sons Ltd, Lincoln City Transport, Tanport Ltd, Basichour Ltd, Yorkshire Terrier Ltd, Kingsman Services Ltd, Yorkshire Traction Co Ltd.

WELLGLADE LTD
MANSFIELD ROAD, HEANOR, DERBY DE75 7BG.
Tel: 01773 536309
Fax: 01773 536310.
Subsidiary companies: Trent-Barton Ltd, Kinchbus Ltd, Nottinghamshire & Derbyshire Traction Co Ltd.

BEDFORDSHIRE

ARRIVA THE SHIRES & ESSEX LTD
487 DUNSTABLE ROAD, LUTON LU4 8DS
Tel: 01582 587000
Fleetname: Arriva the Shires & Essex.
Man Dir: Mark Bowd **Comm Dir:** Brian Drury **Ops Dir:** Heath Williams **Eng Dir:** B. Barraclough. **Fin Dir:** A. Severn
Fleet: 571 - 133 double-deck bus, 273 single-deck bus, 42 coach, 123 minibus.
Ops incl: local bus services, school contracts, excursions & tours, private hire, express.
Livery: Aquamarine and Cream.
Ticket System: Wayfarer 3, Prestige.

BARFORDIAN COACHES LTD
500 GOLDINGTON ROAD, BEDFORD MK41 0DX
Tel: 01234 355440
Fax: 01234 355310
E-mail: barfordiancoaches@btopenworld.com
Ops Man: K. Hargreaves **Sec:** J. Bullard
Fleet: 24 - 4 double-deck bus, 1 single-deck bus, 12 coach, 4 double-deck coach, 1 midicoach, 2 minicoach.
Chassis: 1 Bedford. 9 Bova. 2 Bristol. 1 DAF. 2 Leyland. 1 MCW. 2 Mercedes. 3 Neoplan. 1 Toyota. 2 Volvo.
Bodies: 2 Autobus. 9 Bova. 1 Caetano. 2 Duple. 3 ECW. 1 MCW. 3 Neoplan. 3 Plaxton.
Ops incl: local bus services, school contracts, excursions & tours, private hire, continental tours.
Livery: Orange/Yellow/Blue
Ticket System: Setright

BISHOP COACHES
47 WELLINGTON STREET, LUTON LU1 2QH
Tel: 01582 457008
Prop: R. J. Lush
Fleet: 7 - 6 coaches, 1 minibus.
Chassis: 2 DAF. 1 Dennis. 1 LDV. 1 Leyland. 2 Volvo.
Bodies: 1 Caetano. 2 Duple. 1 LDV. 1 Leyland. 2 Plaxton.
Ops incl: private hire, school contracts, continental tours.
Livery: White

BUFFALO TRAVEL
See Dunn-Line Group, Nottinghamshire

*CEDAR COACHES
ARKWRIGHT ROAD, BEDFORD MK42 0LE.
Tel: 01234 354054
Fax: 01234 219210
E-mail: nikki@cedarcoaches.co.uk
Web site: www.cedarcoaches.co.uk
Prop: Eric Reid **Co Sec:** Nichola Graham
Fleet: 30 - 17 double-deck bus, 4 single-deck bus, 8 coach, 1 double-deck coach.
Chassis: 2 Ayats. 1 Bova. 1 Irisbus. 1 Iveco. 10 Leyland. 1 MAN. 2 Mercedes. 1 Optare. 1 Scania. 2 Volvo.
Bodies: include Alexander. 2 Ayats. 1 Beulas. 1 Berkhof. 1 Bova. 1 Irizar. 1 Jonckheere. 1 Optare.
Ops incl: local bus services, school contracts, excursions & tours, private hire.
Livery: Red/Yellow
Ticket System: Almex

CENTREBUS LTD
DUKEMINSTER INDUSTRIAL ESTATE, DUNSTABLE LU5 4HU
Fleetname: InMotion
Dirs: Ralph Garrett, Peter Harvey
Fleet: 100 - includes double-deck bus, single-deck bus
Chassis: includes Dennis. Leyland. Scania. Volvo.
Bodies: include: Alexander. MCW. Plaxton.
Ops incl: local bus services, school contracts
Livery: White/Blue/Orange

CHILTERN TRAVEL
THE COACH HOUSE, BARFORD ROAD, BLUNHAM MK44 3NA
Tel: 01234 295490
Fax: 01234 295490
E-mail: chilterntravel.coaches@virgin.net
Prop: Trevor Boorman
Fleet: 8 - 6 coach, 2 double-deck coach.
Chassis: 1 Bova. 2 DAF. 3 Mercedes-Benz. 2 Volvo.
Bodies: 1 Bova. 1 Jonckheere. 3 Mercedes-Benz. 3 Van Hool.
Ops incl: private hire, continental tours, school contracts, excursions & tours. **Livery:** White.

*CORPORATE COACHING
EAGLE HOUSE, EAGLE CENTRE WAY, LUTON LU4 9US
Tel: 01525 715872
Fax: 01525 713020
E-mail: sales@corp-coach.co.uk
Web site: www.corp-coach.co.uk
Man Dir: Doreen Colthorpe **Ops Dir:** Peter Collins
Fleet: 8 - 4 midicoach, 4 minicoach.
Chassis: 8 Mercedes-Benz.
Bodies: 4 Optare. 4 Olympus.
Ops incl: private hire.
Livery: Blue/Silver.

DUNN-LINE GROUP
See Nottinghamshire

EXPRESSLINES LTD
UNIT 15, FENLAKE ROAD INDUSTRIAL ESTATE, BEDFORD MK42 0HB
Tel: 01234 268704
Dirs: Richard Harris, Christopher Spriggs
Fleet: 17 – 1 single-deck bus, 5 midicoach, 11 minibus.
Chassis: 10 Ford Transit. 1 Leyland. 5 Mercedes-Benz. 1 Optare.
Bodies: 4 Optare. 1 Reeve Burgess
Ops incl: local bus services, school contracts, private hire.
Livery: Red/White/Silver
Ticket System: Almex Microfare

HERBERTS TRAVEL
SHEFFORD MILL, STANFORD ROAD, SHEFFORD SG17 5LX
Tel: 01462 813240.
Fax: 01462 819425
Dir/Gen Man: M. F. Herbert.
Traf Man/Ch Eng: J. Cobden.
Sec: M. A. Herbert.
Fleet: 14 - 12 coaches, 2 midicoach, 2 minibus, 8 minicoach.
Chassis: Ford. Ford Transit. Freight Rover. Leyland. Mercedes. Neoplan.
Bodies: MCW. Plaxton. Reeve Burgess. Wright. Mercedes.
Ops incl: private hire, school contracts.
Livery: Red/White/Black.

*MARSHALLS COACHES
FIRBANK WAY, LEIGHTON BUZZARD LU7 4YP
Tel: 01525 376077
Fax: 01525 850967
Recovery: 01525 375301
E-mail: info@marshalls-coaches.co.uk

Web site: www.marshalls-coaches.co.uk
Props: F W Marshall, S J Marshall **Ops Man**: I White **Ch Eng**: N Aris
Fleet: 22 - 2 double-deck bus, 19 coach, 1 double-deck coach.
Chassis: 3 Dennis. 7 Iveco. 1 LDV. 1 Neoplan. 10 Volvo.
Bodies: 7 Beulas. 2 East Lancs. 1 Ikarus. 4 Jonckheere. 1 Leyland. 1 Neoplan. 5 Plaxton. 1 Enigma.
Ops incl: private hire, school contracts, local bus services, express, continental tours.
Livery: Blue/Multicoloured.

NEWBOURNE COACHES
See London.

RED KITE COMMERCIAL SERVICES
UNIT 2, LEYS YARD, DUNSTABLE ROAD, TILSWORTH, LEIGHTON BUZZARD LU7 9PU
Tel: 01525 211441.
Props: D. Hoar, R. H. Savage
Fleet: 18 - 15 double-deck bus, 3 coach.
Ops incl: local bus services, school contracts, excursions and tours, private hire, school contracts.
Livery: Red/Blue

*ROLYN TRAVEL
16 STUART ROAD, BARTON-LE-CLAY, BEDFORD MK45 4NG
Tel: 01582 882519
E-mail: coaches@rolyntravel.com
Web site: www.rolyntravel.co.uk
Props: Robin Smith, Lynda Smith.
Fleet: 1 coach
Chassis: Volvo.
Body: Plaxton
Ops incl: excursions & tours, private hire, continental tours.
Livery; White/Pink

RONSWAY COACHES
See Hertfordshire

SAFFORDS COACHES LTD
THE DRIFT, LITTLE GRANSDEN, SANDY SG19 3DW
Tel: 01767 677395
Fax: 01767 677742
Dirs: M. C. Safford, S. I. Gillett.
Fleet: 14 - 1 single-deck bus, 10 coach, 3 midicoach.
Chassis: 2 Mercedes, 12 Volvo.
Bodies: 1 Caetano, 1 Jonckheere, 12 Plaxton.
Ops incl: local bus services, school contracts, excursions & tours, private hire, continental tours.
Livery: White/Blue/Yellow.
Ticket System: Almex.

SHOREYS TRAVEL & TRANSPORT
IVY FARM, 119 CLOPHILL ROAD, MAULDEN MK45 2AE.
Tel: 01525 860694.
Fax: 01525 861850.
Prop: E. C. J. Shorey.
Co Sec/Dir: D. Shorey. **Dir**: G. Shorey.
Fleet: 10 - 9 double deck bus, 1 coach.
Chassis: 2 Daimler. 3 Leyland. 5 MCW.
Bodies: 1 Beulas. 6 MCW. 4 Park Royal.
Ops incl: local bus services, school contracts, private hire, continental tours.
Livery: White/Orange/Blue.
Ticket System: Wayfarer.

*SILVERLINE TRAVEL R
119 DELLS LANE, BIGGLESWADE SG18 8LD
Tel: 01767 314704
Prop: D J Cook
Fleet: 3 - 1 midicoach, 1 minibus, 1 midicoach.
Chassis: 1 Ford Transit. 1 Mercedes. 1 Toyota.

Bodies: 1 Caetano. 1 Mercedes.
Ops incl: school contracts, private hire.
Livery: Red/Silver

STAGECOACH EAST
See Northamptonshire

*TATES COACHES
See Hertfordshire

*THREE STAR (LUTON) LTD
6 HIGH TOWN ROAD, LUTON LU2 0DD
Tel: 01582 722626
Fax: 01582 484034
E-mail: sales@bookthisbus.com
Web site: www.threestar-privatehire.co.uk
Dir: C W Dudley **Gen Man**: D Owens
Fleet: 9 - 4 coaches, 1 midicoach, 1 minibus, 3 minicoach.
Chassis: 2 Dennis. 1 MAN. 5 Mercedes. 7 Volvo.
Bodies: 3 Berkhof. 4 Mercedes. 2 Plaxton.
Ops incl: local bus services, school contracts, private hire, excursions & tours.
Livery: Blue
Ticket system: Almex

VILLAGER MINIBUS (SHARNBROOK) LTD
SHARNBROOK UPPER SCHOOL, ODELL ROAD, SHARNBROOK MK44 1JL
Tel: 01234 781920
Dir: M. Bain
Fleet: 1 minibus
Chassis: Ford
Ops incl: local bus services, private hire
Ticket system: printed book

BERKSHIRE
(WEST BERKSHIRE, BRACKNELL FOREST, READING, SLOUGH, WINDSOR & MAIDENHEAD, WOKINGHAM)

1ST CHOICE SCORPIO TRAVEL
67 WEST END COURT, WEST END LANE, STOKE POGES SL2 4NB
Tel: 01753 648435
Fax: 01753 644878
E-mail: admin@scorpiotravel.net
Web site: www.scorpiotravel.net
Ptnrs: Don Hughes, Gill Hughes.
Fleet: 1 coach
Chassis: Iveco
Body: Beulas
Ops incl: excursions & tours, private hire, continental tours.
Livery: Silver/Cerise/Teal

*ALDERMASTON COACHES
ALDERMASTON, READING RG7 5PP
Tel: 0118 971 3257
Fax: 0118 971 2722
Ptnrs: D. Arlott, T. Arlott, P. Arlott
Fleet: includes 1 midicoach, 1 minicoach.
Chassis: includes 4 Leyland.
Ops incl: private hire, school contracts.
Livery: White

BURGHFIELD MINI COACHES LTD
BURGHFIELD FARM, MILL ROAD, BURGHFIELD BRIDGE, READING RG30 3SS
Tel/Fax: 0118 959 0719
Web site: www.burghfield-coaches.co.uk
E-mail: burghfield.coaches@virgin.net
Dirs: Susan McCouid, Andrew McCouid
Fleet: 34 - 22 minibus, 12 minicoach.
Chassis: 28 Ford Transit. 3 Leyland. 3 Mercedes-Benz
Ops incl: local bus services, school contracts, private hire.

A/c	Air conditioning	
	Vehicles suitable for disabled	
	Coach(es) with galley facilities	
WC	Coach(es) with toilet facilities	
	Seat belt-fitted vehicles	
R	Recovery service available (not 24 hr)	
R24	24hr recovery service	
	Replacement vehicle available	
T	Toilet-drop facilities available	
	Vintage vehicle(s) available	
	Open top vehicle(s)	

COURTNEY COACHES

TERRANOVA HOUSE, KILN LANE, BRACKNELL RG12 1NA
Tel: 01344 412302
Fax: 01344 868980/422278
E-mail: enquiries@courtneycoaches.com
Web site: www.courtneycoaches.com
Prop: Bill Courtney
Fleet: 37 - 5 double-deck bus, 11 coach, 3 double-deck, 4 single-deck bus, 14 minibus.
Chassis: 1 Ayats. 1 Iveco. 7 Leyland. 1 Marshall. 14 Mercedes. 1 Neoplan. 3 Optare. 2 Scania. 7 Volvo.
Ops incl: private hire, local bus services.
Livery: Orange/White.

FIRST IN BERKSHIRE

COLDBOROUGH HOUSE, MARKET STREET, BRACKNELL RG12 1JA
Tel: 01344 868688
Fax: 01344 868332
Web site: www.firstgroup.com
Man Dir: Tony Wilson **Comm Dir**: Andrew Taylor **Business Man**: Chris Dexter
Fleet: 115 - 6 double-deck bus, 68 single-deck bus, 24 midibus, 17 coach.
Chassis: 6 Bluebird. 55 Dennis. 8 Mercedes. 33 Scania. 13 Volvo.
Bodies: 19 Alexander. 8 Berkhof. 6 Bluebird. 1 Irizar. 8 Mercedes. 10 Northern Counties. 43 Plaxton. 20 Wright.
Ops incl: local bus services, school contracts, express.
Livery: FirstGroup/Green Line
Ticket System: Wayfarer

HODGE'S COACHES (SANDHURST) LTD

100 YORKTOWN ROAD, SANDHURST GU47 9BH.
Tel: 01252 873131.
Fax: 01252 874884.
E-mail: enquiries@hodges-coaches.co.uk
Web site: www.hodges-coaches.co.uk
Man Dir: P. R. Hodge. **Dir**: P. Hodge, M. Hodge. M. Hodge.
Fleet: 17 - 12 single-deck coach, 2 midicoach, 1 minibus, 2 minicoach.
Chassis: 3 Bedford. 2 DAF, 4 MAN, 2 Toyota, 5 Volvo. 1 VW.
Bodies: 2 Caetano. 2 Plaxton. 1 Duple. 1 Devon. 11 Berkhof.
Ops incl: excursions & tours, private hire, continental tours, school contracts.
Livery: Blue/Beige.

*HORSEMAN COACHES

WHITLEY WOOD ROAD, READING RG2 8GG
Tel: 0118 975 3811
Fax: 0118 975 3515
E-mail: horsemansales@aol.com
Man Dir: Keith Horseman **Ch Eng**: Derrick Holton **Sales Man**: Neil Timberlake
Personnel Man: Ms Ann Fletcher
Fleet: 49 - 40 coach, 9 minicoach.
Chassis: 6 Dennis. 4 MAN. 9 Toyota. 30 Volvo.

Bodies: 6 Berkhof. 9 Caetano. 15 Jonckheere. 8 MarcoPolo. 10 Plaxton. 1 UVG.
Ops incl: local bus services, school contracts, excursions & tours, private hire, continental tours.
Livery: White with four-colour logo.
Ticket System: Setright

*KINGFISHER MINI COACHES

357 BASINGSTOKE ROAD, READING RG2 0JA
Tel: 0118 931 3454
Prop: Kevin Pope
Fleet: 14 - 6 minibus, 8 minicoach
Chassis: 8 Ford Transit. 2 LDV. 4 Mercedes.
Ops incl: private hire. school contracts
Livery: White/Orange

*MEMORY LANE VINTAGE OMNIBUS SERVICES

78 LILLIBROOKE CRESCENT, MAIDENHEAD SL6 3XQ
Tel: 01628 825050
Fax: 01628 825851
E-mail: admin@memorylane.co.uk
Web site: www.memorylane.co.uk
Prop: M. J. Clarke
Fleet: 5 - 2 double-deck bus, 2 single-deck bus, 1 single-deck coach.
Chassis: 4 AEC. 1 Bristol
Bodies: 1 ECW. 2 MCW. 2 Park Royal.
Ops incl: private hire
Livery: Original operators

READING & WOKINGHAM COACHES

33 MURRAY ROAD, WOKINGHAM RG41 2TA
Tel: 0118 979 3983
Fax: 0118 979 4330
Props: Mark Way, Sharon Way.
Fleet: 10 - 8 coach, 2 minibus
Chassis: 1 Dennis. 1 Iveco. 1 Mercedes. 1 Setra. 1 Toyota. 5 Volvo.
Bodies: 1 Beulas. 2 Berkhof. 1 Caetano. 1 Ikarus. 1 Jonckheere. 1 Mercedes. 1 Setra. 2 Van Hool.
Ops incl: excursions & tours, private hire, school contracts, continental tours.
Livery: White

*READING HERITAGE TRAVEL

PO BOX 147, READING RG1 6BD
Tel: 07850 220151
Prop/Tran Man: M J Russell
Fleet: 2 double-deck bus.
Chassis: 2 AEC
Bodies: 2 Park Royal
Ops incl: private hire
Livery: Red/Cream
Ticket System: Almex

*READING TRANSPORT LTD

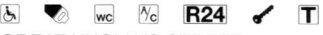

GREAT KNOLLYS STREET, READING RG1 7HH.
Tel: 0118 959 4000
Fax: 0118 957 5379
Recovery: 0118 958 5594
E-mail: info@reading-buses.co.uk
Web site: www.reading-buses.co.uk
Fleetname: Reading Buses, Newbury Buses, Goldline
Chmn: Cllr Tony Page **Man Dir**: Colin Thompson **Fin Dir**: James Carney
Ops/Eng Dir: Sam Simpson **Goldline Man**: Norman Fryer-Saxby **Newbury Man**: Mel Atkinson **Reading Buses Man**: Glynne Davies **Eng Man**: Mark Hodder **Personnel man**: Caroline Anscombe
Fleet: 210 - 82 double-deck bus, 78 single-deck bus, 11 single-deck coach, 36 midibus, 2 minibus, 1 minicoach.
Chassis: 54 DAF. 11 Dennis. 39 Leyland. 22 MCW. 78 Optare. 6 Scania.
Bodies: 6 Irizar. 22 Mercedes. 142 Optare. 10 Park Royal. 6 Plaxton. 13 Roe. 5 Transbus. 5 Van Hool.
Ops incl: local bus services, school contracts, excursions & tours, private hire, continental tours.
Livery: Cream/Maroon
Ticket System: Wayfarer TGX150.

*VINCE COACHES

AYRES HOUSE, AYRES LANE, BURGHCLERE RG20 9HG
Tel: 01635 278308
Prop: D L. Vince
Fleet: 5 coaches
Chassis/Bodies: 2 Berkhof. 3 Dennis.
Ops incl: private hire, school contracts.

*WEAVAWAY TRAVEL

PO BOX 5625, NEWBURY RG20 8EQ
Tel: 01635 820028
Fax: 01635 821128
Partners: Lyn Weaver, Simon Weaver
Fleet: 25 - 1 single-deck bus, 10 coach, 12 double-deck coach, 2 midibus
Chassis: 5 Bova. 1 DAF. 1 MAN. 2 MCW. 2 Mercedes-Benz. 16 Volvo.
Bodies: 5 Bova. 12 East Lancs. 1 Noge. 3 Optare. 4 Transbus.
Ops incl: local bus services, school contracts, private hire.
Livery: Tampa Red.
Ticket system: Wayfarer

WHITE BUS SERVICES

NORTH STREET GARAGE, WINKFIELD, WINDSOR SL4 4TP
Tel: 01344 88262
Fax: 01344 886403
E-mail: reception@whitebus.co.uk
Dir: D. E. Jeatt
Fleet: 12 - 3 single-deck bus, 9 coach.
Chassis: include DAF, Bedford.
Bodies: Duple. Optare. Plaxton. Van Hool.
Ops incl: local bus services, school contracts, private hire.
Livery: White/grey skirt.
Ticket System: Wayfarer Saver, Setright

*WINDSORIAN COACHES

103 ARTHUR ROAD, WINDSOR SL4 1RU
Tel: 01753 860131
Fax: 020 8751 5054
Web site: www.windsoriancoaches.co.uk
Man Dir: Martin Cornell **Gen Man**: Gilbert Parsons
Fleet: 10 - 8 double-deck coach, 2 midicoach.
Chassis: 7 Dennis. 2 Mercedes. 1 Volvo.

Berkshire

Bodies: 2 Mellor. 8 Plaxton.
Ops incl: school contracts, excursions & tours, private hire, continental tours.
Livery: White/Blue.

BRISTOL

ABUS
104 WINCHESTER ROAD, BRISLINGTON BS4 3NL
Tel: 0117 977 6126
Fax: 0117 923 121
Web site: www.abus.co.uk
Chmn/Man Dir: Alan Peters **Co Sec**: Glynis Peters
Fleet: 18 double-deck bus
Chassis: 12 Bristol. 3 DAF. 1 Iveco. 2 Leyland.
Bodies: 2 Alexander. 10 ECW. 4 East Lancs. 2 Optare.
Ops incl: local bus services, school contracts.
Livery: Cream/White/Maroon.
Ticket System: Wayfarer 3 & card.

AZTEC COACH TRAVEL
6/8 EMERY ROAD, BRISLINGTON, BRISTOL BS4 5PF
Tel: 0117 977 0314.
Fax: 0117 977 4431.
Man Dir: I. Fortune. **Fleet Eng**: D. Harvey.
Ops Man: P. Rixon.
Fleet: 15 - 13 midicoach, 2 minibus.
Chassis: 1 Freight Rover. 14 Mercedes.
Bodies: 2 Optare. 7 Reeve Burgess. 4 Autobus Classique.
Ops incl: excursions & tours, private hire, continental tours, school contracts.
Livery: White with diagonal red/orange stripes.

BAKERS DOLPHIN COACH TRAVEL
48 LOCKING ROAD, WESTON-SUPER-MARE BS23 3DN.
Tel: 01934 635635.
Fax: 01934 641162.
E-mail: coach.hire@bakersdolphin.com
Chmn: John Baker.
Man Dir: Tim Newcombe.
Ch Eng: Mark Vearncombe. **Mktg Dir**: Amanda Harrington. **Ops Dir**: Max Fletcher.
Ops Man: Alan White.
Fleet: 75 - single-deck coach, double-deck coach, midibus, minibus, minicoach
Chassis: 20 Bedford. 1 Bova. 15 Leyland. 3 Mercedes. 36 Volvo.
Ops incl: local bus services, excursions & tours, private hire, express, continental tours, school contracts.
Livery: Blue/White/Green/Yellow.

*BERKELEY COACH & TRAVEL LTD
HAM LANE, PAULTON BS39 7PL
Tel: 01761 413196
Fax: 01761 416469
Fleet: 10 coach
Chassis: 10 Volvo
Bodies: 9 Plaxton. 1 Van Hool.
Ops incl: school contracts, private hire.

*BLAGDON LIONESS COACHES LTD
MENDIP GARAGE, STREET END, BLAGDON BS40 7TL
Tel: 01761 462250
Fax: 01761 463237
Dir: T M Lyons
Fleet: 6 coach
Chassis: 2 DAF. 1 Leyland. 1 Mercedes. 1 Toyota. 1 Volvo.
Bodies: 2 Bova. 1 Caetano. 3 Plaxton.
Ops incl: local bus services, excursions & tours, private hire, school contracts.
Livery: White with company logo
Ticket System: Setright

*BLUE IRIS COACHES
25 CLEVEDON ROAD, NAILSEA BS48 1EH
Tel: 01275 851121
Fax: 01275 856522
E-mail: enquiry@blueiris.co.uk
Web site: www.blueiris.co.uk
Dir/Tran Man: P. Hatherall **Dir**: T. Spiller
Fleet: 14 - 1 single-deck bus, 8 single-deck coach, 2 midicoach, 3 minicoach
Chassis: 1 Mercedes. 7 Scania. 5 Toyota. 1 Volvo.
Bodies: 5 Caetano. 5 Irizar. 1 Marshall/MCV. 1 Plaxton. 2 Van Hool.
Ops incl: private hire, local bus services, continental tours, school contracts, excursions & tours.
Livery: Light Blue/Dark Blue/White.
Ticket System: Setright

BRISTOL ELECTRIC RAILBUS LTD
HERON HOUSE, CHISWICK MALLL, LONDON W4 2PR
Tel: 020 8995 3000
Fax: 020 8994 6060
Dir: James Skinner
Fleet: 1 tram.
Chassis/Body: Parry/Clayton

BUGLER COACHES
100 SCHOOL ROAD, BRISLINGTON BS4 4NF
Tel: 0117 977 8759
Fax: 0117 972 3886
E-mail: buglercoaches@yahoo.com
Web site: www.buglercoaches.co.uk
Fleetname: Buglers
Ptnrs: Bob Bugler, Sue Bugler
Fleet: 14 - 2 double-deck bus, 7 coach, 1 midicoach, 4 minibus
Chassis: Bristol, Dennis, Leyland, Volvo
Bodies: Alexander, Plaxton, Van Hool
Ops incl: local bus services, school contracts, private hire.
Livery: Yellow/Red/White

*PETER CAROL PRESTIGE COACHING
BAMFIELD HOUSE, WHITCHURCH BS14 0XD
Tel: 01275 839839
Fax: 01275 835604
E-mail: charter@petercarol.co.uk
Web site: www.luxurycoach.co.uk
Gen Man: Peter Collis
Fleet: 12 - 10 coach, 2 double-deck coach.
Chassis: 2 Bova. 2 DAF. 2 MAN. 4 Neoplan. 1 Scania. 1 Toyota.
Bodies: 1 Berkhof. 2 Bova. 2 Caetano. 4 Neoplan. 1 Noge. 2 Van Hool.
Ops incl: excursions & tours, private hire, continental tours.
Livery: Dark Grey

CROWN COACHES
See Len Munden & Son Ltd (below).

*EAGLE COACHES
FIRECLAY HOUSE, NETHAM ROAD, ST GEORGE BS5 9PJ
Tel: 0117 955 6784/955 7130
Fax: 0117 941 1107
E-mail: office@eagle-coaches.co.uk
Web site: www.eagle-coaches.co.uk
Ptnrs: A J Ball, J A Ball **Fleet Eng**: P Roach
Comm Man: M L Hardiman **Tours Man**: K Burge
Fleet: 27 - 2 double-deck bus, 20 coach, 2 midicoach,1 minicoach, 1 minibus, 1 midibus.
Chassis: DAF. Mercedes.
Bodies: Plaxton. Van Hool.
Ops incl: local bus services, school contracts, excursions & tours, private hire, continental tours.

- Air conditioning
- Vehicles suitable for disabled
- Coach(es) with galley facilities
- Coach(es) with toilet facilities
- Seat belt-fitted vehicles
- **R** Recovery service available (not 24 hr)
- **R24** 24hr recovery service
- Replacement vehicle available
- **T** Toilet-drop facilities available
- Vintage vehicle(s) available
- Open top vehicle(s)

Livery: Yellow/Red with orange stripes
Ticket System: Almex

EASTVILLE COACHES LTD
[wc] [fork] [spanner] [T]
15 ASHGROVE ROAD, REDLAND BS6 6NA
Tel: 0117 971 0657
Fax: 0117 971 5824.
Man Dir: T. Reece.
Fleet: 14 - 6 double-deck bus, 8 coach.
Chassis: 6 Bristol. 1 DAF. 7 Volvo.
Bodies: 6 ECW. 2 Plaxton. 6 Van Hool.
Ops incl: local bus services, school contracts, private hire, continental tours.
Livery: Myosotis Blue/White.

EUROTAXIS
[disabled] [bus] [wc] [N/c] [spanner]
16 HIGHFIELDS CLOSE, HARRY STOKE BS34 8YA
Tel: 01454 320101
Fax: 01454 320011
Web site: www.euro-taxis.co.uk
Dirs: Juan Sanzo, Keith Sanzo, William Sanzo
Fleet: 85 - 3 coach, 82 minibus/minicoach.
Ops incl: school contracts, private hire, excursions & tours
Livery: White

FILER'S COACHES
STANTON WICK, PENSFORD BS39 4BZ.
Tel: 01761 490674, 490465.
Fax: 01761 490861.

FIRST IN BRISTOL [disabled]
ENTERPRISE HOUSE, EASTON ROAD, BRISTOL BS5 0DZ
Tel: 0117 955 8211
Fax: 0117 955 1248
Web site: www.firstgroup.com
Man Dir: Alex Perry **Eng Dir**: Richard Noble **Fin Dir**: Mike Gahan **Ops Dir**: Jenny McLeod
Fleet: 314 - 133 double-deck bus, 44 single-deck bus, 124 midibus, 13 minibus.
Chassis: 115 Dennis. 91 Leyland. 19 Mercedes. 89 Volvo.
Bodies: 29 Alexander. 8 East Lancs. 35 Leyland. 70 Northern Counties. 102 Plaxton. 30 Roe. 40 Wright.
Ops incl: local bus services, school contracts.
Livery: First Bus Barbie 1+2
Ticket System: Wayfarer

GLENVIC OF BRISTOL LTD
[bus]
THE OLD COLLIERY, STANTON WICK, PENSFORD BS39 4BZ
Tel: 01761 490116
Fax: 01761 907 7032
Dirs: Paul Holvey, Philip Holvey **Ops Man/Comp Sec**: Paul Holvey **Eng**: Nick Reed
Fleet: 13 - 4 double-deck bus, 5 coach, 4 minicoach
Chassis: 2 LDV. 7 Leyland. 2 Mercedes-Benz. 2 Volvo.

*GRAHAM'S COACHES
[wc] [bus] [spanner]
7 WYCK BECK ROAD, BRENTRY BS10 7JD
Tel/Fax: 0117 950 9398
Prop: Graham P Smith
Fleet: 8 - 5 double-deck bus, 3 coaches.
Chassis: 1 Bova. 2 Bristol. 1 DAF. 1 Daimler. 2 Leyland. 1 Volvo
Bodies: include 1 Bova. 2 Caetano.
Ops incl: private hire, school contracts.
Livery: White/Red/Maroon.

ARNOLD LIDDELL COACHES [bus]
89 JERSEY AVENUE, BRISLINGTON BS4 4QX.
Tel: 0117 977 2011.
Prop: Michael. Liddell. **Gen Man**: Arnold. Liddell. **Fleet Eng**: Robert Liddell
Fleet: 2 - 1 coach, 1 midicoach.
Chassis: 1 Leyland. 1 Mercedes.
Ops incl: excursions & tours, school contracts.
Livery: Blue/White.

MARTINS SELF DRIVE MINICOACH HIRE [bus]
GRINDELL ROAD GARAGE, 1 GRINDELL ROAD, REDFIELD BS5 9PG.
Tel: 0117 955 1042.
Fax: 0117 939 3383.
Fleet: 12 - 12 minibus.
Chassis: 12 Ford Transit.
Ops incl: Self Drive Minicoach Hire.

LEN MUNDEN & SON LTD
[wc] [bus] [bus] [bus] [spanner]
6 FREESTONE ROAD, ST PHILIPS BS2 0QN.
Tel: 0117 971 0251.
Fax: 0117 972 3121.
Fleetname: Crown Coaches.
Man Dir: Simon Munden
Fleet: 20 - 10 double-deck bus, 7 coach, 1 midibus, 2 minibus.
Chassis: 9 Bristol. 2 DAF. 3 Freight Rover. 6 Leyland.
Bodies: 9 ECW. 1 East Lancs. 1 Leyland. 5 Plaxton.
Ops incl: local bus services, school contracts, excursions & tours, private hire.
Livery: Red/Cream.

*NORTH SOMERSET COACHES [bus]
COATES ESTATE, SOUTHFIELD ROAD, NAILSEA BS48 1JN
Tel/Fax: 01275 859123
Prop: Graham Clements.
Fleet: 3 coach.
Chassis: 1 Dennis. 2 Volvo.
Bodies: 1 Berkhof. 1 Ikarus. 1 Plaxton.
Ops incl: school contracts, private hire.

*PREMIER TRAVEL LTD
[bus] [wc] [N/c] [R24] [spanner] [T]
ALBERT CRESCENT, ST PHILIPS BS2 0SU
Tel: 0117 9300 5550
Fax: 0117 9300 5551
Man Dir: Glenn Bond

Fleet: 5 - 1 double-deck bus, 2 coach, 1 double-deck coach, 1 minicoach.
Chassis: 9 Bova. 1 DAF. 1 Freight Rover. 1 Leyland. 1 Volvo
Bodies: 1 Bova. 1 ECW. 2 Van Hool.
Ops incl: school contracts, continental tours, private hire.
Livery: White/Red with blue lettering.

SOUTH GLOUCESTERSHIRE BUS & COACH COMPANY
STATION ROAD, PATCHWAY BS34 6LR.
Tel: 0117 931 4340.
Partners: R & B. M. Durbin & Sons.
Fleet: 27 - double-deck bus. 8 single-deck bus. 7 coach. 7 minibus.
Chassis: 5 Bristol. 4 Dennis. 7 Leyland. 6 Mercedes. 1 Renault. 4 Volvo.
Bodies: 5 ECW. 2 Leyland. 2 Plaxton. 3 Van Hool. 5 Wadham Stringer.
Ops incl: local bus service, excursions & tours, private hire, continental tours.
Livery: Blue/White.

SOMERBUS [disabled] [bus]
PAULTON, BRISTOL
Tel/Fax: 01761 415456
Web site: www.somerbus.co.uk
E-mail: somerbus@tinyworld.co.uk
Fleet: includes - 4 single-deck bus, 1 midicoach.
Chassis: Leyland. Mercedes. Optare.
Bodies: Alexander. Marshall. Mellor. Optare. Plaxton.
Ops incl: local bus services

*TURNERS COACHWAYS (BRS) LTD
[wc] [bus] [N/c] [R] [spanner] [T]
59 DAYS ROAD, ST PHILIPS BS2 0QS.
Tel: 0117 955 9086
Fax: 0117 955 6948
E-mail: admin@turnerscoachways.co.uk
Web site: www.turnerscoachways.co.uk
Man Dir: A. J. Turner. **Ch Eng**: J Radford **Private Hire Man**: E Venn **Ops Mans**: D Pinches/ A. Harvey
Fleet: 35 - 34 coach, 1 minicoach.
Chassis: 1 Iveco. 1 Mercedes. 4 Scania. 28 Volvo.
Bodies: 1 Beulas. 2 Berkhof. 4 Irizar. 10 Jonckheere. 5 Plaxton. 10 Van Hool.
Ops incl: private hire
Livery: Silver.

Z CARS OF BRISTOL
[wc] [fork] [bus]
32 NORTH STREET, BEDMINSTER BS3 1HW.
Tel: 0117 966 5801.
Fax: 0117 963 3854.
E-mail: zcarsbristol@msn.com
Web site: www.zcars.co.uk
Ptnrs: D. R. Cattermole, N. D. Cattermole.
Ptnr/Ops Man: Ian Cattermole. **Ch Eng**: J. Eason.
Fleet: 13 - 9 coach, 1 midicoach, 3 minicoach.
Chassis: 1 DAF. 2 Iveco. 1 Mercedes. 1 Neoplan. 3 Scania. 2 Toyota.
Bodies: 2 Caetano. 2 Beulas. 1 Neoplan.

1 Optare. 1 Van Hool. 3 Irizar.
Ops incl: Excursions & tours, private hire, continental tours.

BUCKINGHAMSHIRE, MILTON KEYNES

ABBEY COACHES [wc] 🪑
134 DESBOROUGH ROAD, HIGH WYCOMBE HP11 2PU
Tel: 01494 521214.
E-mail: martyn@abbeycoaches.com
Web site: www.abbeycoaches.com
Dirs: Martyn Pearce, John Robinson.
Fleet: 8 - 1 double-deck bus, 5 coach, 2 minicoach.
Chassis: 1 Ford. 1 Ford Transit. 1 Leyland. 1 Mercedes. 4 Volvo.
Bodies: 5 Plaxton. 1 Roe. 2 Other.
Ops incl: School contracts, private hire.
Livery: White/Green lettering.

AUTODOUBLE LTD
90 HAINAULT AVENUE, GIFFARD PARK, MILTON KEYNES MK14 5PE.
Tel: 01908 281350.
Fleetname: Starlight.
Fin Dir/Sec: N. A Gibbard.
Traf Man/Dir: K. G. Gibbard.
Fleet: 5 - 1 coach, 1 midibus, 3 minicoach.
Chassis: 2 Bedford. 1 Bristol. 2 Ford Transit.
Bodies: 1 ECW. 1 Plaxton. 2 Dormobile. 1 Tricentrol.
Ops incl: private hire, school contracts.
Livery: White/Burgundy.

BRAZIERS MINI COACHES
17 VICARAGE ROAD, WINSLOW MK18 3BE
Tel: 01296 712201
Prop: Peter Brazier.
Fleet: 3 minicoach
Chassis: LDV
Ops incl: private hire, school contracts.
Livery: White/Green

CAROUSEL BUSES LTD
🚌 🚐 [R] 🔧
134 DESBOROUGH ROAD, HIGH WYCOMBE HP11 2PU
Tel: 01494 533436
Fax: 01494 533436
E-mail: enquiries@carouselbuses.com
Web site: www.carouselbuses.com
Dirs: Stephen Burns, John Robinson **Ops Man**: N Clark **Ch Eng**: J Blossom
Fleet: 32 - 24 double-deck bus 8 single-deck bus
Chassis: 9 Leyland. 12 MCW. 3 Mercedes.
Bodies: 9 Leyland. 12 MCW. 3 Mercedes.
Ops incl: Local bus services, school contracts, private hire.
Livery: Red/White relief
Ticket system: Wayfarer 3

DERWENT TRAVEL
[wc] 🪑 🍽 [A/c]
UNIT 11, PEMBROKE ROAD, STOCKLAKE, AYLESBURY HP20 1DB
Tel: 01296 415163
Fax: 01296 425938
Recovery: 07775 860511
Ptnrs: Diane Best, David Best **Man**: John Lake **Sec**: Barbara Nash
Fleet: 5 coach
Chassis/bodies: 5 Setra
Ops incl: excursions & tours, private hire, continental tours
Livery: Multicolour (same style)

*DRP TRAVEL 🪑 [A/c] 🔧
1 THE MEADWAY, LOUGHTON, MILTON KEYNES MK5 8AN
Tel: 01908 394141
Mobile: 07979 364968
Web site: www.drptravel.co.uk
E-mail: drptravel@btconnect.com
Man: Darrell Pinnock
Fleet: 3 - 1 minibus, 2 minicoach.
Chassis: 1 Iveco. 1 LDV. 1 Renault
Ops incl: school contracts, excursions and tours, private hire.

HOWLETTS COACHES
🪑 [wc] 🔧
UNIT 2, STATION ROAD INDUSTRIAL ESTATE, WINSLOW MK18 3DZ
Tel: 01296 713201
Fax: 01296 715879
Prop: R. S. Durham
Fleet: 8 - 2 double-deck bus, 6 coach.
Chassis: 1 Bedford. 4 DAF. 2 MCW. 1 Setra.
Ops incl: private hire, continental tours, school contracts.
Livery: Brown/White.

HYLTONE ENTERPRISES
51 GEORGES HILL, WIDMER END, HIGH WYCOMBE HP15 6BH.
Tel: 01494 715298.
Fax: 01494 715298.
Fleetname: Hyltone Coaches.
Prop: R. C. Lockwood.
Dirs: A. Lockwood, A. W. Lockwood.
Fleet: 7 - 4 coach, 3 minicoach.
Chassis: Bedford.
Bodies: Plaxton. Robin Hood.
Ops incl: excursions & tours, private hire, continental tours.
Livery: Red/White.

*LANGSTON & TASKER
🪑 [wc] [A/c]
23 QUEEN CATHERINE ROAD, STEEPLE CLAYDON MK18 2PZ
Tel/Fax: 01296 730347
Ptnrs: Mrs J Langston, Mrs M A Fenner
Man: R Langston **Ops Man**: A Price
Fleet: 18 - 1 double-deck bus, 14 single-deck bus, 3 minibus.
Chassis: 1 Bedford. 4 Dennis. 2 Ford Transit. 1 Iveco. 3 Leyland. 2 Mercedes. 5 Volvo.
Bodies: 1 Caetano. 3 Duple. 1 Jonckheere. 1 Marshall. 8 Plaxton. 2 Reeve Burgess. 1 Transbus. 1 Wadham Stringer.
Ops incl: local bus services, school contracts, private hire
Livery: White/Red

*MAGPIE TRAVEL 🪑
BINDERS INDUSTRIAL ESTATE, CRYERS HILL, HIGH WYCOMBE HP10 0NJ
Tel: 01494 712823
Fax: 01494 715381
E-mail: martinpeterash@supanet.com
Prop: Martin Ash
Fleet: 11 - 1 sinlge-deck bus, 3 coach, 2 midibus, 5 minicoach.
Chassis: 8 Mercedes. 3 Volvo.
Ops incl: local bus services, school contracts, private hire.
Livery: White.
Ticket System: Almex.

MK METRO LTD ♿
UNIT 3-4, ARDEN PARK, OLD WOLVERTON ROAD, MILTON KEYNES MK12 5RN
Tel: 01908 225100
Fax: 01908 313553
Gen Man: Michael Harris
Fleet: 95 - includes 58 midibus/minibus.
Chassis: include: DAF. Dennis. Leyland. Mercedes. Optare. Renault. Scania. Volvo.
Bodies: Caetano. Carlyle. massey. Optare. Plaxton. Reeve Burgess. Rohill. UVG. Wright.
Ops incl: local bus services, school contracts, private hire.
Livery: Dark Blue/Yellow.
Ticket System: Wayfarer 3
Part of Status Bus & Coach.

*MOTTS COACHES (AYLESBURY) LTD
♿ [wc] 🍽 🪑 [A/c] 🔧
15 STATION ROAD, STOKE MANDEVILLE HP22 5UL
Tel: 01296 613831

🪑	Seat belt-fitted vehicles
[R]	Recovery service available (not 24 hr)
R24	24hr recovery service
♿	Vehicles suitable for disabled
🍽	Coach(es) with galley facilities
[wc]	Coach(es) with toilet facilities
[A/c]	Air conditioning
🔧	Replacement vehicle available
[T]	Toilet-drop facilities available
🚌	Vintage vehicle(s) available
	Open top vehicle(s)

Bristol / Buckinghamshire

Fax: 01296 613175
Web site: www.mottstravel.com
E-mail: info@mottstravel.com
Fleetname: Motts Travel
Man Dir: M R Mott **Ops Dir**: C J Mott **Eng Dir**: I Scutt **Tours Dir**: C G Joel **Ops Man**: H J Shanks
Fleet: 43 - 6 double-deck bus, 30 coach, 2 double-deck coach, 3 midicoach, 2 minibus
Chassis: 6 Leyland. 4 MCW. 5 Mercedes. 28 Volvo.
Bodies: ECW. Jonckheere. MCW. Plaxton. Transbus. Van Hool. Sitcar.
Ops incl: local bus services, school contracts, excursions & tours, private hire, continental tours.
Livery: White/Yellow/Green.
Ticket System: Wayfarer.

PASSENGER TRANSPORT LOGISTICS LTD
MILTON KEYNES COACHWAY, BROOK FURLONG, MILTON KEYNES MK10 9AB.
Tel: 01908 676700.
Fax: 01908 694770.
Dir: M. E. Infanti. **Co Sec**: D. M. Infanti.
Gen Man: J. M. Lunt.
Fleet: 40 – 2 double-deck bus. 11 single-deck bus. 10 double-deck coach. 3 midicoach. 14 minicoach.
Chassis: 4 Bedford. 2 Daimler. 1 Ford Transit. 3 Freight Rover. 4 Mercedes-Benz.
Bodies: 3 Carlyle. 3 Mercedes-Benz. 4 Plaxton.
Ops incl: local bus services, school contracts, excursions & tours, private hire.
Livery: Blue/Silver.
Ticket System: AES.
Limousine hire and taxi service.

PAYNES COACHES & CAR HIRE LTD
6 BALMER CUT, BUCKINGHAM INDUSTRIAL ESTATE, BUCKINGHAM MK18 1UL.
Tel: 01280 813108, 817761.
Dirs: J. V. & K. R. Jeffs.
Fleet: 14 - 12 coach, 2 minicoach.
Chassis: Bedford. Ford. Leyland.
Bodies: 4 Caetano. 1 Duple. 2 Jonckheere. 3 Leyland. 1 Mercedes. 2 Optare. 1 Plaxton.
Ops incl: local bus services, excursions & tours, private hire, express, continental tours.
Livery: Green/Cream.
Ticket System: Almex/Wayfarer.
Subsidiary of Jeffs Coaches, Helmdon.

PRESTWOOD TRAVEL
152 WRIGHTS LANE, PRESTWOOD, GREAT MISSENDEN HP16 0LG.
Tel: 01494 864346.
Fax: 01494 864279.
Prop: P. Baird, Mrs G. Baird.
Ch Eng: R. Wood.
Fleet: 15 - 3 double-deck bus, 12 coach.
Ops incl: local bus services, school contracts, excursions & tours, private hire.
Livery: White/Black and Orange reliefs.

RED ROSE TRAVEL LTD
110 OXFORD ROAD, AYLESBURY HP19 2PB.
Tel: 01296 399500.
Fax: 01296 612196.
E-mail: redrose@showbus.com.
Web site: www.showbus.com/redrose
Dir: T. W. Khan. **Co Sec**: C. D. Day.
Fleet: 23 - 9 single-deck bus, 14 minibus.
Chassis: 6 Dennis. 1 Ford Transit. 2 Iveco. 2 Leyland. 8 Mercedes. 4 Optare.
Bodies: Caetano. East Lancs. Mellor. Optare. Plaxton. UVG.
Ops incl: local bus services, school contracts.
Livery: Red/Yellow.
Ticket System: Wayfarer.

ROBINSON'S COACHES
MANOR BUSINESS CENTRE, STEWKLEY, LEIGHTON BUZZARD LU7 0HR.
Tel: 01525 240264.
Fax: 01525 240050.
Fleet: 15 - 10 coach, 5 double-deck bus.
Ops incl: excursions & tours, private hire, continental tours.

SOUL BROS LTD
THE COACH PARK, 2 STILEBROOK ROAD, OLNEY MK46 5EA.
Tel: 01234 711242.
Fleetname: Souls.
Dirs: D. F. Soul (Man), L. Soul, A. Soul.
Fleet Eng: K. J. Ayres. **Gen Man/Co Sec**: K. M. Lyne. **Sales Man**: K. W. Emery.
Traf Man: J. Brown.
Fleet: 43 - 41 coach, 2 midicoach.
Chassis: 15 Bedford. 3 DAF. 2 Dennis. 2 Toyota. 21 Volvo.
Bodies: 3 Caetano. 19 Duple. 21 Plaxton.
Ops incl: local bus services, school contracts, private hire.
Livery: Red/Cream.
Ticket System: Setright.

STUDIO WORKSHOPS LTD
C/O PINEWOOD STUDIOS, PINEWOOD ROAD, IVER HEATH SL0 0NH
Tel: 01753 630364
Fax: 01753 630241
E-mail: transcamera@btconnect.com
Web site: www.studioworkshops.co.uk
Prop: D. Gill. **Man Dir**: B. Gill
Fleet: 18 - 2 coach, 10 minibus, 6 minicoach
Chassis: 1 DAF. 1 Iveco. 5 LDV. 5 Mercedes. 5 Toyota. 1 Volvo
Bodies: 5 Caetano. 1 Jonckheere. 5 Mercedes. 1 Plaxton
Ops incl: private hire. Film & TV work
Livery: White

WINDSORIAN COACHES
See Berkshire

*WOOTTENS LUXURY TRAVEL
THE COACH YARD, LYCROME ROAD, LYE GREEN, CHESHAM HP5 3LG
Tel: 01494 774411
Fax: 01494 784597
E-mail: info@woottens.co.uk
Web site: www.woottens.co.uk
Man Dir: N H Wootten **Dir**: M M Wootten
Ops Man: M J Wootten
Chief Eng: R A Gomm
Fleet: 20 - 3 double-deck bus, 1 single-deck bus, 13 coach, 1 double-deck coach, 1 vintage.
Chassis: 1 Bristol. 6 Irisbus. 6 Leyland. 1 Leyland National. 6 Volvo.
Bodies: 1 Alexander. 6 Beulas. 1 Berkhof. 1 Duple. 3 ECW. 3 Jonckheere. 1 Leyland National. 3 Plaxton. 1 Willowbrook.
Ops incl: local bus services, excursions and tours, continental tours, private hire, school contracts.
Livery: White with coloured swirls.
Ticket System: Wayfarer.

Z & S COACHES
38-40 FLEET STREET, AYLESBURY HP20 2PA.
Tel: 01296 415468.
Fax: 01296 415468.
Prop: U. Zaman.
Fleet: 6 - 2 midibus, 3 midicoach, 1 minibus.
Chassis: 1 AEC. 1 Bedford. 2 Ford Transit. 1 Freight Rover. 1 Scania. 1 Toyota. 2 Volvo.
Bodies: 1 Caetano. 1 Duple. 2 Jonckheere. 1 Plaxton. 1 Van Hool.
Ops incl: local bus services, excursions & tours, private hire.
Livery: Blue and Silver.

CAMBRIDGESHIRE, CITY OF PETERBOROUGH

*ALEC HEAD
See Northamptonshire

*ANDREWS COACHES
20 CAMBRIDGE ROAD, FOXTON
CB2 6SH
Tel: 01223 873002
Fax: 01223 873036
E-mail: andrewscoaches@aol.com
Web site: www.andrewscoaches.co.uk
Prop: Andrew Miller
Fleet: 9 - 1 single-deck bus, 8 coach
Chassis: 1 AEC. 2 Bedford. 1 Ford. 4 Volvo.
1 Seddon.
Bodies: 1 Alexander. 1 Caetano. 7 Plaxton.
Ops incl: private hire, school contracts
Livery: White with Red/Blue arrows

*BURTONS COACHES LTD
See Suffolk

*C & G COACH SERVICES
HONEYSOME LODGE,
HONEYSOME ROAD, CHATTERIS
PE16 6SB
Tel: 01354 692200
Fax: 01354 694433
Web site: www.candgcoaches.co.uk
E-mail: info@candgcoaches.co.uk
Prtnrs: Carole Day, Graham Elliwood,
Robert Day(**Ch Eng**), Chris Smith (**Ops Man**)
Fleet: 26 - 1 double-deck bus, 23 coach,
2 midicoach
Chassis: 3 Bedford. 1 Bristol. 1 MAN.
1 Mercedes. 1 Neoplan. 15 Scania. 4 Volvo.
Bodies: 2 Duple. 1 ECW. 14 Irizar.
1 Neoplan, 6 Plaxton. 2 Van Hool.
Ops incl: school contracts, excursions & tours, private hire, continental tours
Livery: White/Red/Yellow and Burgundy/Gold

*COLLINS COACHES
UNIT 4, CAMBRIDGE ROAD
INDUSTRIAL ESTATE, CAMBRIDGE
CB4 6AZ
Tel: 01223 420462
Fax: 01223 424739
E-mail:
collinscoaches@sagehost.co.uk,
office@collinscoaches.net
Ptnrs: C. R. Collins, R. T. Collins **Off Man**:
Jacky Liptrot **Garage Man**: R D Curtis
Fleet: 19 - 3 coach, 3 midicoach,
13 minibus.
Chassis: 1 Bedford. 2 Dennis. 5 Ford
Transit. 2 Freight Rover. 4 Iveco. 2 LDV.
Ops incl: excursions & tours, school contracts, private hire.
Livery: White/Orange

DEWS COACHES
CHATTERIS ROAD, SOMERSHAM
PE17 3DN.
Tel: 01487 740241.
Fax: 01487 740341.
E-mail: sales@dews-coaches.com
Web site: www.dews-coaches.com
Chmn: David Dew. **Ops Man**: Simon Dew.
Fleet: 10 - 3 single-deck bus, 7 single-deck coach.
Chassis: 2 Bedford, 1 DAF, 5 Scania,
2 Volvo.
Bodies: 2 Berkhof, 3 Irizar, 2 Van Hool.
Ops incl: excursions & tours, private hire, continental tours, school contracts.
Livery: Green/Grey.

EMBLINGS COACHES
BRIDGE GARAGE, GUYHIRN,
WISBECH PE13 4ED.
Tel: 01945 450253.
Fax: 01945 450770
Man Dir: John Embling

*FENN HOLIDAYS
WHITTLESEY ROAD, MARCH
PE15 0AG
Tel: 01354 653329
Fax: 01354 650647
E-mail: info@fennholidays.co.uk
Web site: www.fennholidays.co.uk
Man Dir: P A Fenn **Dir**: Mrs F M Fenn
Fleet: 4 coach
Chassis: 2 Bova. 1 MAN. 1 Scania.
Bodies: 2 Bova. 2 Van Hool.
Ops incl: excursions & tours, private hire, continental tours.
Livery: multicolour

FIRST CHOICE TRAVEL
9 LYTHEMERE, ORTON MALBORNE,
PETERBOROUGH PE2 5NU.
Tel: 01733 753642.
Fleetname: First Choice.
Prop: D. Ely.
Fleet: 2 midibus.
Chassis: 1 Bedford. 1 Renault.
Bodies: 1 Marshall. 1 Wright.
Ops incl: local bus services, school contracts.
Livery: Maroon/Blue.
Ticket System: Setright.

MARGARET GREEN
t/a GREENS COACHES
59 WISBECH ROAD, THORNEY,
PETERBOROUGH PE6 0SA.
Tel: 01733 270327.
Owner: Ms M. Green.
Fleet: 2 coach.
Chassis: Bedford.
Bodies: 1 Duple. 1 Plaxton.

Ops incl: local bus services, school contracts, excursions & tours, private hire.
Livery: Green/Cream.
Ticket System: Setright.

*GRETTON'S COACHES
ARNWOOD CENTRE, NEWARK
ROAD, PETERBOROUGH PE1 5YH
Tel: 01733 311008
Fax: 01733 319859
Prop: Roger Gretton
Fleet: 15 - 13 coach, 1 double-deck coach,
1 minicoach.
Chassis: 2 Bedford. 1 Mercedes. 11 Scania.
1 Volvo.
Bodies: 1 Jonckheere. 2 Van Hool.
12 Plaxton.
Ops incl: school contracts, excursions & tours, private hire.
Livery: Silver/Red/Maroon

GREYS OF ELY
41 SEDGEWAY, WITCHFORD, ELY
CB6 2HY
Tel: 01353 662300.
Fax: 01353 662412
E-mail: richard@greysofely.co.uk
Web site: www.greysofely.co.uk
Prop: D. Grey **Co Sec**: R Grey **Ops Man**:
C Covell
Fleet: 18 - 3 double-deck bus, 9 coach,
2 midibus, 4 midicoach.
Bodies: 5 Plaxton, 4 Berkhof
Ops incl: school contracts, private hire
Livery: Cream/Green

DEREK HIRCOCKS
COACHES
THE OLD BARN, SCHOOL ROAD,
UPWELL PE14 9EW
Tel: 01945 773461.
Fleetname: Upwell & District.
Prop: D. Hircock. **Eng**: W. Hircock.
Sec: Ms. C. Hircock.
Fleet: 7 coach.
Chassis: 4 AEC. 3 Leyland.
Ops incl: excursions & tours, private hire, school contracts.
Livery: Red/White/Blue.

HUNTINGDON & DISTRICT
STUKELEY ROAD, HUNTINGDON
PE29 6HG
Tel: 01480 457036
Web site:
www.huntingdonanddistrictbuses.co.uk
Ops Man: T Mead
Fleet: 30 - 15 double-deck bus, 13 single-deck bus, 2 coach
Chassis: 2 Dennis. 15 Leyland. 13 Volvo.
Bodies: 11 Alexander. 3 ECW. 6 Northern Counties. 2 Plaxton. 8 Wright.
Ops incl: local bus services.
Livery: Blue/Cream

	Air conditioning	
	Vehicles suitable for disabled	
	Coach(es) with galley facilities	
	Coach(es) with toilet facilities	
	Seat belt-fitted vehicles	
R	Recovery service available (not 24 hr)	
R24	24hr recovery service	
	Replacement vehicle available	
T	Toilet-drop facilities available	
	Vintage vehicle(s) available	
	Open top vehicle(s)	

Subsidiary Companies: part of Cavalier Travel, Lincolnshire.

*JANS COACHES
[wc] [restaurant] [leaf] [Nc] [key]

23 TOWNSEND, SOHAM CB7 5DD
Tel: 01353 721344
Fax: 01353 721341
E-mail: janscoaches@aol.com
Dirs: Roland Edwards, Janet Edwards, Stuart Edwards
Fleet: 8 - 3 double-deck bus, 3 coach, 1 double-deck coach, 1 minicoach.
Chassis: 1 Dennis. 1 Iveco. 1 Leyland. 2 MAN. 2 MCW. 1 Neoplan.
Bodies: 1 Berkhof. 2 MCW. 3 Neoplan. 1 Northern Counties. 1 Indcar.
Ops incl: excursions & tours, private hire, continental tours, school contracts.
Livery: White.

*KENZIES COACHES LTD
See Hertfordshire

*MIL-KEN TRAVEL LTD [wc]
[leaf] [Nc] [key] [T]

11 LYNN ROAD, LITTLEPORT CB6 1QG
Tel: 01353 860705
Fax: 01353 863222
E-mail: milken@btconnect.com
Man Dir: Jason Miller **Ch Eng**: Ian Martin
Fleet: 40 - 38 coach, 2 minibus.
Chassis: 6 Bedford. 10 DAF. 6 Dennis. 2 LDV. 16 Volvo.
Bodies: 3 Berkhof. 8 Duple. 3 Jonckheere. 21 Plaxton. 1 Willowbrook. 4 other.
Ops incl: excursions & tours, private hire, continental tours, school contracts.

J. R. MORLEY & SONS LTD
[disabled] [leaf]

WEST END GARAGE, WHITTLESEY PE7 1HR.
Tel: 01733 203520.
Dir/Traf Man: J. R. Morley. **Ch Eng**: W. R. Wright. **Dir/Sec**: Mrs P. E. L. Wright.
Fleet: 19 - 6 double-deck bus, 4 single-deck bus, 7 coach, 1 midicoach, 1 minibus.
Chassis: 7 Bedford, 2 Daimler, 4 Leyland, 2 Mercedes, 1 Volvo, 3 Seddon.
Bodies: 3 Alexander, 4 Duple, 2 Leyland, 1 Northern Counties, 2 Park Royal, 4 Plaxton, 1 Willowbrook, 1 Coachcraft.
Ops incl: local bus services, school contracts, private hire.
Livery: Grey/Red.
Ticket System: Wayfarer.

*NEAL'S TRAVEL LTD
[leaf] [wc] [restaurant] [Nc] [key] [T]

102 BECK ROAD, ISLEHAM CB7 5QP
Tel: 01638 780066
Fax: 01638 780011
E-mail: sales@nealstravel.com
Web site: www.nealstravel.com
Dirs: Bridget Paterson, Graham Neal, Lionel Neal, Nancy Neal
Fleet: 18 - 10 coach, 6 midicoach, 1 midibus, 2 minibus.
Chassis: 3 Dennis. 1 Iveco. 2 MAN. 9 Mercedes. 4 Volvo.
Bodies: 3 Jonckheere. 1 Neoplan. 1 Noge. 3 Optare. 3 Plaxton. 4 Transbus. 2 UVG. 1 Coach Europe. 1 Indcar.

Ops incl: local bus services, school contracts, private hire, continental tours.
Livery: White/Blue.

D A PAYNE COACH HIRE
[leaf] [wc] [restaurant]

UNIT 2, FOUNDRY WAY, LITTLE END ROAD INDUSTRIAL ESTATE, EATON SOCON PE19 8JH.
Tel: 01480 473272.
Fax: 01480 211252
E-mail: david@dapayne.fsnet.co.uk
Web site: dapaynecoachhire.co.uk
Prop: D A Payne **Sec**: Mrs Carole Allen
Ops Man: R Wood
Fleet: 10 - 3 coach, 1 midibus, 1 midicoach, 2 minibus, 3 minicoach.
Chassis: include 3 Setra. 1 Toyota. 1 Volvo.
Bodies: include 1 Caetano. 1 Plaxton. 3 Setra..
Ops incl: school contracts, excursions & tours, private hire.

*PETERBOROUGH TRAVEL CONSULTANTS
[wc] [restaurant] [leaf] [Nc]

12 BUCKLAND CLOSE, NETHERTON, PETERBOROUGH PE3 9UQ
Tel: 01733 267025
Fax: 01733 267025
E-mail: 2 coach, 1 minibus.
Props: Mrs P C Greeves, G M Greeves
Fleet: 2 - 1 coach, 1 midicoach.
Chassis: 1 DAF. 1 MAN. 1 Mercedes-Benz
Bodies: 1 Leyland. 2 Setra.
Ops incl: excursions & tours, private hire, continental tours.
Livery: Blue/White/Red.

PLANET TRAVEL [wc] [leaf] [key]
PLANET HOUSE, MEADOW DROVE, EARITH PE17 3QE.
Tel: 01487 843333.
Fax: 01487 843285.
Prop: D. J. Collier. **Ch Eng**: B. Turnock. **Co Acct**: M. Sloman. **Traf Man**: R. Birchenough. **Ops Man**: Mrs C. Stafford.
Fleet: 9 - 7 coach, 1 double-deck coach, 1 midicoach.
Chassis: 5 Bova. 1 Mercedes. 1 Scania. 2 Seddon.
Bodies: 1 Berkhof. 5 Bova. 2 Setra. 1 RH2000.
Ops incl: private hire, continental tours.

PREMIER TRAVEL SERVICES LTD
[leaf] [wc] [Nc]

PO BOX 178, 100 COWLEY ROAD, CAMBRIDGE CB4 0BB
Tel: 01223 420512
Fax: 01223 424221
E-mail: premier@burtons-bus.co.uk
Web site: www.premierdaybreaks.com
Fleetname: Premier
Man Dir/Co Sec: Paul J Cooper **Fleet Eng**: Mark Naude **Traf Man**: Duncan Barker
Fleet: 7 coaches and minicoaches.
Chassis: 4 Dennis, 1 Mercedes. 2 Volvo.
Bodies: 7 Plaxton
Ops incl: school contracts, excursions & tours, private hire, continental tours.
Livery: Blue/Yellow on white base.

*ROBINSON KIMBOLTON
19 THRAPSTON ROAD, KIMBOLTON PE28 0HW
Tel: 01480 860581
Fax: 01480 860801
Web site: www.robinsonkimbolton.co.uk
Fleet: 10 coach
Chassis: Dennis. Leyland. Toyota.
Bodies: Berkhof. Plaxton.
Ops incl: private hire, school contracts.

SEARLES AUTO SERVICES
[leaf]

10 GREAT NORTH ROAD, THORNHAUGH PE8 6HJ
Tel: 01780 783016
Fax: 01780 783016
Dir: Frank Searle
Fleet: 4 1 coach, 3 minibus
Chassis: 1 Bova. 2 Iveco. 1 Mercedes.
Bodies: 1 Bova. 2 Carlyle. 1 Mercedes-Benz
Ops incl: school contracts, private hire

SHAWS OF MAXEY
[wc] [leaf] [key] [Nc]

31 HIGH STREET, MAXEY PE6 9EF
Tel: 01778 342224
Fax: 01778 380378
Ptnrs: J. Duffelen R. E. Shaw, C. J. Shaw
Fleet: 23 - 1 single-deck bus, 19 coach, 2 midicoach, 1 minicoach.
Chassis: 8 Bedford. 1 Bova. 2 DAF. 1 Mercedes. 1 Renault. 1 Scania. 1 Toyota. 8 Volvo.
Bodies: 15 Plaxton. 1 Van Hool. 3 Jonckheere. 1 Bova. 1 Caetano. 1 Optare. 1 other.
Ops incl: local bus services, school contracts, excursions & tours, private hire, continental tours.
Livery: Blue/White

STAGECOACH EAST
See Northamptonshire

STAGECOACH IN CAMBRIDGE
100 COWLEY ROAD, CAMBRIDGE CB4 4DN
Tel: 01223 423578
Fax: 01223 420065
E-mail: cambridge.enquiries@stagecoachbus.com
Web site: www.stagecoachbus.com/cambridge
Fleetnames: Citi, Stagecoach in Cambridge
Man Dir: Andy Campbell **Ops Dir**: Michelle Hargreaves
Fleet: 125 - 61 double-deck bus, 55 single-deck bus, 7 coach, 2 midibus.
Chassis: 12 Dennis, 2 Leyland. 46 MAN. 2 Optare. 63 Volvo.
Bodies: Alexander. Northern Counties. Optare. Plaxton.
Ops incl: local bus services.
Livery: Stagecoach
Part of Stagecoach East (see Northamptonshire)

*TOURMASTER COACHES LTD
See Lincolnshire

*TOWLERS COACHES LTD
[wc] [Nc]
CHURCH ROAD, EMNETH PE14 8AA
Tel: 01945 583645
Fax: 01945 583645
E-mail: joanne@towlerscoaches.fsnet.co.uk
Dirs: Mark Towler, Wendy Shepherd, Anton Towler, Joanne Walton
Fleet: 7 - 3 double-deck bus, 3 coach, 1 double-deck coach
Chassis: 1 Bova. 1 Bristol. 3 Leyland. 1 Scania. 1 LAG-EOS.
Bodies: 1 Bova. 1 Duple. 1 ECW. 1 East Lancs. 1 Jonckheere. 1 Plaxton. 1 LAG EOS.
Ops incl: school contracts, excursions & tours, private hire.
Livery: Green/Cream/Orange

WEBB'S
[disabled] [seatbelt] [vintage]
ST PETERS FARM, MIDDLE DROVE PE14 8JJ
Tel: 01945 430123
E-mail: webb-s-cant@fsbdial.co.uk
Prop: Barry Webb
Fleet: 3 - 1 midicoach,1 minicoach, 1 minibus.
Ops incl: local bus services

WHIPPET COACHES LTD
[disabled] [wc] [open top] [seatbelt] [R]
CAMBRIDGE ROAD, FENSTANTON PE18 9JB.
Tel: 01480 463792.
Fax: 01480 498534.
Dirs: A. T. Lee, J. T. Lee, J. C. Lee, P. H. Lee, M. H. Lee.
Fleet: 49 - 20 double-deck bus, 6 single-deck bus, 20 coach, 3 minibus.
Chassis: Bedford, Leyland, Scania, Volvo.
Bodies: Duple, East Lancs, Leyland, Northern Counties, Park Royal, Plaxton, Van Hool, Alexander.
Ops incl: local bus service, school contracts, excursions & tours, private hire, express.
Livery: Blue/Cream with logo.
Ticket System: Almex Eurofare.

*W - M TRAVEL
[disabled] [seatbelt] [wc] [Nc]
10 MAIN ROAD, PARSON DROVE, WISBECH PE13 4LF
Tel: 01945 700492
Fax: 01945 700964
Recovery: 01945 700942
Dir: W Norman
Fleet: 6 - 3 single-deck bus, 3 coach
Chassis: Bedford. DAF. Dennis. Scania.
Bodies: Berkhof. Duple. Plaxton. Marcopolo
Ops incl: local bus services, school contracts, excursions & tours, private hire.

CHESHIRE, HALTON & STOCKPORT

A 2 B TRAVEL UK LTD
See Merseyside (Wirral)

ANTHONYS TRAVEL
[wc] [seatbelt] [Nc] [galley] [repl] [T]
8 CORMORANT DRIVE, PICOW FARM ROAD, RUNCORN WA7 4UD
Tel: 01928 561460.
Fax: 01928 561460.
Partners.: Richard Bamber, Anne Bamber, Anthony Bamber. **Ops Man**: Eric Manley.
Fleet: 15 - 4 single-deck coach, 1 midicoach. 2 minibus. 8 minicoach.
Chassis: 2 Iveco, 7 LDV, 2 Setra, 2 Neoplan, 2 Mercedes.
Ops incl: local bus services, school contracts, private hire, excursion & tours.
Livery: Cream/Orange/Brown/White.
Ticket System: Setright.

ARROWEBROOK COACHES
THE OLD COACH YARD, WERVIN ROAD, CROUGHTON CH2 4DA
Tel: 01244 382444
Fax: 01244 379777
Prop: A. G. Parsons
Livery: White/Green.

*BARRATT'S COACHES LTD
[wc] [seatbelt] [galley] [repl] [R] [T] [Nc]
48 LONDON ROAD, NANTWICH CW5 6LT
Tel: 01270 625096
Fax: 01270 627728
E-mail: gilbarratt@aol.com
Web site: www.barrattscoaches.co.uk
Fleetname: Barratt's of Nantwich.
Dirs: G Barratt, D F Bate
Fleet: 20 - 16 coaches, 2 coach, 2 midicoach.
Chassis: Leyland. Mercedes. Neoplan. Scania. Volvo.
Bodies: Jonckheere. Neoplan. Plaxton. Van Hool.
Ops incl: school contracts, excursions & tours, private hire, continental tours.
Livery: White.

BENNETT'S TRAVEL
ATHLONE ROAD, LONGFORD, WARRINGTON WA2 8JJ
Tel/Fax: 01925 415299.
Prop.: B. A. Bennett, D. B. Bennett.
Livery: White/Blue.

BIRCHWOOD TRAVEL
[disabled] [seatbelt] [R24]
106 NEW LANE, CROFT, WARRINGTON WA3 7JL.
Tel: 01925 767962.
Fax: 01925 767073.
Owner: B. Thompson.
Fleet: 8 - 1 single-deck bus, 2 coach, 5 minibus.
Chassis: 1 Bedford. 1 Ford. 3 Iveco. 3 Leyland.
Bodies: 2 Deansgate. 1 Mellor. 1 Dormobile. 1 Galaxy.
Ops incl: local bus services, school contracts, private hire.
Livery: White with Grey/Black stripe.

*A. & H. BOOTH LTD [seatbelt]
See Greater Manchester

BOSTOCK'S COACHES
SPRAGG STREET GARAGE, CONGLETON CW12 1QH
Tel: 01260 273108
Fax: 01260 276338
Dirs: J. F. Aspinall, C. H. Aspinall, D. E. Aspinall, N. J. Forshaw
Mans: M. Bostock, J. Bostock
Fleet: 40 - 1 double-deck bus, 35 coach, 1 double-deck coach, 2 midicoach, 1 minicoach.
Chassis: 2 Bova, 4 DAF, 7 Dennis, 2 Iveco, 4 Mercedes,1 Neoplan, 3 Scania, 12 Volvo.
Bodies: 1 Autobus, 1 Beulas, 3 Berkhof, 3 Caetano, 2 Duple, 1 Irizar, 2 Jonckheere, 3 Mercedes, 1 Neoplan, 14 Plaxton, 6 Van Hool.
Ops incl: excursions & tours, private hire, continental tours, school contracts.
Livery: Green
Subsidiary of: Holmewood Coaches (Lancashire)

*H E BROWN & SONS
[wc] [seatbelt]
8 GREENFIELD ROAD, GREENFIELD FARM INDUSTRIAL ESTATE, CONGLETON CW12 4TR
Tel: 01260 275281
Fax: 01260 280955
Fleetname: Browns Coaches.
Prop: Dennis Brown
Fleet: 5 - 3 coach, 1 double deck coach, 1 minibus.
Chassis: 1 Leyland. 1 Neoplan. 1 Optare.

[Nc]	Air conditioning
[disabled]	Vehicles suitable for disabled
[galley]	Coach(es) with galley facilities
[wc]	Coach(es) with toilet facilities
[seatbelt]	Seat belt-fitted vehicles
[R]	Recovery service available (not 24 hr)
[R24]	24hr recovery service
[repl]	Replacement vehicle available
[T]	Toilet-drop facilities available
[vintage]	Vintage vehicle(s) available
[open top]	Open top vehicle(s)

1 Volvo. 1 Van Hool.
Bodies: 2 Duple. 1 Neoplan.1 Optare. 1 Van Hool.
Ops incl: local bus services, school contract, private hire.
Livery: White/Red.
Ticket System: Setright.

R BULLOCK & CO TRANSPORT

see Greater Manchester

*CHESTER CITY TRANSPORT LTD

STATION ROAD, CHESTER CH1 3AD
Tel: 01244 347452
Fax: 01244 347453
Man Dir: S Hyslop **Eng Dir**: M J Ridge
Fin Dir: R W Pointon **Traf Man**: J R Lee
Fleet: 75 - 26 double-deck bus, 7 open-top bus, 14 single-deck bus, 23 midibus, 5 minibus.
Chassis: 7 Daimler. 35 Dennis. 15 Leyland. 4 Marshall. 4 Optare. 6 Scania. 5 VW. 8 BMC.
Bodies: 4 Alexander. 8 BMC. 5 Constables. 5 East Lancs. 1 Leyland. 11 Marshall. 20 Northern Counties. 4 Optare. 17 Plaxton. 2 Roe. 6 Wright.
Ops incl: local bus services, school contracts.
Livery: Maroon/Cream, Cream/Blue
Ticket System: Wayfarer 3

*DOBSON'S BUSES LTD

WINCHAM PARK, CHAPEL STREET, WINCHAM, NORTHWICH CW9 6DA
Tel/Fax: 01606 350200
Man Dir: I P Dobson **Ch Eng**: P J Dobson
Ops Man: R P Dobson **Co Sec**: R E Dobson
Fleet: 15 - 8 double-deck bus, 2 coach, 5 midibus
Chassis: 2 Daimler. 2 Dennis. 1 Iveco. 6 Leyland. 2 Mercedes. 2 Peugeot.
Bodies: include: 1 Duple. 1 Marshall. 1 Mellor. 2 Plaxton. 2 Peugeot.
Ops Include: local bus services, school contracts, private hire
Ticket system: Datafare

FIRST IN CHESTER & THE WIRRAL

669 NEW CHESTER ROAD, ROCK FERRY CH42 1PZ
Tel: 0151 645 8661
See Merseyside

JOHN FLANAGAN COACH TRAVEL

2 REDDISH HALL COTTAGES, BROAD LANE, GRAPPENHALL, WARRINGTON WA4 3HS
Tel: 01925 266115
Fax: 01925 261100
E-mail: janette@flanagancoaches.co.uk
Web site: www.flanagancoaches.co.uk
Dirs: John Flanagan, Janette Flanagan, Jane Murawski

Fleet: 9 - 4 coach, 1 midicoach, 4 minicoach.
Chassis: 2 Bedford. 1 Ford Transit. 1 Iveco. 2 Mercedes. 1 Volvo. 2 other
Bodies: 1 Jonckheere. 2 Mercedes. 1 UVG. 2 Wright.
Ops incl: excursions & tours, private hire, school contracts, continental tours.
Livery: Red/Black/White

*HALTON BOROUGH TRANSPORT LTD

MOOR LANE, WIDNES WA8 7AF
Tel: 0151 423 3333
Fax: 0151 420 2281
Web site: www.haltontransport.co.uk
E-mail: info@haltontransport.co.uk
Fleetname: Halton Transport
Man Dir/Sec: D J Cunningham **Eng Man**: P Matthews **Traf Man**: C N Adams
Fleet: 61 single-deck bus
Chassis: 55 Dennis. 6 Leyland.
Bodies: 15 East Lancs. 6 Leyland. 40 Marshall.
Ops incl: local bus services.
Livery: Red/Cream.
Ticket System: Wayfarer.

HULME HALL COACHES LTD

1 STANLEY ROAD, CHEADLE HULME SK8 6PL
Tel: 0161 486 1187
Fax: 0161 482 8125
E-mail: hulmehallcoaches@talk21.com
Web site: www.hulmehallcoaches.co.uk
Man Dir: D. Herald **Tran Man**: C. J. O'Neill
Traf Man: I Johnson **Fl Eng**: P Henshall
Fleet: 12 - 7 double-deck bus, 1 single-deck bus, 3 coach, 1 midibus.
Chassis: 6 Bristol. 1 Iveco. 1 Leyland. 1 Leyland National. 3 Volvo.
Bodies: 7 ECW. 1 East Lancs. 1 Mellor. 3 Plaxton.
Ops incl: local bus services, school contracts, private hire.
Livery: Red/Cream
Ticket System: Wayfarer

*HUXLEY COACHES

GREAVES LANE EAST, THREAPWOOD, MALPAS SY14 7AS
Tel: 01948 770661
Fax: 01948 770459
Prop: Fred Huxley
Fleet: 16 - 11 coach. 5 midibus.
Ops incl: local bus services, school contracts, excursions & tours, private hire, continental tours.
Livery: Cream/Yellow/Brown

*LE-RAD COACHES & LIMOUSINES

328 HYDE ROAD, WOODLEY SK6 1PF
Tel: 0161 430 2032
Recovery: 0770 314 5500
E-mail: lerad.travel@virgin.net
Props: Jean Mycock, Dereck Mycock
Fleet: 3 - 2 coach, 1 minicoach.
Chassis: 2 DAF. 1 Ford.

Ops incl: private hire, excursions & tours.

*ROY McCARTHY COACHES

THE COACH DEPOT, SNAPE ROAD, MACCLESFIELD SK10 2NZ
Tel: 01625 425060
Fax: 01625 619853
Senr Ptnr: Andy McCarthy **Ptnr**: M S Lomas
Fleet: 9 coach.
Chassis: 2 Bedford. 2 Dennis. 1 MAN. 4 Volvo.
Bodies: 1 Berkhof. 1 Caetano. 7 Plaxton.
Ops incl: school contracts, excursions & tours, private hire, continental tours.
Livery: Blue/Cream

MARPLE MINI COACHES

5 GROSVENOR ROAD, MARPLE SK6 6PR.
Tel: 0161 881 9111
Owner: G. W. Cross
Fleet: 2 minicoach
Chassis: Ford Transit, LDV.
Ops incl: school contracts, private hire.
Livery: White/Gold.

*MAYNE COACHES LTD

BATTERSBY LANE, WARRINGTON WA2 7ET
Tel: 01925 445588
Fax: 01925 232300
E-mail: warrington@mayne.co.uk
Web site: www.mayne.co.uk
Man Dir: S B Mayne **Gen Man**: R W Vernon **Asst Gen Man**: A Dykes **Traf Man**: J Drake **Ch Eng**: E Sutcliffe
Fleet: 26 - 4 double-deck bus, 22 coach.
Chassis: 1 Daimler. 7 Leyland. 9 Scania. 9 Volvo.
Bodies: 1 Duple. 3 East Lancs. 6 Irizar. 1 Northern Counties. 15 Plaxton.
Ops incl: local bus services, school contracts, private hire.
Livery: Red/Cream
Subsidiary of: Mayne's (Greater Manchester)

*MEREDITHS COACHES

LYDGATE, WELL STREET, MALPAS SY14 8DE
Tel: 01948 860405
Fax: 01948 860162
E-mail: info@merediths.f9.co.uk
Web site: www.meredithscoaches.co.uk
Props: J K Meredith, Mrs M E Meredith, D J Meredith
Fleet: 18 - 1 double-deck bus, 17 single-deck coach.
Chassis: 4 Ford. 4 Leyland. 10 Volvo.
Bodies: Jonckheere. Plaxton. Van Hool. Wadham Stringer.
Ops incl: school contracts, private hire.

MILLMAN'S COACHES [wc]

STATION YARD, GREEN LANE,
PADGATE, WARRINGTON WA1 4JR
Tel: 01925 822298
Fax: 01925 813181
Prop: Eric Millman
Fleet: 8 coach
Chassis: 5 Leyland, 2 Volvo 1 other
Bodies: 1 Berkhof. 3 Duple, 3 Plaxton,
1 Van Hool.
Ops incl: local bus services, school
contracts, excursions & tours, private hire.
Livery: Blue/White

MOORE'S COACHES LTD

53 REES CRESCENT,
HOLMES CHAPEL CW4 7NL.
Tel/Fax: 01477 537004
Dirs: D. M. Moore, J. C. Moore.
Fleet: 4 coach.
Chassis: 1 Dennis. 1 Scania. 1 Volvo.
1 Van Hool.
Bodies: 1 Jonckheere. 1 Plaxton.
2 Van Hool.
Ops incl: excursions & tours, private hire,
express, continental tours, school contracts.
Livery: Moore's Coaches/Nat. Express.

A E & R I NIDDRIE LTD

LEWIN STREET, MIDDLEWICH
CW10 9AS
Tel: 01606 832343.
Fax: 01606 833449.
E-mail: niddries@aol.com
Man Dir: R. I. Niddrie. **Dir/Sec/Tour Man:**
Miss F. J. Niddrie. **Traf man:** P. J. Niddrie.
Fleet: 5 coach.
Chassis: Bedford. 2 DAF. 1 Scania.
1 Volvo.
Bodies: 1 Duple. 3 Plaxton. 1 Van Hool.
Ops incl: excursions & tours, private hire,
continental tours, school contracts.
Livery: Silver/Maroon/Black.

PRESTIGE PEOPLE CARRIERS LTD

131 WESTON LANE, BASFORD CW2 5NJ
Tel/Fax: 01270 650727
Owner: J. J. O'Leary MBE
Fleet: 5 midibus.
Chassis: 1 Ford Transit. 2 Leyland.
2 Toyota.

Ops incl: school contracts, excursions &
tours, private hire.
Livery: Metallic Green/Silver.

ROADLINER TRAVEL

102 VICTORIA STREET, CREWE
CW1 2JT.
Tel/Fax: 01270 250292.
Dir: S. Pyner. **Man:** K. Smedley.
Co Sec: Mrs J. Jones.
Fleet: 6 - 5 coach, 1 midicoach.
Chassis: 5 DAF. 1 Toyota.
Ops incl: excursions & tours, private hire,
school contracts.

*SELWYNS TRAVEL LTD

WESTON, RUNCORN WA7 4LU
Tel: 01928 564515
Fax: 01928 591872
Recovery: 01928 572108
E-mail: sales@selwyns.co.uk
Web site: www.selwyns.co.uk
Fleetname: Selwyns
Man Dir: Selwyn Jones **Ops Man:**
Reno Peers **Fleet Eng:** David Yould **Co
Sec/Acct:** Richard Williams **Sales Man:**
Jayne Furber **Human Resources Man:**
Chris Roach
Fleet: 46 - includes 4 single-deck bus,
1 double-deck coach, 3 midicoach.
Chassis: 36 DAF. 2 Dennis. 2 Mercedes.
1 Neoplan. 1 Toyota. 5 Volvo.
Bodies: 2 Berkhof. 1 Caetano. 3 Ikarus.
1 Neoplan. 7 Plaxton. 29 Van Hool.
4 Wright.
Ops incl: excursions & tours, private hire,
local bus services, school contracts,
continental tours, express.
Livery: White with Blue/Orange relief.
Ticket System: Wayfarer 3

*SHEARINGS LTD

BARLEYCASTLE LANE, APPLETON,
WARRINGTON WA4 4FR.
Tel: 01925 214600
Fax: 01925 262606
Ops Man: Chris Brown
*See also Shearings Ltd, Greater
Manchester.*

SMITHS OF MARPLE LTD

72 CROSS LANE, MARPLE SK6 7PZ
Tel: 0161 427 2825
Fax: 0161 449 7731

E-mail:
julie@smithsofmarple.fsnet.co.uk
Web site:
www.smithsofmarple.fsnet.co.uk
Man Dir: Jason Hibbert. **Co Sec:**
Julie Hibbert
Fleet: 6 - 1 double-deck bus, 3 coach,
2 midibus.
Chassis: 1 Bristol. 1 Irisbus. 2 Setra.
1 Toyota.
Bodies: 1 Beulas. 1 Caetano. 1 ECW.
1 Mellor. 2 Setra
Ops incl: local bus services, school
contracts, excursions & tours, private hire,
continental tours.
Livery: White/Red, Green, Blue, Orange.

*WARRINGTON BOROUGH TRANSPORT LTD

WILDERSPOOL CAUSEWAY,
WARRINGTON WA4 6PT
Tel: 01925 634296
Fax: 01925 418382
Web site:
www.warringtonboroughtransport.co.uk
Man Dir: Nigel Featham **Fin Dir:**
John Bannister **Ops Man:** Charlie Shannon
Eng Man: Damien Graham
Fleet: 115 - 34 double-deck bus, 69 midibus,
12 minibus.
Chassis: 12 Optare. 66 Transbus. 37 Volvo.
Ops incl: local bus services, school
contracts, private hire.
Livery: Red/Ivory
Ticket System: Wayfarer 3

WHITEGATE TRAVEL LTD

15 BEAUTY BANK, WHITEGATE,
NORTHWICH CW8 2BP
Tel: 01606 882760
Fax: 01606 883356
Owner: K. Prince
Fleet: 12 minibus
Chassis: 1 Ford Transit. 2 Freight Rover.
2 Iveco. 2 Mercedes. 5 Leyland DAF.
Ops incl: local bus services, school
contracts, private hire.
Livery: Yellow/White

Cheshire

	Air conditioning
	Vehicles suitable for disabled
	Coach(es) with galley facilities
[wc]	Coach(es) with toilet facilities
	Seat belt-fitted vehicles
R	Recovery service available (not 24 hr)
R24	24hr recovery service
	Replacement vehicle available
T	Toilet-drop facilities available
	Vintage vehicle(s) available
	Open top vehicle(s)

CORNWALL

K T & M BAKER
THE GARAGE, DULOE, LOOE
Tel: 01503 262359
Fleet: about 6 coaches
Ops incl: school contracts

*CURRIAN TOURS AND COACH HIRE
CURRIAN ROAD GARAGE, NANPEAN, ST AUSTELL PL26 7YD
Tel: 01726 822303
Fax: 01726 824848
E-mail: info@currian-coaches.co.uk
Web site: www.currian-coaches.co.uk
Gen Man: T J Stoneman **Ops Man:** J T Stoneman **Ch Eng:** K J Stoneman **Tours Man:** Mrs S Stoneman
Fleet: 12 - 3 double-deck bus, 9 coach.
Chassis: 2 Bova. 3 Bristol. 1 DAF. 1 Iveco. 1 Setra. 4 Volvo.
Bodies: 2 Bova. 3 ECW. 1 Jonckheere. 5 Plaxton. 1 Setra.
Ops incl: excursions & tours, private hire, continental tours, school contracts.
Livery: White.

DAC COACHES   R24
RYLANDS GARAGE, ST ANNE'S CHAPEL, GUNNISLAKE PL18 9HW
Tel: 01822 834571
Fax: 01822 833881
Recovery: 01822 833378
E-mail: dac.coaches@btconnect.com
Web site: www.daccoaches.co.uk
Dirs: Bernard Harding, Nick Smith
Fleet: 10 - 4 coach, 1 double-deck bus, 2 midibus, 3 minicoach.
Chassis: 1 Bedford. 1 Bristol. 1 Ford. 3 Mercedes. 1 Peugeot. 3 Volvo.
Bodies: Duple. ECW. 9 Plaxton. Van Hool.
Ops incl: local bus services, school contracts, excursions & tours, private hire, continental tours.
Livery: Blue/White/Red/Yellow.
Ticket System: Almex.

*DARLEY FORD TRANSPORT
DARLEY FORD, LISKEARD PL14 5AS
Tel: 01579 362272
Fax: 01579 363425
Owner: Albert J Deeble
Fleet: 11 - 10 coach, 1 double-deck coach
Chassis: 1 Leyland. 2 Scania. 1 Toyota. 6 Volvo.
Bodies: 1 Berkhof. 2 Duple. 1 Ikarus. 1 Irizar. 1 Jonckheere. 2 Plaxton. 1 Van Hool
Ops incl: private hire, school contracts, continental tours.

J K DEEBLE
THE GARAGE, UPTON CROSS, LISKEARD PL14 5AX.
Tel: 01579 362226.
Fax: 01579 362220.
Fleetname: Caradon Riviera Tours.
Prop: J. K. Deeble.
Fleet: 13 - 3 single-deck bus, 7 coach, 2 midibus, 1 minibus.

Chassis: 1 Bristol. 1 Freight Rover. 4 Leyland. 2 MCW. 3 Seddon.
Bodies: 5 Alexander. 1 Carlyle. 2 Optare. 5 Plaxton.
Ops incl: local bus services, school contracts, excursions & tours, private hire.
Livery: Ivory/Blue.
Ticket System: Setright.

FIRST IN DEVON & CORNWALL
THE RYDE, CHELSON MEADOW, PLYMOUTH PL9 7JT
Tel: 01752 495250
Web site: www.firstgroup.com
Man Dir: Karl Duncan **Fin Dir:** Simon Harland
Fleet: 474 - 116 double-deck bus, 14 single-deck bus, 56 coach, 116 midibus, 172 minibus.
Chassis: Bristol. Dennis. Leyland. Mercedes. Optare. Volvo.
Bodies: Alexander. Carlyle. ECW. East Lancs. Marshall. Northern Counties. Optare. Plaxton. Reeve Burgess. Roe. Van Hool. Wright. Frank Guy. PMT.
Ops incl: local bus service, school contracts, excursions & tours, private hire, express.
Livery: First livery.
Ticket System: Almex.

GROUP TRAVEL
DUNMERE ROAD, BODMIN PL31 2QN
Tel: 01208 72669
Fax: 01208 77989
Prop: R. K. & R. E. Webber.
Fleet: 24 coach.
Ops incl: local bus services, school contracts, excursions & tours, private hire, continental tours.
Livery: Red/Maroon.

O. J. HAMBLY & SONS LTD
THE GARAGE, PELYNT, LOOE PL13 2JZ.
Tel: 01503 220660.
Gen Man: P. Hambly. **Ch Eng:** P. Yeo.
Sec: A. F. Hambly. **Traf Man:** P. Hambly.
Fleet: 8 - 6 coach, 2 minibus.
Chassis: 3 Bedford. 2 Mercedes. 3 Volvo.
Bodies: 1 Duple. 6 Plaxton. 1 Dormobile.
Ops incl: local bus services, school contracts, excursions & tours, private hire.
Livery: Red/Cream.

HOOKWAYS JENNINGS
LANSDOWNE ROAD, BUDE EX23 8BN.
Tel: 01288 352359.
Fax: 01288 352140.
Prop: C. Hookway. **Gen Man:** B. Coates.
Fleet: 10 coach
Chassis: 10 Volvo.
Bodies: 2 Jonckheere. 8 Plaxton.
Ops incl: local bus services, school contracts, excursions & tours, private hire, continental tours.
Livery: Yellow/Purple/Blue.

Ticket System: Setright
Subsidiary of: Hookways Devon

HOPLEYS BUS & COACH
SUNIC, ROPE WALK, MOUNT HAWKE, TRURO TR4 8DW.
Tel: 01209 890268.
Fax: 01209 890266.
Ptnrs: B. Hopley, D. R. Hopley, N. A. Hopley.
Fleet: 5 - 1 double-deck bus, 2 single-deck bus, 2 coach.
Chassis: 1 Bedford. 1 Bristol. 3 Volvo.
Bodies: 1 Duple. 1 ECW. 1 Jonckheere. 1 Plaxton. 1 Wright.
Ops incl: local bus services, school contracts, excursions & tours, private hire.
Livery: Red/White/Grey.
Ticket System: Wayfarer 3.

*LISKEARD & DISTRICT OMNIBUS COMPANY LTD
HIGHER ST LUKES, BOLVENTOR, LAUNCESTON PL15 7TP
Tel/Fax: 01566 86501
E-mail: cameldist@tesco.net
Fleetname: Camelford & District Omnibus Company
Man/Ops Dir: E R Hobbs **Fin/Co Sec:** C N Hobbs
Fleet: 8 - 2 coach, 1 open-top bus, 4 minibus, 1 minicoach.
Chassis: 1 AEC. 2 Dennis. 1 Ford Transit. 4 Mercedes.
Bodies: 4 Mercedes. 2 Wadham Stringer. 1 Weymann. 1 CDC.
Ops incl: local bus services, private hire.
Livery: Green/Cream, White/Green
Ticket System: Almex

*MOUNTS BAY COACHES   R
4 ALEXANDRA ROAD, PENZANCE TR18 4LY
Tel: 01736 363320
Fax: 01736 366985
Dir: Jeff Oxenham, Kathy Oxenham
Fleet: 9 - 8 coach, 1 midicoach.
Chassis: 1 Scania. 1 Setra. 7 Volvo.
Bodies: 1 Caetano. 8 Van Hool.
Ops incl: school contracts, excursions & tours, private hire.
Livery: Blue/White

*O T S MINIBUS & COACH HIRE
48 FORE STREET, CONSTANTINE TR11 5AB
Tel: 01326 340703
Fax: 01326 340404
E-mail: salots@hotmail.com
Web site: www.otsfalmouth.co.uk
Prop: S B Moore
Fleet: 3 - 1 coach, 1 midicoach, 1 minicoach.
Chassis: 1 Leyland. 2 Mercedes.
Bodies: 1 Plaxton. 2 other.
Ops incl: local bus services, school contracts, excursions & tours, private hire.
Livery: White with blue/brown stripe.

*PENMERE MINIBUS SERVICES

28 BOSMOOR ROAD, FALMOUTH TR11 4PU
Tel: 01326 314165
E-mail: benjamin.moore@tiscali.co.uk
Web site: www.penmereminibusandcoach.co.uk
Man: Benjamin Moore
Fleet: 1 - 1 minicoach.
Chassis: 1 Mercedes.
Ops incl: local bus services, school contracts, private hire.
Livery: White with blue/silver stripes.

PRIMROSE COACHES OF CORNWALL

2 MARKET SQUARE, HAYLE TR27 4EA.
Tel: 01736 754788.
Fax: 01736 754788.
E-mail: wendy@primrose.co.uk
Web site: www.primrosecfreeserve.co.uk
Prop: J. W. Runnalls.
Ops. Man: W. J. Runnalls.
Fleet: 5 - 4 coach, 1 midicoach.
Chassis: 1 Bedford, 1 Setra, 1 Toyota.
Bodies: 1 Caetano, 1 Neoplan, 1 Plaxton, 1 Setra, 1 Van Hool.
Ops incl: excursions & tours, private hire, continental tours, local bus services, school contracts.

ROSELYN COACHES

MIDDLEWAY GARAGE, ST BLAZEY ROAD, PAR PL24 2JA
Tel: 01726 813737
Fax: 01726 813739
Web site: www.roselyncoaches.co.uk
Dirs: J Ede, K. A. Paramor
Fleet: 15 - 10 double-deck bus, 8 coach.
Chassis: 6 Bristol. 1 DAF. 4 Leyland. 7 Volvo.
Bodies: 6 ECW. 4 East Lancs. 1 Jonckheere. 5 Plaxton. 2 Van Hool.
Ops incl: local bus services, school contracts, excursions & tours, private hire, continental tours.
Livery: Green/Gold.
Ticket System: Setright.

SMITHS COACHES

UNIT 11, TREBURGIE WATER, DOBWALLS, LISKEARD
Tel: 01579 321607
Fleet: about 6 coaches
Ops incl: school contracts

*SUN-SET COACHES

BRANE, PENZANCE TR20 8RB
Tel/Fax: 01736 810428
Props: I Topping, S M Topping
Fleet: 10 - 4 midibus, 2 midicoach, 2 minibus, 2 minicoach.
Chassis: 2 Iveco. 8 Mercedes.
Bodies: 4 Mellor. 5 Mercedes. 1 other.
Ops incl: local bus services, school contracts, excursions & tours, private hire, continental tours.
Livery: Sky Blue.
Ticket system: Twin

*TAVISTOCK COMMUNITY TRANSPORT

GREENLANDS, ST ANN'S CHAPEL, GUNNISLAKE PL18 9HW
Tel: 01822 833574
Fleetname: Tavistock Country Bus
Chmn: Robin Pike **Hon Sec**: Keith Potter
Hon Treas: Bob Crosbie
Fleet: 1 minibus
Chassis: Iveco **Body**: G M Coachwork.
Ops incl: local bus services, private hire.
Livery: Red/White
Ticket System: Wayfarer

TILLEY'S COACHES

THE COACH STATION, WAINHOUSE CORNER, BUDE EX23 0AZ.
Tel: 01840 230244.
Prop: P A & L. A. Tilley.
Livery: White/Cream/Maroon.

*TRELEY MOTORS

ST BURYAN, PENZANCE TR19 6DZ
Tel: 01736 810322
Man Dir: J Ley **Ops Man/Ch Eng**: A J Ley
Co Sec: A D Ley
Fleet: 4 - 1 coach, 1 single-deck bus, 1 minicoach
Chassis/Body: 1 Dennis. 1 Mercedes. 1 Volvo.
Bodies: 1 Duple. 1 Plaxton. 1 Jubilee
Ops incl: school contracts, excursions & tours, private hire, continental tours
Livery: Blue/Cream

*TRURONIAN LTD

24 LEMON STREET, TRURO TR1 2LS
Tel: 01872 273453
Fax: 01872 222522
E-mail: enquiries@truronian.co.uk
Web site: www.truronian.com
Joint Man Dirs: David Rabey, Geoff Rumbles **Fleet Eng**: Derek Beck **Ops Man**: Trevor Tobiasen **Coaching Man**: Tracey Parkin

Fleet: 57 - 9 double-deck bus, 30 single-deck bus, 10 coach, 1 midicoach, 5 minibus, 2 minicoach, 1 road train.
Chassis: 1 Bedford. 4 Bristol. 17 Dennis. 1 Ford Transit. 3 Iveco. 7 Leyland. 8 Mercedes. 5 Transbus. 9 Volvo.
Ops incl: local bus services, school contracts, excursions & tours, private hire, continental tours
Livery: Red/Silver.
Ticket System: Almex.

*WESTERN GREYHOUND LTD

14 EAST STREET, NEWQUAY TR7 1BH
Tel: 01637 871871
Fax: 01637 873361
E-mail: enquiries@westerngreyhound.com
Web site: www.westerngreyhound.com
Man Dir: Mark Howarth **Co Sec**: Maria Howarth **Dir**: Robin Orbell **Ops Man**: Brian James **Comm Man**: Hendy Howarth
Fleet: 41 - 4 coach, 6 double-deck bus, 2 open-top bus, 25 midibus, 1 minicoach, 3 heritage.
Chassis: 2 Bristol. 6 Leyland. 26 Mercedes. 4 Volvo.
Bodies: 3 Alexander. 2 ECW. 25 Plaxton. 4 Van Hool. 1 Adamson.
Ops incl: local bus services, school contracts, excursions & tours, private hire.
Livery: Green/White.
Ticket System: Wayfarer 3

*WHEAL BRITON COACHES

BLACKWATER, TRURO TR4 8HH
Tel/Fax: 01872 560281
Prop: C E Palmer **Ch Eng**: G M Palmer
Fleet: 19 - 18 coach, 1 minibus.
Chassis: 1 LDV. 1 Leyland. 4 Scania. 3 Setra. 10 Volvo
Bodies: 1 Duple. 1 Jonckheere. 12 Plaxton. 3 Setra. 1 Van Hool.
Ops incl: school contracts, excursions & tours, private hire.

F. T. WILLIAMS TRAVEL

DOLCOATH INDUSTRIAL PARK, DOLCOATH ROAD, CAMBORNE TR14 8RU
Tel: 01209 717152.
Fax: 01209 612511.
Prop: F. T. Williams.
Livery: White/Gold/Black.

Air conditioning	
Vehicles suitable for disabled	
Coach(es) with galley facilities	
Coach(es) with toilet facilities	
Seat belt-fitted vehicles	
Recovery service available (not 24 hr)	
R24 24hr recovery service	
Replacement vehicle available	
Toilet-drop facilities available	
Vintage vehicle(s) available	
Open top vehicle(s)	

Cornwall

CUMBRIA

*D K & N BOWMAN
BURTHWAITE HILL, BURTHWAITE, WREAY, CARLISLE CA4 0RT
Tel: 01697 473262
Fax: 01697 474800
E-mail: enquiries@bowmans-coaches.co.uk
Web site: www.bowmans-coaches.co.uk
Ptnrs: David K Bowman, Nora Bowman
Fleet: 10 coach.
Chassis: 6 AEC. 1 Dennis. 1 MAN. 2 Scania.
Bodies: 1 Berkhof. 1 Duple. 1 Irizar. 1 Jonckheere. 4 Plaxton. 1 Van Hool. 1 Barnaby.
Ops incl: school contracts, excursions and tours, private hire.
Livery: Ivory/Red

BROWNS LUXURY COACHES
THE COACH & TRAVEL CENTRE, SCOTLAND ROAD, CARNFORTH LA5 9RQ
Tel: 01539 448500.
Fax: 01539 448501.
Fleet: 6 - 4 coach, 2 midicoach.
Chassis: 1 Ford Transit. 1 Mercedes. 4 Volvo.
Bodies: 4 Jonckheere. 1 Plaxton. 1 Mercedes.
Ops incl: excursions & tours, private hire, continental tours, school contracts.
Livery: White with red/yellow/lue stripes.
Part of The Travellers Choice, Carnforth

*S H BROWNRIGG LTD
53 MAIN STREET, EGREMONT CA22 2DB
Tel: 01946 820205
Fax: 01946 822788
Recovery: 01946 822986
Ptnrs: R J Cook, Mrs I M Cook, Mrs L Holliday, B Marshall, Mrs D Marshall
Fleet: 28 - 20 coach, 6 midibus, 2 midicoach.
Chassis: 11 Leyland. 7 Mercedes. 2 Scania. 7 Volvo. 1 VW.
Bodies: Alexander. Duple. Mellor. Plaxton. Reeve Burgess. Van Hool. Wright.
Ops incl: local bus services, school contracts, private hire.
Livery: Purple/White

*CALDEW COACHES LTD
6 CALDEW DRIVE, DALSTON CA5 7NS
Tel/Fax: 01228 711690
E-mail: caldewcoachesltd@aol.com
Web site: www.caldewcoaches.co.uk
Dirs: H B McKerrell, Ann McKerrell, Bill Rogers **Co Sec**: Mandy Rogers
Fleet: 11 - 3 single-deck bus, 4 coach, 3 midicoach, 3 minicoach.
Chassis: 10 Mercedes. 1 Volvo.
Bodies: 6 Mercedes. 2 Plaxton. 1 Van Hool. 1 Eurocoach.
Ops incl: local bus services, school contracts, excursions & tours, private hire, continental tours.
Livery: White/Red
Ticket System: Almex.

*CARR'S COACHES
CONTROL TOWER, THE AIRFIELD, SILLOTH CA7 4NS
Tel: 01697 331276
Fax: 01769 33823
Prop: A J Markley **Ch Eng**: Fred Gill
Fleet: 9 - 4 coach, 2 midibus, 1 midicoach, 2 minibus.
Chassis: 1 Dennis. 3 Ford Transit. 1 Leyland. 2 Mercedes. 2 Scania.
Bodies: 2 Duple. 1 Optare. 2 Van Hool.
Ops incl: local bus services, school contracts, private hire.
Livery: Blue/White.

*CLARKSON COACHWAYS
UNIT 2B, ASHBURNER WAY, WALNEY ROAD INDUSTRIAL ESTATE, BARROW IN FURNESS LA14 5UZ
Tel: 01229 828022
Fax: 01229 828067
E-mail: info@clarksoncoachways.co.uk
Web site: www.clarksoncoachways.co.uk
Chmn: Susan M Clarkson **Co Sec**: Neil Clarkson
Fleet: 11 - 5 single-deck bus, 1 open-top bus, 3 midicoach, 2 minicoach. **Chassis**: 4 Dennis. 1 Ford Transit. 1 Leyland. 3 MAN. 1 Mercedes-Benz. 1 Volvo.
Bodies: 3 Alexander. 3 Berkhof. 3 Caetano. 1 Jonckheere. 1 Marcopolo. 1 Optare. 1 Other.
Ops incl: school contracts, private hire.
Livery: Green two-tone

COAST TO COAST PACKHORSE
WEST VIEW, HARTLEY, KIRKBY STEPHEN CA17 4JH
Tel: 01768 371680
Fax: 01768 371680
E-mail: packhorse@cumbria.com
Web site: www.cumbria.com/packhorse
Operator: J. Bowman.
Fleet: 3 minibus.
Chassis: 2 Ford Transit. 1 Freight Rover.
Ops incl: local bus services, school contracts, private hire.

CUMBRIA COACHES LTD
ALGA HOUSE, BRUNEL WAY, DURRANHILL INDUSTRIAL ESTATE, CARLISLE CA1 3NQ.
Tel: 01228 404300.
Fax: 01228 404309.
Dir: Dennis Smith, H. Humble.
Ops Man: S. Hall.
Fleet: 12 - 8 coach, 4 double-deck coach.
Chassis: 2 Neoplan. 2 Setra. 8 Volvo.
Bodies: 4 Duple. 2 Jonckheere. 2 Neoplan. 2 Plaxton. 2 Setra.
Ops incl: excursions & tours, private hire, express, continental tours, school contracts.

DAGLISH COACHES
BECK LEA, PASTURE ROAD, ROWRAH, FRIZINGTON CA26 3XN
Tel/Fax: 01946 861940
Web site: www.daglishcoaches.co.uk
E-mail: daglish.coaches@bobertd.demon.co.uk
Dir: R. Daglish
Fleet: 13 - 10 coach, 1 double-deck coach, 2 minibus.
Chassis: 3 DAF. 1 Ford Transit. 1 LDV. 4 Leyland. 1 Leyland National. 1 MAN. 1 MCW. 1 Scania.
Ops incl: excursions & tours, private hire, school contracts.
Livery: Yellow/Blue/Red

GRAND PRIX COACHES
MAIN STREET, BROUGH CA17 4AY
Tel: 01768 341328
Web site: www.grand-prix-services.com
E-mail: allison@fsbdial.co.uk
Dirs: Frank Allison, Gilbert Allison, Michael Allison
Fleet: 18 - 4 single-deck bus, 8 coach, 1 midicoach, 4 minibus, 1 minicoach.
Chassis: 1 Bedford. 1 Bristol. 1 Ford Transit. 2 Freight Rover. 1 LDV. 1 MCW. 2 Mercedes. 1 Renault. 4 Volvo.
Bodies: 1 Autobus. 4 Duple. 4 Leyland. 1 MCW. 2 Mercedes. 4 Plaxton. 2 Van Hool.
Ops incl: local bus services, school contracts, excursions & tours, private hire, continental tours.
Livery: White/Blue
Ticket System: Wayfarer 3

*JOHN HOBAN TRAVEL LTD
22 KING STREET, WORKINGTON CA14 4DJ
Tel: 01900 603579
Fax: 01900 605528
E-mail: johnahoban@aol.com
Ptnrs: John Hoban, Allison Hoban
Fleet: 6 minicoach, 4 midicoach.
Chassis/Bodies: 10 Mercedes
Ops incl: local bus services, private hire

*IRVINGS COACH HIRE LTD
JESMOND STREET, CARLISLE CA1 2DE
Tel: 01228 521666
Fax: 01228 521666
Dir: Robert Irving **Dir**: Mrs Joan Harvey
Fleet: 9 coach.
Chassis: 2 DAF. 7 Volvo.
Bodies: 1 Plaxton. 6 Van Hool. 2 Bova.
Ops incl: local bus services, excursions & tours, private hire, school contracts, express, continental tours.
Livery: Orange/White.

*K & B TRAVEL LTD

THE ASHES, CLIBURN, PENRITH CA10 3AL
Tel: 01768 865446
Fax: 01768 862715
E-mail: mail@kbtravel.freeserve.co.uk
Man Dir: G Lund **Dir**: Mrs B Bainbridge
Dir/Co Sec: Mrs T Lund
Fleet: 13 - 6 coach, 2 midicoach, 2 minibus, 1 minicoach, 1 midibus.
Chassis: 1 MAN. 5 Mercedes. 2 Neoplan. 4 Volvo.
Bodies: 1 Berkhof. 5 Mercedes. 2 Neoplan. 4 Van Hool.
Ops incl: local bus services, excursions & tours, private hire, school contracts, continental tours.
Livery: Blue with Green lettering

*KIRKBY LONSDALE COACH HIRE

See Lancashire

*LADYBIRD TRAVEL

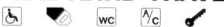

22 CLIFTON COURT, WORKINGTON CA14 3HR
Tel/Fax: 01900 61155
Recovery: 07771 993966
E-mail: ladybirdtravel@virgin.net
Prop: Grahame Stephenson
Fleet: 13 - coach, midicoach, minicoach.
Chassis: 3 DAF. 1 Dennis. 2 Leyland. 1 Mercedes. 4 Renault. 1 Scania. 1 Volvo.
Bodies: 1 Beulas. 1 Caetano. 1 Ikarus. 1 Marcopolo. 1 Optare. 1 Plaxton. 2 Van Hool. 4 Cymric. 1 Iveco.
Ops incl: excursions & tours, private hire, school contracts.
Livery: White with Red/Black stripes.

LAKES SUPERTOURS

1 HIGH STREET, WINDERMERE LA23 1AF.
Tel: 01539 442751.
Fax: 01539 446026.
Dir: R. Minford, A. Dobson. **Ops Man.**: G. Wilkinson.
Fleet: 9 minibus.
Chassis: 8 Renault. 1 Fiat.
Ops incl: excursions & tours.
Livery: White/Purple/Gold.

MESSENGER COACHES LTD

STATION ROAD GARAGE, ASPATRIA CA7 2AJ
Tel: 01697 320244
Fax: 01697 323900
Recovery: 016973 20244
Man: William F Messenger
Co Sec: Jane B Messenger
Fleet: 12 - 11 coach, 1 minibus.
Chassis: 2 Iveco. 6 Leyland. 3 Volvo.
Bodies: 2 Beulas. 9 Plaxton.
Ops incl: local bus services, school contracts, excursions & tours, private hire, continental tours.
Livery: Dual Blue.

MOUNTAIN GOAT LTD

VICTORIA STREET, WINDERMERE LA23 1AD
Tel: 01539 445161.
Fax: 01539 445164.
E-mail: enquiries@mountain-goat.com
Web site: www.mountain-goat.com
Fleetname: Mountain Goat Holidays and Tours
Dirs: Peter Nattrass, Stephen Broughton
Fleet Ops Man: Philip Grundy
Fleet: 12 minicoach
Chassis: 10 Renault. 2 Optare.
Ops incl: local bus services, excursions & tours, private hire, continental tours, school contracts.
Livery: Green/Red on White

REAYS COACHES LTD

R24

UNIT1, MILLER PARK BUSINESS CENTRE, WIGTON CA7 9BA.
Tel: 01697 349999
Fax: 01697 349900
Dirs:: Chris Reay. **Com. Sec**: Nicola Ismay.
Ch Eng: John McGill.
Fleet: 18 - 8 coach, 3 midibus. 3 midicoach, 4 minicoach.
Chassis: 2 Ford Transit. 2 LDV. 2 Leyland. 6 Mercedes. 2 Scania. 4 Volvo.
Bodies: 3 Optare. 6 Plaxton. 5 Van Hool. 4 Crest.
Ops incl: local bus services, school contracts, excursions & tours, private hire, continental tours.
Livery: White/Blue/Gold.
Ticket System: Wayfarer.

*ROBINSONS COACHES

STATION ROAD GARAGE, APPLEBY CA16 6TX
Tel: 01768 351424
Fax: 01768 352199
Prop: S E Graham
Fleet: 9 - 5 coach, 4 minibus.
Chassis: 2 DAF. 3 LDV. 1 Mercedes. 3 Volvo.
Bodies: include: 1 Duple. 2 Plaxton. 2 Van Hool.
Ops incl: local bus services, school contracts, excursions & tours, private hire.
Livery: White/Green

WILLIAM SIM & SON

HUNHOLME GARAGE, BOOT, HOLMROOK CA19 1TF.
Tel: 01946 723227.
Fax: 01946 723158.
E-mail: simstravel@hotmail.com
Fleetname: Sims Travel.
Ptnrs: J. A. Sim, D. P. Sim, B. Sim.
Fleet: 10 - 6 coach, 2 midicoach, 2 minicoach.
Chassis: 1 DAF. 4 Mercedes. 4 Volvo. 1 Van Hool.
Bodies: 2 Autobus, 1 Caetano, 2 Plaxton, 3 Van Hool, 2 Other.
Ops incl: excursions & tours, private hire, continental tours school contracts.
Livery: White/Red/Maroon.

*STAGECOACH NORTH WEST

BROADACRE HOUSE, 16-20 LOWTHER STREET, CARLISLE CA3 8DA
Tel: 01228 597222
Fax: 01228 597888
E-mail: northwest.enquiries@stagecoachbus.com
Web site: www.stagecoachbus.com
Fleetname: Stagecoach in Cumbria/Lancaster/Lancashire
Man Dir: N Barrett **Eng Dir**: P W Lee
Ops Dir: D M Ashworth
Com Dir: C J Bowles
Fleet: 531 - 158 double-deck bus, 155 single-deck bus, 37 coach, 8 open-top bus, 49 midibus, 124 minibus.
Chassis: 1 Bristol, 44 Dennis, 88 Leyland, 26 MAN, 117 Mercedes, 9 Optare, 246 Volvo.
Bodies: 395 Alexander, 4 Duple, 8 ECW, 13 Jonckheere, 6 Northern Counties, 9 Optare, 20 Park Royal, 51 Plaxton, 24 Transbus, 1 Van Hool.
Ops incl: local bus services, school contracts, excursions & tours, private hire, express.
Livery: Stagecoach - Blue/Red/Orange/White.
Ticket System: Wayfarer3/ERG

F W STAINTON & SON LTD

39 BURTON ROAD, KENDAL LA9 7LJ
Tel: 01539 720156.
Fax: 01539 740287.
Fleetname: Staintons Olympic Holidays.
Man Dir: R. S. Stainton. **Ops Man**: C. J. Stainton. **Ch Eng**: I. M Stainton.
Fleet: 14 coach.
Chassis: 1 Mercedes, 7 Setra, 6 Volvo.
Ops incl: excursions & tours, private hire, continental tours.
Livery: Blue/Green/Silver.

STEVE'S OF AMBLESIDE LTD

GALAVA GATE, BORRANS ROAD, AMBLESIDE LA22 0EN
Tel: 01539 433544.
Fax: 01539 432018.
Dir: S. A. Wise. **Sec**: Mrs E. Wise.
Fleet: 2 minibus.
Chassis: 1 Freight Rover. 1 Renault.
Ops incl: excursions & tours, private hire, school contracts. **Livery**: White.

Air conditioning	Replacement vehicle available
Vehicles suitable for disabled	Toilet-drop facilities available
Coach(es) with galley facilities	Vintage vehicle(s) available
Coach(es) with toilet facilities	Open top vehicle(s)
Seat belt-fitted vehicles	
Recovery service available (not 24 hr)	
R24 24hr recovery service	

*E TITTERINGTON & SON
[wc] [access] [N/c] [catering]

THE GARAGE, BLENCOW,
PENRITH CA11 0DG
Tel: 01768 483228
Fax: 01768 483680
Web site:
www.titteringtoncoaches.co.uk
E-mail:
enquiries@titteringtoncoaches.co.uk
Ch Eng: I Titterington **Ops Man**:
P Titterington **Tours Man**: C Titterington
Fleet: 16 coach
Chassis: 1 Iveco. 2 Leyland. 1 MAN.
1 Mercedes-Benz. 11 Volvo.
Bodies: 2 Duple. 1 Beulas. 1 Berkhof.
3 Jonckheere. 2 Neoplan. 5 Plaxton. 2 Van Hool.
Ops incl: excursions & tours, private hire, continental tours, school contracts.
Livery: Mustard/Brown/White.

*TOWER COACHES [access] [disabled]
KENILWORTH, 4 SYKE ROAD,
WIGTON CA7 9LX
Tel: 01697 342744
Props: G B Walker, Mrs D Walker
Fleet: 5 - 2 coach, 2 midibus, 1 minibus.
Chassis: 2 Leyland. 2 Mercedes.
1 Renault.

Bodies: 1 Alexander. 1 Holdsworth.
2 Plaxton. 1 Reeve Burgess.
Ops incl: local bus services, school contracts, excursons & tours, private hire.
Livery: Dark Blue/Admiralty Grey
Ticket System: Almex A

*THE TRAVELLERS CHOICE
[wc] [access] [N/c]

HADWINS TOURS, 71 BUCCLEUCH
STREET, BARROW IN FURNESS
LA14 1QQ
Tel: 01229 824531
Fax: 01229 870515
Fleet: 10 - 9 coach, 1 midibus
Chassis: 1 Leyland. 1 Mercedes. 8 Volvo.
Bodies: 1 Jonckheere. 9 Plaxton.
Ops incl: local bus services, school contracts, excursions & tours, private hire, express, continental tours.
Livery: White with Red/Yellow/Blue stripe.
Part of the Travellers Choice Group,
Carnforth.

TUERS MOTORS LTD
[access] [key] R24

BRIDGE HOUSE, MORLAND,
PENRITH CA10 3AY
Tel: 01931 714224
Fax: 01931 714236

Fleet: 7 - 4 coach, 1 midicoach, 2 minicoach
Chassis: 1 AEC. 1 DAF. 1 Ford Transit.
1 Mercedes. 1 Toyota. 2 Volvo.
Bodies: 1 Caetano. 3 Plaxton. 2 Reeve Burgess. 1 Van Hool.
Ops incl: excursions & tours, private hire, school contracts, continental tours.
Livery: Cream/Red

WRIGHT BROS (COACHES) LTD [wc] [catering] [access] R24 [key] [T]

CENTRAL GARAGE, NENTHEAD,
ALSTON CA9 3NP.
Tel: 01434 381200.
Fax: 01434 382089.
E-mail: wrightbros@btinternet.com
Chmn/Man Dir: J. G. Wright.
Dir: C. I. Wright.
Fleet: 12 - 10 coach, 2 double-deck coach.
Chassis: 5 Bedford. 2 Scania. 5 Volvo.
Bodies: 2 Jonckheere. 7 Plaxton. 2 Van Hool. 1 Ikarus.
Ops incl: local bus services, school contracts, private hire, continental tours.
Livery: Cream/Black/Gold.
Ticket System: Almex.

DERBYSHIRE

ANDREW'S OF TIDESWELL LTD [wc] [access] R24 [key] [T]
ANCHOR GARAGE, TIDESWELL
SK17 8RB
Tel: 01298 871222
Fax: 01298 872412.
E-mail: info@andrews-of-tideswell.co.uk
Web site: www.andrews-of-tideswell.co.uk
Dirs: R. B. Andew, P. D. Andrew.
Fleet: 18 - 2 double-deck bus, 11 coach,
2 double-deck coach, 2 midicoach,
1 minicoach.
Chassis: 2 Ford. 2 Leyland. 3 Mercedes.
1 Scania. 2 Setra. 8 Volvo.
Bodies: 2 Alexander. 3 Mercedes.
5 Plaxton. 2 Setra. 6 Van Hool.
Ops incl: excursions & tours, private hire, continental tours, school contracts
Livery: Cream/Ivory/Red flash.

ARRIVA DERBY LTD [R] [key]
ASCOT DRIVE, OFF LONDON
ROAD, DERBY DE24 8ND
Tel: 01332 861500
Fax: 01332 861501
Fleetname: Arriva Serving Derby.
Prop: ARRIVA Midlands (*see Staffordshire*)
Man Dir: Neil Baker
Fleet: 126 - 74 double-deck bus, 9 single-deck bus, 24 midibus, 19 minibus.
Chassis: 7 Daimler, 26 Dennis,
19 Mercedes, 3 Scania, 71 Volvo.
Bodies: Alexander, 31 East Lancs,
Marshall, Northern Counties, Plaxton.
Ops incl: local bus services,

---

school contracts, private hire.
Livery: Aquamarine/Cotswold Stone
Ticket System: Wayfarer II.

*ASTON BUSES
DAYBIRD ROADLINE LTD, UNIT 10,
BAILEY DRIVE, KILLAMARSH,
SHEFFIELD S21 2JF
Tel: 0114 251 0545
Fax: 0114 251 0545
E-mail: astonbus1@aol.com
Ops Man: Shayne Howarth
Fleet: 22 - 3 double-deck bus, 7 single-deck bus, 12 midibus.
Chassis: 5 Dennis. 3 Leyland. 3 Leyland National. 1 Mercedes. 10 Optare.
Bodies: 3 East Lancs. 3 Northern Counties.
11 Optare. 5 Plaxton.
Ops incl: local bus services, school contracts.
Livery: White with blue band; contract buses: White/Pink/Purple
Ticket system: Wayfarer 3

BAGNALLS COACHES
[wc] [access] [N/c] [T]

THE COACH STOP, GEORGE
HOLMES WAY, SWADLINCOTE
DE11 9DF
Tel: 01283 551964
Fax: 01283 552287
Dir/Ops Man: John Bagnall **Dir/Clerk**:
Pat Bagnall **Dir/Ch Eng**: Karl Bagnall
Dir/Clerk: Gavin Bagnall
Fleet: 12 - single-deck bus, coach
Chassis: 12 Volvo
Bodies: 1 East Lancs. 1 Jonckheere.
1 Plaxton. 10 Van Hool.

Ops incl: local bus services, excursions & tours, private hire, school contracts.
Livery: various

BAKEWELL COACHES
24 MOORHALL, BAKEWELL DE45
1FP
Tel: 01629 813995

RON BANKS COACHES
See Nottinghamshire.

*BOWERS COACHES LTD
[wc] [access] [R] [key]

ASPINCROFT GARAGE, TOWN
END, CHAPEL-EN-LE-FRITH SK23
0NU
Tel: 01298 812204
Fax: 01298 816103
E-mail: mike@bowerscoaches.co.uk
Web site: www.bowerscoaches.co.uk
Man Dir: Michael Bowers
Fleet: 27 - 5 single-deck bus, 6 coach,
12 midibus, 4 midicoach.
Chassis: include 1 DAF, 5 Scania.
Bodies: 5 Leyland National. 12 Mercedes.
4 Optare.
Ops incl: local bus services, school contracts, excursions & tours, private hire, continental tours.
Livery: Red/Yellow and White/Blue/Green.
Ticket System: Wayfarer

CHARNOCK COACHES
See South Yorkshire.

*CLOWES COACHES
A/c | wc | galley | seatbelt | replacement | T

BARROWMOOR, LONGNOR
SK17 0QP
Tel: 01298 83292
Fax: 01298 83838
Props: George Clowes, Kathleen Clowes.
Fleet: 12 - 8 coach, 4 minibus.
Chassis: 3 DAF. 1 Leyland. 4 Mercedes. 4 Neoplan.
Bodies: 3 Alexander. 2 Duple. 4 Neoplan. 1 Plaxton. 1 Reeve Burgess. 1 Smit.
Ops incl: local bus services, school contracts, excursions & tours, private hire.
Livery: Cream/Green/Red

COX'S OF BELPER
seatbelt | wc | replacement

GOODS ROAD, BELPER DE56 1QQ
Tel: 01773 822395
Fax: 01773 821157
Props: Bernard Bembridge, Maureen Bembridge
Fleet: 6 - 2 coach, 1 midicoach, 3 minibus
Chassis: 1 LDV. 3 Mercedes. 2 Volvo
Bodies: 1 Carlyle. 1 Jonckheere. 1 LDV. 1 Mercedes. 1 VanHool. 1 Buscraft
Ops incl: excursions & tours, private hire, school contracts.
Livery: White/blue relief

CRESSWELL'S COACHES
3 SHORTHEATH ROAD, MOIRA,
SWADLINCOTE DE12 6AL
Tel: 01283 217229
Man Dir: David Cresswell
Chassis: includes 4 Iveco
Bodies: includes 4 Beulas

CRISTAL HIRE COACHES OF SWANWICK
wc | seatbelt

19 CROMWELL DRIVE, SWANWICK
DE55 1DB.
Tel: 01773 604932.
Prop: A. Hunt. **Co Sec**: Mrs Christine Hunt.
Fleet: 2 coach.
Chassis: 1 Bova. 1 Leyland.
Ops incl: excursions & tours, private hire, school contract.

DAWSON'S MINICOACHES
disabled | seatbelt

10 HOLLAND CLOSE, MORTON
DE55 6HE
Tel: 01773 873149.
Prop: S. R. Dawson
Fleet: 4 - 2 minibus, 2 minicoach.
Chassis: 2 Ford Transit. 2 Freight Rover.
Ops incl: private hire, school contracts.
Livery: Grey/White/Blue stripe.

*DERBY COMMUNITY TRANSPORT
disabled | seatbelt | R24

MEADOW ROAD GARAGE,
MEADOW ROAD, DERBY DE1 2BH
Tel: 01332 280738
Fax: 01332 203525
Chmn: Rev Graham Maskery **Sec**: K Johnson **Ops Man**: D Taylor
Fleet: 28 minibus

Chassis: LDV. Mercedes.
Bodies: Rohill. Swan.
Ops incl: local bus services, school contracts
Livery: Red/White

K&H DOYLE
190 NOTTINGHAM ROAD, RIPLEY
DE55 3AY
Tel: 01773 745641
Prop. K Doyle. **Livery**: Beige.

*TIM DRAPER HOLIDAYS
SEVERN SQUARE, ALFRETON
DE55 7BQ
Tel: 01773 830921
Fax: 01773 834401

DUNN-LINE GROUP
See Nottinghamshire

'E' COACHES OF ALFRETON
disabled | galley | seatbelt | replacement

1 MANOR COURT, RIDDINGS
DE55 4DG
Tel: 01773 541222
Fax: 01629 825522
Owner: K. Bacon
Fleet: 5 - 2 midicoach, 3 minicoach.
Chassis: 3 Mercedes. 2 LDV.
Bodies: 2 Autobus. 3 Crest.
Ops incl: local bus service, school contract, excursions & tours, private hire.
Livery: Blue/White.

ENNIS COACHES
42 THE LIMES CLOSE, MATLOCK
DE4 3DT
Tel: 01629 582397
E-mail: enniscoaches@yahoo.co.uk
Web site: www.geocities.com/enniscoaches
Fleet: 9 — 5 coaches, 2 single-decker buses, 2 minicoaches.
Chassis: 5 Bova, 2 Leyland, 1 MCW, Mercedes-Benz
Bodies: 1 Advanced, 1 Alexander, 5 Bova, 1 Leyland National, 1 MCW
Ops incl: private hire, school contracts

*FELIX BUS SERVICES LTD
seatbelt | replacement

157 STATION ROAD, STANLEY
DE7 6FJ
Tel/Fax: 0115 932 5332
Ops Man: I Middup
Fleet: 13 - 7 single-deck bus, 3 coach, 2 midibus, 1 minibus.
Chassis: 1 Dennis. 2 Leyland. 1 Mercedes. 2 Optare. 2 Scania. 5 Volvo.
Bodies: 2 Alexander. 2 Leyland. 2 Optare. 5 Plaxton. 2 Wright.
Ops incl: local bus services, school contracts, excursions & tours, private hire, continental tours.
Livery: branded routes
Ticket system: Wayfarer

*GLOVERS COACHES LTD
seatbelt | wc | A/c

MOOR FARM ROAD EAST,
ASHBOURNE DE6 1MD
Tel/Fax: 01335 300043
E-mail: gloverscoaches@aol.com
Dirs: Stephen Mason, Heather Mason
Fleet: 12 - 3 single-deck bus, 8 coach, 1 midicoach.
Chassis: 1 Bedford. 1 Dennis. 4 Leyland. 1 Mercedes. 4 Volvo.
Bodies: 2 Alexander. 3 Duple. 6 Plaxton.
Ops incl: local bus serivces, school contracts, excursions & tours, private hire, continental tours.
Livery: Blue/Cream.

GOLDEN GREEN LUXURY TRAVEL
seatbelt

GOLDEN GREEN GARAGE,
LONGNOR SK17 0QP
Tel: 01298 83583.
Fax: 01298 83584
Props: John and Gill Worth
Fleet: 5 midicoach.
Chassis: 5 Mercedes.
Ops incl: school contracts, excursions & tours, private hire.

HARPUR'S COACHES
WINCANTON CLOSE, DERBY
DE24 8NB
Tel: 01332 757259

HARRISON'S TRAVEL
154 SOMERCOTES HILL,
SOMERCOTES, ALFRETON
DE55 4HU
Tel: 01773 835337

HENSHAWS COACHES
wc | galley | seatbelt | replacement | T

57 PYE HILL ROAD, JACKSDALE
NG16 5LR.
Tel/Fax: 01773 607909.
Ptnrs: D. Henshaw, P. Henshaw, Ms M. Henshaw.
Fleet: 6 - 4 coach, 2 midicoach.
Chassis: 1 DAF. 1 Ford Transit. 2 MAN. 1 MCW. 1 Scania.
Bodies: 3 Van Hool. 1 Berkhof.
Ops incl: local bus services, school contracts, excursions & tours, private hire, express, continental tours.
Livery: Cream/Orange/Brown

G & J HOLMES (COACHES) LTD
124A MARKET STREET, CLAY
CROSS S45 9JY
Tel/Fax: 01246 863232.

*HENRY HULLEY & SONS LTD
seatbelt | wc | galley | A/c | replacement

DERWENT GARAGE, BASLOW,
BAKEWELL DE45 1RP
Tel: 01246 582246

- A/c — Air conditioning
- disabled — Vehicles suitable for disabled
- galley — Coach(es) with galley facilities
- wc — Coach(es) with toilet facilities
- seatbelt — Seat belt-fitted vehicles
- R — Recovery service available (not 24 hr)
- R24 — 24hr recovery service
- replacement — Replacement vehicle available
- T — Toilet-drop facilities available
- — Vintage vehicle(s) available
- — Open top vehicle(s)

Fax: 01246 583161
E-mail: www.hulleys-of-baslow.co.uk
Web site: info@hulleys-of-baslow.co.uk
Fleetname: Hulleys of Baslow
Dirs: P Eades, R W Eades
Fleet: 19 - 11 single-deck bus, 5 coach, 2 minibus, 1 minicoach.
Chassis: 6 Dennis. 5 Leyland. 2 MAN. 3 Mercedes. 1 Optare. 1 Volvo.
Bodies: 1 Caetano. 5 Leyland. 3 Mercedes. 3 Optare. 6 Plaxton. 1 Van Hool.
Ops incl: local bus services, school contracts, private hire, excursions & tours.
Livery: Buses: Cream/Blue; Coaches: White/Blue
Ticket System: Wayfarer 3

LEANDER TRAVEL

7 WORDSWORTH AVENUE, SWADLINCOTE DE11 0DZ
Tel/fax: 01283 213780
E-mail: pat@leandercoaches.co.uk
Web site: www.leandercoaches.co.uk
Fleetname: Leander Coaches
Prop: M. W. Bugden
Fleet: 4 coach, 1 minicoach.
Chassis: 3 DAF. 1 LDV. 1 Volvo.
Ops incl: excursions & tours, private hire, school contracts, continental tours.

JOHNSON'S TOURS

R24

GREEN ACRES, GREEN LANE, HODTHORPE S80 4XR
Tel: 01909 721847/720307
Fax: 01909 722886
E-mail: enquiries@johnsonstours.co.uk
Web site: www.johnsonstours.co.uk
Dir: Tony Johnson **Ops:** Lee Johnson **Ch Eng:** Anthony Johnson **Co Sec:** Coleen Johnson
Fleet: 85 - 40 double-deck bus, 40 single-deck bus, 5 midicoach.
Chassis: 40 Bristol. 1 Ford Transit. 1 Freight Rover. 6 Irisbus. 4 Mercedes. 3 Neoplan. 3 Scania. 2 Toyota. 15 Volvo.
Bodies: 6 Beulas. 2 Caetano. 40 ECW. 2 Irizar. 5 Jonckheere. 3 Neoplan. Noge. 10 Plaxton. 10 Van Hool.
Ops incl: local bus services, school contracts, excursions & tours, continental tours.
Livery: Blue/Gold.
Owns Redfern Coaches, Mansfield.

*KINCHBUS LTD

See Leicestershire

LEGAL MINI BUS HIRE

R24

67 CAMBRIDGE STREET, BLACKWELL DE55 5JX.
Tel/Fax: 01773 580375.
E-mail: legal.minibushire@ntlworld.com
Prop: John. E. Roberts.
Fleet: 1 minibus.
Chassis: 1 Ford Transit.
Ops incl: school contract, private hire.

*LITTLE TRANSPORT LTD

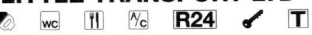

R24

HALLAM FIELDS ROAD, ILKESTON DE7 4AZ
Tel: 0115 932 8581
Fax: 0115 932 5163
Recovery: 07919 020835
Web site: www.littletravel.co.uk
Dirs: Seven Wells, Paul Wright **Ops Man:** Phil Kemp
Fleet: 16 - 2 double-deck bus, 7 single-deck bus, 9 coach
Chassis: 1 Bova. 6 DAF. 2 Dennis. 1 Leyland. 4 Leyland National. 1 MCW. 1 Optare. 2 Volvo.
Bodies: Bova. ECW. Leyland National. Optare. Van Hool.
Ops incl: excursions & tours, private hire, school contracts, local bus services, continental tours.
Livery: White/Cerise/Purple/Burgundy
Ticket system: Almex

*MACPHERSON COACHES LTD

THE GARAGE, HILL STREET, DONISTHORPE DE12 7PL
Tel: 01530 270226
Fax: 01530 273669
E-mail: travel@macphersoncoaches.co.uk
Web site: www.macphersoncoaches.co.uk
Man Dir: Neil MacPherson **Fleet Eng:** Colin Underwood **Sales Man:** Paul Krause
Business Man: Tom Hine
Fleet: 14 - 8 coach, 1 midicoach, 3 midibus. 2 minicoach.
Chassis: 1 Dennis. 6 Mercedes. 7 Setra. 1 Toyota.
Bodies: 1 Alexander. 1 Caetano. 1 Jonckheere. 3 Plaxton. 7 Setra. 1 Excel.
Ops incl: local bus services, school contracts, excursions & tours, private hire, continental tours.
Livery: Cream/Red
Ticket System: Wayfarer.

MYKANN COACH HIRE

29 WARREN DRIVE, LINTON, SWADLINCOTE DE12 6QP
Tel: 01283 762673
Dir: Michael Denton
Fleet: 2 coach
Chassis: 2 Setra.
Bodies: 2 Setra.
Ops incl: private hire, school contracts.
Livery: White/Red & Yellow Relief

*NOTTS & DERBY TRACTION CO LTD

MANSFIELD ROAD, HEANOR DE75 7BG
Fleet: 49 - 5 double-deck bus, 32 single-deck bus, 12 minibus.
Chassis: 18 Dennis. 5 Leyland. 12 Mercedes. 3 Optare. 11 Volvo.
Livery: Blue/Green
Ticket System: Almex

PARKERS COACHES

41 LABURNUM ROAD, NEWHALL, SWADLINCOTE DE11 0NR.
Tel: 01283 550015.
Prop: W. A. Parker.
Fleet: 2 minibus.
Chassis: Ford Transit.
Ops incl: school contracts, private hire.
Livery: Blue/White.

*RINGWOOD LUXURY COACHES

SPEEDWELL GARAGE, CROMPTON ROAD, SPEEDWELL INDUSTRIAL ESTATE, STAVELEY S43 3PG
Tel/Fax: 01246 476366
Prop: David T Brockbank
Fleet: 6 - 2 midicoach, 4 minicoach
Chassis: 5 Mercedes.
Bodies: 1 Caetano. 4 Mercedes. 1 Sitcar
Ops incl: school contracts, private hire

*SLACKS TRAVEL (K V & G L SLACK LTD)

THE TRAVEL CENTRE, LUMSDALE, MATLOCK DE4 5LB
Tel: 01629 582826
Fax: 01629 580519
E-mail: enquiries@slackscoaches.co.uk
Web site: www.slackscoaches.co.uk
Man Dir: G L Slack **Ch Eng:** R M Slack
Co Sec: D R Slack **Tran Man:** T Gough
Fleet: 19 - 15 coach, 1 midicoach, 1 minibus, 1 minicoach.
Chassis: 6 DAF. 3 Dennis. 2 Ford. 2 Ford Transit. 3 Iveco. 2 Mercedes. 1 Scania.
Bodies: 1 Autobus. 3 Beulas. 6 Plaxton. 7 Van Hool.
Ops incl: excursions & tours, private hire, continental tours, school contracts

STAGECOACH EAST MIDLANDS

NEW STREET, CHESTERFIELD S40 2LQ
Tel: 01246 222018
Fax: 01246 232205
Web site: www.stagecoachbus.com
Fleetname: Stagecoach East Midlands
Man Dir: Paul Lynch **Ops Dir:** Richard Kay
Eng Dir: Mike Britten **Com Dir:** John Pope
Service Quality Man: John Curtis
Fleet: 502 - 193 double-deck bus, 76 single-deck bus, 33 single-deck coach, 126 midibus, 3 articulated coach, 71 minibus.
Chassis: 148 Dennis, 1 Ford, 117 Leyland, 71 Mercedes, 16 Optare, 2 Scania, 147 Volvo.
Bodies: 324 Alexander, 2 Duple, 15 ECW, 33 East Lancs, 13 Jonckheere, 33 Northern Counties, 17 Optare, 2 Park Royal, 58 Plaxton, 4 Van Hool, 1 Wadham Stringer.
Ops incl: local bus services, school contracts, private hire, express.
Livery: Stagecoach new.
Ticket System: ERG.

*TM TRAVEL
[wc] [disabled] [seatbelt] [A/c]

FAN ROAD, STAVELEY S43 3PT
Tel: 01246 477331
Fax: 01246 281027
E-mail: info@tmtravel.co.uk
Web site: www.tmtravel.co.uk
Prop: Tim Watts **Tran Man:** Malcolm Watts
Ops Man: Paul Hopkinson
Fleet: 64 - 20 double-deck bus, 13 single-deck bus, 18 coach, 12 midibus, 1 midicoach.
Chassis: 7 DAF, 4 Dennis. 9 Leyland. 12 MCW. 10 Mercedes. 7 Optare. 1 Scania. 14 Volvo.
Bodies: 2 Alexander. 1 ECW. 1 East Lancs. 2 Ikarus. 1 Jonckheere. 4 Leyland. 12 MCW. 1 Mellor. 1 Northern Counties. 10 Optare. 25 Plaxton. 2 UVG. 2 Van Hool.
Ops incl: local bus services, school contracts, excursions & tours, continental tours, private hire.
Livery: Cream/Red/Maroon.
Ticket System: Wayfarer TGX150

*TRENTBARTON
MANSFIELD ROAD, HEANOR DE75 7BG
Tel: 01773 536309
Web site: www.trentbarton.co.uk
Man Dir: B R King **Com Dir:** R I Morgan
Fin Dir: G Sutton
Fleet: 255 - 179 single-deck bus, 7 coach, 69 midibus.
Chassis: 44 Dennis. 16 Mercedes. 121 Optare. 47 Scania. 27 Volvo.
Ops incl: local bus services.

Livery: various
Ticket System: Almex.

VIKING TOURS & TRAVEL
[disabled] [wc] [galley] [seatbelt]

UNIT 2, RYDER CLOSE, SWADLINCOTE DE11 9EU
Tel: 01283 217012
Fax: 01283 550685.
Fleetname: Viking
Gen Man: Graham Allen.
Ch Eng: Farrell Smith.
Fleet: 17 - 16 coach, 1 midicoach.
Chassis: 1 Bova, 1 MCW, 15 Volvo.
Bodies: 1 Bova. 1 ECW. 2 Jonckheere. 9 Plaxton. 4 Van Hool.
Ops incl: excursions & tours, private hire, express, continental tours, school contracts
Livery: Ocean Blue/Orange Band.

*WARRINGTON COACHES
THE COTTAGE, ILAM DE6 2AZ
Tel/Fax: 01335 350204
Web site: www.warringtoncoaches.co.uk
Props: Sheila Warrington, Keith Warrington.
Fleet: 7 - 2 coaches, 2 midicoach, 3 minibus.
Chassis: 2 Dennis. 1 Ford Transit. 2 LDV. 2 Mercedes.

ALBERT WILDE COACHES
[disabled] [wc] [seatbelt] [replacement] [T]

121 PARKSIDE, HEAGE, BELPER DE56 2AF.

Tel/fax: 01773 852374.
Ptnrs: A. Wilde, D. Ward, P. Wilde.
Fleet: 5 coach.
Chassis/bodies: Bova.
Ops incl: excursions & tours, private hire, continental tours, school contracts
Livery: Various.

*WOODWARD'S COACHES LTD [seatbelt]
100 HIGH STREET EAST, GLOSSOP SK13 8QF
Tel: 01457 852651
Fax: 01457 852234
Fleet: 6 - 4 coach, 2 minicoach
Chassis: 3 Denris. 2 Freight Rover. 1 Volvo.
Bodies: Plaxton.
Ops incl: excursons & tours, private hire.
Livery: Blue/White

YESTERYEAR MOTOR SERVICES [vintage]
10 LADY GATE, DISEWORTH, DERBY DE74 2QF
Tel/fax: 01332 810774
E-mail: yesteryear10@hotmail.com
Prop: D. J. Moores
Fleet: 2 - 1 single-deck bus, 1 coach.
Chassis: Bedford, Leyland.
Bodies: Duple, ECW.
Ops incl: private hire.
Livery: Green/Cream.
Ticket System: Bell Punch.

DEVON

*A B COACHES LTD
[wc] [seatbelt] [replacement] [T]

57 TORQUAY ROAD, PAIGNTON TQ3 3DT
Tel: 01803 407270
Fax: 01803 407272
E-mail: abcoaches@btconnect.com
Web site: www.abcoaches.co.uk
Man Dir: Brian Smith **Dir:** Lynn Smith **Ch Eng:** Jim Mounce
Fleet: 17 - 15 coach, 2 double-deck coach.
Chassis: 1 Bova. 4 DAF. 8 Dennis. 2 Neoplan. 1 Scania. 1 Volvo.
Bodies: 1 Bova. 8 Duple. 1 Jonckheere. 2 Neoplan. 1 Plaxton. 4 Van Hool.
Ops incl: local bus services, school contracts, excursions & tours, private hire.

ALANSWAY COACHES LTD
[seatbelt]

61 QUEEN STREET, NEWTON ABBOT TQ12 2AU.
Tel: 01626 334004.
Fax: 01626 362291.

Web site: www.alansway.co.uk
Man Dir/Chmn: A. W. Partridge.
Dir: A. Graham.
Fleet: 18 minibus.
Chassis: 14 Ford Transit. 4 Iveco.
Ops incl: local bus services, school contracts, private hire.
Livery: Orange/White.
Ticket System: Setright.

AXE VALLEY MINI TRAVEL
BUS DEPOT, 26 HARBOUR ROAD, SEATON EX12 2NA
Tel/Fax: 01297 625959
Fleetname: AVMT
Prop: Mrs F. M. Searle **Traf Man:** J. R. Paddon.
Fleet: 9 - 5 double-deck bus, 4 midibus.
Chassis: 1 Dodge. 2 Iveco. 1 Leyland. 4 MCW. 1 Optare.
Bodies: 1 Leyland. 1 Reeve Burgess. 4 MCW. 2 Dormobile. 1 Optare.
Ops incl: local bus services.
Livery: Maroon/White.
Ticket System: Wayfarer.

AYREVILLE COACHES
[disabled] [seatbelt] [replacement]

202 NORTH PROSPECT ROAD, PLYMOUTH PL2 2PR
Tel: 01752 605450.
Fax: 01752 219366.
E-mail: ayrevillecoaches@tinyonline.co.uk
Owner: M. J. Buley.
Fleet: 6 - 3 midiccach, 3 minibus.
Chassis: 1 Ford, I Iveco, 4 Mercedes.
Bodies: 2 Carlyle. 1 Reeve Burgess, 1 Devon Conversion, 2 Pilcher Green.
Ops incl: private hire, school contracts.
Livery: White.

*BOW BELLE OF DEVON
See Dartline Coaches.

BURNHAM PARK COACHES
20 BURNHAM PARK ROAD
PLYMOUTH PL3 5QD
Tel: 01752 703412

A/c	Air conditioning
[disabled]	Vehicles suitable for disabled
[galley]	Coach(es) with galley facilities
wc	Coach(es) with toilet facilities
[seatbelt]	Seat belt-fitted vehicles
R	Recovery service available (not 24 hr)
R24	24hr recovery service
[replacement]	Replacement vehicle available
T	Toilet-drop facilities available
[vintage]	Vintage vehicle(s) available
[opentop]	Open top vehicle(s)

*CARMEL COACHES

STATION ROAD, NORTHLEW,
OKEHAMPTON EX20 3BN
Tel: 01409 221237
Fax: 01409 221226
E-mail: carmelcoaches@hotmail.com
Prop: Tony Hazell.
Fleet: 14 - 8 coach, 1 minicoach,
4 midicoach, 1 midibus.
Chassis: 1 Bova. 2 DAF. 5 Dennis. 1 Iveco.
4 Mercedes. 1 Toyota.
Bodies: 1 Autobus. 1 Bova. 1 Caetano.
1 Duple. 1 Marcopolo. 2 Mellor. 1 Neoplan.
2 Plaxton. 2 Van Hool. 1 Wadham Stringer.
1 Sitcar.
Ops incl: local bus services, school contracts, private hire.
Livery: White with Red lettering
Ticket System: Almex/Wayfarer

*CLH TRAVEL

18 EUGENE ROAD, PAIGNTON
TQ3 2PQ
Tel: 01803 668900
Tran Man: Geoff Wilkins

*DARTLINE COACHES

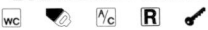

LANGDONS BUSINESS PARK,
CLYST ST MARY, EXETER EX5 1DR
Tel: 01392 872900
Fax: 01392 872909
E-mail: info@dartline-coaches.co.uk
Web site: www.dartlinecoaches.co.uk
Dir: D R P Hounslow **Man Dir:** D M Dart
Tran Man: M Lemin **Gen Man:** K Busby
Fleet: 38 - 21 coach, 5 midibus,
2 midicoach, 10 minicoach.
Chassis: 4 Bova. 2 DAF. 2 Dennis. 4 Iveco.
1 LDV. 12 Mercedes. 12 Volvo.
Bodies: 4 Bova. 1 Autobus. 2 Caetano.
2 Duple. 1 Jonckheere. 4 Marshall. 10 Mercedes. 8 Plaxton. 4 Van Hool. 2 Robin Hood.
Ops incl: local bus services, school contracts, excursions & tours, private hire, continental tours, express.
Livery: White/Green/Yellow.
Ticket System: Almex.
Owns Bow Belle of Devon.

DAWLISH COACHES LTD

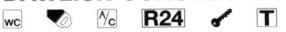

SHUTTERTON INDUSTRIAL
ESTATE, DAWLISH EX7 0NH
Tel: 01626 862525
Fax: 01626 867167
Web site: www.dawlishcoaches.com
Dir: John Weaver
Fleet: 34 - 28 coach, 2 midibus,
4 midicoach.
Chassis: 13 Bova. 2 Iveco. 5 Mercedes.
10 Volvo. 2 other.
Bodies: 2 Beulas. 2 Berkhof. 13 Bova.
1 Caetano. 2 Duple. 1 Plaxton. 9 Van Hool.
Ops incl: local bus services, school contracts, private hire.
Livery: Red/Blue/White
Ticket System: Setright

DOWN'S MOTORS & OTTER COACHES

1 MILL STREET, OTTERY ST MARY
EX11 1AB
Tel: 01404 812002
Tel: 01404 811128
Ptnrs: W M Down, A G Down, C P Down
Fleet: 10 - 9 coach, 1 midicoach.
Chassis: 4 Bedford. 4 Dennis. 1 MAN.
1 Toyota.
Bodies: 1 Bova. 5 Caetano. 1 Duple.
3 Plaxton.
Ops incl: private hire, school contracts, excursions & tours.
Livery: Ivory/Red

EAST TEIGNBRIDGE COMMUNITY TRANSPORT

THE MANOR HOUSE, OLD TOWN
STREET, DAWLISH EX7 9AP
Tel: 01626 888890
Fax: 01626 889253
E-mail: etcta@lineone.net
Man: Jenny Connor **Coordinator:** Jan Green
Fleet: 3 minibus, 3 car.
Chassis: 1 Ford. 1 Ford Transit. 1 LDV.
1 Renault. 1 Fiat. 1 Volkswagen
Ops incl: school contracts, excursions and tours, private hire.

EASTWARD COACHES

See Peninsula Drivers

*FILERS TRAVEL

SLADE LODGE, SLADE ROAD,
ILFRACOMBE EX34 8LB
Tel: 01271 863819
Fax: 01271 867281
E-mail: filers@filers.co.uk
Web site: www.filers.co.uk
Prop: R J Filer **Off & Tours Man:** Christina King **Eng:** J Chesters
Fleet: 18 - 11 coach, 1 open-top bus,
2 midicoach, 4 minibus.
Chassis: 4 Bova. 2 DAF. 2 Freight Rover.
2 Mercedes. 1 Scania. 4 Volvo. 2 VW.
Bodies: 4 Bova. 2 Caetano. 1 Irizar.
4 Plaxton. 2 Van Hool.
Ops incl: excursions & tours, private hire, school contracts.
Livery: White/Blue/Yellow

FIRST IN DEVON & CORNWALL

THE RYDE, CHELSON MEADOW,
PLYMOUTH PL9 7JT
Tel: 01752 495250
Web site: www.firstgroup.com
Man Dir: Karl Duncan **Fin Dir:** Simon Harland
Fleet: 474 – 116 double-deck bus, 14 single-deck bus, 56 coach, 116 midibus,
172 minibus.
Chassis: Bristol. Dennis. Leyland.
Mercedes. Optare. Volvo.
Bodies: Alexander. Carlyle. ECW. East Lancs. Marshall. Northern Counties. Optare. Plaxton. Reeve Burgess. Roe. Van Hool. Wright. Frank Guy. PMT.

Ops incl: local bus service, school contracts, excursions & tours, private hire, express.
Livery: First livery.
Ticket System: Almex.

*GARRETT COACHES LTD

3 STOKES CLOSE,
NEWTON ABBOT TQ12 3YY
Tel: 01626 366580
Fax: 01626 353733
E-mail: garrettcoach@tesco.net
Dir: P Garrett.
Fleet: 3 - 2 coach, 1 minibus.
Chassis/Bodies: 2 Bova. 1 Mercedes.
Ops incl: private hire, school contracts.
Livery: White

*GOLD STAR COACHES

18 WOODVILLE ROAD, TORQUAY
TQ1 1LP
Tel/Fax: 01803 200080
Prop: E Stirk
Fleet: 9 minicoach
Chassis: 2 Ford Transit. 5 LDV.
2 Mercedes.
Ops incl: private hire, school contracts
Livery: Green/Cream

*GUSCOTT'S COACHES LTD

THE GARAGE, CROFT GATE,
HALWILL EX21 5TL
Tel: 01409 221661
Fax: 01409 221435
Dirs: T Guscott, C D Guscott.
Fleet: 8 coach.
Chassis: 3 DAF. 2 Leyland. 3 Volvo.
Bodies: 1 Berkhof. 1 Duple. 1 LAG.
5 Plaxton.
Ops incl: local bus services, school contracts, private hire.
Livery: Cream/Blue/Red

*W L HEARD & SONS LTD

FORE STREET, HARTLAND,
BIDEFORD EX39 6BD
Tel: 01237 441233
Fax: 01237 441789
E-mail: kmheard@aol.com
Web site: www.heardscoaches.co.uk
Fleetname: Heards Coaches.
Dirs: J L Heard, G J Heard,
D G Heard, B W Heard
Co Sec: Miss K M Heard
Fleet: 19 - 18 coach, 1 midicoach
Chassis: 2 Dennis. 3 Ford Transit.1 MAN.
2 Mercedes. 2 Scania. 1 Setra. 9 Volvo.
Bodies: 2 Berkhof. 1 Caetano. 1 Duple. 1 Ikarus. 2 Irizar. 1 Jonckheere. 1 Mercedes. 2 Plaxton. 1 Setra. 3 Van Hool.
Ops incl: school contracts, excursions & tours, private hire
Livery: Blue/White.

*HEMMINGS COACHES

POWLERS PIECE GARAGE,
PUTFORD, HOLSWORTHY
EX22 7XW
Tel: 01237 451282

Fax: 01237 451920
E-mail: hemmingscoaches@aol.com
Props: Ken & Linda Hemmings.
Fleet: 5 coach.
Chassis: 1 DAF. 2 MAN. 2 Volvo.
Bodies: 1 Bova. 1 Neoplan. 1 Noge. 2 Plaxton.
Ops incl: excursions & tours, private hire, continental tours, express, school contracts.
Livery: White

HILLS SERVICES
STIBB CROSS, LANGTREE, TORRINGTON EX38 8LH
Tel: 01805 601203
Fax: 01805 601476
Dirs: David J Hearn, Mary E Hearn
Fleet: 35 - 12 coach, 23 minicoach.
Chassis: 6 Ford Transit. 17 LDV.
Bodies: 1 Duple. 5 Jonckheere. 1 Mellor. 6 Plaxton.
Ops incl: excursions & tours, private hire, school contracts, continental tours.
Livery: White/Green/Orange.

HOOKWAY EDGECUMBES COACHES
ALEXANDRIA INDUSTRIAL ESTATE, SIDMOUTH EX10 9HL.
Tel: 01395 515280.
Fax: 01395 519069.
Web site: www.hookways.com
Prop: C Hookway
Fleet: 11 - 8 coach, 1 midicoach, 1 minibus, 1 minicoach.
Chassis: 2 Bedford. 1 Bristol. 1 DAF. 4 Ford. 1 Leyland. 1 Mercedes. 1 Volvo.
Bodies: 2 Caetano. 2 Duple. 1 Mercedes. 4 Plaxton. 1 Reeve Burges. 1 LAG.
Ops incl: local bus services, school contracts, excursions & tours, private hire.
Livery: White/Purple.
Ticket System: Setright/Almex.

HOOKWAYS GREENSLADES
R24
PINHOE TRADING ESTATE, VENNY BRIDGE, EXETER EX4 8JR.
Tel: 01392 469210.
Fax: 01392 466036.
Web site: www.hookways.com
Prop: C. Hookway. **Traf Man**: Barry Coates
Comm Man: Jim Burch
Fleet: 27 - 23 coach, 4 midicoach.
Chassis: 1 Bedford. 1 Bova. 2 Bristol. 3 DAF. 1 Iveco. 2 Leyland. 2 MAN. 4 Mercedes. 2 Scania. 1 Setra. 6 Volvo.
Bodies: 1 Bova. 2 Caetano. 4 Duple. 6 Jonckheere. 4 Mercedes. 8 Plaxton. 1 Reeve Burgess. 1 Setra. 2 Van Hool.
Ops incl: local bus services, excursions & tours, private hire, continental tours.
Livery: Purple/Yellow/Blue.
Ticket System: Setright.

HOOKWAYS PLEASUREWAYS COACHES
THE GARAGE, MEETH, OKEHAMPTON EX20 3EP
Tel: 01837 810257, 810597.
Fax: 01837 810066.
Web site: www.hookways.com
Prop: C Hookway.
Fleet: 27 - 23 coach, 4 midicoach.
Chassis: 1 Bedford. 1 Bova. 2 Bristol. 3 DAF. 1 Iveco. 2 Leyland. 2 MAN. 4 Mercedes. 2 Scania. 1 Setra. 8 Volvo.
Bodies: 1 Bova. 2 Caetano. 4 Duple. 6 Jonckheere. 4 Mercedes. 8 Plaxton. 1 Reeve Burgess. 1 Setra. 2 Van Hool.
Ops incl: local bus services, excursions & tours, private hire, continental tours.
Livery: Purple/Yellow/Blue.

IVYBRIDGE & DISTRICT COMMUNITY TRANSPORT
DOURO COURT, BROOK ROAD, IVYBRIDGE PL21 0LS.
Tel: 01752 690444.
Fleetname: Ivybridge Ring & Ride.
Co-ordinator: Mrs S. Jenkins.
Chmn: I. Martin.
Fleet: 1 minibus. **Chassis/Body**: LDV.
Ops incl: local bus services, private hire.

KINGDOM'S TOURS LTD
WESTFIELD GARAGE, EXETER ROAD, TIVERTON EX16 5NZ
Tel: 01884 252373
Fax: 01884 252646
Dirs: R. V. Kingdom, S. J. Kingdom (**Sec**).
Fleet: 27 - 11 coach, 3 midibus, 5 midicoach, 1 minibus, 7 minicoach.
Chassis: 2 DAF. 2 Iveco. 4 LDV. 10 Mercedes. 2 Scania. 7 Volvo.
Bodies: 2 Bova. 2 Irizar. 4 Leyland. 10 Mercedes. 7 Van Hool. 2 other.
Ops incl: local bus services, school contracts, excursions & tours, private hire, continental tours.
Livery: Cream/Red/Orange/White
Ticket System: Setright.

MID DEVON COACHES
MIDCO, STATION ROAD, BOW, CREDITON EX17 6JD
Tel/Fax: 01363 82200
Web site: www.mdcoaches.co.uk
E-mail: enquiries@mdcoaches.co.uk
Prop: K. J. Wills **Man**: Mrs L. A. Hamilton
Fleet: 22 - 18 single-deck coach, 2 minicoach, 2 minibus.
Chassis: 2 DAF. 3 Ford. 3 Ford Transit. 5 Leyland. 4 Scania. 2 Toyota. 2 Volvo.
Bodies: 2 Bova.. 2 Caetano. 1 Irizar. 2 Jonckheere. 10 Plaxton.
Ops incl: school contracts, excursions & tours, private hire, continental tours.
Livery: Green/Cream.

MOOR TO SEA
1 SOPHIA WAY, TOTNES ROAD, NEWTON ABEOT TQ12 1YW.
Tel/Fax: 01626 362002.
E-mail: moortosea@eurobell.co.uk
Owner/Operator: Robert Clifford.
Fleet: 1 midicoach.
Chassis: Volvo. **Body**: Plaxton.
Ops incl: private hire. **Livery**: White.

PARAMOUNT MINI-COACHES
6 VENN CRESCENT, HARTLEY, PLYMOUTH PL3 5PJ.
Tel: 01752 767255
Fax: 01752 767255
Prop: B. M. Couch
Fleet: 5 - 1 midicoach, 2 minibus, 2 minicoach.
Chassis: 2 Ford Transit. 1 Leyland. 2 Mercedes.
Ops incl: excursions & tours, private hire, school contracts.

*PENINSULA DRIVERS
TREMATON DRIVE, IVYBRIDGE PL21 0HT
Tel: 01752 896471
Prop: Mike Yedermann
Associated companies: Peninsula Cars & Eastward Coaches (at this address) and DAC Coaches, Callington (see Cornwall)

*PLYMOUTH CITYBUS LTD
MILEHOUSE, PLYMOUTH PL3 4AA
Tel: 01752 264203
Fax: 01752 567209
E-mail: md@plymouthbus.co.uk
Web site: www.citycoach.co.uk
Acting Man Dir: John Ackroyd **Eng Dir**: Chris Webster **Ops Dir**: Phil Smith **Comm Eng Man**: Neal Bourbon **Citycoach Man**: Lesley Smith
Fleet: 182 - 24 double-deck bus, 38 single-deck bus, 17 coach, 4 open-top bus, 58 minibus, 41 minibus.
Chassis: 98 Dennis. 36 Mercedes. 41 Volvo. 7 other.
Bodies: 15 Alexander. 12 East Lancs. 153 Plaxton/Transbus. 1 Van Hool. 1 other.
Ops incl: local bus services, school contracts, excursions & tours, private hire. continental tours
Livery: Red/White/Grey
Ticket System: Wayfarer

*POWELLS COACHES
2 BARRIS, LAPFORD EX17 6PT
Tel/Fax: 01363 83468
Ptnrs: J P & D M Fowell
Fleet: 7 coach.
Chassis: 4 Leyland. 1 Mercedes. 2 Volvo.
Bodies: 1 Duple. 1 Jonckheere. 1 Mercedes. 3 Plaxton. 1 Van Hool.
Ops incl: excursions & tours, private hire,

A/c	Air conditioning
♿	Vehicles suitable for disabled
⛟	Coach(es) with galley facilities
wc	Coach(es) with toilet facilities
💺	Seat belt-fitted vehicles
R	Recovery service available (not 24 hr)
R24	24hr recovery service
✦	Replacement vehicle available
T	Toilet-drop facilities available
🚌	Vintage vehicle(s) available
🚍	Open top vehicle(s)

school contracts.
Livery: Green/Black/White

RADMORES COACHES
4 WOODFORD CRESCENT,
PLYMPTON PL7 4QY
Tel/Fax: 01752 335391
Prop: John Williams.
Fleet: 4 - 1 coach, 2 midibus, 1 midicoach.
Chassis: 1 Ford Transit. 2 Iveco. 1 Leyland.
Bodies: 1 Mellor. 1 Optare. 1 Reeve Burgess.
Ops incl: local bus services, school contracts, excursions & tours, private hire.
Livery: Red/Gold

RAYS COACHES
88 KINGS TAMERTON ROAD,
ST BUDEAUX, PLYMOUTH PL5 2BW
Tel: 01752 369000

REDWOODS TRAVEL
[wc] [symbols]
UNIT 3, STATION ROAD INDUSTRIAL PARK, HEMYOCK
EX15 3SE
Tel: 01823 680288
Fax: 01823 681096
E-mail: paulredwood@redwoodtravel.fsnet.co.uk
Prop: Paul Redwood. **Ops Man:** Mrs Jacquie Redwood **Ch Eng:** Andy Mead
Fleet: 20 - 18 coach, 2 minibus.
Chassis: 3 Bova. 3 DAF. 1 Iveco. 1 Mercedes. 4 Scania. 8 Volvo.
Bodies: 5 Bova. 1 Caetano. 1 Duple. 3 Ikarus. 1 Mercedes. 7 Plaxton. 1 Van Hool. 1 Other
Ops incl: local bus services
Livery: Red/Turquoise/White
Ticket system: Setright

*SEAWARD COACHES
[symbols]
GLENDALE, DALWOOD,
AXMINSTER EX13 7EJ
Tel/Fax: 01404 881343.
Props: I A Seward, R A Seward, C E Seward
Fleet: 21 - 13 coach, 6 midicoach. 2 minibus
Chassis: 3 Bova. 6 Dennis. 1 Irisbus. 2 Leyland. 1 Toyota. 3 MAN. 3 Mercedes. 1 Renault. 1 other.
Bodies: 3 Berkhof. 3 Bova. 3 Caetano. 2 Leyland. 1 Mercedes. 4 Plaxton. 1 Reeve Burgess. 4 other.
Ops incl: local bus services, school contracts, private hire.
Livery: Cream/Orange/Green

H. & A. SLEEP
STATION ROAD, BERE ALSTON
PL20 7EW
Tel: 01822 840244.
Ptnrs: Mrs G. A. Sleep, R. G. Sleep.
Fleet: 6 coach.
Chassis: 4 Bedford. 2 Volvo.
Bodies: 3 Duple. 2 Plaxton. 1 Irizar.
Ops incl: local bus services, excursions & tours, private hire.
Livery: Maroon/Ivory.

*STAGECOACH DEVON
[symbols]
BELGRAVE ROAD, EXETER
EX1 2LB
Tel: 01392 439439
Web site: www.stagecoachbus.com
Man Dir: C G Hilditch **Eng Dir:** M Horide
Co Sec: A Withnall **Dirs:** L B Warneford, C Brown
Fleet: 271 - 62 double-deck bus, 12 single-deck bus, 9 coach, 4 open-top bus, 80 midibus, 105 minibus.
Chassis: 106 Dennis. 15 Iveco. 1 Leyland. 90 Mercedes. 13 Scania. 47 Volvo.
Bodies: 178 Alexander. 5 East Lancs. 28 Marshall. 7 Mellor. 3 Northern Counties. 35 Plaxton. 1 Roe. 8 Wadham Stringer. 6 Wright.
Ops incl: local bus services, school contracts, excursions & tours, private hire, express.
Livery: Blue/Red/Orange/White
Ticket System: Wayfarer 3.

STOKE BUS SERVICES
193 ROSELANDS DRIVE,
PAIGNTON TQ4 7RN
Tel: 01803 554927
Prop.: D. E. R. Hewitt

*STREETS COACHWAYS LTD
[symbols]
THE OLD AERODROME,
CHIVENOR, BARNSTAPLE EX31 4AY
Tel: 01271 815069
Fax: 01271 817333
E-mail: sandra@streetscoachways.com
Chmn: M Street **Man Dir:** S Street **Co Sec:** Mrs S Popham
Fleet: 11 - 7 coach, 2 midicoach, 2 minicoach.
Chassis: 1 Bova. 4 DAF. 2 LDV. 2 Leyland. 2 Mercedes.
Bodies: 1 Bova.. 1 Duple. 2 Marshall. 1 Reeve Burgess. 4 Van Hool. 2 other.
Ops incl: private hire, school contracts.
Livery: White/Yellow/Orange

*TALLY HO! COACHES
[wc] [symbols] R [symbols] T
STATION YARD INDUSTRIAL ESTATE, KINGSBRIDGE TQ7 1ES
Tel: 01548 853081
Fax: 01548 853602
E-mail: info@tallyhocoaches.com
Web site: www.tallyhocoaches.com
Props: S J & S Wellington
Fleet: 50 - 14 single-deck bus, 25 coach, 5 midibus, 2 midicoach, 4 minibus.
Chassis: 1 Bedford. 8 Bristol. 1 DAF. 11 Dennis. 2 Ford. 1 Ford Transit. 3 Freight Rover. 7 Leyland. 2 Leyland National. 7 Mercedes. 3 Scania. 1 Toyota. 3 Volvo.
Bodies: 5 Alexander. 3 Berkhof. 1 Caetano. 3 Duple. 9 ECW. 3 Irizar. 2 Leyland National. 2 Marshall. 2 Mercedes. 17 Plaxton. 1 Van Hool. 2 Wright. 1 other.
Ops incl: local bus services, school contracts, private hire.
Livery: White
Ticket system: Almex

*TAVISTOCK COMMUNITY TRANSPORT
See Cornwall

*TAW & TORRIDGE COACHES LTD incorporating LOVERINGS COACHES
[wc] [symbols] R24 [symbols] T
GRANGE LANE COACH DEPOT, MERTON, OKEHAMPTON EX20 3ED
Tel: 01805 603400
Fax: 01805 603559
Recovery: 01805 603400
E-mail: enquiries@tawandtorridge.co.uk
Web site: www.tawandtorridge.co.uk
Man Dir: Tony Hunt **Dir/Ops Man:** Mark Hunt **Dir/Gen Man:** Chris Laughton **Dir:** Tracey Laughton **Dir/Co Sec:** Linda Hunt **Fleet Eng:** Dennis Petherbridge
Fleet: 39 - 24 coach, 11 midibus, 4 minibus.
Chassis: 2 Bedford. 2 Bova. 4 Bristol. 5 Dennis. 4 LDV. 3 MAN. 2 Scania. 1 Toyota. 1 Van Hool. 15 Volvo.
Bodies: 4 Berkhof. 2 Bova. 1 Caetano. 2 Duple. 4 Jonckheere. 4 LDV. 3 Neoplan. 15 Plaxton. 1 SmithsWhippit. 2 Van Hool. 1 Wadham Stringer.
Ops incl: local bus services, school contracts, excursions & tours, private hire, continental tours.
Livery: Coaches: Miami Blue Buses: Green/Orange/Cream

TOTNES & DARTMOUTH RING & RIDE
[symbols]
C/O RED CROSS CENTRE,
BABBAGE ROAD, TOTNES TQ9 5JA.
Tel: 01803 867878.
Co-ordinator: L. Clark.
Fleet: 3 minibus.
Chassis: 2 Ford Transit. 1 Peugeot.
Ops incl: local bus services, school contracts, excursions & tours, private hire.

*TOWN & COUNTRY COACHES
UNIT 8B, SILVERLANDS ROAD,
DECOY INDUSTRIAL ESTATE,
NEWTON ABBOT TQ12 5ND
Tel: 01626 201052
Tran Man: Geoff Wilkins

TRATHENS TRAVEL SERVICES [wc] [symbols]
BURRINGTON WAY, PLYMOUTH PL5 3LS.
Tel: 01752 794545/790565
Fax: 01752 777931.
Chmn: D. I. Park. **Ch Eng:** P. Holmes.
Fin Dir: G. Donnachie. **Man Dir:** M. Trathen. **Ops Man:** G. Masters.
Fleet: 50 - 15 coach, 35 double-deck coach.
Chassis: 5 MAN. 5 Neoplan. 40 Volvo.
Bodies: 5 Neoplan. 45 Van Hool.
Ops incl: express, continental tours.
Livery: White with Red and Yellow lining; National Express: White.
Subsidiary of Parks of Hamilton

*TURNERS TOURS
[wc] [fork] [A/c] [key] [T]

1 FORE STREET, CHULMLEIGH EX18 7BR
Tel: 01769 580242
Fax: 01769 581281
Recovery: 01769 581256
Web site: www.turnerstours.co.uk
Ptnrs/Props: Mrs P Gilson, S Gilson
Fleet: 30 - coach, single-deck bus, minibus.
Chassis: 1 Bedford. 7 Dennis. 4 Ford. 1 Mercedes. 17 Volvo.
Bodies: 1 Alexander. 1 Caetano. 1 Carlyle. 7 Jonckheere. 15 Plaxton. 3 Reeve Burgess. 2 Wadham Stringer.
Ops incl: local bus services, school contracts, excursions & tours, private hire, express, continental tours.
Livery: Cream/Brown.
Ticket System: Wayfarer.

TW COACHES LTD
75 SOUTH STREET, SOUTH MOLTON EX36 4AG.
Tel: 01769 572139.
Fax: 01769 574183.
Dirs: Chris Tearall, N. Williams, Mrs J. Kelly.
Fleet: 16 coaches.
Ops incl: local bus services, school contracts, excursions & tours, private hire, continental tours.
Livery: Red/Blue/White.
Ticket System: Setright.

WALLACE ARNOLD COACHES LTD
[wc] [A/c] [bus] [seat]

BARTON HILL WAY, TORQUAY TQ2 8JG
Tel: 01803 326016.
Fax: 01803 316059.
Man Dir: K. S. Meddes. **Ops Dir**: S. D. Barber. **Depot Man**: D. Braund.
Fleet: 51 - 1 double-deck bus, 50 coach.
Chassis: 1 Leyland. 50 Volvo.
Bodies: 1 Northern Counties. 50 Plaxton.
Ops incl: excursions & tours, private hire, continental tours.
Livery: Cream/Orange/Brown. *Main depot in Leeds (see West Yorkshire).*

WILLS MINI COACHES
2 LOWER UNION ROAD, KINGSBRIDGE TQ7 1EF
Tel/Fax: 01548 852140.
Man Dir: E. G. Wills. **Dir/Co Sec**: Mrs G. M. Wills.
Fleet: 5 minibus.
Chassis: 4 LDV. 1 Mercedes.
Ops incl: school contracts, private hire.

WOOD BROTHERS TRAVEL LTD
HAREWOOD GARAGE, BOSSELL ROAD, BUCKFASTLEIGH TQ11 0AL.
Tel: 01364 643870.
Fax: 01364 643870.
Livery: Yellow/White.

DORSET, BOURNEMOUTH, POOLE

*BARRY'S COACHES LTD
[wc] [seat] [fork] [A/c] [key]

9 CAMBRIDGE ROAD, GRANBY INDUSTRIAL ESTATE, WEYMOUTH DT4 9TJ
Tel: 01305 784850
Fax: 01305 782252
Man Dir: Mrs M Newsam **Ch Eng**: G Newsam **Co Sec**: Mrs M Hills
Fleet: 25 - 17 coach, 1 minibus, 7 minicoach.
Chassis: 8 Dennis. 1 Iveco. 1 LDV. 2 MAN. 2 Mercedes. 6 Scania. 1 Toyota. 4 Volvo.
Bodies: 3 Berkhof. 1 Caetano. 6 Irizar. 3 Jonckheere. 2 Mercedes. 7 Plaxton. 3 Van Hool.
Ops incl: school contracts, excursions & tours, private hire, continental tours.

*BLUEBIRD COACHES (WEYMOUTH) LTD
[wc] [seat] [fork] [A/c] [R24] [key] [T]

450 CHICKERELL ROAD, WEYMOUTH DT3 4DH
Tel: 01305 786262
Fax: 01305 766223
Recovery: 01305 786262
E-mail: office@bluebirdcoaches.com
Web site: www.bluebirdcoaches.com
Dirs: S F Hoare, M E C Hoare
Fleet: 23 - 20 coach, 1 midicoach, 2 minibus.
Chassis: 1 Bedford. 1 Bova. 3 DAF. 1 Freight Rover. 1 Leyland. 2 MAN. 3 Neoplan. 11 Volvo.
Bodies: 1 Bova. 2 Caetano. 3 Neoplan. 1 Noge. 10 Plaxton. 6 Van Hool.
Ops incl: local bus services, school contracts, excursions & tours, private hire, express, continental tours.
Livery: White/Blue/Orange

*BOURNEMOUTH TRANSPORT LTD
[disabled] [bus] [seat] [wc] [A/c] [T]

MALLARD ROAD, BOURNEMOUTH BH8 9PN
Tel: 01202 636000
Fax: 01202 636001
E-mail: information@yellowbuses.co.uk
Web site: www.yellowbuses.co.uk
Fleetname: Yellow Buses
Chmn: R Symons **Man Dir**: R Edgley **Eng Dir**: G Corrie **Fin Dir/Co Sec**: Mrs C Partridge.
Fleet: 126 - 70 double-deck bus, 6 single-deck bus, 14 coach, 32 midibus, 4 open-top bus.
Chassis: 1 DAF. 63 Dennis. 2 Leyland. 4 Scania. 52 Volvo.
Bodies: 12 Alexander. 90 East Lancs. 1 Ikarus. 2 Plaxton. 11 Van Hool. 6 Wright.
Ops incl: local bus services, school contracts, express.
Livery: Yellow/Blue
Ticket System: Wayfarer 3

COACH HOUSE TRAVEL
[disabled] [wc] [seat]

UNIT 16, POUNDBURY WEST INDUSTRIAL ESTATE, DORCHESTER DT1 2PG
Tel: 01305 267644
Fax: 01305 260608
Prop: Les Watts. **Tran Man**: John Woollen.
Co Sec: Sarah Fursly Taylor **Ch Eng**: Phillip Watts
Fleet: 17 - 7 coach, 3 single-deck bus, 2 midibus, 5 minibus.
Chassis: 3 Dennis, 1 Ford Transit, 2 Iveco, 3 LDV, 3 Mercedes, 1 Renault, 4 Volvo.
Bodies: 1 Berkhof, 1 Duple, 1 Marshall, 1 Mellor, 4 Plaxton, 1 Van Hool, 5 Coach Built, 1 Beaver, 1 Factory Bus.
Ops incl: local bus services, school contracts, excursions & tours, private hire, continental tours.
Livery: Red/White/Blue.
Ticket System: Wayfarer.

*CROSS COUNTRY HIRE
[seat]

64 DORCHESTER ROAD, UPTON, POOLE BH16 5NS
Tel/Fax: 01202 324031
Prop: William. G. Sykes.
Fleet: 1 minicoach.
Chassis: Toyota. **Body**: Caetano.
Ops incl: excursions & tours, private hire.

*DAMORY COACHES
[wc] [seat] [A/c]

UNIT 1, CLUMP FARM, HIGHER SHAFTESBURY ROAD, BLANDFORD FORUM DT11 7TD
Tel: 01258 452545
Fax: 01258 451930
Board Dirs: Martin Ballinger, Chris Moyes, Ian Butcher **Local Man**: I Gray **Man Dir**: Alex Carter **Eng Dir**: Geoff Parsons
Ops Dir: Andrew Wickham
Fleet: 42 - 8 double-deck bus, 8 single-deck bus, 15 coach, 6 midibus, 3 minibus, 2 minicoach.
Chassis: 3 Bova. 8 Bristol. 5 DAF. 5 LDV.

A/c	Air conditioning	key	Replacement vehicle available
disabled	Vehicles suitable for disabled	T	Toilet-drop facilities available
fork	Coach(es) with galley facilities	vintage	Vintage vehicle(s) available
wc	Coach(es) with toilet facilities	bus	Open top vehicle(s)
seat	Seat belt-fitted vehicles		
R	Recovery service available (not 24 hr)		
R24	24hr recovery service		

1 Leyland. 6 Optare. 7 Volvo. 7 Leyland Lynx.
Bodies: 3 Bova. 8 ECW. 1 Ikarus. 1 Jonckheere. 7 Leyland. 6 Optare. 9 Plaxton. 2 Van Hool. 1 Lonsdale. 4 LDV
Ops incl: local bus services, school contracts, excursions & tours, private hire, continental tours.
Livery: Green/White/Maroon
Ticket System: Wayfarer.
Part of the Go-Ahead Group

DORSET QUEEN COACHES

EAST CHALDON DT2 8DN
Tel: 01305 852829
Fax: 01305 852001
E-mail: rha@dorsetqueencoaches.com
Web site: www.dorsetqueencoaches.com
Proprietor: Hookways group
Man Dir: Mrs Rosemary Hodder
Fleet: 8 - 6 coach. 1 minicoach. 1 midicoach.
Chassis: 2 Mercedes. 6 Volvo.
Bodies: 1 Caetano. 5 Plaxton. 1 other, 1 Sitcar.
Ops incl: excursions & tours, private hire, continental tours, school contracts.
Livery: Cream

EXCELSIOR COACHES LTD

BOURNEMOUTH SANDS HOTEL, WEST CLIFFE GARDENS, BOURNEMOUTH BH2 5HR
Tel: 01202 652222
Web site:www.excelsior-coaches.com
Man Dir: Ken Robins **Ops Man**: Peter Downs **Tours Man**: Debbie Howarth
Traf Man: Brian Law
Fleet: 26 - 24 coach, 2 midibus.
Chassis: Toyota, Volvo
Bodies: Caetano, Plaxton, Sunsundegui.
Ops incl: excursions & tours, private hire, express, continental tours.

*FIRST HAMPSHIRE & DORSET

EDWARD STREET, WEYMOUTH DT4 7DP
Tel: 01305 77757
Fax: 01305 760078
Bridport depot: Unit 4, Tannery Road, Bridport DT6 3TP
Main Entry - see Hampshire

MIKE HALFORD MINICOACHES

KISEM, NORTH MILLS, BRIDPORT DT6 3AH
Tel/Fax: 01308 421106
Prop: M. G. Halford.

*HOMEWARD BOUND TRAVEL

137 LYNWOOD DRIVE, WIMBORNE BH21 1UU
Tel: 01202 884491
Fax: 01202 885664
E-mail: enquiries@homewardboundtravel.co.uk
Web site: www.homewardboundtravel.co.uk
Dir: Louisa Fairhead
Fleet: 2 minicoaches
Chassis: Renault
Ops incl: excursions & tours, private hire
Livery: Silver

POWELLS COACHES

THORNFORD GARAGE, THORNFORD, SHERBORNE DT9 6QN
Tel: 01935 872390
Prop: C. Powell, Stella Powell.
Fleet: 3 - 2 coach, 1 midicoach.
Chassis: 2 Ford. 1 Volvo.
Bodies: 3 Plaxton.
Ops incl: local bus services, excursions & tours, private hire.
Livery: Red/White.
Ticket System: Setright.

RAMON TRAVEL

7 HARCOURT ROAD, BOSCOMBE BH5 2JG.
Tel: 01202 432690.
Fax: 01202 432690.
Owner/Ops: C. Rochester.
Fleet: 6 - 1 coach, 1 midicoach, 4 minibus.
Chassis: 1 Bedford. 4 Freight Rover.
Ops incl: excursions & tours, private hire, school contracts.

*ROADLINER PASSENGER TRANSPORT LTD

26 STOURPAINE ROAD, WEST CANFORD HEATH, POOLE BH17 9AT
Tel: 01202 385055
Fax: 01202 690370
Fleetname: Roadliner
Man Dir: M R Self **Co Sec**: N Hargreaves
Traf Man: M Self **Ch Eng**: A Burrage
Fleet: 5 - 3 coach, 1 midicoach, 1 minicoach
Chassis: 2 MAN. 2 Mercedes. 2 Scania.
Bodies: 2 Irizar. 1 Jonckheere. 2 Optare.
Ops incl: school contracts, excursions & tours, private hire, express, continental tours
Livery: Green/Black/Silver

SEA VIEW COACHES (POOLE) LTD

10 FANCY ROAD, POOLE BH12 4QZ.
Tel: 01202 741439
E-mail: seaviewcoaches@eclipse.co.uk
Web site: www.eclipse.co.uk/seaviewcoaches
Man Dir: D. K. Tarr
Fleet: 30 - 19 coach, 10 minibus, 1 midicoach.
Chassis: 13 DAF. 9 Ford. 4 Iveco. 1 LDV. 3 Mercedes.
Bodies: 3 Autobus. 5 Beulas. 9 Ikarus. 3 Van Hool. 10 other.
Ops incl: excursions & tours, private hire.
Livery: Silver/Red/Blue

*SHAFTESBURY & DISTRICT MOTOR SERVICES LTD

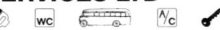

UNIT 2, MELBURY WORKSHOPS, CANN COMMON, SHAFTESBURY SP7 0EB
Tel/Fax: 01747 854359
E-mail: rogerroutemaster@aol.com
Web site: www.shaftesburyanddistrict.co.uk
Prop: Roger Brown
Fleet: 15 - 3 double-deck bus, 1 single-deck bus, 7 coach, 2 midibus, 1 midicoach, 1 minicoach.
Chassis: 4 AEC. 1 Bristol. 1 DAF. 4 Leyland. 1 Mercedes. 2 Optare. 1 Toyota.
Bodies: 1 Alexander. 1 Berkhof. 1 Caetano. 1 Duple. 1 Ikarus. 1 Leyland. 1 MCW. 3 Optare. 2 Park Royal. 2 Plaxton.
Ops incl: local bus services, school contracts, excursions & tours, private hire.
Livery: White with Yellow/Green stripes (double-deck buses: Red).
Ticket System: Setright.

SOUTH DORSET COACHES LTD

VICTORIA AVENUE INDUSTRIAL ESTATE, SWANAGE BH19 1AU.
Tel: 01929 423622.
Fax: 01929 427797.
E-mail: enquiries@southdorset coaches.co.uk
Web site: www.southdorsetcoaches.co.uk
Dirs: J. E. Sheasby, N. J. Sheasby.
Fleet: 10 coach.
Chassis: 2 Bedford. 6 Scania. 2 Volvo.
Bodies: 1 Jonckheere. 3 Plaxton. 6 Van Hool.
Ops incl: excursions & tours, private hire, continental tours, school contracts.
Livery: Burgundy/Cream.

*SOVEREIGN COACHES

PINE LODGE, ROUSDON, LYME REGIS DT7 3RD
Tel: 01297 23000
Fax: 01297 22466
E-mail: rcksovereign@btinternet.com
Ptnrs: R A Keech, C M Keech, R C Keech
Fleet: 9 - 2 coach, 3 midicoach, 4 minicoach.
Chassis: 2 LDV. 3 Mercedes. 2 Toyota. 2 Volvo.
Bodies: 2 Autobus. 2 MCW. 2 Transbus. 1 Crest. 2 Toyota.
Ops incl: school contracts, excursions & tours, private hire.
Livery: Red/White.

SOLENT COACHES

See Hampshire

*VICTORY TOURS

HIGH STREET, HANDLEY SP5 5NR
Tel: 01725 552247
Fax: 01725 552489
E-mail: info@victorytours.co.uk
Web site: www.victorytours.co.uk

Man Dir: N Adams **Dir**: Mrs H Adams **Traf Man**: H Vermaak
Fleet: 17 - 2 double-deck bus, 9 coach, 3 double-deck coach, 1 midicoach, 2 minicoach.
Chassis: 2 Bedford. 2 Bristol. 1 DAF. 4 Irisbus. 4 Iveco. 1 Mercedes. 3 Neoplan. 1 Scania. 1 Setra. 2 Toyota.
Ops incl: school contracts, excursions & tours, private hire, continental tours.
Livery: Blue/Red/White.

*WILTS & DORSET BUS COMPANY LTD

TOWNGATE HOUSE, 2-8 PARKSTONE ROAD, POOLE BH15 2PR
Tel: 01202 680888
Fax: 01202 670244
Web site: www.wdbus.co.uk
Board Dirs: Martin Ballinger, Chris moyes, Ian Butcher **Man Dir**: Alex Carter **Ops Dir**: Andrew Wickham **Eng Dir**: Geoff Parsons
Fleet: 303 - 119 double-deck bus incl 11 convertible open-top) , 33 single-deck bus, 6 coach, 145 minibus.
Chassis: 24 Bristol. 100 DAF. 16 Leyland. 150 Optare. 3 Volvo.
Bodies: 2 Duple. 34 ECW. 3 Ikarus. 7 Northern Counties. 232 Optare. 10 Plaxton. 2 Roe. 3 Van Hool.
Ops incl: local bus services, school contracts, private hire, express.
Livery: Red
Ticket System: Wayfarer TGX

*YELLOW BUSES

See Bournemouth Transport above.

DURHAM

ALFA COACHES LTD

17 RAMSGATE, STOCKTON-ON-TEES TS18 1BS.
Tel: 01642 678066
Fax: 01642 673462
Fleetname: Gladwin Tours
Man Dir: P. Sawbridge. **Man**: M. Gladwin.
Co Sec: P. Sawbridge. **Ops Man**: D. Squire
Fleet: 8 coach
Chassis: DAF
Bodies: 5 Ikarus. 3 Van Hool.
Ops incl: excursions & tours, private hire, continental tours
Livery: Beige with Blue lettering

ALMAR TRAVEL

7 GLENAVON AVENUE, SOUTH PELAW DH2 2JL.
Tel: 0191 388 6752.
Fax: 0191 388 1777.
Prop: A. Rogers.
Fleet: 3 - 2 coach, 1 minicoach.
Chassis: 1 Mercedes. 2 Volvo.
Bodies: 1 Carlyle. 1 Plaxton. 1 Van Hool.
Ops incl: excursions & tours, private hire, continental tours.
Livery: Brown/Orange.

*ARRIVA NORTH EAST LTD

See Tyne & Wear

BEST WAY TRAVEL

21 CHARLTONS, SALTBURN TS12 3DA.
Tel: 01287 635573.
Co Sec: Ann Wakefield. **Business Man**: M. Wakefield. **Ops Man**: B. Wakefield.
Maintenance: C. Wakefield.
Fleet: 4 coach.
Chassis: 2 DAF. 2 Ford.
Ops incl: excursions & tours, private hire, continental tours, school contracts.
Livery: Bronze.

*BROWNS COACHES LTD

R24

1 LEESFIELD DRIVE, MEADOWFIELD, DURHAM DH7 8NG
Tel: 0191 373 4200
Fax: 0191 378 0393
Recovery: 0191 378 0393
E-mail: brownscoachesbv@aol.com
Dir: Ralph Brown
Fleet: 6 coach
Chassis: 1 Bova. 5 DAF.
Ops incl: excursions & tours, private hire, continental tours.

*CLASSIC COACHES LTD

R

CLASSIC HOUSE, MORRISON ROAD, ANNFIELD PLAIN DH9 7RX
Tel: 01207 282288
Fax: 01207 282333
Recovery: 07736 178599
Web site: www.classic-coaches.co.uk
E-mail: sales@classic-coaches.co.uk
Man Dir: Ian Shipley **Ops Man**: Michael Harris **Tran Man**: John Snowball **Fleet Eng**: Eric Bowerbank
Fleet: 66 - 4 double-deck bus, 10 single-deck bus, 50 coach, 2 double-deck coach.
Chassis: 2 DAF. 1 Dennis. 4 MCW. 9 Mercedes. 12 Scania. 36 Volvo.
Bodies: 3 Berkhof. 7 Caetano. 12 Irizar. 4 MCW. 2 Neoplan. 26 Plaxton.
Ops incl: local bus services, school contracts, excursions & tours, private hire, continental tours
Livery: Red/Gold
Part of Status Bus & Coach

COCHRANE'S

R24

4 FARADAY ROAD, NORTH EAST INDUSTRIAL ESTATE, PETERLEE SR8 5AP.
Tel: 0191 586 2136.
Fax: 0191 586 5566.
Fleetname: Cochrane's Kelvin Travel.
Owner: I. P. Cochrane.
Fleet: 7 - 5 single-deck bus, 2 minicoach.
Chassis: 4 Bedford. 1 DAF. 1 Ford. 1 Freight Rover.
Bodies: 5 Plaxton. 2 others.
Ops incl: school contracts.
Livery: Orange/Black.
Ticket System: Setright.

COMPASS ROYSTON TRAVEL LTD

R24   T

BOWESFIELD LANE INDUSTRIAL ESTATE, STOCKTON-ON-TEES TS18 3EG
Tel: 01642 606644
Fax: 01642 608517
Prop: G. Walton. **Ch Eng**: P. Spencer.
Co Sec: Judy Hedger. **Ops**: D. Cass.
Trans Man: M. Metcalfe.
Fleet: 40 - 6 double-deck bus, 31 coach, 3 midicoach.
Chassis: 8 Bristol. 4 Daimler. 2 Ford. 6 Leyland. 3 Mercedes. 31 Volvo.
Bodies: 6 ECW. 7 Jonckheere. 3 Mercedes. 23 Plaxton. 1 Van Hool.
Ops incl: excursions & tours, private hire, express, continental tours, school contracts.
Livery: White with Red/Maroon stripe.
Bus wash and 24 hour parking.

DUNN-LINE GROUP

See Nottinghamshire

DURHAM CITY COACHES LTD

BRANDON LANE, BRANDON, DURHAM DH7 8PL
Tel: 0191 378 0540
Fax: 0191 378 1985
E-mail: sales@durhamcitycoaches.co.uk
Web site: www.durhamcitycoaches.co.uk
Man Dir: Michael Lightfoot. **Dir**: Christine Lightfoot **Dir**: Neil Herbert **Ch Eng**: David Winter
Fleet: 13 - 12 coach, 1 minicoach.
Chassis: 3 Bova. 9 Volvo.
Bodies: 5 Jonckheere, 1 Mercedes,

Ac	Air conditioning
	Vehicles suitable for disabled
	Coach(es) with galley facilities
wc	Coach(es) with toilet facilities
	Seat belt-fitted vehicles
R	Recovery service available (not 24 hr)
R24	24hr recovery service
	Replacement vehicle available
T	Toilet-drop facilities available
	Vintage vehicle(s) available
	Open top vehicle(s)

3 Plaxton, 1 Van Hool.
Ops incl: excursions & tours, private hire, continental tours, school contracts.
Livery: Black/Red/Gold.

DURHAM TRAVEL SERVICES (DTS)
See Dunn-Line Group, Nottinghamshire

*ENTERPRISE TRAVEL
[WC] [☕] [♿] [Nc] [🔧] [T]
14 BLOOMFIELD ROAD, DARLINGTON DL3 6SA
Tel/Fax: 01325 286924
E-mail: coachhire@aol.com
Dirs: B R Brown, Mrs B M Brown
Fleet: 6 - 4 coach, 1 midicoach, 1 minibus.
Chassis: 1 Bedford. 1 DAF. 2 MAN. 2 Mercedes.
Bodies: 2 Caetano. 1 Mercedes. 1 Plaxton. 1 Setra. 1 Van Hool.
Ops incl: private hire, school contracts.
Livery: White with red/green reliefs.

GARDINERS TRAVEL
[♿] [WC] [Nc] [R] [🔧]
COULSON STREET, SPENNYMOOR DL16 7RS
Tel: 01388 814417
Fax: 01388 811466
E-mail: gardiners.travel@virgin.net
Man Dir: John Gardiner **Tran Man**: Harry Revel
Fleet: 8 - 6 coach, 2 midibus.
Chassis: 1 Iveco. 1 Leyland. 2 Optare. 4 Volvo.
Bodies: 1 Beulas. 1 Jonckheere. 2 Optare. 3 Plaxton. 1 Van Hool.
Ops incl: local bus services, school contracts, excursions & tours, private hire, continental tours.
Livery: Cream/Maroon
Ticket system: AES

GARNETT'S INTERNATIONAL [WC]
UNIT E1, ROMAN WAY INDUSTRIAL ESTATE, TINDALE CRESCENT, BISHOP AUCKLAND DL14 9AW.
Tel: 01388 604419.
Fax: 01388 609549.
Man Dir: L. Garnett. **Tran Man**: M. Garnett.
Fleet: 12 - 6 double-deck bus, 6 single-deck bus.
Chassis: 2 Bova. 2 DAF. 1 Daimler. 3 Leyland. 2 Mercedes. 1 Scania. 1 Volvo.
Bodies: 1 Bova. 1 Jonckheere. 1 Leyland. 2 Mercedes. 1 Park Royal. 1 Plaxton. 1 Van Hool.
Ops incl: excursions & tours, private hire, continental tours.
Livery: White/Red/Yellow/Yellow/Black.

GO NORTH EAST
See Tyne & Wear.

GRIERSONS COACHES
[WC] [☕]
SEDGEFIELD ROAD GARAGE, FISHBURN, STOCKTON-ON-TEES TS21 4DD.
Tel: 01740 620209.
Fax: 01740 621243.
Prop: C. & D. Grierson.
Fleet: 20 - 5 double-deck bus, 6 single-deck bus, 4 coach, 1 midicoach, 4 minibus.
Chassis: 1 DAF. 1 Ford. 1 Ford Transit. 2 Freight Rover. 2 Mercedes. 1 Scania. 13 Volvo.
Bodies: 1 Carlyle. 3 Jonckheere. 2 Mercedes. 13 Plaxton. 1 Reeve Burgess. 1 Van Hool.
Ops incl: excursions & tours, private hire, express, continental tours.
Livery: Blue/Red.

H & M COACHES [WC] [♿]
UNIT E1, PARK ROAD INDUSTRIAL ESTATE, CONSETT DH8 5PY.
Tel: 01207 505153.
Fax: 01207 505011.
Prop: H. Bunney.
Fleet: 3 coach.
Chassis: 1 Bova. 1 DAF. 1 Leyland.
Bodies: 1 Bova. 1 Duple. 1 Plaxton.
Ops incl: excursions & tours, private hire, continental tours, school contracts.
Livery: Red/Yellow/White.

HODGSONS COACHES
[WC] [♿] [🔧]
20 GALGATE, BARNARD CASTLE DL12 8BG.
Tel: 01833 630730.
Fax: 01833 630830.
Props: J. K. Hodgson, G. A. Hodgson.
Fleet: 6 - 2 coach, 1 midicoach, 3 minicoach.
Chassis: 1 Bedford. 1 Bova. 1 Leyland. 1 Mercedes.
Bodies: 1 Bova. 1 Plaxton. 1 Elme. 3 Concept Coach Craft.
Ops incl: local bus services, school contracts, excursions & tours, private hire, continental tours.

*HUMBLE'S COACHES
[♿] [WC]
UP YONDER, ROBSON STREET, SHILDON DL4 1EB
Tel: 01388 772772
Fax: 01388 772211
Props: J Malcolm Humble **Tours Man**: P West **Tran Man**: K Towler
Fleet: 6 - 2 coach, 2 midicoach, 2 minicoach.
Chassis: 4 Mercedes. 2 Volvo.
Bodies: 4 Mercedes. 2 Plaxton
Ops incl: school contracts, excursions & tours, private hire.
Livery: Maroon

J & C COACHES
[WC] [☕] [♿] [🔧] [T]
COACH DEPOT, GROAT DRIVE, AYCLIFFE INDUSTRIAL PARK, NEWTON AYCLIFFE DL5 6HY.
Tel: 01325 312728.
Fax: 01325 320385.
Snr Ptnr: J. N. Jones.
Ptnrs: A. Jones, N. Jones, D. Jones.
Fleet: 10 - 6 coach, 1 midicoach, 3 minicoach.
Chassis: 4 DAF. 1 Dennis. 1 Ford Transit. 1 Freight Rover. 2 Mercedes. 1 Setra.
Bodies: 4 Bova. 1 Duple. 1 Leyland. 2 Mercedes. 1 Setra.
Ops incl: school contracts, excursions & tours, private hire, continental tours.
Livery: various

JAYLINE TRAVEL
[♿] [♿] [WC] [☕] [Nc]
UNIT 8A, KILBURN DRIVE, SEAVIEW INDUSTRIAL ESTATE, HORDEN SR8 4TQ
Tel: 0191 586 5787
Fax: 0191 586 5836
E-mail: jaylinetravel@hotmail.com
Web site: jaylinetravel.com
Prop: Jason Rogers
Fleet: 14 - 1 single-deck coach, 1 double-deck coach, 12 midibus.
Chassis: 8 Mercedes, 4 Optare, 2 Scania.
Bodies: 4 Optare, 8 Plaxton, 2 Van Hool
Ops incl: local bus services, continental tours.
Livery: Blue/Orange
Ticket System: AES Datafare 2000

*KINGSLEY COACHES
See Tyne & Wear

*LEE'S COACHES LTD
[♿] [WC] [☕] [Nc] [R24] [🔧] [T]
MILL ROAD GARAGE, MILL ROAD, LANGLEY MOOR DH7 8HE
Tel: 0191 378 0653
Fax: 0191 378 9086
Recovery: 07976 177226
E-mail: info@lee'scoaches.co.uk
Web site: www.lee'scoaches.co.uk
Dirs: Colin Lee, Jean Lee, Malcolm Lee **Ch Eng**: David Welch **Co Sec**: Janice C Jones.
Fleet: 12 - 11 coach, 1 minibus.
Chassis: 1 Mercedes. 11 Volvo.
Bodies: 2 Berkhof. 5 Caetano. 1 Duple. 1 Mellor. 1 Plaxton. 2 Van Hool.
Ops incl: school contracts, excursions & tours, private hire, continental tours.
Livery: Silver/Turquoise.

MAUDES COACHES
[♿] [☕] [🔧]
REDWELL GARAGE, HARMIRE ROAD, BARNARD CASTLE DL12 8QJ
Tel: 01833 637341
Fax: 01833 631888
Prop: Stephen Maude
Fleet: 6 - 4 coach, 1 midicoach, 1 minicoach.
Chassis: 2 Mercedes. 4 Volvo.
Bodies: 1 Jonckheere. 2 Mercedes. 1 Plaxton. 2 Van Hool.
Ops incl: local bus services, school contracts, excursions & tours, private hire.
Livery: Red/White.

METRO COACHES
See North Yorkshire

NORTON MINI TRAVEL [♿]
5 PLUMER DRIVE, NORTON TS20 1HF.
Tel: 01642 555832.
Owner: R. Spears.
Fleet: 2 minicoach.
Chassis: 1 Iveco, 1 Freight Rover.
Ops incl: private hire, school contracts.
Livery: White/Purple.

RICHARDSON COACHES [wc]
3 OXFORD ROAD, HARTLEPOOL
TS25 5SS.
Tel/Fax: 01429 272235.
Man Dir/Ch Eng: T. Richardson.
Dir/Co Sec/Traf Man: D. Richardson.
Fleet: 8 coach.
Chassis: 1 DAF. 4 Leyland. 1 Mercedes.
1 Toyota. 1 Volvo.
Bodies: 1 Caetano. 1 Leyland. 1 Mercedes.
4 Plaxton. 1 Van Hool.
Ops incl: excursions & tours, private hire.
Livery: Green/Red/White.

ROBERTS TOURS
[wc] [fork/knife] [seatbelt] [A/c]

36 NORTH ROAD WEST, WINGATE
TS28 5AP.
Tel: 01429 838268.
Fax: 01429 838228.
Web site: www.robertstours.com
Dirs: T. G. Roberts, D Roberts, C. A. Harper.
Fleet: 14 coach, 1 midibus.
Chassis: 5 Bova. 5 DAF. 2 Leyland 2 Volvo.
Bodies: 5 Bova. 8 Plaxton. 1 Wadham Stringer.
Ops incl: excursions & tours, private hire, express, school contracts.
Livery: Cream/Green.

*SCARLET BAND COACHES
[disabled] [wc] [fork/knife] [seatbelt] [A/c] [replacement]

WELFARE GARAGE, HIGH STREET,
WEST CORNFORTH, FERRYHILL
DL17 9LA
Tel: 01740 654247
Fax: 01740 656068
E-mail: sband@freeuk.com
Web site: www.scarletbandcoaches.co.uk
Fleet: 18 - 11 coach, 7 midibus.
Chassis: 2 Bova. 1 DAF. 3 Dennis.
6 Leyland. 1 MAN. 1 MCW. 3 Optare.
1 Volvo.
Bodies: 2 Bova. 1 MCW. 3 Optare.
9 Plaxton. 3 Van Hool.
Ops incl: local bus services, school contracts, excursions & tours, private hire, continental tours.
Livery: White/Red/Yellow
Ticket System: AES Datafare

SHERBURN VILLAGE COACHES
[seatbelt] [fork/knife] [wc] [replacement]

FRONT ST, SHERBURN VILLAGE
DH6 1QY.
Tel: 0191 372 1531.
Fax: 0191 386 1970.
Prop: J. Cousins.
Fleet: 6 - 3 coach, 1 midibus, 2 minicoach.
Chassis: 1 Leyland. 1 Mercedes. 2 Volvo.
Bodies: 2 Duple. 1 Plaxton. 2 Reeve Burgess. 1 Wadham Stringer.
Ops incl: local bus services, school contracts, excursions & tours, private hire.
Livery: Yellow/Red.
Ticket System: AES.

SNOWDON COACHES
[wc] [seatbelt] [replacement]

SEASIDE LANE, EASINGTON SR8 3TW.
Tel: 0191 527 0535.
Fax: 0191 527 3280.
Prop: A. Snowdon. **Man:** G. Parkin.
Ch Eng: J. R. Main. **Sec:** V. Dowson.
Fleet: 16 coach.
Chassis: 1 Bova. 1 MAN. 14 Volvo.
Bodies: 1 Bova. 14 Plaxton. 1 Van Hool.
Ops incl: private hire, school contracts.
Livery: White with Pink reliefs.

STAGECOACH IN DARLINGTON, STAGECOACH IN HARTLEPOOL, STAGECOACH ON TEESIDE
see Stagecoach North East (Tyne & Wear)

STANLEY TAXIS & MINICOACHES
THE BUS STATION, STANLEY
DH9 OTD
Tel: 01207 237424.
Fax: 01207 233233.
E-mail: stanleytaxis@btinternet.com
Ptnr: Ian Scott.

TOWN & COUNTRY MOTOR SERVICES LTD [seatbelt]
UNIT 2, HENSON ROAD, YARM
ROAD BUSINESS PARK,
DARLINGTON DL1 4QD.
Tel: 01325 489966.
E-mail: sales@townanccountrycoaches.co.uk
Web site: www.townandcountrycoaches.co.uk
Fleetname: Town & Country.
Man Dir: Philip Notman.
Co Sec: Jaqulene. Notman.
Fleet: 3 - 1 single-deck bus, 1 midibus, 1 midicoach.
Chassis: 2 Leyland. 2 Mercedes.
Bodies: 1 Duple. 1 Marshall, 1 Plaxton.
Ops incl: local bus services, school contracts, private hire.
Livery: White/Blue.
Ticket System: Almex.

PAUL WATSON TRAVEL
BRIDGE HOUSE, MOOR ROAD,
STAINDROP DL2 3LF
Tel/Fax: 01833 660471
E-mail: paul@pwatsontravel.fslife.co.uk
Web site: www.paulwatsontravel.co.uk
Man Dir: Paul Watson,
Ops Man: Joanne Watson
Fleet: 8 - 2 single-deck coach, 2 midicoach, 1 minibus.
Chassis: 1 LDV, 2 Mercedes, 2 Volvo.
Bodies: 1 Jonckheere, 1 Mercedes, 1 Optare, 1 Plaxton, 1 other.
Ops incl: excursions & tours, private hire, continental tours, school contracts.

*WEARDALE MOTOR SERVICES LTD
STANHOPE DL13 2YQ
Tel: 01388 528235
Fax: 01388 526080
Dirs: R S Gibson, A M Hewitson, Anthony Gibson, Ian Gibson
Fleet: 22 - 6 double-deck bus, 6 single-deck bus, 9 coach, 1 double-deck coach.
Chassis: 1 Bova. 1 Iveco. 5 Leyland. 3 Mercedes. 1 Optare. 7 Volvo.
Bodies: Alexander. Bova. East lancs. Mercedes. Optare. Plaxton. Van Hool.
Ops incl: local bus services, excursions & tours, school contracts, private hire, express, continental tours.
Livery: Red/White
Ticket System: Wayfarer

A/c	Air conditioning	♥ Seat belt-fitted vehicles	✓ Replacement vehicle available
♿	Vehicles suitable for disabled	R Recovery service available (not 24 hr)	T Toilet-drop facilities available
🍴	Coach(es) with galley facilities		Vintage vehicle(s) available
wc	Coach(es) with toilet facilities	R24 24hr recovery service	Open top vehicle(s)

EAST SUSSEX, BRIGHTON & HOVE

AUTOPOINT COACHES

THE CAUSEWAY YARD, BODLE STREET BN27 4UA
Tel: 01323 832430
Fax: 01323 833434
Ptners: B. P. Rodemark, G. Rodemark, Miss D. Rodemark **Ch Eng**: G. Rodemark.
Fleet: 18 - 2 single-deck bus, 6 coach, 3 midibus, 3 midicoach, 4 minibus.
Chassis: 2 Bedford. 1 Ford Transit. 2 Volvo. 2 Leyland. 1 Leyland National. 10 Mercedes.
Bodies: 1 Leyland National. 1 Mellor. 3 Mercedes. 4 Plaxton. 2 Reeve Burgess. 2 UVG. 1 Van Hool. 3 Wadham Stringer. 1 Wright.
Ops incl: local bus services, school contracts, excursions & tours, private hire.
Livery: Blue/White.
Ticket System: Wayfarer.

*BARCROFT TOURS & EVENTS

60 QUEENS ROAD, HASTINGS TN34 1RE
Tel: 01424 200201
Fax: 01424 648250
Web site: www.barcrofttours.co.uk
Ptnrs: Peter Warren, Catherine Barcroft
Man: Keith Henderson
Fleet: 2 - includes coach & midibus
Chassis: 1 Ford. 1 Setra.
Ops incl: excursions & tours, private hire, continental tours.
Livery: Silver/Blue squares

*BRIGHTON & HOVE BUS & COACH CO

43 CONWAY STREET, HOVE BN3 3LT
Tel: 01273 886200
Fax: 01273 822073
E-mail: info@buses.co.uk
Web site: www.buses.co.uk
Chmn: Martin Ballinger **Man Dir**: Roger French **Fin Dir**: Phil Woodgate **Eng Dir**: Tony Griffiths **Ops Dir**: Paul Williams
Fleet: 252 - 159 double-deck bus, 83 single-deck bus, 10 coach.
Chassis: 1 Bristol. 138 Dennis. 83 Scania. 30 Volvo.
Bodies: 1 ECW. 122 East Lancs. 1 Irizar. 14 Marshall. 18 Optare. 75 Plaxton. 21 Wright.
Ops incl: local bus services, school contracts, excursions & tours, private hire, continental tours.
Livery: Red/Cream with Black
Ticket System: WayfarerTGX

*BRIGHTONIAN COACHES

3 THE AVENUE, BRIGHTON BN2 4GF
Tel: 01273 696195
Props: Laurence R Walker, Susan M Walker
Fleet: 2 coach
Chassis: 2 Volvo.
Bodies: 1 Duple 1 Plaxton.
Ops incl: school contracts, private hire.
Livery: White

*C & S COACHES

STATION ROAD, HEATHFIELD TN21 8DF
Tel: 01435 866600
Fax: 01435 868264
E-mail: info@candscoaches.co.uk
Ptnrs: Chris Hicks, Geoff Shaw **Ch Eng**: Paul Matthews
Fleet: 36 - 34 coach, 1 double-deck coach, 1 midicoach.
Chassis: 10 DAF. 4 Leyland. 1 Neoplan. 10 Scania. 2 Setra. 9 Volvo.
Bodies: 4 Jonckheere. 1 Neoplan. 10 Plaxton. 1 Reeve Burgess. 2 Setra. 18 Van Hool.
Ops incl: school contracts, private hire.
Livery: White with red/black graphics

*COASTAL COACHES

18 WEST POINT, NEWICK BN8 4NU
Tel: 01825 723024
Prop: Peter Jenkins
Fleet: 11 - single-deck bus and minibus.
Chassis: 10 Dennis. 1 Transbus.
Bodies: 1 Marshall/MCV. 1 Plaxton. 9 Transbus.
Ops incl: local bus services
Livery: Green/White/Blue
Ticket System: Wayfarer 3

CUCKMERE COACHES

3 MARK LANE, EASTBOURNE BN21 4RJ
Tel: 01323 639890.
Fax: 01323 639448.
Prop: John Dearnley.
Fleet: 3 coach.
Chassis: 2 Scania, 1 Volvo.
Bodies: 3 Van Hool.
Ops incl: excursions & tours, private hire, continental tours.
Livery: White.

*CUCKMERE COMMUNITY BUS

THE OLD RECTORY, LITLINGTON BN26 5RB
Tel/Fax: 01323 870032
Chmn: Mrs Beryl Smith **Organiser**: Philip Ayers **Hire Organiser**: Geoffrey Maynard **Sec**: Mrs Susan de Angeli **Treasurer**: Michael Sutton
Fleet: 3 minibus
Chassis: 3 Mercedes.
Bodies: 1 Mercedes, 2 Constables
Ops incl: local bus services, excursions & tours, private hire.
Livery: Green/Cream
Ticket system: Setright

*EASTBOURNE BUSES LTD

BIRCH ROAD, EASTBOURNE BN23 6PD.
Tel: 01323 416416
Fax: 01323 643034
E-mail: mailbox@eastbournebuses.co.uk
Web site: www.eastbournebuses.co.uk
Man Dir/Co Sec: Steve Barnett **Dir of Ops**: Vernon Barfoot **Fin & Admin Man**: Chris Ormsby **Coaching Man**: Mark Willis **Wkshp Man**: Ian Stringer
Fleet: 66 - 12 double-deck bus, 45 single-deck bus, 9 coach.
Chassis: 1 AEC. 32 DAF. 6 Dennis. 5 Leyland. 10 Optare. 6 Scania. 6 Volvo.
Ops incl: local bus services, school contracts, excursions & tours, private hire, continental tours.
Livery: Blue.
Ticket System: Wayfarer 3

*L. J. EDWARDS COACH HIRE

BELLBANKS CORNER, MILL ROAD, HAILSHAM BN27 2AH
Tel: 01323 440622
Fax: 01323 442555
Recovery: 07974 369570 (24hrs)
E-mail: info@ljedwards.co.uk
Web site: www.ljedwards.co.uk
Props: John Edwards, Liz Edwards **Co Sec**: David Maynard
Fleet: 9 - 7 coach, 2 midicoach
Chassis: 5 Bova. 1 Irisbus. 1 Neoplan. 1 Scania. 1 Toyota.
Bodies: 5 Bova. 1 Caetano. 1 Irisbus. 1 Optare. 1 Van Hool.
Ops incl: local bus services, school contracts, excursions & tours, private hire, continental tours.
Livery: White with red detail

*EMPRESS COACHES LTD

10/11 ST MARGARETS ROAD, ST LEONARDS-ON-SEA TN37 6EH
Tel/Fax: 01424 430621
Web site: www.empressofhastings.co.uk
Prop: Stephen Dine
Fleet: 8 - 1 coach, 3 midicoach, 2 minicoach, 2 midicoach.
Chassis: 2 Ford Transit. 3 Mercedes. 3 Omni.
Bodies: 1 Autobus. 1 Mercedes. 1 Plaxton. 2 Dormobile. 2 Omni.
Ops incl: local bus services, school contracts, private hire.
Livery: Maroon/Ivory
Ticket system: Wayfarer

J & H COACHES

UNIT 2, SIMPSONS YARD, HARBOUR ROAD, RYE TN31 7TE.
Tel: 01797 225881.
Prop: J. Campbell

OCEAN COACHES

19 STONERY CLOSE, PORTSLADE BN41 2TD.
Tel/Fax: 01273 278385.
Web site: www.oceancoaches.net
E-mail: info@oceancoaches.net
Prop: Peter Woodcock.
Fleet: 1 coach.
Chassis: Volvo. **Body**: Ikarus.

Ops incl: private hire, school contracts.
Livery: Cream/Red.

*PAVILION COACHES
144 NEVILL AVENUE, HOVE BN3 7NH
Tel: 01273 732405
Fax: 01273 732405
Web site: www.pavilioncoaches.co.uk
Props: Peter Hammer, Nicola Hammer
Fleet: 3 - 1 double-deck bus, 2 coach
Chassis: 1 Leyland. 2 Volvo.
Bodies: 1 Jonckheere, 1 Plaxton, 1 Park Roayal (London RT)
Ops incl: school contracts, excursions & tours, private hire, continental tours.

R D H SERVICES
WESTCROFT, PLUMPTON LANE, PLUMPTON BN7 3AH
Tel: 01273 890477
Fax: 01273 890743
E-mail: info@rdhservices.co.uk
Web site: www.rdhservices.co.uk
Ptnrs: Tom Hawthorne, Derek Hunnisett
Ch Eng: Martin Wisk. Ops Man: Doug Brooks.
Fleet: 27 - 9 single-deck bus, 10 coach, 8 midibus. 4 midicoach, 1 minicoach.
Chassis: 6 Dennis. 11 Leyland. 8 Mercedes. 2 Volvo.
Bodies: 1 Caetano. 1 Carlyle. 1 Ikarus. 1 Jonckheere. 1 LAG. 2 Neoplan. 2 Optare. 4 Plaxton. 4 Reeve Burgess. 1 Van Hool. 6 Wadham Stringer. 2 Wright.
Ops incl: local bus services, school contracts, excursions & tours, private hire.
Livery: White/Orange/Blue.
Ticket System: Wayfarer 3.

RAMBLER COACHES
WESTRIDGE MANOR, WHITWORTH ROAD, HASTINGS TN37 7PZ
Tel: 01424 52505
Fax: 01424 751815
Ptnrs: C. Rowland, J. Goodwin.
Fleet: 38 - 5 single-deck bus, 26 coach, 1 midibus, 3 midicoach. 1 minicoach.
Chassis: 8 Bedford. 4 Dennis. 2 Leyland National. 5 Mercedes. 1 Scania. 18 Volvo.
Bodies: 5 Berkhof. 1 Duple. 2 Leyland National. 2 Optare. 17 Plaxton. 7 Van Hool. 1 Reeve Burgess. 1 Wadham Stringer. 1 Wright. 1 Hispano.
Ops incl: local bus services, school contracts, excursions & tours, private hire, continental tours.

Livery: Green/Black.
Ticket System: Wayfarer.

RENOWN COACHES
13 SEA ROAD, BEXHILL-ON-SEA TN40 1EE
Tel: 01424 210744
Fleet: 18 - 4 double-deck bus, 4 single-deck bus, 10 coach
Chassis: 1 DAF. 1 Dennis. 11 Leyland. 1 Setra. 4 Volvo.
Bodies: 2 Caetano. 2 Duple. 6 Leyland. 1 Plaxton. 1 Reeve Burgess. 1 Setra. 4 Van Hool. 1 Wadham Stringer.
Ops incl: local bus services, school contracts, excursions & tours, private hire, continental tours.

STAGECOACH IN HASTINGS
BEAUFORT ROAD, SILVERHILL, ST LEONARDS ON SEA TN37 6PL
Tel: 01424 445600
Fax: 01424 435340
E-mail: enquiries.southeast@stagecoachbus.com
Web site: www.stagecoachbus.com/hastings
Man Dir: Paul Southgate Ops Dir: Neil Instrall Eng Dir: Keith Dyball
Fleet: 63 - 23 double-deck bus, 40 single-deck bus.
Chassis: 27 Dennis. 4 Leyland. 6 Scania. 26 Volvo
Bodies: 45 Alexander. 18 Northern Counties.
Ops incl: local bus services.
Livery: Stagecoach

SUSSEX COUNTRY COACH HIRE LTD
See West Sussex.

SUSSEX PIONEER COACHES
3 THE AVENUE, BRIGHTON BN2 4GF.
Tel: 01273 696195.
Fax: 01273 696195.
Ptnrs: L. R. Walker, Mrs S. M. Walker.
Fleet: 3 coach.
Chassis: 3 Leyland.
Bodies: 1 Duple. 1 Plaxton. 1 Roe.
Ops incl: private hire.

WARREN'S COACHES (KENT & SUSSEX) LTD
HIGH STREET, TICEHURST TN5 7AN.
Tel: 01580 200226.
Fax: 01580 201126.
E-mail: warrenscoa@aol.com
Web site: www.warrens.uk.com
Man Dir: G. R. Fry. Dir/Co Sec: M. Fry.
Dir: P. Warren.
Fleet: 18 - 17 coach, 1 minicoach.
Chassis: 1 Bedford. 4 Iveco. 2 Setra. 1 Toyota. 10 Volvo.
Bodies: 4 Beulas. 1 Caetano. 1 Duple. 10 Plaxton. 2 Setra.
Ops incl: local bus services, school contracts, private hire, continental tours.
Livery: Primrose/Blue/Red.
Ticket System: Almex.

WATERHOUSE TOURS LTD
R24
DITTONS ROAD, POLEGATE BN26 6JG
Tel: 01323 485251/2/3.
Fax: 01323 484712.
E-mail: privatehire@wannacoach.com
Web site: www.wannacoach.com
Fleetname: Waterhouse.
Man Dir: K. Waterhouse. Gen Man: B. Wells. Co Sec: Ms J. Waterhouse. Tours Man: N. Grice. Dir: D. Bond.
Fleet: 12 - 8 coach. 2 double-deck coach. 1 midicoach, 1 minicoach.
Chassis: 1 Ayats 4 Iveco. 1 MAN. 3 Mercedes. 2 Neoplan. 1 Setra.
Ops incl: excursions & tours, private hire, continental tours.
Livery: White/Blue/Turquoise.

*WISE COACHES LTD
74 HIGH STREET, HAILSHAM BN27 1AU
Tel: 01323 844321
Fax: 01323 845321
E-mail: info@wisecoaches.co.uk
Web site: www.wisecoaches.co.uk
Dirs: J S G Wise, J E Wise
Fleet: 4 coach.
Chassis: 3 DAF. 1 Iveco
Bodies: 1 Beulas 1 Ikarus. 1 Ovi. 1 Smit.
Ops incl: excursions & tours, private hire, continental tours, school contracts.
Livery: White/Red/Black.

A/c	Air conditioning
	Vehicles suitable for disabled
	Coach(es) with galley facilities
wc	Coach(es) with toilet facilities
	Seat belt-fitted vehicles
R	Recovery service available (not 24 hr)
R24	24hr recovery service
	Replacement vehicle available
T	Toilet-drop facilities available
	Vintage vehicle(s) available
	Open top vehicle(s)

East Sussex

EAST RIDING OF YORKSHIRE, CITY OF KINGSTON UPON HULL

*ABBEY COACHWAYS LTD
See main entry in North Yorkshire

*ACKLAMS OF BEVERLEY

39 LADYGATE, BEVERLEY
HU17 8BX
Tel: 01482 887666
Fax: 01482 874949
Web site: www.acklams-coaches-beverley.co.uk
Prop: Paul Acklam
Fleet: 10 - 5 coach, 2 midicoach, 3 minicoach.
Chassis: 2 DAF. 3 Dennis. 2 LDV. 2 Mercedes.
Bodies: 1 Optare. 6 Plaxton.
Ops incl: local bus services, school contracts, private hire.
Livery: Red/Grey

*ALPHA COACH CO

DAIRYCOATES INDUSTRIAL ESTATE, WILTSHIRE ROAD, HULL HU4 6PA
Tel: 01482 353941
Fax: 01482 353771
Partners: Craig Porteous, Jean Porteous.
Fleet: 84 - 22 double-deck bus, 13 single-deck bus, 26 coach, 3 double-deck coach, 7 midibus, 7 midicoach, 6 minicoach.
Chassis: 2 Ayats. 2 Bedford. 1 Bova. 1 Daimler. 7 Dennis. 1 Ford Transit. 2 Iveco. 19 Leyland. 2 Leyland National. 1 MAN. 2 MCW. 22 Mercedes. 3 Scania. 1 Toyota. 13 Volvo.
Bodies: 5 Alexander. 2 Ayats. 2 Beulas. 1 Berkhof. 1 Bova. 2 Caetano. 3 Duple. 1 ECW. 2 East Lancs. 1 Jonckheere. 7 Leyland National. 1 MCW. 6 Mercedes. 9 Northern Counties. 3 Optare. 1 Park Royal. 29 Plaxton. 3 Roe. 2 Van Hool. 1 Dormobile. 1 Crest.
Ops incl: local bus services, school contracts, private hire, excursions & tours, continental tours.
Livery: various
Ticket system: Almex

R DRURY COACHES

CARTER STREET, GOOLE
DN14 6SL
Tel/Fax: 01405 763440
Dirs: Roland Drury, Richard Drury
Fleet: 5 coach, 1 midicoach
Chassis: 1 Toyota. 5 Volvo.
Bodies: 1 Caetano. 5 Plaxton.
Ops incl: local bus services, school contracts, private hire.
Livery: White/Green/Yellow

EAST YORKSHIRE MOTOR SERVICES LTD

252 ANLABY ROAD, HULL HU3 2RS
Tel: 01482 327142
Fax: 01482 212040
E-mail: admin@eyms.co.uk
Web site: www.eyms.co.uk
Fleetname: East Yorkshire
Chmn/Ch Exec: Peter Shipp **Fin Dir**: Peter Harrison **Com Man**: Bob Rackley **Eng&Ops Man**: Robert Graham **Co Account**: Paul Jenkinson **Business Man, Coaching**: Mark Ellis
Fleet: 360 - 168 double-deck bus, 104 single-deck bus, 33 coach, 5 open-top bus, 34 midibus, 16 minibus.
Chassis: 3 AEC. 1 Bedford. 16 Bristol. 1 DAF. 46 Dennis. 102 Leyland. 3 Leyland National. 12 MAN. 4 MCW. 43 Mercedes. 1 Neoplan. 16 Optare. 1 Scania. 111 Volvo.
Bodies: 45 Alexander. 3 Berkhof. 3 Caetano. 3 Duple. 29 ECW. 4 East Lancs. 9 Leyland. 4 MCW. 4 Mercedes. 1 Neoplan. 81 Northern Counties. 35 Optare. 1 Park Royal. 127 Plaxton. 2 Reeve Burgess. 3 Roe. 5 Van Hool. 1 Willowbrook.
Ops incl: local bus services, school contracts, private hire, excursion & tours, private hire, express, continental tours.
Livery: Burgundy/Cream
Ticket System: Wayfarer TGX150

FRODINGHAM COACHES

MIDDLE STREET SOUTH, DRIFFIELD YO25 6PY
Tel: 0870 4430473
Fax: 01482 212040
E-mail: alan@frodinghamcoaches.co.uk
Web site: www.frodinghamcoaches.co.uk
Chmn: P J S Shipp **Fin Dir**: P Harrison **Man**: A Wilkonson
Fleet: 5 coach
Chassis: 1 MAN. 2 Mercedes. 1 Scania. 1 Volvo.
Bodies: 2 Mercedes. 1 Neoplan. 1 Plaxton. 1 Van Hool.
Ops incl: local bus services, school contracts, excursion & tours, private hire.
Livery: White/Blue/Grey
Part of East Yorkshire Motor Services

GREY DE LUXE COACHES

DAIRYCOTES INDUSTRIAL ESTATE, WILTSHIRE ROAD, HULL HU4 6PA.
Tel: 01482 571711.
Fax: 01482 353771.
Props: Craig Porteous, Jean Porteous.
See Alpha Coach Co, Hull.

BEN JOHNSON COACHES

THE GRANGE, CATFOSS LANE, BRANDESBURTON YO25 8EJ.
Tel: 01964 542475.
Prop: Ben Johnson.
Fleet: 8 - 7 coach, 2 minibus.
Chassis: 1 DAF. 2 LDV. 2 Leyland. 1 Setra. 2 Volvo.
Bodies: 4 Plaxton. 1 Setra. 1 Van Hool.
Ops incl: local bus services, school contracts, private hire.

MANOR TRAVEL

2 MANOR DRIVE, MAIN STREET, BEEFORD YO25 8BB.
Tel: 01262 488431.

*PEARSON COACHES

9 HEADLANDS ROAD, ALDBROUGH HU11 4RR
Tel: 01964 527260 **Fax**: 01964 527774
Ptnrs: Mrs V Pearson C Pearson
Fleet: 9 - 5 coach, 4 minicoach.
Chassis: 5 Volvo. 4 Mercedes.
Ops incl: local bus services, school contracts, excursions & tours, private hire.
Livery: Light Grey with Red/Burgundy stripes.
Ticket system: Wayfarer 2

*COLLIN PHILLIPSON MINI-COACHES

1 HILLCREST, OUSEFLEET, GOOLE DN14 8HP
Tel: 01405 704394
Prop: Collin Phillipson **Tran Man**: Tracey Phillipson
Fleet: 1 minicoach
Chassis: 1 Mercedes
Bodies: 1 Excell
Ops incl: school contracts, private hire

SILVERWING & UKAN GO HOLIDAYS LTD

THE CABIN, 141 SOUTHCOATES AVENUE, HULL HU9 3HF
Tel/Fax: 01482 794119
Props: R. Bristow, Mrs H. Goodwin
Fleet: 6 - 4 coach (two with lifts), 1 double-deck coach, 1 minicoach.
Chassis: 1 Bedford. 1 Leyland. 1 Optare. 4 Volvo.
Bodies: 3 Duple. 1 Leyland. 1 Optare. 1 Plaxton.
Ops incl: excursions & tours, private hire continental tours, school contracts.
Livery: White with sea/sun decal.

STAGECOACH IN HULL

FOSTER STREET, HULL HU8 8BT
Tel: 01482 222333
Fax: 01482 217623
Web site: www.stagecoachbus.com
Dirs: as Stagecoach East Midland
Fleet: 133 - 71 double-deck bus, 17 single-deck bus, 6 coach, 3 articulated coach, 24 midibus, 12 minibus.
Chassis: 36 Dennis. 50 Leyland. 12 Mercedes. 58 Volvo.
Bodies: 45 Alexander. 12 ECW. 10 East Lancs. 3 Jonckheere. 49 Northern Counties. 14 Plaxton. 1 Wadham Stringer.
Ops incl: local bus services, express.
Livery: Stagecoach
Ticket system: Wayfarer 3.

East Yorkshire

SWEYNE COACHES
LONGSHORES, REEDNESS ROAD, SWINEFLEET DN14 8ER.
Tel: 01405 704263

WOLD TRAVEL wc ⅋ ♥ ✔
THE OLD FORGE, NORTH DALTON, DRIFFIELD YO25 9UY.
Tel: 01377 217461.
Fax: 01377 217810.
Dirs: D. Rowland, J. Rowland.
Fleet: 6 - 2 coach, 1 double-deck coach, 1 midicoach, 1 minicoach, 1 minibus.
Ops incl: excursions & tours, private hire, continental tours, school contracts.
Livery: Grey, Yellow with Red lines.

ESSEX

AMBASSADOR COACHES
AMBASSADOR HOUSE, 39 BOURNEMOUTH PARK ROAD, SOUTHEND ON SEA SS2 5JH
Tel: 01702 315830
Props: M & D Murray

*ANITAS BRITISH & CONTINENTAL TOURS LTD
ROOM 4/5, AIRWAYS HOUSE, FIRST AVENUE, STANSTED AIRPORT CM24 1RY
Tel: 01279 681551
Fax: 01279 661771
Man Dir/Chmn: E Wheeler **Dir/Sec:** Mrs V Wyatt **Ch Eng:** V M Wheeler
Fleet: 7 - 5 coach, 2 minicoach.
Chassis: 1 DAF. 1 Dennis. 1 MAN. 1 Mercedes. 3 Volvo.
Bodies: 1 Bova. 5 Caetano. 1 Plaxton
Ops incl: contracts, private hire, excursions & tours.
Livery: White/Marigold/Brown

APT COACHES LTD
⅋ wc ♥ ❆c ✔ T
UNIT 27, RAWRETH INDUSTRIAL ESTATE, RAWRETH LANE, RAYLEIGH SS6 9RL
Tel: 01268 783878
Fax: 01268 782656
E-mail: apt.holidays@virgin.net
Man.Dir: Peter Thorn.
Fleet: 13 - 2 double-deck bus, 7 coach, 1 double-deck coach. 2 midicoach. 1 minibus.
Chassis: 5 DAF. 1 Ford Transit. 2 Leyland. 1 MAN. 1 Scania. 1 Toyota. 2 Volvo.
Bodies: 2 Berkhof. 4 Bova. 1 Irizar. 2 Van Hool. 1 Optimo. 2 Olympian.
Ops incl: school contracts, excursions & tours, private hire, continental tours

ARRIVA COLCHESTER LTD
♿ 🚌 ♥ R T
38 MAGDALEN STREET, COLCHESTER CO1 2LD.
Tel: 01206 764029.
Fax: 01206 766345.
E-mail: www.arriva.co.uk
Fleetname: ARRIVA serving Colchester.
Gen Man: David Shelley. **Ops Man:** Chris Moseley. **Eng Man:** Ray Giles.
Fleet: 48 - 11 double-deck bus, 23 single-deck bus, 4 coach, 10 midibus.
Chassis: 4 DAF. 11 Dennis. 15 Leyland. 10 Mercedes. 2 Scania. 6 Volvo.
Ops incl: local bus services, school contracts, private hire.
Livery: Aquamarine/Cotswold Stone
Ticket System: Wayfarer 3

ARRIVA SOUTHEND ♿
20 SHORT STREET, SOUTHEND-ON-SEA SS2 5BY.
Tel: 01702 442444.
Fax: 01702 442450.
Ops Man: G. Newman. **Eng Man:** Graham Brierley.
Fleet: 76 - 35 double-deck bus, 30 single-deck bus, 11 midibus.
Chassis: 55 Dennis. 6 Leyland. 11 Mercedes. 5 Volvo.
Bodies: Alexander. East Lancs. Northern Counties. Plaxton. Wright.
Ops incl: local bus services, school contracts, express.
Livery: Aquamarine/Cotswold Stone
Ticket System: Wayfarer 3.

B J S TRAVEL wc ♥ ✔
61A HIGH STREET, GREAT WAKERING SS3 0EF
Tel: 01702 219403
Fax: 01702 216472
Prop: Brian Snow
Fleet: 5 - 3 single-deck coach, 2 midicoach.
Chassis: 1 Bova, 2 Mercedes, 2 Volvo.
Bodies: 1 Bova, 1 Plaxton, 1 Reeve Burgess, 1 Van Hool. 1 other.
Ops incl: school contracts, private hire.
Livery: White/Red/Gold.

BLUE DIAMOND COACHES ♥
37 HOLMES MEADOW, HARLOW CM19 5SG.
Tel: 01279 427524.
Fax: 01279 427525.
Prop: J. Robilliard. **Sec:** A. Robilliard.
Fleet: 4 - 1 coach, 2 minibus, 1 minicoach.
Chassis: 1 Bedford. 2 Freight Rover. 1 Toyota.
Bodies: 1 Caetano. 2 Carlyle. 1 Plaxton.
Ops incl: excursions & tours, private hire, continental tours, school contracts.
Livery: Blue/White.

BLUE TRIANGLE BUSES LTD 🚌
UNIT 3C, DENVER INDUSTRIAL ESTATE, RAINHAM RM13 9BU
Tel: 01708 631001
E-mail: contacts@bluetrianglebuses.co.uk
Web site: www.bluetrianglebuses.co.uk
Man Dir: Roger Wright
Fleet: 101 - 78 double-deck bus, 23 single-deck bus
Chassis: 8 AEC. 51 Dennis. 15 Leyland. 11 Leyland National. 23 MCW. 5 Volvo.
Bodies: 5 Alexander. 8 Caetano. 34 East Lancs. 6 Leyland. 23 MCW. 13 Park Royal. 20 Plaxton. 1 Saunders. 3 Weymann.
Ops incl: local bus services, excursions & tours
Livery: Red/Cream

*BORDACOACH ♥ ✔
25B ULFA COURT, EASTWOOD ROAD, RAYLEIGH SS6 7JD
Tel: 01268 747608
Gen Man: D J Stubbington.
Fleet: 1 coach.
Chassis: 1 Leyland
Bodies: 1 Plaxton
Ops incl: local bus services, school contracts, excursions & tours, private hire.
Livery: White/Blue
Ticket System: Almex

BRENTWOOD COACHES
wc ♥ 🚌 ✔ T
79 WASH ROAD, HUTTON, BRENTWOOD CM13 1DL.
Tel: 01277 233144.
Fax: 01277 201386.
Prop: A. J. Brenson. **Ch Eng:** K. Wright.
Sec: Mrs P. Alexander. **Traf Man:** B. Pierce.
Fleet: 30 - 15 double-deck bus, 14 coach. 1 midibus.
Chassis: Daimler, Volvo.
Bodies: Caetano, Jonckheere, Plaxton.
Ops incl: excursions & tours, private hire, school contracts, continental tours.
Livery: White/Brown/Orange/Yellow.
Ticket System: Almex.

❆c	Air conditioning	♥	Seat belt-fitted vehicles	✔ Replacement vehicle available
♿	Vehicles suitable for disabled	R	Recovery service available (not 24 hr)	T Toilet-drop facilities available
⅋	Coach(es) with galley facilities	R24	24hr recovery service	🚌 Vintage vehicle(s) available
wc	Coach(es) with toilet facilities			🚌 Open top vehicle(s)

C I COACHLINES
[WC] [coach] [food] [A/C]

POOLS LANE, HIGHWOOD, CHELMSFORD CM1 3QL
Tel: 01245 248669
Fax: 01245 248185
E-mail: cicoachlines@btopenworld.com
Props: S Lodge, I Lodge, C Femer
Fleet: 4 coach
Chassis: 1 Iveco. 3 Volvo
Ops incl: private hire

*C N ENTERPRISES (COACH HIRE) [coach]

9 BARTHOLOMEW DRIVE, HAROLD WOOD RM3 0WB
Tel/Fax: 01708 379700
E-mail: cnenterprise1@aol.com
ManDir: Colin Nossek **Dir:** Vena Nossek
Fleet: 1 coach.
Chassis: 1 Volvo.
Bodies: 1 Jonckheere.
Ops incl: excursions & tours, private hire.

*CEDRIC COACHES

1 THE AVENUE, WIVENHOE CO7 9AH
Tel: 01206 824363
Fax: 01206 822253
Fleet: 27 - 12 double-deck bus, 12 coach, 2 double-deck coach. 1 minibus.
Chassis: 3 Bova. 1 Bristol. 1 Dennis. 1 LDV. 11 Leyland. 3 Neoplan. 3 Setra. 7 Volvo.
Bodies: 1 Berkhof. 3 Bova. 12 ECW. 3 Jonckheere. 2 Neoplan. 2 Plaxton. 3 Setra. 1 Van Hool.
Ops incl: local bus services, school contracts, private hire, continental tours.
Livery: White
Ticket System: Wayfarer

CHADWELL HEATH COACHES [WC] [coach]

30 REYNOLDS AVENUE, CHADWELL HEATH RM6 4NT
Tel: 020 8590 7505
Fax: 020 8597 8883
Props: John Thompson, Lynn Thompson.
Fleet: 5 coach.
Chassis: 2 Leyland. 3 Volvo.
Bodies: 3 Berkhof. 1 Duple. 1 Plaxton.
Ops incl: excursions & tours, private hire, school contracts.
Livery: Country cream

*CHARIOTS OF ESSEX LTD
[disabled] [WC] [coach]

THE COACH HOUSE, 1 ONE TREE HILL, STANFORD-LE-HOPE SS17 9NH
Tel: 01268 581444
Fax: 01268 581555
Man Dir: K T Flavin **Dir:** W J Collier
Fleet: 18 - 3 double-deck bus, 2 single-deck bus, 4 single-deck coach, 1 midicoach, 7 minibus, 1 minicoach.
Chassis: Bova. DAF. Freight Rover. Iveco. Mercedes. Toyota.
Bodies: Bova. Caetano. Marshall/MCV. MCW.
Ops incl: local bus services, school contracts, private hire, express.
Livery: Orange/Yellow
Ticket system: Wayfarer

*CLINTONA MINICOACHES
[coach] [key]

LITTLE WARLEY HALL LANE, BRENTWOOD CM13 3HA
Tel: 01277 215526
Fax: 01277 200038
E-mail: enquiries@clintona.co.uk
Web site: www.clintona.co.uk
Dirs: Robin Staines, Barbara J Staines.
Fleet: 28 - 11 midibus, 10 midicoach, 4 minibus, 3 minicoach.
Chassis: 1 Ford Transit. 9 Iveco. 4 LDV. 14 Mercedes.
Ops incl: local bus services, school contracts, private hire.
Livery: White/Blue.
Ticket System: Wayfarer 3

*COOKS COACHES
[WC] [coach] [A/C] [T]

607 LONDON ROAD, WESTCLIFF-ON-SEA SS0 9PE
Tel: 01702 344702
Fax: 01702 436887
E-mail: info@cookscoaches.co.uk
Web site: www.cookscoaches.co.uk
Prop: W E Cook
Fleet: 12 - 10 coach, 2 minibus.
Chassis: 10 Bova. 2 LDV.
Bodies: includes 10 Bova.
Ops incl: excursions & tours, private hire, continental tours.
Livery: Red/White

*COUNTY COACHES
[WC] [coach] [A/C]

2 CRESCENT ROAD, BRENTWOOD CM14 5JR
Tel: 01277 201505
Fax: 01277 225918
Dirs: A R Pratt, R J Pratt, C A Jee, S M Best
E-mail: enquiries@countycoaches.com
Fleet: 10 coach.
Chassis: 1 Dennis. 1 Mercedes. 1 Scania. 1 Toyota. 6 Volvo.
Bodies: 1 Berkhof. 2 Caetano. 2 Duple. 1 Irizar. 1 Mercedes. 1 Plaxton. 2 Van Hool.
Ops incl: excursions & tours, private hire, school contracts.
Livery: White/Green.

CROWN COACHES [WC] [coach]

35 DANDIES DRIVE, EASTWOOD, LEIGH-ON-SEA SS9 5R4.
Tel/Fax: 01702 420201.
Owners: T. Cox, P. Cox.
Fleet: 8 - 3 coach, 1 midicoach, 4 minibus.
Chassis: 1 Bedford. 1 Bova. 1 DAF. 4 Iveco.
Bodies: 1 Bova. 4 Carlyle. 1 Duple. 1 Ikarus.
Ops incl: local bus services, excursions & tours, private hire.
ivery: Silver/Red/Orange/Grey stripes.
Ticket System: Wayfarer.

CRUSADER HOLIDAYS
[WC] [food] [A/C] [coach]

CRUSADER BUSINESS PARK, CLACTON-ON-SEA CO15 4HP
Tel: 01255 425453
Fax: 01255 222683
Web site: www.crusader-holidays.co.uk
Ops incl: excursions & tours, continental tours

CUNNINGHAM CARRIAGE COMPANY
[WC] [coach] [food] [A/C] [key]

THE CARRIAGE HOUSE, FOBBING ROAD, CORRINGHAM SS17 9BG
Tel: 01375 676578.
Fax: 01375 679719.
Prop: Pat Cunningham **Junior Ptnr:** Sarah Cunningham
Fleet: 1 coach.
Chassis: 1 Scania.
Bodies: 1 Irizar.
Ops incl: private hire, express.
Livery: White
Ticket System: Setright.

*DONS COACHES DUNMOW LTD
[WC] [A/C]

PARSONAGE DOWNS, GREAT DUNMOW CM6 2AT
Tel: 01371 872644
Dirs: D T Hale S D Harvey **Man:** W H Cooper
Fleet: 20 - 6 double-deck bus, 14 coach.
Chassis: 12 Dennis. 6 Leyland. 2 Toyota.
Bodies: Alexander. Duple. Marcopolo. Neoplan.
Ops incl: private hire, continental tours, school contracts.

EDS MINIBUS & COACH HIRE

257 PRINCESS MARGARET ROAD, EAST TILBURY RM18 8SB
Tel/Fax: 01375 858049
Props: E Sammons, Mrs S Sammons
Fleet: 2 - 1 coach, 1 minibus.
Chassis/Body: MAN/Algarve
Ops incl: Private hire, excursions & tours

ENSIGNBUS COMPANY
[bus] [coach] [bus] [R24] [key]

PURFLEET INDUSTRIAL PARK, JULIETTE WAY, PURFLEET RM15 4YA
Tel: 01708 865656.
Fax: 01708 864340.
E-mail: sales@ensignbus.com
Web-site: www.ensignbus.com
Fleetname: Ensignbus.
Chman: Peter Newman. **Ops Dir:** Ross Newman. **Eng Dir:** Brian Longley.
Fleet: 19 - 16 double-deck bus, 2 single-deck bus, 1 articulated bus.
Chassis: 1 AEC. 1 Daimler. 1 Leyland-DAB. 2 Leyland National. 16 MCW.
Bodies: 1 Leyland-DAB. 2 Leyland National. 1 Park Royal. 16 MCW. 1 Weymann.
Ops incl: private hire.
Livery: Blue/Silver
Ticket System: Almex.
Also owns City Sightseeing, Stratford Blue.

EXCALIBUR COACH TRAVEL [coach] [WC] [key]

44 MOUNTVIEW CRESCENT, ST LAWRENCE BAY, SOUTHMINSTER CM0 7NR

Tel: 01621 779980
Fax: 01621 778928
E-mail: info@excaliburcoach.co.uk
Web site: www.excaliburcoach.co.uk
Prop: Trevor Wynn
Fleet: 4 - 2 coach, 1 midicoach, 1 minicoach.
Chassis: 1 DAF. 1 Iveco. 1 Leyland. 1 Talbot.
Bodies: 1 Caetano. 1 Plaxton. 1 LAG. 1 Talbot.
Ops incl: private hire, school contracts, excursions and tours.
Livery: White with Burgundy/Grey

*EXCEL PASSENGER LOGISTICS LTD

AIRWAYS HOUSE, FIRST AVENUE, STANSTED AIRPORT NORTH CM24 1RY
Tel: 01279 681800
Fax: 01279 681900
E-mail: excelcoaches@hotmail.com
Man Dir: Graham Hayden **Fin Dir**: Lyn Watson
Fleet: 24 - 4 double-deck bus, 6 single-deck bus, 8 coach, 1 open-top bus, 9 midibus, 1 minibus, 1 minicoach.
Chassis: 2 Leyland. 11 Mercedes. 2 Scania. 14 Volvo.
Bodies: include: 6 Carlyle. 2 Irizar. 2 MCW. 8 Plaxton.
Ops incl: local bus services, private hire.

FARGO COACHLINES

ALLVIEWS, SCHOOL ROAD, RAYNE, BRAINTREE CM7 8SS
Tel: 01376 321817
Fax: 01376 551236
E-mail: fargocoachlines@btconnect.com
Prop: L J Smith
Fleet: 30 - 12 double-deck bus, 11 single-deck coach, 2 double-deck coach, 4 midicoach, 1 minicoach.
Chassis: 3 DAF. 2 Daimler. 4 Dennis. 1 Freight Rover. 5 Leyland. 5 Mercedes. 2 Optare. 8 Scania.
Bodies: 5 Bova. 1 Irizar. 4 Leyland. 2 Optare. 1 Plaxton. 5 Van Hool. 2 other. 1 LDV Convoy.
Ops incl: private hire, school contracts.
Livery: White

FERRERS COACHES LTD

117B HULLBRIDGE ROAD, SOUTH WOODHAM FERRERS CM3 5LL
Tel: 01245 320456.
Dir: A. Read, G. Read.
Fleet: 4 - 2 coach, 2 minibus.
Chassis: 2 Dennis. 1 Ford Transit. 1 Freight Rover.
Ops incl: excursions & tours, private hire, school contracts.

FIRST IN ESSEX

STAPLEFORD CLOSE, NEW WRITTLE STREET, CHELMSFORD CM2 0SD
Tel: 01245 256159
Fax: 01245 492763
Dir & Gen Man: Steve Smith
Fleet: 180 - double-deck bus, single-deck bus, midibus, minibus.
Chassis: Dennis. Leyland. Mercedes-Benz. 11 Optare. Scania.
Bodies: ECW. Leyland. Optare. Plaxton. Wright.
Ops incl: local bus service, school contracts, private hire, express.
Livery: White/Blue/Magenta
Ticket System: Wayfarer

*FORDS COACHES

THE GARAGE, FAMBRIDGE ROAD, ALTHORNE CM3 6BZ
Tel: 01621 740326
Fax: 01621 742781
E-mail: info@fordscoaches.co.uk
Web site: www.fordscoaches.co.uk
Prop: Anthony A W Ford **Ch Eng**: Anthony Ford
Fleet: 25 - 10 double-deck bus, 11 coach, 2 double-deck coach, 2 midicoach.
Chassis: 4 Bedford. 1 Bova. 2 Bristol. 1 DAF. 3 Daimler. 6 Dennis. 2 Iveco. 4 Leyland. 1 MAN. 1 Mercedes. 1 Scania.
Bodies: 2 Berkhof. 1 Bova. 2 Caetano. 1 Duple. 6 ECW. 1 Jonckheere. 1 Mellor. 3 Northern Counties. 2 Plaxton. 3 Van Hool. 1 Indcar.
Ops incl: local bus services, school contracts, excursions & tours, private hire.
Ticket System: Wayfarer/Setright

GATWICK FLYER LTD

DANES ROAD, ROMFORD RM7 0HL
Tel: 01708 730555
Fax: 01708 751231
Web site: www.gatwickflyer.co.uk
Fleetnames: Gatwick Flyer, Avon Coaches
Fleet: 15 - 6 coach, 9 minicoach.
Ops incl: private hire, express.

*GENIAL TRAVEL

43 PEACE ROAD, STANWAY, COLCHESTER CO3 0HL.
Tel/Fax: 01206 571513
Prop: Trevor Brookes
Fleet: 1 coach.
Chassis: 1 DAF
Body: 1 Van Hool
Ops incl: excursions & tours, private hire.
Livery: White/Blue/Yellow.

*PETER GODWARD COACHES

4 EDWIN HALL VIEW, SOUTH WOODHAM FERRERS CM3 5QL
Tel: 01268 591834
Fax: 01268 591835
Prop: Peter Godward

Fleet: 12 - 8 single-deck coach, 1 double-deck coach, 1 midibus, 2 minicoach.
Chassis: 1 Ford Transit. 1 Mercedes-Benz. 6 Irisbus. 6 Ivecc. 1 LDV. 1 Scania.
Ops incl: school contracts, excursions & tours, private hire, express, continental tours.

*GOLDEN BOY COACHES (JETSIE LTD)

See Hertfordshire

GOODWIN'S COACHES

ALWYNN, LONDON ROAD, BLACK NOTLEY, BRAINTREE CM7 8QQ
Tel: 01376 321096
Prop: A. M. Goodwin. **Sec**: I. B. Goodwin.
Fleet: 6 - 5 coach, 1 minibus.
Chassis: 3 Bedford. 2 Volvo.
Bodies: 1 Berkhof. 4 Plaxton. 1 Crystal.
Ops incl: excursions & tours, private hire.
Livery: White/Blue/Grey stripes.

GRAHAM'S

19 CHURCH ROAD, KELVEDON CO5 9JH
Tel: 01376 570150.
Fax: 01376 570657
Prop: G. Ellis.
Livery: White/Blue.

HAILSTONE TRAVEL

82 BRACKLEY CRESCENT, BASILDON SS13 1RA
Tel: 01268 550635
E-mail: info@hailstonetravel.co.uk
Web site: www.hailstonetravel.co.uk
Dir: Lawrence Hailstone. **Dir**: Tina Hailstone.
Fleet: 5 minicoach.
Chassis: 5 Mercedes.
Ops incl: school contracts, private hire.

HARRIS COACHES

MANOR ROAD WEST THURROCK RM20 4EH
Tel: 01708 864911
Fax: 01708 865715
Chmn: F. W. Harris. **Man Dir**: F. D. Harris.
Dirs: N. S. Harris, D. J. Harris, D. E. Harris.
Gen Man: J. Turner. **Fleet Eng**: R. Littlefield.
Fleet: 15 - 12 coach, 2 double-deck coach, 1 midicoach.
Chassis: 9 DAF. 3 Neoplan. 2 Volvo.
Bodies: 3 Neoplan. 2 Plaxton. 6 Van Hool. 3 Ikarus.
Ops incl: excursions & tours, private hire, continental tours.
Livery: Blue/Green.
Ticket System: Wayfarer 3/Wayfarer Graphics.

IMPERIAL BUS CO LTD

FROG ISLAND, FERRY LANE, RAINHAM RM13 9YN
Tel: 01708 550320
Man Dir: M Biddel
Fleet: 37 - 27 double-deck bus, 9 single-deck bus, 1 coach

- Air conditioning
- Vehicles suitable for disabled
- Coach(es) with galley facilities
- Coach(es) with toilet facilities
- Seat belt-fitted vehicles
- Recovery service available (not 24 hr)
- R24 24hr recovery service
- Replacement vehicle available
- Toilet-drop facilities available
- Vintage vehicle(s) available
- Open top vehicle(s)

Livery: Green.

*HEDINGHAM & DISTRICT OMNIBUSES LTD

WETHERSFIELD ROAD, SIBLE HEDINGHAM CO9 3LB
Tel: 01787 460621
Fax: 01787 262852
Fleetname: Hedingham
Man Dir: R J MacGregor **Dir**: D R MacGregor
Fleet: 104 - double-deck bus, single-deck bus, coach.
Chassis: 26 Bristol. 10 Dennis. 35 Leyland. 33 Volvo.
Bodies: 11 Alexander. 1 Duple. 37 ECW. 1 East Lancs. 8 Leyland. 2 Northern Counties. 37 Plaxton. 2 Transbus. 1 Willowbrook. 2 Wright.
Ops incl: local bus services, school contracts, excursions & tours, private hire.
Livery: Red/Cream.
Ticket System: Wayfarer 3.

*KINGS COACHES

364 LONDON ROAD, STANWAY, COLCHESTER CO3 8LT
Tel: 01206 210332
Fax: 01206 213861
E-mail: kings-coaches@fsnet.co.uk
Web site: www.kings-coaches.co.uk
Prop: Andrew B Cousins
Fleet: 7 single-deck coach.
Chassis: 7 Bova.
Bodies: 7 Bova.
Ops incl: excursions & tours, private hire, continental tours.
Livery: Green/Cream

KIRBYS COACHES

PRINCESS ROAD, RAYLEIGH SS6 8HR.
Tel: 01268 777777.
Fax: 01702 202555.
Prop: Edward Kirby, Elizabeth A Kirby.
Fleet: 9 coach.
Chassis/bodies: 9 Setra.
Ops incl: excursions & tours, private hire, continental tours.
Livery: Multi Lilac/Turquoise.

LEE-ROY COACHES

58 LIME GROVE, DODDINGHURST, BRENTWOOD CM15 0QY.
Tel: 01277 636110.
Fax: 01277 224836.
Owners: M. Neal, Ms T. Tyrill, L. Scott.
Fleet: 3 - 1 coach, 1 midicoach, 1 minicoach.
Chassis: Leyland, Mercedes.
Bodies: Caetano, Mercedes.
Ops incl: local bus services, school contracts, private hire.
Livery: White.

LINKFAST LTD T/A S&M COACHES

93 ROSEBERRY AVENUE, BENFLEET SS7 4JF.
Tel/Fax: 01268 795763.

Essex

Props: B. W. Smith (Ch Eng), W. N. May (Sec).
Fleet: 10 - 9 double-deck bus, 1 coach.
Chassis: Daimler, Leyland.
Bodies: ECW, Northern Counties, Park Royal, Plaxton.
Ops incl: school contracts, private hire.
Livery: Mixed.

LODGE COACHES

THE GARAGE, HIGH EASTER, CHELMSFORD CM1 4QT
Tel: 01245 231262
Fax: 01245 231825
E-mail: lodgecoaches@btconnect.com
Web site: www.lodgecoaches.co.uk
Dirs: R C Lodge, A D Lodge, C J Lodge.
Fleet: 10 - 10 coach, 1 midicoach, 3 minibus, 1 minicoach, 1 vintage
Chassis: 3 Bedford. 1 Ford Transit. 3 Mercedes. 8 Scania. 1 Toyota.
Bodies: 1 Caetano, 2 Carlyle, 3 Duple. 1 Plaxton. 7 Van Hool, 2 other.
Ops incl: local bus services, school contracts, excursions & tours, private hire, continental tours.
Livery: Blue/Cream

MIKES COACHES

THE GRANARY, PIPPS HILL ROAD NORTH, CRAYS HILL, BASILDON CM11 2UJ.
Tel: 01268 525900.
Fax: 01268 453654.
Ptnrs: M. Orphan, D. Orphan, P. Brown.
Fleet: 6 - 5 coach, 1 midicoach.
Chassis: 2 Bedford. 1 DAF. 3 Volvo.
Bodies: 5 Plaxton. 1 Van Hool.
Ops incl: local bus services, school contracts, private hire.

W. H. NELSON (COACHES) LTD

THE COACH STATION, BRUCE GROVE, WICKFORD SS11 8BZ.
Tel: 01268 767870. .
Fleetname: Nelsons Independent Bus Services.
Livery: Yellow.

OLYMPIAN COACHES LTD

UNIT 9, BURNT MILL INDUSTRIAL ESTATE, ELIZABETH WAY, HARLOW CM20 2HT.
Tel: 01279 868868.
Fax: 01279 868867.
Dirs: C. Marino. **Co Sec**: Mrs D. K. Higgins.
Ops Dir: B. Gunton.
Fleet: 5 - 4 coach, 1 double-deck coach.
Chassis: 2 Bova. 2 DAF. 2 Leyland. 1 MAN. 1 Setra.
Ops incl: local bus services, school contracts, excursions & tours, private hire, continental tours.

P & M COACHES

74 CHURCHEND LANE, WICKFORD SS11 7JG.
Tel: 01268 763616.

PHILLIPS COACHES

117B HULLBRIDGE ROAD, SOUTH WOODHAM FERRERS CM3 5LL.
Tel/Fax: 01245 323039.
Prop: L. Phillips.
Fleet: 3 - 2 coach, 1 minibus.
Chassis: 1 Freight Rover. 2 Volvo.
Bodies: Plaxton. Van Hool.
Ops incl: excursions & tours, private hire, school contracts.
Livery: Cream/Maroon.

REGAL BUSWAYS

LANDVIEW, ONGAR ROAD, COOKSMILL GREEN, CHELMSFORD CM1 3SR
Tel: 01702 291001
Ops incl: local bus services, school contracts.
Livery: Maroon/White

*RELIANCE LUXURY COACHES

54 BROOK ROAD, BENFLEET SS7 5JF
Tel/Fax: 01268 758426
Prop: Martyn J Titchen
Fleet: 4
Chassis: 1 Dennis. 1 Leyland. 2 Scania.
Bodies: 1 Berkhof. 1 ECW. 2 Van Hool.
Ops incl: excursions & tours, private hire, school contracts.
Livery: Yellow/White/Orange/Red.

STAGECOACH EAST LONDON

See London.

STALLION COACHES

STACEYS FARM BUNGALOW, BROOMFIELD, CHELMSFORD CM1 7HF.
Tel/Fax: 01245 443500.
Ptnrs: D. A. Brewster, Miss J. C. Pinkerton.
Fleet: 2 midicoach.
Chassis: 1 Mercedes. 1 Toyota.
Bodies: 1 Caetano. 1 Reeve Burgess.
Ops incl: school contracts, private hire.

STAN'S COACHES

THE COACH-HOUSE, BECKINGHAM ROAD, GREAT TOTHAM, MALDON CM9 8DY.
Tel: 01621 891959.
Fax: 01621 891365.
Prop: S. J. Porter.
Fleet: 6 - 5 coach, 1 minibus.
Chassis: 1 Bedford. 3 Bova. 1 Mercedes. 1 Volvo.
Bodies: 3 Bova. 1 Duple. 1 Mercedes. 1 Plaxton.
Ops incl: excursions & tours, private hire, continental tours.
Livery: White with Blue/Grey stripes.

*STEPHENSONS OF ESSEX LTD

RIVERSIDE INDUSTRIAL ESTATE, SOUTH STREET, ROCHFORD SS4 1BS

Tel: 01702 541511
Fax: 01702 549461
Web site:
www.stephensonsofessex.com
E-mail:
sales@stephensonsofessex.com
Man Dir: W Hiron **Fin Dir**: L Watson
Fleet: 28 - 13 double-deck bus, 7 coach, 1 double-deck coach, 2 open-top bus, 5 midibus.
Chassis: 1 Bristol. 5 Dennis. 15 Leyland. 7 Volvo.
Bodies: 16 ECW. 8 Plaxton. 4 Transbus.
Ops incl: local bus services, school contracts, private hire, express.
Livery: White/Green
Ticket System: Wayfarer

SWALLOW COACH CO LTD
wc 🎫 R ✓

RAINHAM HOUSE, MANOR WAY, RAINHAM RM13 8RE.
Tel: 01708 630555.
Fax: 01708 555135.
Chmn: D. R. Webb. **Man Dir**: K. I. Webb.
Sec: Mrs. S. D. Webb.
Fleet: 26 - 17 coach. 5 midicoach. 4 minicoach.
Chassis: 1 DAF. 1 Dennis. 1 Ford. 1 Ford Transit. 3 Freight Rover. 3 Leyland. 1 MAN. 2 Mercedes. 1 Setra. 1 Toyota. 11 Volvo.
Bodies: 5 Caetano. 1 Carlyle. 4 Jonckheere. 2 Mercedes. 6 Plaxton. 1 Setra. 2 Van Hool. **Ops incl**: Private hire.
Livery: Various.

TOWN & COUNTRY TRAVEL
ASKEW HOUSE, ASKEW LANE, GRAYS RM17 5XR
Tel: 01375 3999388
Ptnrs: B. Waters.
Livery: Light/Dark Blue

T. F. MINI COACHES 🎫
1 SCRATTONS TERRACE, RIPPLE ROAD, BARKING IG11 0TY.
Tel: 020 8593 6205.
Fax: 020 8592 7182.
Man Dir: T. Farrugia.
Fleet: 7 midicoach.
Chassis: 7 Renault.
Ops incl: excursions & tours, private hire, airport transfer.

TRUSTLINE SERVICES LTD
🎫 wc
See Hertfordshire

VICEROY OF ESSEX LTD
wc 🎫 🍽 /c ✓ R

12 BRIDGE STREET, SAFFRON WALDEN CB10 1BU.
Tel: 01799 508010.
Fax: 01799 506106.
Email:
enquiries@viceroycoaches.co.uk
Web site: www.viceroycoaches.co.uk
Dir: A. Moore. **Dir/Chief Eng**: S. Moore.
Fleet: 12 - 5 coach, 2 single-deck bus, 2 double-deck coach. 1 midibus. 2 minibus.
Chassis: 1 Bedford. 1 Dennis, 1 Ford Transit, 1 Freight Rover, 2 Mercedes, 2 Neoplan. 2 Setra, 3 Volvo.
Bodies: 2 Duple. 1 Jonckheere. 2 Plaxton. 1 Mercedes, 2 Setra. 1 Van Hool.

Ops incl: local bus services, school contracts, excursions & tours, private hire.
Livery: Blue/White.
Ticket System: Wayfarer 2.

*WALDEN TRAVEL LTD
🎫 /c ✓

126 THAXTED ROAD, SAFFRON WALDEN CB11 3BJ
Tel/Fax: 01799 516878
Man Dir: P B Blanchard **Non-exec Dirs**: J M Wilson, D C Grimmett, J N Raynham
Fleet: 7 - 5 coach, 1 midibus, 1 midicoach.
Chassis: 3 Dennis. 1 Leyland. 2 Mercedes. 1 Volvo
Bodies: 1 Duple. 1 Jonckheere. 5 Plaxton.
Ops incl: local bus services, school contracts, excursions & tours, private hire.
Livery: White
Ticket System: AEG

WEST'S COACHES LTD
198/200 HIGH ROAD, WOODFORD GREEN IG8 9EF
Tel: 020 8504 9747
Fax: 020 8559 1085
Man Dir: R West
Fleet: 16 coach.
Ops incl: excursions & tours, private hire, school contracts.
Livery: White with red/blue stripes

GLOUCESTERSHIRE

ALEXCARS LTD
♿ wc 🎫 /c

LOVE LANE INDUSTRIAL ESTATE, CIRENCESTER GL7 1YG
Tel: 01285 653985
Fax: 01285 652964
E-mail: rod@alexcars.co.uk
Man Dir: Rod Hibberd **Dirs**: Jenny Jarvis, Barbara Hibberd **Tran Man**: Will Jarvis **Co Sec**: Glyn Daye **Ch Eng**: Steve Hall
Fleet: 20 - 1 single-deck bus, 13 coach, 3 midicoach, 3 minicoach.
Chassis: 1 Bedford. 11 Dennis. 3 MAN. 2 Scania. 3 Toyota.
Bodies: 1 Berkhof. 5 Caetano. 1 Duple. 3 Irizar. 1 Noge. 3 Plaxton. 3 Wadham Stringer. 3 Marco Polo.
Ops incl: local bus services, school contracts, excursions & tours, private hire, continental tours.
Livery: Duo Blue
Ticket System: Almex

*K. W. BEARD LTD
wc 🎫 🍽 ✓ T

VALLEY ROAD, CINDERFORD GL14 2PD
Tel: 01594 823031
Fax: 01594 825965
E-mail:
beardscoaches.co@btconnect.com
Man Dir: David K Beard **Ch Eng**: Andrew Baker **Co Sec**: Megan Beard.
Fleet: 10 - 9 coach, 1 midicoach.
Chassis: 1 Bedford. 2 Bova. 2 DAF. 2 Leyland. 1 Mercedes. 2 Volvo.
Bodies: 2 Bova. 1 Duple. 1 Jonckheere. 4 Plaxton. 1 Van Hool. 1 Onyx.
Ops incl: local bus services, school contracts, excursions & tours, private hire.
Livery: White/Blue
Ticket System: Setright.

B. E. W. BEAVIS/BEAVIS HOLIDAYS wc 🎫 /c
BUSSAGE GARAGE, BUSSAGE, STROUD GL6 8BA

Tel: 01453 882297
Fax: 01453 731019
E-mail:
beavisholidays@btopenworld.com
Props/Ptnrs: Brian Beavis, Anita Baxter
Ch Eng: Chris Beavis
Fleet: 8 - 5 coach, 1 midicoach, 1 minicoach, 1 minibus.
Chassis: 1 DAF. 4 Neoplan. 1 Scania. 1 Toyota. 1 Volkswagen.
Bodies: 1 Caetano, 1 Irizar, 4 Neoplan. 1 Volkswagen. 1 EOS.
Ops incl: excursions & tours, private hire, school contracts, continental tours.
Livery: Gold/Orange/Red/Yellow.

BENNETT'S COACHES
EASTERN AVENUE, GLOUCESTER GL4 7LP.
Tel: 01452 527809.
Fax: 01452 384448.
Prop: P. & R. Bennett. **Ch Eng**: R. Bennett.
Gen Man: P. Bennett.
Fleet: 24 - 6 double-deck bus, 18 coach.
Chassis: 6 Bristol. 12 DAF. 4 Ford. 2 Leyland.

/c	Air conditioning
♿	Vehicles suitable for disabled
🍽	Coach(es) with galley facilities
wc	Coach(es) with toilet facilities
🎫	Seat belt-fitted vehicles
R	Recovery service available (not 24 hr)
R24	24hr recovery service
✓	Replacement vehicle available
T	Toilet-drop facilities available
🚌	Vintage vehicle(s) available
🚐	Open top vehicle(s)

Bodies: 3 Duple. 6 ECW. 12 Plaxton. 3 Van Hool.
Ops incl: local bus services, excursions & tours, private hire, continental tours.
Livery: Blue/Grey/Orange.

*JAMES BEVAN (LYDNEY) LTD

THE BUS STATION, HAMS ROAD, LYDNEY GL15 5PE
Tel/Fax: 01594 842859
E-mail: bevanbus@tiscali.co.uk
Fleetname: James Bevan
Man Dir: J A Bevan **Co Sec/Dir:** J G Bevan.
Fleet: 9 - 1 single-deck bus, 6 coach, 2 midicoach.
Chassis: 3 Dennis. 1 MAN. 1 Optare. 4 Volvo.
Bodies: 1 Caetano. 1 Optare. 3 Plaxton. 1 Sunsundegui. 3 Wadham Stringer.
Ops incl: local bus services, school contracts, excursions & tours, private hire.
Livery: Silver
Ticket System: Setright/Wayfarer

*CASTLEWAYS LTD

CASTLE HOUSE, GREET ROAD, WINCHCOMBE GL54 5PU
Tel: 01242 603715
Fax: 01242 604454
Web site: www.castleways.co.uk
Man Dir: John Fogarty **Co Sec:** Rowena McCubbin **Ch Eng:** Trevor Wood
Fleet: 12 - 2 single-deck bus, 9 coach, 1 midicoach
Chassis: 1 Dennis. 2 Leyland. 8 Mercedes. 1 Toyota.
Bodies: 1 Caetano. 1 Mercedes. 3 Plaxton. 6 Setra. 1 Transbus.
Ops incl: local bus services, private hire.
Livery: Blue/Silver
Ticket System: Wayfarer

*COTTRELLS COACHES

MILL END, MITCHELDEAN GL17 0HP
Tel: 01594 542224
Fax: 01594 542740
Prop: Edgar R Cottrell
Fleet: 12 - 4 double-deck bus, 2 single-deck bus, 5 coach, 1 double-deck coach
Chassis: 1 Dennis. 4 Leyland. 4 MCW. 3 Volvo.
Bodies: 1 Alexander. 1 Duple. 4 MCW. 5 Plaxton. 1 Wadham Stringer.

*EAGLE LINE TRAVEL

ANDOVERSFORD TRADING ESTATE, ANDOVERSFORD, CHELTENHAM GL54 4LB
Tel: 01242 820535
Fax: 01242 820637
E-mail: brian@eaglelinetravel.co.uk
Web site: www.eaglelinetravel.co.uk
Man Dirs: BrianDavis Martin Davis Wayne Hodge **Ch Eng:** Tony Mezzone
Fleet: 22 - 10 coach, 2 double-deck coach, 2 midibus, 4 midicoach, 2 minicoach, 2 minibus.
Chassis: 2 DAF. 2 Dennis. 4 Ford Transit. 6 Mercedes. 1 Neoplan. 1 Scania. 1 Setra.1 Toyota. 5 Volvo.
Bodies: 2 Autobus. 2 Berkhof. 1 Caetano.

2 Mercedes. 4 Ford Transit. 1 Neoplan. 2 Plaxton. 6 Van Hool. 2 VW.
Ops incl: school contracts, excursions & tours, private hire, continental tours.
Livery: Dark Blue/Silver/Silver Blue

*EBLEY COACHES LTD

UNIT 27, NAILSWORTH MILLS ESTATE, AVENING ROAD, NAILSWORTH GL6 0BS
Tel/Fax: 01453 839333
Dirs: C C Levitt, G A Jones.
Fleet: 19 - 6 double-deck bus, 7 coach, 5 minibus, 1 minicoach
Chassis: 6 Bristol. 5 DAF. 1 Leyland. 1 MAN. 6 Mercedes.
Bodies: 4 Alexander. 1 Duple. 6 ECW. 1 Plaxton. 2 Reeve Burgess. 5 Van Hool.
Ops incl: local bus services, school contracts, excursions & tours, private hire, continental tours.

DAVID FIELD

WHEATSTONE HOUSE, WATERY LANE, NEWENT GL18 1PY
Tel: 01531 820979
Dir: David Field.
Fleet: 8 - 6 coach, 2 midicoach.
Chassis: 1 Bedford. 1 DAF. 1 Iveco. 1 Leyland. 1 Setra. 1 Toyota.
Ops incl: school contracts,private hire.
Livery: Black/White.
Ticket System: Setright.

GRINDLES COACHES LTD

4 DOCKHAM ROAD, CINDERFORD GL14 2DD.
Tel: 01594 822110.
Fax: 01594 823189.
Man Dir: P. R. Grindle. **Co Sec:** W. H. R. Grindle.
Fleet: 7 coach.
Chassis: 3 Bedford. 1 Bova. 3 DAF.
Bodies: 1 Bova. 5 Plaxton. 1 Van Hool.
Ops incl: local bus services, private hire.

*COLIN HOSKINS MINI COACHES

4 COTSWOLD AVENUE, EASTINGTON, STONEHOUSE GL10 3AR
Tel: 01453 825243
Fax: 01453 825243
Dirs: C. J. Hoskins, B. R. Davis.
Fleet: 3 - 1 midicoach, 2 minibus.
Chassis: 2 Mercedes, 1 LDV.
Bodies: local bus services, school contracts, private hire
Livery: Green/White
Ticket system: Setright

MARCHANTS COACHES LTD

61 CLARENCE STREET, CHELTENHAM GL50 3LB
Tel: 01242 257714
Fax: 01242 251360
Recovery: 01242 226267
E-mail: info@marchants-coaches.com
Web site: www.marchants-coaches.com
Man Dir: Roger Marchant **Dir:** Richard Marchant
Fleet: 24 - 6 double-deck bus, 3 single-deck

bus, 12 coach, 2 double-deck coach, 1 midicoach.
Chassis: 4 Bristol. 2 Leyland. 1 Mercedes. 2 Neoplan. 15 Volvo.
Bodies: 6 ECW. 2 Neoplan. 15 Plaxton. 1 Van Hool.
Ops incl: local bus services, school contracts, excursions & tours, private hire, continental tours.
Livery: Red/Gold
Ticket System: Setright

*ROVER EUROPEAN TRAVEL

THE COACH HOUSE, HORSLEY, STROUD GL6 0PU
Tel: 01453 832121
Fax: 01453 832722
Dir: David Hand
Fleet: 8 coach
Chassis: 1 Bedford. 7 Bova.
Ops incl: school contracts, excursions & tours, private hire, continental tours.
Livery: Blue/Cream/Orange.

*STAGECOACH WEST

3RD FLOOR, 65 LONDON ROAD, GLOUCESTER GL1 3HF
Tel: 01452 418630
Fax: 01452 304857
Web site: www.stagecoachbus.com
Man Dir: Ian Manning **Comm Dir:** Rupert Cox **Eng Dir:** Peter Sheldon **Ops Dir:** Sholto Thomas
Fleet: 209 - double-deck bus, single-deck bus, coach, midibus, minibus.
Chassis: 24 Leyland. 13 Mercedes. 118 Transbus. 54 Volvo.
Bodies: 140 Alexander. 1 ECW. 4 Marshall. 5 Northern Counties. 3 Optare. 33 Plaxton. 11 Roe. 4 Wright.
Ops incl: local bus services.
Livery: Stagecoach
Ticket System: Wayfarer

*SWANBROOK BUS

GOLDEN VALLEY, STAVERTON, CHELTENHAM GL51 0TE
Tel: 01452 712386
Fax: 01452 859217
E-mail: enquiries@swanbrook.co.uk
Web site: www.swanbrook.co.uk
Dirs: D J Thomas, K J Thomas (**Co Sec**), K J West, **Ch Eng:** G Hooper
Fleet: 33 - 12 double-deck bus, 12 single-deck bus, 5 coach, 4 midibus.
Chassis: 3 Dennis. 1 Iveco. 5 Leyland. 9 MCW. 4 Mercedes. 5 Optare. 1 Scania. 5 Volvo.
Bodies: 1 Berkof. 1 East Lancs. 1 Irizar. 2 Marshall. 9 MCW. 3 Northern Counties. 5 Optare. 5 Plaxton. 1 Dormobile. 3 Reeve Burgess. 1 UVG.
Ops incl: local bus services, school contracts.
Livery: red/Orange/Yellow
Ticket System: Wayfarer 2

F R WILLETTS & CO (YORKLEY) LTD

DEAN RISE, MAIN ROAD, PILLOWELL GL15 4QY
Tel: 01594 562511
Fax: 01594 564373

Man Dir: Geoff Willetts **Sec**: Sue Willetts
Fleet: 6 - 4 coach, 1 minicoach, 1 minibus.
Chassis: 1 Dennis. 1 Leyland. 2 Mercedes. 1 Setra. 1 Volvo.
Bodies: 1 Mercedes. 4 Plaxton. 1 Setra.
Ops incl: local bus services, school contracts, excursions & tours, private hire.
Livery: Red
Ticket System: Setright.

MAL WITTS EXECUTIVE TRAVEL 🚌 ᴬc R24 ✒
1 YEW TREE COTTAGE, BRISTOL ROAD, HARDWICK, GLOUCESTER GL2 4QZ
Tel/Fax: 01452 724072
E-mail: mal@malwittstravel.co.uk
Web site: www.malwittstravel.co.uk
Prop: Mal Witts
Fleet: 4 minicoach
Chassis: 2 Mercedes. 2 Volkswagen
Ops incl: school contracts, excursions & tours, private hire, continental tours.

GREATER MANCHESTER
(INCL: BOLTON, BURY, OLDHAM, ROCHDALE, SALFORD, TAMESIDE, WIGAN)

ADLINGTON TAXIS AND MINICOACHES ♿ R24
LODGE FARM, SANDY LANE, HORWICH BL6 6RS
Tel: 01204 697577
Prop: F. Johnson. **Sec**: Mrs D. Johnson.
Fleet: 5 - 1 coach, 1 midibus, 1 minibus, 2 minicoach.
Chassis: Dodge. Ford Transit. Freight Rover. Leyland National.
Bodies: Leyland. Leyland National. Plaxton.
Ops incl: local bus services, excursions & tours, private hire.
Livery: White with Blue/Red stripe.
Ticket System: Almex.

*ASHALL'S COACHES
♿ wc 🚌
612 ASHTON NEW ROAD, CLAYTON M11 4SG
Tel: 0161 231 7777
Fax: 0906 528 0920
Prop: D S Ashall
Fleet: 20 - 6 double-deck bus, 4 single-deck bus, 8 single-deck coach, 2 midicoach.
Chassis: 15 Dennis. 2 Mercedes. 1 Scania. 2 Volvo.
Bodies: 2 Duple. 2 Mellor. 6 Northern Counties. 2 Plaxton. 2 Transbus. 6 Wadham Stringer.
Ops incl: local bus services, school contracts, private hire.
Livery: Red
Ticket system: Wayfarer 2

ATHERTON BUS COMPANY
33 LANDEDMANS, WESTHOUGHTON BL5 2QJ.
Tel: 01942 791535
Prop: P. G. Hughes.

BATTERSBY'S COACHES
wc 🚌 ᴬc
73 BRIDGEWATER ROAD, WALKDEN M28 3AF
Tel/Fax: 0161 790 2842
Dirs: R W Griffiths, S. J. Griffiths
Fleet: 3 coach.
Chassis: 1 Leyland. 2 Setra.
Ops incl: private hire, school contracts.

*BLUE BUS & COACH SERVICES LTD
See Lancashire

BLUEBIRD BUS & COACH
ALEXANDER HOUSE, GREENGATE, MIDDLETON M24 1RU
Tel: 0161 653 1900
Fax: 0161 653 6602
Web site: www.bluebirdbus.co.uk
Chmn: T. A. Dunstan **Gen Man**: Michael Dunstan. **Ptnr**: Moira Dunstan
Fleet: 32 - 2 double-deck bus, 22 single-deck bus, 2 coach, 6 minibus.
Chassis: 20 Dennis, 2 Iveco, 4 Leyland, 4 Mercedes, 2 Scania.
Bodies: 2 Caetano, 9 East Lancs, 2 Marshall, 11 Plaxton, 8 Wright.
Ops incl: local bus services.
Livery: two tone Blue.
Ticket System: ERG

BMT (MAYFIELD)
🚌 wc ᴬc ✒
THE COACH COMPOUND, LOWER GREEN LANE, ASTLEY M29 7JZ
Tel/Fax: 01942 884844
Owner: W B Maye
Fleet: 10 coach
Chassis: 5 Leyland. 1 MAN. 4 Volvo
Ops incl: excursions & tours, private hire, school contracts.
Livery: White/Green

*A & H BOOTH LTD
🚌 🚐 ✒
GROSVENOR GARAGE, DOWSON ROAD, HYDE SK14 5BN
Tel: 0161 368 2413
Tel(24hr): 0161 430 2032
Dirs: J Mycock, D Mycock
Fleet: 3 - 2 coach, 1 minicoach.
Chassis: 1 DAF. 1 Ford. 1 LDV.
Bodies: include 1 Caetano. 1 Plaxton.
Ops incl: excursions & tours, private hire, continental tours.

R BULLOCK & CO (TRANSPORT) LTD ♿ 🚌
COMMERCIAL GARAGE, STOCKPORT ROAD, CHEADLE SK8 2AG
Tel: 0161 428 5265.
Fax: 0161 428 9074.
E-mail: bullockscoaches@talk21.com
Web site: www.bullockscoaches.co.uk
Fleet: 63 - double-deck bus, single-deck bus, coach, minibus
Livery: Red/White.

BU-VAL
UNIT 5, PARAGON INDUSTRIAL ESTATE, WALSDEN OL15 8QF
Tel: 01706 372787
Prop: M. Bull.
Livery: Red/White/Black.

LES BYWATER & SONS LTD
wc 🚌
SPARTH BOTTOMS ROAD, ROCHDALE OL11 4HT.
Tel: 01706 648573.
Man Dir: M. T. Bywater. **Dir**: N. L. Bywater.
Fleet: 3 - 1 coach, 1 midicoach, 1 minibus.
Chassis: 1 Dennis. 2 Iveco.
Bodies: 1 Duple. 2 Robin Hood.
Ops incl: private hire, school contracts.
Livery: White/Blue/Black.

CARSVILLE COACHES
wc 🚌 R
51A HIGHER ROAD, URMSTON M41 9AP
Tel: 0161 748 2698
Fax: 0161 747 2694
Dirs: S. Hughes, D. Hughes. **Ch Eng**: I. Hughes. **Co Sec**: E. Hughes.
Fleet: 10 coach.
Chassis: 5 Ford. 2 Leyland. 2 Volvo. 1 Ward. **Bodies**: 3 Duple. 7 Plaxton. 1 Van Hool.
Ops incl: private hire, school contracts.
Livery: Yellow/White.

*COACH OPTIONS
See Lancashire

ᴬc	Air conditioning	
♿	Vehicles suitable for disabled	
🍴	Coach(es) with galley facilities	
wc	Coach(es) with toilet facilities	
🚌	Seat belt-fitted vehicles	
R	Recovery service available (not 24 hr)	
R24	24hr recovery service	
✒	Replacement vehicle available	
T	Toilet-drop facilities available	
🚐	Vintage vehicle(s) available	
🚌	Open top vehicle(s)	

109

Greater Manchester

*COACHWAYS LTD
MANDALE PARK, CORPORATION ROAD, ROCHDALE OL11 4HJ
Tel: 01706 712321
Fax: 01706 632875
Web site: www.coachways.co.uk
E-mail: coachhire@coachways.co.uk
Man Dir: Edgar Oldham **Comm Dir**: Barry Drelincourt **Coach Man**: Ian Smithson
Fleet: 6 coach
Chassis: 1 Dennis. 5 Volvo.
Bodies: 3 Plaxton. 3 Sunsundegui.
Ops incl: school contracts, private hire, express.
Livery: White

CROPPER COACHES
316 BURY ROAD, TOTTINGTON BL8 3DT
Tel: 01204 885322.
Prop: L. Donnell.
Fleet: 7 minibus.
Chassis: 5 Ford Transit. 1 Freight Rover.
Ops incl: private hire, school contracts.

DAM EXPRESS
GROVE HOUSE, 27 MANOR STREET, ARDWICK GREEN M12 6HE.
Tel: 0161 273 1234.
Fax: 0161 274 4141.
Fleetname: Don Travel.
Prop/Ops Man: D. Francis.
Sales Man: W. Lee. **Co Sec**: Miss T. Wilding.
Fleet: 3 - 1 coach, 2 double-deck coach.
Ops incl: excursions & tours, private hire, express, continental tours.

DENNIS'S COACHES
UNIT 4, CHARLES STREET, DUKINFIELD SK16 4SG
Tel: 0161 339 8575
Fax: 0161 343 6561
E-mail: sales@denniscoaches.co.uk
Web site: www.denniscoaches.co.uk
Ptnr: Ray Cooper **Eng**: Graham Broadbent
Accounts: Mrs Kelly Baggot
Fleet: 49 - 6 double-deck bus, 35 single-deck bus, 1 coach, 7 midibus.
Chassis: 1 Bedford. 41 Dennis. 7 Mercedes.
Bodies: 8 East Lancs. 26 Plaxton. 17 Wright.
Ops incl: local bus services, private hire, school contracts.

*EAVESWAY TRAVEL LTD
See Greater Manchester.

ELITE SERVICES LTD
UNIT 6, ADSWOOD ROAD INDUSTRIAL ESTATE, ADSWOOD ROAD, STOCKPORT SK3 8LF.
Tel: 0161 480 0617.
Fax: 0161 480 3099.
Dirs: D. R. Nickson, A. J. Short.
Fleet: 10 - 8 coach, 2 double-deck coach.
Chassis: Ford. Leyland. Mercedes. Scania. Volvo.

Bodies: Duple. Jonckheere. Mercedes. Plaxton. Van Hool.
Ops incl: excursions & tours, private hire, continental tours, school contracts.
Livery: Silver/Blue/Purple.

FINGLAND'S COACHWAYS LTD
261 WILMSLOW ROAD, RUSHOLME M14 5LJ
Tel: 0161 224 3341
Fax: 0161 257 3154
E-mail: enquiry@finglands.co.uk.
Web site: www.finglands.co.uk.
Fleetname: Finglands
Chmn: P J S Shipp **Man Dir**: G Rayner.
Dirs: P Harrison, D Shurden **Fleet Eng**: T C Jenkins
Fleet: 55 - 41 double-deck bus, 4 single-deck bus, 10 coach.
Chassis: 2 Dennis. 53 Volvo.
Bodies: 28 Alexander, 1 Berkhof, 1 Caetano, 11 Northern Counties, 14 Plaxton, 1 Van Hool.
Ops incl: local bus services, school contracts, excursions & tours, private hire.
Livery: White with Orange/Brown/Beige stripes.
Ticket System: Wayfarer TGX150

*FIRST NORTH WEST
WALLSHAW STREET, OLDHAM OL1 3TR
Tel: 0161 627 2929
Fax: 0161 627 5845
Fleetname: First
Co Dirs: Colin Stafford (**Regional Eng Dir**), Russell Gard (**Regional Comm Dir**), Nigel Armitt (**Regional Fin Dir**).
Fleet: 1269 - 294 double-deck bus, 457 single-deck bus, 418 midibus, 18 articulated bus, 82 minibus.
Chassis: DAF. Dennis. Ford. Iveco. Leyland. MAN. MCW. Mercedes-Benz. Neoplan. Optare. Scania. Volvo.
Bodies: ECW. East Lancs. Ikarus. Leyland. Marshall. MCW. Mercedes-Benz. Optare. Transbus. Wright. Technobus.
Ops incl: local bus services, school contracts, private hire.
Livery: First - Magenta/Blue & Grey/White
Ticket System: ERG TP4004 (Manchester East and Manchester West), Almex (Potteries)
Subsidiary Companies:
First in Manchester East, Boyle Street, Cheetham, Manchester M8 8UT
First in Manchester West, Weston Street, Bolton BL3 2AW
First in Potteries, Dividy Road, Adderley Green, Stoke-on-Trent ST3 5YY

*FREEBIRD
REVERS STREET GARAGE, WOODHILL BL8 1AQ
Tel: 0161 797 6633
Fax: 08712 773214
Recovery: 0161 797 6633
E-mail: info@freebirdcoaches.co.uk
Web site: www.freebirdcoaches.co.uk
Owner: Paul Dart **Man**: Rob Dart
Fleet: 15 - 6 coach, 4 midicoach, 5 minibus.
Chassis: 1 DAF. 1 Dennis. 2 Ford Transit. 3 LDV. 4 Mercedes. 4 Volvo.
Bodies: 1 Berkhof. 3 Plaxton. 2 Van Hool. 4 Balmoral.

Ops incl: excursions & tours, private hire, school contracts, continental tours.
Livery: White with maroon writing

G P D TRAVEL
See Greater Manchester.

*HAYTON'S EXECUTIVE TRAVEL LTD
12 ACORN CLOSE, BURNAGE M19 2HS
Tel: 0161 223 3103
Fax: 0161 223 9528
Prop: Barry Hayton **Dir/Sec**: Barry A Hayton
Fleet: 17 - 3 double-deck bus, 3 single-deck bus, 10 coach, 1 midibus.
Chassis: 3 MAN. 1 Neoplan. 1 Optare. 1 Setra. 10 Volvo.
Bodies: 2 East Lancs. 2 Jonckheere. 1 Noge. 2 Optare. 4 Plaxton. 1 Setra. 4 Van Hool.
Ops incl: local bus services, school contracts, excursions & tours, private hire, express, continental tours.
Livery: White

HEALINGS INTERNATIONAL COACHES
See Lancashire

HURST'S COACHES
440 WARRINGTON ROAD, GOOSE GREEN, WIGAN WN3 6QF.
Tel: 01942 243167, 247703.
Fax: 01942 820400.
Props: A. Hurst, M. Hurst, V. Leak.
Fleet: 21 - 19 coach, 2 minicoach.
Chassis: 1 Bedford. 1 Bova. 4 DAF. 1 MAN. 2 Mercedes. 5 Scania. 4 Volvo.
Bodies: 1 Bova. 1 Caetano. 1 Duple. 2 Mercedes. 1 Plaxton. 8 Van Hool. 3 EOS. 3 Irizar. 1 Ikarus.
Ops incl: school contracts, excursions & tours, private hire.
Livery: Orange/Blue/White.

*JONES EXECUTIVE COACHES LTD
THE COACH STATION, SHARP STREET, WALKDEN M28 3LX
Tel: 0161 790 9495
Fax: 0161 790 9400
Web site: www.jonesexecutive.co.uk
E-mail: simonjones@supanet.com
Man Dir: Simon Jones **Tran Man**: Peter Wragg
Fleet: 7 - 6 coach, 1 minicoach
Chassis: 2 DAF. 2 Iveco. 1 Mercedes. 1 Scania. 1 Volvo.
Bodies: 2 Beulas. 1 Duple. 1 Mercedes. 1 Plaxton. 2 Van Hool.
Ops incl: local bus services, school contracts, private hire.
Livery: Blue/Red/Gold

*LAMBS COACHES
2A BUXTON STREET, HAZEL GROVE, STOCKPORT SK7 4BB
Tel/Fax: 0161 483 5011
E-mail: lambs139@aol.com

Dir: Geoffrey Lamb
Fleet: 7
Chassis: 6 Bova.
Bodies: include 1 Jonckheere.
Ops incl: private hire, school contracts.
Livery: Blue/White

*LENDOR MINI COACHES
17 VALLEY CLOSE, MOSSLEY OL5 0NH
Tel/Fax: 01457 832845
Prop: Leonard E Glynn
Fleet: 7 minibus.
Chassis: 2 Ford Transit. 2 Iveco. 2 Mercedes. 1 Vauxhall.
Ops incl: private hire, school contracts.

MARPLE MINI COACHES
5 GROSVENOR ROAD, MARPLE SK6 6PR.
Tel: 0161 881 9111.
Owner: G. W. Cross.
Fleet: 2 minicoach.
Chassis: Ford Transit. LDV.
Ops incl: school contracts, private hire.
Livery: White/Gold.

A MAYNE & SON LTD
ASHTON NEW ROAD, CLAYTON M11 4PD
Tel: 0161 2235 2035
Fax: 0161 231 7980
E-mail: coaches@mayne.co.uk
Web site: www.mayne.co.uk
Fleetname: Mayne of Manchester
Man Dir: S B Mayne **Dir/Gen Man**: G R Thompson **Dirs**: A A Mayne, D Mayne **Dir/Co Sec**: O Mayne **Ch Eng**: C F Pannell
Fleet: 55 - 28 double-deck bus, 8 single-deck bus, 19 coach.
Chassis: 3 Bova, 2 DAF, 15 Dennis, 1 Leyland, 29 Scania, 5 Volvo.
Bodies: 3 Bova, 21 East Lancs, 6 Irizar, 6 Marshall, 9 Northern Counties, 8 Plaxton, 2 UVG.
Ops incl: local bus services, school contracts, excursions & tours, private hire, express, continental tours.
Livery: Red/Cream

METROLINK
SERCO METROLINK, METROLINK HOUSE, QUEENS ROAD, MANCHESTER M8 0RY
Tel: 0161 205 8685
Fax: 0161 205 8699
Web site: www.gmpte.com
Man Dir: Phil Smith
Fleet: 28 - tram
Chassis: GEC Alstom
Bodies: Firema
Ops incl: tram service

OLYMPIA TRAVEL
See Lancashire

*DAVID PLATT COACHES & MINITRAVEL OF LEES
8 THE WOODS, GROTTON, OLDHAM 0L4 4LP
Tel/Fax: 0161 633 4845
Props: David Platt, Marlene J Platt
Fleet: 2 - 1 coach, 1 midicoach.
Chassis: 1 Bedford. 1 Toyota.
Bodies: 1 Caetano. 1 Plaxton.
Ops incl: private hire.
Livery: Black/Aqua on white

*ROSSENDALE TRANSPORT
See Lancashire

*SELWYNS TRAVEL
BUILDING 77, TERMINAL 2, MANCHESTER AIRPORT M90 1QX
Tel: 0161 489 9157
Fax: 0161 499 9157
E-mail: sales@selwyns.co.uk
Web site: www.selwyns.co.uk
Man Dir: Selwyn Jones **Co Sec/Acct**: Richard Williams **Fleet Eng**: Dave Yould
Sales Man: Jayne Furber **Ops Man**: Reno Peers **Human Res Man**: Chris Roach
Fleet: 15 - 3 coach, 4 midibus, 3 minicoach, 5 midicoach.
Chassis: 1 DAF. 3 Dennis. 1 Ford. 8 Mercedes. 2 Optare.
Bodies: 2 Autobus. 2 Berkhof. 1 Iveco. 3 Mercedes. 2 Optare. 3 Plaxton. 1 Transbus. 1 Van Hool.
Ops incl: local bus services, private hire.
Livery: White with Blue/Orange/Green stripes
Ticket System: Wayfarer 3

*SHEARINGS LTD
MIRY LANE, WIGAN WN3 4AG
Tel: 01942 244246
Fax: 01942 242518
Web site: www.shearingsholidays.com
Ch Exec: D J Slatcher
Fin Dir: D R Newbold **Ops Dir**: J H King
Fleet: 226 coach
Chassis: 226 Volvo.
Bodies: 52 Jonckheere, 55 Plaxton, 119 Van Hool.
Ops incl: excursions & tours, private hire, continental tours.
Livery: Miami Blue/Orange

SMITHS COACHES (MARPLE) LTD
72 CROSS LANE, MARPLE SK6 7PZ
Tel: 0161 427 2825.
Fax: 0161 449 7731.
Man Dir: K. Smith. **Co Sec**: Mrs J. Smith.
Ops Man: Mrs G. Lillis.
Fleet: 6 - 2 double-deck bus, 3 coach, 1 midibus.
Chassis: 2 Bristol. 2 Dennis. 1 Iveco. 1 Volvo.
Bodies: 1 Caetano. 2 ECW. 2 Neoplan.

Ops incl: local bus services, school contracts, excursions & tours, private hire, continental tours.
Livery: White/Orange-Rose.

SOUTH LANCS TRAVEL
UNIT 22/23, CHANTERS INDUSTRIAL ESTATE, ATHERTON M46 9BP
Tel: 01942 888893
Fax: 01942 884010
Man Dir: M L R Bott **Eng Dir**: D A Stewart
Tran Man: W Peach
Fleet: 35 - 3 double-deck bus, 20 single-deck bus, 12 midibus
Chassis: 22 Dennis. 2 Iveco. 2 Leyland. 7 Mercedes. 2 Volvo.
Bodies: 5 Alexander. 4 Duple. 3 East Lancs. 18 Plaxton. 1 UVG. 4 Wright.
Ops incl: local bus services, tram service, school contracts
Livery: Yellow/Blue
Ticket System: Wayfarer 3

*STAGECOACH MANCHESTER
HYDE ROAD, MANCHESTER M12 6JS
Tel: 0161 273 3377
Fax: 0161 276 2594
E-mail: manchester.enquiries@stagecoachbus.com
Web site: www.stagecoachbus.com
Man Dir: Mark Threapleton **Ops Dir**: Elisabeth Tasker. **Comm Dir**: Ray Cossins
Eng Dir: Darren Roe
Fleet: 623 - 304 double-deck bus, 245 single-deck bus, 22 midibus, 52 minibus.
Chassis: 159 Dennis. 100 Leyland. 105 MAN. 52 Mercedes. 5 Scania. 202 Volvo.
Bodies: 441 Alexander. 13 Duple. 114 Northern Counties. 55 Plaxton.
Ops incl: local bus services, school contracts.
Livery: Stagecoach (White/Blue/Orange)
Ticket System: ERG System 4000

STOTT'S TOURS (OLDHAM) LTD
144 LEES ROAD, OLDHAM OL4 1HT
Tel: 0161 624 4200.
Fax: 0161 628 2969.
Prop: A. Stott.
Ops incl: school contracts.
Livery: Cream/Red/Black.

TIMELINE TRAVEL
MOOR LANE, BOLTON BL1 4TD
Tel: 01204 557800
Fax: 01204 365176
E-mail: sales@timelinetravel.co.uk
Web site: www.timelinetravel.co.uk
Man Dir: Ian Longworth
Fleet: 12 - coach
Chassis: 1 Iveco. 4 Scania. 7 Volvo.
Bodies: 1 Beulas. 6 Plaxton. 5 Van Hool.
Ops incl: local bus services, tram service, school contracts, excursions & tours, private hire, express, continental tours.
Livery: Off-white/Orange/Yellow
Subsidiary Companies: also at Walsall (See West Midlands)

A/c	Air conditioning	✓	Replacement vehicle available
♿	Vehicles suitable for disabled	T	Toilet-drop facilities available
R	Recovery service available (not 24 hr)	🚌	Vintage vehicle(s) available
¶	Coach(es) with galley facilities		Open top vehicle(s)
WC	Coach(es) with toilet facilities		
R24	24hr recovery service		

VALES COACHES (MANCHESTER) LTD
49 BROUGHTON STREET, MANCHESTER M8 8AN
Tel: 0161 832 9445.
Fleetname: Vale of Manchester.
Dir: P. D. Green. **Dir/Sec**: G. L. Green
Fleet: 20 midibus.
Chassis: 20 Mercedes.
Bodies: 2 Alexander. 1 Carlyle. 13 Plaxton. 4 Reeve Burgess.
Ops incl: local bus services, school contracts, private hire.
Livery: Blue/Cream
Ticket System: Wayfarer 2

VIKING COACHES [wc]
DOCTOR FOLD FARM, DOCTOR FOLD LANE, BIRCH, HEYWOOD 0L10 2QE.
Tel: 01706 368999.
Fax: 01706 620011.
E-mail: viking@coaches76.freeserve
Web site: www.coach-day-trips
Owners: A. Warburton, Ms A. Warburton.
Fleet: 4 coach.
Chassis: Volvo. Iveco.
Bodies: Beulas. Plaxton. Van Hool.
Ops incl: excursions & tours, private hire, continental tours, school contracts.
Livery: Viking Ship.

*WRIGLEY'S COACHES LTD
4 FIDDLERS LANE, IRLAM M44 6QE
Tel: 0161 775 2414
Fax: 0161 775 1558
24hr: 07802 552415
E-mail: sales@wrigleyscoaches.com
Web site: www.wrigleyscoaches.com
Man Dir: Colin Wrigley **Co Sec/Dir**: Lesley Wrigley **Gen Man**: Alan Grice
Fleet: 10 - 1 double-deck bus, 6 coach, 2 double-deck coach, 1 midicoach.
Chassis: 1 Leyland. 4 MAN. 1 MCW. 2 Neoplan. 1 Setra. 1 Toyota.
Bodies: 1 Caetano. 1 ECW. 1 Jonckheere. 1 Leyland. MCW. 4 Neoplan. 1 Noge. 1 Plaxton. 1 Setra.
Ops incl: excursions & tours, school contracts, private hire, continental tours.
Livery: Blue/White

HAMPSHIRE

*AIRLYNX LTD
THE SYCAMORES, OAKLEY ROAD, SHIRLEY, SOUTHAMPTON SO16 4LJ
Tel: 023 8039 9078
Fax: 023 8077 7724
E-mail: airlynxbuses@hotmail.com
Web site: www.airlynx.co.uk
Man Dir: Dominic Brown **Co Sec**: Michael Rudder.
Fleet: 10 - 1 single-deck bus, 1 midicoach, 8 minicoach.
Chassis/bodies: Carlyle. Mercedes. Faro.
Ops incl: private hire, excursions & tours, school contracts, local bus services.
Livery: Blue/Yellow

ALTONIAN COACHES
MILL LANE, ALTON GU34 2QJ.
Tel: 01420 84839
Fax: 01420 84803
Dirs: G. H. Warren, R. Turner. **Chmn**: R. L. Warren. **Ch Eng**: K. Tillin. **Sec**: S. Austen.
Fleet: 16 -12 coach, 2 midicoach, 2 minibus.
Chassis: 3 Bedford. 5 Dennis. 2 Mercedes. 1 Scania. 1 Renault. 4 other.
Bodies: 1 Caetano. 3 Duple. 1 Irizar. 3 Neoplan. 1 Optare. 3 Plaxton. 1 Wadham Stringer. 3 other.
Ops incl: local bus services, school contracts, excursions & tours, private hire, continental tours.
Livery: Orange.
Ticket System: Almex.

*AMK CHAUFFUER DRIVEN
PASSFIELD BUSINESS PARK, MILL LANE, PASSFIELD, LIPHOOK GU30 7RP
Tel: 01428 751711
Fax: 01428 751677
E-mail: simon.moger@amkxl.com
Web site: www.amkxl.com
Ptnrs: Kevin Moger, Angela Moger,
Simon Moger.
Fleet: 80 - 60 minibus, 20 minicoach.
Chassis: 10 Ford Transit. 5 Mercedes. 60 Renault

AMPORT & DISTRICT COACHES LTD
EASTFIELD HOUSE, THRUXTON, ANDOVER SP11 8ED.
Tel: 01264 772307.
Fax: 01264 773020.
Chmn: P. J. Tedd. **Sec**: A. M. Tedd. **Man**: N. B. Tedd.
Fleet: 9 - 8 coach, 1 midicoach.
Chassis: 3 Mercedes. 6 Volvo.
Bodies: 1 Berkhof. 2 Jonckheere. 2 Mercedes. 3 Plaxton. 1 Van Hool.
Ops incl: excursions & tours, private hire, continental tours, school contracts.
Livery: White/Orange/Brown.

*ANGELA COACHES LTD
OAKTREE HOUSE, LOWFORD, BURSLEDON SO31 8ES
Tel: 023 8040 3170
Fax: 023 8040 6487
E-mail: info@angelacoaches.co.uk
Web site: www.angelacoaches.co.uk
Man Dir: M J Pressley **Co Sec**: Mrs H M Pressley **Ops Dir**: R J Pressley
Ch Eng: G Nichols.
Fleet: 10 - 3 coach, 1 midicoach, 6 minicoach.
Chassis: 5 Irisbus. 2 Mercedes. 3 Toyota.
Bodies: 4 Beulas. 3 Caetano. 1 Indcar. 2 Robin Hood.
Ops incl: excursions & tours, private hire, continental tours, school contracts.

BYNGS INTERNATIONAL COACHES
1B ANGERSTEIN ROAD, NORTH END, PORTSMOUTH PO2 8HJ.
Tel: 023 9266 2223
Fax: 023 9267 8464
Dirs: Paul Grant, Trevor Grant. **Fleet Eng**: John Hampton.
Fleet: 40 - 1 single-deck bus, 37 coach, 1 midicoach, 1 minicoach.
Chassis: 10 Bova. 2 DAF. 2 Dennis. 4 Leyland. 4 Mercedes. 7 Scania. 1 Toyota. 10 Volvo.
Bodies: 10 Bova. 2 DAF. 2 Dennis. 4 irizar. 2 Jonckheere. 4 mercedes. 11 Plaxton. 7 Van Hool.
Ops incl: excursions & tours, private hire, school contracts.
Livery: Silver/Brown.

A. S. BONE & SONS
LONDON ROAD, HOOK RG27 9EQ
Tel: 01256 761388, 762106
Fleetname: Newnham Coaches
Man Dir: J. E. Bone. **Co Sec**: Mrs M. Bone.
Fleet: 5 - 3 double-deck bus, 2 single-deck bus.
Chassis: 1 Bristol. 2 Daimler. 2 Leyland National.
Ops incl: private hire.
Livery: Cream/Blue.

*BRIJAN TOURS R24
THE COACH STATION, ABBEY MILL, BISHOPS WALTHAM SO32 1DH
Tel: 01489 892942
Fax: 01489 896361
E-mail: info@brijantours.com
Man Dir: Brian Botley **Co Sec**: Janet Botley
Ops Man: Brian Bedford
Ch Eng: Colin Batten
Fleet: 23 - 5 double-deck bus, 9 coach, 8 midibus, 1 midicoach.
Chassis: 2 Bristol. 1 DAF. 5 Dennis. 1 Leyland. 2 MCW. 10 Mercedes. 1 Scania. 1 Volvo.
Bodies: 1 Alexander. 3 Autobus. 1 Berkhof.

2 ECW. 1 Irizar. 1 Leyland. 2 MCW.
8 Plaxton. 1 Sunsundegui. 1 UVG. 1 Van
Hool. 1 Onyx.
Ops incl: local bus services, school
contracts, excursions & tours, private hire,
continental tours.
Livery: coaches: Cream/Red/Burgundy.
Buses: Solent Blue Line livery
Ticket System: Wayfarer.

BUDDENS COACHES

29 PREMIER WAY, ABBEY PARK,
ROMSEY SO51 9AQ
Tel: 01794 515260
Fax: 01794 512260
E-mail: sales@buddens-coaches.co.uk
Web site: www.buddens-coaches.co.uk
Chmn: A P Budden **Fin Dir**: Mrs M Michels
Ops Dir: K Harding **Ops Man**: M Connolly
Wkshp Man: L Leadley
Fleet: 45 - 38 coach, 6 double-deck coach,
1 minicoach.
Chassis: 1 Iveco. 5 Mercedes. 34 Scania.
2 Volvo.
Bodies: 15 Berkhof. 21 Irizar. 2 Jonckheere.
5 Setra.
Ops incl: school contracts, excursions &
tours, private hire, continental tours.
Livery: Yellow/Purple

CLEGG & BROOKING LTD

WHITE HORSE SERVICE STATION,
MIDDLE WALLOP SO20 8DZ
Tel: 01264 781283.
Fax: 01264 781679.
Man Dirs: K. R. J. Brooking, J. A. Cook.
Co Sec: Mrs T. J. Brooking. **Dirs**:
R. R. Brooking, P. U. Brooking, J. P. Cook.
Fleet: 7 - 1 single-deck bus, 2 coach,
1 midicoach, 3 minibus.
Chassis: 1 Dennis. 1 Dodge. 1 Freight
Rover. 1 Mercedes. 1 Renault. 1 Toyota.
Bodies: 2 Caetano. 1 Jonckheere.
1 Wadham Stringer. 1 Cymric. 1 M2M.
Ops incl: excursions & tours, private hire,
school contracts.
Livery: Blue/White.

*COLISEUM COACHES LTD

BOTLEY ROAD GARAGE, WEST
END, SOUTHAMPTON SO30 3JA
Tel: 023 8047 2377
Fax: 023 8047 6537
E-mail: info@coliseumcoaches.co.uk
Web site:
www.coliseumcoaches.co.uk
Dirs: David Pitter, Kerry Pitter
Ch Eng: Dave Rowsell
Fleet: 12 coach.
Chassis: 13 MAN
Bodies:. 12 Neoplan
Ops incl: excursions & tours, private hire,
continental tours.
Livery: Silver

*COOPERS COACHES

31-35 LAKE ROAD, WOOLSTON
SO19 9EB
Tel: 023 8039 3393
Fax: 023 8044 4929.
Prop: Stephen Cooper
Fleet: 8 - 5 coach, 2 minibus, 1 midicoach.
Chassis: 1 DAF. 1 Ford Transit. 1 LDV.
1 Mercedes. 4 Volvo.
Bodies: 1 Caetano. 1 Ikarus. 2 Plaxton.
1 Van Hool. 1 Robin Hood.
Ops incl: local bus services, school
contracts, private hire.
Livery: Cream/Pine/Burgundy

RAY DUNN COACH TRAVEL

COACH HOUSE, 48 BRITANNIA
GARDENS, HEDGE END SO30 2RP
Tel: 01489 797990.
Fax: 01489 797900.
Props: R. R. Dunn, S. L. Dunn..

EASSONS COACHES LTD

44 WODEHOUSE ROAD, ITCHEN
SO19 2EQ
Tel: 023 8044 8153
Fax: 023 8044 1635
Dirs: R. A. Easson, D. H. Easson.
Fleet: 10 - 7 coach, 2 midicoach, 1 minibus.
Chassis: 3 Mercedes. 1 Neoplan. 3 Setra.
2 Volvo. 1 Van Hool.
Bodies: 1 Mercedes. 1 Neoplan. 2 Plaxton.
3 Setra. 1 Van Hool. 2 Robin Hood.
Ops incl: excursions & tours, private hire,
continental tours.
Livery: Cream/Khaki Brown.

*EMSWORTH & DISTRICT MOTOR SERVICES LTD

THE BUS GARAGE, CLOVELLY
ROAD, SOUTHBOURNE PO10 8PE
Tel: 01243 378337
Web site:
www.emsworth+district.co.uk
Fleet: 26 - 3 double-deck bus, 12 single-deck bus, 6 coach, 1 midicoach, 3 minibus,
2 minicoach. 1 midibus.
Chassis: Bedford. Dennis. Ford Transit.
Leyland. Mercedes. Optare.
Bodies: Mercedes. Optare. Van Hool.
Ops incl: local bus services, school
contracts, excursions & tours, private hire,
continental tours.
Livery: Green/Cream
Ticket System: Wayfarer 3

*FIRST HAMPSHIRE & DORSET LTD

226 PORTSWOOD ROAD,
SOUTHAMPTON SO17 2BE
Tel: 023 8058 4321
Fax: 023 8067 1448
Web site: www.firstgroup.com
E-mail:
contacthampshire@firstgroup.com
Fleetname: First
Man Dir: Richard Soper **Eng Dir**: David Toy
Fin Dir: Ian Stone **Ops Dir**: Mike Smith
Com Dir: Marc Reddy
Fleet: 428 - 88 double-deck bus, 81 single-deck bus, 155 midibus, 105 minibus.
Livery: FirstGroup
First Hampshire & Dorset Ltd is a subsidiary
company of First Group Ltd
Depots:
Fareham: Gosport Road, Fareham
PO16 0ST
Tel: 01329 232208 **Fax**: 01329 234189
Portsmouth: London Road, Hilsea,
Portsmouth PO2 9RP
Tel: 023 9265 0413 **Fax**: 023 9265 1023
Southampton: 226 Porstwood Road,
Southampton SO17 2BE
Tel: 023 8058 4321 **Fax**: 023 8067 1448
Weymouth, Bridport see Dorset

FLYGHT TRAVEL

3A SPUR ROAD, COSHAM PO6
3DY.
Tel: 023 9232 7703.
Fax: 023 9238 2900.
Chairm: J. Stewart. **Tran Man**: T. Byng.
Admin/Fin: Ms P. Stewart.
Fleet: 13 - 7 coach, 2 midibus, 1 midicoach,
2 minibus, 1 minicoach.
Chassis: 3 DAF. 2 MAN, 2 Mercedes.
1 Optare. 5 Scania.
Ops incl: excursions & tours, private hire,
express, continental tours, school contracts.
Livery: White/Red Pegasus.

*GEMINI TRAVEL SOUTHAMPTON LTD

MARCHWOOD INDUSTRIAL PARK,
NORMANDY WAY, MARCHWOOD
SO40 4PB
Tel: 023 8066 0066
Fax: 023 8087 1308
Dirs: R A Nunn, P F Nunn **Gen Man**:
N B Smith **Traf Mans**: K J Hatch, M
Bennett.
Fleet: 23 - 2 single-deck coach.
4 midicoach, 17 minicoach.
Chassis: 6 LDV. 4 Mercedes. 2 Volvo.
7 Citroen. 4 Plaxton.
Bodies: include 1 Mercedes. 3 Optare.
2 Park Royal.
Ops incl: private hire, school contracts.
Livery: White with Blue stripes.

*HELLYERS OF FAREHAM

FORT FAREHAM BUSINESS PARK,
NEWGATE LANE, FAREHAM
PO14 1AH
Tel: 01329 285432
Fax: 01329 205267
E-mail: info@hellyers-coaches.co.uk
Web site: www.hellyers-coaches.co.uk
Dir: Paul Grant **Dir/Co Sec**: Trevor Grant
Fleet Eng: Rob Ingram
Fleet: 38 - 1 single-deck bus, 37 coach.
Chassis: 8 Bova. 2 Dennis. 4 Leyland.
4 Mercedes. 4 Scania. 6 Setra. 1 Toyota.
9 Volvo.
Bodies: 8 Bova. 1 Caetano. 4 Ikarus.

A/c	Air conditioning
	Vehicles suitable for disabled
	Coach(es) with galley facilities
wc	Coach(es) with toilet facilities
	Seat belt-fitted vehicles
R	Recovery service available (not 24 hr)
R24	24hr recovery service
	Replacement vehicle available
T	Toilet-drop facilities available
	Vintage vehicle(s) available
	Open top vehicle(s)

Hampshire

1 Irizar. 3 Jonckheere. 4 Mercedes. 10 Plaxton. 6 Setra. 4 Van Hool.
Ops incl: excursions & tours, private hire, school contracts, express, continental tours.

*HERRINGTON COACHES LTD

MANOR FARM, SANDLEHEATH ROAD, ALDERHOLT, FORDINGBRIDGE SP6 3EG
Tel: 01425 652842
Props: A G Herrington, Mrs J Herrington
Fleet: 6 - 3 coach, 3 minibus.
Chassis: 1 Dennis. 3 Mercedes. 2 Volvo.
Bodies: 1 Crest. 1 Jonckheere. 2 Mercedes. 1 Plaxton. 1 Van Hool.
Ops incl: local bus services, school contracts, private hire.
Livery: Grey/Red.

*HYTHE & WATERSIDE COCHES LTD

1A HIGH STREET, HYTHE SO45 6AG
Tel: 023 8084 4788
Fax: 023 8020 7284
E-mail: enquiries@watersidetours.co.uk
Web site: www.watersidetours.co.uk
Fleetname: Waterside Tours
Man Dir: Roy Barker **Co Sec**: Jackie Withey **Ch Eng**: Bob Johns
Fleet: 7 - 4 coach, 1 minibus, 2 minicoach.
Chassis: 2 Mercedes. 1 Toyota. 4 Volvo.
Bodies: 1 Autobus. 3 Berkhof. 1 Caetano. 1 Plaxton. 1 Tawe.
Ops incl: excursions & tours, private hire, continental tours, school contracts.
Livery: White/Burgundy/Gold.

LUCKETTS TRAVEL

BROADCUT, WALLINGTON, FAREHAM PO16 8TB
Tel: 01329 823755
Fax: 01329 823855
E-mail: info@lucketts.co.uk
Web site: www.lucketts.co.uk
Chmn: D. F. Luckett **Dirs**: S. Luckett, I. Luckett, R. A. P. McLean
Fleet: 32 - 26 coach, 2 double-deck coach, 1 minibus, 3 minicoach.
Chassis: 10 Dennis. 1 LDV. 4 Mercedes. 12 Scania. 3 Toyota. 2 Volvo.
Bodies: 8 Berkhof. 3 Caetano. 12 Irizar. 2 Neoplan. 4 Plaxton. 3 other.
Ops incl: excursions & tours, private hire, continental tours, school contracts.
Livery: Grey/White/Orange

*MARCHWOOD MOTORWAYS LTD

200 SALISBURY ROAD, TOTTON SO40 3PE
Tel: 023 8066 3700
Fax: 023 8066 7762
Dirs: D P Osborne, I C W Osborne, S E Welbourn, P F Lane (**Tran Man**)
Fleet: double-deck bus, single-deck bus, coach, midibus, midicoach, minibus.
Chassis: Bova. DAF. Iveco. Ford Transit. Optare. Toyota.
Bodies: Bova. Caetano. Ikarus. Optare. Van Hool. Wright.
Ops incl: local bus services, school contracts, private hire.

Livery: Silver
Ticket system: Wayfarer

*MERVYN'S COACHES

THE NEW COACH HOUSE, INNERSDOWN, MICHELDEVER SO21 3BW
Tel/Fax: 01962 774574
Web site: www.mervynscoaches.com
Ptnrs: Mervyn Annetts, Carol Annetts, Linda Porter, James Annetts.
Fleet: 6 - 5 coach, 1 minibus.
Chassis: 6 Bedford.
Chassis: 1 Duple. 4 Plaxton. 1 Churchill
Ops incl: local bus services, school contracts, excursions & tours, private hire.
Livery: Brown/Cream
Ticket System: Setright.

OWEN'S COACHES LTD

11 CRANFORD PARK DRIVE, YATELEY GU46 6JR
Tel: 01252 872267
Fax: 01252 874898
Dirs: C Owen, Mrs D Owen **Tran Man**: D Devine
Fleet: 6 coach
Chassis: 1 Bedford. 1 Dennis. 4 Volvo.
Bodies: 4 Plaxton, 2 Van Hool.
Ops incl: private hire, school contracts.
Livery: Blue/Beige

JOHN PIKE COACHES

77 SCOTT CLOSE, WALWORTH INDUSTRIAL ESTATE, ANDOVER SP10 5NU.
Tel: 01264 334328.
Fax: 01264 334329.
Props: J. S. Pike, Jenny Pike, C. Pike, R. Pike.
Fleet: 15 - 4 double-deck bus, 5 coach, 2 midicoach, 4 minibus.
Chassis: Bristol. Ford Transit. Iveco. Mercedes. Volvo.
Bodies: Mercedes. Plaxton. ECW.
Ops incl: local bus services, school contracts, excursions & tours, private hire, continental tours.
Livery: White.
Ticket System: Setright.

PRINCESS SUMMERBEE COACHES

BOTLEY ROAD, WEST END, SOUTHAMPTON SO30 3HA.
Tel: 023 8047 2150.
Fax: 023 8039 9944.
Prop: J. Barfoot.
Fleet: 16 - 12 coach, 1 double-deck coach, 3 minibus.
Chassis: 2 DAF. 2 Ford. 3 Ford Transit. 1 Iveco. 1 MAN. 1 Mercedes. 3 Scania. 2 Volvo.
Bodies: 1 Caetano. 4 Duple. 2 Jonckheere. 2 Plaxton. 3 Van Hool.
Ops incl: excursions & tours, private hire, school contracts.

SOLENT BLUE LINE

BARTON PARK, EASTLEIGH SO50 6RR
Tel: 023 8061 4459

Fax: 023 8061 4234
E-mail: enquiries@solentblueline.swinternet.co.uk
Web site: www.solentblueline.com
Chmn: S. G. Linn **Man Dir**: Phil Stockley
Ops Dir: P. J. J. Shelley. **Eng Man**: D. King
Ops Man: Marc Morgan-Huws **Comm Man**: P. C. Curtis
Fleet: 64 - 42 double-deck bus, 16 single-deck bus, 6 midibus.
Chassis: 20 Dennis. 6 Iveco. 20 Leyland. 18 Volvo.
Bodies: 4 Alexander. 7 ECW. 18 East Lancs. 12 Leyland. 6 Mellor. 4 Northern Counties. 12 Plaxton.
Ops incl: local bus services, school contracts.
Livery: Blue/Yellow/Turquoise
Ticket System: Wayfarer 3/Magnetic
Subsidiary of Southern Vectis, Isle of Wight

SOLENT COACHES LTD

11 WHITEFIELD ROAD, NEW MILTON BH25 6DE.
Tel: 01425 611330
Fax: 01425 622555
E-mail: enquiries@solentcoaches.co.uk
Web site: www.solentcoaches.co.uk
Dirs: John Skew, Paul Skew.
Fleet: 12 - 9 coach, 2 minibus 1 minicoach.
Chassis: 1 Ford Transit. 2 Mercedes. 1 Neoplan. 6 Scania. 1 Setra 1 Toyota.
Bodies: 1 Caetano. 1 Irizar. 2 Mercedes. 1 Neoplan. 1 Setra. 5 Van Hool.
Ops incl: excursions & tours, private hire, continental tours, school contracts.
Livery: White and two Blues.

STAGECOACH IN HAMPSHIRE

BUS STATION, FESTIVAL PLACE, CHURCHILL WAY, BASINGSTOKE RG21 9 7HZ
Tel: 01256 464501
Fax: 01256 811931
Man Dir: Andrew Dyer. **Eng Dir**: Richard Alexander. **Fin Dir**: Martin Stoggell.
Div Man: Matthew Callow.
Fleet: 150 - 47 double-deck bus. 86 single-deck bus. 17 minibus.
Chassis: 4 Bristol, 53 Dennis, 16 Leyland, 15 Mercedes, 2 Optare. 60 Volvo.
Bodies: 138 Alexander. 4 ECW. 2 Optare. Plaxton.
Ops incl: local bus services, school contracts.
Livery: Blue/Red/Orange
Ticket System: Wayfarer.

STAGECOACH HANTS & SURREY

HALIMOTE ROAD, ALDERSHOT GU11 1NJ
Tel: 01256 464501.
Man Dir: Andrew Dyer. **Eng Dir**: Richard Alexander. **Fin Dir**: Martin Stoggell. **Div Man**: Philip Medlicott.
Fleet: 80 - 13 double-deck bus, 43 single-deck bus, 24 minibus.
Chassis: 37 Dennis. 6 Leyland. 24 Mercedes. 13 Volvo.
Bodies: Alexander. Plaxton.

Ops incl: local bus services, school contracts.
Livery: Blue/Red/Orange
Ticket System: Wayfarer

SUMMERFIELD COACHES LTD
💺 🍴 wc A/c R24 ✔ T

247 ALDERMOOR ROAD, SOUTHAMPTON SO16 5NU
Tel: 023 8077 8717
Fax: 023 8032 0327
Web site: www.summerfieldcoaches.co.uk
E-mail: summerfield@tcp.co.uk
Man Dir: Tracey Ralph Chmn: Colin Ralph
Ops Man: Karen Bright
Fleet: 8 - 5 coach, 1 midicoach, 2 minicoach.
Chassis: 1 LDV. 1 MAN. 1 Mercedes. 1 Toyota. 4 Volvo.
Bodies: 1 Berkhof. 3 Caetano. 1 Leyland. 2 Plaxton. 1 Robin Hood.
Ops incl: school contracts, excursions & tours, private hire, continental tours.
Livery: Green

TAYLORS OF SUTTON SCOTNEY LTD
wc 💺 A/c ✔

THE GARAGE, OXFORD ROAD, SUTTON SCOTNEY SO21 3JL
Tel: 01962 760222
Fax: 01962 760658
E-mail: sales@taylors-coaches.co.uk
Web site: www.taylors-coaches.co.uk
Man Dir: Maxim Taylor Co
Sec: Alexandra Taylor
Fleet: 19 - 4 double-deck bus, 10 coach, 5 midicoach.
Chassis: 5 Bristol. 5 Dennis. 1 Ford. 3 MAN. 1 Setra. 2 Toyota. 2 Volvo.
Bodies: 5 Berkhof. 2 Caetano. 5 ECW. 1 Jonckheere. 2 Neoplan. 2 Plaxton. 1 Setra. 1 Van Hool.
Ops incl: excursions & tours, private hire, continental tours, school contracts.
Livery: White/Green/Orange

*TEST VALLEY TRAVEL
See Wiltshire

TRUEMANS TRAVEL
wc 💺 A/c

3 CROOKHAM ROAD, FLEET GU51 8DL

Tel: 01252 624404.
Dir: R. Trueman
Fleet: 6 coach.
Chassis: Iveco.
Bodies: Beulas.
Ops incl: excursions & tours, private hire, continental tours, school contracts.
Livery: Orange, Silver, Green

VISION TRAVEL
💺 wc A/c R24 ✔

12 BUNTING GARDENS, COWPLAIN, WATERLOOVILLE PO8 9UN
Tel: 07771 682389
Fax: 023 9225 3553
Recovery: 07810 800 989
E-mail: visiontravels@aol.com
Web site: www.visiontravel.biz
Dirs: Peter R Sharpe, Carolyn M Sharpe, Rebecca Simmons
Fleet: 9 - 8 coach, 1 midicoach
Chassis: 2 DAF. 1 Leyland. 1 Mercedes. 3 Scania. 1 Cummins.
Bodies: 2 Irizar. 2 LAG. 1 Mercedes. 1 Plaxton. 2 Van Hool.
Ops incl: school contracts, excursions & tours, private hire, continental tours.

HEREFORDSHIRE

BOWYER'S COACHES 💺
QUARRY GARAGE, PETERCHURCH HR2 0TF.
Tel: 01981 550206.
Prop: Fernley C. Anning, Anthony H. Anning.
Fleet: 9 - 5 coach, 4 minibus.
Chassis: Bedford. LDV.
Ops incl: private hire, school contracts.
Livery: White/Red.

BROMYARD OMNIBUS COMPANY ♿ 💺 🚌 R
STREAMHALL GARAGE, LINTON TRADING ESTATE, BROMYARD HR7 4QL
Tel: 01885 482782
Fax: 01885 482127
Prop: Martin Perry Fleet Eng: Michael Simcock
Fleet: 11 - 6 single-deck bus, 3 coach, 1 midibus, 1 minicoach.
Chassis: 1 Bedford. 2 Leyland. 2 Mercedes. 4 Optare. 1 Volvo. 1 Trojan.
Bodies: 2 Autobus. 1 Caetano. 1 Duple. 4 Optare. 2 Plaxton. 1 Trojan.
Ops incl: local bus services, school contracts, private hire.
Livery: Red/Cream
Ticket System: Wayfarer Saver

*COACH COMPANIONS LTD
See London

*D R M COACHES ♿ 💺
THE COACH GARAGE, BROMYARD HR7 4NT
Tel: 01885 483219
Fax: 01885 482927
Prop: David R. Morris
Fleet: 9 - 8 single-deck bus, 1 single-deck coach.
Chassis: 2 Scania. 7 Volvo.
Bodies: 1 Alexander. 2 East Lancs. 1 Jonckheere. 1 Leyland National. 1 Wright. 1 Scania. 2 other.
Ops incl: local bus services, school contracts.
Livery: Blue/White
Ticket System: Wayfarer

*GOLDEN PIONEER TRAVEL wc 💺 A/c T
BRANDON, REDHILL, HEREFORD HR2 8BH
Tel: 01432 274307
Fax: 01432 275809
Dirs: B Crockett, J Crockett.
Fleet: 5 coach, 1 midicoach.
Chassis: 2 Iveco. 1 MAN. 1 Mercedes. 1 Scania. 1 Toyota.
Bodies: 2 Beulas. 1 Caetano. 1 Irizar. 1 Mercedes. 1 Van Hool.
Ops incl: school contracts, excursions & tours, private hire, continental tours.
Livery: Black/Gold/Red/Green

*GOLD STAR TRAVEL
See Worcestershire

*P. W. JONES COACHES
wc 💺 A/c 🍴 R ✔ T

HILBREY GARAGE, BURLEY GATE, HEREFORD HR1 3OL
Tel: 01432 820214
Fax: 01432 820521
Prop: Philip W Jones
Fleet: 19 - 17 single-deck coach, 2 minicoach.
Chassis: 5 Bedford. 1 Bova. 8 Dennis. 2 Freight Rover. 1 MAN. 1 Neoplan. 1 Toyota.
Bodies: 1 Bova. 2 Caetano. 1 Marcopolo. 1 Neoplan. 12 Plaxton.
Ops incl: excursions & tours, private hire, continental tours, school contracts.
Livery: White with multi colours

*LUGG VALLEY PRIMROSE TRAVEL
♿ wc 💺 🍴 A/c R24 ✔

SOUTHERN AVENUE, LEOMINSTER HR6 0QF
Tel/Fax: 01568 616747
Recovery: 01568 612279
Man Dir: Mrs E Sankey

A/c	Air conditioning	✔	Replacement vehicle available
♿	Vehicles suitable for disabled	T	Toilet-drop facilities available
🍴	Coach(es) with galley facilities	🚌	Vintage vehicle(s) available
wc	Coach(es) with toilet facilities		Open top vehicle(s)
💺	Seat belt-fitted vehicles		
R	Recovery service available (not 24 hr)		
R24	24hr recovery service		

Fleet Eng: Steve Palmer
Fleet: 28 - 16 single-deck bus, 12 coach.
Chassis: 2 Bedford. 8 Dennis. 1 Leyland. 1 Marshall. 9 Optare. 6 Volvo.
Bodies: 1 Berkhof. 3 Caetano. 1 Duple. 1 Jonckheere. 1 Marshall. 1 Northern Counties. 9 Optare. 10 Plaxton. 1 Transbus.
Ops incl: local bus services, school contracts, excursions & tours, private hire, continental tours, express.
Livery: Beige
Ticket System: Wayfarer

*M&S LUXURY MINI-COACHES

CROFTWELL HOUSE, KIMBOLTON, LEOMINSTER HR6 0HD
Tel: 01568 612803
Mobile: 07947 156350
Props: Maurice Peruffo, Susan Peruffo
Fleet: 6 - midicoach, minicoach.
Chassis: 3 Mercedes. 3 Toyota.
Bodies: 3 Caetano. 3 Mercedes.
Ops incl: school contracts, excursions & tours, private hire, continental tours.
Livery: White with gold lettering and red flash

NEWBURY COACHES

LOWER ROAD TRADING ESTATE, LEDBURY HR8 2DJ.
Tel: 01531 633483.
Fax: 01531633650.
Livery: Blue/White.

SARGEANTS BROS LTD

MILL STREET, KINGTON HR5 3AL
Tel/Fax: 01544 230481
E-mail: mike@sargantsbros.com
Web site: www.sargantsbros.com
Prop: Michael Sargeant
Fleet: 29 - 1 double-deck bus, 2 single-deck bus, 6 single-deck coach, 10 midibus, 1 midicoach, 9 minibus.
Chassis: 4 Bedford, 1 DAF, 1 Dodge, 4 Ford Transit, 1 LAG, 2 Leyland, 7 Mercedes, 4 Optare, 2 Renault, 1 Volvo, 2 Talbot.
Bodies: 1 Alexander, 2 Jonckheere, 7 Optare, 6 Plaxton, 2 Reeve Burgess, 2 PMT, 1 LAG, 1 Cymric, 2 Freeway, 4 Ford. 1 Renault.
Ops incl: local bus services, school contracts, private hire.
Livery: Red
Ticket System: Wayfarer

SMITHS MOTORS (LEDBURY) LTD

COACH GARAGE, HOMEND, LEDBURY HR8 1BA.
Tel: 01531 632953.
Dirs: F. W. B. Sterry, M. Sterry.
Fleet: 11 - 8 coach, 2 midicoach, 1 minibus.
Chassis: 3 Bedford. 1 Ford. 1 Iveco. 4 Leyland. 2 Mercedes.
Bodies: 1 Caetano. 3 Duple. 3 Plaxton. 2 Van Hool. 1 PMT. 1 Devon.
Ops incl: local bus services,

continental tours.
Livery: White with Green/Blue/Red stripe.
Ticket System: Setright.

*STAGECOACH IN SOUTH WALES

See Torfaen

YEOMANS CANYON TRAVEL LTD R24 T

21-23 THREE ELMS TRADING ESTATE, HEREFORD HR4 9PU.
Tel: 01432 356201.
Fax: 01432 356206.
Dirs: N. D. & G. H. Yeomans
Sec: S. M. T. Yeomans
Traf Man: N. Yeomans.
Fleet: 35 - 1 double-deck bus, 10 single-deck bus, 20 coach, 1 midicoach, 2 minibus ,1 minicoach.
Chassis: 4 Bedford. 8 Dennis. 2 Ford Transit. 2 Leyland. 2 Mercedes. 1 Neoplan. 4 Optare. 2 Scania. 7 Volvo.
Bodies: 1 Alexander. 2 Berkhof. 3 Carlyle. 3 Duple. 2 Irizar. 2 Jonckheere. 1 Neoplan. 1 Northern Counties. 4 Optare. 6 Plaxton. 2 Van Hool.
Ops incl: local bus services, school contracts, excursions & tours, express, continental tours.
Livery: Green and Cream.
Ticket System: Wayfarer.

HERTFORDSHIRE

*ABBEY TRAVEL LTD

58 BURYMEAD ROAD, HITCHIN SG5 1RT
Tel: 01462 421777/421888
Fax: 01462 421999
E-mail: rich@abbeytravel.co.uk
Web site: www.abbeytravel.co.uk
Man Dir: Peter Malyon **Dir**: Patricia Malyon
Co Man: Richard Window.
Co Sec: Leigh Featherstone
Fleet: 14 - 2 single-deck bus, 8 coach, 1 midibus, 2 minibus, 1 minicoach.
Chassis: 1 Dennis. 1 Ford Transit. 4 Mercedes. 1 Peugeot. 7 Volvo.
Bodies: 1 Berkhof. 1 Duple. 2 Jonckheere. 1 Mercedes. 4 Plaxton. 3 Reeve Burgess. 1 Van Hool. 1 Peugeot.
Ops incl: excursions & tours, private hire, continental tours, school contracts.
Livery: White/Blue.

*ACE TRAVEL

11 MAYFLOWER GARDENS, BISHOPS STORTFORD CM23 4PA
Tel/Fax: 01279 658056
Dir: Frank Gowen
Fleet: 1 coach.
Chassis: 1 Scania.
Body: 1 Irizar.
Ops incl: excursions & tours, private hire.
Livery: Blue

ALPHA PERSONALISED TRAVEL LTD

300 HIGH ROAD, LEAVESDEN WD25 7EB
Tel/Fax: 01923 202052.
Chmn: G. Picton. **Man Dir**: D. Green.
Co Sec: J. Foster.
Fleet: 3 - 1 midicoach, 2 minibus.
Chassis: 2 Ford Transit. 1 Toyota.
Bodies: 1 Caetano.
Ops incl: excursions & tours, private hire, continental tours.
Livery: Blue/Orange/White.

A R TRAVEL LTD

40 PERRY GREEN, HEMEL HEMPSTEAD HP2 7ND
Tel: 01992 501337
Fax: 01992 501662
E-mail: artravelltd@hotmail.com
Web site: www.artravelltd.co.uk
Dir: T A Hill **Fin Dir**: Mrs L J Hill
Fleet: 7 - 2 midicoach, 5 minicoach
Chassis: 1 LDV. 1 MAN. 4 Optare.
Body: 1 Berkhof. 1 Leyland. 4 Optare. 1 Caravelle.
Ops incl: excursions & tours, private hire, continental tours, school contracts.
Livery: White

B & F COACHWAYS

See Middlesex.

*CANTABRICA COACH HOLIDAYS R24 T

9 ELTON WAY, WATFORD WD25 8HH
Tel: 01923 230526
Fax: 01923 817066
Fleet: 20
Chassis: 1 Freight Rover. 3 Mercedes. 16 Volvo.
Ops incl: excursions & tours, private hire, continental tours.
Livery: Blue/Red.
Coach wash, workshop facilities.

*CHAMBERS COACHES (STEVENAGE) LTD

38 TRENT CLOSE, STEVENAGE SG1 3RT
Tel: 01438 352920
Fax: 01462 486616
E-mail: chamberscoaches@btconnect.com
Man Dir: Cyril Chambers **Dir**: M Chambers
Co Sec: Debra Tidey.
Fleet: single-deck coach, midicoach, minicoach
Chassis: Dennis. Ford. Leyland. Mercedes. Optare. Scania.
Bodies: Caetano. Leyland. Marcopolo. Mercedes. Optare. Plaxton. Transbus.
Ops incl: school contracts, private hire

*GALLEON TRAVEL LTD
🪑 wc 🍴 A/c

THE GARAGE, FILLETS FARM,
STANSTEAD ROAD, HUNSDON
SG12 8QA
Tel: 01920 870700
Fax: 01279 877079
E-mail:
galleontravel@btopenworld.com
Web site: www.galleontravel.com
Man Dir: Helen Bowden **Ops Dir**: Mark Bowden
Fleet: 4 - 2 coach, 2 double-deck coach
Chassis: 3 Scania. 1 Volvo.
Bodies: 1 Berkhof. 1 East Lancs. 2 Irizar.
Ops incl: school contracts, private hire, continental tours.
Livery: White.

*GOLDEN BOY COACHES (JETSIE LTD)
wc 🪑 A/c 🔧 T

JOHN TERENCE HOUSE,
GEDDINGS ROAD, HODDESDON
EN11 0NT
Tel: 01992 465747
Fax: 01992 450957
E-mail: sales@goldenboy.co.uk
Web site: www.goldenboy.co.uk
Joint Man Dirs: G A McIntyre, T P McIntyre
Tran Man: G Jaikens **Ch Eng**: P Murdoch
Fleet: 32 - 1 single-deck bus, 18 coach, 10 midicoach, 3 minicoach.
Chassis: 1 Dennis. 13 Mercedes. 18 Volvo.
Bodies: 1 Mellor. 9 Plaxton. 18 Van Hool. 2 Sitcar. 2 Crest.
Ops incl: local bus services, private hire, school contracts.
Livery: Black/Red/Gold.
Ticket System: Almex.

*GRAVES COACHES & MINIBUSES 🪑

134 WINFORD DRIVE DRIVE,
BROXBOURNE EN10 6PN
Tel/Fax: 01992 445556
E-mail: m.graves@btinternet.com
Prop: Michael Graves
Fleet: 2 -1 minicoach, 1 minibus
Chassis: 1 Mercedes. 1 Toyota.
Bodies: 1 Caetano. 1 Mercedes.
Ops incl: private hire, school contracts.

*GROVE COACHES 🪑

101 MANDEVILLE ROAD,
HERTFORD SG13 8JL
Tel: 01992 583417
Fleetname: Pride of Hertford
Driver/operator: R A Bowers
Fleet: 1 coach.
Chassis: Volvo. **Body**: Plaxton.
Ops incl: private hire, school contracts.
Livery: Brown/Orange

*KENZIES COACHES LTD
wc 🪑 A/c

6 ANGLE LANE, SHEPRETH
SG8 6QH

Tel: 01763 260288
Fax: 01763 262012
Fleet: 25 coach.
Chassis: 2 Bedford. 1 Scania. 22 Volvo.
Bodies: 6 Plaxton. 19 Van Hool.
Ops incl: private hire, school contracts.

*THE LITTLE BUS COMPANY 🪑
See Hertfordshire

*LITTLE JIM'S BUSES 🪑
1 CASTLE STREET, BERKHAMSTED
HP4 2BQ
Tel: 07736 705520
Fax: 01442 877217
E-mail: littlejimbuses@aol.com
Prop: Jim Petty
Fleet: 2 - 1 midibus, 1 midicoach.
Chassis: 2 Mercedes.
Bodies: 2 Mercedes.
Ops incl: local bus services, school contracts, excursions & tours, private hire.
Livery: Variable.
Ticket System: Almex.

*MASTER TRAVEL ♿ wc 🍴
🪑 A/c 🔧

9-11 PEARTREE FARM, WELWYN
GARDEN CITY AL7 3UW
Tel: 01707 334040
Fax: 01707 334366
Ptnrs: R J Goulden, S Goulden
Fleet: 16 - 1 single-deck bus, 3 coach,
1 double-deck coach, 2 midicoach,
6 minibus, 3 midibus.
Chassis: 1 DAF. 3 Dennis. 2 Ford. 2 Iveco.
3 LDV. 3 Optare. 1 Renault.
Bodies: 1 Berkhof. 1 Jonckheere.
1 Jonckheere. 1 Marcopolo. 1 Neoplan.
4 other.
Ops incl: private hire, school contracts, excursions & tours.
Livery: White/Blue.

*MINIBUS SERVICES 🪑
773 ST ALBANS ROAD, WATFORD
WD25 9LA
Tel: 01923 219107
Fax: 01923 219108
E-mail:
minibusservices@btconnect.com
E-mail: www.minibusservices.uk.com
Prop: Russell Crowson
Fleet: 5 - 1 coach, 2 minibus, 2 midicoach
Chassis: 1 Iveco. 1 LDV. 1
Mercedes.1 Renault. 1 Volvo.
Bodies: include Plaxton
Ops incl: school contracts, private hire, excursions & tours

PARKSIDE TRAVEL ♿

PARADISE WILDLIFE PARK,
WHITE STUBBS LANE,
BROXBOURNE EN10 7QA
Tel: 01992 444477
Fax: 01992 465441
Fleetname: Parkside Travel

Dirs: P C Sampson, G F Sampson
Fleet: 7 minibus.
Chassis: 7 Ford Transit.
Ops incl: school contracts, private hire.
Livery: Light Blue

PROVENCE PRIVATE HIRE
🪑 wc A/c 🔧

HEATH FARM LANE, ST ALBANS
AL3 5AE
Tel: 01727 864988
Fax: 01727 855275
E-mail: office@pphcoaches.com
Web site: www.pphcoaches.com
Dirs: A. K. Hayes, R. F. Hayes
Ch Eng: D. Higgins
Fleet: 31 - 2 double-deck bus, 22 coach,
6 double-deck coach, 1 minibus.
Chassis: 1 Bedford. 2 DAF. 4 Dennis.
1 Ford Transit. 4 Leyland. 5 MCW.
3 Neoplan. 6 Scania. 4 Volvo.
Bodies: 1 Caetano. 2 Duple. 3 East Lancs.
2 Irizar. 6 MCW. 3 Neoplan. 9 Plaxton.
2 UVG. 1 Unicar. 1 Van Hool.
Ops incl: excursions & tours, private hire, continental tours, school contracts.
Livery: Yellow.

*REG'S COACHES LTD
🪑 A/c 🔧

C/O FOXHOLES FARM, LONDON
ROAD, HERTFORD SG13 7NT
Tel: 01992 586302
Fax: 01992 501952
E-mail: regscoaches@btconnect.com
Web site: www.regscoaches.co.uk
Man Dir: Terry Hunt **Dir**: Beverly Hunt
Man: Gary Kingsbury **Asst Man**: John
Paget **Ch Eng**: Bill Parlow
Fleet: 19 - 2 single-deck bus, 16 coach,
1 midicoach.
Chassis: 12 Dennis. 1 Leyland.
1 Mercedes. 5 Volvo.
Bodies: 1 Optare. 14 Plaxton. 1 Transbus.
2 Van Hool. 1 Wright.
Ops incl: local bus services, school contracts, excursions & tours, private hire.
Livery: Black/Green
Ticket System: Wayfarer 2/Almex

*REYNOLDS DIPLOMAT COACHES wc 🪑 A/c

185 LOWER HIGH STREET,
WATFORD WD17 2HY
Tel: 01923 296877
Fax: 01923 210020
E-mail: reynoldscoaches@lineone.net
Web site: www.reynoldscoaches.com
Props: R Reynolds Mrs S Reynolds
Fleet: 14 - 10 coach, 3 double-deck coach,
1 minibus.
Chassis: 1 Ford. 1 MAN. 2 Mercedes.
10 Volvo.
Bodies: 10 Jonckheere. 3 Neoplan.
Ops incl: excursions & tours, private hire, continental tours, school contracts.
Livery: Green/Gold/White

A/c	Air conditioning
♿	Vehicles suitable for disabled
🍴	Coach(es) with galley facilities
wc	Coach(es) with toilet facilities
🪑	Seat belt-fitted vehicles
R	Recovery service available (not 24 hr)
R24	24hr recovery service
🔧	Replacement vehicle available
T	Toilet-drop facilities available
	Vintage vehicle(s) available
	Open top vehicle(s)

RICHMOND'S COACHES

THE GARAGE, BARLEY, ROYSTON SG8 8JA
Tel: 01763 848226
Fax: 01763 848105
E-mail: postbox@richmonds-coaches.co.uk
Web site: www.richmonds-coaches.co.uk
Dirs: D. M. Richmond, M. J. Richmond, A. P. Richmond **Sales & Mktg Man**: R. Ellis
Coaching Man: B. Sellars.
Fleet: 25 - single-deck bus, coach, midicoach, midibus, minibus.
Chassis: 4 Dennis. 7 Mercedes. 1 Optare. 13 Volvo.
Bodies: 4 Berkhof. 1 Marshall. 1 Optare. 7 Plaxton. 10 Van Hool. 1 Beluga. 1 Ferqui.
Ops incl: local bus services, school contracts, excursions & tours, private hire, express, continental tours.
Livery: Chocolate/Cream
Ticket System: Wayfarer

RONSWAY COACHES

FIRBANK WAY, LEIGHTON BUZZARD LU7 4YP
Tel: 01442 242641
Fax: 01525 850967
Recovery: 01525 375301
Web site: www.marshalls-coaches.co.uk
E-mail: info@marshalls-coaches.co.uk
Props: F W Marshall, Mrs S J Marshall
Ops Man: Ian White
Fleet: 20 - 1 double-deck bus, 18 coach, 1 minicoach.
Chassis: 3 Dennis. 7 Iveco. 1 Mercedes. 3 Scania. 6 Volvo.
Bodies: 2 Berkhof. 7 Beulas. 1 Caetano. 1 Irizar. 5 Jonckheere. 4 Plaxton.
Ops incl: private hire, school contracts, local bus services.
Livery: Blue/Multicoloured
Subsidiary of Marshalls Coaches (Bedfordshire)

*SHIRE COACHES

31 FROGMORE, PARK STREET, ST ALBANS AL4 0SX
Tel: 01727 874494
Fax: 01727 873370
E-mail: shirecoaches@supanet.com
Ptnrs: Lynda Maney Michael Maney **Man**: Steven Impey **Travel Cnsltnt**: Matthew Maney
Fleet: 1 0 coach.
Chassis: 3 Dennis. 1 MAN. 5 Scania. 1 Volvo.
Ops incl: local bus services, school contracts, excursions & tours, private hire, express, continental tours.
Livery: Various colours and designs.

SIMMONDS COACHES LTD

9 BROADWATER AVENUE, LETCHWORTH SG6 3HE.
Tel: 01462 684729.
Fax: 01462 683879.
Garage: NORTON WAY NORTH, LETCHWORTH
Tel: 01462 683879 (night 01462 730517).
Dirs: M. J. Simmonds, B. J. Simmonds, S. M. Simmonds.
Fleet: 12 - 1 double-deck bus, 7 coach, 2 midicoach, 2 minicoach.
Chassis: 1 Daimler. 1 MAN. 2 Mercedes. 1 Toyota. 7 Volvo.
Bodies: 1 Caetano. 2 Optare. 1 Park Royal. 4 Plaxton. 4 Van Hool.
Ops incl: local bus services, school contracts, excursions & tours, private hire.
Livery: Fawn/Orange/Brown.
Ticket System: Setright.

SMITH BUNTINGFORD

CLAREMONT, BALDOCK ROAD, BUNTINGFORD SG9 9DJ
Tel/Fax: 01763 271516
Prop: Graham Smith.
Fleet: 6 minicoach.
Chassis: 1 Ford Transit. 1 LDV. 1 Citroen. 1 Peugeot.
Bodies: Autobus, Courtside, Advance
Ops incl: private hire
Livery: White/Orange/Brown

G. A. SMITHS COACHES LTD

THE GARAGE, WIGGINTON HP23 6EJ
Tel: 01442 823163.
Fax: 01442 824799.
Dirs: G. A. Smith (**Man Dir**), Mrs S. N. Smith, J. Smith.
Fleet: 8 - 6 coach, 1 midicoach, 1 minicoach. **Chassis**: 2 Mercedes. 6 Volvo.
Bodies: 2 Mercedes. 1 Plaxton. 1 Reeve Burgess.
Ops incl: local bus services, excursions & tours, private hire, continental tours.
Livery: Red/Cream.

SOUTH MIMMS TRAVEL LTD

21 GOWERFIELD, SOUTH MIMMS EN6 3NT.
Tel: 01707 660664.
Fax: 01923 859396.
Man Dir: S. J. Griffiths.
Fleet: 8 coach.
Chassis: 3 Ford. 3 Leyland. 1 Volvo.
Bodies: Duple. Plaxton. Van Hool.
Ops incl: school contracts, excursions & tours, private hire, continental tours.
Livery: Red/Black/Gold.

SOVEREIGN BUS & COACH CO LTD

BABBAGE ROAD, STEVENAGE SG1 2EQ
Tel: 01438 746066
Fax: 01438 318255
E-mail: enquiry@sovereignbus.co.uk
Web site: www.sovereignbus.co.uk
Fleetname: Sovereign, GreenLine
Man Dir: S D Wilde **Ops Dir**: J A Joslin
Comm Dir: D J Hurry **Gen Man**: H Barrington
Fleet: 86 - 76 single-deck bus, 5 coach, 5 midibus.
Chassis: 33 Dennis. 5 Mercedes. 48 Volvo.
Bodies: 9 Alexander. 43 Plaxton. 34 Wright.
Ops incl: local bus services, school contracts
Livery: Blue/Cream (Green Line - green/white; school - yellow)
Ticket System: Wayfarer 3.

STANSTED TRANSIT

OFFICE 17, BUILDING 44, STANSTED BUSINESS PARK, STANSTED AIRPORT CM24 1RY
Tel: 01229 681786
Prop: André Morris. **Co Sec**: Gillian Morris.
Ops Man: Sîan Morris. **Ch Eng**: Suzanne Morris.
Fleet: 33 - 5 double-deck bus, 22 single-deck bus, 6 midibus.
Chassis: 1 DAF, 12 Dennis, 1 Leyland National, 5 MCW. 7 Optare.
Bodies: 1 Alexander, 2 Caetano, 7 Leyland, 1 Leyland National, 5 MCW. 7 Optare. 7 Plaxton. 1 UVG. 2 Wright.
Ops incl: local bus services, school contracts, private hire.
Livery: White.
Ticket system: ERG.

*SULLIVAN BUSES LTD

FIRST FLOOR, DEARDS HOUSE, ST ALBANS ROAD, POTTERS BAR EN6 3NE
Tel: 01707 646803
Fax: 01707 646804
E-mail: admin@sullivanbuses.com
Web site: www.sullivanbuses.com
Man Dir: Dean Sullivan
Fleet: 36 - 26 double-deck bus, 10 single-deck bus
Chassis: 3 AEC.11 Leyland. 9 MCW. 10 Transbus. 2 Volvo.
Bodies: 7 Caetano. 1 Carlyle. 2 East Lancs. 11 Leicester. 9 MCW. 3 Park Royal. 3 Plaxton.
Ops incl: local bus services
Livery: Red
Ticket system: Wayfarer TGX

*TATES COACHES

44 HIGH STREET, MARKYATE, ST ALBANS AL3 8PA
Tel: 01582 840297
Fax: 01582 840014
E-mail: tates-coaches@fsbdial.co.uk
Web site: www.tates-coaches.co.uk
Chmn: Alan M Tate **Dirs**: Antony Tate, Stephen Tate
Fleet: 10 - 2 single-deck bus, 8 coach
Chassis: 1 Bedford. 1 Bova. 3 DAF. 2 Mercedes. 1 Neoplan. 2 Scania.
Bodies: 1 Bova. 2 Caetano. 2 Irizar. 1 Neoplan. 2 Plaxton. 2 Hispano.
Ops incl: school contracts, excursions & tours, private hire, continental tours.
Livery: Cream/Blue/Orange

TERRY'S COACHES

2 HIGH STREET GREEN, HEMEL HEMPSTEAD HP2 7AQ
Tel: 01442 265850
Ptnrs: T. Bunyan, Mrs S. Bunyan.
Fleet: 5 - 1 single-deck bus, 3 midicoach, 1 minicoach.
Chassis: 1 DAF. **Bodies**: 1 Caetano, 1 Leicester, 1 Optare.

Ops incl: local bus services, school contracts, private hire, excursions & tours.
Livery: Blue/White

*TRUSTLINE SERVICES LTD
THE DEPOT, FILLETS FARM, STANSTEAD ROAD, HUNSDON SG12 8QA
Tel: 01920 877877
Fax: 01279 877079
E-mail: trustlineservices@talk21.com
Fleetname: Trustline
Man Dir: Helen Bowden **Ops Dir**: Mark Bowden **Ch Eng**: Bob Campbell **Fleet Eng**: Derek Collier
Fleet: 15 - 2 double-deck bus, 9 single-deck bus, 4 minibus.
Chassis: 8 Dennis. 1 MAN. 1 MCW. 4 Mercedes. 1 Volvo.
Bodies: 2 Alexander. 2 Optare. 10 Plaxton. 1 Transbus.
Ops incl: local bus services, school contracts.
Livery: Yellow/Red/Blue.
Ticket System: Almex A90

UNICORN COACHES LTD
[wc] [seatbelt] [A/c]
PO BOX 45, HATFIELD AL9 5LD
Tel: 0845 658 5000
E-mail: info@unicorncoaches.com
Web site: www.unicorncoaches.com
Man Dir: Mrs J E Pleshette **Co Sec**: S T Saltmarsh
Fleet: 3 - 2 coach, 1 minibus.
Chassis: 1 Scania. 1 Volvo.
Bodies: 1 Irizar. 1 Van Hool. 1 other.
Ops incl: excursions & tours, continental tours.
Livery: White

UNIVERSITYBUS LTD [disabled]
GYPSY MOTH AVENUE, HATFIELD BUSINESS PARK, HATFIELD AL10 9BS
Tel: 01707 255764
Fax: 01707 255761
Web site: www.universitybus.co.uk
Chmn: T. Wilson. **Gen Man**: M. Finn.
Fleet Eng: S. Buckland. **Co Sec**: P. Waters.
Ops Man: P. Campbell **Dir**: P. Neville.
Fleet: 42 single-deck bus.
Chassis: 4 Bluebird, 8 DAF, 19 Dennis, 1 Leyland, 1 Marshall, 4 Mercedes, 3 Optare.

Bodies: 4 Bluebird, 1 Mercedes, 1 East Lancs, 1 Leyland, 5 Marshall, 2 Northern Counties, 4 Optare, 1 Reeve Burgess, 20 Wright.
Ops incl: local bus services, school contracts.
Livery: White/Grey skirt.
Ticket System: Wayfarer 3 Inform.

LEN WRIGHT BAND SERVICES LTD
[wc] [galley] [key] [T]
9 ELTON WAY, WATFORD WD2 8HH.
Tel: 01923 238611.
Fax: 01923 230134.
E-mail: lwbs1@aol.com
Web site: www.lenwright.co.uk
Ops Dir: L. Collins.
Fleet: 13 - 6 coach, 5 double-deck coach (all sleeper), 2 minibus.
Chassis: 1 Bova. 2 Mercedes. 4 Scania. 6 Volvo.
Bodies: 1 Bova. 2 Irizar. 2 Jonckheere. 2 Plaxton. 4 Van Hool. 2 Autobus.
Ops incl: specialist private hire.
Livery: Grey.

ISLE OF WIGHT

*AWAY DAYS
[wc] [galley] [seatbelt] [A/c] [key]
56 WILTON ROAD, SHANKLIN PO37 7BZ
Tel: 01983 862774
Fax: 01983 864315
E-mail: awaydays@supanet.com
Website: www.awaydaysiowco.uk
Props: Roy Townend, Hedda Townend
Fleet: 3 coach
Chassis: 2 Iveco. 1 Scania.
Bodies: 2 Beulas. 1 Berkhof.
Ops incl: school contracts, excursions & tours, private hire, continental tours.
Livery: White with orange lettering and multi-coloured kite.

GANGES COACHES [seatbelt]
77 PLACE ROAD, COWES PO31 7AE
Tel: 01983 296666
Fax: 01983 296666
Prop: John Gange
Fleet: 9 - 4 coach, 3 midicoach, 1 minibus, 1 minicoach.
Chassis: 1 AEC. 1 Bedford. 1 Ford. 1 Leyland. 3 Mercedes. 1 Renault. 1 Peugeot/Talbot
Bodies: 2 Duple. 1 Mercedes. 3 Plaxton. 3 other.
Ops incl: private hire
Livery: Red/Cream and Blue/Cream

GRAND HOTEL TOURS LTD (KIM'S COACHES) [wc]
GRAND HOTEL, CULVER PARADE, SANDOWN PO36 8QA.
Tel: 01983 402236.
Fax: 01983 406784.
Fleetname: Grand Tours.
Prop: R. J. H. & M. A. Hayter.
Sec: Mrs Marilyn Gerrard. **Traf Man**: G. Worrall. **Gen Man**: R. H. J. Hayter.
Fleet: 3 coach.
Chassis: DAF. Dennis. Scania.
Bodies: Duple. Van Hool. LAG.
Ops incl: excursions & tours, private hire.
Livery: Yellow/White.

ISLAND COACH SERVICES LTD [wc] [galley] [seatbelt] [key]
UNIT D10, SPITHEAD BUSINESS CENTRE, NEWPORT ROAD, LAKE PO36 9PH
Tel: 01983 408080
Fax: 01983 408808
Website: www.islandcoachservices.co.uk
E-mail: info@islandcoachservices.co.uk
Dir: R J Long **Tran Man**: D Draper
Fleet: 11 coach
Chassis: 1 DAF. 1 Dennis. 1 Mercedes. 8 Volvo.
Bodies: 2 Caetano. 2 Jonckheere. 1 Mercedes. 1 Neoplan. 3 Plaxton. 2 Van Hool.

Ops incl: excursions & tours, private hire, continental tours, school contracts.
Livery: Blue flash/White.

ISLE OF WIGHT COUNTY TRANSPORT DEPARTMENT
[disabled] [seatbelt]
21 WHITCOMBE ROAD, NEWPORT PO30 1YS
Tel: 01983 823734.
Fax: 01983 825818.
Fleetname: Wightbus.
Tran Man: A. A. Morris. **Ops Man**: J. Lamb.
Fleet: 27 - 1 double-deck bus, 13 single-deck bus, 2 coach, 11 midibus.
Chassis: 13 Dennis. 1 Ford. 2 Leyland. 11 Mercedes.
Bodies: 2 Caetano. 1 Duple. 1 ECW. 1 Reeve Burgess. 15 Wadham Stringer. 1 Wright. 2 LCB. 1 Mellor. 1 Steedrive. 2 Withey.
Ops incl: local bus services, school contracts, excursions & tours, private hire.
Livery: White with Orange and Blue stripes.
Ticket System: Setright.

*KARDAN TRAVEL
[wc] [galley] [seatbelt] [A/c] [key]
490 NEWPORT ROAD, COWES PO31 8QU
Tel/Fax: 01983 520995
Web site: www.kardan.co.uk
E-mail: info@kardan.co.uk
Dirs: R L Hodgson, L Hodgson

[A/c]	Air conditioning	
[disabled]	Vehicles suitable for disabled	
[galley]	Coach(es) with galley facilities	
[wc]	Coach(es) with toilet facilities	
[seatbelt]	Seat belt-fitted vehicles	
[R]	Recovery service available (not 24 hr)	
[R24]	24hr recovery service	
[key]	Replacement vehicle available	
[T]	Toilet-drop facilities available	
[vintage]	Vintage vehicle(s) available	
[bus]	Open top vehicle(s)	

Ops Man: P Cooper
Fleet: 5 coach
Chassis: 1 Leyland. 2 Setra. 2 Volvo.
Bodies: 3 Plaxton. 2 Setra.
Ops incl: private hire

*SEAVIEW SERVICES LTD
R24

SEAFIELD GARAGE, COLLEGE FARM, FAULKNER LANE, SANDOWN PO36 9AZ
Tel: 01983 407070
Fax: 01983 407045
Recovery: 01983 613100
E-mail: mail@seaview-services.com
Web site: www.seaview-services.com
Chmn: Philip Robinson **Dirs**: Albert Robinson, Mary Robinson **Ops Man**: Karen Heathfield **Ch Eng**: Jim Woods
Co Tour Man: Mairi Robinson
Fleet: 10 - 8 coach, 1 open-top bus, 1 midicoach.

Chassis: 1 Bristol. 2 Iveco. 1 Toyota. 6 Volvo.
Bodies: 2 Beulas. 1 Caetano. 1 Jonckheere. 1 MCW. 5 Van Hool.
Ops incl: excursions & tours, private hire, continental tours, express, school contracts.
Livery: Green/Red

*THE SOUTHERN VECTIS OMNIBUS CO LTD
R24

NELSON ROAD, NEWPORT PO30 1RD
Tel: 01983 522456
Fax: 01983 524961
E-mail: a.white@southernvectis.com
Web site: www.svoc.co.uk
Chmn: Stuart Linn **Man Dir**: Alan White
Ops Man: Mick Poole
Fleet: 84 - 45 double-deck bus, 11 single-deck bus, 1 coach, 8 open-top bus, 19 midibus.
Chassis: 6 Bristol. 12 Dennis. 19 Iveco. 25 Leyland. 22 Volvo.

Bodies: 2 Duple. 6 ECW. 16 Leyland. 9 Marshall. 8 Mellor. 24 Northern Counties. 9 Plaxton. 2 Reeve Burgess. 6 UVG. 1 Dormobile. 1 Robin Hood.
Ops incl: local bus services, school contracts, excursions and tours, private hire, continental tours.
Livery: Red/Blue/Orange & Yellow.
Ticket system: Wayfarer

*JOHN WOODHAMS VINTAGE TOURS

GROVE ROAD, RYDE PO33 3LH
Tel/Fax: 01983 812147
E-mail: vintagetours@btconnect.com
Web site: www.vintagetours.net
Prop: John Woodhams
Fleet: 2 midicoach.
Chassis: 2 Bedford.
Bodies: 2 Duple.
Ops incl: excursions & tours, private hire.
Livery: Two tone Green.

KENT

AMBERLEE UK LTD
56 HOLLY ROAD, WAINSCOTT, ROCHESTER ME2 4LH
Tel: 01634 356000
Fax: 01634 338989
E-mail: enquiries@amberlee.co.uk
Fleet: 20 - 7 double-deck bus, 6 single-deck bus, 7 coach
Ops incl: local bus services

ARRIVA SOUTHERN COUNTIES LTD
INVICTA HOUSE, ARMSTRONG ROAD, MAIDSTONE ME15 6TX
Tel: 01622 697000
Fax: 01622 697001.
Web site: www.arriva.co.uk/southerncounties
Man Dir: Bob Scowen **Ch Eng**: Tony Ward
Fin Dir: Beverley Lawson. **Comm Dir**: Kevin Hawkins **Ops Dir**: Steve Fearns
Fleet: 680 - 171 double-deck bus, 344 single-deck bus, 132 midibus, 33 coach.
Chassis: Dennis. Optare. Volvo.
Bodies: Alexander. Optare. Plaxton. Wright.
Ops incl: local bus services, private hire.
Livery: Blue/Stone (red in London area).
Ticket System: Wayfarer 3.

DOUGLAS C. ALLEN (t/a D.C. Travel)
FRENSHAM, WHITEPOST LANE, SOLE STREET DA13 9AX
Tel/Fax: 01474 814298
Fleetname: D. C. Travel. **Prop**: D. C. Allen.
Fleet: 6 coach.
Chassis: 1 AEC. 1 Ford. 4 Leyland.
Bodies: 2 Duple. 4 Plaxton.
Ops incl: local bus services, excursions & tours, private hire, continental tours.
Livery: Maroon/White.

*ASM COACHES
8 THE OAZE, THANET WAY, WHITSTABLE CT5 4TQ
Tel/Fax: 01227 280254
E-mail: asmcoaches@eurobell.co.uk
Web site: www.asmcoaches.co.uk
Props: Steven R Morrish, Alison Morrish.
Fleet: 2 minibus
Chassis: 1 Ford Transit. 1 LDV.
Ops incl: school contracts, excursions & tours, private hire, continental tours.
Livery: White/Mauve

*AUTOCAR BUS & COACH SERVICES LTD
64 WHETSTED ROAD, FIVE OAK GREEN, TONBRIDGE TN12 6RT
Tel: 01892 833830
Fax: 01892 836977
Dir: Eric Baldock **Fleet Eng**: Ray Tompsett
Fleet: 8 - 4 single-deck bus, 2 coach, 1 double-deck coach, 1 midicoach.
Chassis: 1 DAF. 1 Dennis. 4 Leyland. 1 Mercedes. 1 Scania.
Bodies: 1 Alexander. 1 Duple. 2 East Lancs. 2 Plaxton. 1 Wadham Stringer. Wright.
Ops incl: local bus services, school contracts, private hire.
Livery: White/Purple (two shades)
Ticket System: Wayfarer 2

BEXLEY COACHLINES
3 HATHERLEY ROAD, SIDCUP DA14 4BH
Tel/Fax: 020 8302 7551.
Web site: www.bexleycoach.co.uk
Gen Man: Glyn Matthews.
Fleet: 5 coach.
Chassis: 1 AEC. 2 Dennis. 2 Volvo.
Bodies: 5 Plaxton.
Ops incl: excursions & tours, private hire.
Livery: Green/Cream.

*BRITANNIA COACHES
R

BRITANNIA HOUSE, HOLLOW WOOD ROAD, DOVER CT17 0UB
Tel: 01304 228111
Fax: 01304 215350
E-mail: enquiries@britannia-coaches.co.uk
Web site: www.britannia-coaches.co.uk.
Ptnrs: Barry Watson, Danny Lawson.
Fleet: 23 minicoach.
Chassis/bodies: 15 Mercedes. 8 Renault.
Ops incl: private hire, school contracts, express, excursions & tours.

BROWNS COACHES
MANOR POUND, BRABOURNE, ASHFORD TN25 5LG.
Tel: 01303 813555.
Prop: P. L. Browne.
Fleet: 7 - 6 coach, 1 minibus.
Chassis: 6 Bedford. 1 Mercedes.
Bodies: 1 Duple. 1 Plaxton.
Ops incl: excursions & tours, private hire.
Livery: Red/Ivory.

BUZZLINES
R24

UNIT G1, LYMPNE INDUSTRIAL PARK, LYMPNE CT21 4LR
Tel: 01303 261870 (out of hours 07767 475625)
Fax: 01303 230093
E-mail: sales@:buzzlines.co.uk
Web site: www.buzzlines.co.uk
Dir: Mrs K Busbridge **Man Dir**: N. P. Busbridge **Eng Man**: L Mant **Ops Man**: K Barraclough **Traf Man**: G Creasey
Fleet: 42 - 3 single-deck bus, 26 coach, 2 double-deck coach, 5 minbus, 3 minicoach, 3 people carriers.

Chassis: 1 AEC. 1 Bedford.
1 Ford. 1 Leyland. 7 Mercedes. 4 Neoplan.
6 Scania. 10 Setra. 2 Toyota, 7 Volvo.
2 Volkswagen.
Bodies: 2 Caetano. 2 Duple. 4 Irizar.
1 Jonckheere, 4 Neoplan, 9 Plaxton, 10
Setra, 3 Mercedes, 3 Cheetah, 1 Citaro,
2 Caravelle, 1 Galaxy.
Ops incl: local bus services, school
contracts, excursions & tours, private hire,
continental tours.
Livery: Modern multicoloured.

CARDINAL COACHES

43 CHERRY TREE AVENUE, DOVER
CT16 2NL
Tel: 01304 212859
Fax: 01304 207890
E-mail:
cardinal.travel@btinternet.com
Prop: Tony Alexander **Tran Man**: Lawrence
MacGregor **Office Man**: Diane Matthews
Fleet: coach, minibus, midicoach.
Chassis: DAF. Iveco. Mercedes. Optare.
Scania. Volvo.
Bodies: Berkhof. Jonckheere. Mercedes.
Optare. Plaxton. other
Ops incl: local bus services, school
contracts, excursions & tours, private hire,
continental tours.
Livery: White with red logo
Ticket System: Almex.

CENTRAL MINI COACHES

177 LOWER ROAD, DOVER
CT17 0RE.
Tel/Fax: 01304 823030.
Prop: P. Hull.
Fleet: 6 - 5 minibus, 1 minicoach.
Chassis: 3 Bedford. 1 Mercedes. 1 Renault.
Ops incl: private hire, school contracts.

*CHALKWELL COACH HIRE & TOURS

195 CHALKWELL ROAD,
SITTINGBOURNE ME10 1BJ
Tel: 01795 423983
Fax: 01795 431855
E-mail: coachhire@chalkwell.co.uk
Web site: www.chalkwell.com
Man Dir: Clive Eglinton **Ops Man**: Roland
Eglinton **Coach Reservations Man**:
Richard Senior
Fleet: 31 - 18 coach, 3 midibus,
6 midicoach, 4 minicoach.
Chassis: 9 Dennis. 1 Iveco. 3 LDV.
9 Mercedes. 9 Volvo.
Bodies: 5 Alexander. 1 Caetano.
18 Plaxton. 2 UVG. 1 Wadham Stringer.
Ops incl: local bus services, school
contracts, excursions & tours, private hire,
express, continental tours.
Livery: White/Red/Black
Ticket System: Almex A90

*CONISTON COACHES LTD
See London

CRAKERS COACHES

52 BIRDWOOD AVENUE, DEAL
CT14 9SF
Tel: 01304 362002
Prop: Alf Craker
Fleet: 1 coach.
Chassis: 1 Volvo.
Bodies: 1 Van Hool.
Ops incl: private hire.
Livery: Cream/Red.

*CROSSKEYS COACHES

ASHFORD ROAD, NEWINGREEN,
HYTHE CT21 4JB
Tel: 01303 266533
Fax: 01303 262357
E-mail: coachhire@crosskeys.uk.com
Web site: www.crosskeys.uk.com
Props: A Johnson
Fleet: 16 - 4 single-deck bus, 11 coach,
1 minicoach.
Chassis: 1 Bedford. 9 Bova. 9 DAF.
2 Dennis. 3 Leyland National.
Bodies: 9 Bova. 3 Leyland National.
3 Plaxton. 1 Wright.
Ops incl: school contracts, excursions &
tours, private hire, continental tours.
Livery: White/Orange/Brown

*CROWN COACHES
See London

*ALAN DAWNEY HOLIDAYS LTD

UNIT 6, TRANSIT WORKS, POWER
STATION ROAD, HALFWAY,
SHEPPEY ME12 3AD
Tel/Fax: 01795 662688
E-mail: dawneyholidays@aol.com
Dirs: Alan Dawney, Carole Dawney (**Tran Man**)
Fleet: 10 - 4 coach, 1 minicoach, 5 midibus.
Chassis: 1 Dennis. 1 Ford Transit. 4 LDV.
1 MAN. 1 Toyota. 2 Volvo.
Bodies: include - 4 Caetano. 1 Plaxton.
Ops incl: excursions & tours, private hire.
Livery: White/Green with green/yellow flash

EASTONWAYS LTD

MANSTON ROAD, RAMSGATE
CT12 6HJ
Tel: 01843 588944
Fax: 01843 582300
E-mail:
ele@eastonways.demon.co.uk
Web site:
www.eastonways.demon.co.uk
Chmn/Co Sec E. L. Easton.
Man Dir: D. Austin **Dir**: Y. M. Easton.
Ops Man: S. Lee. **Eng**: E. Easton.
Fleet: 15 - 2 double-deck coach, 8 single-
deck bus, 3 coach, 2 midicoach.
Chassis: 2 Bristol. 1 DAF. 1 Optare. 2
Toyota. 1 Volvo.
Bodies: 1 Caetano. 1 Duple. 2 Northern
Counties. 8 Optare. 1 Van Hool.

Ops incl: local bus services, school
contracts, private hire.
Livery: Coaches: Blue/Silver. Buses: Red.
Ticket System: Wayfarer.

*EUROLINK FOKESTONE

GREATWORTH, CANTERBURY
ROAD, ETCHINGHILL,
FOLKESTONE CT18 8BS
Tel: 01303 862767
Fax: 01303 862484
Ptnrs: A S Williams
Fleet: 8 - 4 midicoach, 4 minibus.
Chassis: 1 Ford Transit. 2 MAN.
3 Mercedes. 1 Renault. 1 Toyota.
Bodies: 3 Caetano. 1 Mercedes. 1 Optare.
3 Robin Hood.
Ops incl: school contracts, private hire.
Livery: White/Orange.

FARLEIGH COACHES

ST PETERS WORKS, HALL ROAD,
WOULDHAM, ROCHESTER
ME1 3XL
Tel: 01634 201065.
Fax: 01634 660350.
Prop: J. M. Smith.
Livery: White/Yellow/Red/Black.

FERRYMAN TRAVEL

RECTORY LANE NORTH,
LEYBOURNE ME19 5HD.
Tel/Fax: 01732 843396
Fleet: 4 minibus.
Chassis: 3 DAF. 1 Ford Transit.
Ops incl: school contracts, excursions &
tours, private hire, continental tours.

G & S TRAVEL

14 PYSONS ROAD, RAMSGATE
CT12 6TS.
Tel: 01843 591105.
Fax: 01843 596274.
E-mail: malc@pysons.freeserve.co.uk
Web site: www.g-s-travel.co.uk
E-mail: malc@g-s-travel.freeserve.co.uk
Dirs: Mrs Shirley Rimmer, George Rimmer,
Malcolm Wood.
Fleet: 13 - 2 double-deck bus, 9 coach,
1 minibus, 1 midicoach.
Chassis: 1 Leyland. 1 Toyota. 8 Volvo.
1 Van Hool Integral. 1 LDV.
Bodies: 1 Alexander. 4 Caetano. 1 MCW.
5 Plaxton. 1 Van Hool. 1 LDV.
Ops incl: school contracts, excursions &
tours, private hire, continental tours.
Livery: Green/White.

JAYCREST LTD

14 BAYFORD ROAD,
SITTINGBOURNE ME10 3AD
Tel: 01795 438400
Fleet: 22 - 1 single-deck bus, 3 coach,
18 midibus
Ops incl: local bus services

- A/c — Air conditioning
- Vehicles suitable for disabled
- Coach(es) with galley facilities
- wc — Coach(es) with toilet facilities
- Seat belt-fitted vehicles
- R — Recovery service available (not 24 hr)
- R24 — 24hr recovery service
- Replacement vehicle available
- T — Toilet-drop facilities available
- Vintage vehicle(s) available
- Open top vehicle(s)

*KENT COACH TOURS LTD

THE COACH STATION,
MALCOLM SARGENT ROAD,
ASHFORD TN23 6JW
Tel/Recovery: 01233 627330
Fax: 01233 612977
Web site: www.kentcoachtours.co.uk
Dirs: David Farmer, Ann Farmer, Andrew Farmer (**Co Sec**), Brian Farmer (**Ch Eng**)
Fleet: 13 - 1 single-deck bus, 7 coach, 5 minibus.
Chassis: 1 MAN. 5 Mercedes. 1 Optare. 7 Volvo
Bodies: 1 Optare. 12 Plaxton.
Ops incl: local bus services, school contracts, excursions & tours, private hire.
Livery: Blue
Ticket System: Wayfarer

KENT COUNTY COUNCIL

COMMERCIAL SERVICES,
PASSENGER SERVICES, FORSTAL ROAD, AYLESFORD ME20 7HB
Tel: 01622 605935.
Fax: 01622 790338.
Tran Man: Darien Goodwin. **Ops Contr:** Roger Faunch. **Asst Ops Contr:** Mick Curd.
Fleet: 48 - 2 double-deck bus, 12 single-deck bus, 4 coach, 2 midibus, 1 midicoach, 27 minibus.
Chassis: 5 Dennis. 27 Iveco. 4 Leyland. 3 Mercedes. 4 Optare. 1 Volvo.
Bodies: 1 Alexander. 1 Caetano. 7 Leicester. 2 Leyland. 4 Optare. 6 Plaxton.27 Euromotive.
Ops incl: local bus services, school contracts, private hire.
Livery: Red on White.
Ticket System: Almex.

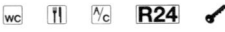

*THE KINGS FERRY

THE TRAVEL CENTRE,
EASTCOURT LANE, GILLINGHAM ME8 6HW
Tel: 01634 377577
Fax: 01634 370656
Recovery: 01634 265508
E-mail: sales@thekingsferry.co.uk
Web site: www.thekingsferry.co.uk
Fleetname: The Kings Ferry
Chmn: Peter O'Neill **Man Dir:** Steven O'Neill **Eng Man:** Danny Elford **Group Ops Man:** Ian Fraser
Fleet: 58 - 4 double-deck bus, 3 single-deck bus, 39 coach, 6 double-deck coach, 2 midicoach, 2 minicoach, 2 minibus.
Chassis: 1 DAF. 2 Dennis. 2 Iveco. 5 Mercedes. 1 Neoplan. 31 Scania. 6 Setra. 10 Volvo.
Bodies: 2 Alexander.16 Berkhof. 1 Bova. 1 Castrosua. 2 East Lancs. 3 Hispano. 6 Irizar. 5 Mercedes. 1 Neoplan. 2 Plaxton. 6 Setra. 1 Sunsundegui. 12 Van Hool.
Ops incl: local bus services, school contracts, excursions & tours, private hire, express, continental tours.
Livery: Yellow/Green

*KINGSMAN INTERNATIONAL TRAVEL

57 BRAMLEY AVENUE, FAVERSHAM ME13 8LP
Tel: 01795 531553
Fax: 01795 536798
E-mail: isoutherside@tiscali.co.uk
Prop: John Mancini **Ops Dir:** Jonathan Mancini
Fleet: 8 - 4 single-deck bus, 3 coach, 1 minibus.
Chassis: Mercedes. Neoplan.
Bodies: Mercedes. Neoplan.
Ops incl: local bus services, school contracts, excursions & tours, private hire, continental tours.
Livery: Blue/White

*LOGANS TOURS LTD

1 AND 2 THE COTTAGES,
NORTHFLEET GREEN DA13 9PT
Tel: 01474 833876
Fax: 01474 832038
E-mail: dave@loganstours.co.uk
Web site: www.loganstours.co.uk
Dir: David Logan.
Fleet: 2 coach.
Chassis: 1 Dennis. 1 Raba.
Bodies: 1 Caetano. 1 Ikarus.
Ops incl: excursions & tours, private hire, continental tours
Livery: Pink blending to White

LONDINIUM CHARTER

See David Watts, below

*LONDON LINK

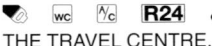

THE TRAVEL CENTRE,
EASTCOURT LANE, GILLINGHAM ME8 6HW
Tel: 020 8807 1177
Fax: 01634 370656
Recovery: 01634 265508
E-mail: sales@thelondonlink.com
Web site: www.thelondonlink.com
Fleetname: The Kings Ferry
Chmn: Peter O'Neill **Man Dir:** Steven O'Neill **Eng Man:** Danny Elford **Group Ops Man:** Ian Fraser
Ops incl: school contracts, private hire, express.
Livery: Green

MARTIN'S MINI-COACHES

See London.

NEW ENTERPRISE COACHES

CANNON LANE, TONBRIDGE TN9 1PP.
Tel: 01732 355256.
Fax: 01732 357716.
Prop: Arriva Southern Counties.
Gen Man: Chris Lawrence.
Eng Man: Andy Weber.
Fleet: 24 - 5 double-deck bus, 2 single-deck bus, 17 coach.
Chassis: 8 DAF. 3 Leyland. 4 MCW. 3 Scania. 6 Volvo.
Bodies: 2 Caetano. 3 Duple. 4 MCW. 1 PMT. 11 Plaxton. 1 Reeve Burgess. 3 Van Hool.
Ops incl: local bus services, school contracts, excursions & tours, private hire, continental tours.
Livery: White/Red/Blue.
Ticket System: Wayfarer II.

NU-VENTURE COACHES LTD

86 MILL HALL, AYLESFORD ME20 7JN
Tel: 01622 882288
Fax: 01622 718070
E-mail: nu-venture@breathemail.net
Web site: www.nu-venture.co.uk
Dirs: N. Kemp, D Quick.
Fleet: 37 - 10 double-deck bus, 12 single-deck bus, 4 coach, 11 midibus.
Chassis: Dennis. Leyland. Leyland National. MAN. Mercedes. Optare. Scania.
Bodies: Alexander. ECW. East Lancs. Irizar. Leyland. Leyland National. Marshall. Optare. Plaxton. Roe. UVG. Van Hool. Marcopolo.
Ops incl: local bus services, school contracts, private hire, continental tours.
Livery: White/Blue/Red
Ticket System: Wayfarer 3.

POYNTERS COACHES

WYE COACH DEPOT,
CHURCHFIELD WAY, ASHFORD TN25 5EQ.
Tel: 01233 812002.
Fax: 01233 813210.
Dir/Man: R. J. Poynter. **Dir:** B. J. Poynter.
Co Sec: M. J. P. Poynter.
Fleet: 16 - 2 double-deck bus, 6 single-deck bus, 7 coach, 1 double-deck coach.
Ops incl: local bus services, school contracts, excursions & tours, private hire, continental tours.
Livery: Cream/Orange.
Ticket System: Setright.

R. K. F. TRAVEL

19 COBB CLOSE, STROOD ME2 3TY
Tel/Fax: 01634 715897.
Dir: Ray Fraser.
Fleet: 2 minibus.
Chassis: 1 LDV, 1 VW.
Ops incl: private hire.

THE RAINHAM COACH CO

1A SPRINGFIELD ROAD,
GILLINGHAM ME7 1YJ
Tel/Fax: 01634 852020
Recovery: 07850 657653
E-mail: sales@rainhamcoach.co.uk
Web site: www.rainhamcoach.co.uk
Ptnrs: David Graham, Ronald Wisbey **Tran Man:** Alan Lorenston
Fleet: 18 - 4 midicoach, 14 minicoach.
Chassis/Bodies: 4 Ford Transit. 12 Mercedes, 2 Optare.
Ops incl: school contracts, excursions & tours, private hire, continental tours.
Livery: White with Magenta/Grey.

REDROUTE BUSES

GRANBYCOACHWORKS, GROVE ROAD, NORTHFLEET DA11 9AX
Hool.
Ops incl: local bus services, school contracts, excursions & tours, private hire, continental tours.

Tel: 01474 353896
Web site: www.redroutebus.com
Fleet: 25 - 14 double-deck bus, 3 single-deck bus, 1 coach, 7 minibus.
Ops incl: local bus services
Livery: Red

*REGENT COACHES
[wc] [seat] [Nc]

UNIT 16, ST AUGUSTINES BUSINESS PARK, SWALECLIFFE, WHITSTABLE CT5 2QJ
Tel: 01227 794345
Fax: 01227 795127
E-mail: info@regentcoaches.com
Web site: www.regentcoaches.co.uk
Props: Paul Regent, Kerry Regent **Tran Mans**: Garry Moore, Ken Bishop, Sam Regent **Wkshp Man**: Robert Wildish
Fleet: 23 - 2 midibus, 7 midicoach, 14 minicoach.
Chassis: 4 Iveco. 6 LDV. 11 Mercedes. 1 Renault. 1 other.
Ops incl: local bus services, school contracts, private hire.

RELIANCE TRAVEL
45 DARNLEY ROAD, GRAVESEND DA11 0SD
Tel: 01474 322002
Fax: 01474 536998
E-mail: info@reliance-travel.co.uk
Web site: www.reliance-travel.co.uk
Props: Redwing Coaches (*See London*)

ROUNDABOUT BUSES LTD
[bus] [bus]

3 HATHERLEY ROAD, SIDCUP DA14 4BH.
Tel/Fax: 020 8302 7551.
E-mail: info@roundaboutbuses.co.uk
Web site: www.roundaboutbuses.co.uk
Man Dir: Glyn Matthews.
Fleet: 6 - 1 single-deck bus, 1 minibus.
Chassis: 1 AEC. 2 Iveco. 5 Leyland.
Bodies: 3 ECW. 1 Marshall. 1 Park Royal. 1 Roe. 1 Robin Hood.
Ops incl: local bus services, school contracts.

Livery: Green/Cream.
Ticket System: Wayfarer.

SCOTLAND & BATES
[wc] [seat] [Nc] [✓]

HEATH ROAD, APPLEDORE TN26 2AJ
Tel: 01233 758325.
Fax: 01233 758611.
E-mail: info@scotlandandbates.co.uk
Werbsite: www.scotlandandbates.co.uk
Ptnrs: D. C. R. Bates, R. M. Bates, G. A. Bates.
Fleet: 17 coach.
Chassis: 17 Volvo.
Bodies: 9 Plaxton. 8 Van Hool.
Ops incl: private hire, school contracts.

SEATH COACHES [seat] [✓]
FIELDINGS, STONEHEAP ROAD, EAST STUDDAL CT15 5BU
Tel/Fax: 01304 620825.
Owner: P. Seath.
Fleet: 4 coach.
Chassis: Ford. Iveco. Leyland. Volvo.
Bodies: Caetano. Plaxton
Ops incl: school contracts, private hire.
Livery: Pink/White/Beige.

*SMITHS CONTINENTAL TRAVEL [wc] [galley] [seat] [✓] [T]

THE COACH STATION, KING STREET, BRENZETT TN29 9UD
Tel: 01797 344228
Fax: 01797 344248
Man Dir: Dave Smith **Ops Man**: Steve Rees **Ch Eng**: F C Ovenden
Fleet: 17 - 16 coach, 1 double-deck coach.
Chassis: 1 DAF. 9 Leyland. 7 Scania.
Bodies: 2 Jonckheere. 11 Plaxton. 4 Van Hool.
Ops incl: local bus services, school contracts, excursions & tours, private hire, continental tours.
Livery: Blue/White
Ticket system: Wayfarer

*SOUTHLANDS TRAVEL LTD [wc] [seat] [Nc]
THE COACH STATION, LONDON ROAD, SWANLEY BR8 8BY
Tel: 01322 660661
Fax: 01322 665610
Web site: www.southlandstravel.co.uk
Dir: N Kemp **Gen Man**: D Booker **Eng Man**: N Hogg
Fleet: 20 - 2 double-deck bus, 11 coach, 3 midibus, 3 minibus, 1 minicoach.
Chassis: 9 Dennis. 8 Leyland. 3 Optare.
Bodies: 2 Duple. 5 East Lancs. 2 Leyland. 6 Northern Counties. 3 Optare. 2 Plaxton.
Ops incl: local bus services, excursions & tours, private hire, school contracts.
Livery: Yellow/Blue
Ticket system: Wayfarer 2

SOUTHNOR COACHES [seat]
91 DARTFORD ROAD, DARTFORD DA1 3ES.
Tel/Fax: 01322 228963.
Owner: D. Hucker.
Fleet: 2 - 1 coach, 1 minibus.
Chassis: Volvo. **Body**: Plaxton.
Ops incl: excursions & tours, private hire, continental tours.

*SPOT HIRE TRAVEL [seat] [Nc]
STATION APPROACH, BEARSTED RAILWAY STATION, MAIDSTONE ME14 4PH
Tel: 01622 738932
Fax: 01622 630406
Prop: Roger Young
Fleet: 11 - 6 coach, 1 midicoach, 4 minicoach.
Chassis: 5 Mercedes. 6 Volvo.
Bodies: 2 Autobus. 1 Jonckheere. 2 Mercedes. 5 Plaxton. 1 Van Hool.
Ops incl: school contracts, private hire.
Livery: Cream

STAGECOACH IN EAST KENT & HASTINGS [disabled] [wc] [seat]

BUS STATION, ST GEORGE'S LANE, CANTERBURY CT1 2SY
Tel: 01227 828103
Fax: 01227 828150
Web site: www.stagecoachbus.com
Ch Exec: Brian Souter **Man Dir UK Bus**: L Warneford **Group Fin Dir**: M Griffiths **Co Sec**: A Whitnall **Man Dir**: Paul Southgate **Ops Dir**: Neil Install **Eng Dir**: Keith Dyball
Fleet: 302 - 143 double-deck bus, 45 single-deck bus, 17 coach, 45 midibus, 52 minibus.
Chassis: 48 Dennis. 3 Dodge. 1 Ford. 4 Ford Transit. 43 Leyland. 9 MAN. 52 Mercedes. 44 Scania. 106 Volvo.
Bodies: 182 Alexander. 4 Leyland. 7 Leyland. 74 Northern Counties. 40 Plaxton. 3 Wadham Stringer. 3 Wright.
Ops incl: local bus services, express.
Livery: Stagecoach (Blue,Orange,White,Red); National Express (White).
Ticket System: ERG/Wayfarer.

The Grasshopper Inn

13th Century Tudor Inn, 21st Century hospitality
Coffee, Drinks, Lunch or Dinner Stops
Kent/Surrey's Best Carvery
We welcome Coach Parties
Complimentary meal/refreshment
for driver with each coach party
Massive car park with coach bays
Just give us a call. . . .
Rural location but close to M25 (between Junction 5 & 6)
The Grasshopper Inn, Moorhouse (A25) Nr Westerham Kent/Surrey Border
Tel: 01959 563136   Fax: 01959 564823
website: www.grasshopperinn.co.uk   e-mail: info@grasshopperinn.co.uk

---

Nc	Air conditioning
[disabled]	Vehicles suitable for disabled
[galley]	Coach(es) with galley facilities
wc	Coach(es) with toilet facilities
[seat]	Seat belt-fitted vehicles
R	Recovery service available (not 24 hr)
R24	24hr recovery service
✓	Replacement vehicle available
T	Toilet-drop facilities available
[vintage]	Vintage vehicle(s) available
[bus]	Open top vehicle(s)

STREAMLINE (MAIDSTONE) LTD

WEST STATION APPROACH, MAIDSTONE ME16 8RJ
Tel: 01622 750750
Fax: 01622 750751
Web site: www.streamlinetaxis.co.uk
Dir: Ron Parker **Gen Man**: Andrew Parker
Fleet: coach, minicoach, midicoach.
Chassis/Bodies: 1 DAF. 1 LDV. 4 Mercedes Benz. 2 Setra.

TANGNEY TOURS

PILGRIM HOUSE, STATION COURT, BOROUGH GREEN TN15 8AF
Tel: 01732 885688.
Fax: 01732 886885.
Propr: P. J. Tawney. **Ops Man**: S. L. Hedley
Fleet: 5 - 4 single-deck coach, 1 midicoach.
Chassis: 4 Setra.
Bodies: 1 Caetano. 4 Setra.
Ops incl: excursions & tours, private hire, continental tours.

THOMSETT'S COACHES

50 GOLF ROAD, DEAL CT14 6QB
Tel/Fax: 01304 374731
E-mail: sythomsett@thomsettscoaches.fsnet.co.uk
Web site: www.thomsettscoaches.co.uk
Prop: S. J. Thomsett
Fleet: 5 - 4 coach, 1 midicoach.
Chassis: 3 Bedford. 1 MAN. 1 Scania.
Bodies: 1 Caetano. 3 Plaxton. 1 Van Hool.
Ops incl: school contracts, private hire.
Livery: White/Black/Red.

*TIM'S TRAVEL R24

THE COACH STATION, DORSET, SHEERNESS ME12 1LT
Tel: 01634 265511
Fax: 01634 370656
Recovery: 01634 265508
Fleetname: The Kings Ferry
Chmn: Peter O'Neill **Man Dir**: Steven O'Neill **Eng Man**: Danny Elford **Group Ops Man**: Ian Fraser
Fleet: 13 - 11 coach, 2 double-deck coach.
Chassis: 1 DAF. 4 Mercedes. 2 Scania. 6 Volvo.
Bodies: 1 Berkhof. 1 Caetano. 4 Mercedes. 6 Plaxton. 1 Van Hool.
Ops incl: local bus services, school contracts, excursions & tours, private hire, express.
Livery: Green

*TRACKS VEHICLE SERVICES LTD

THE FLOTS, BROOKLAND, TN29 9TF
Tel: 01797 344164
Fax: 01797 344135
E-mail: info@tracks-travel.com
Web site: tracks-travel.com
Man Dir: Andrew Toms.
Fleet: 6 - 5 coach, 1 double-deck coach.
Chassis: 1 DAF. 1 Mercedes. 1 Scania. 2 Setra.
Bodies: 1 Caetano. 1 Mercedes. 2 Setra. 1 Van Hool.
Ops incl: excursions & tours, continental tours.
Livery: White

*TRAVEL RITE R24

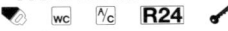

THE TRAVEL CENTRE, EASTCOURT LANE, GILLINGHAM ME8 6HW
Tel: 01634 265511
Fax: 01634 370656
Recovery: 01634 265508
E-mail: sales@travelrite.co.uk
Web site: www.travelrite.co.uk
Fleetname: The Kings Ferry
Chmn: Peter O'Neill **Man Dir**: Steven O'Neill **Eng Man**: Danny Elford **Group Ops Man**: Ian Fraser
Fleet: 7 - 5 coach, 1 double-deck coach, 1 minibus.
Chassis: 1 DAF. 1 Mercedes. 5 Scania.
Bodies: 2 Berkhof. 2 Irizar. 1 Mercedes. 1 Plaxton. 1 Van Hool.
Ops incl: school contracts, private hire.
Livery: Yellow

*VIKING MINICOACHES

UNIT 1, LYSANDER CLOSE, PYSONS ROAD INDUSTRIAL ESTATE, BROADSTAIRS CT10 2YJ
Tel/Fax: 01843 860876
Fax: 01843 866975
Prop: P A Troke
Fleet: 6 - 2 midicoach, 4 minicoach.
Chassis/bodies: 1 Mercedes. 2 Renault. 1 Toyota. 1 Caetano
Ops incl: school contracts, private hire.
Livery: White/Green

WARREN'S COACHES (TENTERDEN) LTD R24

CRAYTHORNE GARAGE, BEACON OAK ROAD, TENTERDEN.
Tel: 01580 763212.
Fax: 01580 762414.
Man Dir: G. R. Fry. **Ch Eng**: M. Freer.
Sec: Mrs A. Holdstock.
Fleet: 8 - 6 coach, 1 minibus, 1 minicoach.
Chassis: 1 Bedford. 1 Leyland. 1 Toyota. 1 Volvo.
Bodies: 1 Berkhof. 3 Plaxton. 2 Van Hool.
Ops incl: excursions & tours, private hire, continental tours.
Livery: Blue/Primrose.
Also at Ticehurst (West Sussex)

*WESTERHAM COACHES

See Surrey

LANCASHIRE (ALSO BLACKBURN WITH DARWEN, BLACKPOOL, WIGAN)

ADLINGTON TAXIS & MINICOACHES

See Greater Manchester.

*ALFA TRAVEL

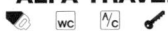

EUXTON LANE, CHORLEY PR7 6AF
Tel: 0845 130 5777
Fax: 0845 130 3777
E-mail: req@alfatravel.co.uk
Web site: www.alfatravel.co.uk
Man Dir: Paul Sawbridge **Tours Man**: Neil McMurdy **Ops Man**: Tom Smith **Fin Dir**: Peter Sawbridge
Fleet: 29 coach
Chassis: 15 DAF. 14 Transbus
Bodies: 15 Ikarus. 14 Plaxton. 1 Van Hool.
Ops incl: excursions & tours, private hire, continental tours.
Livery: Cream

J & F ASPDEN (BLACKBURN) LTD R

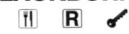

LANCASTER STREET, BLACKBURN BB2 1UA.
Tel: 01254 52020.
Fax: 01254 57474.
Fleetname: Aspdens Coaches.
Fleet: 14 - 1 double-deck bus, 13 coach.
Chassis: 1 Bristol. 13 Leyland.
Bodies: 5 Duple. 1 Northern Counties. 8 Plaxton.
Ops incl: school contracts, excursions & tours, private hire, continental tours.
Livery: Yellow/Black.
Subsidiary of Holmeswood Coaches

*BATTERSBY SILVER GREY COACHES R24 T

THE COACH & TRAVEL CENTRE, MIDDLEGATE, WHITE LUND BUSINESS PARK, MORECAMBE LA3 3PE
Tel: 01524 380000
Fax: 01524 380800
E-mail: sales@battersbys.co.uk
Web-site: www.battersbys.co.uk
Chair: J A Harrison **Co Sec**: M F Harrison
Ops Dir: M R Harrison **Ch Eng**: D McKinley
Fleet: 30 - 20 coach, 10 midicoach.
Chassis: 10 Mercedes, 20 Volvo.
Bodies: 30 Plaxton.
Ops incl: local bus services, excursions & tours, private hire, continental tours, school contracts.
Livery: White

*BLACKBURN BOROUGH TRANSPORT LTD

[&] [R]

INTACK, BLACKBURN BB1 3JD.
Tel: 01254 51112
Fax: 01254 662637
E-mail: info@blackburntransport.co.uk
Web site: www.blackburntransport.co.uk
Fleetname: Blackburn Transport
Man Dir: Michael Morton. **Fin Dir/Co Sec**: Ted Buckley. **Eng Dir**: Jim Hilton.
Eng Man: Glenn Dearden. **Ops Man**: Alastair Nuttall
Fleet: 114 - 52 double-deck bus. 23 single-deck bus. 39 midibus.
Chassis: 15 Dennis. 47 Leyland. 9 Leyland National. 23 Optare. 6 Transbus. 14 Volvo.
Bodies: 29 ECW. 23 East Lancs. 13 Leyland. 4 Northern Counties. 23 Optare. 10 Plaxton. 1 Roe. 5 Wright. 6 Transbus.
Ops incl: local bus services, school contracts, private hire.
Livery: Green/Cream/Yellow
Ticket System: Almex Optima Smartcard.

BLACKPOOL TRANSPORT LTD

[&] [bus] [R] [✓] [T]

RIGBY ROAD, BLACKPOOL FY1 5DD
Tel: 01253 473001
Fax: 01253 473101
E-mail: directors@blackpooltransport.com
Web site: www.blackpooltransport.com
Fleetname: MetroCoastlines
Man Dir: Steve Burd **Eng Dir**: Bill Gibson
Ops Dir: David Eaves **Fin Dir**: Allan Leach
Business Development Man: Liz Esnouf
Human Res Man: Annie Nancollis
Fleet: 229 - 72 double-deck bus, 39 single-deck bus, 46 midibus, 72 tram.
Chassis: 30 DAF. 18 Dennis. 48 Leyland. 55 Optare. 6 Volvo.
Bodies: 10 ECW. 44 East Lancs. 15 Northern Counties. 85 Optare. 3 Roe. (also 8 Optare Solos jointly owned by Blackpool Borough Council and Lancashire County Council)
Ops incl: local bus services, tram services, school contracts, private hire.
Livery: Yellow plus route branded route colours.
Ticket System: Almex A90

*BLUE BUS AND COACH SERVICES LTD [&] [♥]

MOOR LANE BUS STATION, BLACK HORSE STREET, BOLTON BL1 1SY
Tel: 01204 388125
Fax: 01204 396257
Web site: www.blue-bus.co.uk
Man Dir: Roger Jarvis **Ops Mans**: Ian Laing, Ben Jarvis **Fleet Eng**: John Nixon
Comm Man: Andrew Jarvis
Fleet: 98 - 16 double-deck bus, 53 single-deck bus, 2 coach, 10 midibus, 17 minibus.
Chassis:16 DAF. 33 Dennis. 14 Leyland. 5 MAN. 5 Mercedes. 15 Optare. 10 Volvo.
Bodies: 24 Alexander. 2 Duple. 17 East Lancs. 10 Ikarus. 3 Leyland. 15 Optare. 22 Plaxton. 6 Wright.
Ops incl: local bus services, school contracts, private hire.
Livery: two-tone Blue
Ticket System: ERG TP4000

*BRADSHAWS TRAVEL ♥

46 WESTBOURNE ROAD, KNOTT END ON SEA FY6 0BS
Tel: 01253 810058
Prop: Mrs Jill Swift
Fleet: 5 - 4 coach, 1 minibus.
Chassis: 1 Dennis. 3 Leyland. 1 Mercedes.
Ops incl: private hire, school contracts.
Livery: White.
Ticket System: Almex

BURNLEY & PENDLE

QUEENSGATE BUS DEPOT, COLNE ROAD, BURNLEY BB10 1HH
Tel: 01282 427778
Web site: www.burnleyandpendle.co.uk
Prop: Blazefield Holdings Ltd.
Chmn: Giles Fearnley. **Man Dir**: Stuart Wilde. **Dir (Lancs)**: George Scrymgeour.
Fleet: 97 - 41 double-deck buses, 52 single-deck buses, 4 midibuses.
Chassis: Dennis, Leyland, Mercedes-Benz, Volvo.
Bodies: Alexander, ECW, Northern Counties, Plaxton, Wright.
Livery: Red/Cream.
Ticket System: ERG.

CENTRAL GARAGE

See West Yorkshire (Calderdale)

*COACH OPTIONS LTD

[wc] [♨] [♥] [A/c] [✓]

UNIT 1, FINLAN ROAD, STAKEHILL INDUSTRIAL PARK, MIDDLETON M23 4RW
Tel: 0161 654 7444
Fax: 0161 654 7555
E-mail: coach.options@freeuk.com
Web site: www.travelwithoptions.co.uk
Prop: Paul R Stone
Fleet: 11 - 6 single-deck coach. 2 midicoach. 3 minicoach.
Chassis: 1 Bova. 2 Ford Transit. 3 Irisbus. 1 Mercedes. 1 Neoplan. 1 Scania. 1 Toyota.
Body: 3 Beulas. 1 Bova. 1 Caetano. 1 Irizar. 1 Jonckheere. 1 Neoplan. 4 other.
Ops incl: excursions & tours, private hire,continental tours, school contracts.
Livery: Blue

COLRAY COACHES

14 PRESTBURY AVENUE, BLACKPOOL FY4 1PT
Tel: 01253 349481.
Owner: G. Shaw
Fleet: coach, midibus.
Chassis: 2 Mercedes. 1 Setra. 2 Toyota.
Bodies: 2 Caetano. 1 Mercedes. 1 Setra

DARWEN COACH SERVICES

5 WESTVIEW KNOWLE LANE, DARWEN BB3 0EG.
Tel: 01254 776877
Prop: D. R. Russell.
Ops incl: local bus services.
Livery: Red/White.

*DUCKWORTH COACHES

[wc] [♨] [♥] [A/c] [✓]

STATION ROAD, GISBURN BB7 4JT
Tel: 01200 445210
Fax: 01200 445570
E-mail: ianduckworth@ukonline.co.uk
Prop: Ian Duckworth.
Fleet: 9 - 4 coach, 3 minicoach, 2 midicoach.
Chassis: 1 Dennis. 2 MAN. 4 Mercedes. 1 Neoplan. 1 VW.
Bodies: 1 Berkhof. 1 Marcopolo. 4 Mercedes. 1 Neoplan. 1 Van Hool. 1 VW.
Ops incl: school contracts, excursions & tours, private hire, continental tours.
Livery: Lilac (metallic).

*EAVESWAY TRAVEL LTD

[wc] [♨] [♥] [A/c] [✓] [T]

BRYN SIDE, ERYN ROAD, ASHTON-IN-MAKERFIELD WN4 8BT
Tel: 01942 727985
Fax: 01942 271234
E-mail: sales@eaveswaytravel.com
Web site: www.eaveswaytravel.com
Man Dir: M Eaves **Dir**: P Rogers.
Fleet: 20 - coach
Chassis: 12 DAF. 8 MAN.
Bodies: 20 Van Hool.
Ops incl: excursions & tours, private hire.
Livery: Silver/Blue/Green.

JOHN FISHWICK & SONS

[wc] [♨] [♥] [A/c]

GOLDEN HILL GARAGE, LEYLAND PR25 3LE.
Tel: 01772 421207.
Fax: 01772 622407.
Web site: www.fishwicks.co.uk
E-mail: enquiries@fishwicks.co.uk
Dir: J. C. Brindle **Dir**: J. F. Hustler. **Ch Eng**: J. Cave. **IT Man**: A Clenshaw **Coach Man**: A Aldam.
Fleet: 47 - 7 double-deck bus, 31 single-deck bus, 8 coach, 1 minibus.
Chassis: 12 DAF. 4 Dennis. 5 EOS. 15 Leyland. 8 Leyland National. 2 Mercedes.
Bodies: 6 Alexander. 2 ECW. 8 Leyland. 9 Leyland National. 1 Plaxton. 1 Reeve Burgess. 7 Van Hool. 8 Wright.
Ops incl: local bus services, school contracts, excursions & tours, private hire, continental tours.
Livery: Green.
Ticket System: Wayfarer.

A/c	Air conditioning
&	Vehicles suitable for disabled
♨	Coach(es) with galley facilities
wc	Coach(es) with toilet facilities
♥	Seat belt-fitted vehicles
R	Recovery service available (not 24 hr)
R24	24hr recovery service
✓	Replacement vehicle available
T	Toilet-drop facilities available
	Vintage vehicle(s) available
bus	Open top vehicle(s)

FOCUS COACHES LTD
UNIT 4, LONGTON BUSINESS PARK, MUCH HOOLE PR4 5LE
Tel: 01772 616699
Fax: 01772 616677
Web site: www.focuscoaches.co.uk
Chmn: Christopher W Reay **Man Dir:** Darren J Critchley
Fleet: 12 - 4 double-deck bus, 6 coach, 1 midicoach, 1 minicoach.
Chassis: 4 Leyland. 2 Mercedes. 6 Volvo.
Bodies: 4 Northern Counties. 6 Van Hool. 2 other.
Ops incl: school contracts, excursions & tours, private hire, continental tours.
Livery: White/Purple/Pink/Gold.
Ticket System: Wayfarer/Almex
Associated with Reay's Coaches (Cumbria)

FRASER EAGLE LTD
THE COACH HOUSE, SHUTTLEWORTH MEAD, PADIHAM BB12 7NG
Tel: 01254 231100
Fax: 01254 872719
E-mail: coaching@frasereagle.co.uk
Web site: www.frasereagle.com
Fleetname: Fraser Eagle
Chmn: Alan Dyson **Man Dir:** Ken Savage
Fleet: 20 - 16 coach, 1 midicoach, 3 minibus.
Chassis: 3 DAF, 2 Renault, 1 Peugeot, 1 Scania, 1 Toyota, 12 Volvo.
Bodies: 1 Berkhof, 3 Bova, 1 Caetano, 12 Van Hool.
Ops incl: school contracts, excursions & tours, private hire, continental tours.
Livery: Blue/White/Green.

FREEBIRD
9-11 SPRINGVALE STREET, TOTTINGTON BL8 3LR.
Tel: 01204 887344.
Fax: 01204 885757.
Web site: www.freebirdcoaches.co.uk
Owner: Paul Dart. **Ops Man:** Gary Jennings.
Fleet: 10 - 1 coach, 4 midicoach, 3 minibus, 2 minicoach.
Chassis: 2 Ford Transit. 1 Iveco. 2 LDV. 1 Leyland. 4 Mercedes.
Bodies: 1 Mellor 1 Plaxton. 4 Balmoral. 1 Cunliffe.
Ops incl: excursions & tours, private hire, school contracts, continental tours.
Livery: White.

G B COACHES
44 BEAUFORT ROAD, MORECAMBE LA4 5SE
Tel: 01524 424529
Fax: 01524 424146
E-mail: office@gbcoaches.co.uk
Web site: www.gbcoaches.co.uk
Prop: Rich Blaikie
Fleet: 3 - 2 coach, 1 midicoach.
Chassis: 1 Bedford. 1 DAF. 1 Mercedes.
Bodies: 1 Jonckheere, 1 Plaxton, 1 Reeve Burgess.
Ops incl: private hire, school contracts.
Livery: White/Red/Blue
Ticket System: Almex.

GPD TRAVEL
27 HARTFORD AVENUE, HEYWOOD OL10 4XH
Tel: 01706 622297
Fax: 01706 361494
Web site: www.gpdtravel.freeserve.co.uk
E-mail: gary@gpdtravel.freeserve.co.uk
Props: Gary Dawson, Janine Dawson
Fleet: 7 - 3 coach, 2 minicoach. 2 midibus.
Chassis: 2 DAF. 4 Mercedes. 1 Volvo.
Bodies: 1 Autobus, 1 Caetano. 2 Plaxton.
Ops incl: school contracts, excursions & tours, private hire, continental tours.
Livery: Red/Gold stripes.

*JEFF GRIFFITHS COACHES
22 MYERSCOUGH AVE, ST ANNES-ON-SEA FY8 2HY
Tel: 01253 714230
Fax: 01253 640560
E-mail: jeff-griffiths@comserve.com
Dir: Jeff Griffiths
Fleet: coach
Chassis: Volvo.
Bodies: Plaxton
Ops incl: excursions & tours, private hire.
Livery: White

GRIMSHAW COACHES
14 RAEBURN AVENUE, BURNLEY BB11 2AE.
Tel/Fax: 01282 413539.
Prop: I. Grimshaw.
Fleet: 6 coach.
Chassis: 3 Leyland. 2 Scania. 1 Setra.
Bodies: 3 Duple. 1 Setra. 2 Van Hool.
Ops incl: school contracts, excursions & tours, private hire, continental tours.
Livery: Multi-colour.

HEALINGS INTERNATIONAL COACHES
251 HIGGINSHAW LANE, ROYTON, OLDHAM OL2 6HW
Tel: 0161 624 8975.
Fax: 0161 652 0320.
Web site: www.healingscoachhire.co.uk
Prop: E Healing **Fleet Eng:** P Healing
Tours Man: Mrs M Woodward **Ops Man:** R Healing.
Fleet: 10 - 7 coach, 3 midicoach.
Chassis: 1 Ayats. 2 DAF. 1 Mercedes. 1 Scania. 1 Toyota. 1 Volvo.
Bodies: 1 Ayats. 5 Duple. 1 Irizar 1 Plaxton. 1 Pegasus
Ops incl: school contracts, excursions & tours, private hire, continental tours.
Livery: White with blue decals.

*HODDER MOTOR SERVICES LTD
3 ALDERFORD CLOSE, CLITHEROE BB7 2QP
Tel: 01200 422473
Fax: 01200 422590
E-mail: hodder@talk21.com
Dir: Paul Hodgson **Co Sec:** Janice Hodgson.
Fleet: 1 coach
Chassis: Volvo.
Body: Jonckheere.
Ops incl: private hire, excursions & tours.
Livery: Green/Blue/White

*HOLMESWOOD COACHES LTD
SANDY WAY, HOLMESWOOD, ORMSKIRK L40 1UB
Tel: 01704 821245
Fax: 01704 822090
E-mail: sales@holmeswood.uk.com
Web site: www.holmeswood.uk.com
Fleet: 128 - 20 double-deck bus, 97 coach, 3 double-deck coach, 2 midibus, 5 midicoach, 1 minicoach.
Chassis: 2 Ayats. 2 Bova. 19 DAF. 14 Dennis. 8 Iveco. 16 Leyland. 9 MAN. 5 Mercedes. 1 Neoplan. 21 Scania. 31 Volvo.
Bodies: 5 Alexander. 1 Autobus. 2 Ayats. 4 Beulas. 5 Berkhof. 2 Bova. 7 Caetano. 5 ECW. 4 East Lancs. 10 Ikarus. 2 Irizar. 5 Jonckheere. 11 Marcopolo. 2 Neoplan. 4 Northern Counties. 3 Optare. 28 Plaxton. 22 Van Hool. 6 other.
Ops incl: school contracts, excursions & tours, private hire, continental tours.
Livery: Green

J & Y COACHES
9 MILLTHORNE AVENUE, CLITHEROE BB7 2LE.
Tel/Fax: 01200 426269.
Web site: www.uk-coachtours.co.uk
Ptnrs: J. Robinson, Yvonne Robinson.
Fleet: 1 coach. **Chassis/body:** Setra.
Ops incl: excursions & tours, private hire, continental tours.
Livery: Blue/White.

JACKSON'S COACHES
JACKSON HOUSE, BURTON ROAD, BLACKPOOL FY4 4NW
Tel: 01253 792222.
Props: J. P. Jackson, Mrs M Jackson
Fleet: 6 coach.
Chassis: 4 DAF. 1 MAN. 1 Scania.
Bodies: 1 Caetano. 3 Plaxton. 2 Van Hool.
Ops incl: school contracts, private hire.
Livery: White/Blue.
Ticket System: Setright

*KIRKBY LONSDALE COACH HIRE
TWENTY ACRES, MOOR END, HUTTON ROOF, CARNFORTH LA6 2PF
Tel: 01524 272239
E-mail: sutton@klchbbfree.co.uk
Man Dir: Mrs J M Sutton **Sec:** S J Sutton
Fleet: 18 - 3 coach, 10 midibus, 2 midicoach, 2 minibus, 1 minicoach.
Chassis: 1 Cannon. 3 DAF. 13 Mercedes. 1 Renault.
Bodies: 1 Alexander. 1 Caetano. 1 Leicester. 5 Mercedes. 2 Optare. 3 Plaxton. 1 Rohill. 2 Van Hool. 1 Dormobile.
Ops incl: local bus services, school contracts, excursions & tours, private hire.
Livery: Service: Maroon/White Private Hire:

White/Blue/Maroon
Ticket System: Wayfarer

LAKELAND COACHES
SMITHY ROW, HURST GREEN.
Tel: 01254 826646.
Fax: 01254 826610.
Prop: J. R. Lakeland.
Livery: Blue/White.

LANCASHIRE UNITED
MANNER SUTTON STREET,
BLACKBURN BB1 5DT.
Tel: 01254 260661
Web site: www.lancashireunited.co.uk
Prop: Blazefield
Chairman: Giles Fearnley. Man Dir: Stuart Wilde. Dir (Lancs): George Scrymgeour.
Fleet: 131 - 45 double-deck buses, 68 single-deck buses, 18 minibuses.
Chassis: Dennis, Leyland, Mercedes-Benz, Optare, Volvo.
Bodies: Alexander, Berkhof, East Lancs, National, Northern Counties, Plaxton, Wright.
Livery: Blue/Cream.
Ticket System: ERG.

LENDOR TAXIS & LUXURY MINICOACH TRAVEL
See Greater Manchester

LONSDALE COACHES
THE COACH & TRAVEL CENTRE, SCOTLAND ROAD, CARNFORTH LA5 9RQ
Tel: 01524 720544.
Fax: 01524 720044.
Prop: Part of The Travellers Choice Group.
Fleet: 6 - 4 coach, 2 minicoach.
Chassis: 1 Ford Transit. 1 Mercedes. 4 Volvo.
Bodies: 4 Jonckheere, 1 Mercedes, 1 Plaxton.
Ops incl: local bus services, school contracts, excursions & tours, private hire, express, continental tours.
Livery: White with red/yellow/blue stripe

McLAUGHLIN'S TOURS
UNIT 1A PORTA CABIN, FACTORY LANE, PENWORTHAM PR1 9TZ
Tel/Fax: 01772 749358
Prop: Anthony McLaughlin
Fleet: 7 - 4 coach, 3 minibus.
Chassis: 2 Leyland, 3 Volvo.
Bodies: 3 Mercedes.
Ops incl: local bus services, school contracts, excursions & tours, continental tours.
Livery: Blue/White/Yellow.
Ticket System: Almex

*NORTHERN BLUE
UNIT 7, DEAN MILL, PLUMBE STREET, BURNLEY BB11 3AG
Tel: 01282 456351
Fax: 01282 439386
Web site: www.northernblue.co.uk
Man Dir: P Beaumont Com Dir/Co Sec: Michael Robinson Eng Dir: Lee Welton
Coaching Man: Norman Peele Comm Man: Colin Cropper Bus Ops Man: Brendan O'Reilly.
Fleet: 40 - 10 double-deck bus, 10 single-deck bus, 7 coach, 12 midibus, 1 midicoach.
Chassis: 3 Iveco. 13 Leyland. 12 Optare. 1 Toyota. 8 Volvo.
Bodies: 3 Beulas. 2 Caetano. 1 Ikarus. 13 Leyland. 3 Leyland National. 2 Northern Counties. 12 Optare. 4 Van Hool.
Ops incl: local bus services, school contracts, excursions & tours, private hire, express, continental tours.
Livery: Blue/White.
Ticket System: Wayfarer 3

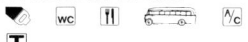

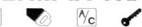

OLYMPIA TRAVEL
44 ARGYLE STREET, HINDLEY WN2 3PH
Tel: 01942 522322
Fax: 01942 254666
E-mail: olympia@coach-hire.net
Web site: www.olympiatravel.co.uk
Props: Joseph Lewis, Shaun Lewis.
Fleet: 18 - 12 coach, 4 midicoach, 2 minibus.
Chassis: 1 Bedford. 6 Dennis. 1 Ford Transit. 1 LDV. 6 Volvo.
Bodies: 5 Duple. 2 Jonckheere. 2 Mercedes. 4 Plaxton. 1 Reeve Burgess.
Ops incl: local bus services, school contracts, private hire, continental tours.
Livery: White with blue stripes

*PRESTON BUS LTD
R24
221 DEEPDALE ROAD, PRESTON PR1 6NY
Tel: 01772 253671
Fax: 01772 555840
E-mail: peter.bell@prestonbus.co.uk
Web site: www.prestonbus.co.uk
Man Dir: Peter Bell Traf Man: John Asquith. Eng Dir: Jack Hornby. Fin Dir: Margaret Ingram
Fleet: 112 - 50 double-deck bus, 16 single-deck bus, 1 coach, 45 minibus.
Chassis: 18 Dennis. 48 Leyland. 45 Optare. 1 Volvo.
Bodies: 2 Alexander. 1 ECW. 28 East Lancs. 5 Northern Counties. 45 Optare. 1 Van Hool.
Ops incl: local bus services, school contracts, excursions & tours, private hire.
Livery: Blue/Cream
Ticket System: Wayfarer TGX150

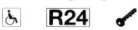

REDLINE COACHES
83 BISHAM AVENUE, LEYLAND PR5 3QE.
Tel: 01772 611612.
Fax: 01772 611613.
Prop: R. G. H. & S. R. Nuttall.

REEVES COACH HOLIDAYS
34 MONKS DRIVE, WITHNELL, CHORLEY PR6 8SG.
Tel/Fax: 01254 830545.
E-mail: info@reevescoachholidays.co.uk
Web site: www.reevescoachholidays.co.uk
Props: John E Reeves, Kathryn Reeves
Fleet: 1 coach.
Chassis/body: Setra.
Ops incl: excursions & tours, continental tours.
Livery: Amethyst with purple relief

RIGBY'S, KIRKHAM'S, GRIMSHAWS
THE COACH CENTRE, MOORFIELD INDUSTRIAL ESTATE, MOORFIELD DRIVE, ALTHAM, ACCRINGTON BB5 5WG
Tel: 01254 388366
Fax: 01254 232505
E-mail: coachcentre@btconnect.com
Co Sec/Dir: D. Moorhouse Engs/Dirs: M. Mellor, K. Hoyle Traffic/Dir: A M. Knowles
Fleet: 23 - 20 coach, 1 midicoach, 2 minicoach
Chassis: 3 Leyland. 3 Mercedes. 3 Scania. 14 Volvo.
Bodies: 1 Autobus. 4 Duple. 2 Neoplan. 7 Plaxton. 9 Van Hool.
Ops incl: school contracts, excursions & tours, private hire, continental tours.
Livery: Blue/Orange/Red
Ticket system: Almex

ROBINSONS HOLIDAYS
PARK GARAGES, GREAT HARWOOD BB6 7SP
Tel: 01254 889900
Fax: 01254 884708
E-mail: sales@robinsons-holidays.co.uk
Web site: www.robinsons-holidays.co.uk
Dirs: D. D. Lord, E. Shutt (Sec) Ops Man: C. Skeen Workshop Foreman: P Godwin Office Man: B Cooke Accounts Man: E Barnsley
Fleet: 26 - 23 coach, 1 midicoach, 2 minibus.
Chassis: 3 DAF. 2 Ford Transit. 4 MAN. 4 Scania. 13 Volvo.
Bodies: 4 Ikarus. 3 Jonckheere. 4 Noge. 10 Plaxton. 3 Van Hool. 2 Ford Transit.
Ops incl: excursions & tours, private hire, continental tours, school contracts.

A/c	Air conditioning	
	Vehicles suitable for disabled	
	Coach(es) with galley facilities	
WC	Coach(es) with toilet facilities	
	Seat belt-fitted vehicles	
R	Recovery service available (not 24 hr)	
R24	24hr recovery service	
	Replacement vehicle available	
T	Toilet-drop facilities available	
	Vintage vehicle(s) available	
	Open top vehicle(s)	

*ROSSENDALE TRANSPORT LTD

35 BACUP ROAD, RAWTENSTALL, ROSSENDALE BB4 7NG
Tel: 01706 212337
Fax: 01706 229515
Web site: www.rossendalebus.co.uk
E-mail: b.drelincourt@rossendalebus.co.uk
Fleetname: Handyrider, Easyride+.
Man Dir: Edgar Oldham **Comm Dir**: Barry Drelincourt **Ch Eng**: Stephen Wolfe **Co Sec**: Matthew Parkes **Bus Ops Man**: Robert Edwards
Fleet: 110 - 15 double-deck bus, 62 coach, 11 midibus, 22 minibus.
Chassis: 62 Dennis. 17 Leyland. 5 Mercedes. 7 Optare. 20 Volvo.
Bodies: 2 Alexander. 13 Carlyle. 3 Duple. 22 East Lancs. 17 Leyland. 4 Marshall. 4 Mercedes. 8 Northern Counties. 7 Optare. 21 Plaxton. 2 Reeve Burgess. 8 Wright.
Ops incl: local bus services, school contracts.
Livery: White/Red/Cream.
Ticket System: Wayfarer TGX150

*SANDGROUNDER COACHES

28 WARWICK STREET, SOUTHPORT PR8 5ES
Tel: 01704 541194
Recovery: 01704 541194
E-mail: gerry@sandgrounder.fsbusiness.co.uk
Prop: Gerald Doherty
Fleet: 3 coaches.
Chassis: 2 DAF. 1 Dennis.
Ops incl: school contracts, excursions & tours, private hire.
Livery: White/Gold/Red

*STAGECOACH NORTH WEST

See Cumbria

*THE TRAVELLERS CHOICE

THE COACH & TRAVEL CENTRE, SCOTLAND ROAD, CARNFORTH LA5 9RQ
Tel: 01524 720033
Fax: 01524 720044
E-mail: info@travellerschoice.co.uk
Web site: www.travellerschoice.co.uk
Chmn: R. Shaw **Man Dir**: J Shaw **Dir**: D Shaw **Co Sec**: P Shaw
Fleet: 28 - 20 coach, 1 double-deck coach, 6 midicoach, 1 minicoach.
Chassis: 1 Ford Transit. 6 Mercedes. 1 Neoplan. 20 Volvo.
Bodies: 16 Jonckheere. 6 Mercedes. 1 Neoplan. 4 Plaxton. 4 Sunsundegui.
Ops incl: local bus services, school contracts, excursions & tours, private hire, continental tours, express.
Livery: White with blue/yellow/red stripe

R. S. TYRER & SON

51 CHORLEY ROAD, HEATH CHARNOCK, CHORLEY PR6 9JT.
Tel: 01257 480979.
Fax: 01257 480951.
Props: Ms S. Buckle, G. Buckle.
Fleet: 3 - 2 coach, 1 minibus.
Chassis: 1 Leyland. 1 Mercedes. 1 Volvo.
Bodies: 1 Plaxton. 1 Van Hool.
Ops incl: excursions & tours, private hire, continental tours, school contracts, .

*TYRER TOURS LTD

16 KIRBY ROAD, LOMESHAYE INDUSTRIAL ESTATE, NELSON BB9 6RS
Tel: 01282 611123
Fax: 01282 615541
E-mail: tyrertours@btconnect.com
Web site: www.tyrertours.com
Man Dir: Robert Tyrer **Tran Mans**: Trevor Hancock, David Carson

Fleet: 19 - 4 double-deck bus, 6 single-deck bus, 9 coach.
Chassis: 8 DAF. 3 Dennis. 1 MAN. 5 Mercedes. 1 Optare. 2 Volvo.
Ops incl: local bus services, school contracts, excursions & tours, private hire, continental tours.
Livery: White/Blue/Red
Ticket System: ERG

VIKING COACHES

HEYWOOD. See Greater Manchester.

VISCOUNT CENTRAL COACHES LTD

6 DEAN MILL, PLUMB STREET, BURNLEY BB11 2AG
Tel: 01282 456351
Fax: 0 1282 421925
Man Dir: P Beaumont
Fleet: 10 - coach, 1 midicoach.
Chassis: 1 Iveco.1 Toyota. 9 Volvo.
Bodies: 1 Beulas. 3 Caetano. 1 Ikarus. 2 Jonckheere. 1 Ramseies&Jenser. 3 Van Hool.
Ops incl: private hire

JAMES HACKING (YELLOW ROSE COACHES) LTD

WEST LEA, DIXON'S FIELD, CRAG BANK, CARNFORTH LA5 9JN
Tel: 01524 735853.
Fleetname: Yellow Rose Coaches
Co Sec/Dir: G Brocken **Dir**: Mrs C. M. Brocken **Fleet Eng**: C. R. Ardis
Fleet: 4 - 2 coach, 1 midicoach, 1 minicoach.
Chassis: 1 MAN, 1 Mercedes, 2 Volvo.
Bodies: 1 Caetano, 1 Duple, 1 Van Hool, 1 Crest.
Ops incl: excursions & tours, private hire.
Livery: Yellow/White
Ticket System: Almex.

LEICESTERSHIRE, CITY OF LEICESTER, RUTLAND

ABC EUROPEAN TRAVEL

5 WOODSIDE CLOSE, LEICESTER LE4 9UJ.
Tel: 0116 276 7020
Fax: 0116 224 0060
Prop: Mr Mani. **Ch Eng**: Mr Anant.
Co Sec: Mrs Niki.
Fleet: 9 - 5 coach, 1 double-deck coach, 1 midicoach, 2 minibus.
Chassis: 1 Dennis. 2 Ford Transit. 1 MAN. 2 Mercedes. 1 Neoplan. 1 Scania. 1 Volvo.
Bodies: 1 Duple. 1 Jonckheere. 1 Neoplan. 1 Plaxton. 1 Reeve Burgess. 1 Van Hool.
Ops incl: private hire, continental tours, school contracts.
Livery: Yellow/Orange/Red stripes.

ARRIVA MIDLANDS

PO BOX 613, LEICESTER LE4 8BT
Tel: 0116 264 0400
Fax: 0116 260 5605

Web site: www.arriva.co.uk
Man Dir: Neil Barker **Fin Dir**: John Barlow **Eng Dir**: Richard Dyball **Comm Dir**: Kevin Belfield **Ops Dirs**: Stuart McIntosh, John Marrow **Eng Dir**: Jason Chalk
Fleet: 650 - double-deck bus, single-deck bus, coach, midibus.
Chassis: 46 DAF. 58 Dennis. 21 Leyland. 99 Mercedes. 58 Scania. 49 Volvo.
Bodies: Alexander. ECW. East Lancs. Leicester. Leyland. Northern Counties. Optare. Plaxton. Reeve Burgess.
Ops incl: local bus services, school contracts, private hire, express.
Livery: Acquamarine/Cotswold Stone
Ticket System: Wayfarer

ASMAL COACHES

70 KEDLESTONE ROAD, LEICESTER LE5 5HW
Tel/Fax: 0116 249 0443
Man Dir: Mehboob M. Asmal.

AUSDEN CLARK LTD

DYSART WAY, LEICESTER LE1 2JY
Tel: 0116 262 9492
Fax: 0116 251 5551
Man Dir: Paul Ausden-Clark.
Dir: Danny Smith. **Co Sec**: Susan Ward.
Fleet: 32 - 1 double-deck bus, 24 coach, 1 double-deck coach, 6 minicoach.
Chassis: 13 Bedford. 1 Leyland. 6 Mercedes. 11 Scania. 1 Volvo.
Ops incl: local bus services, school contracts, excursions & tours, private hire, continental tours.

BAGNALLS COACHES

See Derbyshire

BAILISS TOURS

21 ODSTONE ROAD, BARTON-IN-THE-BEANS CV13 0DF.

Tel: 01455 290253.
Fax: 01455 292700.
Prop: G. Treadwell.
Fleet: 1 coach. **Chassis:** DAF. **Body:** Duple.
Ops incl: excursions & tours, private hire, continental tours.
Livery: Blue/Cream.

*CONFIDENCE BUS & COACH HIRE
30 SPALDING STREET, LEICESTER LE5 4PH
Tel: 0116 276 2171
Fax: 0116 276 2171
E-mail: confidencebus@btclick.com
Web site: www.confidencebus.co.uk
Dirs: K M Williams, A P Williams **Ch Eng:** M Crawford
Fleet: 29 - 18 double-deck coach, 11 coach.
Chassis: 1 AEC. 27 Leyland. 1 Volvo.
Bodies: 10 ECW. 3 East Lancs. 1 Optare. 1 Park Royal. 10 Plaxton. 3 Roe. 1 Van Hool.
Ops incl: local bus services, school contracts, private hire.
Livery: Buses: Black/Grey, Coaches: Black/Red.
Ticket System: Setright

COUNTY MINI COACHES
31 EDENHURST AVENUE, LEICESTER LE3 2PH.
Tel/Fax: 0116 289 7205.
Owner: F. Bradshaw.
Fleet: 3 - 2 midicoach, 1 minibus.
Chassis: 1 DAF. 1 Freight Rover. 1 Iveco.
Ops incl: school contracts, private hire.

COUNTRY HOPPER
213 MELBOURNE ROAD, IBSTOCK LE67 6NQ
Tel: 01530 260888

DUNN-LINE GROUP
See Nottinghamshire

FIRST IN LEICESTER
ABBEY PARK ROAD, LEICESTER LE4 5AH.
Tel: 0116 251 6691.
Fax: 0116 253 8270.
Man Dir: I. Humphreys. **Eng Dir:** C. Stafford. **Fin Dir:** J. Hollis. **Gen Man Ops:** C. Lara.
Fleet: 116 - double-deck bus, single-deck bus, coach, midibus, minibus.
Chassis: Bristol. Dennis. Mercedes. Optare. Scania. Volvo.
Bodies: 8 Alexander. 71 East Lancs. 10 Marshall. 20 Northern Counties. 19 Optare. 3 Plaxton. 11 Wright.
Ops incl: local bus services, school contracts, excursions & tours, private hire, express, continental tours.
Livery: Multicoloured.
Ticket System: Wayfarer 3

*BRYAN GARRATT/ COACHMASTER
RMC YARD, THURMASTON FOOTPATH, HUMBERSTONE LANE, LEICESTER LE4 9JU
Tel: 0116 276 7228
Fax: 0116 246 1338
Prop: Bryan A Garratt
Fleet: coach, midicoach.
Chassis: Dennis. Leyland. Scania. Toyota. Volvo.
Ops incl: school contracts, excursions & tours, private hire.
Livery: White/Blue/Red.

HYLTON & DAWSON
CHESTNUT ROAD, GLENFIELD, LEICESTER LE3 8DB
Tel: 0116 233 0222.
Fax: 0116 233 1011
Web site: www.hyltonanddawson.co.uk
Prop: A. E. Hylton.
Fleet: 8 - 3 single-deck bus, 5 coach.
Chassis: 6 Bedford. 2 Dennis.
Bodies: 4 Duple. 4 Plaxton.
Ops incl: local bus services, school contracts, private hire.
Livery: Maroon/Cream/Grey.
Ticket System: Wayfarer.

PAUL JAMES COACHES
UNIT 5, GRANGE FARM BUSINESS PARK, GRANGE ROAD, HUGGLESCOTE, COALVILLE LE67 2BT
Tel: 01530 832399
Fax: 01530 836128
E-mail: info@pauljamescoaches.co.uk
Web site: www.pauljamescoaches.co.uk
Ptnrs: S. O'Brien, P. O'Brien **Coaching Man:** D Wood
Fleet: 27 - 2 single-deck bus, 15 coach, 12 midibus.
Chassis: 3 Bedford. 2 Bova. 1 Dennis. 2 Leyland. 6 Mercedes. 6 Optare. 1 Setra. 6 Volvo.
Bodies: 5 Alexander. 1 Autobus. 2 Bova. 6 Optare. 10 Plaxton. 2 Van Hool.
Ops incl: excursions & tours, private hire, local bus services, school contracts, continental tours.
Livery: Ivory
Ticket System: Wayfarer 3

*KINCHBUS LTD
MANSFIELD ROAD, HEANOR DE75 7BG
Tel: 01775 536309
Web site: www.kinchbus.co.uk
Fleet: 35 - 8 double-deck bus, 9 single-deck bus, 18 minibus.
Chassis: 2 Dennis. 8 Leyland. 11 Mercedes. 11 Optare. 3 Volvo.
Ops incl: local bus services
Livery: Blue/Yellow
Ticket System: Wayfarer

MACPHERSON COACHES LTD
See Derbyshire

NESBIT BROS LTD
BURROUGH ROAD, SOMERBY, MELTON MOWBRAY LE14 2PP.
Tel: 01664 454284.
Fax: 01664 454106.
Dirs: I. Foster, J. Townsend.
Ch Eng: J. Townsend. **Sec:** E. Tomes.
Ops Man: I. Foster.
Fleet: 13 coach.
Chassis: 1 AEC. 1 Leyland. 11 Volvo.
Bodies: 6 Duple. 7 Plaxton.
Ops incl: school contracts, excursions & tours, private hire.
Livery: Blue/Cream.
Ticket System: Setright.

*NIGEL JACKSON TRAVEL
R24
5 NEW ZEALAND LANE, QUENIBOROUGH LE7 3FU
Tel: 0116 260 0839
Fax: 0116 276 1969
Prop: Nigel Jackson.
Fleet: 5 - 3 double-deck bus, 2 coach
Chassis: 1 Bristol. 2 MCW. 2 Scania.
Bodies: 1 ECW. 1 Jonckheere. 2 MCW. 1 Plaxton.
Ops incl: local bus services, school contracts, private hire, continental tours.
Livery: Blue/Rec.
Ticket System: Wayfarer

RELIANT COACHES LTD
MILL LANE, HEATHER LE67 2QE.
Tel: 01530 260468.
Fax: 01530 263685.
Man Dir: M. Stannard. **Traf Man:** B. Moors.
Dir: M. Bishop. **Ops Dir:** H. King.
Co Sec: J. Highton.
Fleet: 17 - 16 coach, 1 midicoach.
Chassis: 2 Bedford. 4 Bova. 4 DAF. 1 Mercedes. 6 Volvo.
Bodies: 4 Bova. 8 Caetano. 1 Duple. 3 Plaxton. 1 Coach Kraft.
Ops incl: excursions & tours, private hire, express, continental tours.
Livery: Bachelor Blue/Larkspur Blue.

*ROBERTS COACHES
THE LIMES, MIDLAND ROAD, HUGGLESCOTE LE67 2FX
Tel: 01530 817444
Fax: 01530 817666
E-mail: info@robertscoaches.co.uk
Web site: www.robertscoaches.co.uk
Man Dir: Jonathan Hunt **Ops Man:** Clive Houldsworth **Ops Asst:** Charles Eaton
Fleet: 18 - 6 double-deck bus, 7 coach, 1 midibus, 1 midicoach, 3 minibus.
Chassis: 2 MCW. 4 Mercedes. 4 Scania. 8 Volvo.
Bodies: 1 Caetano. 4 East Lancs. 2 MCW.

A/c	Air conditioning
&.	Vehicles suitable for disabled
¶	Coach(es) with galley facilities
WC	Coach(es) with toilet facilities
❤	Seat belt-fitted vehicles
R	Recovery service available (not 24 hr)
R24	24hr recovery service
✔	Replacement vehicle available
T	Toilet-drop facilities available
🚌	Vintage vehicle(s) available
🚌	Open top vehicle(s)

Leicestershire

4 Plaxton. 7 Van Hool.
Ops incl: local bus services, school contracts, excursions & tours, private hire, continental tours, express.
Livery: Gold
Ticket System: Wayfarer.

*ROMDRIVE LTD

17 NORFOLK DRIVE, MELTON MOWBRAY LE13 0AJ
Tel: 01664 563498
Fax: 01664 568568
Man Dirs: John Penniston, Peter Penniston
Fleet: 20 - 2 single-deck bus, 8 coach, 8 midibus, 2 minibus.
Chassis: 1 Dennis. 1 MAN. 12 Mercedes. 1 Scania. 3 Setra.
Bodies: 4 Alexander. 1 Jonckheere. 3 Mercedes. 4 Park Royal. 2 Reeve Burgess. 3 Setra.
Ops incl: local bus services, school contracts, excursions & tours, private hire.
Livery: Blue/White
Ticket System: Wayfarer 3

SCHOFIELD TRAVEL LTD

PRINCE WILLIAM ROAD, LOUGHBOROUGH LE11 0GU.
Tel: 01509 611045
Fax: 01509 611012
Man Dir: E. B. Mee **Dir/Ch Eng**: K. W. Greasley. **Gen Man**: R. A. Schofield.
Fleet: 6 - 4 coach, 2 midicoach.
Chassis: 1 Bedford. 2 Bova. 2 DAF. 1 Ford.
Bodies: 2 Bova. 4 Plaxton.
Ops incl: school contracts, private hire, express.
Livery: Blue/Pale Grey.

*T LINE TRAVEL

76 PARK ROAD, MELTON MOWBRAY LE13 1TT
Tel/Fax: 01664 565040

Fleet: 3 midicoach.
Chassis/Bodies: 3 Mercedes.
Ops incl: excursions & tours, private hire, continental tours, school contracts.

TRAVEL-WRIGHT

64 ROCKHILL DRIVE, MOUNTSORREL LE12 7DT.
Tel: 0116 230 2887.
Fax: 0116 230 2223.
E-mail: trwright@demon.co.uk
Dir: C. Wright.
Fleet: 5 minibus.
Chassis: 1 DAF. 2 Mercedes. 2 VW.
Bodies: 2 Crystals. 2 VW. 1 Advanced.
Ops incl: private hire, school contracts.

WIDE HORIZON LUXURY TRAVEL

48 COVENTRY ROAD, BURBAGE, HINCKLEY LE10 2HP
Tel: 01455 615915
Fax: 01455 230767
Ptnrs: Reg Clarke, Elaine Clarke, Jon Clarke.
Fleet: 1 double-deck bus, 1 single-deck bus, 8 coach, 1 double-deck coach
Chassis: 1 Bova. 2 DAF. 1 Daimler. 1 Dennis. 1 Leyland. 1 Neoplan. 1 Scania. 2 Setra. 1 Volvo.
Bodies: 1 Berkhof. 1 Bova. 3 Carlyle. 1 East Lancs. 1 Jonckheere. 4 Plaxton. 2 Setra.
Ops incl: local bus services, excursions & tours, school contracts, private hire, continental tours.
Livery: White with logo

PAUL S WINSON COACHES LTD

ROYAL WAY, LOUGHBOROUGH LE11 5XR

Tel: 01509 232354
Fax: 01509 265110
Recovery: 01509 237999
Web site: www.winsoncoaches.co.uk
E-mail: sales@winsoncoaches.co.uk
Chmn: Paul S Winson **Ch Eng**: Paul B Winson **Dir**: Mrs M A Winson
Ops Man: Anthony J Winson
Fleet: 28 - 6 double-deck bus, 18 coach, 4 minibus.
Chassis: 4 Bova. 1 DAF. 3 Dennis. 6 Leyland. 7 Mercedes. 8 Volvo.
Bodies: 1 Autobus. 4 Bova. 1 Caetano. 3 Jonckheere. 2 Northern Counties. 12 Plaxton. 3 Roe.
Ops incl: local bus services, school contracts, excursions & tours, private hire, continental tours.
Livery: Red/White/Blue.
Ticket system: Wayfarer

WOODS COACHES LTD

211 GLOUCESTER CRESCENT, WIGSTON LE18 4YH
Tel: 0116 278 6374
Fax: 0116 247 7819
E-mail: sales@woods-coaches.co.uk
Web site: woods-coaches.com
Dirs: Mark Wood, Kevin Brown **Mktg Exec**: Alison Trunkfield **Eng Dir**: Ian Trigg
Fleet: 32 - 14 single-deck bus, 18 midibus.
Chassis: 18 Mercedes. 14 Volvo.
Bodies: 8 Alexander. 1 Caetano. 1 Duple. 1 Marshall. 1 Mellor. 1 Mercedes. 19 Plaxton.
Ops incl: local bus services, excursions, tours, private hire, continental tours.
Livery: Blue base – orange/yellow/white relief
Ticket System: Wayfarer.

LINCOLNSHIRE

BARNARDS COACHES

NORTH CLIFF ROAD, KIRTON LINDSEY DN21 4NJ
Tel: 01652 648381
Fax: 01652 640377
E-mail: barnardscoaches@fsmail.net
Ptnrs: John S. Barnard, K. M. Barnard, M. Barnard.
Fleet: 17 - 15 coach, 2 double-deck bus.
Chassis: 3 Bedford. 3 Bristol. 3 DAF. 3 Ford. 2 Leyland. 3 Scania. 1 Volvo.
Bodies: 5 Duple. 3 Irizar. 4 Plaxton. 1 Van Hool. 4 other.
Ops incl: local bus services, school contracts, private hire, continental tours.
Livery: Maroon/White.

BRYLAINE TRAVEL

291 LONDON ROAD, WYBERTON PE21 7DD.
Tel: 01205 364087.
Fax: 01205 359504.

Prop: Brian W. Gregg. **Ch Eng**: Brian Paul Gregg. **Ops Dir**: Malcolm Wheatley.
Fleet: 38 - 7 double-deck bus, 25 single-deck bus, 6 midibus.
Chassis: Dennis. Ford. Leyland National. Mercedes. Optare.
Bodies: Alexander. ECW. East Lancs. Leyland National. Marshall. Mercedes. Northern Counties. Optare. Plaxton.
Ops incl: local bus services, school contracts.
Livery: Blue/White.
Ticket System: Wayfarer 3.

J W CARNELL LTD

72 BRIDGE ROAD, SUTTON BRIDGE PE12 9UA.
Tel: 01406 350482.
Fax: 01406 350600.
E-mail: carnellcoaches@ukonline.co.uk
Dirs: John Grindwood, Mervyn Emmet
Fleet: 22 - 3 double-deck bus, 16 coach, 2 midicoach, 1 minicoach.
Chassis: 2 Bedford. 1 Bova. 2 DAF. 5 Leyland. 1 MAN. 3 MCW. 2 Toyota 6 Volvo.

Bodies: 1 Bova. 3 Caetano. 8 Duple. 3 MCW. 6 Plaxton. 1 Van Hool.
Ops incl: local bus services, school contracts, excursions and tours.
Livery: Silver/Red/Orange.
Ticket system: Setright.

CAVALIER TRAVEL

SEAGATE ROAD, LONG SUTTON PE12 9AD.
Tel: 01406 362518
Fax: 01406 362418
Props: A. D. Ladbrook, C. J. Boor.
Man Dir: Dennis Upton
Fleet: 40 double deck/single deck buses
Livery: Blue
Ops incl: local bus services, school contracts

CROPLEY BROS TOURS (FOSDYKE) LTD

MAIN ROAD, FOSDYKE PE20 2BH.
Tel: 01205 260226.
Fax: 01205 260246.

Web site: www.cropleycoach.co.uk
E-mail: enquiries@cropleycoach.co.uk
Fleetname: Cropley
Man Dir: J. R. Cropley.
Co Sec: S. R. Cropley.
Ch Eng: D. W. Hogg
Fleet: 12 coach.
Chassis: 2 Setra, 10 Volvo.
Bodies: 10 Plaxton. 2 Setra.
Ops incl: school contracts, excursions & tours, private hire, continental tours.
Livery: White.

*DELAINE BUSES LTD

8 SPALDING ROAD, BOURNE
PE10 9LE
Tel: 01778 422866
Fax: 01778 425593
Web site: www.delainebuses.com
Chmn: I Delaine-Smith. **Man Dir:** A Delaine-Smith **Dirs:** M Delaine-Smith, K Delaine-Smith **Co Sec:** Mrs B P Tilley
Fleet: 20 - 14 double-deck bus, 6 single-deck bus.
Chassis 6 Leyland. 14 Volvo.
Bodies: 2 Duple. 12 East Lancs. 4 Northern Counties. 2 Wright.
Ops incl: local bus services, school contracts.
Livery: Light Blue/Dark Blue/Ivory.
Ticket System: Almex A90

*EAGRE COACHES LTD

CROOKED BILLET STREET,
MORTON, GAINSBOROUGH
DN21 3AG
Tel: 01427 612098
Fax: 01427 811340
Man Dir: Rob Eaglen **Ch Eng:** M Thrower
Co Sec: A Lee
Fleet: 8 coaches
Chassis: 6 Iveco. 2 MAN.
Bodies: 6 Beulas. 1 Noge. 1 Marcopolo.
Ops incl: excursions & tours, private hire, continental tours
Livery: Multicolours

EMMERSON COACHES LTD

See North Lincolnshire

*W H FOWLER & SONS (COACHES) LTD

155 DCG DROVE SOUTH,
HOLBEACH DROVE, SPALDING
PE12 0SD
Tel: 01406 330232
Fax: 01406 330923
E-mail: andrewfowler67@aol.com
Fleetname: Fowlers Travel
Man Dir John Fowler **Dir:** Andrew Fowler
Co Sec: Jackie Fowler
Fleet: 22 - 6 double-deck bus, 4 single-deck bus, 12 coach.
Chassis: 1 Bedford. 1 DAF. 7 Leyland. 1 Leyland National. 4 Scania. 8 Volvo.
Ops incl: local bus services, school contracts, excursions & tours, private hire.
Livery: Cream/Orange.
Ticket System: Wayfarer.

*GRAYSCROFT BUS SERVICES LTD

15A VICTORIA ROAD,
MABLETHORPE LN12 2AF
Tel: 01507 473236
Fax: 01507 477073
E-mail: grayscroft.buses@btinternet.com
Web site: www.grayscroftbuses.co.uk
Dirs: C W Barker, N Barker, N W Barker
Fleet: 14 - 2 double-deck bus, 2 single-deck bus, 9 coach, 1 double-deck coach.
Chassis: 2 Leyland. 1 Mercedes. 1 Neoplan. 1 Optare. 9 Volvo.
Bodies: 2 Alexander. 1 Caetano. 1 Duple. 1 Jonckheere. 1 Mellor. 1 Neoplan. 1 Optare. 5 Plaxton. 2 Van Hool.
Ops incl: local bus services, school contracts, excursions & tours, private hire, express, continental tours.
Livery: White/Blue/Orange
Ticket system: Setright

PHIL HAINES COACHES

RALPHS LANE, FRAMPTON WEST,
BOSTON PE20 1QU.
Tel/Fax: 01205 722359.
Props: N. A. & F. E. Haines.

HODSON COACHES LTD

CHAPEL LANE, NAVENBY LN5 0ER
Tel: 01522 810262
Fax: 01522 810793
E-mail: jg.hodsoncoaches@btinternet.com
Web Site: www.hodsoncoaches.co.uk
Dirs: S. Carter, J. Carter.
Fleet: 10 - 6 single-deck coach, 1 midicoach, 3 minicoach.
Chassis: 1 MAN. 5 Mercedes. 4 Setra.
Bodies: 3 Mercedes. 1 Neoplan. 1 Optare. 4 Setra. 1 Solera.
Ops incl: local bus services, school contracts, excursions & tours, private hire, continental tours.
Livery: Cream/Purple Pink/Maroon.
Ticket system: Almex Microfare 2

*HUNTS COACHES

2-3 WEST STREET, ALFORD
LN13 9DG
Tel/Fax: 01507 463000
E-mail: hunts@huntstravel.fsnet.co.uk
Web site: www.hunts-coaches.co.uk
Dirs: Michael Hunt, Charles Hunt **Traf Man:** Alistair Bell
Fleet: 19 - 5 single-deck bus, 9 coach, 4 midibus, 1 midicoach.
Chassis: 3 Dennis. 4 Leyland. 5 Mercedes. 7 Volvo.
Bodies: 5 Alexander. 5 Mercedes. 1 Plaxton. 8 Van Hool.
Ops incl: local bus services,

school contracts, excursions & tours, private hire, express, continental tours.
Livery: Cream/White.
Ticket System: Almex

R KIME & CO LTD

3 SLEAFORD ROAD, FOLKINGHAM,
SLEAFORD NG34 0SB
Tel: 01529 497251
Fax: 01529 497554
Fleetname: Kimes Coaches.
Man Dir: Paul Brown
Fleet: 20 - 10 double-deck bus, 6 single-deck bus, 3 coach, 1 midicoach.
Chassis: 4 DAF. 12 Leyland. 1 Mercedes. 3 Volvo.
Bodies: 2 Alexander. 12 Leyland. 3 Northern Counties. 1 Optare. 2 Plaxton.
Ops incl: local bus services, school contracts, excursions & tours, private hire.
Livery: Cream/Green
Ticket System: Almex

LINCOLNSHIRE ROAD CAR CO LTD

PO BOX 15, DEACON ROAD,
LINCOLN LN2 4JB
Tel: 01522 522255
Fax: 01522 533229
E-mail: roadcar@roadcar.co.uk
Web site: www.roadcar.co.uk
Fleetname: RoadCar, Superbuzz
Chmn: Frank Carter **Man Dir:** Paul Hill
Eng Dir: Derek Eradley **Fin Dir:** Mark Adamson
Fleet: 285 - 92 double-deck bus, 137 single-deck bus, 6 coach, 6 open-top bus, 44 midibus.
Chassis: 1 Bova. 1 Bristol. 10 DAF. 42 Dennis. 86 Leyland. 26 Leyland National. 6 MAN. 35 MCW. 6 Mercedes. 8 Optare. 29 Renault. 6 Scania. 29 Volvo.
Bodies: 14 Alexander. 1 Bova. 4 Duple. 29 ECW. 90 East Lancs. 23 Leyland National. 4 Marshall. 35 MCW. 1 Northern Counties. 17 Optare. 24 Plaxton. 24 Reeve Burgess. 1 Wadham Stringer. 16 Wright. 11 Europa. 1 Safle.
Ops incl: local bus services, school contracts, excursions & tours, private hire.
Livery: Green/Yellow/White; Blue/Yellow/Red
Ticket System: Almex.

MEMORY LANE COACHES

ELM HOUSE, OLD BOLINGBROKE,
SPILSBY PE23 4HF
Tel: 01790 763394
Prop: John B Dorey
Fleet: 5 - 3 coach, 2 midicoach.
Chassis: 2 Bedford. 1 Iveco. 1 Leyland. 1 Mercedes.
Bodies: 1 Carlyle. 3 Duple. 1 Plaxton.
Ops incl: school contracts, private hire.
Livery: White/Green/Red.

MILLMAN COACHES

See North Lincolnshire

- Air conditioning
- Vehicles suitable for disabled
- Coach(es) with galley facilities
- Coach(es) with toilet facilities
- Seat belt-fitted vehicles
- **R** Recovery service available (not 24 hr)
- **R24** 24hr recovery service
- Replacement vehicle available
- **T** Toilet-drop facilities available
- Vintage vehicle(s) available
- Open top vehicle(s)

*PC COACHES OF LINCOLN LTD
R24 T
17 CROFTON ROAD, ALLENBY TRADING ESTATE, LINCOLN LN3 4NL
Tel: 01522 533605
Fax: 01522 560402
E-mail: pctravel@aol.com
Web site: www.pc-coaches.co.uk
Man Dir: P C Smith **Off Man**: S Pickering
Wkshp Man: D Longmate
Fleet: 57 - 15 double-deck bus, 9 single-deck bus, 28 coach, 2 midicoach, 2 minibus, 1 minicoach.
Chassis: 5 Bedford. 1 DAF. 2 Ford Transit. 1 LDV. 1 Leyland. 5 MCW. 4 Mercedes. 1 Optare. 32 Scania.
Bodies: 2 Autobus. 1 Berkhof. 15 East Lancs. 1 Ford. 13 Irizar. 1 LDV. 2 Optare. 13 Plaxton. 4 Van Hool.
Ops incl: local bus services, school contracts, private hire, excursions & tours, continental tours.
Livery: White/Orange/Maroon.
Ticket System: Wayfarer.

COLLIN PHILLIPSON
See South Yorkshire.

PULFREYS COACHES
1 WILKINSON ROAD, FOSTON, GRANTHAM NG32 2JX.
Tel: 01476 564144.
Fax: 01476 593700.
Ptnrs: J. Pulfrey, A. J. Pulfrey.
Fleet: 3 coach.
Chassis: 1 Bedford. 1 DAF. 1 Volvo.
Bodies: 3 Plaxton.
Ops incl: school contracts, excursions & tours, private hire, continental tours.
Livery: Cream.
Ticket System: Setright.

RELIANCE TRAVEL
T
47 HIGH STREET, GREAT GONERBY, GRANTHAM NG31 8JR.
Tel: 01476 563118.
Fax: 01476 591033.

Fleet: 17 - 8 single-deck bus, 6 coach, 1 double-deck coach, 2 minibus.
Chassis: 1 Bova. 3 Dennis. 5 Leyland. 2 MAN. 1 MCW. 1 Mercedes. 1 Scania. 2 Volvo.
Bodies: 1 Bova. 4 Duple. 1 East Lancs. 1 Leyland. 1 MCW. 3 Optare. 3 Plaxton. 3 Van Hool.
Ops incl: local bus services, school contracts, excursions & tours, private hire, continental tours.
Livery: Coach: Silver/Blue. Bus: Red/White.
Ticket System: Wayfarer 3.
Subsidiary of Mass Transit (South Yorkshire)

ROADCAR
See Lincolnshire Road Car

ROY PHILLIPS
69 STATION ROAD, RUSKINGTON NG34 9DF
Tel/Fax: 01526 832279
Prop: R Phillips.
Fleet: 6 coach.
Chassis: 2 DAF. 1 Leyland. 3 Volvo.
Bodies: 2 Bova. 3 Plaxton. 2 Van Hool.
Ops incl: private hire, school contracts.

SLEAFORDIAN COACHES
49 WESTGATE, SLEAFORD NG34 7PU
Tel: 01529 303333
Fax: 01529 300324
E-mail: office@sleafordian.co.uk
Web site: www.sleafordian.co.uk
Dirs: D. Broughton, Mrs J Broughton, M Broughton, C J Broughton **Ops Man**: M Broughton **Ch Eng**: P Kerr
Fleet: 9 - 8 coach, 1 miidicoach.
Chassis: 1 Mercedes. 8 Volvo.
Bodies: 1 Autobus. 3 Plaxton. 5 Van Hool.
Ops incl: local bus services, school contracts, excursions & tours, private hire, continental tours.
Livery: White/Orange/Yellow
Ticket System: Setright

SMITHS COACHES, CORBY GLEN
THE GREEN, CORBY GLEN NG33 4NR.
Tel: 01476 550285.

Fax: 01476 550032.
Ptnrs: H. J. and Mary J. Smith.
Fleet: 7 - 5 coach, 1 double-deck coach, 1 minibus.
Chassis: 1 Bedford. 1 Bova. 1 Ford. 1 Freight Rover. 2 MAN. 1 Mercedes.
Bodies: 1 Bova. 1 Carlyle. 1 Duple. 2 MAN. 1 Neoplan. 1 Plaxton.
Ops incl: excursions & tours, private hire, continental tours, school contracts.
Livery: Blue/White.

*TOURMASTER COACHES LTD
R
51 PETERBOROUGH ROAD, CROWLAND PE6 0BB
Tel: 01733 211710
Fax: 08712 423623
E-mail: tourmaster@lineone.net
Man Dir: David A Dinsey
Fleet: 10
Chassis: 2 DAF. 8 Volvo.
Bodies: 1 Jonckheere. 5 Plaxton. 4 Van Hool.
Ops incl: local bus services, school contracts, excursions & tours, private hire, express, continental tours.

TRAVEL PATH
PO BOX 32, GRANTHAM NG31 8DN
Tel: 01476 592966

*TRANSLINC LTD
JARVIS HOUSE, 157 SADLER ROAD, LINCOLN LN6 3RS
Tel: 01522 552999
Fax: 01522 552997
E-mail: logistics@translinc.co.uk
Web site: www.translinc.co.uk
Man Dir: Brian West. **Dir of Logistics**: Carole Smith **Ops Man**: Trish Wilson
Fleet: 22 - 15 coach. 7 midicoach.
Chassis: 6 Dennis. 3 Mercedes. 1 Scania. 4 Toyota. 4 Transbus. 3 Volvo.
Bodies: 10 Caetano. 6 Plaxton. 2 Setra. 4 Transbus. 1 Van Hool.
Ops incl: school contracts, excursions & tours, private hire, express.

LONDON

This section includes those operators in the London postal areas, as well as operators who have asked to appear under this heading. Other operators within Greater London with a non-London postal address, eg Kingston, Surrey; Bromley, Kent; Enfield, Middlesex, etc, may be found under their respective postal counties.

AA, KNIGHTS OF THE ROAD
R
WREN ROAD, SIDCUP DA14 4NA
Tel: 020 8309 7741
Prop: J. V. H. Knight. **Ch Eng**: D. Knight
Fleet: 10 - 6 coach, 2 double-deck coach, 2 minibus.
Chassis: 6 DAF. 2 Mercedes. 2 Volvo.
Bodies: 6 Bova. 2 Jonckheere. 2 Mercedes.
Ops incl: excursions & tours, private hire, continental tours, school contracts.
Livery: Cream/Beige.

ABBEY TRAVEL (LONDON) LTD
See Hertfordshire.

ACE TRAVEL
See Hertfordshire.

AIRLINKS
HEATHROW COACH CENTRE, SIPSON ROAD, WEST DRAYTON UB7 0HN

Tel: 020 8990 6300
Fax: 020 8997 3626
Man Dir: Bill Cahill. **Fin Dir**: Richard Smith.
Dir of Eng: Steve Perks.
Fleet: 329 - includes 19 double-deck bus.
Chassis: 76 DAF. 54 Dennis. 3 MAN. 57 Mercedes. 16 Scania. 12 Toyota. 111 Volvo.
Bodies: 14 Alexander. 32 Berkhof. 15 Caetano. 6 Cobus. 17 East Lancs. 8 Jonckheere. 2 LDV. 11 Frank Guy. 16 Mercedes. 2 Northern Counties. 6 Optare. 99 Plaxton. 13 UVG. 32 Van Hool. 36 Wright.

Ops incl: local bus services, excursions & tours, private hire, express.
Livery: Various.
Subsidiary of National Express

*ALLIED COACHLINES LTD
See Middlesex

*ANDERSON TRAVEL LTD
[icons]
178A TOWER BRIDGE ROAD, LONDON SE1 3LS
Tel: 020 7403 8118
Fax: 020 7403 8421
E-mail: sales@andersontravel.freeserve.co.uk
Web site: www.andersontravel.co.uk
Man Dir: Mark Anderson Gen Man: Stephen Lee Tran Man: Peter Gilbert
Fleet: 21 - 17 coach, 2 midicoach, 2 minicoach.
Chassis: 7 Bova. 12 Mercedes. 2 Toyota.
Bodies: 7 Bova. 2 Caetano. 2 Mercedes. 10 Setra.
Ops incl: excursions & tours, private hire, continental tours, express.
Livery: White/Green.

ANGEL MOTORS (EDMONTON) LTD
1 CONSTABLE STREET, LONDON N15 4QZ
Tel: 020 8808 2000
Fax: 020 8808 0008
Fleet: 19 - 17 coach, 2 minicoach.
Livery: White/Blue/Yellow.

ARMCHAIR PASSENGER TRANSPORT CO LTD
See Middlesex.

ARRIVA LONDON NORTH, ARRIVA LONDON SOUTH, ARRIVA LONDON NORTH EAST
[icons]
16 WATSONS ROAD LONDON N22 7TZ
Tel: 020 8271 0101
Fax: 020 8271 0120.
Web site: arriva.co.uk
Man Dir: Mark Yexley. Fin Dir: Alan Sewell
Eng Dir: Ian Tarrran Ops Dir: Jeff Quantrell
Comm Dir: Peter Batty
Fleet: 1460 - 1172 double-deck bus, 200 single-deck bus, 14 coach, 74 midibus.
Chassis: 209 AEC. 526 DAF. 218 Dennis. 246 Leyland. 95 MCW. 166 Volvo.
Bodies: 464 Alexander. 149 ECW. 11 East Lancs. 1 Ikarus. 95 MCW. 52 Northern Counties. 209 Park Royal. 275 Plaxton. 202 Wright. 2 Van Hool.
Ops incl: local bus services, excursions & tours, private hire.
Livery: Red.
Ticket System: London Transport.

*BACK ROADS TOURING COMPANY LTD [icons]
14A NEW BROADWAY, LONDON W5 2XA.
Tel: 020 8566 5312
Fax: 020 8566 5457
E-mail: info@backroadstouring.co.uk
Web site: www.backroadstouring.co.uk
Man Dir: Bruce Cherry
Fleet: 27 - 12 minibus, 15 minicoach.
Chassis: 7 Mercedes. 20 Renault
Ops incl: excursions & tours, private hire, continental tours.
Livery: White

BEXLEY COACHLINES
[icons]
See Kent

*BIG BUS COMPANY [icon]
GROSVENOR GARDENS HOUSE, 35-37 GROSVENOR GARDENS, LONDON SW1W 0BS
Tel: 020 7233 8722
Fax: 020 7233 8766
E-mail: pgriffith@bigbustours.com
Web site: www.bigbustours.com
Man Dir: R P Maybury Exec Dir: E M Maybury Eng: D V Maybury Bus Dev: P Waterman Ops Man: M Forde
Fleet: 155 - 79 double-deck bus, 76 open-top bus.
Chassis: 4 AEC. 16 Dennis. 59 Leyland.
Ops incl: private hire, excursions & tours.

BLUE TRIANGLE
See Essex

BLUEWAYS GUIDELINE COACHES LTD
[icons]
49 WINDERS ROAD, LONDON SW11 3HE
Tel: 020 7228 3515
Fax: 020 7228 0290
E-mail: blueways@clara.co.uk
Web site: www.bluewaysguideline.co.uk
Dirs: Philip Bruton, Janet Bruton, Thomas McKechnie.
Fleet: 6 - 4 coach. 2 minicoach.
Chassis: 1 Mercedes. 3 Scania. 2 Toyota
Bodies: 2 Caetano. 3 Irizar. 1 Mercedes.
Ops incl: excursions & tours, private hire, continental tours, school contracts.
Livery: 2 White/two-tone Blue, 2 White, 2 England sponsors.

BRENTONS OF BLACKHEATH [icons]
55-57 INVICTA ROAD, LONDON SE3 7HD
Tel: 020 8858 9210
Fax: 020 8858 0264
Prop: C. Clark. Tran Man: D. Eaton.
Ch Eng: I. Powell.

Fleet: 15 - 12 coach, 3 midicoach.
Chassis: 2 Dennis. 8 Leyland. 3 Mercedes. 2 Volvo.
Ops incl: private hire, school contracts, excursions and tours.
Livery: Red/Cream/Grey

BRYANS OF ENFIELD
[icons]
19 WETHERLEY ROAD, ENFIELD EN2 0NS.
Fax: 020 8366 0062.
Owner: B. Nash.
Fleet: 6 - 3 double-deck bus, 1 single-deck bus, 1 coach, 1 double-deck coach.
Chassis: 1 AEC. 1 DAF. 2 Daimler. 1 Leyland. 1 MCW.
Bodies: 1 ECW. 2 MCW. 2 Park Royal. 1 Van Hool.
Ops incl: school contracts, private hire.
Livery: Red.

*PETER CAROL PRESTIGE COACHING
See Bristol

*CAVALIER TRAVEL SERVICES [icons]
ARMCHAIR HOUSE, COMMERCE ROAD, BRENTFORD TW8 8ES
Tel: 020 8847 5362
Fax: 020 8758 1914
Recovery: 07734 55050
E-mail: bookings@cavaliercoaches.com
Dir: Andrew W Pagan
Fleet: 11 - 7 coach, 2 midicoach, 3 minicoach.
Chassis: 4 Iveco. 4 Mercedes. 2 Neoplan. 1 Scania. 1 Toyota.
Bodies: 4 Beulas. 1 Caetano. 1 Mercedes. 2 Neoplan. 3 Optare. 1 Van Hool.
Ops incl: private hire

CENTAUR TRAVEL MINICOACHES [icons]
188 HALFWAY STREET, SIDCUP DA15 8DJ.
Tel: 020 8300 3001.
Fax: 020 8302 5959.
Man Dir: M. Sims. Ch Eng: R. Raison.
Ops Man: Kay Priestley.
Fleet: 14 - 2 midicoach, 5 minibus, 7 minicoach.
Chassis: 7 Freight Rover. 2 Mercedes. 5 Renault.
Ops incl: private hire, school contracts.

C I COACHLINE
See Essex.

C W B EXECUTIVE COACH HIRE
See Kent.

*CABIN COACHES
See Middlesex.

[icon] Ac	Air conditioning
[icon]	Vehicles suitable for disabled
[icon]	Coach(es) with galley facilities
[icon] wc	Coach(es) with toilet facilities
[icon]	Seat belt-fitted vehicles
R	Recovery service available (not 24 hr)
R24	24hr recovery service
[icon]	Replacement vehicle available
T	Toilet-drop facilities available
[icon]	Vintage vehicle(s) available
[icon]	Open top vehicle(s)

*CALL-A-COACH
See Surrey.

CAVALIER
See Middlesex.

CENTAUR TRAVEL MINICOACHES
See Kent.

CHALFONT LINE LTD
[icons] R24
4 PROVIDENCE ROAD, WEST DRAYTON UB7 8HJ
Tel: 01895 459540
Fax: 01895 459549
E-mail: holidays@chalfont-line.co.uk
Web site: www.chalfont-line.co.uk
Chmn: Terry Reynolds **Dir**: Tim Parsons
Tran Man: Tom Barrett
Ch Eng: Dave Stockford
Fleet: 75 - 3 single-deck bus, 2 coach, 70 minibus.
Chassis: 1 Ford Transit. 12 Leyland. 6 Mercedes. 3 Optare. 50 Renault. 2 Volvo.
Bodies: include 2 Van Hool
Ops incl: local bus services, excursions & tours, private hire, continental tours, school contracts.
Livery: White/Green

*CHERRY BRIAR LTD
[icons] R
SUPREME HOUSE, STOUR WHARF, STOUR ROAD, LONDON E3 2NT
Tel: 020 8985 8888
Fax: 020 8936 2444
Man Dir: Clifford Humphreys **Ops Man/Co Sec**: Helen Humphreys **Ch Eng**: B Raif.
Fleetname: Channel Coachways
Fleet: 5 - 4 coach. 1 midicoach.
Chassis: Scania. Toyota.
Bodies: Caetano. Irizar.
Ops incl: school contracts, excursions & tours, private hire, continental tours.
Livery: White/Red/Blue.

*CHARIOTS OF ESSEX LTD
See Essex

*CITY CIRCLE UK LTD
[icons] T
WEST LONDON COACH CENTRE, NORTH HYDE GARDENS, HAYES UB3 4DT
Tel: 020 8561 2112
Fax: 020 8561 2010
Dir: Neil Pegg **Ops Man**: Mike Fletcher
Fleet: 16 coach
Chassis: 11 Neoplan. 5 Setra.
Bodies: 11 Neoplan. 5 Setra.
Ops incl: excursions & tours, private hire, continental tours.
Livery: White/Blue/Grey
Ticket System: Almex, Wayfarer 3, Setright

*CLARKES OF LONDON
[icons] T
KANGLEY BRIDGE ROAD, LONDON SE26 5AT
Tel: 020 8778 6697
Fax: 020 8778 0389
E-mail: info@clarkescoaches.co.uk
Web site: www.clarkescoaches.co.uk
Man Dir: Mrs D Newman **Comm Dir**: J Devacmaker **Fin Dir**: S Reeve
Fleet: 57 - 53 coach, 4 minicoach.
Chassis: 20 Setra. 15 Scania . 4 Toyota. 18 Volvo.
Bodies: 4 Caetano. 15 Irizar. 10 Jonckheere. 20 Setra. 8 Mistral.
Ops incl: excursions & tours, private hire, express, continental tours.
Livery: Green/Silver.

*COACH COMPANIONS LTD
[icons]
MAGNOLIA HOUSE, 12 ST BOTOLPH'S GREEN, LEOMINSTER HR6 8ER
Tel: 01568 620279
Fax: 01568 616906
E-mail: enquiries@coachcompanions.co.uk
Web site: www.coachcompanions.co.uk
Dir: Richard Asghar-Sandys
Fleet: 1 midicoach.
Chassis: 1 Mercedes.
Bodies: 1 other.
Ops incl: private hire.
Livery: White

*COLLINS COACHES LTD [icons]
WATERSIDE TRADING CENTRE, TRUMPERS WAY, LONDON W7 2QD
Tel: 020 8843 2145
Fax: 020 8843 2375
E-mail: collinscoaches@aol.com
Web site: www.collins-coaches.co.uk
Man Dir: Eric Collins
Fleet: 9 coach.
Chassis: 9 Volvo.
Bodies: 1 Jonckheere. 7 Plaxton. 1 Van Hool.
Ops incl: continental tours, private hire, school contracts.
Livery: Red/White.

*CONISTON COACHES LTD
[icons]
88 CONISTON ROAD, BROMLEY BR1 4JB.
Tel/Fax: 020 8460 3432
Web site: www.conistoncoaches.co.uk
Dir: Richard Smock
Fleet: 5 coach
Chassis: 5 Volvo
Bodies: 1 Caetano. 4 Plaxton.
Ops incl: excursions & tours, private hire, continental tours, school contracts.
Livery: White/Red.

*COUNTY COACHES
See Essex

DAVID CORBEL OF LONDON LTD [icons]
6 CAMROSE AVENUE, EDGWARE HA8 6EG
Tel: 020 8952 1300.
Fax: 020 8952 8641
E-mail: corbeloflondon@aol.com
Dir: Robert Whelan
Fleet: 9 coach

Chassis: 4 Dennis. 1 Setra. 4 Volvo.
Bodies: 4 Plaxton. 1 Setra. 4 UVG.
Ops incl: school contracts, private hire.
Livery: Pink/Yellow.

*CROWN COACHES
68 CANON ROAD, BICKLEY BR1 2SP
Tel: 020 8313 3020
Fax: 020 8464 2375

CROYDON TRAMLINK
TRAMLINK CROYDON LTD, COOMBER WAY, CROYDON CR0 4TQ
Tel: 020 8665 9695
Fax: 020 8665 7347
Web site: www.tfl.gov.uk/trams
Ops Dir: John Ryman.
Fleet: 24 Tram
Chassis/bodies: Bombardier
Ops incl: local tram services
Livery: Red/White

CRYSTALS COACHES LTD
[icons]
HORTENSIA ROAD, CHELSEA SW10 0QP.
Tel: 020 7376 3015.
Fax: 020 7376 3019.
Ops Man: G. Betts.
Fleet: 30 - 15 minibus, 15 minicoach.
Chassis: Ford Transit. Freight Rover. Mercedes.
Ops incl: local bus services, school contracts, private hire.

CUMFI-LUX COACHES
See Middlesex.

DANS MINI-BUS HIRE LTD
[icons]
ROYAL FOREST COACH HOUSE, 109 MAYBANK ROAD, LONDON E18 1EZ.
Tel: 020 8505 8833.
Fax: 020 8519 1937.
Man Dir: D. J. Brown. **Dir**: S. A. Brown.
Fleet: 43 mini/midicoaches.
Chassis: 19 Ford Transit. 24 Mercedes.
Bodies: 24 Mercedes. 7 Optare. 5 Reeve Burgess. 1 Ford.
Ops incl: school contracts, excursions & tours, private hire, continental tours.

DOCKLANDS MINIBUS
FACTORY ROAD, SILVERTOWN, LONDON E16 2EW
Tel: 0207 474 9933
Dir: F Cheroomi **Sec**: R F Charoomi
Ops incl: local bus services, contracts, private hire
Livery: Red/Blue/White

EALING COMMUNITY TRANSPORT LTD [icon]
97 BOLLO LANE, ACTON, LONDON W3 8QN
Tel: 020 8753 7810
Web site: www.ectgroup.co.uk
Pass Ops Dir: Anna Whitty
Fleet: 28 - 13 single-deck bus, 15 minibus
Ops incl: local bus services
Livery: Red/Yellow

EAST LONDON COACHES
STAGECOACH EAST LONDON ROMFORD GARAGE, NORTH STREET, ROMFORD RM1 1DS.
Tel: 01708 731088.
Fax: 01708 765436.
Coaching division of Stagecoach East London.

EAST THAMES BUSES
See London Buses Ltd

P & J ELLIS LTD [wc] [Ac]
UNIT 3, RADFORD ESTATE, OLD OAK LANE, LONDON NW10 6UA.
Tel: 020 8961 1141.
Fax: 020 8965 5995.
Chmn: M. Ellis. **Dir**: J. Ellis.
Fleet: 10 coach.
Chassis: Volvo.
Bodies: 9 Jonckheere. 1 Berkhof.
Ops incl: excursions & tours, private hire, continental tours.
Livery: White/Red.

*ELTHAM EXECUTIVE CHARTER LTD
21-23 CROWN WOODS WAY, LONDON SE9 2NL
Tel: 020 8850 2011
Fax: 020 8850 5210
E-mail: enquiries@eec-minicoaches.co.uk
Web site: www.eec-minicoaches.co.uk
Dirs: Ray Lawrence, Jill Lawrence, Fiona Lawrence
Fleet: 6 - 1 midicoach, 4 minibus, 1 minicoach
Chassis: 1 Ford. 4 Iveco. 1 Fiat.
Bodies: 1 Indcar. 1 Optare. 4 other
Ops incl: private hire.
Livery: White/Blue/Gold

EMPRESS MOTORS LTD
3 CORBRIDGE CRESCENT, LONDON E2 9DS.
Tel: 020 7739 5454. **Fax**: 020 7729 0237
E-mail: info@empresscoaches.co.uk
Web site: www.empresscoaches.co.uk
Fleetmane: Empress of London
Dirs: P D Stanton(**Man Dir**), T A Stanton (**Co Sec**), L M R Stanton
Op Mans: J C Stanton, M E Stanton
Fleet: 18 - 13 coach, 3 midicoach, 2 minibus.
Chassis: 2 Ford Transit. 1 MAN. 1 Mercedes. 1 Toyota. 13 Volvo.
Bodies: 1 Caetano. 1 Jonckheere. 1 Optare. 13 Plaxton.
Ops incl: private hire.
Livery: Cream/Maroon.

ENFIELD TOWN COACHES
See Middlesex

*EPSOM COACHES GROUP
See Surrey.

*EXCALIBUR COACHES
1A BRABOURN GROVE, LONDON SE15 2BS
Tel: 020 7358 1441
Fax: 020 7358 1661
Web site: www.excaliburcoaches.com
Man Dir: Gary Zacca **Ops Man**: Ian Green
Fleet Eng: C Patel
Fleet: 13 - 12 coach, 1 minibus.
Chassis: 3 Iveco. 9 Scania.
Bodies: 2 Beulas. 9 Irizar.
Ops incl: excursions & tours, private hire, express, continental tours, school contracts.
Livery: Blue

FAHRENWIDE
See Kent.

FINCHLEY COACHES LTD
231A COLNEY HATCH LANE, LONDON N11 3DG.
Tel: 020 8368 0040.
Fax: 020 8361 1934.
Web site: www.coaches.org.uk
Man Dir: M. P. Rice. **Dirs**: Mrs V. M. Rice, P. M. Rice, Mrs E. B. Scrivens.
Fleet: 11 coach.
Chassis: 6 Leyland. 5 Volvo.
Bodies: 1 Duple. 10 Plaxton.
Ops incl: school contracts, excursions and tours, private hire, continental tours.
Livery: Yellow/Blue/Orange.
Associated with Southgate Coaches Ltd

FIRST IN LONDON
3RD FLOOR, MACMILLAN HOUSE, PADDINGTON STATION, LONDON W2 1TY
Tel: 020 7298 7300.
Fax: 020 7706 8789.
Web site: www.firstlondon.co.uk
Div Dir: Leon Daniels. **Man Dir**: Tony Wilson. **Div Fin & Comm Dir**: David Quinn.
Eng Dir: John Whitworth. **Eng Ops Dir**: Alan Coney.
Fleet: 1204 - 699 double-deck bus, 12 single-deck bus, 476 midibus, 15 minibus, 2 open-top bus.
Chassis: 59 AEC. 924 Dennis. 21 Leyland. 24 MCW. 24 Mercedes. 149 Volvo.
Bodies: 67 Alexander. 3 Carlyle. 49 East Lancs. 1 Leyland. 450 Marshall. 30 MCW. 14 Mercedes. 89 Northern Counties. 59 Park Royal. 429 Plaxton. 2 Reeve Burgess. 11 Wright.
Ops incl: local bus services, school contracts, private hire.
Livery: Red with Yellow/Grey stripes.

Ticket System: Prestige (TfL).

FOREST COACHES [wc]
THE COACH HOUSE, NELSON STREET, LONDON E6 2QA.
Tel: 020 8472 5954.
Fax: 020 8472 6098.

*FORESTDALE COACHES LTD
68 VINEY BANK, COURTWOOD LANE, FORESTDALE, ADDINGTON CR0 9JT
Tel/Fax: 020 8651 1359
Chmn/Man Dir: V Holub
Co Sec: Mrs P R Holub
Fleet: 1 coach.
Chassis/Body: Bova.
Ops incl: excursions & tours, private hire, continental tours.
Livery: Red/Gold signwriting.

*GOLDENSTAND SOUTHERN LTD
13 WAXLOW ROAD, LONDON NW10 7NY
Tel: 020 8961 8541
Fax: 020 8961 9949
Man Dir: J Chivrall **Ch Eng**: J O'Donovan
Sec: Mrs K Kemp
Fleet: 27 - coach, midibus, minibus.
Chassis: 1 DAF. 20 LDV. 5 Scania. 1 Volvo.
Bodies: include: 5 Jonckheere. Goldenstand.
Ops incl: school contracts, excursions & tours, private hire
Livery: Red/White

THE GOLD STANDARD
94A HORSENDEN LANE NORTH, GREENFORD UB6 7QH
Tel: 020 8795 0075.
Fax: 020 8900 9630.
E-mail: paul@luxuryminicoaches.co.uk
Web site: www.luxuryminicoach.co.uk
Prop: Paul Grant.
Fleet: 1 minicoach.
Chassis: Optare.
Ops incl: excursions & tours, private hire.

A GREEN COACHES LTD
357A HOE STREET, LONDON E17 9AP
Tel: 020 8520 1138.
Fax: 020 8520 1139.
E-mail: agreencoaches357@aol.com
Dirs: Keith Richards, Janis Grover.
Fleet: 6 coach.
Chassis: 6 Volvo.
Ops incl: private hire, school contracts.

Ac	Air conditioning
	Vehicles suitable for disabled
	Coach(es) with galley facilities
wc	Coach(es) with toilet facilities
	Seat belt-fitted vehicles
R	Recovery service available (not 24 hr)
R24	24hr recovery service
	Replacement vehicle available
T	Toilet-drop facilities available
	Vintage vehicle(s) available
	Open top vehicle(s)

HACKNEY COMMUNITY TRANSPORT
ASH GROVE BUS DEPOT, MARE STREET, LONDON E8 4RH
Tel: 020 7275 2400
Fax: 020 7275 2450
E-mail: info@hackneyct.org
Web site: www.hackneyct.org
Fleet: 38 - 13 double-deck bus, 21 single-deck bus, 4 minibus.
Chassis: includes Transbus
Bodies: includes Caetano
Ops incl: local bus services
Livery: Red/Yellow

HAILSTONE TRAVEL
See Essex

HAMPTON COACHES (WESTMINSTER) LTD
54B TRUNDLEYS ROAD, DEPTFORD SE8 5JG.
Tel: 020 8692 5182.
Fax: 020 8692 9304.
Dirs: A. T. Cocklin, Mrs M. E. Cocklin (**Co Sec**): I. Cocklin. **Gen Man**: I. Cocklin. **Ch Eng**: D. Francis. **Sec**: Mrs W. E. Cocklin. **Traf Man**: R. Leicester.
Fleet: 15 coach.
Chassis: 4 Bedford. 1 Ford. 4 Leyland. 1 Scania. 5 Volvo.
Bodies: Duple. Jonckheere. Plaxton.
Ops incl: excursions & tours, private hire, continental tours.
Livery: Blue/Grey.

HEARNS COACHES
(See Middlesex)

*JOHN HOUGHTON LUXURY MINI COACHES
2 ELGAR AVENUE, LONDON W5 3JU.
Tel: 020 8567 0056
Fax: 020 8567 5781
E-mail: jrhoughton@connectfree.co.uk
Web site: www.luxury-mini-coaches.co.uk
Man Dir: John Houghton
Sec: Marlene Houghton
Fleet: 3 minicoach.
Chassis/bodies: Mercedes.
Ops incl: private hire.
Livery: White

HOUNSLOW MINI COACHES
HIGH STREET, FELTHAM TW13 4HQ.
Tel: 020 8890 8429.
Fax: 020 8893 1736.
Prop: Gerry Willing.
Fleet: 16 - 2 midicaoch, 14 minibus.
Chassis: 5 Ford Transit, 3 LDV, 6 Mercedes.
Ops incl: school contracts, excursions & tours, private hire.

HOUSTON'S OF LONDON
83 GLADESMORE ROAD, LONDON N15 6TL.
Tel/Fax: 020 8800 4576.
Prop: H. Jones.
Fleet: 2 coach. **Chassis**: Leyland.
Ops incl: school contracts, excursions & tours, private hire.

IMPACT OF LONDON
R24
7-9 WADSWORTH ROAD, GREENFORD UB6 7JD
Tel: 020 8579 9922
Fax: 020 8840 4880.
E-mail: info@impactgroup.co.uk
Web site: www.impactgroup.co.uk
Prop: A. Hill. **Gen Man**: A. Palmer.
Engs: H Louis, L. Singh.
Fleet: 44 - 14 coach, 20 midicoach, 10 minibus.
Chassis: 2 Bova. 2 Dennis. 10 LDV. 20 Mercedes. 10 Volvo.
Bodies: 7 Berkhof. 2 Bova. 1 Caetano. 2 Mellor. 24 Mercedes. 3 Optare. 3 Plaxton. 2 Van Hool.
Ops incl: excursions & tours, private hire, express, continental tours, school contracts.
Livery: White.

INTERNATIONAL COACH LINES LTD
19 NURSERY ROAD, THORNTON HEATH CR7 8RE.
Tel: 020 8684 2995.
Fax: 020 8689 3483.
Dir: Mrs S. Bailey.
Fleet: 18 - 3 double-deck bus, 1 single-deck bus, 10 coach, 4 minicoach.
Ops incl: excursions & tours, private hire, express, continental tours.
Livery: Blue/White.

ISLEWORTH COACHES
See Middlesex

*THE KINGS FERRY
See Kent

*LONDON LINK
See Kent

*LEWIS TRAVEL UK PLC
2-10 DENHAM STREET, LONDON SE1 0RY
Tel: 020 8858 0031
Fax: 020 8858 7631
Chmn: T Lewis **Man Dir**: P Legworthy
Chief Eng: P Letchcorn **Traff Man**: J Harpic
Fleet: 19 - 17 coach, 2 midicoach.
Chassis: 5 Dennis. 2 Mercedes. 4 Scania. 8 Volvo.
Bodies: Berkhof. Caetano. Neoplan. Plaxton. Setra. Van Hool.
Ops incl: local bus services, school contracts, excursions & tours, private hire, continental tours.

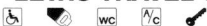

LINK LINE COACHES LTD
1 WROTTESLEY ROAD, LONDON NW10 5XA.
Tel: 020 8965 2221.
Fax: 020 8961 3680.
E-mail: info@linkline-coaches.co.uk
Web site: wwwlinkline-coaches.co.uk
Man Dir: T. J. Russell.
Fleet: 10 - 3 coach, 4 midicoach, 3 midibus.
Chassis: 2 Dennis. 1 Iveco. 2 Mercedes. 3 Volvo.
Bodies: 2 Caetano. 1 Optare. 3 Plaxton. 1 Reeve Burgess. 3 Irisbus.
Ops incl: private hire, continental tours.
Livery: White/Maroon/Gold
Subsidiary of Tellings Golden Miller (Middlesex)

*THE LITTLE BUS COMPANY
HOME FARM, ALDENHAM ROAD, ELSTREE WD6 3AZ
Tel: 020 8953 0202
Fax: 020 8953 9553
E-mail: enquiry@littlebus.co.uk
Web site: www.littlebus.co.uk
Fleet: includes single deck coach, midicoach, minibus, minicoach
Chassis: LDV. Leyland. Mercedes.
Bodies: Mercedes.
Prop: Jeremy Reese
Fleet: 7 minibus.
Chassis: 5 LDV. 2 Ford Transit.
Ops incl: school contracts, private hire.

LONDON BUSES LTD t/a EAST THAMES BUSES
ASH GROVE, MARE STREET, LONDON E8 4RH
Tel: 020 7241 7220.
Fax: 020 7241 7239.
Fleet Name: East Thames Buses.
Man Dir: Alan Barrett **Fin Dir**: David Bowen. **Eng. Dir**: Gary Filbey.
Gen Man: Norman Priestly.
Fleet: 128 - 77 double-deck bus. 51 single-deck bus.
Chassis: 12 DAF, 15 Dennis. 10 Optare. 14 Scania. 77 Volvo.
Bodies: 40 East Lancs. 10 Optare. 21 Plaxton. 3 Wright.
Ops incl: local bus services.
Livery: Red.
Ticket System: Prestige
Part of Transport for London

*LONDON CENTRAL BUS CO LTD
25 RALEIGH GARDENS, MITCHAM CR4 3NS
Tel: 020 8646 1747
Fax: 020 8640 2317
E-mail: enq@go-ahead-london.com
Web site: www.go-ahead-london.com
Ch Exec (London): David Brown. **Eng Dir**: Phil Margrave. **Fin Dir**: Paul Reeves.
Ops Dir: John Trayner.
Fleet: 637 - 457 double-deck bus, 153 single-deck bus, 27 articulated bus.
Chassis: 83 AEC. 17 DAF. 136 Dennis. 1 Leyland. 27 Mercedes. 373 Volvo.
Bodies: 46 Alexander. 17 East Lancs. 28 Marshall. 27 Mercedes. 63 Northern Counties. 83 Park Royal. 240 Plaxton. 129 Transbus. 1 Wright.
Ops incl: local bus services, school contracts, excursions & tours, private hire.
Livery: Red

*LONDON GENERAL TRANSPORT SERVICES LTD

25 RALEIGH GARDENS, MITCHAM CR4 3NS.
Tel: 020 8646 1747.
Fax: 020 8640 2317.
E-mail: enq@go-ahead-london.com
Web site: www.go-ahead-london.com
Ch Exec (London): David Brown **Eng Dir**: Phil Margrave **Fin Dir**: Paul Reeves.
Fleet: 656 - 428 double-deck bus, 197 single-deck bus, 31 articulated bus.
Chassis: 51 AEC. 175 Dennis. 1 MCW. 31 Mercedes. 14 Transbus. 369 Volvo.
Bodies: 52 East Lancs. 1 MCW. 31 Mercedes. 39 Northern Counties. 51 Park Royal. 240 Plaxton. 83 Transbus. 159 Wright.
Ops incl: local bus services, school contracts, excursions & tours, private hire.
Livery: Red

*LONDON LINK
See Kent.

LONDON TRANSIT
See Hertfordshire

*LONDON UNITED BUSWAYS LTD
See Middlesex

LUXURY MINI COACH

94A HORSENDEN LANE, GREENFORD UB6 7QH
Tel: 020 8795 0075.
Fax: 020 8900 9630.
E-mail: paul@luxuryminicoach.co.uk
Web site: www.luxuryminicoach.co.uk
Dir: Paul Grant
Fleet: minicoaches.
Ops incl: private hire.

*MARTIN'S MINI COACHES

THE GAS WORKS, 709 OLD KENT ROAD, LONDON SE15 1JJ
Tel: 020 7732 1000
Fax: 020 7732 1011
E-mail: info@martinsminicoachesco uk
Web site: www.martinsminicoaches.co.uk
ManDir: Steve Martin Ashdown **Acc Man**: H Buck
Fleet: 10 minicoach
Chassis: Mercedes
Bodies: Transbus
Ops incl: excursions & tours, private hire.

MCH MINIBUSES LTD
See Middlesex.

METROBUS LTD
FARNBOROUGH HILL, ORPINGTON BR6 6DA.
Tel: 01689 861432.
Fax: 01689 857324.
Web site: www.metrobus.co.uk
Fleetname: Metrobus.
Man Dir: A. Eatwell. **Ops Dir**: G. Wood.
Fleet Eng Man: C. C. Prowse.
Fleet: 268 - 111 double-deck bus, 155 single-deck bus, 2 midibus.
Chassis: 176 Dennis. 17 Leyland. 2 Optare. 53 Volvo.
Bodies: Alexander. Caetano. East Lancs. Leyland. Northern Counties. Optare. Plaxton. Scania.
Ops incl: local bus services.
Livery: Blue/Yellow, Red/Yellow/Blue
Ticket System: Wayfarer Prestige.
Subsidiary of Go-Ahead Group

*METROLINE
HYGEIA HOUSE, 66 COLLEGE ROAD, HARROW HA1 1BE
Tel: 020 8218 8888
Fax: 020 8218 8899
E-mail: info@metroline.co.uk
Web site: www.metroline.co.uk
Man Dir: Steve McAleavy **Fin Dir**: Steve Ellis **Comm Dir**: Sean O'Shea **Dir Safety Standards**: Eddie Ledwith
Communications Dir: Kevin Barnett
Fleet: 998 - 644 double-deck bus, 333 single-deck bus, 1 open-top bus.
Chassis: 23 AEC. 665 Dennis. 1 MAN. 11 MCW. 1 Mercedes. 5 Optare. 302 Volvo.
Bodies: 107 Alexander. 81 Marshall. 11 MCW. 16 Northern Counties. 5 Optare. 23 Park Royal. 742Plaxton. 13 Wright.
Ops incl: local bus services, school contracts
Livery: Red/Blue.
Ticket System: Prestige.

MINI-BUS SHUTTLE SERVICE
68 LUPUS STREET, LONDON SW1V 3EH.
Tel: 020 7821 1157.
Fax: 020 7834 6748.
Prop: Kaye Stoyles. **Man**: R. Stoyles.
Fleet: 16 minibus.
Ops incl: school contracts, excursions & tours, private hire.

MITCHAM BELLE
223 STREATHAM ROAD, MITCHAM CR4 2AJ
Tel: 020 8640 0140
Fax: 020 8687 0716
Fleet: 95 - 80 single-deck bus, 12 coach, 3 double-deck bus
Chassis: 82 Dennis. 2 Iveco. 2 Leyland. 3 MCW. 2 Mercedes. 4 Optare.
Bodies: 2 Beulas. 34 Caetano. 2 Hispano. 3 MCW. 4 Neoplan. 4 Optare. 46 Plaxton.
Ops incl: local bus services, school contracts, private hire.
Livery: Red/White/Blue

M&M COACHLINES
See Middlesex

*M T P CHARTER COACHES
39 GROSVENOR ROAD, LONDON E11 2EW
Tel/Fax: 020 8989 0211
Prop: M Powis
Fleet: 2 - 1 coach, 1 minicoach.
Chassis: 1 Setra. 1 Toyota.
Bodies: 1 Caetano. 1 Setra.
Ops incl: private hire, excursions & tours, continental tours.
Livery: White

NEW BHARAT COACHES LTD
1A PRIORY WAY, SOUTHALL UB2 5EB
Tel: 020 8574 6810
Fax: 020 8813 9555
E-mail: admin@newbharat.co.uk
Web site: www.newbharat.co.uk
Dir: Surjit Singh Dhaliwal **Ch Eng**: Alan Littlemore
Fleet: 4 coach
Chassis: 4 Volvo
Ops incl: school contracts, excursions & tours, private hire, express, continental tours.
Livery: Red/Yellow/Blue on white base.

NEWBOURNE COACHES
FIRBANK WAY, LEIGHTON BUZZARD LU7 4YP
Tel: 020 7837 6663
Fax: 01525 850967
Web site: www.marshalls-coaches.co.uk
E.mail: info@marshalls-coaches.co.uk
Props: F. W. Marshall, S. J. Marshall
Ops Man: Ian White.
Fleet: 20 - 18 coach, 1 double-deck coach, 1 minicoach
Chassis: 3 Dennis. 7 Iveco. 1 Mercedes. 3 Scania. 6 Volvo.
Bodies: 7 Beulas. 2 Berkhof. 1 Caetano. 1 Irizar. 5 Jonckheere. 4 Plaxton.
Ops incl: private hire, school contracts, local bus services.
Livery: Blue/Multicoloured.

*THE ORIGINAL LONDON TOUR
JEWS ROW, LONDON SW18 1TB
Tel: 020 8877 1722
Fax: 020 8877 1968
E-mail: info@theoriginaltour.com
Web site: www.theoriginaltour.com
Fleet: 94 - 24 double-deck bus, 70 open-top bus.
Chassis: 2 Dennis. 13 Leyland. 41 MCW. 14 Volvo.
Bodies: 13 Alexander. 41 MCW. 2 Northern Counties. 14 Transbus.
Ops incl: local bus services.
Livery: Red/Cream
Ticket system: Almex/Wayfarer

Ac	Air conditioning	
♿	Vehicles suitable for disabled	
🍴	Coach(es) with galley facilities	
wc	Coach(es) with toilet facilities	
♥	Seat belt-fitted vehicles	
R	Recovery service available (not 24 hr)	
R24	24hr recovery service	
✓	Replacement vehicle available	
T	Toilet-drop facilities available	
	Vintage vehicle(s) available	
🚌	Open top vehicle(s)	

OWENS COACHES
See Kent

PARKSIDE TRAVEL
See Hertfordshire.

PEMICO TRAVEL/PECKHAM MINI COACHES
9-11 VERNEY ROAD, LONDON SE16 3DH
Tel: 020 7231 8525
Fax: 020 7252 1018.
Dirs: R. G. Sault, P. R. Roff
Fleet: 28 - 2 single-deck bus, 9 coach, 3 midicoach, 12 minibus, 2 minicoach.
Chassis: 9 Dennis. 11 LDV. 8 Mercedes.
Bodies: 2 Alexander. 6 Autobus. 9 Plaxton.
Ops incl: local bus services, school contracts, excursions & tours, private hire, continental tours.
Livery: White

REDWING COACHES
10 DYLAN ROAD (OFF MILKWOOD ROAD), LONDON SE24 0HL.
Tel: 020 7733 1124.
Fax: 020 7733 5194.
E-mail: keith@redwing-coaches.co.uk
Web site: www.redwing-coaches.co.uk.
Man Dir: Paul Campana. **Acc Man**: Suzanne Jones. **Ch Eng**: Robbie Hodgkiss. **Tran Man**: Paul Frankland. **Sales & Mktg Man**: Keith Payne. **Com Man**: Steve Hillier. **Res Man**: Jef Johnson. **Ops Man**: Dave Hunt.
Fleet: 44 - 41 coach. 3 midicoach.
Chassis: 22 Iveco. 1 MAN. 20 Mercedes. 1 Neoplan.
Bodies: 22 Beulas. 1 Berkhof. 20 Mercedes. 1 Neoplan.
Ops incl: excursions & tours, private hire, continental tours, school contracts.
Livery: Red/Cream

ROUNDABOUT BUSES LTD
See Kent

*SILVERDALE LONDON LTD
UNIT 3, RADFORD ESTATE, OLD OAK LANE, LONDON NW10 6UA
Tel: 020 8961 1812
Fax: 020 8961 5677
Email: silverdalelondon@aol.com
Web site: www.silverdalelondon.com
Dir: Robert Green **Ops Man**: Richard Cassell
Fleet: 13 - 11 coach, 2 midicoach.
Chassis: 1 MAN. 2 Mercedes. 10 Volvo.
Bodies: 7 Caetano. 1 Marcopolo. 2 Optare. 3 Plaxton.
Ops incl: school contracts, excursions & tours, private hire, express, continental tours.
Livery: White/Black/Red

SOUTHGATE COACHES LTD
231A COLNEY HATCH LANE, LONDON N11 3DG.
Tel: 020 8368 0040.
Fax: 020 8361 1934.
Web site: www.coaches.org.uk
Man Dir: M. P. Rice. **Dirs**: Mrs V. M. Rice, P. M. Rice, Mrs E. B. Scrivens.
Fleet: 11 coach.
Chassis: 6 Leyland. 5 Volvo.
Bodies: 1 Duple. 10 Plaxton.
Ops incl: school contracts, excursions and tours, private hire, continental tours.
Livery: Yellow/Blue/Orange
Associated with Finchley Coaches Ltd

STAGECOACH LONDON
2 CLEMENTS ROAD, ILFORD IG1 1BA
Tel: 020 8695 0707/3420
Fax: 020 8477 7200
Web site: www.stagecoachbus.com
Man Dir: Barry Arnold **Eng Dir**: Peter Sumner **Ops Dir**: Barry Beckham
Fleet: 1767 - 828 double-deck bus, 50 single-deck bus, 4 coach, 35 articulated bus, 350 midibus.
Chassis: DAF. Dennis. Leyland. Mercedes. Scania. Volvo.
Bodies: Alexander. Mercedes. Optare. Park Royal. Plaxton. Wright.
Ops incl: local bus services, excursions & tours, private hire.
Livery: Red.
Ticket System: Wayfarer.

*SULLIVAN BUSES
See Hertfordshire

TELLINGS GOLDEN MILLER
See Middlesex (TGM Buses – See Surrey).

F E THORPE & SONS LTD
UNIT 5, FOURTH WAY, WEMBLEY HA9 0LH
Tel: 020 8998 1155
Man Dir: F. Thorpe. **Dir**: J. Thorpe.
Fleet: 106 - 84 single-deck bus, 19 double-deck bus, 3 minibus
Chassis: 60 Dennis. 15 MCW. 3 Mercedes. 28 Volvo.
Bodies: 2 Alexander. 28 East Lancs. 15 MCW. 60 Plaxton. 1 Wadham Stringer.
Livery: Red/Yellow
Ops incl: local bus services, school contracts

TOMORROWS TRANSPORT
GIBBS STORAGE, GIBBS ROAD, LONDON N18 3PU
Tel: 020 8807 4555
Fax: 020 8807 4603
Prop: V A Daniels
Fleet: 3 - 2 coach, 1 midicoach
Chassis: 1 DAF. 1 Leyland. 1 Toyota.
Bodies: 1 Caetano. 1 Duple. 1 Van Hool.
Ops incl: private hire

*T W H TRAVEL
THE GAS WORKS, 709 OLD KENT ROAD, LONDON SE15 1JJ
Tel: 020 7639 6600
Fax: 020 7639 6677
E-mail: terryh@twhlondon.freeserve.co.uk
Web site: www.ukcoachhire.com
Man Dir: T Hawthorne **Ops Man**: A Brignull
Co Sec: D Pugh **Dir**: P Campana
Fleet: 12 coach
Chassis: 10 Iveco. 2 Volvo.
Bodies: 10 Beulas. 2 Sunsundegui.
Services include: school contracts, excursions & tours, private hire, express continental tours
Livery: Maroon/Gold

*TRAVEL LONDON LTD
301 CAMBERWELL NEW ROAD, LONDON SE5 0TF
Tel: 020 8683 7060
Fax: 020 8665 1264
Man Dir: Paul McGowan
Ops Dir: Bill Weatherley
Fleet: 181 - 128 double-deck bus, 31 single-deck bus, 22 midibus.
Chassis: 159 Dennis. 22 Optare.
Ops incl: local bus services
Livery: Red

WESTBUS (UK) LTD
27A SPRING GROVE ROAD, HOUNSLOW TW19 9RH
Tel: 020 8572 6348.
Fax: 020 8570 2234.
Recovery: 07850 773328
Web site: www.westbus.co.uk
E-mail: reservations@westbus.co.uk
Ch Eng: Graham Bessant. **Acct**: Robert Davies. **Ops Man**: Tim Miles
Fleet: 26 - 23 coach, 3 minibus.
Chassis: 11 DAF. 4 Mercedes. 11 Volvo.
Bodies: 2 Berkhof. 6 Jonckheere. 11 Van Hool. 1 Hispano. 6 Plaxton.
Ops incl: private hire, continental tours, express.
Livery: Red/Cream

WESTWAY COACH SERVICES
7A RAINBOW INDUSTRIAL ESTATE, STATION APPROACH, RAYNES PARK, LONDON SW20 0JY
Tel: 020 8944 1277.
Fax: 020 8947 5339.
E-mail: david@westway-coaches.co.uk
E-mail: www.westwaycoachservices.com
Prop: David West. **Gen Man**: Arthur Richardson.
Fleet: 16 - 7 coach, 7 double-deck coach, 2 midicoach.
Chassis: 2 Mercedes. 14 Volvo
Bodies: 6 Jonckheere. 1 Plaxton. 6 Van Hool. 2 other.
Ops incl: school contracts, excursions & tours, private hire, continental tours.
Livery: Blue/Orange

WHITE ROSE TRAVEL LTD
See Surrey.

WINGS LUXURY TRAVEL LTD wc 🚌 A/c
WEST LONDON COACH CENTRE, HAYES UB3 4QT
Tel: 020 8573 8388
Fax: 020 8573 7773
Web site: www.wingstravel.co.uk
E-mail: info@wingstravel.co.uk
Gen Man: Bill Gritt
Fleet: 34 - 17 single-deck bus, 7 midicoach, 4 minicoach, 6 exec. minicoach.
Chassis/Bodies: Mercedes. East Lancs. Optare. Setra.
Ops Incl: local bus services, school contracts, excursions and tours, private hire.

MERSEYSIDE (ST HELENS, KNOWSLEY, LIVERPOOL, SEFTON, WIRRAL)

A1A LTD
373 CLEVELAND STREET, BIRKENHEAD CH41 4JW.
Tel: 0151 650 1616
Fax: 0151 650 0007
Web site: www.a1atravel.co.uk
Props: John and Barbara Ashworth
Fleet: 26 - 7 single-deck bus, 8 midibus, 11 minibus.
Chassis: 7 Dennis. 8 LDV. 1 Mazda. 5 Mercedes. 1VW.
Ops incl: local bus services, school contracts, private hire.
Livery: White/Blue

A2B TRAVEL (UK) LTD ♿ 🚌 wc 🔧
5 PRENTON WAY, NORTH CHESHIRE TRADING ESTATE, PRENTON CH43 3DU
Tel: 0151 609 0600
Fax: 0151 609 0601
E-mail: info@a2b-travel.com
Web site: www.a2b-travel.com
Man Dir: G Evans **Co Sec:** Mrs M Evans
Dirs: D Evans, Miss J Evans
Fleet: includes single-deck coach, midicoach, minibus, minicoach
Chassis: DAF, Dennis, LDV, MAN, Mercedes.
Bodies: include Caetano
Ops incl: school contracts, private hire, continental tours, excursions & tours.

AINTREE COACHLINE
11 CLARE ROAD, BOOTLE L20 9LY.
Tel: 0151 922 8630.
Fax: 0151 933 6994.
Livery: Red/Cream.
Owns Helms of Eastham.

ARRIVA NORTH WEST
♿ 🚌 🚌 R 🔧
73 ORMSKIRK ROAD, AINTREE L9 5AE.
Tel: 0151 522 2880
Fax: 0151 525 9556
Web site: www.arriva.co.uk
Man Dir: R. A. Hind. **Fin Dir:** Phil Stone
Eng Dir: M. Gilkerson.
Fleet: 1350 - 231 double-deck, 864 single-deck, 263 minibus.
Chassis: 95 DAF. 514 Dennis. 142 Leyland. 18 MCW. 145 Mercedes. 15 Neoplan. 3 Optare. 97 Scania. 326 Volvo. 3 others.
Ops incl: local bus services, school contracts, excursions & tours, private hire.

Livery: Aquamarine/Stone.
Ticket System: Wayfarer.

*G. ASHTON COACHES
wc 🚌 A/c
WATERY LANE, ST HELENS WA9 3JA
Tel: 01744 733275
Fax: 01744 454122
Prop: George Ashton
Fleet: 8
Chassis: 5 Scania. 1 Toyota. 2 Cummins.
Bodies: 1 Caetano. 2 Duple. 5 irizar.
Ops incl: excursions & tours, private hire, continental tours.
Livery: Blue/Grey/Red.

AVON COACH AND BUS COMPANY ♿
10 BROOKWAY, NORTH CHESHIRE TRADING ESTATE, PRENTON CH43 3DT.
Tel: 0151 608 8000.
Fax: 0151 608 9955.
Prop: L. W. Smith.
Tran/Ops Man: P. Harwood.
Fleet: 10 - 7 double-deck bus, 2 single-deck bus, 1 coach.
Chassis: 1 Bedford. 2 Daimler. 4 Leyland. 2 Leyland National. 1 Volvo.
Ops incl: local bus services, school contracts, excursions & tours, private hire.
Livery: Cream with Blue and Gold stripe.
Ticket System: Wayfarer.

BLUELINE COACHES
♿ wc 🚌
54 STATION ROAD, MAGHULL L31 3DB.
Tel/Fax: 0151 526 8888.
Prop: C. P. Carr.
Fleet: 12 - 3 coach, 4 midicoach, 5 minicoach.
Ops incl: private hire, school contracts.

CMT BUSES ♿
LIVER INDUSTRIAL ESTATE, LONG LANE, AINTREE L9 7ES.
Tel: 0151 523 3118
Fax: 0151 525 0432
Fleetname: C&M Travel
Man Dir: Jeff Grant
Fleet: 104 - single-deck bus, midibus, minibus.
Ops incl: local bus services
Livery: Red with Yellow
Ticket System: Wayfarer 3

CMT is a subsidiary companies of Glenvale Transport (se below)

CUMFY COACHES wc 🚌
49 MILL LANE, SOUTHPORT PR9 7PL.
Tel: 01704 227321.
Fax: 01704 505781.
Prop: M. R. Vickers. **Admin:** Mrs P. Lyon.
Fleet: 12 - 1 midicoach, 3 minibus, 8 minicoach.
Chassis: 1 Bedford. 3 Dodge. 1 Iveco. 1 Mercedes. 5 Renault.
Bodies: 1 Duple. 1 Wright. 3 Reeve Burgess. 6 van conversions.
Ops incl: excursions & tours, private hire, school contracts.

EMS BUS & COACH
OLD MILL WORKSHOPS, BEAUFORT ROAD, BIRKENHEAD CH41 1HE.
Prop: R. Benson.

FIRST IN CHESTER & THE WIRRAL
659 NEW CHESTER ROAD, ROCK FERRY CH42 1PZ
Tel: 0151 645 8661
Web site: www.firstgroup.com
Fleet: 203 double-deck bus, single deck bus, coach, minibus.
Ops incl: local bus services

*FIVE STAR GROUP TRAVEL
wc 🚌 A/c 🔧
6 ORCHARD AVENUE, LIVERPOOL L14 3NQ
Tel: 0151 481 0000
Fax: 0151 493 9999
Web site: www.fivestartravel.co.uk
Prop: Phil Riley.
Fleet: 3 coach.
Bodies: 3 Bova.
Ops incl: excursions & tours, private hire, continental tours.

FORMBY COACHWAYS LTD T/A FRESHFIELD COACHES
🚌
38 STEPHENSON WAY, FORMBY L37 8EW.
Tel: 01704 834448.
Fax: 01704 878820.

A/c	Air conditioning	🚌	Seat belt-fitted vehicles	🔧 Replacement vehicle available
♿	Vehicles suitable for disabled	R	Recovery service available (not 24 hr)	T Toilet-drop facilities available
🍴	Coach(es) with galley facilities			🚍 Vintage vehicle(s) available
wc	Coach(es) with toilet facilities	R24	24hr recovery service	🚌 Open top vehicle(s)

Fleetname: Freshfield Coaches.
Man Dir/Tran Man: K. W. Bradley.
Sec: D. A. Bradley.
Chassis: 1 minibus. **Chassis:** Ford Transit.
Ops incl: school contracts, private hire.
Livery: Two-tone Green.

GLENVALE TRANSPORT LTD

GILMOSS GARAGE, EAST LANCASHIRE ROAD, LIVERPOOL L11 0BB
Tel: 0151 330 6200
Web site: www.glenvale-transport.co.uk
Man Dir: Dominic Brady
Fleet: 173 - double-deck bus, single-deck bus, midibus
Chassis: MCW, Leyland, Optare, Dennis Scania.
Bodies: MCW, Park Royal, Plaxton, Marshall, Optare
Ops incl: local bus services
Subsidiary Company: CMT Buses (see above)

HAPPY AL'S COACHES
wc ‖ R ✂ T

40 CLEVELAND STREET, BIRKENHEAD L41 8EQ
Tel: 0151 653 0053
Fax: 0151 670 0509
E-mail: dan@happyals.com
Web site: www.happyals.com
Fleetname: Happy Al's
Owner: T. A. Cullinan. **Ops Man:** M. Cullinan
Fleet: 51 - 39 double-deck bus, 3 single-deck bus, 8 coach, 1 double-deck coach.
Chassis: 20 Bristol. 3 DAF. 5 Dennis. 14 Leyland. 6 Leyland National. 1 Neoplan. 3 Volvo.
Bodies: 5 Alexander. 2 ECW. 2 Ikarus. 14 Leyland. 6 Leyland National. 1 Neoplan. 2 Optare. 4 Van Hool. 3 others.
Ops incl: local bus services, school contracts, excursions & tours, private hire, express, continental tours.
Livery: Multi-coloured.
Ticket System: Wayfarer 3.

*HARDINGS TOURS
🚫 ‖ wc Nc

60 ST JOHNS ROAD, HUYTON L36 5SY
Tel: 0151 489 1228

Fax: 0151 480 2030
Web site: www.hardingstours.co.uk
Dir: K. O'Sullivan **Ops Man:** K Pickavance
Fleet: 11 - coach
Chassis: 1 Mercedes. 8 Scania. 2 Volvo.
Bodies: 1 Berkhof. 7 Irizar. 1 Mercedes. 2 Van Hool.
Ops incl: excursions & tours, private hire, continental tours.
Livery: White/Red/Orange/Yellow.

K G & R HATTON

ST HELENS CENTRAL STATION YARD, SHAW STREET, ST HELENS WA10 1DQ
Fleetname: Hattons Travel, Nip on Transport.
Prop: K.G. & R. Hatton.
Livery: Red/White.

LIVERPOOL CITY COACHES/CITY BUS ♿

99-103 STANHOPE STREET, LIVERPOOL L8 5RE.
Tel: 0151 708 6201.
Fax: 0151 708 7201.
Prop: J. Bleasdale.
Fleet: 13 - 2 double-deck bus, 6 single-deck bus, 2 coach, 1 midibus, 2 minibus.
Chassis: 2 Bristol. 1 Ford Transit. 1 Freight Rover. 4 Leyland. 5 Leyland National.
Bodies: 2 ECW. 1 Leyland. 5 Leyland National. 1 Optare. 2 Plaxton.
Ops incl: local bus services, private hire.
Livery: Blue/White.
Ticket System: Wayfarer.

GAVIN MURRAY & ELLISONS COACHES
wc ‖ 🚫 Nc ✂ T

QUEENS GARAGE, 61 BOUNDARY ROAD, ST HELENS WA10 2LX.
Tel: 01744 22882.
Fax: 01744 24402.
Dirs: A. Magowan, M. Magowan.
Fleet: 10 coach.
Chassis: 6 Bova. 3 Mercedes. 1 Volvo.
Bodies: 6 Bova. 3 Neoplan. 1 Van Hool.
Ops incl: private hire.
Livery: White/Red/Yellow.

*DAVID OGDEN COACHES
wc 🚫 Nc R24 ✂ T

BAXTERS LANE, SUTTON, ST HELENS WA9 3DH
Tel/Recovery: 01744 606176

Fax: 01744 850903
E-mail: ogdenssutton@btconnect.com
Web site: www.davidogdenholidays.co.uk
Dirs: David Ogden, Carol Ogden.
Fleet: 19 - 2 single-deck bus, 14 coach, 3 minibus.
Chassis: 16 DAF. 2 Ford Transit. 1 Mercedes.
Bodies: 3 Ikarus. 3 Plaxton. 10 Van Hool.
Ops incl: excursions & tours, private hire, express, continental tours.
Livery: Red/White/Blue.

*SANDGROUNDER COACHES
See Lancashire

SUPERTRAVEL MINICOACHES ♿ 🚫

STC HOUSE, SPEKE HALL ROAD, SPEKE L24 9HD.
Tel: 0151 486 3994.
Fax: 0151 448 1216.
Sole Prop: G. Bolderson.
Fleet: 36 - 8 single-deck bus, 10 midibus, 7 midicoach, 8 minibus, 3 minicoach.
Chassis: include Dennis, Fiat, Ford Transit, Freight Rover, Iveco, LDV, Mercedes-Benz, 2 Optare, Renault, Talbot.
Bodies: include Carlyle, East Lancs, Mellor, 2 Optare, Plaxton, Reeve Burgess, Fiat, Talbot.
Ops incl: local bus services, school contracts, private hire.
Livery: Purple/White/Green.

WINGATES TOURS
🚫 R24 ✂ T

SPENCERS LANE, MELLING, LIVERPOOL L31 1HB.
Tel: 0151 547 2713.
Fax: 0151 548 2849.
Man Dir: John F. Donnelly
Fleet: 9 - 4 double-deck bus, 4 coach, 1 minibus.
Chassis: 4 Leyland. 1 Mercedes. 4 Volvo.
Bodies: 2 Jonckheere. 1 Mercedes. 2 Van Hool.
Ops incl: school contracts, excursions & tours, private hire, express, continental tours.
Livery: White.
Ticket System: Wayfarer 2.

MIDDLESEX

*ALLIED COACHLINES LTD
wc 🚫 Nc

THE BULLS BRIDGE CENTRE, NORTH HYDE GARDENS, HAYES UB3 4QT
Tel: 020 8573 2626
Fax: 020 8561 6636
E-mail: sales@alliedcoachlines.co.uk
Web site: www.alliedcoachlines.co.uk
Dirs: S Robinson, R Charles
Fleet: 7 coach.
Chassis: 5 Mercedes. 2 Setra

Bodies: 5 Mercedes. 2 Setra.
Ops incl: private hire.

ARMCHAIR PASSENGER TRANSPORT CO LTD
wc ‖ 🚫 Nc ✂ T

ARMCHAIR HOUSE, COMMERCE ROAD, BRENTFORD TW8 8LZ.
Tel: 020 8568 8227.
Fax: 020 8847 2679.
E-mail: coach@armchair.co.uk
Web site: www.armchair.co.uk

Joint Man Dirs: Ann Newman, Ronnie Whitefield **Fleet Eng:** Graham Lashbrook. **Coach Ops Dir:** David Phillips.
Fleet: 107 - 32 double-deck bus, 53 single-deck bus, 13 coach, 2 minicoach. 6 midicoach.
Chassis: 2 Bova. 85 Dennis. 2 Toyota. 18 Volvo.
Bodies: 2 Caetano. 85 Plaxton. 18 Van Hool.
Ops incl: local bus services, excursions & tours, private hire, continental tours.
Livery: Orange/White

*ARON COACHLINES LTD

THE BULLS BRIDGE CENTRE, NORTH HYDE GARDENS, HAYES UB3 4QT
Tel: 020 8569 2949
Fax: 020 8561 2829
E-mail: sales@aroncoachlines.co.uk
Web site: www.aroncoachlines.co.uk
Dirs: S. Robinson, R. Charles
Fleet: 6 - 4 coach, 2 minibus.
Chassis: 6 Mercedes.
Bodies: 6 Mercedes.
Ops incl: private hire.

*ASHFORD LUXURY COACHES

373 HATTON ROAD, FELTHAM TW14 9QS
Tel: 020 8890 6394
Fax: 020 8751 5054
Web site: www.ashfordluxurycoaches.co.uk
Man Dir: Martin Cornell
Fleet: 10 - 1 single-deck bus, 6 coach, 2 midicoach, 1 minicoach.
Chassis: 7 Dennis. 3 Mercedes.
Bodies: 3 Mellor. 7 Plaxton.
Ops incl: private hire, school contracts, local bus services.

BEECHES TRAVEL

23 POWDER MILL LANE, TWICKENHAM TW2 6EE.
Tel/Fax: 020 8898 7048.
Prop: C. Miller.
Fleet: 4 minicoach.
Chassis: Ford Transit. Freight Rover.
Ops incl: school contracts, excursions & tours, private hire.
Livery: White/Yellow.

BESSWAY TRAVEL

16 TINTERN WAY, WEST HARROW HA2 0SA.
Tel: 020 8422 3128.
Prop: Michael Heffernan.
Fleet: 6 - 1 coach, 3 midicoach, 2 minicoach.
Chassis: 1 Dennis. 5 Mercedes.
Bodies: 5 Autobus. 1 UVG.
Ops incl: private hire, school contracts.

*CABIN COACHES

1 PARSONAGE CLOSE, HAYES UB3 2LZ
Tel: 020 8573 1100
Fax: 020 8573 8604
E-mail: cabincoaches@aol.com
Props: P Martin
Fleet: 5 - 4 coach, 1 midicoach.
Chassis: 1 Dennis. 1 Mercedes. 1 Scania. 2 Setra.
Bodies: 1 Duple. 1 Mercedes. 2 Setra. 1 Van Hool.
Ops incl: excursions & tours, school contracts, private hire.
Livery: White

*CALL-A-COACH
See Surrey

*CARAVELLE COACHES

9 CHESTNUT AVENUE, EDGWARE HA8 7RA
Tel/Fax: 020 8952 4025
Dir: Harvey Lawrence.
Fleet: 2 - 1 midicoach, 1 minicoach.
Chassis: 1 Freight Rover. 1 Mercedes.
Ops incl: school contracts, excursions & tours, private hire.

*CAVALIER TRAVEL SERVICES
See London

*CHALFONT COACHES OF HARROW LTD

200 FEATHERSTONE ROAD, SOUTHALL UB2 5AQ
Tel: 020 8843 2323
Fax: 020 8574 0939
E-mail: chalfont.coaches@btopenworld.com
Web site: www.chalfontcoaches.co.uk
Man Dir: C J Shears **Dirs**: I Shears, M Shears **Ops Man**: P Williams **Ch Eng**: R Arents **Co Sec**: G Shears
Fleet: 18 - 15 coach, 1 midicoach, 2 minibus.
Chassis: 2 LDV. 1 Mercedes. 15 Volvo.
Bodies: 3 Autobus. 15 Van Hool.
Ops incl: school contracts, excursions & tours, private hire, express, continental tours.
Livery: Mauve/White

CHALFONT LINE LTD
See London

*CITY CIRCLE UK LTD
See London

COLLINS COACHES LTD
See London.

CUMFI-LUX COACHES

69 CORWELL LANE, HILLINGDON UB8 3DE.
Tel: 020 8561 6948.
Fax: 020 8569 3809.
Prop: N. R. Farrow (**Traf Man**).
Sec: Mrs T. K. Lovell.
Fleet: 3 - 1 coach, 1 minibus, 1 minicoach.
Chassis: 2 Mercedes. 1 Scania
Ops incl: excursions & tours, private hire.
Livery: Orange/White (coach); White (minibuses).

*FALCON TRAVEL

123 NUTTY LANE, SHEPPERTON TW17 0RQ
Tel: 01932 787752
Fax: 01932 785521
Fleet: 6 - 5 coach 1 midicoach.
Chassis: 1 Leyland. 1 Mercedes. 4 Volvo.
Bodies: 1 Plaxton. 4 Van Hool. 1 Sitcar.
Ops incl: private hire, excursions & tours, school contracts.
Livery: White/Black/Crimson

THE GOLD STANDARD

94A HORSENDEN LANE NORTH, GREENFORD UB6 7QH.
Tel: 020 8795 0075.
Fax: 020 8900 9630.
Owner/driver: P. Grant.
Fleet: 1 minicoach.
Chassis: Mercedes.**Body**: Soroco.
Ops incl: excursions & tours, private hire, continental tours.

HAMILTON OF UXBRIDGE

589-591 UXBRIDGE ROAD, HAYES END UB4 8HP
Tel: 01895 232266
Fax: 01895 810454.
Ops Man: D. L. Bennett.
Fleet: 10 - 8 coach, 2 double-deck coach.
Chassis: 10 MAN.
Bodies: 5 Ayats. 4 Noge. 1 Marco Polo
Ops incl: private hire, express, continental tours.

HEARNS COACHES

801 KENTON LANE, HARROW WEALD HA3 6AH
Tel: 020 8954 0444.
Fax: 020 8954 5959.
Prop: R J & P E Hearn
Fleet: 30 - 27 double-deck bus, 1 minibus, 1 minicoach, 1 minibus.
Chassis: 9 Leyland. 3 Mercedes. 3 Scania. 8 Setra. 7 Volvo.
Bodies: 3 Irizar. 3 Mercedes. 15 Plaxton. 8 Setra. 1 Van Hool.
Ops incl: school contracts, private hire
Livery: Blue/Grey/White.

HOUNSLOW COMMUNITY TRANSPORT

9 MONTAGUE ROAD, HOUNSLOW TW3 1JY.
Tel: 020 8572 8204.
Fax: 020 8572 0997.
Ch Exec: Val Merritt. **Flt Co-ord**: Guy King.
Fleet: 7 minibus.**Chassis**: 4 Ford Transit. 2 Freight Rover. 1 Renault.
Bodies: 3 Dormobile. 1 Eurostyle.
Ops incl: private hire.
Livery: Rhubarb/Custard.

A/c	Air conditioning	
♿	Vehicles suitable for disabled	
🍽	Coach(es) with galley facilities	
WC	Coach(es) with toilet facilities	
♥	Seat belt-fitted vehicles	
R	Recovery service available (not 24 hr)	
R24	24hr recovery service	
✓	Replacement vehicle available	
T	Toilet-drop facilities available	
	Vintage vehicle(s) available	
	Open top vehicle(s)	

HOUNSLOW MINI COACHES
HIGH STREET, FELTHAM TW13 4HQ.
Tel: 020 8890 8429.
Fax: 020 8893 1736.
Prop: G. Willing. **Ops Man**: A. Nugent.
Fleet: 16 - 3 midicoach, 8 minibus, 5 minicoach.
Chassis: 5 Ford Transit. 8 Mercedes. 3 LDV.
Bodies: 4 Mercedes. 5 Ford. 5 Autobus. 2 Devon.
Ops incl: local bus services, school contracts, excursions & tours, private hire.
Livery: White with logo.

VIC HUGHES & SON LTD
61 FERN GROVE, FELTHAM TW14 9AY.
Tel: 020 8831 0770.
Fax: 020 8831 0660.
Man Dir: V. B. Hughes.
Co Sec: Mrs V. Hughes. **Dir**: K. Hughes.
Fleet: 21 - 4 midicoach, 5 minibus, 12 ambulance.
Chassis: Ford, Mercedes.
Ops incl: school contracts, excursions & tours, private hire.
Livery: White/Black.

IMPACT OF LONDON
See London

ISLEWORTH COACHES
2 STOURTON AVENUE, HANWORTH TW13 6LG
Tel: 0845 128 4132
Fax: 0845 128 4133
E-mail: reservations@luxurycoachtravel.com
Web site: www.luxurycoachtravel.com
Man Dir: Andy Blackford
Fleet: 4 coach.
Chassis: 4 Volvo.
Bodies: 4 Plaxton.
Ops incl: private hire.
Livery: Blue with red relief.

J & D EURO TRAVEL
58 WEALD LANE, HARROW HA3 5EX.
Tel: 020 8861 1829, 8933 2961.
Fax: 020 8424 2585.
Sole Trader: J. T. Thomas.
Fleet: 9 - 2 coach, 1 midicoach, 4 minibus, 2 minicoach.
Chassis: 1 Bedford. 1 DAF. 1 Ford. 1 Ford Transit. 1 Freight Rover. 1 Iveco. 1 Mercedes. 1 Renault. 1 Volvo.
Bodies: 1 Alexander. 1 Carlyle. 1 Jonckheere. 1 Leyland. 1 Van Hool. 2 Pentiplan.
Ops incl: school contracts, excursions & tours, private hire, continental tours.
Livery: Black/White.

*LEOLINE TRAVEL
UPPER SUNBURY ROAD, HAMPTON TW12 2DW
Tel: 020 8941 3370
Fax: 020 8941 3372
Prop: David Baker **Ops Man**: Judy Dale
Fleet: 6 - 5 coach, 1 minibus.
Chassis: 1 Toyota. 5 Volvo.
Bodies: 1 Caetano, 5 Jonckheere
Ops incl: excursions & tours, private hire, school contracts.
Livery: Blue with orange letters

*LONDON UNITED BUSWAYS LTD
BUSWAYS HOUSE, WELLINGTON ROAD, TWICKENHAM TW2 5NX
Tel: 020 8400 6665
Fax: 020 8943 2688
E-mail: customer@lonutd.co.uk
Web site: www.lonutd.co.uk
Man Dir: Charlie Beaumont **Eng Dir**: Les Birchley **Fin Dir**: Richard Casling
Ch Op Off: Derek Lott **Head of Human Resources**: Miss Karen Fuller
Fleet: 655- 319 double-deck bus, 336 single-deck bus.
Chassis: 33 AEC. 452 Dennis. 8 MAN. 22 MCW. 108 Volvo. 32 other.
Bodies: 238 Alexander. 1 Carlyle. 8 Optare. 335 Plaxton. 21 Wright. 52 other.
Ops Incl: local bus services
Livery: Red/Grey

LUXURY MINI COACH
94A HORSENDEN LANE, GREENFORD UB6 7AH
Tel: 020 8795 0075.
Fax: 020 8900 9630.
Web site: www.luxuryminicoach.co.uk
Dir: Paul Grant
Fleet: minicoaches.
Ops incl: private hire.

M&M COACHLINES
33 HITHERWELL DRIVE, HARROW WEALD HA3 6JD.
Tel: 020 8863 2085.
Fax: 020 8861 6175.
Props: M. C. Burcombe, Mrs M. Burcombe.
Fleet: 1 coach.

Chassis: Scania. **Body**: Berkhof.
Ops incl: private hire, continental tours.

MCH MINIBUSES
126-127 WATERLOO ROAD, UXBRIDGE UB8 2QZ
Tel: 01895 230643.
Fax: 01895 234891.
Web site: mch-coaches.co.uk
E-mail: info@mch-coaches.co.uk
Dirs: P. N. Webber (**Tran Man**), E. Gavin.
Fleet: 32 - 5 coach, 10 midibus, 17 minibus.
Chassis: 29 Mercedes. 3 Neoplan.
Bodies: 27 Autobus. 2 Mercedes. 3 Neoplan.
Ops incl: private hire, school contracts.
Livery: White.

*METROLINE
See London.

NEW BHARAT COACHES LTD
See London

SUNBURY COACHES
204A CHARLTON ROAD, SHEPPERTON TW17 0RG.
Tel: 01932 785153.
Fax: 01932 761923.
Dir: P. Jones.
Fleet: 5 coach.
Chassis: Iveco, Leyland, Volvo.
Bodies: Berkhof, Beulas, Jonckheere.
Ops incl: excursions & tours, private hire.
Livery: White/Turquoise.

*TELLINGS GOLDEN MILLER LTD
See Surrey

VENTURE TRANSPORT (HENDON) (1965) LTD
307 PINNER ROAD, HARROW HA1 4HG.
Tel: 020 8427 0101.
Fax: 020 8427 1707.
Ops incl: private hire
Subsidiary of Hearns Coaches

WESTBUS UK LTD
See London.

*WINDSORIAN COACHES
See Berkshire

WINGS LUXURY TRAVEL LTD
See London.

NORFOLK

*AMBASSADOR TRAVEL (ANGLIA) LTD
[icons] R24 T

JAMES WATT CLOSE, GAPTON HALL INDUSTRIAL ESTATE, GREAT YARMOUTH NR31 0NX
Tel: 01493 440350
Fax: 01493 440367
Man Dir: M Gree **Ops Man**: M Pleasants
Dep Ops Man: B Picton
Fleet: 51 - 13 single-deck bus, 36 coach, 2 minibus.
Chassis: 2 Dennis. 5 Leyland. 2 Mercedes. 4 Scania. 38 Volvo.
Bodies: 2 Caetano. 2 Irizar. 36 Plaxton. 4 Van Hool. 7 Wright.
Ops incl: local bus services, school contracts, excursions & tours, private hire, express, continental tours.
Livery: White.
Ticket System: Setright/Almex.

ANGLIAN COACHES LTD
See Suffolk

BRITTAINS COACHES LTD
See Northants.

*CHENERY TRAVEL
[icons] R24 T

THE GARAGE, IPSWICH ROAD, DICKLEBURGH, DISS IP21 4NJ
Tel: 0870 8900545
Fax: 01379 740728
Recovery: 01379 741656
E-mail: Julia@chenerytravel.co.uk
Web site: www.chenerytravel.co.uk
Prop: Mrs P G Chenery **Gen Man**: Mrs J M McGraffn **Tran Man**: P Croxson **Ch Eng**: M Leeder
Fleet: 22 coach.
Chassis: 1 Bedford. 1 Leyland. 18 Setra. 2 Volvo.
Bodies: 1 Leyland. 2 Plaxton. 18 Setra.
Ops incl: school contracts, excursions & tours, private hire, express, continental tours.
Livery: Silver/Blue.

*COACH SERVICES LTD
[icons]

CROXTON ROAD, THETFORD IP24 1AG
Tel: 01482 752226
Fax: 0 1482 750498
E-mail: cochservicesltd@btconnect.com
Dir: Allen Crawford **Gen Man**: Ian Taylor
Tran Man: Rick Martin
Fleet: 22 - 18 coach. 3 midibus. 1 minibus.
Chassis: 4 Bova. 3 DAF. 3 Dennis. 1 LDV. 3 Leyland. 1 Mercedes. 2 Optare. 6 Volvo.
Bodies: 4 Bova. 5 Jonckheere. 2 Optare. 7 Plaxton. 3 UVG. 1 LDV.

Ops incl: local bus services, school contracts, excursions & tours, private hire, continental tours.
Livery: White
Ticket System: Wayfarer

CRUSADER HOLIDAYS
See Essex.

D/WAY TRAVEL COACHES
[icons] T

GREENWAYS, THE STREET, EARSHAM, BUNGAY NR35 2TZ
Tel: 01986 895375
Fax: 01986 891110.
E-mail: david@dwaytravel.com
Web site: www.dwaytravel.com
Prop: David Thompson
Fleet: 10 - 8 coach, 1 minibus, 1 hire car.
Chassis: 3 Ford. 1 Ford Transit. 5 MAN. 1 Renault.
Bodies: 1 Duple. 2 Plaxton. 5 MAN.
Ops incl: school contracts, excursions & tours, private hire, continental tours.
Livery: White with orange/yellow/brown.

A W EASTON'S COACHES LTD T [icons]

THE OLD COACH HOUSE, STRATTON STRAWLESS, NORWICH NR10 5LR.
Tel: 01603 754253.
Fax: 01603 754133.
Fleetname: Easton's Coaches.
Dirs: Robert Easton, Derek Easton. **Sec**: Christine Easton.
Fleet: 12 - 11 coach, 1 minicoach.
Chassis: 1 Bedford. 6 DAF. 3 Iveco. 1 Volvo.
Ops incl: local bus services, excursions & tours, private hire, continental tours.
Livery: Red/White/Yellow.
Ticket System: Almex.

EUROSUN COACHES
[icons] T

THORPE MARKET ROAD, UNIT 1, GREENWAYS, SOUTH REPPS, CROMER NR11 8NQ.
Tel: 01263 834483
Fax: 01263 834482.
E-mail: eurosuncoaches@hotmail.com
Web site: www.eurosun.net
Ch Eng: Adam Goffin **Sales & Mktg Man**: Tony Porter **Dirs**: Phil Overy, Jack Overy
Fleet: 19 - 16 coach, 3 double-deck coach.
Chassis: 7 DAF. 4 Leyland. 3 MAN. 2 Mercedes. 5 Neoplan.
Bodies: 3 Bova. 2 Leyland. 5 Neoplan. 6 Plaxton. 2 Van Hool. 1 other.
Ops incl: school contracts, excursions & tours, private hire, continental tours.
Livery: Red and Gold

FARELINE COACH SERVICES
See Suffolk.

FENN HOLIDAYS LTD
See Cambridgeshire.

FIRST EASTERN COUNTIES
[icons]

ROUEN HOUSE, ROUEN ROAD, NORWICH NR1 1RB.
Tel: 01603 760076
Fax: 01603 615439
Man Dir: John Pope
Fleet: 414 - 56 double-deck bus, 261 single-deck bus, 46 coach, 51 minibus.
Chassis: Dennis. Leyland. Mercedes. Scania. Volvo.
Bodies: Alexander. Duple. ECW. East Lancs. Frank Guy. Leyland. Northern Counties. Plaxton. Reeve Burgess. Wright.
Ops incl: local bus services, school contracts, private hire, express.
Livery: White/Blue/Magenta
Ticket System: Wayfarer.

FREESTONES COACHES
GREEN LANE, BEETLEY NR20 4DL.
Tel: 01362 860236.
Fax: 01362 860276.
Dir: B. Feeke.

GRANGEWOOD TRAVEL [icon]
GRANGEWOOD, CHAPEL ROAD, POTTER HEIGHAM NR29 5LS.
Tel: 01692 670944.
Prop: Phil Burgin.
Fleet: 1 minibus.
Chassis: 1 Toyota.
Ops incl: private hire.

*D&H HARROD COACHES LTD [icons]

BUS STOP, CASTLE ROAD, WORMEGAY, KING'S LYNN PE33 0SG
Tel: 01553 840492
Fax: 01553 841318
E-mail: harrodcoaches@eidosnet.co.uk
Web site: www.harrodcoachesltd.co.uk
Man Dir: David Reeve **Dir**: Mrs D Harrod
Co Sec: Mrs J Reeve **Ch Eng**: D Harrod
Fleet: 12.
Chassis: 1 Bedford. 2 DAF. 4 Dennis. 5 Volvo.
Bodies: 3 Jonckheere. 6 Plaxton. 1 Van Hool. 2 Wadham Stringer.
Ops incl: local bus services, school contracts, excursions & tours, private hire, continental tours.
Livery: White with blue writing

A/c	Air conditioning
[icon]	Vehicles suitable for disabled
[icon]	Coach(es) with galley facilities
wc	Coach(es) with toilet facilities
[icon]	Seat belt-fitted vehicles
R	Recovery service available (not 24 hr)
R24	24hr recovery service
✓	Replacement vehicle available
T	Toilet-drop facilities available
[icon]	Vintage vehicle(s) available
[icon]	Open top vehicle(s)

*KONECTBUS LTD
JOHN GOSHAWK ROAD, DEREHAM
NR19 1SY
Tel: 01362 851210
Fax: 01362 851215
E-mail: enquiries@konectbus.co.uk
Web site: www.konectbus.co.uk
Dirs: Julian Patterson, Steve Challis
Fleet: 23
Chassis: 6 DAF. 2 Leyland. 4 Leyland National. 1 Mercedes. 10 Optare. **Bodies**: 4 Leyland National. 16 Optare. 3 Plaxton.
Ops incl: local bus services
Livery: Blue/Yellow/Grey
Ticket system: Almex A90

*MATTHEWS COACHES
WESTGATE STREET GARAGES, SHOULDHAM, KING'S LYNN
PE33 0BN
Tel: 01366 347220
Fax: 01366 347293
Recovery: 07771 763365
E-mail: matthewscoaches@aol.com
Dir: John Lloyd
Fleet: 10 - 9 coach, 1 minibus
Chassis: 2 DAF. 6 Dennis. 1 LDV. 1 Leyland.
Bodies: 7 Plaxton. 2 Van Hool. 1 Convoy
Ops incl: school contracts, excursions & tours, private hire.
Livery: White/Blue

*NORFOLK GREEN
HAMLIN WAY, KINGS LYNN
PE30 4NG
Tel: 01553 776980
Fax: 01553 770891
Web site: www.norfolkgreen.co.uk
Man Dir: Ben Colson **Dirs**: A R Batchelor, K Shayshutt **Fleet Eng**: N Firth **Ops Man**: P Pengelly **Accounts Man**: R Hindley
Fleet: 39 - 1 double-deck bus, 5 single-deck bus, 33 midibus
Chassis: 1 Leyland. 1 MCW. 22 Mercedes. 15 Optare.
Bodies: 5 Alexander. 1 Leyland. 1 MCW. 2 Mercedes. 15 Optare. 12 Plaxton. 3 Reeve Burgess.
Ops incl: local bus services
Livery: two-tone Green
Ticket System: Wayfarer.

*PEELINGS COACHES
THE GARAGE, CLAY HILL, TITTLESHALL, KING'S LYNN
PE32 2RQ
Tel/Fax: 01328 701531
E-mail: jr@peelingscoaches.fsnet.co.uk
Prop: Jonathan Joplin **Ch Eng**: Jonathan Sayer
Fleet: 6 - coach.
Chassis: 1 Bedford. 1 DAF. 1 Dennis. 1 Van Hool. 2 Volvo.
Bodies: 4 Plaxton. 2 Van Hool.

Ops incl: local bus services, school contracts, excursions & tours, private hire, express.
Livery: White
Ticket System: Setright

*REYNOLDS COACHES OF CAISTER
THE GARAGE, ORMESBY ROAD, CAISTER-ON-SEA NR30 5QJ
Tel: 01493 720312/720050
Fax: 01493 721512
E-mail: reynolds.coaches@gtyarmouth.co.uk
Prop: Charles Reynolds
Fleet: 16 - 13 coach, 2 midicoach, 1 minibus.
Chassis: 2 Bedford. 4 DAF. 4 Dennis. 1 Ford Transit. 1 Mercedes. 1 Setra. 3 Volvo.
Bodies: 2 Caetano. 1 Duple. 7 Plaxton. 1 Reeve Burgess. 1 Setra. 3 Van Hool.
Ops incl: school contracts, excursions & tours, private hire, continental tours.
Livery: Blue/Grey/Yellow.

*SANDERS COACHES
HEATH DRIVE, HEMPSTEAD ROAD INDUSTRIAL ESTATE, HOLT
NR25 6JU
Tel: 01263 712800
Fax: 01263 710920
Website: www.sanderscoaches.com
Dirs: Charles Sanders, Paul Sanders
Fin Controller: Carole Willimott **Fleet Eng**: Andrew Sanders **Ops Man**: James Panton
Fleet: 86 - 8 double-deck bus, 27 single-deck bus, 38 coach, 10 midibus, 3 minicoach.
Chassis: 11 Bedford. 47 DAF. 7 Dennis. 4 Leyland. 13 Mercedes. 2 Setra. 2 Volvo.
Bodies: 5 Autobus. 2 Caetano. 4 ECW. 20 Ikarus. 2 Neoplan. 7 Optare. 27 Plaxton. 7 Reeve Burgess. 2 Setra. 10 Van Hool.
Ops incl: local bus services, school contracts, excursions & tours, private hire, continental tours.
Livery: Blue/Orange
Ticket System: Wayfarer 3

*H SEMMENCE & CO LTD
34 NORWICH ROAD, WYMONDHAM
NR18 0NS
Tel: 01953 602135
Fax: 01953 605867
E-mail: enquiries@semmence.co.uk
Web site: www.semmence.co.uk
Chairm: R H Green **Man Dir**: Sean Green **Co Sec**: M C Green **Tran Man**: Brian Lafferty **Eng Man**: Kevin Hughes
Fleet: 30 - 26 coach, 2 midicoach, 2 minibus.
Chassis: 8 Bedford. 10 Dennis. 4 Mercedes. 1 Scania. 7 Volvo.
Ops incl: local bus services, school contracts, excursions & tours, private hire, continental tours.
Livery: White.

Ticket System: Almex

*SIMONDS COACH & TRAVEL
R24
THE GARAGE, BOTESDALE, DISS
IP22 1BX
Tel: 01379 898202
Fax: 01379 898910
E-mail: bookings@simonds.co.uk
Web site: www.simonds.co.uk
Chmn: D O Simonds **Man Dir**: M S Simonds **Dir**: R S Simonds **Ops Man**: C Lummis **Eng Man**: A Tant
Fleet: 40 - 6 single-deck bus, 32 coach, 2 midicoach.
Chassis: 1 DAF. 1 Ford. 5 Leyland. 2 Mercedes. 1 Optare. 4 Transbus. 26 Volvo.
Bodies: 1 Autobus. 26 Plaxton. 5 Transbus. 10 Van Hool.
Ops incl: local bus services, school contracts, excursions & tours, private hire, continental tours.
Livery: White base with gold/green/red leaves
Ticket System: Wayfarer

*SPRATTS COACHES (EAST ANGLIAN & CONTINENTAL) LTD
THE GARAGE, WRENINGHAM, NORWICH NR16 1AZ
Tel: 01508 489262
Fax: 01508 489404
E-mail: sprattscoaches@aol.com
Web site: www.sprattscoaches.com
Dir/Gen Man: Richard Spratt **Dirs**: Christine Bilham, Gwen Spratt
Fleet: 11 - 8 coach, 2 midicoach, 1 minicoach.
Chassis: 1 Bedford. 1 Bova. 1 Mercedes. 7 Scania. 1 Volvo.
Bodies: 1 Autobus. 2 Berkhof. 1 Bova. 1 Caetano. 1 Duple. 6 Van Hool.
Ops incl: private hire, school contracts, excursions and tours.
Livery: White.

*SUNBEAM COACHES LTD
WESTGATE STREET, HEVINGHAM, NORWICH NR10 5NH.
Tel/Fax: 01603 754211
E-mail: sunbeamcoaches@aol.com
Dirs: G M Coldham, J M Cole.
Fleet: 8 - 6 coach, 2 midicoach.
Chassis: 1 DAF. 2 Dennis. 1 MAN. 1 Mercedes. 1 Toyota. 2 Volvo.
Bodies: 1 Caetano. 1 Neoplan. 1 Optare. 4 Plaxton. 1 Van Hool.
Ops incl: school contracts, excursions & tours, private hire.
Livery: White/Orange/Blue/Yellow

NORTH & NORTH EAST LINCOLNSHIRE

EMMERSON COACHES LTD
[wc] [seatbelt] [A/c] [key]

BLUESTONE LANE, IMMINGHAM
DN40 2EL.
Tel: 01469 578166
Fax: 01469 575278
E-mail: emmersoncoaches.ukf.net
Web site:
www.emmersoncoaches.ukf.net
Dirs: Alan Brumby, O. M. Stocks,
Allen Stocks.
Fleet: 12 - 11 coach, 1 minibus.
Chassis: 1 Bedford. 1 DAF. 1 Ford. 2 MAN.
3 Mercedes. 1 Scania. 3 Volvo.
Bodies: 2 Duple. 1 Ikarus. 1 Jonckheere.
2 Mercedes. 4 Plaxton. 1 other.
Ops incl: school contracts, private hire.
Livery: Cream with orange and brown stripes.

*EXPERT COACH SERVICES LTD
[wc] [seatbelt] [A/c]

2 PASTURE STREET, GRIMSBY
DN31 1QD
Tel: 01472 350650
Fax: 01472 351926
E-mail: sales@expertcoaches.co.uk
Web site: www.expertcoaches.co.uk
Man Dir: L A Harniess **Dir**: C J Cator
Fleet: 2 coach
Chassis: 2 Scania.
Bodies: 1 Berkhof. 1 Plaxton.
Ops incl: excursions & tours, private hire, continental tours.
Livery: Blue/White.

HOLLOWAY COACHES LTD
COTTAGE BECK ROAD,
SCUNTHORPE DN16 1TP.
Tel: 01724 282277, 281177.
Fax: 01724 289945.
Dirs: F. S. Holloway (**Man Dir**),
P. A. Holloway.
Fleet: 14 - 7 double-deck bus, 6 coach, 1 minicoach.
Chassis: 1 Bedford. 2 Dennis. 11 Leyland.
Bodies: 7 Alexander. 6 Plaxton. 1 other.
Ops incl: excursions & tours, express.
Livery: Red/White/Blue.

HORNSBY TRAVEL
[wc] [seatbelt] [T]

51 ASHBY HIGH STREET,
SCUNTHORPE DN16 2NB.
Tel: 01724 282255

Fax: 01724 282788.
E-mail: office@hornsbytravel.co.uk
Man Dir: R Hornsby, **Gen Man**: N J Hornsby
Eng: P Gawley
Fleet: 35 - 6 double-deck bus, 15 single-deck bus, 11 coach, 2 minibus, 1 midicoach.
Chassis: 6 DAF. 2 Daimler. 10 Dennis.
1 Iveco. 3 Leyland. 2 MAN. 2 MCW.
2 Mercedes. 2 Renault. 1 Volvo. 1 Citroen.
1 Vauxhall.
Bodies: 1 Berkhof. 1 Caetano. 3 Ikarus.
1 Marshall. 2 MCW. 1 Mellor. 4 Northern Counties. 1 Optare. 2 Park Royal.
14 Plaxton. 3 Wright.
Ops incl: local bus services, excursions & tours, private hire, school contracts, continental tours.
Livery: Silver/Blue.
Ticket System: Almex/Metric.

MILLMAN COACHES
[wc] [seatbelt] [key]

17 WILTON ROAD INDUSTRIAL
ESTATE, HUMBERSTON, GRIMSBY
DN36 4AW
Tel/Fax: 01472 210297
E-mail:
enquiries@millmancoaches.co.uk
Web site: www.millmancoaches.co.uk
Ptnrs: M. Millman, D. Millman, A. J. Millman
Ch Eng/Joint Tran Man: D Millman **Joint Tran Man**: A J Millman
Fleet: 11 - 8 coach, 1 midicoach, 2 minibus.
Chassis: 1 Bedford. 1 DAF. 1 Dennis.
5 Leyland. 2 Mercedes. 1 Volvo.
Bodies: 4 Duple. 1 Jonckheere.
2 Mercedes. 3 Plaxton.
Ops incl: private hire, school contracts.
Livery: White/Blue/Yellow

*RADLEY COACH TRAVEL
[seatbelt] [wc] [A/c] [key]

50 WRAWBY STREET, BRIGG
DN20 8JB
Tel: 01652 653583
Fax: 01652 656020
E-mail: info@radleytravel.co.uk
Owner: Kevin M Radley.
Fleet: 2 coach
Chassis: 2 Scania. **Bodies**: 2 Irizar.
Ops incl: excursions & tours, private hire, continental tours.
Livery: Gold/Maroon

SHERWOOD TRAVEL
[disabled] [wc] [key]

19 QUEENS ROAD, IMMINGHAM
DN40 1QR.
Tel: 01469 571140.
Fax: 01469 574937.
Fleetname: Sherwood Travel.
Man Dir: S. V. Oakland.
Fleet: 12 - 5 coach, 2 midicoach, 5 minibus.
Chassis: 2 DAF. 1 Ford. 2 Ford Transit.
4 Mercedes. 1 Toyota. 1 Volvo.
Bodies: 1 Autobus. 1 Duple. 2 Jonckheere.
1 Plaxton. 2 Reeve Burgess. 1 Panel Van Conversion. 1 Previa (Toyota).
Ops incl: school contracts, excursions & tours, private hire
Livery: Black Tulip/Skymist Grey.

SOLID ENTERTAINMENTS
[wc]

46 WELLOWGATE, GRIMSBY
DN32 0RA.
Tel: 01472 349222.
Fax: 01472 362275.
Prop: S. J. Stanley.
Fleet: 2 - 1 coach 1 minibus.
Chassis: 1 Scania.
Bodies: 1 Irizar.
Ops incl: excursions & tours, private hire, continental tours.
Livery: Black.

*WILBYS COACHES
[wc] [seatbelt] [vintage] [R24] [key]

BRICKHILLS, BROUGHTON, BRIGG
DN20 0BZ
Tel: 01652 654681
Fax: 01652 350396
Dirs: John K Wilby, Trixie A Wilby
Fleet: 31 - 5 double-deck bus, 7 coach,
1 double-deck coach, 1 midicoach,
3 minibus.
Chassis: 3 AEC. 3 Bedford. 1 Bristol.
1 Daimler. 1 Dennis. 2 Leyland. 2 MAN.
3 Mercedes. 1 Neoplan.
Bodies: 1 Alexander. 3 Duple. 1
Jonckheere. 2 Leyland. 3 Mercedes.
1 Neoplan. 3 Plaxton.
Ops incl: local bus services, school contracts, excursions & tours, private hire, continental tours.
Livery: Red/White/Blue

[A/c] Air conditioning	[seatbelt] Seat belt-fitted vehicles	[key] Replacement vehicle available
[disabled] Vehicles suitable for disabled	[R] Recovery service available (not 24 hr)	[T] Toilet-drop facilities available
[galley] Coach(es) with galley facilities	[R24] 24hr recovery service	[vintage] Vintage vehicle(s) available
[wc] Coach(es) with toilet facilities		[opentop] Open top vehicle(s)

NORTH YORKSHIRE, YORK

*ABBEY COACHWAYS LTD

MEADOWCROFT GARAGE, LOW STREET, CARLTON DN14 9PH
Tel: 01405 860337
Fax: 01405 869433
Dirs: Mrs L E Baker, J. Stockdale.
Fleet: 4 coaches.
Chassis: 1 DAF. 1 Scania. 2 Volvo.
Bodies: 4 Plaxton.
Ops incl: school contracts, excursions & tours, private hire.
Livery: Blue/White.

*G. ABBOTT & SONS

AUMANS HOUSE, LEEMING, NORTHALLERTON DL7 9RZ
Tel: 01677 422858
Fax: 01677 427435
Web site: www.abbottscoaches.co.uk
Props: D C Abbott, C G Abbot.
Fleet: 67 - 1 double-deck bus, 48 coach, 9 midibus, 1 midicoach, 8 minicoach.
Chassis: 3 Bedford. 5 DAF. 4 Ford Transit. 1 Freight Rover. 1 Iveco. 3 LDV. 15 Leyland. 1 MCW. 7 Mercedes. 4 Optare. 1 Renault. 20 Scania. 4 Volvo.
Bodies: 1 Beulas. 13 Duple. 4 Ford Transit. 12 Irizar. 1 MCW. 4 Optare. 14 Plaxton. 5 Reeve Burgess. 7 Van Hool. 1 other.
Ops incl: local bus services, school contracts, excursions & tours, private hire, continental tours.
Livery: Cream/Red

ALTERNATIVE TRAVEL

53 NAPIER CRESCENT, SCARBOROUGH YO12 4HX
Tel/Fax: 01723 863885.
Prop: Malcolm Chambers
Fleet: 2 - 1 coach, 1 minicoach
Chassis: 1 Mercedes. 1 Volvo.
Bodies: 2 Optare. 1 Plaxton.
Ops incl: private hire, school contracts

*ARRIVA NORTH EAST LTD

See Tyne & Wear

*H ATKINSON & SONS

INGLEBY ARNCLIFFE, NORTHALLERTON DL6 3LN.
Tel: 01609 882222
Fax: 01609 882476
E-mail: h.atkinson@orange.net
Web site: www.atkinsoncoaches.co.uk
Dirs: Mrs N. Atkinson, T S Atkinson, R. Atkinson
Fleet: 12 - 11 coach, 1 midibus
Chassis: 1 DAF. 4 Irisbus. 1 Leyland. 1 Setra. 5 Volvo.
Bodies: 3 Beulas. 2 Berkhof. 1 Duple. 1 Indcar. 1 Ikarus. 1 Jonckheere. 1 Marcopolo. 1 Plaxton. 1 Setra.
Ops incl: school contracts, excursions & tours, private hire, continental tours.

BALDRY'S COACHES

LEYLANDII, SELBY ROAD, HOLME-ON-SPALDING-MOOR YO43 4HB.
Tel: 01430 860992.
Prop: A. Baldry.
Fleet: 9 - 8 coach, 1 midicoach.
Chassis: 1 AEC. 1 Bedford. 5 Ford.
Ops incl: school contracts, excursions & tours, private hire.
Livery: Two-tone Green.

BEECROFT COACHES

POST OFFICE, FEWSTON HG3 1SG.
Tel/Fax: 01943 880206.
Prop: D. Beecroft.
Fleet: 6 - 3 coach, 1 midicoach, 2 minibus.
Chassis: 1 DAF. 1 Dodge. 2 Freight Rover. 1 Scania. 1 Volvo.
Bodies: 1 Alexander. 1 Bova. 3 Carlyle. 1 Duple. 1 Plaxton. 1 Van Hool.
Ops incl: local bus services, school contracts, excursions & tours, private hire, continental tours.
Livery: Green/Orange/White.

*BIBBY'S OF INGLETON

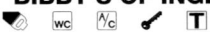

NEW ROAD, INGLETON LA6 3NU.
Tel: 01524 241330
Fax: 01524 242216
E-mail: bibbys_travel@talk21.com
Man Dir: P Bibby **Co Sec**: Mrs S Holcroft
Ch Eng: M Stephenson.
Fleet: 22 - 17 coach, 5 minibus.
Chassis: 17 DAF. 3 LDV. 3 Mercedes.
Bodies: 6 Ikarus. 3 LDV. 2 Mercedes. 4 Plaxton. 7 Van Hool. 1 Ovi.
Ops incl: school contracts, excursions & tours, private hire, continental tours.
Livery: Blue/Grey/Red with white stripes.

*BOTTERILLS

HIGH STREET GARAGE, THORNTON DALE YO18 7QW
Tel: 01751 474210
E-mail: botterills@hotmail.com
Web site: www.botterills.org.uk
Fleet: 4 minibus
Chassis/bodies: 4 Mercedes
Ops incl: local bus services, private hire.
Livery: White with black/gold lettering

*EDDIE BROWN TOURS LTD

BAR LANE, ROECLIFFE, YORK YO51 9LS
Tel: 01423 321240
Fax: 01423 326213
E-mail: operations@eddiebrowntours.com
Web site: www.eddiebrowntours.com
Ops Dir: Philip Brown **Tours Dir**: Diedre Brown
Fleet: 32 - 26 coach, 3 midicoach, 3 minicoach.
Chassis: 1 Freight Rover. 4 Leyland. 1 Mercedes. 4 Scania. 1 Toyota. 21 Volvo.
Bodies: 15 Plaxton. 14 Van Hool.
Ops incl: school contracts, excursions & tours, private hire, continental tours.
Livery: White/Red/Maroon

*BARNARD CASTLE COACHES (BURRELL'S)

SOUTH VIEW GARAGE, NEWSHAM, RICHMOND DL11 7RA
Tel: 01833 621302
Fax: 01833 621431
Dirs: Mrs M Burrell, A Burrell, Mrs S Burrell
Fleet: 6 - 5 coach, 1 minibus.
Chassis: 1 Leyland. 1 Mercedes. 4 Volvo.
Bodies: 1 Duple. 1 Mercedes. 1 Plaxton. 3 Van Hool.
Ops incl: school contracts, excursions & tours, private hire, express, continental tours.
Livery: Yellow/White

CHARTER COACH LTD

THE CONTROL TOWER OFFICES, THE AIRFIELD, TOCKWITH YO26 7QF
Tel: 01423 359655.
Fax: 01423 359459.
E-mail: expert.coaches@btinternet.com
Dir: Antoni LaPilusa.

COASTAL & COUNTRY COACHES LTD

THE GARAGE, FAIRFIELD WAY, STAINSACRE INDUSTRIAL ESTATE, WHITBY YO22 4PU.
Tel: 01947 602922.
Fax: 01947 600830
E-mail: enquiries@coastalandcountry.co.uk
Web site: www.coastalandcountry.co.uk
Fleet: 16 - 13 coach, 1 open-top bus. 2 minicoach.
Chassis: 1 Bedford. 1 Bristol. 2 Dennis. 5 Leyland. 2 Mercedes. 6 Volvo.
Bodies: 1 Duple. 1 ECW. 1 Jonckheere. 10 Plaxton. 1 Reeve Burgess. 2 Van Hool. 1 Adamson
Ops incl: local bus services, school contracts, excursions & tours, private hire.
Livery: White and two blues.

*COLLINS COACHES

CLIFFE SERVICE STATION, YORK ROAD, CLIFFE, SELBY YO8 6NN
Tel: 01757 638591
Fax: 01757 630196
Recovery: 01757 638591
E-mail: collins@coaches.fsworld.co.uk
Web site: www.collinscoaches.co.uk
Prop: Alan Collins.
Fleet: 5 - 4 coach, 1 midicoach
Chassis: 1 Mercedes. 4 Volvo.
Bodies: 1 Plaxton. 3 Van Hool. 1 Sitcar.
Ops incl: school contracts, private hire.
Livery: White

*COUNTRYSIDE BUS SERVICES

SOUTH GOWLAND, GOWLAND LANE, HARWOOD DALE, SCARBOROUGH YO13 0DU
Tel: 01723 870790
Fax: 01273 870790
Props: Piers A Turner, Jasmin M Turner.
Fleet: 2 minibus.
Chassis: 2 LDV
Ops incl: local bus services, school contracts, private hire.

J. DODSWORTH (COACHES) LTD

WETHERBY ROAD, BOROUGHBRIDGE YO5 9HS.
Tel: 01423 322236.
Fax: 01423 324682.
Dirs: J. W. Dodsworth.
Fleet: 13 - 10 coach, 2 midicoach, 1 minicoach.
Chassis: 3 Mercedes. 10 Volvo.
Bodies: 10 Plaxton. 2 Reeve Burgess. 1 Onyx.
Ops incl: excursions & tours, private hire, continental tours, school contracts.
Livery: Cream/Orange.

FIRST IN YORK

7 JAMES STREET, YORK YO10 3HH
Tel: 01904 435600.
Fax: 01904 431888.
E-mail: info@firstyork.co.uk
Web site: www.firstyork.co.uk
Man Dir: Jonathan May **Eng Man**: D. Liston. **Comm Man**: A. Walmsley.
Ops Man: J. Fletcher.
Fleet: 100 - 12 double-deck bus, 86 single-deck bus, 2 midibus.
Chassis: 98 Volvo, 2 Optare
Bodies: 12 Alexander. 2 Optare. 86 Wright.
Ops incl: local bus services, school contracts.
Livery: Grey/Magenta/Blue.
Ticket System: Wayfarer.

R HANDLEY & SONS LTD

NORTH ROAD, MIDDLEHAM, LEYBURN DL8 4PJ
Tel: 01969 623216
Fax: 01969 624546
Dirs: Mrs J Anderson, M Anderson.
Fleet: 8 - 6 coach, 1 minibus, 1 minicoach.
Chassis: 1 Ford Transit. 3 Leyland. 1 Mercedes. 2 Scania. 1 Volvo.
Bodies: 1 Berkhof. 1 Mercedes. 2 Van Hool. 1 Tiger. 2 Leopard.
Ops incl: private hire, school contracts, excursions & tours.
Livery: Black/White.

*HARGREAVES COACHES

BRIDGE HOUSE, HEBDEN, SKIPTON BD23 5DE
Tel: 01756 752567
Fax: 01756 753768
E-mail: hargreaves.coaches@ukonline.co.uk
Prop: Andrew C Howick
Fleet: 7 - 4 coach, 2 midicoach, 1 minibus.
Chassis: 1 LDV. 2 MAN. 3 Mercedes. 1 Scania.
Bodies: 2 Mercedes. 2 Neoplan. 1 Noge. 1 Van Hool. 1 LDV.
Ops incl: school contracts, excursions & tours, private hire, continental tours.
Livery: Pink/Silver

HARROGATE & DISTRICT TRAVEL LTD

PROSPECT PARK, BROUGHTON WAY, STARBECK, HARROGATE HG2 2NY
Tel: 01423 884020
Fax: 01423 885670
Web site: www.harrogateanddistrict.co.uk
www.the36.co.uk
Fleetname: Harrogate & District.
Chmn: G R Fearnley **Man Dir**: Dave Alexander
Fleet: 66 - 8 double-deck bus, 45 single-deck bus, 13 coach.
Chassis: 13 Dennis. 6 Leyland. 47 Volvo.
Bodies: 7 Alexander. 4 Northern Counties. 13 Plaxton. 42 Wright.
Ops incl: local bus services, school contracts.
Livery: Red/Cream.
Ticket System: Wayfarer 3
Subsidiary of Blazefield Holdings.

P HOPWOOD

22 MAIN STREET, ASKHAM BRYAN YO23 3QU
Tel: 01904 707394
Prop: P Hopwood
Fleet: 3 coach.
Chassis: 3 Dennis.
Bodies: 2 Duple. 1 Plaxton.
Ops incl: school contracts, private hire.

INGLEBY'S LUXURY COACHES LTD

24 HOSPITAL FIELDS ROAD, FULFORD ROAD INDUSTRIAL ESTATE, FULFORD ROAD, YORK YO10 4DZ
Tel: 01904 637620
Fax: 01904 612944
Dir: Chris Ingleby **Ops**: Maggie Evans
Fleet: includes coach, midicoach, minicoach.
Ops incl: private hire.
Livery: Blue/Cream

J. R. TRAVEL

36 CALF CLOSE, HAXBY YO3 3NS.
Tel: 01904 766233.
Ptnrs: R. Flatt, J. Smith.
Fleet: 10 - 3 double-deck bus, 3 coach, 4 double-deck coach.
Chassis: 3 Daimler. 3 Mercedes. 4 Neoplan.
Bodies: 1 East Lancs. 2 Neoplan. 2 Northern Counties. 2 Plaxton. 3 Taz.
Ops incl: local bus services, school contracts, excursions & tours, private hire, continental tours.
Livery: White with green/red stripes.

JOHNSON'S TOURS
See Derbyshire

KINGS LUXURY COACHES

FERRY ROAD, MIDDLESBROUGH TS2 1PL.
Tel: 01642 243387.
Prop: K. E. King.
Fleet: 5 - 2 double-deck bus, 3 coach.
Chassis: 2 Scania. 3 Setra.
Bodies: 1 Jonckheere. 3 Setra. 1 Van Hool.
Ops incl: private hire, continental tours.
Livery: Yellow/White.

METRO COACHES

51 LANGLEY AVENUE, THORNABY TS17 7HG.
Tel: 01642 643322.
Fax: 01642 805639.
Prop: Michael Davies.
Fleet: 4 - 3 coach 1 midibus.
Chassis: 2 Leyland, 1 Volvo.
Bodies: include 1 Mercedes.
Ops incl: private hire, school contracts.
Livery: Blue/white.

PENNINE MOTOR SERVICES

GROUSE GARAGE, GARGRAVE BD23 3RB.
Tel: 01756 749215.
Props: N. J. & M. Simpson.
Chassis: Leyland National, Leyland.
Ops incl: local bus services.
Livery: Orange/Black.

*PERRY'S COACHES

RICCAL DRIVE, YORK ROAD INDUSTRIAL PARK, MALTON YO17 6YE.
Tel: 01653 690500
Fax: 01653 690500
Web site: www.perrystravel.com
E-mail: info@perrystravel.com
Ptnrs: D J Perry (**Gen Man/Ch Eng**)
Mrs A Holtby (**Co Sec**)
Fleet: 19 - 11 coach, 6 midicoach, 2 minicoach.
Chassis: 1 Dennis. 7 Mercedes. 1 Toyota. 9 Volvo.
Bodies: 1 Caetano. 2 Crest. 1 Jonckheere. 9 Plaxton. 3 Van Hool. 2 Sitcar.
Ops incl: local bus services, school contracts, excursions & tours, private hire, continental tours.
Livery: Red/White.

A/c	Air conditioning
♿	Vehicles suitable for disabled
🍽	Coach(es) with galley facilities
wc	Coach(es) with toilet facilities
🚌	Seat belt-fitted vehicles
R	Recovery service available (not 24 hr)
R24	24hr recovery service
✓	Replacement vehicle available
T	Toilet-drop facilities available
🚍	Vintage vehicle(s) available
🚐	Open top vehicle(s)

*PROCTERS COACHES (NORTH YORKS) LTD

TUTIN ROAD, LEEMING BAR INDUSTRIAL ESTATE, LEEMING BAR DL7 9UJ
Tel: 01677 425203
Fax: 01677 426550
E-mail: enquiries@procterscoaches.co.uk
Web site: www.procterscoaches.co.uk
Man Dir: Kevin Procter **Fleet Eng**: Philip Kenyon **Tran Man**: Andrew Fryatt
Bus Ops Man: Stephen Dyne
Fleet: 41 - 2 double-deck bus, 2 single-deck bus, 24 coach, 5 midibus, 2 midicoach, 3 minibus, 3 minicoach.
Chassis: 2 DAF. 3 Dennis. 2 Ford Transit. 1 LDV. 8 Mercedes. 5 Optare. 22 Volvo.
Bodies: 4 Alexander. 2 Duple. 1 Ikarus. 3 Jonckheere. 1 Mercedes. 5 Optare. 16 Plaxton.
Ops incl: local bus services, school contracts, private hire, continental tours.
Livery: White
Ticket System: Wayfarer 3

*RELIANCE MOTOR SERVICES

RELIANCE GARAGE, YORK ROAD, SUTTON-ON-FOREST, YORK YO61 1ES.
Tel/Fax: 01904 768262.
Prop: John H Duff.
Fleet: 10 - 3 double-deck bus, 4 single-deck bus, 2 coach, 1 midicoach.
Chassis: 2 DAF. 1 Dennis. 7 Volvo.
Ops incl: local bus services, school contracts, private hire.
Livery: Cream/Green
Ticket System: Wayfarer.

*RONDO TRAVEL

LEVENS HALL PARK, LUND LANE, KILLINGHALL, HARROGATE HG3 2BG
Tel: 01423 526800
Fax: 01423 527800.
E-mail: sales@rondotravel.co.uk
Web site: www.rondotravel.co.uk
Man Dir: J D Bullock **Ch Eng**: A P Driffield
CPC holder: M Theakston
Fleet: 2 coach
Chassis/Bodies: 2 Setra
Ops incl: private hire, excursions & tours, continental tours.
Livery: Red/Gold.

SCARBOROUGH & DISTRICT

BARRY'S LANE, SCARBOROUGH YO12 4HA
Tel: 01723 500064
Fax: 01723 370064
E-mail: sd@eyms.co.uk
Web site: www.eyms.co.uk
Chmn: P J S Shipp **Fin Dir**: P Harrson
Com Man: R Rackley **Eng&Ops Man**: R Graham
Ops incl: local bus services, school contracts, excursions & tours, private hire, express, continental tours.
Livery: Burgundy/Cream
Ticket system: Wayfarer TGX150
A division of East Yorkshire Motor Services Ltd

*SIESTA INTERNATIONAL HOLIDAYS

158 LINTHORPE ROAD, MIDDLESBROUGH TS1 3RB
Tel: 01642 227711
Fax: 01642 225067
Web site: www.siestaholidays.co.uk
Dir: Paul R Herbert **Co Sec**: Julie Marsh
Fleet Man: Brian Watson
Fleet: 14 - 3 coach, 10 double-deck coach, 1 minibus.
Chassis: 1 DAF. 1 Ford Transit. 12 Scania.
Bodies: 12 Berkhof. 1 Bova.
Ops incl: excursions & tours, private hire, continental tours.
Livery: Blue.

*JOHN SMITH & SONS

THE AIRFIELD, DALTON, THIRSK YO7 3HE
Tel: 01845 577250
Fax: 01845 577752
SenrPtnr: Mrs A M Smith **Ptnrs**: A N Smith, J G Smith
Fleet: 24 - 2 double-deck bus, 10 coach, 3 midibus, 4 midicoach, 4 minicoach, 1 vintage.
Chassis: 2 Bedford. 4 DAF. 2 Dennis. 1 Ford. 2 Ford Transit. 1 LDV. 5 Leyland. 2 MAN. 5 Mercedes.
Bodies: 1 Caetano. 8 Duple. 2 Leyland. 5 Mercedes. 2 Neoplan. 6 Plaxton. 1 Reeve Burgess. 2 UVG. 1 Van Hool.
Ops incl: local bus services, school contracts, excursions & tours, private hire, continental tours.
Livery: Green/Cream.
Ticket system: Wayfarer 3

STAGECOACH TRANSIT

See Durham.

*STEPHENSONS OF EASINGWOLD LTD

MOOR LANE INDUSTRIAL ESTATE, THOLTHORPE, YORK YO61 1SR
Tel: 01347 838990
Fax: 01347 830189
E-mail: sales@stephensonsofeasingwold.co.uk
Web site: www.stephensonsofeasingwold.co.uk
Dirs: Harry J Stephenson, David Stephenson
Ops Man: Jonathan Hill
Fleet: 37 - 13 double-deck bus, 7 single-deck bus, 17 coach.
Chassis: 1 Bristol. 5 DAF. 9 Leyland. 3 MCW. 18 Volvo.
Bodies: 1 Caetano. 1 Duple. 8 leyland. 1 Leyland National. 3 MCW. 12 Plaxton.
Ops incl: local bus services, school contracts, private hire.

STEVE STOCKDALE COACHES (t/a Validford Ltd)

76 GREEN LANE, SELBY YO8 9AW
Tel: 01757 703549
Fax: 01757 210956
Dirs: S. Stockdale, J. Stockdale
Dir/Co Sec: Julie O'Neill
Fleet: 6 - 2 double-deck bus, 4 coach
Chassis: 2 Bedford. 2 Bristol. 2 Leyland.
Bodies: 2 Alexander. 2 Duple. 2 Plaxton.
Ops incl: local bus services, school contracts, private hire.
Livery: Red/White.
Ticket System: Almex.

G. E. SYKES & SON

SOUTHFIELD, APPLETON ROEBUCK YO5 7DG.
Tel: 01904 484231.

*THORNES INDEPENDENT LTD

THE COACH STATION, HULL ROAD, HEMINGBROUGH, SELBY YO8 6QG
Tel: 01757 630777
Fax: 01757 630666
Man Dir: Philip Thornes **Ch Eng**: Steve Cotton **Co Sec**: Christine Thornes.
Fleet: 17 - 2 double-deck bus, 1 single-deck bus, 8 coach, 2 midicoach, 4 heritage.
Chassis: 1 AEC. 1 Bedford. 1 Bristol. 1 DAF. 2 Dennis. 1 Ford Transit. 1 Leyland. 1 Mercedes. 7 Volvo. 1 Seddon.
Bodies: 1 Duple. 3 East Lancs. 1 Optare. 9 Plaxton. 1 Harrington. 1 Dormobile. 1 Van Hool.
Ops incl: local bus services, school contracts, excursions & tours, private hire, continental tours.
Livery: Blue/Grey
Ticket System: Wayfarer Saver

*TOP LINE TRAVEL OF YORK LTD

23 HOSPITAL FIELDS ROAD, FULFORD INDUSTRIAL ESTATE, YORK YO10 4EW
Tel: 01904 655585
Fax: 01904 655587
E-mail: toplinetravel@aol.com
Web site: www.city-sightseeing.com
Man Dir: Peter Dew **Dir/Co Sec**: Susan Dew.
Fleet: 17 - 6 double-deck bus, 1 single-deck bus, 10 open-top bus.
Chassis: 1 Bristol. 1 DAF. 5 Leyland. 10 MCW.
Bodies: 1 Alexander. 1 ECW. 10 MCW. 1 Optare. 3 Park Royal. 1 Wright.
Ops incl: local bus services, school contracts, private hire.
Livery: Red (City Sightseeing), Green/Cream (Guide Friady), White/Blue & Blue/Yellow (Top Line)
Ticket System: Almex A90

WINN BROS

8 MILL HILL CLOSE, BROMPTON, NORTHALLERTON DL6 2QP.
Tel: 01609 773520.
Fax: 01609 775234.

WISTONIAN COACHES

PLANTATION GARAGE, CAWOOD ROAD, WISTOW, SELBY YO8 0XB.
Tel: 01757 269303.
Props: John Firth, Gordon Firth.
Fleet: 3 coach, 1 midicoach.
Chassis: 1 Bedford. 3 Volvo.

Bodies: 4 Plaxton.
Ops incl: school contracts, private hire.
Livery: Cream, Red/Orange/Yellow stripes.

WRAYS OF HARROGATE
♿ wc Ac ✂ T

THE COACH DEPOT, MANSE LANE, KNARESBOROUGH HG1 2TQ.
Tel: 01423 522868
Fax: 01423 520609.
E-mail: operations@wrays.co.uk
Web site: www.eddiebrowntours.com
Dir: Philip Brown **Tours Dir:** Deidre Brown
Ch Eng: Tony Hainsworth **Ops Man:** Paul Johnson.

Fleet: 15 - 12 coach, 1 midicoach, 2 midicoach
Chassis: 1 Dennis. 1 Mercedes, 1 Toyota. 12 Volvo.
Bodies: 1 Duple. 1 Optare. 9 Plaxton. 4 Van Hool.
Ops incl: school contracts, excursions & tours, private hire, continental tours.
Livery: White with silver/maroon swirls.
Subsidiary of Eddie Brown Tours Ltd.

YORKSHIRE COASTLINER LTD
BUS STATION, RAILWAY STREET, MALTON YO17 7NR.

Tel: 01653 692556.
Fax: 01653 695341.
Web site: www.yorkshirecoastliner.co.uk
Prop: Blazefield Holdings Ltd.
Ops Man: Brian Kneeshaw.
Fleet: 19 - 12 double-deck bus, 7 single-deck bus.
Chassis: 26 Volvo.
Bodies: 11 Alexander. 1 Northern Counties. 3 Plaxton. 13 Wright.
Ops incl: local bus services.
Livery: Cream/Blue.
Ticket System: Wayfarer 3.
A Blazefield Group company.

NORTHAMPTONSHIRE

*ALEC HEAD ♿ wc ▼
🚌 Ac R24 ✂ T

LUTTON, PETERBOROUGH PE8 5NE
Tel: 01832 272546
Fax: 01832 273077
Web site: www.alecheadcoaches.co.uk
Ptnrs: A M Head, Mrs J Head, Mrs S J Johns
Fleet: 39 - 7 double-deck bus, 10 single-deck bus, 15 coach, 4 double-deck coach, 1 open-top bus, 1 midicoach, 1 minicoach.
Chassis: 24 Bedford. 7 Dennis. 4 Iveco. 1 Leyland. 2 MAN. 2 Mercedes. 7 Scania. 1 Toyota. 5 Volvo.
Bodies: 7 Alexander. 4 Ayats. 1 Caetano. 2 Marcopolo. 4 MCW. 2 Neoplan.
Ops incl: local bus services, school contracts, excursions & tours, private hire, continental tours.

GEOFF AMOS COACHES LTD
wc ▼ 🍴 Ac R24 ✂ T

THE COACH STATION, WOODFORD ROAD, DAVENTRY NN11 3PL
Tel: 01327 260522.
Fax: 01327 262883
E-mail: sales@geoffamos.co.uk
Web site: www.geoffamos.co.uk
Dir: B G Amos **Ch Eng:** K. Wilson. **Dir/Co Sec:** Mrs S. Smith. **Ops Man:** B Ellard
Fleet: 23 - 8 double-deck bus, 1 single-deck bus, 9 coach, 5 midibus.
Chassis: 3 DAF. 4 Dennis. 11 Leyland. 1 Marshall. 4 Mercedes.
Bodies: 3 Berkhof. 2 Bova. 7 ECW. 1 East Lancs. 2 Marshall. 3 Plaxton. 3 Reeve. 1 Smit. 1 Wadham Stringer.
Ops incl: local bus services, school contracts, excursions & tours, private hire, continental tours.

BASFORDS COACHES LTD
wc ▼ ✂

HIGH STREET, GREENS NORTON NN12 8BA.
Tel: 01327 350493.
Dirs: J. V. & K. R. Jeffs.
Fleet: 15 - 3 double-deck bus, 12 single-deck bus.
Chassis: 3 Bedford. 1 Ford. 3 Leyland. 8 Volvo.
Bodies: 6 Caetano. 4 Duple. 2 Jonckheere. 3 Leyland National.
Ops incl: school contracts, excursions & tours, private hire, continental tours.
Livery: Red/White/Green.
Ticket System: Bellgraphic.
Subsidiary of Jeffs Coaches Ltd.

BRITTAINS COACHES LTD
SOUTHBRIDGE, COTTON END, NORTHAMPTON NN4 8BS.
Tel: 01604 765708.
Fax: 01604 700481.
Dirs: W. J. Cunningham, Mrs P. M. Brittain, Mrs J. Cunningham.
Co Sec: Miss C. Brittain. **Off Man:** M. Kelly.
Fleet: 7 - 3 double-deck bus, 4 coach.
Chassis: 3 Bristol. 2 DAF. 2 Scania.
Bodies: 3 Alexander. 2 Caetano. 2 Van Hool.
Ops incl: private hire.
Livery: White with Black lettering.

BUCKBY'S COACHES
3 FOX STREET, ROTHWELL NN14 6AN.
Tel: 01536 710344.
Prop: H. F. Cooper.
Gen Man/Ch Eng/Ops Man: R. W. Cooper.
Fleet: 5 - 4 coach, 1 midicoach.
Chassis: 3 Bedford. 1 Dennis. 1 Toyota.
Bodies: 1 Caetano. 4 Plaxton.
Ops incl: local bus services, excursions & tours, private hire, continental tours.
Livery: Blue/Red/Cream.
Ticket System: Setright.

COOPERS COACHES ▼
FOX STREET, ROTHWELL NN14 6AN
Tel: 01536 710227.
Fax: 01536 712244.
Ptnrs: H. F. Cooper, J. M. Cooper
Fleet: 2 coach.
Chassis: 1 Volvo, 1 Dennis.
Body: 2 Plaxton.
Ops incl: school contracts, private hire.
Livery: White with blue/red flash

*COUNTRY LION (NORTHAMPTON) LTD
▼ wc Ac

87 ST JAMES MILL ROAD, NORTHAMPTON NN5 5JP
Tel: 01604 754566
Fax: 01604 755800
Dirs: J S F Bull, A J Bull
Fleet: 40
Chassis: 1 Bristol 5 Dennis. 4 Iveco. 7 Mercedes. 2 Scania. 16 Volvo.
Bodies: 4 Alexander. 4 Beulas. 2 East Lancs. 2 Irizar. 1 Jonckheere. 1 Optare. 19 Plaxton. 1 Van Hool. 2 Wadham Stringer. 3 other.
Ops incl: local bus services, school contracts, private hire.
Livery: White/Yellow/Orange/Brown.
Ticket System: Almex.

FIRST NORTHAMPTON
♿ wc ▼ ✂

THE BUS DEPOT, ST JAMES' ROAD, NORTHAMPTON NN5 5JD.
Tel: 01604 751431.
Man Dir: I. Humphreys. **Eng Dir:** C. Stafford. **Fin Dir:** J. Hollis.
Fleet: 75 - 42 double-deck bus, 24 single-deck bus, 5 coach, 4 minibus.
Chassis: 3 Bristol. 9 MCW. 4 Renault. 6 Scania. 45 Volvo.
Bodies: Alexander, East Lancs, Northern Counties, Wright.
Ops incl: local bus services, school contracts, private hire.

Ac	Air conditioning		▼	Seat belt-fitted vehicles
♿	Vehicles suitable for disabled		R	Recovery service available (not 24 hr)
🍴	Coach(es) with galley facilities		R24	24hr recovery service
wc	Coach(es) with toilet facilities			
✂	Replacement vehicle available			
T	Toilet-drop facilities available			
🚌	Vintage vehicle(s) available			
	Open top vehicle(s)			

Livery: Cream/Red.
Ticket System: Wayfarer 3

GOODE COACHES

47 BURFORD AVENUE,
BOOTHVILLE, NORTHAMPTON
NN3 6AF.
Tel: 01604 862700.
Night emergency: 01604 645369.
Prop/Ch Eng: David Goode. **Traf Man**: Andrew Wall.
Fleet: 4 - 1 midicoach, 3 coach.
Chassis: 4 Leyland.
Bodies: 3 Plaxton. 1 Wadham Stringer.
Ops incl: local bus services, school contracts, private hire.
Livery: Cream/Maroon.
Ticket System: Almex.
Breakdown relief to CPT members.

*J. C. S. COACHES

2 THE JAMB, CORBY NN17 1AY
Tel: 01536 202660
Props: Jaqueline Burton, Michael Burton
Fleet: 7 - 5 coach, 2 midicoach.
Chassis: 5 DAF. 2 Mercedes.
Bodies: 1 Autobus. 3 Bova. 2 Caetano. 1 Marshall.
Ops incl: excursions & tours, private hire, school contracts.
Livery: Silver

J. R. J. COACHES

24 STALBRIDGE WALK, CORBY
NN18 0DT.
Tel: 01536 200317.
Fax: 01536 394387.
Prop: J. D. Judge.
Fleet: 6 - 3 coach, 1 midicoach, 2 minibus.
Chassis: 1 Bedford. 1 Ford Transit. 1 Mercedes.
Bodies: 1 Caetano. 1 Carlyle. 1 Duple. 1 Mercedes.
Ops incl: local bus services, school contracts, excursions & tours, private hire.

*JEFFS COACHES LTD

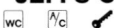

HIGH STREET, GREENS NORTON,
TOWCESTER NN12 8BA.
Tel: 01327 350493
Fax: 01327 353538.
Dir: K. R. Jeffs **Man**: I R Higham.
Fleet: 14 - 3 double-deck bus, 11 coach.
Fleet: 1 Bedford. 3 Leyland . 10 Volvo.
Bodies: 1 Alexander. 8 Caetano. 1 Duple. 2 ECW. 1 Jonckheere. 1 Plaxton.
Ops incl: school contracts, excursions & tours, private hire, continental tours.
Livery: White /Red/Green.

*R B TRAVEL

ISHAM ROAD, PYTCHLEY NN4 1EW
Prop: Roger Bull
Tel/Fax: 01536 791066
Fleet: 10 coach
Chassis: 6 DAF. 4 MAN.
Bodies: 2 Plaxton. 8 Van Hool.

MARTINS COACHES

6 HAZEL ROAD, KETTERING
NN16 7AL.
Prop: G. H. Martin.

*RODGER'S COACHES

102 KETTERING ROAD, WELDON
NN17 3GG
Tel: 01536 200500
Fax: 01536 407407
E-mail: rodger'scoaches@hotmail.com
Props: James Rodger, Linda Rodger
Fleet: 14 - 7 double-deck bus, 6 coach, 1 double-deck coach.
Chassis: 3 Dennis. 1 Iveco. 1 Neoplan. 9 Volvo.
Bodies: 1 Alexander. 1 Beulas. 3 East Lancs. 1 Neoplan. 2 Northern Counties. 2 Plaxton. 3 UVG.
Ops incl: private hire, school contracts.
Livery: Red

*STAGECOACH EAST

ROTHERSTHORPE AVENUE,
NORTHAMPTON NN4 8UT
Tel: 01604 702112
Fax: 01604 701807
Web site: www.stagecoachbus.com
Man Dir: Inglis Lyon **Eng Dir**: Iain Ferguson **Ops Dir**: Michelle Hargreaves
Fleet: 312 - 154 double-deck bus, 36 coach, 1 open-top bus, 45 midibus, 76 minibus.
Chassis: 2 Bristol. 56 Dennis. 66 Leyland. 59 Mercedes. 16 Optare. 1 Renault. 5 Scania. 107 Volvo.
Bodies: 162 Alexander. 4 ECW. 2 Jonckheere. 49 Northern Counties. 16 Optare. 36 Plaxton. 1 Roe. 42 Transbus.
Ops incl: local bus services, school contracts.
Livery: Stagecoach (white/blue/red/orange)
Ticket System: ERG

*YORKS COACHES

SHORT LANE, COGENHOE NN7 1LT
Tel: 01604 890210
Fax: 01604 891153
E-mail: yorksta@yorks-travel.co.uk
Web site: www.yorkstravel.com
Chmn: A Moseley **Ch Exec**: K Lower
Dirs: W Concannon, C J Padbury, K G York
Ch Eng: D Hoy **Traf Man**: N G Tetley
Fleet: 30 - 27 coach, 2 minicoach, 1 minibus.
Chassis: 2 Bova. 3 Dennis. 1 LDV. 9 MAN. 1 Neoplan. 7 Setra. 2 Toyota. 5 Volvo.
Bodies: 2 Caetano. 2 Bova. 6 Marcopolo. 6 Noge. 1 Neoplan. 3 Plaxton. 7 Setra. 2 Van Hool. 1 other.
Ops incl: local bus services, school contracts, excursions & tours, private hire, express, continental tours.
Livery: Silver
Ticket System: Almex

NORTHUMBERLAND

*ADAMSON'S COACHES

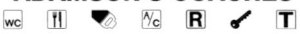

8 PORLOCK COURT, NORTHBURN
CHASE, CRAMLINGTON NE23 3TT
Tel/Fax: 01670 734050
Prop: Allen Mullen
Fleet: 4 coach
Chassis: 4 DAF
Bodies: 4 Van Hool
Ops incl: private hire
Livery: Cream

*ARRIVA NORTH EAST LTD
See Tyne & Wear

*HENRY COOPER
See Tyne & Wear

*CRAIGGS TRAVEL EUROPEAN

1 CENTRAL AVENUE, AMBLE
NE65 0NQ
Tel/Fax: 01665 710614
E-mail: classicalholiday@aol.com
Web site: www.craiggstravel.co.uk
Props: Joan Craiggs, Ian Craiggs, Lawrence Craiggs.
Fleet: 4 coach.
Chassis: 1 Leyland. 2 Setra. 1 Volvo.
Bodies: 2 Plaxton. 2 Setra.
Ops incl: school contracts, excursions & tours, private hire, continental tours.
Livery: Red

GO NORTH EAST
See Tyne & Wear.

*HILLARYS COACHES

20 CASTLE VIEW, PRUDHOE
NE42 6NG
Tel/Fax: 01661 832560
Props: Lawrence Hillary, Violet Hillary
Fleet: 5 - 1 coach. 3 midicoach, 1 minibus.
Chassis/Bodies: 1 DAF. 1 MAN. 3 Mercedes.
Ops incl: local bus services, school contracts, excursions & tours, private hire.

LONGSTAFF'S COACHES

UNIT 107, AMBLE INDUSTRIAL
ESTATE, AMBLE, MORPETH
NE65 0PE
Tel: 01665 713300
Fax: 01665 710987
Man Dir: Frederick Longstaff

Co Sec: Alison Longstaff **Ops Man**: Frederick Longstaff
Fleet: 9 - 7 coach, 1 midicoach
Chassis: 1 Leyland. 1 Mercedes. 1 Neoplan. 7 Volvo
Bodies: 1 Jonckheere. 1 Neoplan. 3 Plaxton. 3 Van Hool. 1 other
Ops incl: local bus services, excursions & tours, private hire, continental tours, school contracts.
Livery: Blue/Cream/Yellow.

*ROWELL COACHES
[wc] [🪑] [A/c] [🔧] [T]

3B DUKES WAY, PRUDHOE NE42 5BJ
Tel: 01661 832316
Fax: 01661 834485
E-mail: sales@rowellcoaches.co.uk
Web site: www.rowellcoaches.co.uk
Ptnrs: S H Gardiner, Mrs B Gardiner
Fleet: 10 coach
Chassis: 2 Bedford. 6 Bova. 2 Leyland.
Ops incl: school contracts, excursions & tours, private hire.

SERENE TRAVEL
[wc] [🍴] [🪑] [🚌] [R] [T]

86A FRONT STREET EAST, BEDLINGTON NE22 5AB.
Tel: 01670 829636.
Fax: 01670 827961.
Web site: www.yell.co.uk/sites/serenetravel
Man Dir: Mrs C. E. Fielding. **Flt Eng**: G. J. Balsdon. **Co Sec**: D. A. Fielding.
Fleet: 17 - 7 single-deck bus, 6 coach, 2 midicoach, 2 minibus.
Chassis: 1 AEC. 2 Bedford. 1 Ford Transit. 1 Iveco. 3 Leyland. 6 Leyland National. 2 MCW. 1 Volvo.
Bodies: 2 Carlyle. 2 Duple. 6 Leyland National. 2 Optare. 4 Plaxton. 1 Burlingham.
Ops incl: local bus services, school contracts, excursions & tours, private hire, express.
Livery: Blue/Cream.
Ticket System: Wayfarer II.

TARGET TRAVEL GROUP LTD
[🪑] [wc] [🪑] [🔧] [T]

STATION ROAD, CRAMLINGTON NE23 9DL.
Tel: 01670 712244, 0191 261 1126
Fax: 01670 734794
E-mail: enquiries@target-group.co.uk
Website: www.target-group.co.uk
Dir: J. Reed.
Fleet: 6 - 2 coach, 1 midibus, 1 minibus, 2 minicoach.
Chassis: 1 DAF. 1 Ford Transit. 1 LAG. 1 MCW. 2 Mercedes.
Bodies: 1 Duple. 2 Mercedes. 1 LAG. 1 Plaxton. 1 Ford Transit.
Ops incl: local bus services, school contracts, excursions & tours, private hire, express, continental tours.
Livery: Red.
Ticket System: Almex

*TRAVELSURE
[wc] [🍴] [🪑] [A/c] [R24] [🔧]

25 MAIN STREET, SEAHOUSES NE68 7RE.
Tel: 01665 720907
Fax: 01665 721381
E-mail: travelsure@travelsure.co.uk
Web site: www.travelsure.co.uk
Jnt Owners: Barrie Patterson, Karen Patterson
Ch Eng: Mark Patterson.
Fleet: 23 - 1 double-deck bus, 4 single-deck bus, 7 coach, 1 double-deck coach, 7 midibus, 3 minibus.
Chassis: 3 Bova. 1 DAF. 1 Ford Transit. 2 Iveco. 1 LDV. 4 Leyland. 3 MCW. 5 Mercedes. 1 Scania. 1 Volkswagen. 1 Volvo.

Bodies: 1 Autobus. 2 Beulas. 3 Bova. 1 Duple. 1 Irizar. 1 Jonckheere. 3 MCW. 4 Mercedes. 3 Plaxton. 1 LDV. 1 Van Hool. 1 VW.
Ops incl: local bus services, school contracts, excursions & tours, private hire, continental tours.
Livery: Blue metallic.
Ticket System: Wayfarer.

TYNEDALE GROUP TRAVEL
[wc] [🍴] [🪑] [A/c] [🔧]

TOWNFOOT GARAGE, HALTWHISTLE NE49 0EJ.
Tel: 01434 322944.
Fax: 01434 322955.
E-mail: admin@tynedalegrouptravel.co.uk
Web site: www.tynedalegrouptravel.co.uk
Ptnr: Andy Sinclair.
Fleet: 6 - 1 single-deck coach, 3 midibus, 2 midicoach.
Chassis: 5 Mercedes. 1 Volvo.
Bodies: 4 Plaxton 1 Van Hool, 1 other.
Ops incl: local bus servcices, school contracts, excursions & tours, private hire, continental tours.

TYNE VALLEY COACHES LTD [🪑]

ACOMB, HEXHAM NE46 4QT.
Tel: 01434 602217.
Fax: 01434 608146.
Dirs: H. D. Weir, Mrs K. M. Weir.
Fleet: 20 - 4 single-deck bus, 16 coach.
Chassis: 15 Leyland. 2 Leyland National. 3 Volvo.
Ops incl: local bus services, school contracts, excursions & tours, private hire, express, continental tours.
Livery: Blue/Silver.
Ticket System: Setright.

NOTTINGHAMSHIRE, NOTTINGHAM

BAILEY'S COACHES LTD
[wc] [🪑] [🔧] [T]

EEL HOLE FARM, LONG LANE, WATNALL NG16 1HY.
Tel: 0115 968 0141
Fax: 0115 968 1101.
Dirs: T. Bailey (**Gen Man & Traf Man**), Mrs J. Bailey (**Sec**).
Ch Eng: G. Payne.
Fleet: 10 - 2 double-deck bus, 6 coach 2 double-deck coach.
Chassis: Bristol. DAF. Duple. Volvo.
Bodies: 10 Duple. 3 Others.
Ops incl: local bus services, school contracts, excursions & tours, private hire, continental tours.
Livery: White with Yellow/Brown/Orange stripes.

BARTON BUSES LTD
See Trent Barton Buses, Derbyshire

*EDDIE BROWN TOUR GROUP [wc] [🪑] [A/c] [🔧] [T]

UNIT 10, CANALSIDE INDUSTRIAL PARK, CROPWELL BISHOP, NOTTINGHAM NG12 3BE
Tel: 0115 989 4466
Fax: 0115 989 0327
Recovery: 0115 989 4117
Email: trevor.sharpe@eddiebrowntours.com
Web site: www.eddiebrowntours.com
Dirs: Mrs D Brown, P Brown **Gen Man**: Trevor Sharpe
Fleet: 18 - 4 single-deck bus, 13 coach, 1 minicoach

Chassis: 3 Dennis. 1 Scania. 1 Toyota. 13 Volvo.
Bodies: 1 Caetano. 7 Plaxton. 10 Van Hool.
Ops incl: school contracts, excursions & tours, private hire, continental tours.
Livery: White/Red/Orange/Maroon
Ticket System: Wayfarer 2

BUTLER BROTHERS COACHES [wc] [🪑]

60 VERNON ROAD, KIRKBY IN ASHFIELD NG17 8ED
Tel: 01623 753260.
Fax: 01623 754581
E-mail: butlerscoaches@btconnect.co.uk
Dirs: Robert Butler, Anita Butler.
Fleet: 8 - 7 coach, 1 midicoach.
Chassis: 3 DAF. 3 Dennis. 1 MAN. 1 Volvo.

A/c	Air conditioning
🪑	Vehicles suitable for disabled
🍴	Coach(es) with galley facilities
wc	Coach(es) with toilet facilities
🪑	Seat belt-fitted vehicles
R	Recovery service available (not 24 hr)
R24	24hr recovery service
🔧	Replacement vehicle available
T	Toilet-drop facilities available
🚌	Vintage vehicle(s) available
🚌	Open top vehicle(s)

Bodies: 1 Caetano. 1 Duple. 4 Plaxton. 2 Van Hool.
Ops incl: school contracts, excursions & tours, private hire.
Livery: Dual Blue.
Ticket System: Wayfarer 3

*DUNN-LINE

THE COACH STATION, PARK LANE, BASFORD NG6 0RD
Tel: 0115 916 9000
Fax: 0115 942 0578
E-mail: sales@dunn-line.com
Web site: www.dunn-line.com
Chmn: Robert Dunn **Co Sec:** Carol Dunn
Man Dir: Scott Dunn **Ops Man:** Paul Van Staden **Ch Eng:** Steve Green
Fleet: 108 - 29 double-deck bus, 25 single-deck bus, 53 coach, 1 open-top bus.
Chassis: 1 Bova. 3 Dennis. 6 Leyland. 16 MCW. 11 Mercedes. 25 Scania. 46 Volvo.
Bodies: 2 Autobus. 1 Bova. 7 East Lancs. 13 Irizar. 8 Jonckheere. 16 MCW. 26 Plaxton. 1 Reev Burgess. 4 Transbus. 7 Van Hool. 1 Wadham Stringer. 6 Wright.
Ops incl: local bus services, school contracts, excursions & tours, private hire, express.
Livery: Purple/Silver
Ticket System: Wayfarer 3

*GOSPEL'S COACHES

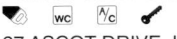

27 ASCOT DRIVE, HUCKNALL NG15 6JA
Tel: 0115 963 3894
Dirs: T Gospel, G Gospel, G T Gospel
Fleet: 4 - 2 double-deck bus, 2 coach.
Chassis: 2 Leyland. 2 Volvo.
Bodies: 1 Alexander. 1 Northern Counties. 2 Plaxton.
Ops incl: excursions & tours, private hire, school contracts.
Livery: White/Blue.

HENSHAWS COACHES

57 PYE HILL ROAD, JACKSDALE NG16 5LR.
Tel/Fax: 01773 607909
Ptnrs: Paul Henshaw
Fleet: 6 - 5 coach. 1 midicoach.
Chassis: includes Volvo
Bodies: 1 Leyland, 2 Mercedes, 2 Van Hool.
Ops incl: excursions & tours, private hire, school contracts, continental tours.
Livery: Cream/Orange/Brown.

JOHNSON'S TOURS

See Derbyshire

JUMBO MINI COACHES

338 THE WELLS ROAD, NOTTINGHAM NG3 3AA.
Tel: 0115 958 4730.
Owner: J. Talbot.
Fleet: 2 minibus. **Chassis:** 2 LDV.
Ops incl: school contracts, private hire.
Livery: White/Blue.

K & S COACHES

21 CLIFTON GROVE, MANSFIELD NG18 4HY.
Tel/Fax: 01623 656768.
Prop: K. & Sue Burnside.
Fleet: 4 - 1 midicoach, 3 minicoach.
Chassis/bodies: Ford Transit. Mercedes. Renault. Talbot.
Ops incl: school contracts, excursions & tours, private hire.
Livery: White/Red/Grey.

*KETTLEWELL (RETFORD) LTD

GROVE STREET, RETFORD DN22 6LA.
Tel: 01777 860360
Fax: 01777 710351
Chmn: A J Kettlewell **Man Dir:** P C Kettlewell **Tours Dir:** C C Kettlewell
Tours Man: M Burton
Fleet: 19 - 3 double-deck bus, 1 single-deck bus, 13 coach, 1 double-deck coach, 1 minibus.
Chassis: 1 Bristol. 1 Daimler. 2 Leyland. 1 Leyland National. 1 Mercedes. 2 Neoplan. 10 Scania. 1 Volvo.
Bodies: 2 East Lancs. 8 Irizar. 1 Jonckheere. 1 Leyland National. 1 Mercedes. 2 Neoplan. 2 Park Royal. 2 Plaxton. 1 Ajokki.
Ops incl: school contracts, excursions & tours, private hire, continental tours.
Livery: White/Yellow.
Ticket System: Wayfarer.

LEGAL MINI BUS HIRE

67 CAMBRIDGE STREET, BLACKWELL DE55 5JX.
Tel: 01773 580375.
Prop: J. E. Roberts. **Sec:** D. Roberts.
Fleet: 2 minibus.
Chassis: 1 Ford Transit. 1 Freight Rover.
Ops incl: school contract, private hire.

*MARSHALLS OF SUTTON-ON-TRENT

11 MAIN STREET, SUTTON-ON-TRENT NG23 6PF.
Tel: 01636 821138
Fax: 01636 822227
Web site: www.marshallscoaches.co.uk
Prop: J. A. Marshall. **Flt Eng:** P. J. Marshall
Ops Man: K G Tagg
Fleet: includes double-deck bus, single-deck bus, coach, midibus, midicoach.
Chassis: Dennis. Leyland. MAN. Mercedes. Optare. Transbus. Volvo.
Bodies: Alexander. Berkhof. Caetano. East Lancs. Northern Counties. Optare. Plaxton. Transbus. Van Hool.
Ops incl: local bus services, school contracts, excursions & tours, private hire, continental tours.
Livery: Blue/Cream.
Ticket System: Almex

MAUN CRUSADER TOURS

NEW CROSS HOUSE, 8-10 MANSFIELD ROAD, SUTTON-IN-ASHFIELD NG17 4GR.
Tel: 01623 555621.

Fax: 01623 555671.
Dirs: R. A. Read (**Gen Man/Traf Man**), N. G. Barks (**Sec**). **Ch Eng:** S. Palmer.
Fleet: 17 - 8 double-deck bus, 8 single-deck bus. 1 midicoach.
Chassis: 3 DAF, 1 Daimler. 5 Dennis. 2 Leyland. 1 MAN. 1 Mercedes. 4 Integral.
Bodies: 1 Alexander. 1 Caetano. 6 Duple. 1 East Lancs. 1 Jonckheere. 1 Marco Polo. 4 Northern Counties. 1 Plaxton. 1 SC.
Ops incl: private hire, continental tours, school contracts.
Livery: Multi-coloured.

C. W. MOXON LTD

MALTBY ROAD, OLDCOTES, WORKSOP S81 8JN.
Tel: 01909 730345.
Fax: 01909 733670.
Web site: www.moxons-tours.co.uk
Fleetname: Moxons Coaches.
Dirs: Mrs L. Marlow, Mrs M. Moxon, **Co Sec:** Mrs J. Holder, **Ch Eng:** M. Marlow.
Fleet: 15 - 3 double-deck bus, 12 coach.
Chassis: 2 Bedford. 3 Bristol. 7 DAF. 2 Leyland. 1 Iveco.
Bodies: 2 Bova. 1 Duple. 3 MCW. 5 Plaxton. 3 Van Hool. 1 Eos.
Ops incl: excursions & tours, private hire, continental tours, school contracts.
Livery: Cream/Red.

*NOTTINGHAM CITY TRANSPORT LTD

LOWER PARLIAMENT STREET, NOTTINGHAM NG1 1GG
Tel: 0115 950 5745
Fax: 0115 950 4425
E-mail: info@nctx.co.uk, sheila.swift@nctx.co.uk
Web site: www.nctx.co.uk
Chmn: Brian Parbutt **Man Dir:** Mark Fowles
Eng Dir: Barry Baxter **Fin Dir/Co Sec:** Rob Hicklin **Mktg & Communications Dir:** Nicola Tidy **Ops Man:** Barrie Burch **Senior Eng Dir:** Pete Smith
Fleet: 365 - 151 double-deck bus, 83 single-deck bus, 14 coach, 6 double-deck coach, 5 articulated bus, 96 midibus.
Chassis: 1 Bova. 58 Dennis. 4 Leyland. 2 Mercedes. 110 Optare. 84 Scania. 96 Volvo.
Bodies: 31 Alexander. 1 Beulas. 149 East Lancs. 5 Northern Counties. 110 Optare. 23 Plaxton. 22 Scania. 14 Wright.
Ops incl: local bus services, school contracts, excursions & tours, private hire.

NOTTINGHAM EXPRESS TRANSIT

THE GUILDHALL, SOUTH SHERWOOD STREET, NOTTINGHAM NG1 4BT
Tel: 0115 915 6600
E-mail: tram@nottinghamcity.gov.uk
Web site: www.nottinghamcity.gov.uk, www.nottinghamexpresstransitco.uk
Concession Co: Arrow Light Rail (Bombardier, Carillon, Transdev, Nottingham City Transport, Inisfree, CDC Projects)
Fleet: 15 tram
Chassis/bodies: Bombardier
Ops incl: tram service
Livery: Green/White

*PATRON TRAVEL
wc 🌀 ⚲

GLEBE COTTAGE, 1 FOSSE WAY, FLINTHAM NG23 5LH
Tel: 01636 525725.
Fax: 01636 525499.
Fleet: 1 double-deck bus, 2 coach.
Chassis: 1 MCW (107 seats). 2 Volvo
Ops incl: continental tours, private hire, school contracts, excursions & tours.
Livery: Cream.

PEGASUS COACHWAYS LTD
wc 🌀 A/c

GROVE STREET, RETFORD DN22 6LA.
Tel: 01777 860360.
Fax: 01777 710351.
Chmn: A. J. Kettlewell. **Man Dir**: P C. Kettlewell. **Tours Dir**: C. C. Kettlewell.
Tours Man: M. Burton **Ops Man**: G. Palmer
Fleet: 8 - 7 coach, 1 minicoach.
Chassis: 1 Mercedes. 7 Scania.
Bodies: 7 Irizar. 1 Mercedes.
Ops incl: private hire, excursions and tours, continental tours.
Livery: White/Yellow
Subsidiary of Kettlewells, Retford

REDFERN COACHES (MANSFIELD) LTD ♿ 🌀 wc
🍽 🚌 A/c R24 ⚲ T

LINDLEY STREET, MANSFIELD NG18 1QE
Tel: 01623 27653
Fax: 01623 25787
Web site: www.johnsontours.co.uk
E-mail: enquiries@johnsontours.co.uk
Fleet: 29 - 18 double-deck bus, 4 single-deck bus, 4 coach, 1 midibus, 1 midicoach, 1 minicoach.
Chassis: 18 Bristol. 1 Ford. 1 Freight Rover. 1 Scania. 2 Volvo.
Bodies: include 2 Irizar.
Ops incl: local bus services, excursions & tours, private hire, express, continental tours, school contracts.
Livery: Green/Faded Green/Gold
Subsidiary of Johnsons Tours (Derbyshire)

SILVERDALE TOURS LTD
wc 🍽 🌀 A/c ⚲

LITTLE TENNIS STREET SOUTH, NOTTINGHAM NG2 4EU
Tel: 0115 912 1000
Fax: 0115 912 1558
Dir: John Doherty **Dir**: Shaun Doherty

Dir/Ops Man: Pete Hallam **Ch Eng**: Pete Reddish
Fleet: 35 - 6 double-deck bus, 4 single-deck bus, 20 coach, 3 double-deck coach, 2 midicoach.
Ops incl: private hire, school contracts.

SKILLS MOTOR COACHES
🌀 wc 🍽 A/c R24 ⚲ T

BELGRAVE ROAD, BULWELL, NOTTINGHAM NG6 8LY
Tel: 0115 977 7424
Fax: 0115 977 7464
Recovery: 0115 977 7424
E-mail: nigel@skills.co.uk
Web site: www.skillsholidays.co.uk
Man Dir: Nigel Skill
Fleet: 41 - 37 coach, 1 midicoach, 3 minibus.
Chassis/bodies: 4 DAF, 1 Bova, 1 Leyland, 2 Mercedes, 1 Neoplan, 17 Setra, 15 Van Hool.
Ops incl: school contracts, excursions & tours, private hire, express, continental tours.
Livery: Green.

*SPENCERS COACHES 🌀
20 THORNHILL DRIVE, BOUGHTON, NEWARK NG22 9JG
Tel/Fax: 01623 860394
Dirs: R C Spencer.
Fleet: 2 midibus.
Chassis: 2 Mercedes.
Bodies: 2 Plaxton
Ops incl: school contracts
Livery: Cream/Green

F T TAGG COACHES
wc 🌀 A/c ⚲ T

QUARRY YARD, SUTTON-IN-ASHFIELD NG17 1BQ
Tel/Fax: 01623 554458
E-mail: ft.taggcoaches@virgin.net
Props: F T Derbyshire, Mrs D J Derbyshire
Fleet: 3 coach.
Chassis: 1 DAF. 1 MAN. 1 Scania.
Bodies: 1 Irizar. 2 Van Hool.
Ops incl: excursions & tours, private hire, continental tours.
Livery: White with red and blue

*TRANSIT EXPRESS TRAVEL 🌀 ⚲
UNIT 7, EVANS BUSINESS PARK, RADMARSH ROAD, LENTON, NOTTINGHAM NG7 2GN
Tel: 0115 970 2900

Fax: 0115 970 5515
Fleetname: Transit Express
Prop: G M Crosby
Fleet: 9 - 1 single-deck bus, 3 coach, 2 midicoach, 2 minibus, 1 minicoach.
Chassis: 2 Ford. 4 Ford Transit. 2 Leyland. 1 MAN.
Bodies: 1 Caetano. 1 Carlyle. 2 Duple. 3 Ford. 1 Plaxton. 1 Reeve Burgess.
Ops incl: school contracts, excursions and tours, private hire.
Livery: Blue/White

TRAVEL WRIGHT LTD
🌀 wc A/c ⚲

LINCOLN ROAD, NEWARK-ON-TRENT NG24 2DR.
Tel: 01636 703613.
Fax: 01636 674541.
Web site: www.travelwright.co.uk
E-mail: info@travelwright.fsnet.co.uk
Prop: T. D. Wright. **Tran Man**: C. A. Wright.
Tours Man: D. C. Wright. **Ass Tran Man**: S. Bunting. **Ch Eng**: D. Walker. **Acc Man**: P. Allen.
Fleet: 30 - 1 double-deck bus, 1 single-deck bus, 22 coach, 2 minicoach, 4 minibus.
Chassis: 2 Bedford, 4 Dennis, 1 Leyland, 1 MAN, 4 Mercedes, 3 Neoplan, 1 Scania, 14 Volvo.
Ops incl: local bus services, school contracts, excursions & tours, private hire, continental tours.
Livery: Cream/Red and Brown/Black.
Ticket System: Wayfarer.

UNITY COACHES
BECK GARAGE, CLAYWORTH DN22 9AG.
Tel: 07777 817556.
Ptnrs: F. Marriott, Mrs J. Marriott.
Livery: Blue/Grey/Cream.

*WALLIS COACHWAYS
wc 🌀 🍽 A/c

BRAIL WOOD ROAD, BILSTHORPE NG22 8UA
Tel/Fax: 01623 870655
E-mail: jennifer.wallis@tesco.net.
Prop: Stephen Wallis
Fleet: 3 - 2 coach, 1 minicoach.
Chassis/bodies: 1 Mercedes. 1 Setra.
Ops incl: local bus services, school contracts, excursions & tours, private hire
Livery: White with cocktail glass and stars
Ticket system: Smartcard

A/c	Air conditioning
♿	Vehicles suitable for disabled
🍽	Coach(es) with galley facilities
wc	Coach(es) with toilet facilities
🌀	Seat belt-fitted vehicles
R	Recovery service available (not 24 hr)
R24	24hr recovery service
⚲	Replacement vehicle available
T	Toilet-drop facilities available
🚌	Vintage vehicle(s) available
🚐	Open top vehicle(s)

OXFORDSHIRE

*BAKERS COMMERCIAL SERVICES
UNIT 5A, ENSTONE BUSINESS PARK, ENSTONE, CHIPPING NORTON OX7 4NP
Tel: 01608 677415/6
Fax: 01608 677150
E-mail: enquiries@bakerscoaches.co.uk
Web site: www.bakerscoaches.co.uk
Prop: Mike Baker **Ops Man**: Dave Goodall
Ch Eng: Dave Nappin
Fleet: 12 - 11 coach, 1 minibus, 2 minicoach.
Chassis: 6 Dennis. 3 Mercedes. 5 Volvo.
Bodies: 1 Berkhof. 1 Caetano. 11 Plaxton.
Ops incl: local bus services, school contracts, excursions & tours, private hire, continental tours.
Livery: Red on White.

BANBURYSHIRE ETA LTD
UNIT 17, BEAUMONT BUSINESS CENTRE, BEAUMONT CLOSE, BANBURY OX16 7TN
Tel: 01295 263777
Fax: 01295 273086
E-mail: bcta@msn.com
Fleetname: Cherwell District Dial-A-Ride
Fleet: 3 minibus
Chassis/Bodies: 2 Mercedes. 1 Peugeot
Ops incl: local bus services, private hire

*BLUNSDON'S COACH TRAVEL
73 GROVE ROAD, BLADON OX20 1RJ
Tel/Fax: 01993 811320
Prop: Merlyn Blunsdon
Fleet: 4 coach.
Chassis: 4 Dennis.
Bodies: 1 Neoplan. 3 Plaxton.
Ops incl: private hire, school contracts.

CHARLTON-ON-OTMOOR SERVICES
THE GARAGE, CHARLTON-ON-OTMOOR OX5 2UQ.
Tel: 01865 331249.
Fax: 01865 316189.

CHENEY COACHES LTD
CHANEY HOUSE, THORPE MEAD, BANBURY OX16 8RZ.
Tel: 01295 254254.
Fax: 01295 271990.
E-mail: travel@cheneycoaches.co.uk
Web site: www.cheneycoaches.co.uk
Chmn/Man Dir: Graham W. Peace. **Fin Dir**: Mark R. Peace. **Co Sec**: Shirley A. K. Peace. **Fleet Eng**: Tony Piotrowski.
Fleet: 63 - 3 double-deck bus, 10 single-deck bus, 45 coach, 1 minicoach, 4 minibus.
Chassis: 2 Bedford, 1 Bova, 10 Dennis. 3 Ford Transit. 1 LDV. 15 Leyland. 4 Leyland National. 1 MAN. 8 Mercedes. 18 Volvo.
Bodies: 5 Caetano. 10 Duple. 3 Leyland. 4 Leyland National. 5 Mercedes. 30 Plaxton. 6 Van Hool.
Ops incl: local bus services, school contracts, excursions & tours, private hire, continental tours.
Livery: White.
Ticket System: Wayfarer.

*GRAYLINE COACHES (HARTWOOL) LTD
STATION APPROACH, BICESTER OX26 6HU
Tel: 01869 246461
Fax: 01869 240087
E-mail: sales@grayline.co.uk
Web site: www.grayline.co.uk
Dirs: A Gray, B Gray. **Traf Man**: P Gray
Ch Eng: G Willoughby
Fleet: 17 - 10 coach, 6 midibus, 1 midicoach.
Chassis: 1 Bedford. 1 Bova. 4 Dennis. 1 Iveco. 2 MAN. 3 Mercedes. 3 Optare. 1 Scania.
Bodies: 1 Beulas. 2 Berkhof. 1 Bova. 1 Caetano. 1 Noge. 4 Optare. 5 Plaxton. 1 Hispano.
Ops incl: school contracts, excursions & tours, private hire, continental tours.
Livery: White/Red/Blue

HEYFORDIAN TRAVEL LTD
MURDOCK ROAD, BICESTER OX26 4PP.
Tel: 01869 241500.
Fax: 01869 360011.
E-mail: info@heyfordian.co.uk
Web site: www.heyfordian.co.uk
Man Dir: R. D. Smith. **Tech Dir**: A. M. Smith. **Chmn**: J. T. Smith. **Sales Dir**: J. J. Smith. **Chief Eng**: D. F. James.
Fleet: 85 - 4 double-deck bus, 11 70 coach, 2 double-deck coach, 3 minibus. 3 minicoach.
Chassis: 8 Bova. 8 DAF. 2 Dennis. 27 Leyland. 1 MAN. 4 Optare. 20 Scania. 15 Volvo.
Bodies: 7 Alexander. 8 Bova. 4 Caetano. 31 Jonckheere. 2 Neoplan. 4 Optare. 25 Plaxton. 4 Van Hool.
Ops incl: local bus services, school contracts, excursions & tours, private hire, continental tours.
Livery: White/Red/Orange/Black.
Ticket System: Wayfarer.

JEFFS COACHES LTD
See Northamptonshire

McLEANS COACHES
UNIT 5, TWO RIVERS INDUSTRIAL ESTATE, STATION LANE, WITNEY OX28 6BH.
Tel: 01993 771445.
Fax: 01993 779556
Man Dir: Brian Constable.
Dirs: Mark Hepden, Ian Lewis
Fleet: 18 - 14 coach. 4 midicoach.
Chassis: 3 Ford. 1 MAN. 1 Mercedes.
1 Neoplan. 12 Volvo.
Ops incl: local bus services, school contracts, excursions & tours, private hire.
Livery: White/Red.

*THE OXFORD BUS COMPANY
395 COWLEY ROAD, OXFORD OX4 2DJ
Tel: 01865 785400
Fax: 01865 711745
E-mail: info@oxfordbus.co.uk
Web site: www.oxfordbus.co.uk
Fleetname: Cityline, Oxford Express, Oxford Park and Ride, The Airline
Man Dir: Philip Kirk **Eng Dir**: Ray Woodhouse **Com Dir**: Nigel Eggleton
Fleet: 158 - 20 double-deck bus, 85 single-deck bus, 41 coach, 12 midibus.
Chassis: 32 Dennis. 17 Mercedes. 13 Scania. 99 Volvo.
Bodies: 20 Alexander. 13 Irizar. 6 Jonckheere. 2 Marshall. 17 Mercedes. 13 Northern Counties. 56 Plaxton. 31 Wright.
Ops incl: local bus services, express.
Ticket System: Wayfarer

PEARCES PRIVATE HIRE
TOWER ROAD INDUSTRIAL ESTATE, BERINSFIELD, WALLINGFORD OX10 7LN
Tel: 01865 340560.
Fax: 01865 341582.
Props: Clive Pearce, Martin Pearce.
Fleet: 12 - 8 coach, 2 midicoach, 2 minicoach.
Chassis: 1 Bova. 6 Dennis. 2 Mercedes. 1 Scania. 2 Toyota.
Bodies: 1 Bova . 2 Caetano. 2 Neoplan. 6 Plaxton. 1 Van Hool.
Ops incl: school contracts, excursions and tours, private hire.
Livery: Yellow/White

*PLASTOWS COACHES
134 LONDON ROAD, WHEATLEY OX33 1JH
Tel: 01865 872270
Fax: 01865 875066
Recovery: 01865 872270
Fleet: 11 - 9 coach, 2 car.
Chassis: Dennis. Volvo.
Bodies: Jonckheere. Plaxton
Ops incl: excursions & tours, private hire, continental tours, school contracts.
Livery: White /Orange/Yellow

*STAGECOACH IN OXFORDSHIRE
HORSEPATH ROAD, COWLEY, OXFORD OX4 2RY
Tel: 01865 772250
Fax: 01865 747879
E-mail: oxford.enquiries@stagecoachbus.com
Web site: www.stagecoachbus.com
Man Dir: Martin Sutton **Service Delivery Dir**: Paul O'Callaghan

Fleet: 179 - 26 double-deck bus, 63 single-deck bus, 28 double-deck coach, 25 minibus, 33 midibus.
Chassis: 18 Dennis. 72 MAN. 25 Mercedes. 28 Transbus. 36 Volvo.
Bodies: 123 Alexander. 28 Jonckheere. 28 Transbus.
Ops incl: local bus services, express.
Livery: Stagecoach
Ticket system: Wayfarer 3

*TAPPINS COACHES
wc ♿ 🚌 A/c R24 ✂
T

COLLETT ROAD, SOUTHMEAD PARK, DIDCOT OX11 7ET
Tel: 01235 819393
Fax: 01235 816464.
Recovery: 01235 819393

E-mail: coaches@tappins.co.uk
Web site: www.tappins.co.uk
Man Dir: P. T. Tappin **Fin Controller**: K Russell **Comm Man**: D Brown
Fleet: 66 - 1 double-deck bus, 2 single-deck bus, 50 coach, 1 double-deck coach, 1 minicoach, 11 open top double-deck bus.
Chassis: 11 Leyland. 1 Leyland National. 1 MCW. 1 Neoplan. 2 Toyota. 50 Volvo.
Bodies: 1 Leyland National. 36 Plaxton. 14 Van Hool.
Ops incl: local bus services, school contracts, excursions & tours, private hire, express, continental tours.
Livery: Orange/Black

*WORTHS MOTOR SERVICES LTD
wc A/c ✂

ENSTONE, CHIPPING NORTON OX7 4LQ

Tel: 01608 677322
Fax: 01608 677298
Web site: www.worthscoaches.co.uk
E-mail: worths.coaches@ukonline.co.uk
Chmn: R Worth **Dir**: P Worth **Co Sec**: Mrs P Worth **Ch Eng**: M Florey
Fleet: 26 - 2 double-deck bus, 3 single-deck bus, 20 coach, 1 midibus.
Chassis: 2 Dennis. 2 Leyland. 1 Mercedes. 1 Optare. 20 Volvo.
Bodies: 1 Berkhof. 1 Duple. 1 Jonckheere. 1 Mercedes. 1 Optare. 20 Plaxton.
Ops incl: local bus services, continental tours, private hire.
Livery: Silver/Blue
Ticket System: Wayfarer 3.

SHROPSHIRE

ARRIVA MIDLANDS NORTH
See Staffordshire

ASTONS OF NEWPORT
STATION GARAGE, NEWPORT TF10 7EN
Tel/Fax: 01952 811285
Dirs: E. H. Aston, J. E. Aston, P. T. H. Aston
Fleet: 4 - 1 single-deck bus, 2 coach, 1 minibus.
Chassis: 2 Bedford. 1 Ford Transit. 1 Renault
Bodies: 1 Duple. 1 Northern Counties. 1 Plaxton. 1 Ford.
Ops incl: school contracts, private hire.

*BOULTONS OF SHROPSHIRE LTD
♿ wc ♿ 🚌 A/c ✂

SUNNYSIDE, CARDINGTON, CHURCH STRETTON SY6 7JZ
Tel: 01694 771226
Fax: 01694 771296
Prop: M Boulton
Fleet: 20 - 7 single-deck bus, 5 coach, 4 midicoach, 1 minibus, 3 midibus.
Chassis: Bova. Dennis. Ford Transit. Leyland. Mercedes. Optare.
Bodies: Bova. Leyland. Mercedes-Benz. Optare.
Ops incl: local bus services, school contracts, excursions & tours, private hire, continental tours.
Livery: Cream/Orange/Brown.
Ticket System: Almex.

*BRIAN'S TRAVEL ♿
CANTLOP GARAGE, PITCHFORD ROAD, CONDOVER, SHREWSBURY
Tel: 01743 761700
Fax: 01743 761374
E-mail: courtesy@tiscali.co.uk
Prop: Brian Davies.

Fleet: 1 minibus.
Chassis: 1 LDV.
Ops incl: school contracts, private hire.
Livery: White.

BRITANNIA INTERNATIONAL TRAVEL
See Lionspeed/Petes Travel, West Midlands

BRITANNIA (PROBUS MANAGEMENT LTD)
UNITE, HORTON ENTERPRISE PARK, HORTONWOOD, TELFORD
Tel/Fax: 01952 608578
Man: Mr Wall
Fleet: 22

*A T BROWN COACHES
81 TRENCH ROAD, TRENCH, TELFORD TF2 6PF
Tel: 01952 605331
Fax: 01952 608011
Prop: Alex Macleod
Fleet: 8 coach
Chassis: 5 DAF. 2 Dennis. 1 Mercedes.
Bodies: includes Caetano, Plaxton
Ops incl: school contracts, private hire.
Livery: Pale Blue with dark-blue lettering

BUTTERS COACHES
♿ wc A/c

VILLAGE ROAD, CHILDS ERCALL, MARKET DRAYTON TF9 2DG.
Tel: 01952 840216
Fax: 01952 840498
Dirs: Roger Taylor, Karen Taylor, Lesley Mackintosh, Erica Mackintosh, Barry Managh.
Fleet: 14 - 1 single-deck bus. 12 coach, 1 minibus.

Chassis: 2 Bedford, 5 DAF, 2 Dennis, 1 LDV, 2 Leyland,1 Optare, 1 Volvo.
Bodies: 2 Duple, 1 Jonckheere, 1 LDV, 1 Optare, 2 Plaxton, 1 UVG, 6 Van Hool.
Ops incl: local bus services, school contracts, excursions & tours, private hire.
Livery: Blue/White.
Ticket system: Wayfarer

CARADOC COACHES
3 CROSSWAYS, CHURCH STRETTON SY6 6PQ
Tel: 01694 724522
Mobile: 07967 210008
Prop: Mr Goff
Fleet: 8
Chassis: 1 Bedford. 3 LDV. 1 Leyland. 1 Renault. 1 Toyota. 1 Volvo.
Bodies: 1 Caetano. 1 LDV. 3 Plaxton. 1 Rosehill.
Ops incl: local bus services, school contracts, private hire.
Livery: White with blue flash & lettering.

*COURTESY TRAVEL ♿
2 WOODFIELD AVENUE, SHREWSBURY SY3 8HT
Tel: 01743 358209
Fax: 08712 425821
E-mail: courtesy@tiscali.co.uk
Prop: John Amies.
Fleet: 2 - 1 minicoach, 1 midicoach.
Chassis: 1 Ford Transit, 1 Toyota
Ops incl: excursions & tours, private hire.
Livery: Blue/White

CRAVEN ARMS TRAVEL
TOWNSEND COTTAGE, ABCOTT, CLUNGUNFORD SY7
Tel: 01588 660448
Dir: Mr Newton
Fleet: 6
Chassis: Bedford. DAF. Mercedes.
Bodies: Mercedes. Plaxton.

A/c	Air conditioning	✂ Replacement vehicle available
♿	Vehicles suitable for disabled	T Toilet-drop facilities available
🍳	Coach(es) with galley facilities	🚌 Vintage vehicle(s) available
wc	Coach(es) with toilet facilities	Open top vehicle(s)
♿	Seat belt-fitted vehicles	
R	Recovery service available (not 24 hr)	
R24	24hr recovery service	

Ops incl: school contracts, private hire.
Livery: Red with gold lettering.

*ELCOCK REISEN

THE MADDOCKS, MADELEY, TELFORD TF7 5HA
Tel: 01952 585712
Fax: 01952 582577
Recovery: 07767 250246
Web site: www.elcockgroup.co.uk
Man Dir: J C Elcock **Dirs**: J H Prince, J Ashley.
Fleet: 37 - 1 single-deck bus, 30 coach, 4 midicoach, 2 minicoach.
Chassis: 1 Dennis. 6 Mercedes. 30 Volvo.
Bodies: 2 Autobus. 35 Plaxton.
Ops incl: local bus services, school contracts, excursions & tours, private hire, continental tours.
Livery: Silver/Red

*GROUP TRAVEL LTD

11 FRANKWELL, SHREWSBURY
also at: AMBLECOTE, STOURBRIDGE, WORCESTERSHIRE
Tel: 01743 243366
Fleet: 4 coaches.
Chassis: 4 Volvo.
Ops incl: excursions & tours, continental tours, private hire.
Livery: Dark Green with gold letters

*HAPPY DAYS COACHES

LITTLE GREEN, BRONINGTON, WHITCHURCH SY13 3HQ.
Tel: 01948 780269.
Fax: 01948 780271
E-mail: info@happydayscoaches.co.uk
Web site: www.happydayscoaches.co.uk
Chmn/Man Dir: B V Austin **Tran Dir**: N G Austin **Tours Dir**: H B Austin **Ser Dir/Flt Eng**: R A Austin
Fleet: 28 - 2 single-deck bus, 23 coach, 1 midicoach, 2 minicoach.
Chassis: 2 Leyland, 18 Mercedes, 8 Volvo.
Bodies: 8 Irizar, 4 Plaxton, 18 Van Hool.
Ops incl: school contracts, excursions & tours, continental tours, private hire.
Livery: White with rising sun
Ticket System: Setright.

*HOLMES GROUP TRAVEL

CHAPEL HOUSE, 6 STAFFORD ROAD, NEWPORT TF10 7LY
Tel: 01952 820477
Fax: 01952 270607
Fax: 07831 258084
Dir: C Holmes
Fleet: 3 - coach
Chassis: includes 1 Mercedes, 1 Volvo.
Bodies: 1 Mercedes. 1 Plaxton.
Ops incl: excursions & tours, private hire.
Livery: White with flag emblem

*HORROCKS

IVY HOUSE, BROCKTON, LYDBURY NORTH SY7 8BA.
Tel: 01588 680364
Prop: A P Horrocks
Fleet: 9 - 2 double-deck bus, 2 single-deck bus, 5 midibus.
Chassis: 1 Bedford. 1 Bristol. 1 Daimler. 1 Dodge. 1 LDV. 4 Mercedes. 1 Volvo.
Ops incl: school contracts, private hire
Livery: White/Blue

*K N M MINIBUS SERVICES

WOODLANDS, CHAPEL LANE, KNOCKIN HEATH, OSWESTRY
Tel: 01691 682681
Mobile: 07801 624694
Prop/Dir: K Newport
Fleet: 5 - 5 minicoach.
Chassis: 3 Ford. 2 Iveco.
Bodies: 3 Ford. 2 Holloway
Ops incl: private hire.
Livery: White with gold letters

*KEL KIR COACHES

SANDY CROFT, COTTAGE FIELDS, ST MARTINS OSWESTRY
Tel/Fax: 01691 778464
Prop: R Jones
Fleet: 6 - 5 coach, 1 minibus
Chassis: 1 Iveco. 1 LDV. 1 Mercedes. 1 MAN. 1 Noge. 1 Scania.
Bodies: 1 Azair. 1 Euro. 1 LDV. 1 Noge. 1 Setra. 1 Van Hool.
Ops incl: school contracts, private hire, tours & excursions.
Livery: Purple

*LAKESIDE COACHES LTD

BROAD OAKS, ELSON ROAD, ELLESMERE SY12 9EH
Tel: 01691 622761
Fax: 01691 623694
E-mail: mailbox@hireacoach.co.uk
Web site: www.lakesidecoaches.co.uk
Dirs: John Davies, Dorothy Davies **Gen Man**: Neil Hall
Fleet: 17 - 11 coach, 2 midicoach, 2 minicoach, 2 midibus
Chassis: 5 Dennis. 2 LDV. 2 Mercedes. 2 Toyota. 6 Volvo.
Bodies: Caetano. Concept. Mercedes. Optare. Plaxton. Van Hool.
Ops incl: local bus services, school contracts, excursions & tours, private hire, continental tours.
Livery: White with two-tone green
Ticket System: Almex

*LONGMYND TRAVEL

THE COACH DEPOT, LEA CROSS, SHREWESBURY SY5
Tel: 01743 861999
E-mail: enquiries@longmyndtravel.co.uk
Web site: www.longmyndtravel.co.uk
Dirs: T G Evans, F J Evans, V M Sheppard Evans **Tran Man**: D M Sheppard.
Fleet: 23
Chassis: 1 Dennis. 1 Iveco. 2 Mercedes. 1 Toyota. 16 Volvo.

Bodies: 1 Beulas. 2 Berkhof. 1 Caetano. 4 Jonckheere. 2 Mercedes. 13 Plaxton.
Ops incl: school contracts, excursions & tours, private hire, continental tours.
Livery: White with red/black decals

MYTTON TRAVEL

MYTTON DINGLE, STIPERSTONES, MINSTERLEY, SHREWSBURY SY5 0LZ
Tel: 01743 791309/ 01588 520358
Prop: D J Bradbury
Fleet: 8
Chassis: 2 Ford Transit . 4 LDV. 1 Freight Rover. 1 Mercedes. .
Ops incl: school contracts, private hire.
Livery: White with yellow/red stripes

*M &B COACHES & MINIBUSES

UNIT 22, HADLEY PARK INDUSTRIAL ESTATE, TELFORD TF1 2PY
Tel: 01952 251125
Fax: 01952 619619
Mobile: 07812 178163
Prop: Brian Bull
Fleet: 6 - 5 midicoach. 1 coach
Chassis: 1 Dennis. 1 DAF. 4 Mercedes.
Bodies: 1 Duple. 1 LDV. 3 Mercedes. 1 Robin Hood.
Ops incl: school contracts, private hire.
Livery: Red (metallic) with gold and silver letters

M & J TRAVEL

COACH GARAGE, NEWCASTLE, CRAVEN ARMS SY7 8QL.
Tel: 01588 640273.
Prop: W. M. Price.
Fleet: 13 - 7 coach, 1 midicoach, 5 minibus
Chassis: 4 Bedford. 2 Dennis. 1 Toyota. 1 Talbot.
Bodies: 1 Caetano. 2 Duple. 4 Plaxton.
Ops incl: school contracts, excursions & tours, private hire, continental tours.
Livery: White/Black/Gold.
Ticket System: Setright.

*M P MINICOACHES

14 REDBURN CLOSE, KETLEY BANK, TELFORD TF2
Tel: 01952 415607
Fax: 01952 619188
Prop: Mark Perkins
Fleet: 3 - 1 midbus. 2 minicoach.
Chassis/bodies: 1 LDV. 2 Mercedes.
Ops incl: school contracts, excursions & tours, private hire.
Livery: Blue (two-tone metallic)

*MINSTERLEY MOTORS SERVICES LTD

STIPERSTONES, MINSTERLEY SY5 0LZ
Tel: 01743 791208
Fax: 01743 790101
E-mail: john@minsterley-motors.co.uk
Web site: www.minsterley-motors.co.uk
Props: John Jones
Fleet: 30 - 4 single-deck bus, 25 coach,

1 midicoach.
Chassis: 5 Bedford. 2 DAF. 1 Dennis. 1 Mercedes. 22 Volvo.
Bodies: 2 Bova. 5 Jonckheere. 1 Mercedes. 14 Plaxton. 2 Sunsundegui. 3 Wright.
Ops incl: local bus services, school contracts, excursions & tours, private hire, continental tours.
Livery: Blue/Dark Blue
Ticket system: Wayfarer

*N. C. B. MOTORS LTD
💺 wc 🍴 ✏ T

EDSTASTON GARAGE, WEM SY4 5RF
Tel: 01939 232379
Fax: 01939 234892
E-mail: mail@ncb-motors.co.uk
Dirs: Derek N Brown, Paul R Brown.
Fleet: 10 coach.
Chassis: 10 Volvo.
Bodies: 4 Jonckheere. 6 Plaxton.
Ops incl: private hire, school contracts, excursions & tours.
Livery: Brown/Cream.

*OWENS OF OSWESTRY LTD wc 🍴 💺 R ✏

36 BEATRICE STREET, OSWESTRY SY11 1QG
FOXEN PARK BUSINESS ESTATE, FOUR CROSSES
Tel: 01691 652126
Fax: 01691 670047.
E-mail: owenstravel@compuserve.com
Web site: www.owenstravel.co.uk
Fleetname: Travelmaster.
Dirs: F G Owen (**Man Dir**), M Owen, D A Owen
Fleet: 14
Chassis: 1 Dennis. 1 LDV. 4 MAN. 1 Mercedes. 1 Scania. 1 Toyota. 4 Volvo. 1 VW.
Bodies: includes: Berkhof. Caetano. Plaxton. Van Hool.
Ops incl: excursions & tours, private hire, continental tours, school contracts.
Livery: Red/White/Blue
Subsidiary company: Stratos Coaches, Newtown

*R & B TRAVEL
PLEASANT VIEW, KNOWLE, LUDLOW SY8 3NE.
Tel/Fax: 01584 890770.
Prop: A T Radnor, L Radnor.
Fleet: 11 - midibus.
Chassis: 2 Bedford. 2 Leyland DAF. 1 Ford Transit. 2 VW. 1 Iveco. 2 Volvo.
Bodies: Duple. Optare. Plaxton. Robin Hood. Wright.
Ops incl: Local bus services, school contracts, private hire, excursions & tours.
Livery: Silver/Red/Orange/White

RIVERSIDE COACHES R
HEATH HILL, DAWLEY TF4 2JU
Tel: 01952 505490
Fax: 01952 505590
Prop: K H Pollen
Fleet: 13 - included 2 double-deck buses, 1 double-deck coach
Chassis: includes - Bristol. Ford. Volvo.
Ops Incl: private hire, school contracts
Livery: Blue/Silver and Blue/White

*SALOPIA COACHES
UNIT D6, WEM INDUSTRIAL ESTATE, SOULTON ROAD, WEM
Tel: 01939 236682
Fax: 01939 236137
Dirs: Helen Heath, Ian Blake, Alison Chambers
Fleet: 8 coaches
Chassis: 3 Dennis. 2 Ford. 2 Leyland. 1 Volvo.
Bodies: include Jonckheere, Plaxton
Ops Incl: local bus service, private hire, excursions & tours, school contracts
Livery: White/Blue/Orange and Fawn with green stripes
Ticket system: Almex

*SHROPSHIRE COUNTY COUNCIL ♿
INTEGRATED TRANSPORT UNIT, 107 LONGDEN ROAD, SHREWSBURY SY3 9DS.
Tel: 01743 245300
Fax: 01743 253279
E-mail: peter.ralphs@shropshire-cc.gov.uk
Web site:

www.shropshireonline.gov.uk
Fleetname: Fleet Operations
Ch Exec: Carolyn Downs **Gen Man Transp**: Adrian Millard **Fleet Ops Off**: Peter Ralphs.
Fleet: 55 - 1 single-deck bus, 51 minibus, 2 midicoach, 1 midibus.
Chassis: 1 Ford Transit. 30 Iveco. 13 LDV. 8 Mercedes. 1 Optare. 2 Renault.
Ops incl: local bus services, school contracts.
Livery: White
Ticket system: Almex

*TOWN & COUNTRY TRAVEL 💺
13 ROSEMARY, LEINTWARDINE, CRAVEN ARMS SY7
Tel/Fax: 01547 540420
Prop: Roy Taylor
Fleet: 3 - 2 midicoach, 1 minicoach.
Chassis: 1 LDV. 1 Mercedes. 1 Toyota.
Bodies: 1 Caetano. 1 LDV. 1 Mercedes.
Ops incl: school contracts, private hire
Livery: White with maroon stripe and silver/blue lettering.

WHITTLE COACH, BUS & HOLIDAYS
See Worcestershire.

*WORTHEN TRAVEL
💺 wc 🍴 R24 T

STATION ROAD, LITTLE MINSTERLEY SY5 0BW
Tel: 01743 792622
Fax: 01743 791053
Recovery: 01743 792622
E-mail: jackie@worthentravel.freeserve.co.uk
Prop: D A Pye **Gen Man**: C L Robinson
Sec: J Davies
Fleet: 20 - 2 single-deck bus, 15 coach, 3 minibus.
Chassis: 5 DAF. 1 Ford Transit. 7 other.
Bodies: 3 Caetano. 4 Leyland. 3 Van Hool.
Ops incl: local bus services, school contracts, excursions & tours, private hire, express, continental tours.
Livery: White/Blue
Ticket system: Wayfarer 2

SOMERSET (ALSO BATH & N E SOMERSET, N SOMERSET)

*A1 TRAVEL 💺 wc 🍴 🍴
80 HIGHFIELD ROAD, YEOVIL BA21 4RJ
Tel/Fax: 01935 477722
Web site: www.a1travelservices.com
Dir: Ian Watson
Fleet: 5 - 2 midibus, 3 minibus.
Chassis: 1 Ford. 2 Freight Rover. 2 LDV. 1 Mercedes. 1 Setra.
Bodies: include 1 Plaxton. 1 Setra.
Ops incl: school contracts, private hire.

*ARLEEN COACH HIRE & SERVICES LTD
wc 💺 🍴 ✏

14 BATH ROAD, PEASEDOWN ST JOHN BA2 8DH
Tel: 01761 434625
Fax: 01761 436578
E-mail: arleen.coach-hire@virgin.net
Web site: www.arleen.co.uk
Dirs: A W Spiller, A A Spiller

Co Sec: Mrs M K Spiller
Fleet: 24 - 19 single-deck bus, 2 midicoach, 3 minibus.
Chassis: 2 Bedford. 1 Bova. 4 DAF. 1 Dennis. 1 Freight Rover. 2 Leyland. 2 MAN. 7 Mercedes. 1 Optare. 1 Volvo.
Bodies: 1 Autobus. 1 Berkhof. 2 Duple. 1 Mercedes. 2 Neoplan. 4 Plaxton. 1 Reeve Burgess. 3 Van Hool. 1 Wadham Stringer.
Ops incl: local bus services, school contracts, excursions & tours, private hire, continental tours.
Livery: Red/White/Blue

💺	Seat belt-fitted vehicles	✏	Replacement vehicle available
🍴	Vehicles suitable for disabled	T	Toilet-drop facilities available
🍴	Coach(es) with galley facilities		Vintage vehicle(s) available
wc	Coach(es) with toilet facilities	R	Recovery service available (not 24 hr)
		R24	24hr recovery service
			Open top vehicle(s)

AXE VALE COACHES
[WC] [icons]

BIDDISHAM, AXBRIDGE BS26 2RD.
Tel: 01934 750321.
Fax: 01934 750334.
Dirs: A. L. Bailey, C. P. Bailey.
Fleet: 14 - 10 coach, 2 midicoach, 1 minicoach, 1 midibus.
Chassis: 7 Bova. 2 DAF. 1 Ford. 1 LDV. 2 Mercedes.
Bodies: 7 Bova. 1 Carlyle. 4 Plaxton.
Ops incl: school contracts, excursions & tours, private hire, continental tours.
Livery: White with Red/Blue

BAKERS COACHES
[WC] [R24] [icons]

8 BUCKLAND ROAD, YEOVIL BA21 5EA.
Tel: 01935 428401.
Fax: 01935 410423
Recovery: 01935 428401
E-mail: carol@moonway.fsnet.co.uk
Web site: www.moonway.fsnet.co.uk
Dirs: S Baker, A Palmer
Fleet: 15 - 12 coach, 3 minibus
Chassis: 1 Bova. 8 DAF. 4 Ford Transit. 1 Mercedes. 1 Setra. 1 Volvo.
Bodies: 1 Berkhof. 1 Caetano. 2 Jonckheere. 1 Mercedes. 1 Setra. 2 Van Hool.
Ops incl: school contracts, private hire, continental tours.
Livery: White

BAKERS DOLPHIN COACH TRAVEL
[WC] [icons] [T]

48 LOCKING ROAD, WESTON-SUPER-MARE BS23 3DN.
Tel: 01934 635635.
Fax: 01934 641162.
E-mail: coach.hire@bakersdolphin.com
Chmn: John Baker.
Man Dir: Tim Newcombe. **Ch Eng:** Mark Vearncombe. **Mktg Dir:** Amanda Harrington.
Ops Dir: Max Fletcher.
Ops Man: Alan White.
Fleet: 75 - single-deck coach, double-deck coach, midibus, minibus, minicoach
Chassis: 20 Bedford. 1 Bova. 15 Leyland. 3 Mercedes. 36 Volvo.
Ops incl: local bus services, excursions & tours, private hire, express, continental tours, school contracts.
Livery: Blue/White/Green/Yellow.

BATH BUS COMPANY [icon]

1 PIERREPONT STREET, BATH BA1 1LB.
Tel: 01225 330444.
Fax: 01225 330727.
E-Mail: hq@bathbuscompany.com
Web site: www.bathbuscompany.com
Chmn: Peter Newman **Man Dir:** Martin Curtis. **Dir:** Dr. Mike Walker. **Eng Dir:** Collin Brougham-Field. **Co Sec/Dir:** Rob Bromley.
Com Dir: Keith Tazewell.
Fleet: 11 double-deck bus, 7 single-deck bus, 3 minibus.
Chassis: 1 AEC, 6 Bristol, 6 Dennis, 3 Leyland-DAB, 3 Leyland, 3 MCW. 4 Mercedes.
Bodies: 1 Alexander. 6 ECW. 1 Leyland.

3 MCW. 1 Park Royal. 3 Plaxton. 6 Wright.
Ops incl: local bus services, excursions & tours, private hire.
Livery: Red/Primrose.
Ticket System: Wayfarer/BBC punch system.
Subsidiary of Ensignbus

*BERRY'S COACHES (TAUNTON) LTD [WC] [icons]

CORNISHWAY WEST, NEW WELLINGTON ROAD, TAUNTON TA1 5NA
Tel: 01823 331356
Fax: 01823 322347
E-mail: info@berryscoaches.co.uk
Web site: www.berryscoaches.co.uk
Dirs: S A Berry, P I Berry
Fleet: 28 - 23 coach, 5 double-deck coach.
Chassis: 28 Volvo.
Bodies: 2 Jonckheere. 8 Plaxton. 18 Van Hool.
Ops incl: local bus services, school contracts, excursions & tours, private hire, express, continental tours.
Livery: White/Red/Orange.
Ticket System: Setright.

*BLAGDON LIONESS COACHES LTD
See Bristol

*BLUE IRIS COACHES
See Bristol

CENTURION TRAVEL LTD
[WC] [icons] [R24] [icon]

WEST ROAD GARAGE, WELTON, MIDSOMER NORTON BA3 2TP.
Tel: 01761 417372.
Fax: 01761 417369.
E-mail: coach-hire@centuriontravel.co.uk
Web site: www.centuriontravel.co.uk
Man Dir: Martin Spiller.
Fleet: 20 - 17 coach, 1 minibus, 2 minicoach.
Chassis: 6 Bedford, 4 DAF, 1 Freight Rover, 1 Leyland. 11 Mercedes.
Bodies: 1 Bova, 5 Duple, 1 Jonckheere, 2 Optare, 5 Plaxton, 2 Van Hool, 1 other.
Ops incl: school contracts, excursions & tours, private hire, continental tours.
Livery: Red/Cream/Burgundy.

*CLAPTON COACHES [WC] [icon]

1 HAYDON ESTATE, RADSTOCK, BATH BA3 3RD
Tel: 01761 431936
Fax: 01761 431935
E-mail: claptonholidays@btconnect.com
Dirs: S C Lippet, M C Lippet, C Higgs
Fleet: 12 - 6 coach, 6 minicoach.
Bodies: 2 Beulas. 4 Bova.
Ops incl: excursions & tours, private hire, continental tours.
Livery: Lilac

*COOKS COACHES [icons]

WHITEBALL GARAGE, WELLINGTON TA21 0LT
Tel: 01823 672247
Fax: 01823 673101

E-mail: landylines@aol.com
Web site: www.cookscoaches-somerset.co.uk
Man Dir: Paul Landymore
Ops Dir: Nigel Billinger.
Fleet: 60 - 10 single-deck bus, 2 coach, 10 midicoach, 22 minibus, 11 midibus, 5 minicoach.
Chassis: 15 LDV. 34 Mercedes. 10 Optare. 1 Volvo.
Bodies: 6 Alexander. 5 Autobus. 1 Duple. 11 Optare. 18 Plaxton. 2 Reeve Burgess. 1 Wadham Stringer. 9 G&M Conversion. 4 Crest. 4 Onyx. 4 Trucksmith.
Ops incl: local bus services, school contracts, private hire.
Livery: White, some with red/blue stripes, some with blue/yellow
Ticket System: Almex

COOMBS TRAVEL
[icons] [R] [icons] [T]

SEARLE CRESCENT, WINTERSTOKE COMMERCIAL CENTRE, WESTON-SUPER-MARE BS23 3YX
Tel: 01934 632612
Fax: 01934 635853
E-mail: coombscoaches@aol.com
Prop: B. F. Coombs **Gen Man:**
W. R. Davies. **Traf Man:** C. Winser
Ch Eng: J. J. Ellis.
Sec: Mrs M. Lillie
Fleet: 45 - 2 double-deck bus, 4 single-deck bus, 16 coach, 8 midibus, 3 midicoach, 12 minibus.
Chassis: 3 Bedford. 1 Bristol. 2 Dennis. 2 Dodge. 9 Ford Transit. 3 LDV. 4 Mercedes. 2 Renault. 8 Scania. 1 Toyota.
Bodies: 2 Autobus. 1 Caetano. 1 Irizar. 2 Northern Counties. 6 Plaxton. 2 Reeve Burgess. 8 Van Hool. 3 Wadham Stringer. 2 Wright.
Ops incl: local bus services, school contracts, excursions and tours, private hire, continental tours.
Livery: Yellow/White
Ticket System: Setright

*FIRST SOMERSET & AVON LTD
[icons] [R24] [icons] [T]

OLDMIXON CRESCENT, WESTON-SUPER-MARE BS24 9AY
Tel: 01934 620122
Fax: 01934 415859
Recovery: 0117 955 4442
Web site: www.firstgroup.com
Fleet: 472 - 69 double-deck bus, 111 single-deck bus, 7 coach, 10 articulated bus, 12 open-top bus, 117 midibus, 146 minibus.
Chassis: 7 Bristol. 173 Dennis. 2 Iveco. 46 Leyland. 134 Mercedes. 10 Optare. 3 Scania. 97 Volvo.
Bodies: 32 Alexander. 1 Caetano. 7 ECW. 25 East Lancs. 35 Leyland. 4 MCW. 16 Northern Counties. 10 Optare. 265 Plaxton. 10 Roe. 4 Van Hool. 52 Wright. 3 Derwent. 2 City Star.
Ops incl: local bus services, school contracts, excursions & tours, express, private hire.
Livery: First
Ticket System: Wayfarer

W. H. FOSTER & SON (AVALON COACHES)
NORTHLOAD GARAGE, GLASTONBURY BA6 9JJ.
Tel/Fax: 01458 832293.
Ptnrs: R. A. Foster, M. Foster (**Traf Man**).
Fleet: 12 - 10 coach, 1 midicoach, 1 minicoach.
Chassis: 1 Bova. 2 Dennis. 1 LDV. 1 Mercedes. 7 Volvo.
Bodies: 1 Autobus. 1 Bova. 4 Plaxton. 6 Van Hool.
Ops incl: excursions & tours, private hire, continental tours.
Livery: Red/White.

GLENVIC OF BRISTOL LTD
See Somerset/Bath & N E Somerset

HUTTON COACH HIRE
95 MOORLAND ROAD, WESTON-SUPER-MARE BS23 4HS.
Tel: 01934 627080.
Fax: 01934 641362.
E-mail: avtel-net.co.uk/superhire.html
Prop: J. R. Lawrence.
Fleet: 7 - 2 double-deck bus, 1 single-deck bus, 2 coach, 1 midibus, 1 minicoach.
Chassis: 2 Bristol. 1 Ford Transit. 1 Iveco. 2 Leyland. 1 Volvo.
Bodies: 1 Plaxton. 1 Reeve Burgess. 1 Iveco. 1 Renault. 2 ECW.
Ops incl: excursions & tours, private hire, school contracts.
Livery: Maroon/Ivory.

KINGFISHER COACHES OF YEOVIL LTD
28 TURNERS BARN LANE, YEOVIL BA20 2LW.
Tel: 01935 411511.
Fax: 01935 411911.
Chmn: C. R. Bettiss. **Tran Man**: S. Taylor.
Sec: D. K. Cloake.
Fleet: 2 - 1 coach, 1 minibus.
Chassis: DAF. Leyland.
Ops incl: private hire, school contracts.

REXQUOTE HERITAGE COACHES
STATION WORKS, STATION ROAD, BISHOPS LYDEARD TA4 3BU
Tel: 01823 433398.
Fax: 01823 433725.
E-mail: sales@rexquote.co.uk
Web site: www.rexquote.co.uk
Fleetname: Quantock Motor Services.
Man Dir: Stephen Morris
Fleet: 57 - 6 double-deck bus, 20 single-deck bus, 30 single-deck coach. 1 double-deck coach.
Chassis: 19 AEC. 11 Bristol. 2 Daimler. 3 Dennis. 14 Leyland.
Bodies: 1 Alexander. 5 Duple. 18 ECW. 6 East Lancs. 2 Leyland. 10MCW. 4 Park Royal. 6 Willowbrook..
Ops incl: local bus services, excursions &

tours, private hire, school contracts.

*RIDLERS LTD
JURY ROAD GARAGE, DULVERTON TA22 9EJ
Tel: 01398 323398
Fax: 01398 324398
Dirs: G A Ridler, S R Ridler **Ops Man**: M Jamieson
Fleet: 17 - 14 coach, 2 midicoach, 1 minicoach.
Chassis: Bedford. Ford. Iveco. Leyland. Scania. Toyota.
Bodies: Berkhof. Duple. Plaxton. Van Hool.
Ops incl: local bus services, school contracts, excursions & tours, private hire, continental tours.
Livery: White/Red/Silver.
Ticket system: Almex

D. W. SKELTON
90 BROADWAY, CHILTON POLDEN TA7 9EQ.
Tel: 01278 722066.
Fax: 01278 722608.
Fleetname: Skelton Tours.
Prop: D. W. Skelton.
Fleet: 3 coach.
Chassis: 1 Ford. 2 MAN.
Bodies: 1 Neoplan. 1 Plaxton. 1 MAN.
Ops incl: excursions & tours, private hire, continental tours.
Livery: Black/Green/Gold.

*SMITH'S COACHES (B.E. & G.W. SMITH)
BYFIELDS, PYLLE, SHEPTON MALLET BA4 6TA.
Tel: 01749 830126
Fax: 01749 830888
Ptnr/Ch Eng/Prop: Graham Smith **Ptnr/Co Sec**: Betty Smith
Fleet: 17 - 16 coach, 1 midicoach.
Chassis: 5 Bedford. 3 Leyland. 1 Toyota. 8 Volvo.
Bodies: 1 Caetano. 16 Plaxton.
Ops incl: local bus services, school contracts, private hire.
Livery: Maroon/Cream
Ticket System: Setright.

*SOUTH WEST COACHES LTD
SOUTHGATE ROAD, WINCANTON BA9 9EB
Tel/Fax: 01963 33124
E-mail: southwestcoachesltd@hotmail.com
Web site: www.southwestcoaches.co.uk
Man Dir: A M Graham **Dir**: S Graham.
Fleet: 69 - 7 single-deck bus, 28 coach, 6 midibus, 3 midicoach, 25 minibus.
Chassis: 5 Bedford. 1 DAF. 1 Dennis. 16 Ford Transit. 15 Leyland. 2 Marshall. 10 Mercedes. 1 Optare. 3 Setra. 9 Volvo. 6 VW.

Bodies: 1 Alexander. 11 Duple. 1 East Lancs. 6 Marshall. 6 Mercedes. 1 Optare. 15 Plaxton. 3 Setra. 2 Van Hool. 1 Wadham Stringer.
Ops incl: local bus services, school contracts, excursions & tours, private hire, continental tours.
Livery: Blue/White.
Ticket System: Wayfarer/Setright/Almex.

STARLINE BAND SERVICES
THE BUS DEPOT, TWEED ROAD, CLEVEDON BS21 6UU
Tel/Fax: 01275 876543
Fax: 01275 340280
E-mail: chris@star-line.co.uk
Web site: www.star-line.co.uk
Owner: M D C Langson. **Dirs**: J Langson, R Langson
Fleet: 19 - 2 coach, 17 double-deck coach.
Chassis: 4 Ayats. 2 DAF. 8 Mercedes. 9 Volvo.
Bodies: 4 Ayats. 1 Bova. 4 Neoplan. 2 Plaxton. 8 Van Hool.
Ops incl: excursions & tours, private hire
Livery: Silver.

*STONES OF BATH
LOWER BRISTOL ROAD, BATH BA2 3DR
Tel: 01225 422267
Fax: 01225 442209
E-mail: stonescoaches@compuserve.com
Senior Ptnr: D G Stone, **Ops Man**: C G Stone, **Ch Eng**: S M Stone, **Sec/Fin**: Mrs N R Russell
Fleet: 13 - 10 double-deck coach, 3 midicoach
Chassis: DAF. Neoplan. Scania. Toyota.
Bodies: Bova. Irizar. Neoplan. Van Hool.
Ops incl: excursions & tours, school contracts, private hire, continental tours.
Livery: Cream/Red

*TOP COACHES
NORTH ROAD, TIMSBURY BA2 0JH
Tel/Fax: 01761 470240
Prop: C Gregory, M Gregory
Fleet: 1 minibus
Chassis: 1 Peugeot Talbot
Ops incl: school contracts

TRANS-CONTINENTAL COACHES
STRODE ROAD, CLEVEDON BS21 6Q.
Tel: 01275 893349, 87413.
Fax: 01275 340280.
Reg name: Clevedon Motorways Ltd.
Dir/Gen Man: R. Langson.
Ch Eng: C. S. Doran. **Co Sec**: M. E. Thompson. **Ops Man**: C. J. Langson.
Fleet: 13 - 3 double-deck bus, 1 single-deck bus, 7 coach, 2 minicoach.
Chassis: 1 Bedford. 2 DAF. 2 Mercedes. 5 Neoplan.
Bodies: 1 Alexander. 5 Neoplan. 3 Plaxton.

A/c	Air conditioning
♿	Vehicles suitable for disabled
🍴	Coach(es) with galley facilities
WC	Coach(es) with toilet facilities
♥	Seat belt-fitted vehicles
R	Recovery service available (not 24 hr)
R24	24hr recovery service
✔	Replacement vehicle available
T	Toilet-drop facilities available
🚌	Vintage vehicle(s) available
🚍	Open top vehicle(s)

3 LAG. 1 Ford.
Ops incl: local bus services, excursions & tours, private hire, express, continental tours.
Livery: White/Red/Black, plus others.

TRAVELINE [wc] [🍴] [♻] [R24]
SUMMERLAND CAR PARK, MINEHEAD TA24 5BN.
Tel: 01643 704774, 821883.
Fax: 01643 821883.
Dirs: D. C. & P. A. Grimmett.
Fleet: 1 coach. **Chassis/Body**: Bova.
Ops incl: excursions & tours, private hire, continental tours.

*VISTA COACHWAYS
[♻] [🚌] [🔧]
ROSE VISTA, 261 STOWEY ROAD, YATTON BS49 4QX
Tel: 01934 832074
E-mail: terry@vistacoach.co.uk
Web site: www.vistacoach.co.uk
Prop: T P Jones
Fleet: 8 - 2 coach, 5 midicoach, 1 midibus.
Chassis: 3 Bedford. 1 Bristol. 1 Iveco. 1 Leyland. 2 Mercedes.
Bodies: 1 Carlyle. 1 Duple. 4 Plaxton. 1 Dormobile. 1 PMT.
Ops incl: local bus services, school contracts, private hire.
Livery: Cream with green/red

WAKES COACHES
See SOUTH WEST COACHES LTD

*WEBBER BUS
BRUE AVENUE, COLLEY LANE INDUSTRIAL ESTATE, BRIDGWATER TA6 5LT
Tel: 0800 096 3039
Fax: 01278 455250
Web site: www.webberbus.com
Dirs: D J Webber, D A Webber, T Gardner, E Gardner.
Fleet: 29 - 15 coach, 2 midicoach, 10 minibus, 2 minicoach.
Chassis: 1 Bova. 2 DAF. 5 Ford Transit.7 LDV. 1 Neoplan. 1 Scania. 6 Volvo.
Bodies: 2 Bova. 1 Caetano. 4 Duple. 1 Mellor. 1Neoplan. 5 Plaxton. 2 Van Hool. 8 other.
Ops incl: local bus services, school contracts, excursions & tours, private hire, continental tours.

SOUTH YORKSHIRE

*ANDERSON COACHES LTD
[wc] [♻]
4 HOLLY BANK AVENUE, SHEFFIELD S12 2BL
Tel: 0114 239 9231
Dir: D Anderson
Fleet: 5 - 1 coach, 2 midicoach, 2 minicoach.
Chassis: 1 Dennis. 1 Ford Transit. 1 LDV. 1 Neoplan. 1 Volvo.
Ops incl: excursions & tours

ASHLEY TRAVEL LTD
t/a GRANT & McALLIN
8A STATION ROAD, MOSBOROUGH, SHEFFIELD S19 5AD.
Tel: 0114 251 1234.
Fax: 0114 251 1900.
Dirs: R. Atack (**Gen Man/Traf Man**), T. F. Atack (**Ch Eng/Sec**).
Fleet: 3 coach.
Chassis: 1 Bedford. 2 Volvo.
Bodies: 3 Plaxton.
Ops incl: excursions & tours, private hire.
Livery: Turquoise/Blue/White.

ASTON EXPRESS COACHES
See Derbyshire

*BARNSLEY & DISTRICT TRACTION CO
WAKEFIELD ROAD, BARNSLEY S71 1NU
Tel: 01226 299288
Fax: 01226 779079
Gen Man: K Allison
Fleet: 46 - 45 single-deck bus, 1 midibus.
Chassis: 21 DAF. 1 Optare. 24 Volvo.
Bodies: 23 Alexander. 1 East Lancs. 22 Optare.
Ops incl: local bus services.
Livery: White/Blue.
Ticket System: Wayfarer 3

*BILLIES COACHES LTD
[♿] [wc] [🍴] [♻] [T]
CHESTERTON ROAD, EASTWOOD TRADING ESTATE, ROTHERHAM S65 1SU
Tel: 01709 382912
Chassis/Bodies: Volvo. Plaxton
Ops Incl: excursions & tours, private hire
Livery: White

BUCKLEYS
[wc] [♻] [🍴] [♻]
STONEHAVEN, GATEHOUSE LANE, AUCKLEY, DONCASTER DN9 3EJ
Tel: 01302 770379.
Man Dir: R. Buckley.
Fleet: 2 coach.
Chassis/Bodies: Mercedes/Hispano.
Ops incl: excursions & tours.

BURDETTS COACHES LTD
[wc] [♻] [🔧]
8 STATION ROAD, MOSBOROUGH, SHEFFIELD S20 5AD.
Tel: 0114 248 2341.
Fax: 0114 247 5733.
Ptnrs: F. Burdett, K. J. Burdett, D. W. Burdett.
Fleet: 12 coach. **Chassis**: 2 Leyland. 10 Volvo.
Bodies: 3 Jonckheere. 5 Plaxton. 4 Van Hool.
Ops incl: excursions & tours, private hire, continental tours, school contracts.
Livery: White/Red/Green.

BYRAN COACHES LTD [♻]
[wc] [R]
31 SUSSEX STREET, SHEFFIELD S4 7YY
Tel/Fax: 0114 270 0060
Dir/Owner: Julie Scott **Dir**: Dennis Heaton
Fleet: 6 - 3 minibus, 3 minicoach.
Chassis: 1 Ford. 4 Mercedes.
Bodies: include 1 Setra.
Ops incl: school contracts, excursions & tours, private hire.
Livery: White/Jade/Black.

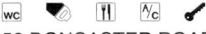

CLARKSONS COACHES
[wc] [♻] [🍴] [♻] [🔧]
52 DONCASTER ROAD, SOUTH ELMSALL WF9 2JN.
Tel: 01977 642385.
Fax: 01977 640158.
E-mail: info@clarksonscoaches.co.uk
Web site: www. clarksonscoaches.co.uk
Dirs: K. Clarkson, P. Clarkson, J. Hancock.
Ops Man: J. Donniss.
Fleet: 9 - 8 single-deck coach. 1 midicoach.
Chassis: 4 Mercedes, 2 Neoplan, 3 Volvo.
Bodies: 4 Mercedes. 2 Neoplan. 3 Van Hool.
Ops incl: local bus services, school contracts, excursions & tours, private hire, continental tours.
Livery: Blue.
Ticket System: Wayfarer.

COOPERS TOURS LTD
[♿] [wc] [♻] [🍴] [♻] [🚌]
[R24] [🔧] [T]
ALDRED CLOSE, NORWOOD INDUSTRIAL ESTATE, KILLAMARSH S21 2JH
Tel: 0114 248 2859.
Fax: 0114 248 3867.
E-mail: sales@cooperstours.co.uk
Web site: www.cooperstours.co.uk
Dirs: Alan Cooper, Graham Cooper.
Fleet: 8 coach.
Chassis: 1 AEC. 2 Leyland. 1 MAN. 3 Volvo.
Bodies: 2 Berkhof. 4 Plaxton. 2 Van Hool.
Ops incl: excursions & tours, private hire, continental tours.
Livery: Yellow/White.

COSY COACHES [🚌]
5 MEYNELL WAY, KILLAMARSH, SHEFFIELD S21 1HG
Tel: 0114-248 9139
E-mail: enquiries@cosycoach.co.uk
Web site: www.cosycoach.co.uk
Fleet: 1 Bedford/Duple vintage coach

ELLENDERS COACHES
wc | ¶ | ● | ✓

71 HURLFIELD AVE, SHEFFIELD
S12 2TL.
Tel: 0114 264 1837.
Ptnrs: Mrs P. J. D. Ellender, C. S. Ellender.
Fleet: 2 coach.
Chassis: Volvo. **Bodies:** Jonckheere.
Ops incl: excursions & tours, private hire, continental tours, school contracts.

EXPRESSWAY COACHES
& | wc | ● | ✓

THE MISSION, BREWERY ROAD,
WATH UPON DEARNE S63 7BX.
Tel: 01709 875358.
Fax: 01709 879919.
Owner: P. Regan.
Fleet: 10 - 2 coach 3 midicoach, 5 minicoach.
Chassis: 1 Dennis. 1 Ford Transit. 1 MAN. 7 Mercedes.
Bodies: 2 Berkhof. 2 Optare. 6 Onyx.
Ops incl: private hire, continental tours, school contracts.

FIRST IN SOUTH YORKSHIRE & 🚌 R24

MIDLAND ROAD, ROTHERHAM
S60 1TF.
Tel: 01709 566000
E-mail: enquiries@firstgroup.com
Web site: www.firstmainline.co.uk
Man Dir: Gary Nolan **Ops Dir:** Bob Hamilton
Eng Dir: Mark Hargreaves **Fin Dir:** Martin Wilson **Comm Dir:** Brandon Jones
Fleet: 630 - 146 double-deck bus, 351 single-deck bus, 74 midibus, 59 minibus.
Chassis: 148 Dennis. 8 Leyland. 49 Mercedes. 10 Optare. 12 Scania. 403 Volvo.
Bodies: 297 Alexander. 6 Carlyle. 6 ECW. 7 East Lancs. 16 Northern Counties. 10 Optare. 121 Plaxton.185 Wright.
Ops incl: local bus services, school contracts
Livery: FirstGroup corporate liveries
Ticket System: Wayfarer 3

L. FURNESS & SONS

THOMPSON HILL, HIGH GREEN,
SHEFFIELD S30 4JU.
Tel: 0114 284 8365.
Ptnrs: G. Furness, A. Furness.
Ch Eng: P. Hayes.
Fleet: 8 - 7 coach 1 minicoach.
Chassis: 3 DAF. 3 Ford. 1 Leyland. 1 Mercedes.
Bodies: 1 Duple. 7 Plaxton.
Ops incl: excursions & tours, private hire.
Livery: Red/Cream.

GEE-VEE TRAVEL
wc | ● | A/c | ✓ | T

173 DONCASTER ROAD,
BARNSLEY S70 1UF
Tel: 01226 287403
Fax: 01246 284783
Owner: G. C. H. Clark
Fleet: 16 - 11 coach, 5 minibus.

Chassis: 11 DAF. 5 Mercedes.
Bodies: 11 Bova. 5 Mercedes.
Ops incl: excursions & tours, private hire, continental tours.

*W GORDON & SONS
& | ● | wc | ¶ | A/c | T

EASTWOOD TRADING ESTATE,
CHESTERTON ROAD, ROTHERHAM
S65 1SU
Tel: 01709 363913
Fax: 01709 838209
Dir: D Gordon
Fleet: 14 coach
Chassis: Dennis. Volvo.
Bodies: Plaxton
Ops incl: excursions & tours, private hire.
Livery: Red/Ivory
Ticket System: Almex.

GRAYS LUXURY TRAVEL ●

30-32 SHEFFIELD ROAD, HOYLAND
COMMON S74 0DQ.
Tel: 01226 743109.
Fax: 01226 749430.
E-mail: stephen@grays-travel.co.uk
Web site: www.grays-travel.co.uk
Man Dir: S. Gray. **Ch Eng:** P. Winter.
Fleet: 10 - 7 coach 1 midicoach, 1 minibus, 1 minicoach.
Chassis: 1 Bova. 6 DAF. 2 Dennis. 1 Toyota.
Bodies: 1 Berkhof. 1 Caetano. 2 Duple. 6 Plaxton.
Ops incl: excursions & tours, private hire, school contracts.
Livery: White/Blue/Yellow.

*HAGUES COACHES
& | ● | wc | ¶ | A/c | T

CHESTERTON ROAD, EASTWOOD
TRADING ESTATE, ROTHERHAM
S65 1SU
Tel: 01709 363913
Fleet: 1 coach
Chassis/Bodies: Volvo. Plaxton.
Ops incl: excursions & tours, private hire.
Livery: Red/Ivory

HEATON'S OF SHEFFIELD
● | wc | ✓ | T

46 CANTERBURY CRESCENT,
FULWOOD, SHEFFIELD S10 3RX
Tel/Fax: 0114 230 9184
Fleet: 10 - 4 coach, 2 midicoach, 4 minicoach.
Chassis: 1 Ford. 4 Mercedes. 5 Setra.
Bodies: 4 Mercedes. 1 Plaxton. 5 Setra.
Ops incl: school contracts, excursions & tours.
Livery: White.

HOGG EUROPEAN COACHES

50 DOVERCOURT ROAD,
SHEFFIELD S2 1UA.
Tel: 0114 272 0895.
Prop: A. Hogg.
Fleet: 1 coach.

Chassis: DAF. **Body:** Moseley.
Ops incl: excursions & tours, continental tours.
Livery: Blue/Blue.

INTEGRATED TRANSPORT GROUP LTD 🚌 🚌 R

See Mass Transit

ISLE COACHES wc

97 HIGH STREET, OWSTON FERRY
DN9 1RL
Tel: 01427 728227.
Props: J. & C. Bannister.
Ch Eng: E. Scotford. **Sec:** Jill Bannister.
Fleet: 12 - 2 double-deck bus, 3 single-deck bus, 6 coach 1 minibus.
Chassis: 2 Daimler. 1 Ford. 4 Leyland. 3 Leyland National. 1 Mercedes. 1 Volvo.
Bodies: 1 Alexander. 1 Duple. 3 Leyland National. 4 Plaxton. 1 Reeve Burgess. 1 Roe. 1 Van Hool.
Ops incl: local bus services, excursions & tours, private hire.
Livery: Blue/Cream.
Ticket System: Almex.

JEMS TRAVEL ●

23 STANWOOD CRESCENT,
STANNINGTON S6 5JA
Tel: 0800 298 1938.
Fax: 0114 233 5329.
E-mail: info@jemstravel.co.uk
Web site: www.jemstravel.co.uk
Prop: Malcolm S Mallender.
Fleet: 2 minibus.
Chassis/bodies: 2 Mercedes
Ops incl: school contracts, excursions & tours, private hire.
Livery: White/Blue.

KINGSMAN SERVICES LTD
wc | ¶ | ✓

YORKSHIRE TERRIER GARAGE,
ROTHER VALLEY WAY, HOLBROOK
INDUSTRIAL ESTATE, SHEFFIELD
S19 5RW.
Tel: 0114 247 0777.
Fax: 0114 248 9085.
Fleetname: Kingsman Travel.
Dirs: W. Baldwin, G. Keeling, T. Dixon.
Ch Eng: J. B. Knight. **Man:** P. Beardsley.
Fleet: 8 - 4 single-deck bus, 4 coach.
Chassis: 4 Leyland. 4 Leyland National.
Bodies: 4 Leyland National. 4 Plaxton.
Ops incl: local bus services, school contracts, excursions & tours, private hire, continental tours.
Livery: White/Yellow/Green.
Ticket System: Wayfarer 3.
(Part of the Yorkshire Traction Group).

*K. M. MOTORS LTD
wc | ● | A/c

WILSON GROVE, LUNDWOOD,
BARNSLEY S71 5JS
Tel: 01226 245564
Fax: 01226 213005
Man Dir: Kith Meynell

A/c	Air conditioning
&	Vehicles suitable for disabled
¶	Coach(es) with galley facilities
wc	Coach(es) with toilet facilities
●	Seat belt-fitted vehicles
R	Recovery service available (not 24 hr)
R24	24hr recovery service
✓	Replacement vehicle available
T	Toilet-drop facilities available
🚌	Vintage vehicle(s) available
🚌	Open top vehicle(s)

South Yorkshire

Fleet: 9 - 8 coach, 1minibus.
Chassis: 2 Bova. 1 Dennis. 1 LDV. 5 Scania.
Ops incl: excursions & tours, continental tours, private hire.
Livery: Gold/Maroon/White.

LADYLINE
47 BERNARD STREET, RAWMARSH S62 5NR.
Tel: 01709 522422.
Fax: 01709 525558.
Owner: C. B. Goodridge.
Fleet: 6 coach.
Chassis: 2 AEC. 3 Bova. 1 DAF.
Bodies: 3 Bova. 1 Caetano. 2 Plaxton.
Ops incl: local bus services, school contracts, excursions & tours, private hire, continental tours.
Livery: Blue/White.

LEON MOTOR SERVICES LTD
FINNINGLEY DN9 3DE.
Tel: 01302 770273.
Fax: 01302 770483.
Traf Man: E. McGuinness.
Fleet: 38 - 19 double-deck bus, 10 single-deck bus, 9 coach.
Chassis: Dennis, Leyland.
Bodies: Alexander, Duple, East Lancs, ECW, Northern Counties, Plaxton, Optare, Van Hool.
Ops incl: local bus services, excursions & tours, express, continental tours.
Livery: Blue/Cream.
Ticket System: Almex, A90
Subsidiary of Mass Transit

*WALTER MARTIN COACHES
57 OLD PARK AVENUE, GREENHILL, SHEFFIELD S8 7DQ
Tel: 0114 274 5004
Props:
Walter Martin, John Martin, June Martin.
Fleet: 3 coach.
Chassis: 3 Volvo.
Ops incl: excursions & tours, private hire.

MARTINS COACHES
58 ARUNDEL ROAD, CHAPELTOWN, SHEFFIELD S35 2RD.
Tel: 0114 246 0111.

MASS TRANSIT
HOUGHTON ROAD, THE NORTH ANSTON TRADING ESTATE, ANSTON, SHEFFIELD S25 4JJ.
Tel: 01909 550480.
Fax: 01909 550486.
E-mail: masseng@aol.com
Man Dir: M. Strafford.
Fleet: 45 double-deck bus.
Chassis: 3 Dennis, 42 Leyland.
Bodies: 3 Alexander. 42 Leyland.
Ops incl: local bus services, school contracts, private hire.
Livery: Red/White/Green.
Ticket System: Wayfarer.
Also offers a complete maintenance/ refurbishment service to bus and coach operators.

MAYFIELD COACHES
172 AUGHTON ROAD, AUGHTON, SHEFFIELD S26 3XE
Tel: 0114 287 2622
Fax: 0114 287 5003
E-mail: info@mayfieldtravel.co.uk
Web site: www.mayfieldstravel.co.uk

MOSLEYS TOURS
LEES HALL ROAD, THORNHILL LEES, DEWSBURY WF12 9EQ.
Tel: 01226 382243.
Fax: 01924 458665.
Dirs: A. Gath-Bragg, J. R. Bragg. **Gen Man**: P. R. Emerton.
Fleet: 3 - 2 coach, 1 midicoach.
Chassis: 1 Dennis, 1 Leyland, 1Volvo.
Ops incl: school contracts, private hire, continental tours, excursions and tours, express
Livery: Grey/Cream.

*NIELSEN TRAVEL SERVICES
23 WINN GROVE, MIDDLEWOOD, SHEFFIELD S6 1UW
Tel/Fax: 0114 234 2961
Recovery: 07803 758063
E-mail: niel@nielsenstravel.co.uk
Web site: www.nielsenstravel.co.uk
Fleet: 2 minibus
Chassis: 1 Iveco. 1 Mercedes.
Ops incl: school contracts, private hire

COLLIN PHILLIPSON
1 HILLCREST, OUSEFLEET, GOOLE DN14 8HP.
Tel: 01405 704394.
Prop: C. Phillipson. **Traf Man**: Miss T. Phillipson.
Fleet: 1 minicoach.
Chassis: Mercedes.
Bodies: Autobus Classique.
Ops incl: excursions & tours, private hire.
Livery: White.

*JOHN POWELL TRAVEL
R24
UNIT 2, 6 HELLABY LANE, HELLABY, ROTHERHAM S66 8HN
Tel: 01709 700900
Fax: 01709 701521
Recovery: 07850 051763
Dirs: John Powell, Pauline Powell, Ian Powell, Jane Powell, John Evans **Man**: Lynn Oliver **Ch Eng**: Ian Slater **Co Acct**: Pat Godber
Fleet: 32 - 10 double-deck bus, 10 single-deck bus, 7 coach, 1 midicoach, 4 minibus.
Chassis: 11 Dennis. 6 Leyland. 6 MCW. 2 Mercedes. 1 Setra. 10 Volvo.
Ops incl: local bus services, school contracts, excursions & tours, private hire, continental tours.
Livery: Blue/Orange/Red/Yellow.
Ticket System: Wayfarer 3

ROEVILLE TOURS LTD
APEX HOUSE, CHURCH LANE, ADWICK-LE-STREET DN6 7DY.
Tel: 01302 330330.
Fax: 01302 330204.
Dirs: W. A. & S. M. Scholey. **Ch Eng**:
N. G. Haxby. **Gen Man**: P. G. Haxby.
Fleet: 7 - 1 double-deck bus, 4 coach 2 minibus. Also nine taxis able to carry disabled passengers.
Chassis: 1 AEC. 1 DAF. 2 Ford. 1 Leyland. 1 Mercedes. 1 Scania.
Bodies: 1 Duple. 1 Mercedes. 3 Plaxton. 1 Reeve Burgess. 1 Roe.
Ops incl: local bus services, excursions & tours, private hire, continental tours.
Livery: Green/Blue/White.
Ticket System: Almex.
Subsidiary of Wilfreda Beehive.

*ROYLES TRAVEL
114 TUNWELL AVENUE, SHEFFIELD S5 9FG.
Tel: 0114 245 4519
Fax: 0114 257 8585
Ptnrs: Rick C Gales, Roy V Gales.
Fleet: 2 coach.
Chassis: 1 DAF. 1 Iveco.
Bodies: 1 Beulas. 1 Van Hool.
Ops incl: excursions & tours.

SLEIGHTS COACHES
87 STATION STREET, SWINTON S64 8PZ.
Tel: 01709 584561.
Fax: 01709 582016.
Owner: J. Sleight.
Fleet: 3 coach.
Chassis: DAF. **Bodies**: Jonckheere.
Ops incl: excursions & tours, private hire, continental tours, school contracts.
Livery: Orange/Cream.

*STAGECOACH SUPERTRAM
NUNNERY DEPOT, WOODBURN ROAD, SHEFFIELD S9 3LS
Tel: 0114 275 9888
Fax: 0114 279 8120
Web site: www.supertram.com
Man Dir: Andy Morris **Gen Man**: Carl Williams
Fleet: 25 tramcars
Chassis/bodies: Siemens
Ops incl: tram services.

*SWIFTS HAPPY DAYS TRAVEL
HAPPY DAYS, THORNE ROAD, BLAXTON DN9 3AX
Tel/Fax: 01302 770999
Ptnrs: Stuart & Joyce Swift
Fleet: 3 coach.
Chassis: 3 DAF.
Bodies: 3 Van Hool.
Ops incl: local bus services, school contracts, excursions and tours, private hire.
Livery: Red/White/Blue
Ticket System: Almex

THOMPSON TRAVEL
THE NEW DEPOT, NAYLOR STREET, PARKGATE S62 6BP.
Tel/Fax: 01709 524985.
Ptnr: T. Thompson.
Fleet: 11 - 1 double-deck bus, 3 single-deck bus, 7 coach.
Chassis: 2 DAF. 7 Leyland. 2 Volvo.
Bodies: 1 Ikarus. 1 Optare. 8 Plaxton. 1 Van Hool.

Ops incl: local bus services, school contracts, excursions & tours, private hire.
Livery: Red/Black/Gold.
Ticket System: Wayfarer 3

*TRAVELGREEN COACHES
CANDA LODGE, HAMPOLE BALK LANE, SKELLOW, DONCASTER DN6 8LF
Tel/Fax: 01302 722227
Owner: David Green
Fleet: double-deck bus, midicoach, minicoach.
Chassis: 1 AEC. 6 Mercedes. 2 Optare. 3 Crest.
Bodies: include: 2 Mercedes. 1 AEC Routemaster
Ops incl: private hire.
Livery: Maroon/White

WILFREDA BEEHIVE
APEX HOUSE, CHURCH LANE, ADWICK-LE-STREET DN6 7AY
Tel: 01302 330330
Fax: 01302 330204
E-mail: sales@wilfreda.co.uk
Web site: www.wilfreda.co.uk
Chmn: W. A. Scholey. **Man Dir/Co sec:** S. M. Scholey. **Dev Man:** P. Haxby.
Com Man N. Haxby. **Ch Eng:** P. Whitaker.
Fleet: 25 - 3 double-deck bus, 12 coach, 5 midibus. 1 minicoach, 4 minibus.
Chassis: 3 Bova. 1 Daimler. 2 Dennis. 2 Ford Transit. 2 Leyland. 2 Mercedes. 6 Optare. 7 Scania.
Bodies: 3 Bova. 2 Duple. 2 East Lancs. 3 Irizar. 2 Mercedes. 4 Plaxton. 6 Optare..
Ops incl: local bus services, school contracts, excursions & tours, private hire, continental tours.
Livery: Blue/White/Yellow.
Ticket System: Wayfarer.

*WILKINSONS TRAVEL
2 REDSCOPE CRESCENT, KIMBERWORTH PARK, ROTHERHAM S61 3LX
Tel: 01709 553403
Fax: 01709 550550
Owner: M. D. Wilkinson.
Fleet: 9 - 2 coach 3 minibus, 4 minicoach.
Chassis: AEC. Volvo.
Bodies: Berkhof. Duple. Ikarus. Jonckheere.
Ops incl: excursions & tours, private hire, continental tours, school contracts.

WILLIAMSONS OF ROTHERHAM
19 VICTORIA STREET, CATCLIFFE S60 5SJ.
Tel: 01709 366856.
Fax: 01709 828241.
Prop: P. Williamson.
Fleet: 3 coach.
Chassis: 1 Bedford. 1 DAF. 1 Leyland.
Bodies: 1 Duple. 1 Leyland. 1 Van Hool.
Ops incl: school contracts, excursions & tours, private hire, continental tours.
Livery: White.

*WILSON'S COACHES
PLOT 5, BANKWOOD LANE INDUSTRIAL ESTATE, ROSSINGTON, DONCASTER DN11 0PS.
Tel/Fax: 01302 866193
Fleet: 4 coach.
Chassis: 4 Volvo.
Bodies: 1 Ikarus. 1 Jonckheere. 2 Van Hool.
Ops incl: excursions & tours, private hire.

YORKSHIRE TERRIER
ROTHER VALLEY WAY, HOLBROOK INDUSTRIAL ESTATE, SHEFFIELD S20 3RW.
Tel: 0114 247 0777 (buses), 0114 248 7588 (coaches).
Fax: 0114 248 9085.
Chmn: F. A. Carter. **Man Dir:** W. Baldwin.
Eng Man: J. B. Knight.
Ops Man: P. Beardsley.
Fleet: 131 – 14 double-deck bus, 110 single-deck bus, 6 coach, 2 midibus.
Chassis: 2 DAF. 35 Dennis. 13 Leyland. 46 Leyland National. 5 MCW. 1 6 Optare. 1 Renault. 27 Volvo.
Bodies: 44 Alexander. 28 East Lancs. 46 Leyland National. 6 MCW. 2 Optare. 6 Plaxton. 1 Reeve Burgess.
Ops incl: local bus services, school contracts.
Livery: Green/White/Yellow.
Ticket System: Wayfarer.
(Part of the Yorkshire Traction Group)

YORKSHIRE TRACTION CO
UPPER SHEFFIELD ROAD, BARNSLEY S70 4PP.
Tel: 01226 202555
Fax: 01226 282313
Fleetname: Yorkshire Traction
Man Dir: Frank Carter
Dirs: N. Cooke, M. F. Carter, P. N. Hill, M. Adamson.
Fleet: 295 - double-deck bus, single-deck bus, coach, double-deck coach, midibus.
Chassis: DAF. Dennis. Duple. Kirn. Leyland. MAN. MCW. Mercedes. Optare. Scania. Volvo. Spartan.
Bodies: Alexander. Duple. ECW. East Lancs. Leyland. MCW. Marshall. Northern Counties. Optare. Plaxton. Reeve Burgess. Van Hool. Wright.
Ops incl: local bus services, school contracts, excursions & tours, private hire, express, continental tours.
Livery: White, Red and Blue.
Ticket System: Wayfarer 3.

STAFFORDSHIRE

ACE TRAVEL
10 BIDDULPH PARK, IRONSTON ROAD, BURNTWOOD WS7 8LG.
Tel: 01543 279068.
Prop: G. E. Elson.
Fleet: 1 midicoach. **Chassis:** Toyota.
Ops incl: excursions & tours, private hire, continental tours, school contracts.

ARRIVA MIDLANDS LTD
DELTA WAY, CANNOCK WS11 3XB.
Tel: 01543 466123.
Fax: 01543 570900.
Web site: www.arriva.co.uk
Fleetname: ARRIVA serving the North Midlands.
Man Dir: N. J. Barker. **Fin Dir:** M. G. Doyle.
Eng Dir: B. J. Baxter. **Com Dir:** K. J. Belfield. **Ops Dir:** J. Morrow.
Fleet: 386 - 19 double-deck bus, 289 single-deck bus, 78 midibus.
Chassis: 38 DAF. 151 Dennis. 44 Leyland. 78 Mercedes. 2 Optare. 24 Scania. 49 Volvo.
Bodies: Alexander. Carlyle. ECW. East Lancs. Leyland. Marshall. Northern Counties. Optare. Plaxton. Reeve Burgess. Wright.
Ops incl: local bus services, school contracts.
Livery: Aquamarine/Cotswold Stone.
Ticket System: Wayfarer 3.

ASTONS OF NEWPORT
See Shropshire.

BAGNALLS COACHES
See Derbyshire.

	Air conditioning		Seat belt-fitted vehicles		Replacement vehicle available
	Vehicles suitable for disabled	R	Recovery service available (not 24 hr)	T	Toilet-drop facilities available
	Coach(es) with galley facilities				Vintage vehicle(s) available
WC	Coach(es) with toilet facilities	R24	24hr recovery service		Open top vehicle(s)

*BAKERS COACHES

SPRING GROVE, CONGLETON ROAD, BIDDULPH ST8 7RQ
Tel: 01782 522101
Fax: 01782 513106
E-mail: sales@bakerbus.co.uk
Web site: www.bakerbus.co.uk
Man Dir: Philip Baker **Ch Eng**: Steve Marsh
Ops Mans: Nigel Whalley, David Machin
Fleet: 34 - 5 single-deck bus, 18 coach, 9 midibus, 2 midicoach.
Chassis: 3 DAF. 2 Dennis. 10 Mercedes. 1 Optare. 2 Scania. 17 Volvo.
Bodies: 4 Caetano. 2 Irizar. 1 Optare. 22 Plaxton. 5 Wright. 1 Europa.
Ops incl: local bus services, school contracts, excursions & tours, private hire, continental tours.
Livery: Duo-green/White
Ticket System: AES/ETM

BENNETTS TRAVEL (CRANBERRY) LTD

CRANBERRY, GATES HEATH ST21 6SQ.
Tel: 01782 791468.
Prop/Gen Man: J. P. McDonnell.
Fleet: 27
Chassis: Bedford. Ford Transit. Leyland. Mercedes.
Bodies: Mercedes. Plaxton.
Ops incl: local bus services, excursions & tours, private hire.
Livery: Blue/White

L F BOWEN LTD

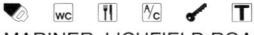

MARINER, LICHFIELD ROAD, TAMWORTH B79 7UL
Tel: 01827 60011
E-mail: coach@bowenstravel.com
Web site: www.bowenstravel.co.uk
Man Dir: W. Concannon. **Ops Man**: Colin Rowe **Fleet Eng**: David Hoy **Traf Man**: Tony York.
Fleet: 35 - 33 coach, 2 minicoach.
Chassis: 8 Bova, 11 MAN, 14 Scania, 2 Toyota.
Bodies: 8 Bova, 2 Caetano, 14 Irizar, 9 Noge, 2 Marco Polo.
Ops incl: excursions & tours, private hire, express, continental tours.
Livery: Silver or Cream

*M BOYDON & SONS

ASHBOURNE ROAD, WINKHILL, LEEK ST13 7PP
Tel: 01538 308255
Fax: 01538 308849
E-mail: lynton@boydons.freeserve.co.uk
Fleetname: Boydons Coaches.
Ptnrs: R M Boydon, G M L Boydon
Man: L Boydon **Ch Eng**: G N Boydon.
Fleet: 16 - 14 coach, 2 midicoach.
Chassis: 2 DAF. 4 Dennis. 7 Leyland. 1 Toyota. 2 Volvo.
Bodies: 1 Caetano. 5 Duple. 1 Jonckheere. 7 Plaxton. 1 Van Hool. 1 other.
Ops incl: school contracts, excursions & tours, private hire.
Livery: Maroon/Gold
Ticket system: Wayfarer

*TERRY BUSHELL TRAVEL

13 DERBY STREET, BURTON-ON-TRENT DE14 2LA
Tel/Fax: 01283 538242.
Prop: T Bushell
Fleet: 4 - 3 coach, 1 minicoach.
Chassis: 2 Volvo. 2 Mercedes.
Bodies: 1 Jonckheere. 1 Neoplan. 1 Van Hool. 1 Mercedes.
Ops incl: excursions & tours, private hire, continental tours.
Livery: Red/Gold/Orange

BUTTER'S COACHES

See Shropshire.

*CHASE COACHES LTD

NO NAME ROAD, CHASETOWN, BURNTWOOD WS7 8FS
Tel: 01543 686937
Fax: 01543 686432
E-mail: andrew@chase-coaches.co.uk
Web site: www.chase-coaches.co.uk
Fleetname: Chase Bus Service
Fleet: 40 - 35 single-deck bus, 4 coach, 1 minibus.
Chassis: DAF. Dennis. Leyland National. Setra. Volvo.
Bodies: Ikarus. Leyland National. Van Hool.
Ops incl: local bus services, private hire.
Livery: Coaches: Blue. Buses: Orange/Brown/White.
Ticket System: Almex

COPELAND TOURS (STOKE-ON-TRENT) LTD

UTTOXETER ROAD, MEIR, STOKE-ON-TRENT ST3 6HE.
Tel: 01782 324466
Fax: 01782 319401
Recovery: 01782 324466
E-mail: mb@copelandtours.co.uk
Web site: www.copelandtours.co.uk
Chmn/Man Dir: J E M Burn **Dir**: Mrs P Burn **Ch Eng**: J C Burn **Co Sec**: J E M Burn
Fleet: 26 - 1 single-deck bus, 22 coach, 2 midibus, 1 midicoach.
Chassis: 1 AEC. 14 DAF. 1 Dennis. 7 Leyland. 1 MAN. 2 Mercedes.
Bodies: 1 Duple. 1 Jonckheere. 1 Marshall. 17 Plaxton. 4 Van Hool. 2 Wadham Stringer.
Ops incl: local bus services, school contracts, excursions & tours, private hire, express, continental tours.
Livery: Blue-Blue/Orange.
Ticket System: Wayfarer.

CRUSADE TRAVEL

PINFOLD LANE, PENKRIDGE ST19 5AS.
Tel/Fax: 01785 714124
Web site: www.crusade-travel.com
Prop/Gen Man: J. P. McDonnell.
Fleet: 6 - 2 coach, 2 midicoach, 2 minibus.
Chassis: 1 Dennis. 1 Ford Transit. 2 Mercedes. 2 Volvo.
Bodies: 2 Plaxton. 1 Reeve Burgess. 1 Van Hool. 2 other.

Ops incl: school contracts, excursions & tours, private hire.

*D & G COACH AND BUS LTD

MOSSFIELD ROAD, OFF ANCHOR ROAD, LONGTON, STOKE ON TRENT ST3 5BW
Tel: 01782 332337
Fax: 01782 337864
E-mail: dreeves@dgbus.co.uk
Man Dir: D Reeves **Ops Dir**: G Henderson
Fleet Eng: M Johnson **Depot Eng**: K Mitchell
Fleet: 49 - 14 coach, 35 midibus.
Chassis: 10 Dennis. 1 Ford. 33 Mercedes. 5 Optare.
Bodies: 7 Alexander. 2 Carlyle. 3 East Lancs. 1 Marshall. 6 Optare. 12 Plaxton. 2 Reeve Burgess. 1 Wadham Stringer. 4 Wright. 11 other.
Ops incl: local bus services, school contracts.
Livery: Cream/Blue
Ticket system: Wayfarer

*D H CARS OF DENSTONE LTD

9 HAWTHORN CLOSE, DENSTONE, UTTOXETER ST14 5HB.
Tel: 01889 590096
Fax: 01889 591888
Dir: D Handley **Sec**: A Williams
Fleet: 3 - 1 coach, 2 minicoach.
Chassis: 1 Leyland. 2 Mercedes.
Bodies: 1 Plaxton. 2 Van Conversions.
Ops incl: private hire
Livery: White with blue/gold stripes

D R M MINIBUS & COACH TRAVEL

43 HIGH STREET, CHASE TERRACE WS7 8LR.
Tel: 01543 410223 (day), 01543 276655 (night).
Fax: 01543 416223.
Prop: D. R. Morgan.
Fleet: 8 - 6 coach, 2 minibus.
Chassis: 3 Bedford. 1 DAF. 1 Ford Transit. 1 Freight Rover. 1 Leyland. 1 Volvo.
Bodies: 3 Duple. 2 Plaxton. 1 LAG.
Ops incl: school contracts, excursions & tours, private hire, express, continental tours.
Livery: White/Silver.

DUNN-LINE GROUP

See Nottinghamshire

FIRST IN POTTERIES

ADDERLEY GREEN GARAGE, DIVIDY ROAD, STOKE-ON-TRENT ST3 0AJ
Tel: 01782 592500
Fax: 01782 592541
Man Dir: Bob Hamilton **Ops Dir**: Christopher Blyth **Fin Dir**: Simon Dorris
Eng Dir: Alf Bligh
See First North West, Greater Manchester

GREEN BUS SERVICE

See Warstone Motors Ltd.

HAPPY DAYS COACHES
[&] [♥] [wc] [¶] [A/c] [R24] [✓] [T]

GREYFRIARS COACH STATION,
GREYFRIARS WAY, STAFFORD
ST16 2SH
Tel: 01785 229797.
Fax: 01785 229791
Recovery: 07973 940555
E-mail:
info@happydayscoaches.co.uk
Web site:
www.happydayscoaches.co.uk
Man Dir: Brian Austin **Dirs**: Neil Austin,
Huw Austin, Richard Austin.
Fleet: 32 - 30 coach, 2 minicoach.
Chassis: Leyland. Mercedes. Scania. Volvo.
Bodies: Plaxton. Van Hool.
Ops incl: excursions & tours, private hire,
express, continental tours, school contracts.
Livery: White with rising sun motif

HOLLINSHEAD COACHES LTD
MEADOWCROFT, WHARF ROAD,
BIDDULPH ST8 6AQ.
Tel/Fax: 01782 512209.
Man Dir: D. Haydon.

*JOSEPHS MINI COACHES
[♥] [A/c]

171 CRACKLEY BANK,
CHESTERTON, NEWCASTLE-
UNDER-LYME ST5 7AB
Tel: 01782 564944
Dir: Joseph Windsor
Fleet: 2 minicoach.
Chassis: 2 Mercedes.
Ops incl: private hire
Livery: White.

*LEONS COACH TRAVEL (STAFFORD) LTD
[&] [wc] [♥] [A/c] [✓]

DOUGLAS HOUSE, TOLLGATE
PARK, BEACONSIDE, STAFFORD
ST16 3EE
Tel: 01785 244575
Fax: 01785 258444
E-mail: info@leons.co.uk
Web site: www.leons.co.uk
Chmn/Man Dir: L H Douglas **Co Sec**:
S Douglas **Dirs**: R L Douglas, A Douglas
Fleet: 29 - 26 coach, 1 midicoach,
1 midibus, 1 minicoach.
Chassis: 3 Bova. 4 Mercedes. 12 Scania.
5 Setra. 5 Volvo.
Bodies: 1 Berkhof. 3 Bova. 1 Duple. 3 Irizar.
4 Mercedes. 2 Plaxton. 5 Setra. 10 Van Hool.
Ops incl: school contracts, excursions &
tours, continental tours, private hire.
Livery: Yellow/Orange/Red

MACPHERSON COACHES LTD
[wc] [¶] [♥] [A/c] [✓]

THE GARAGE, HILL STREET,
DONISTHORPE DE12 7PL
Tel: 01530 270226
Fax: 01530 273669
E-mail: macpherson@coach-tours.co.uk
Web site: www.coach-tours.co.uk/macpherson
(*See Derbyshire*)

*KEN MILLER TRAVEL
See West Midlands

MOORLAND BUSES
WESTON SERVICE STATION,
WESTON COYNEY ST3 6QB.
Tel: 01782 334202.
Prop: A Titterton.
Ops incl: local bus services
Livery: Blue/White.

*PARAGON TRAVEL LTD
[wc] [¶] [♥] [A/c] [✓] [R24]

WESTFIELD, BARNWELL CLOSE,
STRAMSHALL, UTTOXETER
ST14 5AW
Tel: 01889 569899
Fax: 01889 563518.
E-mail: phil@paragontravel.co.uk
Web site: www.paragontravel.co.uk
Dir: Philip Smith
Fleet: 7 - 6 coach, 1 midicoach.
Chassis: 1 Mercedes. 1 Scania. 5 Volvo
Bodies: 1 Alexander. 2 Jonckheere.
4 Van Hool.
Ops incl: local bus services, school
contracts, excursions & tours, continental
tours, private hire.
Livery: White with Blue/Red writing.
Ticket system: Wayfarer

PARRYS INTERNATIONAL TOURS LTD
[wc] [¶] [♥]

LADYWOOD GREEN, CHESLYN
HAY WS6 7QX
Tel: 01922 414576.
Fax: 01922 413416
E-mail: info@parrys-international.co.uk
Web site: www.parrys-international.co.uk
Man Dir: David Parry
Fleet: 11 - 9 coach, 1 midicoach,
1 minicoach.
Chassis: 9 Neoplan. 1 Renault. 1 Toyota.
Bodies: 1 Caetano. 9 Neoplan. 1 Jubilee.
Ops incl: excursions & tours
Livery: Red/Gold

*PLANTS LUXURY TRAVEL
[&] [♥] [¶] [A/c] [✓]

167 TEAN ROAD, CHEADLE
ST10 1LS
Tel: 01538 753561
Fax: 01538 757025
E-mail:
julie.plant@plantsluxurytravel.co.uk
Web site:
www.plantsluxurytravel.co.uk
Ptnrs: T J Plant, M Plant.
Fleet: 7 - 1 coach, 1 midicoach,
5 minicoach.
Chassis: 1 LDV. 6 Mercedes.
Bodies: 1 Optare. 3 Onyx. 2 Crest. 1 Unvi.
Ops incl: private hire, excursions & tours,
continental tours, school contracts.
Livery: Silver with Burgundy/Gold/Mustard
stripes.

F PROCTER & SON LTD
[wc] [♥] [A/c]

DEWSBURY ROAD, FENTON,
STOKE-ON-TRENT ST4 2HS.
Tel: 01782 846031.
Fax: 01782 744732.
Dirs: R Walker, J Walker.
Fleet: 16
Chassis: 2 Bova. 5 DAF. 1 Iveco. 6 Leyland.
2 Scania.
Ops incl: local bus services, school
contracts, excursions & tours, private hire.
Livery: Blue/White
Ticket System: Wayfarer

*ROBIN HOOD TRAVEL LTD
[wc] [¶] [♥] [A/c] [T]

HIGHWAY GARAGE, RUDYARD
ST13 8PS
Tel: 01538 306618
Fax: 01538 306079
Dirs: R T Eyre, M Eyre
Fleet: 14 - 3 single-deck bus, 10 coach,
1 minibus.
Chassis: Bedford. Bova. DAF. Iveco.
Leyland National. Setra. Transbus.
Ops incl: school contracts, excursions &
tours, private hire, continental tours.
Livery: Green

*SHIRE TRAVEL INTERNATIONAL LTD
[wc] [♥] [A/c] [✓]

4:02 CANNOCK ENTERPRISE
CENTRE, WALKERS RISE,
HEDNESFORD WS12 0QU
Tel/Fax: 01543 871605
E-mail: shiretravel@totalise.co.uk
Web site: www.shire-travel.co.uk
Dir: Robert P Garrington **Co Sec**: Anthony Holford
Fleet: 9 - 5 coach, 2 minicoach, 2 minibus.
Chassis: 1 LDV. 3 Leyland. 4 Mercedes.
1 Scania.
Bodies: 1 Leyland. 3 Plaxton. 1 Setra.
1 Van Hool. 3 other
Ops incl: private hire, school contracts,
excursions & tours, continental tours.
Livery: White/Red/Gold with England flag

[A/c]	Air conditioning	[✓]	Replacement vehicle available
[&]	Vehicles suitable for disabled	[T]	Toilet-drop facilities available
[¶]	Coach(es) with galley facilities		Vintage vehicle(s) available
[wc]	Coach(es) with toilet facilities		Open top vehicle(s)
[♥]	Seat belt-fitted vehicles		
[R]	Recovery service available (not 24 hr)		
[R24]	24hr recovery service		

STANWAYS COACHES

THE OLDGASWORKS INDUSTRIAL ESTATE, HARDINGSWOOD ROAD, KIDSGROVE ST7 1EF
Tel: 01782 786232
Fax: 01782 786040
E-mail: stanwaycoaches@yahoo.co.uk
Dirs: A J Fenwick, Mrs J Tankard, P Smith.
Fleet: 12 - 10 coach, 1 minibus, 1 minicoach.
Chassis: includes 8 Volvo.
Bodies: 2 Jonckheere. 3 Plaxton. 3 Van Hool.
Ops incl: excursions & tours, private hire, continental tours, school contracts.

*STODDARDS LTD

GREENHILL GARAGE, LEEK ROAD, CHEADLE ST10 1JF
Tel: 01538 752253
Fax: 01538 750375
Man Dir: Judith Myatt **Vehicle/Ops Dir**: Paul Stoddard **Offica Man**: Julia Smith
Fleet: 4 - 2 single-deck bus, 2 coach.
Chassis: 4 DAF
Bodies: 4 Bova.
Ops incl: excursions & tours, private hire, school contracts.
Livery: Silver/Blue

*SWIFTSURE TRAVEL (BURTON UPON TRENT) LTD

3/4 GUILD STREET, BURTON-UPON-TRENT DE14 1NA.
Tel: 01283 512974
Fax: 01283 516728
E-mail: richard@swiftsure.co.uk
Web site: www.swiftsure.co.uk
Man Dir: R J Hackett **Co Sec**: K Hackett
Dirs: B Kershaw, J Peddle
Fleet: 7 - 4 coach, 1 midicoach, 1 minibus, 1 minicoach.
Chassis: 1 Bova. 3 DAF. 1 Mercedes. 1 Toyota. 1 Mazda.
Bodies: 1 Bova. 1 Caetano. 1 Optare. 3 Van Hool. 1 Howletts.
Ops incl: local bus services, excursions & tours, express, private hire, continental tours, school contracts.
Livery: White/Blue/Green
Ticket system: Setright

WARSTONE MOTORS LTD

THE GARAGE, LANDYWOOD WS6 6AD.
Tel: 01922 414141.
Fleetname: The Green Bus Service.
Dir: G. Martin
Fleet: 25 - 3 double-deck bus, 18 single-deck bus, 4 minibus.

Chassis: Leyland, Mercedes.
Bodies: Alexander. Carlyle. Duple. East Lancs. Massey. Roe.
Ops incl: local bus services.
Livery: Green/Cream.
Ticket System: Wayfarer.

*WINTS COACHES

MONTANA, WETTON ROAD, BUTTERTON ST13 7ST
Tel/Fax: 01538 304370
Props: Andrew Wint, Maxine Wint.
Fleet: 10 - 8 coach, 2 minicoach.
Chassis: 1 DAF. 1 Dennis. 6 Mercedes. 1 Optare. 1 Volvo.
Bodies: 1 Bova. 6 Mercedes. 1 Neoplan. 1 Optare. 1 Plaxton.
Ops incl: school contracts, excursions & tours, private hire, continental tours.

J. P. A. WORTH R24

GOLDEN GREEN GARAGE, LONGNOR SK17 0QP.
Tel: 01298 83583.
Fleet: 2 - 1 midicoach, 1 minicoach.
Chassis: 1 Leyland. 1 Mercedes.
Ops incl: school contracts, private hire.

SUFFOLK

ANGLIAN COACHES LTD

BECCLES BUSINESS PARK, BECCLES NR34 7TH
Tel: 01502 711109
Fax: 01502 711161
E-mail: andrew@angliancoaches.co.uk
Man Dir: David Pursey **Dirs**: Christine Pursey, Andrew Pursey **Ops Man**: Kelvin Searle **Eng Man**: David Marshall
Fleet: 33 - 5 single-deck bus, 8 single-deck coach, 20 minibus.
Chassis: 2 Dennis. 27 Mercedes. 3 Scania. 1 Volvo.
Bodies: 7 Mercedes. 21 Plaxton. 1 Van Hool. 1 Wadham Stringer. 3 Wright.
Ops incl: local bus services, private hire, school contracts.
Livery: Yellow
Ticket System: Wayfarer 3

*AWAYDAYS LTD T/A GEMINI TRAVEL

UNIT 20, STERLING COMPLEX, FARTHING ROAD, IPSWICH IP1 1AP
Tel: 01473 462721
Fax: 01473 462731
E-mail: sales@geminiofipswich.co.uk
Web site: www.geminiofipswich.co.uk
Chmn: Edmund Nicholls **Co Sec**: Keith Nicholls **Tran Man**: Bob Fletcher
Fleet: 10
Chassis: 2 Iveco. 7 Mercedes. 1 LDV.
Bodies: include: 4 Autobus. 3 Plaxton.
Ops incl: local bus services, excursions & tours, private hire, school contracts, continental tours.
Livery: Red/White

IAN BALDRY PUBLIC TRANSPORT SERVICES

43 CAGE LANE, FELIXSTOWE IP11 9BJ
Tel: 01394 672344
E-mail: ic.baldry@talk21.com
Man Dir: Ian Baldry

*BEESTONS COACHES LTD R24

LONG BESSELS, HADLEIGH IP7 5DB
Tel: 01473 823243
Fax: 01473 823608
Recovery:01473 823243
E-mail: info@beestons.co.uk
Web site: www.beestons.co.uk
Man Dir: P R Munson **Co Sec**: S J Munson
Ops Man: T Munson
Fleet: 19 - 7 double-deck bus, 8 single-deck bus, 20 coach, 4 minibus.
Chassis: 1 Bedford. 1 Ford Transit. 7 Leyland. 2 Leyland National. 1 MCW. 3 Mercedes. 1 Neoplan. 2 Optare. 10 Scania. 1 Setra. 8 Volvo.
Bodies: 1 Alexander. 1 Duple. 1 ECW. 3 East Lancs. 1 Leyland. 2 Leyland National. 1 MCW. 1 Neoplan. 2 Optare. 4 Plaxton. 1 Setra. 13 Van Hool. 4 Wright.
Ops incl: local bus services, school contracts, excursions & tours, private hire, continental tours.
Livery: Gold/Black
Ticket System: Wayfarer

*BURTONS COACHES LIMITED

DUDDERY HILL, HAVERHILL CB9 8DR
Tel: 01440 702257
E-mail: hire@burtons-bus.co.uk
Web site: www.burtoncoaches.com
Fleetname: Burtons
Man Dir: Paul J Cooper **Wkshp Man**: Steve Legate **Traf Man**: Duncan Barker
Fleet: 43 - 3 double-deck bus, 5 single-deck bus, 25 coach, 10 midibus.
Chassis: 2 Bova. 15 Dennis. 6 Leyland. 20 Volvo.
Bodies: 2 Alexander. 14 Caetano. 1 East Lancs. 26 Mercedes
Ops incl: local bus services, school contracts, excursions & tours, private hire, express, continental tours.
Livery: Blue/Yellow on white base.
Ticket system: Almex A90

*H C CHAMBERS & SON LTD

KNOWLE HOUSE, BURES CO8 5AB
Tel: 01787 227233
Fax: 01787 227042
E-mail: info@chamberscoaches.co.uk
Web site: www.chamberscoaches.co.uk
Fleet: 26 - 12 double-deck bus, 2 single-

deck bus, 7 coach, 4 midibus, 1 minibus.
Chassis: 3 DAF. 6 Leyland. 2 MAN.
5 Mercedes. 4 Scania. 4 Volvo. 1 Van Hool.
Bodies: 6 Alexander. 4 East Lancs.
2 Jonckheere. 4 Marshall. 1 Mercedes.
2 Northern Counties. 3 Plaxton. 4 Van Hool.
Ops incl: local bus services, school contracts, excursions & tours, private hire, continental tours.
Livery: Red/Cream
Ticket System: Wayfarer

D-WAY TRAVEL
See Norfolk

*FARELINE BUS & COACH SERVICES
OLD ROSES, SYLEHAM ROAD, WINGFIELD IP21 5RF.
Tel: 01379 668151
Prop: Jeff Morss
Fleet: 1 coach
Chassis: Bedford. **Body**: Plaxton
Ops incl: local bus services, school contracts, excursions & tours, private hire.
Livery: Red/White.
Ticket System: Setright Mk 3

*FORGET-ME-NOT (TRAVEL) LTD
R24
CHAPEL ROAD, OTLEY, IPSWICH IP6 9NT
Tel: 01473 890268
Fax: 01473 890748
Fleetname: Soames
E-mail: sales@forgetmenot-travel.co.uk
Web site: www.forgetmenottravel.co.uk
Dirs: A F Soames, M A Soames, A M Soames
Fleet: 17 - 16 coach, 1 midicoach.
Chassis: 1 Mercedes. 16 Volvo.
Bodies: 1 Autobus. 1 Jonckheere. 14 Plaxton. 1 Van Hool.
Ops incl: private hire, school contracts.
Livery: three-tone Blue

*GALLOWAY EUROPEAN COACHLINES
DENTERS HILL, MENDLESHAM IP14 5RR
Tel: 01449 766323
Fax: 01449 766241
Recovery: 01449 766323
E-mail: coach@galloway-travel.co.uk
Dirs: D Cattermole, J Miles, R Stedman, J Stocker, G Calver, E Palfrey, I Webber, A Kemp, R Abbott
Fleet: 35 - 1 double-deck bus, 1 single-deck bus, 27 coach, 4 minicoach, 2 minibus.
Chassis: 1 Bedford. 24 DAF. 1 Dennis. 1 Iveco. 1 Leyland. 6 Mercedes. 1 Scania.
Bodies: 1 Autobus. 1 Beulas. 1 ECW. 3 Ikarus. 2 Optare. 7 Plaxton. 1 UVG. 19 Van Hool.
Ops incl: local bus services, school contracts, excursions & tours, private hire, express, continental tours.
Livery: White
Ticket System: Setright/Wayfarer.

HAPPY WANDERER TOURS
15 HIGH STREET, LEISTON IP16 4EL.
Tel: 01728 830358.
Fax: 01728 833149.
E-mail: sales@happywanderertours.co.uk
Web site: www.happywanderertours.co.uk
Dir: B W Finch. **Man Dir**: P D Scott **Ch Eng**: M W Chappell **Dir/Co Sec**: Mrs A S Chappell.
Fleet: 12 - 11 coach, 1 midicoach.
Chassis: Leyland. MAN. Mercedes. Volvo.
Bodies: Jonckheere. Leyland. Mercedes. Plaxton. Van Hool.
Ops incl: excursions & tours, private hire, continental tours, school contracts.
Livery: Black/White/Orange.

*HARLEQUIN TRAVEL
77 LANERCOST WAY, IPSWICH IP2 9DP.
Tel: 01473 407408
Fax: 01473 407408
E-mail: paul.lewis80@ntlworld.com
Web site: www.harlequin.travel.co.uk
Ptnrs: Paul Lewis
Fleet: 2 midicoach.
Chassis: Mercedes.
Ops incl: school contracts, private hire
Livery: Maroon/White

IPSWICH BUSES LTD
7 CONSTANTINE ROAD, IPSWICH IP1 2DL.
Tel: 01473 232600.
Fax: 01473 232062.
E-mail: info@ipswichbuses.co.uk
Web site: www.ipswichbuses.co.uk
Fleetname: Ipswich Buses
Fleet: 92 - 20 double-deck bus, 1 open-top bus, 54 single-deck bus, 16 midibus.
Chassis: 5 Bristol. 12 DAF. 29 Dennis. 7 Leyland. 35 Optare. 3 Volvo.
Bodies: 5 Alexander. 39 East Lancs. 46 Optare. 1 Roe.
Ops incl: local bus services, school contracts, excursions & tours, private hire.
Livery: Green/Cream/White
Ticket System: Wayfarer TGX150

*LAMBERT'S COACHES (BECCLES) LTD
UNIT 4A, MOOR BUSINESS PARK, BECCLES NR34 7TQ
Tel: 01502 717579
Fax: 01502 711209
E-mail: enquiries@lambertscoaches.co.uk
Web site: www.lambertscoaches.co.uk
Man Dir: D M Reade
Fleet: 10 coach.
Chassis: 2 Bedford. 4 DAF. 1 Leyland. 3 Volvo.
Bodies: 7 Plaxton. 3 Van Hool.
Ops incl: private hire, school contracts.
Livery: Blue/White

*MAX SERVICES LTD
155 OULTON ROAD, LOWESTOFT NR32 4QR
Tel: 01502 516409
Fax: 01502 589302
E-mail: coachguide@btinternet.com
Dirs: Tony Porter Pat Lennox
Fleet: 3
Chassis: 1 Bova 1 DAF. 1 Dennis.
Bodies: 1 Bova. 2 Plaxton.
Ops incl: school contracts, excursions & tours, private hire, continental tours.

*MIL-KEN TRAVEL LTD
GRASSMERE, BURY ROAD, KENTFORD, NEWMARKET CB8 7PZ
Tel: 01638 750201
Fax: 01638 750439
E-mail: milken@btconnect.com
Man: Mark Rogers **Traf Man**: Dan Rogers
Fleet: 40 - 38 coach, 2 minibus.
Chassis: 6 Bedford. 10 DAF. 6 Dennis. 2 LDV. 16 Volvo.
Bodies: 3 Berkhof. 8 Duple. 3 Jonckheere. 21 Plaxton. 1 Willowbrook. 4 other.
Ops incl: excursions & tours, private hire, continental tours, school contracts.

MINIBUS & COACH HIRE
LINGS FARM, BLACKSMITHS LANE, FORWARD GREEN, EARL STONHAM IP14 5ET.
Tel: 01449 711117.
Fax: 01449 711977.
Owner: Mrs L. J. Eustace.
Fleet: 11 - 3 coach, 8 minibus.
Chassis: 3 Bedford, 1 Iveco. 6 LDV. 1 Nissan.
Bodies: Plaxton.
Ops incl: local bus services, school contracts, excursions & tours, private hire.

*MULLEYS MOTORWAYS LTD
STOW ROAD, IXWORTH, BURY ST EDMUNDS IP31 2JB.
Tel: 01359 230234
Fax: 01359 232451
E-mail: enquiries@mulleys.co.uk
Web site: www.mulleys.co.uk
Dir/Co Sec: Jayne D Munson **Dir**: David J Munson
Fleet: 39 - 4 double-deck bus, 26 coach, 2 double-deck coach, 3 midicoach, 4 midibus.
Chassis: 4 Iveco. 6 Leyland. 4 Mercedes. 7 Scania. 4 Setra. 2 Volvo.
Bodies: 1 Alexander. 3 Beulas. 2 Duple. 4 ECW. 11 Jonckheere. 11 Plaxton. 4 Setra. 6 Van Hool. 2 Indcar. 1 Euro Coach.

A/c	Air conditioning
🦽	Vehicles suitable for disabled
🍳	Coach(es) with galley facilities
WC	Coach(es) with toilet facilities
💺	Seat belt-fitted vehicles
R	Recovery service available (not 24 hr)
R24	24hr recovery service
✓	Replacement vehicle available
T	Toilet-drop facilities available
🚌	Vintage vehicle(s) available
🚐	Open top vehicle(s)

Suffolk

Ops incl: local bus services, school contracts, excursions & tours, private hire.
Livery: Orange/Silver.
Ticket System: Wayfarer.

B R SHREEVE & SONS LTD/BELLE COACHES

RIVERSIDE ROAD, LOWESTOFT NR33 0TU.
Tel: 01502 564384.
Fax: 01502 532009.
E-mail: robert@bellecoaches.co.uk
Web site: www.bellecoaches.co.uk
Fleetname: Belle Coaches.
Joint Man Dirs: K J Shreeve, R B Shreeve.
Dir: J E Shreeve **Chmn**: E B Shreeve
Co Sec: Mrs S Speed **Tran Man**: A White
Tours Man: D Dickinson

Fleet: 44 - 38 coach, 4 midicoach, 2 minicoach.
Chassis: 10 Bedford. 5 DAF. 3 Mercedes. 13 Scania. 3 Setra. 1 Toyota. 7 Volvo. 1 VW.
Bodies: 3 Berkhof. 1 Caetano. 6 Duple. 14 Plaxton. 3 Setra. 12 Van Hool. 1 VW. 1 Olympus. 2 Euro Coachbuilders.
Ops incl: local bus services, school contracts, excursions & tours, private hire, continental tours.
Livery: Blue.

SQUIRRELL'S COACHES

OLD MILL GARAGE, HITCHAM, IPSWICH IP7 7NF.
Tel/Fax: 01449 740582.
Dir: Richard Squirrell.
Fleet: 7 - 5 coach, 2 midicoach.
Chassis: 2 Leyland. 1 MAN. 2 Mercedes.

2 Volvo.
Bodies: 1 Duple. 1 Mercedes. 2 Plaxton. 1 Reeve Burgess. 4 Van Hool.
Ops incl: local bus services, school contracts, private hire.
Livery: Silver/Blue.
Ticket System: Setright.

THOMPSON'S REMOVALS & COACH HIRE

DORMICK HOUSE, NEW STREET, FRAMLINGHAM IP13 9RF.
Tel: 01728 723403.
Prop: M. A. Rogers, D. J. Rogers (**Sec**).
Fleet: 3 coach.
Chassis: 1 Ford. 2 Volvo.
Bodies: 1 Duple. 2 Jonckheere.
Ops incl: local bus services, excursions & tours, private hire, continental tours.
Livery: Blue/White.

SURREY

*A & D COACHES

14 COLBORNE WAY, WORCESTER PARK KT4 8NG.
Tel: 020 8337 6912
Recovery: 07885 025950
E-mail: dennis@griffithsd4.fsnet.co.uk
Prop: Dennis Griffiths
Fleet: 3 - 1 midicoach, 2 minibus.
Chassis/bodies: 2 LDV. 1 Mercedes.
Ops incl: private hire

ARRIVA GUILDFORD & WEST SURREY

FRIARY BUS STATION, GUILDFORD GU1 4YP
Tel: 01483 505693
Fleetname: Arriva serving Guildford & West Surrey.
Acting Man Dir: Kevin Hawkins
Eng Dir: I. Tarran. **Fin Dir**: Ms E. Limm.
Gen Man: R. Thornton.
Fleet: 59 - 3 double-deck bus, 56 single-deck bus.
Chassis: 29 DAF. 39 Dennis.
Bodies: East Lancs. Plaxton. Wright.
Ops incl: local bus services.
Livery: Aquamarine and Stone.
Ticket System: Wayfarer 3

BANSTEAD COACHES LTD

1 SHRUBLAND ROAD, BANSTEAD SM7 2ES.
Tel: 01737 354322.
Fax: 01737 371090.
E-mail: sales@bansteadcoaches.co.uk
Web site: www.bansteadcoaches.co.uk
Chairm: Dudley Haynes. **Dir**: Christine Haynes. **Dir**: Matthew Haynes.
Fleet: 15 coach.
Chassis: 3 Bedford. 12 Dennis.
Bodies: 4 Berkhof. 11 Plaxton.
Ops incl: school contracts, excursions and tours, continental tours, private hire.
Livery: Pink/White.

*CALL-A-COACH

CAPRI HOUSE, WALTON-ON-THAMES KT12 2LY

Tel: 01932 223838
Fax: 01932 269109
Prop: Arthur Freakes
Fleet: 9 - 1 coach, 1 midicoach, 1 minibus, 6 minicoach.
Chassis/bodies: 1 Bova. 7 LDV. 1 Mercedes.
Ops incl: school contracts, excursions & tours, private hire.

CARS INTERNATIONAL A. C. T.

4 WYCHWOOD CLOSE, ASH GU12 6RA.
Tel: 01252 328774.
Fax: 01252 332337.
Prop: G. Hawkins. **Traf Man**: J. Baker.
Fleet: 3 coach.
Chassis: 1 Leyland. 2 Setra.
Bodies: 1 Leyland, 2 Setra.
Ops incl: excursions & tours, private hire, continental tours, school contracts.

CHEAM COACHES

11 FREDERICK CLOSE, CHEAM SM1 2HY.
Tel: 01372 742527.
Fax: 01372 742528.
Props: M Mower, L Cyr-Mower.
Fleet: 5 - 1 coach, 1 midicoach, 3 minibus.
Chassis: 3 Mercedes. 2 Volvo.
Bodies: 3 Mercedes. 2 Plaxton.
Ops incl: private hire, school contracts.

*CHIVERS COACHES LTD

13A ROSS PARADE, WALLINGTON SM6 8QG
Tel: 020 8647 6648
Fax: 020 8647 6649
E-mail: chivers@aol.com
Dirs: Mrs Lynne Lucas, Miss Melanie Chivers, Mrs Pam Chivers
Fleet: 4 - 2 coach, 1 midicoach, 1 minibus.
Chassis: 1 DAF. 1 LDV. 1 Mercedes. 1 Volvo.
Bodies: include: 1 Plaxton. 1 Van Hool. 1 Robin Hood.

Ops incl: private hire, school contracts.
Livery: Blue and White.

COUNTRYLINER COACH HIRE LTD

GB HOUSE, WESTFIELD ROAD, GUILDFORD GU1 1RR
Tel: 01483 506919
Fax: 01483 306395
E-mail: info@countryliner-coaches.com
Web site: www.countryliner-coaches.co.uk
Dirs: R Hodgetts, R Belcher, C Brands
Gen Man: N Natcher
Ops Mans: M Lambley, M Chadwick
Fleet: 34 - 4 double-deck bus, 15 single-deck bus, 12 coach, 2 minibus, 1 minicoach.
Chassis: 1 Bristol. 4 DAF. 14 Dennis. 8 Leyland. 1 MCW. 1 Mercedes. 1 Optare. 1 Setra. 1 Toyota. 1 Volvo.
Bodies: 1 Alexander. 3 Caetano. 4 ECW. 1 Ikarus. 1 Leyland. 1 MCW. 1 Optare. 16 Plaxton. 1 Setra. 3 Van Hool. 2 other.
Ops incl: local bus services, school contracts, excursions & tours, private hire.
Livery: Green/White.
Ticket System: Wayfarer/Almex.

CRUISERS LTD

UNIT M, KINGSFIELD BUSINESS CENTRE, REDHILL RH1 4DP.
Tel: 01737 770036.
Fax: 01737 770046.
Web site: www.cruisersltd.co.uk
Fleet: 30 - coach, midicoach, minibus.
Chassis: Citroen, Ford Transit, Iveco, LDV, Mercedes, Renault.
Bodies: Mellor, Optare, Plaxton
Ops incl: local bus services, school contracts, private hire.
Livery: multi metallic.
Ticket System: Almex.

*EPSOM COACHES GROUP

BLENHEIM ROAD, EPSOM
KT19 9AF
Tel: 01372 731700
Fax: 01372 731740
E-mail: sales@epsomcoaches.com
Web site: www.epsomcoaches.com
Fleetname: Epsom Coaches, Quality Line
Chman: R B Richmond **Man Dir**: A J Richmond **Comm Dir**: S R Whiteway
Bus Services Man: G Wernham **Coach Services Man**: S Green **Vehicle Services Man**: I Golder
Fleet: 83 - 53 single-deck bus, 21 coach, 9 minibus.
Chassis: 26 Dennis. 2 Iveco. 11 Mercedes. 21 Optare. 9 Setra. 5 Volvo. 9 Volkswagen.
Bodies: 13 Alexander. 5 Berkhof. 5 Jonckheere. 7 Mercedes. 21 Optare. 8 Plaxton. 9 Setra. 7 Transbus. 9 VW Caravelle.
Ops incl: local bus services, school contracts, excursions & tours, private hire, express, continental tours.
Livery: Coach: Red/Cream. Bus: Red

FARNHAM COACHES

ODIHAM ROAD, EWSHOT,
FARNHAM GU10 5AE.
Tel/Fax: 01252 724010.
Dir: B. Newman. **Gen Man**: K. L. Pullen.
Dir: G. Button.
Fleet: 14 - 13 coach, 1 midicoach.
Chassis: 4 MAN. 2 Mercedes. 4 Setra. 4 Volvo.
Bodies: 1 Optare. 4 Plaxton. 4 Setra. 2 EOS, 2 Neoplan, 1 Mercedes.
Ops incl: excursions & tours, private hire, school contracts, continental tours.
Livery: Purple/White.
(*Owned by Safeguard Coaches, Guildford*)

FERNLEAF COACHES

7 MARTIN GROVE, MORDEN
SM4 5AJ.
Tel: 020 8715 1839.
Fax: 020 8543 0722.
Owners: K. J. Leigh, L. M. Leigh.
Fleet: 4 - 2 coach, 2 minicoach.
Ops incl: excursions & tours, private hire, continental tours.

G J TRAVEL LTD

BARGE LODGE, BROX ROAD,
OTTERSHAW KT16 0LG
Tel: 01932 872282.
Fax: 01932 873197.
Dirs: S. Adams, Mrs B. Adams.
Fleet: 6 - 2 minibus, 4 midicoach.
Chassis: 1 LDV. 5 Mercedes.
Bodies: 1 Leyland. 2 Mercedes. 3 Optare.
Ops incl: excursions & tours, private hire, school contracts, continental tours.
Livery: Red/Blue

GALES COACHES LTD

SPRINGFARM ROAD,
CAMELSDALE, HASLEMERE
GU27 3RH.
Tel: 01428 643837.
Fax: 01428 658809.
Dir: J. P. Pirard. **Co Sec**: R. L. Pirard.
Fleet: 5 - 3 coach, 2 midicoach.
Chassis: 1 Mercedes. 1 Toyota. 3 Volvo.
Bodies: 1 Caetano. 3 Jonckheere. 1 Plaxton.
Ops incl: private hire, school contracts.
Livery: White/Red/Gold.

HARDINGS COACHES

WELLHOUSE ROAD,
BETCHWORTH RH3 7HH.
Tel: 01737 842103.
Fax: 01737 842831.
Owner: D J Harding
Fleet: 12 - 7 coach, 2 midicoach. 3 minicoach.
Chassis: 4 Mercedes. 1 Toyota. 7 Volvo.
Bodies: 2 Berkhof. 2 Autobus. 1 Caetano. 2 Jonckheere. 2 Optare. 3 Plaxton.
Ops incl: private hire, school contracts, excursions & tours.
Livery: Red/Orange on White

HARWOOD COACHES

51 ELLESMERE ROAD,
WEYBRIDGE KT13 0HW.
Tel: 01932 842073, 227272.
Prop: R. W. Harwood, G. A. Harwood.
Fleet: 5 coach.
Chassis: 2 Bedford. 3 Volvo.
Bodies: 2 Duple. 3 Van Hool.
Ops incl: private hire.
Livery: Beige/Red/Brown.

HI-DECK CRUISERS

COULSDON. *See London.*

HILLS

129 BURWOOD ROAD, HERSHAM
KT12 4AN
Tel: 01932 254795
Fax: 01932 222671
Fleet: 4 - 3 coach, 1 minicoach.
Chassis: 1 Toyota. 3 Volvo.
Ops incl: school contracts, excursions & tours, private hire, continental tours.
Livery: White/Red

HODGE'S COACHES (SANDHURST) LTD

See Berkshire.

K-VALLEY MINI-COACHES

WOODPECKERS, CARLTON ROAD,
WOKING GU21 4HE.
Tel: 01483 769462.
Mobile: 0771 368 1207.
Fax: 01483 769462.
Prop: F. E. Trotman.
Fleet: 1 minibus.
Chassis/body: DAF.
Ops incl:

M&E COACHES

11 VAUX CRESCENT, HERSHAM
KT12 4HE.
Tel: 01932 244664.
Prop/Gen Man: M. W. Oram.
Sec: Mrs A. E. Oram.
Fleet: 3 coach.
Chassis: 1 MAN. 2 Mercedes.
Ops incl: school contracts, excursions & tours, private hire.
Livery: Blue/White.

*MEMORY LANE VINTAGE OMNIBUS SERVICES

See Berkshire

METROBUS

See Kent

MITCHAM BELLE

See London.

PICKERING COACHES

R24

12 HAYSBRIDGE COTTAGES,
WHITE WOOD LANE, SOUTH
GODSTONE RH9 8JN.
Tel/Fax: 01342 843731.
Props: R. Pickering, Ms D. Pickering.
Fleet: 5 coach.
Chassis: Volvo.
Bodies: 2 Duple. 1 Jonckheere. 2 Plaxton.
Ops incl: private hire, school contracts.

RANGER TRAVEL

PO BOX 805, SOUTH CROYDON
CR8 2XY.
Tel: 020 8673 0077.
Fleet: 5 - 3 coach, 1 midibus, 1 minibus.
Chassis: 1 Bedford. 1 DAF. 1 LDV. 1 MCW. 1 Volvo.
Bodies: 1 Leicester. 1 MCW. 2 Plaxton. 1 Van Hool.
Ops incl: private hire.
Livery: White.

REDWOOD TRAVEL

UNIT 8, MARTLANDS INDUSTRIAL
ESTATE, SMARTS HEATH LANE,
MAYFORD GU22 0RQ.
Tel: 01483 235333.
Prop: Sean Brady
Fleet: 10 - 1 single-deck bus, 7 coach, 2 minibus.
Chassis: 1 Bedford. 2 Dennis. 1 MCW. 2 Mercedes. 4 Setra.
Bodies: 1 Duple. 2 Mercedes. 1 MCW. 1 Neoplan. 1 Plaxton. 4 Setra.
Ops incl: excursions & tours, private hire, continental tours, school contracts.
Livery: White.

A/c	Air conditioning
	Vehicles suitable for disabled
	Coach(es) with galley facilities
wc	Coach(es) with toilet facilities
	Seat belt-fitted vehicles
R	Recovery service available (not 24 hr)
R24	24hr recovery service
	Replacement vehicle available
T	Toilet-drop facilities available
	Vintage vehicle(s) available
	Open top vehicle(s)

SAFEGUARD COACHES

RIDGEMOUNT GARAGE,
GUILDFORD PARK ROAD,
GUILDFORD GU2 5TH
Tel: 01483 561103
Fax: 01483 455865
E-mail:
enquiries@safeguardcoaches.co.uk
Web site:
www.safeguardcoaches.co.uk
Man Dir: Mark Newman
Fleet: 39 - includes single-deck bus, coach, double-deck coach, midicoach.
Livery: Red/White.
Ops incl: local bus services, private hire, excursions & tours.

*SKINNERS OF OXTED

15 BARROW GREEN ROAD, OXTED
RH8 0NJ
Tel: 01883 713613
Fax: 01883 730079
E-mail: skinners@skinners.net
Web site: www.skinners.net
Ptnrs: Stephen Skinner, Debora Skinner.
Fleet: 16 - 13 coach, 1 midicoach, 2 minicoach.
Chassis: 1 Bedford. 2 Dennis. 1 MCW. 2 Mercedes. 1 Neoplan. 7 Setra. 2 Volvo.
Bodies: 2 Duple. 1 MCW. 1 Neoplan. 3 Plaxton. 7 Setra. 1 other.
Ops incl: excursions & tours, private hire, school contracts, continental tours.

STAGECOACH HANTS & SURREY

See Hampshire

SUNRAY TRAVEL LTD

70 ASHLEY RD, EPSOM KT18 5BN
Tel: 01372 740400/07778 120298
Fax: 01372 800778
Web site: www.sunraytravel.co.uk
Dir: Noel Millier **Traf Man**: Piers Millier
Fleet: 7 coach
Chassis: 3 Dennis. 1 Leyland. 3 Volvo.
Bodies: include: 2 Carlyle. 4 Plaxton
Ops incl: local bus services, school contracts, excursions & tours, private hire, continental tours.
Livery: Blue with yellow/orange/red sun rays

SURELINE COACHES

UNIT 8, MARTLANDS INDUSTRIAL
ESTATE, SMARTS HEATH LANE,
MAYFORD GU22 0RQ.
Tel/Fax: 01483 234649
Web site: www.surelinecoaches.com
E-mail: surelinecoaches@btclick.com
Prop: Les Heaton **Ops Man**: D Goderham
Fleet: 9 - 6 coach, 3 midicoach.
Chassis: 6 Bova. 3 Mercedes.

Bodies: 6 Bova. 3 Plaxton.
Ops incl: excursions & tours, private hire, continental tours, school contracts.
Livery: White

SURREY & HANTS TRAVEL

See Hampshire.

*SUTTON COMMUNITY TRANSPORT

HALLMEAD DAY CENTRE, ANTON
CRESCENT, COLLINGWOOD ROAD,
SUTTON SM1 2NT
Tel: 020 8644 6001
Fax: 020 8644 2247
Ch Exec: Turner Duff **Ops Man**: Malcolm Sailing
Fleet: 17 minibus.
Chassis/bodies: 1 Fiat. 5 Ford Transit. 4 VW. 5 LDV. 1 Mercedes.
Ops incl: local bus services, school contracts, excursions & tours, private hire.
Livery: White with purple logo

*TELLINGS GOLDEN MILLER BUSES LTD

THE OLD TRAM DEPOT, STANLEY
ROAD, TWICKENHAM TW2 5NP
Tel: 020 8755 7050
Fax: 020 8977 3340
E-mail: sales@tellings.co.uk
Web site: www.tellingsgoldenmiller.co.uk
Ch Exec: Stephen Telling **Dir Buses**: Bill Hiron **Eng Man**: Ian Foster **Ops Dir Group**: Richard Telling **Fin Dir**: Bob Hodgetts
Fleet: 181 single-deck bus
Chassis: 141 Dennis. 2 Freight Rover. 18 Mercedes. 7 Volvo.
Bodies: 7 Alexander. 44 Caetano. 13 Optare. 112 Plaxton.
Ops incl: local bus services, school contracts.
Livery: White/Blue/Yellow/Red
Ticket System: Almex

*TELLINGS GOLDEN MILLER COACHES LTD

THE OLD TRAM DEPOT, STANLEY
ROAD, TWICKENHAM TW2 5NP
Tel: 020 8755 7050
Fax: 020 8977 1926
E-mail: sales@tellings.co.uk
Web site: www.tellingsgoldenmiller.co.uk
Ch Exec: Stephen Telling **Ops Dir Coaches**: Paul Cowell **Eng Man**: Ian Foster **Ops Dir Group**: Richard Telling **Fin Dir**: Bob Hodgetts
Fleet: 35 - 34 coach, 1 minicoach
Chassis: 2 Iveco. 39 Volvo.
Bodies: includes 32 Plaxton.

Ops incl: school contracts, excursions & tours, private hire, express, continental tours.
Livery: White/Blue/Yellow

*EDWARD THOMAS & SON

442 CHESSINGTON ROAD, WEST
EWELL KT19 9EJ
Tel: 020 8397 4276
Fax: 020 8397 5276
Prop: I E Thomas **Ch Eng**: E Seager
Sec: Mrs S Gray **Ops Man**: N Seager
Fleet: 26 - 4 double-deck bus, 2 single-deck bus, 20 coach
Chassis: 26 Leyland, 6 Volvo.
Bodies: 4 East Lancs. 20 Plaxton. 2 Van Hool.
Ops incl: local bus services, school contracts, private hire.

TRINGWOOD TRAVEL

TRINGWOOD, 28 NEW ZEALAND
AVENUE, WALTON ON THAMES
KT12 1PT
Tel: 01932 242900.
Fax: 01932 252829.
E-mail: tringwood.travel@virgin.net
Props: Jean Bell
Fleet: 1 minicoach.
Chassis: 1 Mercedes
Ops incl: excursions & tours, private hire.
Livery: White/Green/Gold.

TRUEMANS TRAVEL

See Hampshire.

W & H COMMERCIALS T/A W & H MOTORS

See West Sussex.

*WESTERHAM COACHES

15 BARROW GREEN ROAD, OXTED
RH8 0NJ
Tel: 01883 713613
Fax: 01883 730079.
Ptnrs: Stephen Skinner, Deborah Skinner.
Fleet: 16 - 13 coach, 1 midicoach, 2 minicoach.
Chassis: 1 Bedford. 3 Dennis. 1 MCW. 2 Mercedes. 1 Neoplan. 7 Setra. 2 Volvo.
Bodies: 2 Duple. 1 MCW. 1 Neoplan. 3 Plaxton. 1 Reeve Burgess. 7 Setra. 1 other.
Ops incl: excursions & tours, private hire, school contracts, continental tours.

WILTAX

CANAL BRIDGE INDUSTRIAL
ESTATE, BYFLEET ROAD, NEW
HAW, ADDLESTONE KT15 3JE
Tran Man: Chris Sullivan
Fleet: 3 - double-deck bus.
Chassis: MCW
Bodies: MCW
Livery: Orange/Yellow

TYNE & WEAR

*A & J COACHES OF WASHINGTON CO LTD

6 SKIRLAW CLOSE, GLEBE VILLAGE, WASHINGTON NE38 7RE
Tel/Fax: 0191 417 2564
E-mail: jean@ajcoaches.fsnet.co.uk
Dir: Ian Ashman **Co Sec**: Jean Ashman
Fleet: 1 coach
Chassis: 1 Volvo
Bodies: 1 Duple
Ops incl: school contracts, private hire.
Livery: White/Blue

*A-LINE COACHES

UNIT 1, PELAW INDUSTRIAL ESTATE, GATESHEAD NE10 0UW
Tel/Fax: 0191 495 2424
E-mail: les@a-linecoaches.co.uk
Web site: www.a-linecoaches.co.uk
Ptnrs: David C Annis, Leslie B Annis **Sec**: S Reay **Eng**: E Weightman
Fleet: 8 - 1 double-deck bus, 1 single-deck bus, 2 coach, 4 midibus.
Chassis: 1 DAF. 3 Dennis. 1 Leyland. 1 MCW. 2 Mercedes.
Bodies: 1 Duple. 1 Leyland. 1 MCW. 1 Plaxton. 2 Reeve Burgess. 1 Van Hool. 1 Wright.
Ops incl: local bus services, school contracts, excursions & tours, private hire, continental tours.
Livery: Red/White
Ticket System: Datafare2000

ALTONA COACH SERVICES & TRAVEL CONSULTANT

UNIT K4, SKILLION BUSINESS CENTRE, GREEN LANE, FELLING NE10 0QW.
Tel: 0191 469 2193.
Fax: 0191 469 3025.
Fleetname: Altona Travel.
Prop: A. C. Hunter. **Ops Man**: A. I. Hunter.
Office Man: R. Dudding.
Fleet: 9 - 5 coach, 2 midicoach, 2 minicoach.
Chassis: 1 DAF. 1 Dennis. 2 Mercedes. 1 Toyota. 3 Volvo.
Bodies: 2 Caetano. 2 Duple. 1 LAG. 2 Plaxton. 1 Robin Hood. 1 Bus Craft Impala.
Ops incl: excursions & tours, private hire, continental tours.
Livery: Two tone Blue and Orange.

AMBERLINE

EARSDON ROAD, WEST MONKSEATON NE25 9SX
Tel/Fax: 0191 253 2286.
Prop: D. Boyd.
Fleet: 12 - 8 minibus, 4 minibus.
Chassis: 2 Ford Transit. 3 Freight Rover. 6 Iveco. 1 Mercedes.

Ops incl: local bus services, school contracts, private hire.
Livery: Red/Orange.
Ticket System: Wayfarer Saver.

*ARRIVA NORTH EAST

ADMIRAL WAY, DOXFORD INTERNATIONAL BUSINESS PARK, SUNDERLAND SR3 3XP
Tel: 0191 520 4200
Fax: 0191 520 4222
Web site: www.arriva.co.uk
Man Dir: S. L. Noble **Eng Dir**: J Greaves
Fin Dir: Mrs S Richardson **Ops Dir**: I McInroy **Comm Dir**: Mrs L Esnouf
Fleet: 650 - 117 double-deck bus, 326 single-deck bus, 8 coach, 199 minibus.
Chassis: DAF. Dennis. Iveco. Leyland. MCW. MAN. Mercedes. Optare. Scania. Transbus. Volvo.
Bodies: Alexander. ECW. East Lancs. Ikarus. Leyland. MCW. Mercedes. Northern Counties. Optare. Plaxton. Transbus. Van Hool. Wright.
Ops incl: local bus services, school contracts, private hire, express.
Livery: Aquamarine/Stone
Ticket System: Wayfarer 3

ASHLEY COACHES PSV

1 THORNLEY VIEW, ROWLANDS GILL NE39 1PL.
Tel: 01207 543118.
Owner: D. Murphy.
Co Sec: Mrs B. Stephenson.
Fleet: 8 - 2 coach, 2 minibus, 2 midicoach, 2 minibus.
Ops incl: local bus services, school contracts, private hire.
Livery: Blue.

*CAMPBELL'S COACHES

37 MORPETH AVENUE, SOUTH SHIELDS NE34 0SF
Tel: 0191 455 4295
Prop: Gordon Campbell
Fleet: 1 coach
Chassis: 1 Bedford
Body: 1 Duple
Ops incl: excursions & tours, private hire.

COACHLINERS OF TYNESIDE

16 BRANDLING COURT, SOUTH SHIELDS NE34 8PA
Tel/Fax: 0191 427 1515
Fleet: 2 - 1 midicoach, 1 minicoach
Chassis: 2 Mercedes.
Bodies: 2 Plaxton.
Ops incl: school contracts, excursions & tours, private hire.
Livery: White with red stripes

*HENRY COOPER

LANE END GARAGE, ANNITSFORD NE23 7BD
Tel: 0191 250 0260
Fax: 0191 250 1820
Ptnrs: Graham & Lily Greaves
Fleet: 8 coach
Chassis: 1 Leyland. 7 Volvo.
Ops incl: school contracts, private hire.

DERWENT COACHES LTD

MORRISON ROAD, ANNFIELD PLAIN DH9 7RX
Tel: 0191 488 7248.
Fax: 01207 281333.
E-mail: derwentc@aol.com
Man Dir: I. Shipley. **Dir**: A. Fox.
Comm Exec: D. Allan.
Garage Foreman: B. Thurgood.
Fleet: 10 coach.
Chassis: Volvo.
Bodies: 5 Plaxton. 5 Van Hool.
Ops incl: local bus services, school contracts, excursions & tours, private hire, express, continental tours.
Livery: White, Red & Blue.
Ticket System: Almex.

ERB SERVICES LTD

HANNINGTON PLACE, BYKER, NEWCASTLE UPON TYNE NE6 1JU
Tel: 0191 224 0002
Fax: 0191 276 7177
Prop: E Brown
Fleet: 15 minicoach
Chassis: 2 Ford Transit. 1 Leyland. 11 Mercedes. 1 Volvo
Ops incl: school contracts, excursions & tours, private hire

*GO NORTH EAST

117 QUEEN STREET, GATESHEAD NE8 2UA.
Tel: 0191 420 5050
Fax: 0191 420 0225
E-mail: customerservices@gonortheast.co.uk
Web site: www.simplygo.co.uk
Man Dir: D P Mathews **Ops Dir**: K Carr
Fin Dir: G C McPherson
Comm Dir: M P Harris
Fleet: 731 - 173 double-deck bus, 184 single-deck bus, 19 coach, 4 articulated bus, 189 midibus, 162 minibus.
Chassis: 100 DAF. 254 Dennis. 27 Leyland. 13 MCW. 108 Optare. 50 Scania. 179 Volvo.
Bodies: 33 Alexander. 17 ECW. 27 East Lancs. 33 Marshall. 13 MCW. 79 Northern Counties. 182 Optare. 156 Plaxton. 68 Transbus. 123 Wright.
Ops incl: local bus services, school contracts.

- Air conditioning
- Vehicles suitable for disabled
- Coach(es) with galley facilities
- Coach(es) with toilet facilities
- Seat belt-fitted vehicles
- **R** Recovery service available (not 24 hr)
- **R24** 24hr recovery service
- Replacement vehicle available
- **T** Toilet-drop facilities available
- Vintage vehicle(s) available
- Open top vehicle(s)

Livery: Red/Blue/Yellow
Ticket System: Wayfarer 3.

*JIM HUGHES COACHES
[wc] [A/c]

WEAR STREET, LOW SOUTHWICK, SUNDERLAND SR5 2BH
Tel: 0191 548 9600
Fax: 0191 549 3728
Man Dir: James Hughes
Dir: Valerie Hughes **Sec**: Jean Fisher
Ch Eng: Stephen McCuinness
Fleet: 8 - 7 coach, 1 minicoach.
Chassis: 1 Bedford. 1 Mercedes. 6 Volvo.
Bodies: 4 Plaxton. 1 Reeve Burgess. 3 Van Hool.
Ops incl: private hire, excursions & tours, continental tours.
Livery: Cream

*KINGSLEY COACHES
[wc] [A/c]

UNIT 20, PENSHAW WAY, PORTOBELLO, BIRTLEY DH3 2SA
Tel: 0191 492 1299
Fax: 0191 410 9281
E-mail: kingsleycoaches@aol.com
Chmn: David Kingsley **Sec**: Eileen Kingsley

Ops Man: David Kingsley Jnr **Fleet Eng**: Ian Kingsley
Fleet: 20 - 12 double-deck bus, 2 double-deck coach, 4 coach, 2 minicoach.
Chassis: 1 LDV. 2 Leyland. 14 MCW. 1 Mercedes. 1 Volvo.
Bodies: 1 Berkhof. 2 Duple. 1 Leyland. 14 MCW. 1 Reeve Burgess. 1 Van Hool.
Ops incl: school contracts, excursions & tours, private hire, continental tours
Livery: Blue/White.
Ticket System: Wayfarer 3

PRIORY MOTOR COACH CO LTD

59 CHURCHWAY, NORTH SHIELDS NE29 0AD.
Tel: 0191 257 0283.
Man Dir: S. H. Lee. **Eng**: G. Hatley.
Fleet: 8 coach.
Chassis: Bedford.
Bodies: 2 Duple. 6 Plaxton.
Ops incl: excursions & tours, private hire, school contracts.

REDBY TRAVEL LTD
HENDON ROAD, HENDON, SUNDERLAND SR2 8NT.

Tel: 0191 514 2294.
Fax: 0191 565 8822.

SIESTA INTERNATIONAL
See North Yorkshire

*STAGECOACH NORTH EAST
WHEATSHEAF, SUNDERLAND SR5 1AQ
Tel: 0191 567 5251
Fax: 0191 566 0202
Web site: www.stagecoachbus.com
Man Dir: John Conroy **Ops Dir**: Graham Brown **Eng Dir**: David Kirsopp
Fleet: 617 - 112 double-deck bus, 302 single-deck bus, 160 midibus, 43 minibus.
Chassis: 143 Dennis. 72 Leyland. 128 Marshall. 38 Mercedes. 3 Optare. 2 Renault. 46 Scania. 185 Volvo.
Bodies: 474 Alexander. 31 Leyland. 61 Northern Counties. 49 Plaxton. 2 Reeve Burgess.
Ops incl: local bus services, school contracts.
Livery: Stagecoach (White/Blue/Orange/red)
Ticket System: ERGsystem4000

WARWICKSHIRE

BAILISS TOURS
See Leicestershire.

*CATTERALLS OF SOUTHAM
[wc] [A/c] [T]

74A COVENTRY STREET, SOUTHAM CV47 0EA
Tel: 01926 813840
Fax: 01926 813915
E-mail: travelcatteralls@aol.com
Dir: Paul Catterall **Tran Man**: Stan Griffin
Fleet Eng: Paul Rhodes **Garage**: Dave Ould **Office**: Maureen Allison **(Tours)**, Tracey Connors **(Excursions)**, Lynda Barber **(Acc)**
Fleet: 20 - 15 coach, 3 double-deck coach, 2 midicoach
Chassis: 4 MAN. 1 Mercedes. 1 Neoplan. 2 Scania. 2 Setra. 10 Volvo.
Bodies: 1 Irizar. 2 Jonckheere. 1 Marcopolo. 1 Neoplan. 2 Noge. 10 Plaxton. 2 Setra. 1 Van Hool.
Ops incl: local bus services, school contracts, excursions & tours, private hire, continental tours.
Livery: Blue/Yellow on White

*CHAPEL END COACHES
[wc] [A/c]

WINSON HOUSE, 3 OASTON ROAD, NUNEATON CV11 6JX
Tel: 024 7635 4588
Fax: 024 7635 6406
E-mail: cecoaches@ukonline.co.uk
Man Dir: Malcolm Wilson **Dir**: Tracey Wilson **Dir**: Noel Philips **Chmn**: Malcolm Wilson

Fleet: 15 coach.
Chassis: 3 Dennis. 12 Volvo.
Ops incl: excursions & tours, private hire, continental tours, school contracts.
Livery: Cream/White, various

COURTLINE THE 'MINI' COACH CO
107 CAMP HILL ROAD, NUNEATON CV10 0JR.
Tel: 024 7639 3939.
Fax: 024 7639 7900.
Man Dir: R. A. Court. **Sec**: Ms V. Court.
Fleet: 3 minicoach.
Chassis: Mercedes.
Bodies: Autobus Classique.
Ops incl: private hire.
Livery: Silver/Maroon.

L. S COURT LTD [wc]
RED HILL, FILLONGLEY CV7 8DA.
Tel: 01676 40282.
Dirs: G. E. Purchase, J. Purchase.
Co Sec: J. Swift.
Fleet: 10 coach.
Chassis: Leyland. Scania. Volvo.
Bodies: Van Hool. Joncheere. Plaxton. Reeve Burgess.
Ops incl: local bus services, school contracts, excursions & tours, private hire, continental tours.
Livery: White/Green or Red/Cream.

*MIKE DE COURCEY TRAVEL LTD
See West Midlands.

HALLMARK COACHES
See West Midlands.

LEWIS'S COACHES [wc]
CENTRAL GARAGE, PAILTON CV23 0QE.
Tel: 01788 832261.
Fax: 01788 832558.
Prop: N. E. Lewis.
Fleet: 13 coach.
Chassis: Dennis. Ford. Iveco.
Bodies: Plaxton.
Ops incl: excursions & tours, private hire, continental tours, school contracts.
Livery: Multi colour.

MARTIN'S OF TYSOE
20 OXHILL ROAD, MIDDLE TYSOE CV35 0SX
Tel: 01295 680642.
Prop: Martin Thomas.

SKYLINERS LTD [wc] [T]
19 BOND STREET, NUNEATON CV11 4NX.
Tel: 024 7632 5682
Fax: 024 7635 4626
E-mail: haydn@skyliners.co.uk
Dir: Haydon J. Dawkins
Fleet: 1 double-deck coach.
Body: Neoplan.
Ops incl: excursions & tours, private hire, continental tours.

*STAGECOACH IN WARWICKSHIRE
[wc] [A/c] [T]

RAILWAY TERRACE, RUGBY CV21 3HS
Tel: 01788 562036

Fax: 01788 546907
E-mail:
warks.enquiries@stagecoachbus.com
Web site:
www.stagecoachbus.com/warwickshire
Man Dir: James Freeman
Fleet: 167 - 39 double-deck bus, 33 single-dek bus, 11 coach, 34 midibus, 50 minibus.
Chassis: 8 Dennis. 25 Leyland.
27 Mercedes. 18 Optare. 9 Transbus.
132 Volvo.
Bodies: 107 Alexander. 23 ECW. 6 Northern Counties. 18 Optare. 15 Plaxton.
9 Transbus. 2 Wright.
Ops incl: local bus services, school contracts, express.

Livery: Stagecoach corporate livery
Ticket System: ERG

STRATFORD BLUE
See Ensignbus Company, Purfleet.

TERRYS COACH HIRE
COVENTRY. *See West Midlands*

*WAINFLEET MOTOR SERVICES LTD
💺 A/c ✂ T

OASTON ROAD, NUNEATON
CV11 6JX

Tel: 024 7638 3243
Fax: 024 7638 3160
E-mail: wainfleetuk2000@yahoo.com
Dirs: K Clifford **Man**: K Wood
Ch Eng: D Ridgway.
Fleet: 12 coach
Chassis: 12 Volvo.
Bodies: 12 Plaxton.
Ops incl: local bus services, school contracts, excursions & tours, private hire, express.
Livery: Green/Cream.

WEST MIDLANDS

*ADAMS TOURS 💺 A/c R ✂

75 SANDBANK, BLOXWICH
WS3 2HL
Tel: 01922 406469
Fax: 01922 406469
Ptnr: Dave Adams
Fleet: 8 - 4 coach, 2 midicoach, 2 minibus.
Chassis: 4 DAF. 4 Mercedes.
Bodies: 2 Autobus. 1 Mercedes. 1 Plaxton. 4 Van Hool.
Ops incl: private hire, excursions & tours, school contracts.
Livery: Cream/Green

ALBION COACHES
TUNNEL ROAD, HILL TOP, WEST BROMWICH B70 0RD.
Tel: 0121 556 1780, 2563.
Prop: J. T. Smith (**Gen Man/Ch Eng**).
Co Sec: M. Shepherd.
Fleet: 9 coach.
Chassis: 5 AEC. 4 Ford.
Bodies: 5 Duple. 4 Plaxton.
Ops incl: excursions & tours, private hire, continental tours.
Livery: Cream/Multicolour.

ARRIVA FOX COUNTY
See Leicestershire

ASTONS OF NEWPORT
See Shropshire.

*B B COACHES 💺 A/c ✂
22 VICTORIA AVENUE,
HALESOWEN B62 9BL
Tel: 0121 422 4501
Dir/Sec: Barbara Blewitt **Dir**: Mick Bird
Fleet: 2 coach.
Chassis: 2 Volvo
Bodies: 2 Plaxton
Ops incl: excursions & tours, private hire.
Livery: White/Crimson/Gold

BEACON COACHES
wc 💺 ✂

24 CHICHESTER GROVE,
CHELMSLEY WOOD B37 5RZ.
Tel: 0121 783 2221
Fax: 0121 680 2582
E-mail: enquiries@beaconcoaches
Web site: www.beaconcoaches.co.uk
Fleet: 6 - 2 double-deck coach,
1 midicoach, 1 minicoach, 2 minibus.
Chassis: 1 MAN, 2 Scania, 1 Toyota. LDV.
Bodies: 3 Jonckheere.
Ops incl: excursions & tours, private hire, school contracts, continental tours.
Livery: White /Red/Grey.

BEARWOOD COACHES
♿ wc 💺

316 BEARWOOD ROAD,
SMETHWICK B66 4HJ.
Tel/Fax: 0121 429 5126.
Owner: W. J. Burnett.
Fleet: 38 - 3 double-deck coach,
35 minibus.
Chassis: 5 DAF. 1 Ford. 10 Ford Transit. 2 Iveco. 10 Leyland. 8 Mercedes.
Ops incl: school contracts, excursions & tours.

B. D. BENNETT ♿
28 MARMION STREET, TAMWORTH B79 7JG.
Tel: 01827 54444, 62919.
Fax: 01827 64286.
Fleetname: Bennetts.
Prop: B. D. Bennett.
Fleet: 3 - 2 midicoach, 1 minicoach.
Chassis: 1 LDV. 2 Mercedes.
Ops incl: excursions & tours, continental tours.
Livery: White/Red/Yellow.

BENNETS TRAVEL
See Warwickshire

THE BIRMINGHAM COACH COMPANY LTD
💺 wc 🍽 A/c ✂

CROSS QUAYS BUSINESS PARK,
HALLBRIDGE WAY, TIPTON ROAD,
TIVIDALE, OLDBURY B69 3HY.
Tel: 0121 557 7337
Fax: 0121 520 4999
E-mail: enquiries@birmingham-coach.co.uk
Web site: www.birmingham-coach.co.uk
Chairman: G H Howle **Man Dir**: Dr J D Craggs **Traf Mar**: P Blackmoor **Bus Div Man**: D Best **Ch Eng**: C James
Fleet: 112 - 90 single-deck bus, 22 coach.
Chassis: 14 DAF 56 Dennis. 4 Leyland.
10 Leyland National. 10 Optare. 15 Scania. 3 Volvo.
Bodies: 1 Duple. 1 Jonckheere. 10 Leyland National. 26 Northern Counties. 45 Plaxton.
15 Van Hool. 14 Wright.
Ops incl: local bus services, private hire, express.
Livery: Red/White/Black (buses),
Red/White/Yellow (coaches).
Ticket System: Wayfarer TGX

*BIRMINGHAM & MIDLAND MOTOR OMNIBUS TRUST
🚌

THE TRANSPORT MUSEUM,
CHAPEL LANE, WYTHALL B47 6JX
Tel: 01564 826471
E-mail: enquiries@bammot.org.uk
Web site: www.bammot.org.uk
Trustees: David Taylor, Paul Gray, Philip Ireland, Malcolm Keeley
Fleet (hire only): 7 - 4 double-deck bus,
3 single-deck bus.
Chassis: 3 BMMO. 2 Bristol. 1 Guy.
1 Leyland.
Bodies: 3 BMMO. 2 ECW. 1 Leyland.
1 MCW.
Ops incl: local bus services, excursions & tours, private hire
Livery: of original operator/historic
Ticket System: Setright

A/c	Air conditioning	
♿	Vehicles suitable for disabled	
🍽	Coach(es) with galley facilities	
wc	Coach(es) with toilet facilities	
💺	Seat belt-fitted vehicles	
R	Recovery service available (not 24 hr)	
R24	24hr recovery service	
✂	Replacement vehicle available	
T	Toilet-drop facilities available	
🚌	Vintage vehicle(s) available	
🚐	Open top vehicle(s)	

*BIRMINGHAM INTERNATIONAL COACHES

10 FORTNUM CLOSE, TILE CROSS, BIRMINGHAM B33 0JT.
Tel/Fax: 0121 783 4004
E-mail: birmingham@intlcoaches.freeserve.co.uk
Web site: www.birminghaminternationalcoaches.co.uk
Man Dir: A Watkiss **Co Sec:** M Watkiss **Dir:** N Watkiss
Fleet: 9 - 8 coach, 1 minicoach.
Chassis: 7 Bova. 1 Toyota.
Bodies: including 1 Duple.
Ops incl: excursions & tours, private hire, continental tours, express, school contracts.
Livery: Dark Silver/Red

*COURTESY TRAVEL
See Shropshire

DEN CANEY COACHES LTD

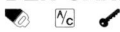

THE COACH STATION, 182 STONE HOUSE LANE, BARTLEY GREEN, BIRMINGHAM B32 3AH
Tel: 0121 427 2078
Fax: 0121 427 8905
Dirs: D. Stevens, Mrs W. Caney, M. Stevens
Ch Eng: A Doggett **Ops Man:** J Clarke
Administrator: Mrs D Johnston
Fleet: 13 - 10 coach, 3 minicoach.
Chassis: 2 Dennis. 2 Leyland. 3 Toyota. 5 Volvo.
Bodies: 3 Caetano. 9 Plaxton. 1 Van Hool.
Ops incl: excursions & tours, private hire, school contracts.
Livery: White/Yellow/Beige/Green

*CARELINE BIRMINGHAM LTD

1018 COVENTRY ROAD, HAY MILLS, BIRMINGHAM B25 8DP
Tel: 0121 771 3558
Fax: 0121 773 3990
Fleetname: Careline
Dir: Angela Denham **Gen Man/Ch Eng:** D Denham
Fleet: 6 - 2 coach, 2 midicoach, 2 midibus.
Chassis: 2 LDV. 2 Mercedes-Benz. 2 Volvo
Bodies: 1 Caetano. 2 Plaxton. 1 Van Hool.
Ops incl: private hire, school contracts
Livery: White with blue stripe

*CENTRAL BUSES LTD

191 CORPORATION STREET, BIRMINGHAM B4 6RG
Tel/Fax: 0121 236 5431
E-mail: geoff.cross@centralbuses.com
Web site: www.centralbuses.com
Dirs: G Cross, S Cross
Fleet: 5 - 2 single-deck bus, 3 midibus
Chassis: Dennis. MAN. Optare.
Bodies: Duple. Optare. Plaxton.
Ops incl: local bus services, school contracts, private hire
Livery: Red/Silver
Ticket System: Almex A90

CHAUFFEURS OF BIRMINGHAM

CREST HOUSE, 7 HIGHFIELD ROAD, EDGBASTON, BIRMINGHAM B15 3ED.
Tel: 0121 456 3355.

*CLARIBEL COACHES

10 FORTNUM CLOSE, TILE CROSS, BIRMINGHAM B33 0JT
Tel: 0121 789 7878
Dirs: A Watkiss, M Watkiss, N Watkiss **Co Sec:** Margaret Watkiss
Fleet: 18 - 17 single-deck bus, 1 coach.
Chassis: 6 DAF. 1 Dennis. 11 Optare.
Bodies: 1 Caetano. 1 Duple. 11 Optare. 5 Wright.
Ops incl: local bus services, school contracts, private hire, excursions & tours, express, continental tours.
Livery: Blue/White.
Ticket System: Wayfarer 3

*COFTON COACHES

1631 BRISTOL ROAD SOUTH, REDNAL, BIRMINGHAM BH45 9UA
Tel: 0121 453 5151
Fax: 0121 453 5504
E-mail: info@euroliners.co.uk
Fleetname: Euroliners
Prop: Tony Armstrong **Gen Man:** Glen Styles
Fleet: 24 - 8 coach, 4 midicoach, 8 minibus, 4 minicoach.
Chassis: 24 Mercedes.
Bodies: 8 Mercedes. 7 Olympus. 8 Optare.
Ops incl: local bus services, school contracts, excursions & tours, private hire, continental tours.

COURTLINE THE 'MINI' COACH CO
See Warwickshire.

DAIMLER

99 SAREHOLE ROAD, HALL GREEN, BIRMINGHAM B28 8ED.
Tel: 0121 778 2837.
Fax: 0121 702 2843.
Prop: Roy Picken
Fleet: 1 coach. **Chassis/Body:** MAN.
Ops incl: excursions & tours, continental tours.
Livery: Red/Charcoal Grey.

*MIKE DE COURCEY TRAVEL LTD

ROWLEY DRIVE, COVENTRY CV3 4FG
Tel: 024 7630 2656
Fax/Recovery: 024 7660 2656
E-mail: coaches@decourceytravel.com
Web site: www.decourceytravel.com
Man Dir: Michael de Courcey **Co Sec:** Bernadette de Courcey **Gen Man:** Bob Wildman **Ch Eng:** Neville Collins **Ops Man:** John Browns **Bus Services Man:** Alex Miller
Fleet: 57 - 22 double-deck bus, 19 single-deck bus, 12 coach, 4 midibus.

Chassis: 9 Dennis. 3 MAN.3 Marshall. 22 MCW. 4 Mercedes. 12 Volvo.
Bodies: 4 Alexander. 4 Caetano. 4 Ikarus. 4 Jonckheere. 4 Leyland. 7 Marshall. 22 MCW. 4 Plaxton. 3 Van Hool.
Ops incl: local bus services, school contracts, excursions & tours, private hire, express, continental tours.
Livery: White/Blue/Orange.
Ticket System: Wayfarer

DIRECT COACH TOURS

68 BERKELEY ROAD EAST, HAY MILLS, BIRMINGHAM B25 8NP
Tel: 0121 772 0664.
Fax: 0121 773 8649.
Tours Man: Brian Bourne.
Fleet: 7 - 6 coach, 1 midicoach.
Chassis: 1 Toyota. 6 Volvo.
Bodies: 1 Caetano. 6 Plaxton.
Ops incl: excursions & tours, private hire.

DRM MINIBUS & COACH TRAVEL
See Staffordshire.

*DUNN-LINE (FLIGHTS) LTD

FLIGHTS COACH STATION, LONG ACRE, BIRMINGHAM B7 5JJ
Tel: 0121 322 2222
Fax: 0121 322 2224
E-mail: sales@motorcoach.co.uk
Web site: www.motorcoach.co.uk
Fleetname: Flights
Man Dir: Simon Dunn
Gen Man: Paul Williams
Fleet: 39 - 14 single-deck bus, 23 single-deck coach, 2 midicoach.
Chassis: 10 Dennis. 1 Neoplan. 5 Scania. 2 Toyota. 21 Volvo.
Bodies: 2 Caetano. 1 Neoplan. 29 Plaxton. 2 Sunsundegui. 1 Van Hool. 4 Wright.
Ops incl: local bus services, school contracts, excursions & tours, private hire, express, continental tours.
Livery: Cream/Black/Silver.

*ENDEAVOUR COACHES

30 PLUME STREET, ASTON, BIRMINGHAM B6 7UW
Tel: 0121 326 4994
Fax: 0121 326 4999
E-mail: johnm@endeavour172.fsnet.co.uk
Web site: www.endeavourcoaches.co.uk
Dirs: J Mitchell, G Mitchell**(Ch Eng)**, D Mitchell**(Ch Eng)**
Fleet: 8 single-deck bus.
Chassis: 1 DAF. 7 Volvo.
Bodies: 1 Bova. 1 Plaxton. 7 Van Hool.
Ops incl: private hire, excursions and tours, school contracts, express, continental tours.
Livery: Silver/Green

GLIDER TRAVEL

13 HILLSIDE, BROWNHILLS WS8 7AE.
Tel/Fax: 01543 375801.
Owner: S. J. Mealey.
Fleet: 1 coach.
Chassis: Volvo. **Body:** Jonckheere.
Ops incl: excursions & tours, private hire.
Livery: Cream/Red.

GLOWBELLE COACHES LTD
wc ⓣ 🛇 🚌 R ✓

11 HALL GREEN ROAD, WEST BROMWICH B71 3JS.
Tel: 0121 588 4535.
Fax: 0121 588 4536.
Dir/Tran Man: J. Griffith, W. O. Griffith.
Sec: P. Edwards. **Traf Man:** R. Brown.
Fleet: 20 - 1 double-deck bus, 16 coach, 1 midicoach, 2 minibus.
Chassis: 1 Bristol. 12 DAF. 1 Dennis. 1 Ford. 1 Mercedes. 1 Toyota. 3 Volvo.
Bodies: 13 Caetano. 2 Duple. 1 Mercedes. 3 Plaxton. 1 Van Hool.
Ops incl: school contracts, excursions & tours, private hire, express, continental tours.
Livery: Green/Orange/Yellow.
Ticket System: Bell Punch.

GOODES COACHWAYS
wc ⓣ 🛇 Ac ✓ T

150 CRANKHALL LANE, WEDNESBURY WS10 0ED.
Tel: 0121 556 0706.
Fax: 0121 505 1619.
E-mail: info@goodebus.com
Web site: www.goodebus.com
SeniorPtnr/CEO: P W Goode. **Ops/Ptnr:** K Goode **Tran Man:** G McGowan **Fleet Man:** M Eaton
Fleet: 11 - 9 coach. 1 midicoach. 1 minicoach.
Chassis: 1 Mercedes. 9 Volvo. 1 Toyota. .
Bodies: 1 Caetano, 3 Jonckheere, 1 Optare. 5 Plaxton, 1 Van Hool.
Ops incl: excursions & tours, private hire, continental tours.

GRAY'S TRAVEL OF COVENTRY
12 MONMOUTH CLOSE, MOUNT NOD, COVENTRY CV5 7JA.
Tel/Fax: 024 7647 4481.
Prop: E. Gray.
Fleet: 3 coach. **Chassis:** Bedford.
Ops incl: local bus services, school contracts, private hire.
Livery: Name Black with Red shadow; Black/Red stripes.
Ticket System: Setright.

HAPPY WANDERER TRAVEL
♿ 🛇

17 COLLEGE ROAD, HANDSWORTH WOOD, BIRMINGHAM B20 2HU.
Tel: 0121 554 2533.
Fax: 0121 523 5068
Senior Ptnr: Mrs E. M. G. Charnock **Ptnr:** J. R. Charnock.
Fleet: 1 coach.
Chassis: Volvo
Body: Plaxton
Ops incl: excursions & tours, private hire.
Livery: Yellow/Black

*HARDINGS COACHES
wc ⓣ 🛇 Ac ✓ T

319 EVESHAM ROAD, CRABBS CROSS, REDDITCH B97 5HL.
Tel: 01527 542590
Fax: 01527 545691
Recovery: 01527 545590
E-mail: john@hardingscoaches.co.uk
Web site: www.hardingscoaches.co.uk
Man Dir: John Dyson
Co Sec: Malcolm Playford
Fleet: 45 - 5 single-deck bus, 36 coach, 4 midicoach.
Chassis: 6 DAF. 6 Leyland. 2 MAN. 8 Mercedes. 18 Scania. 1 Toyota. 4 Volvo.
Bodies: 3 Berkhof. 1 Caetano. 1 East Lancs. 1 Ikarus. 10 Irizar. 5 Mercedes. 1 Optare. 3 Plaxton. 2 Reeve Burgess. 6 Transbus. 12 Van Hool.
Ops incl: local bus services, school contracts, excursions & tours, private hire, continental tours.
Livery: Silver/Grey

J. R. HOLLYHEAD INTERNATIONAL
32 CROSS STREET, WILLENHALL WV13 1PG.
Tel: 01902 607364.
Fax: 01902 609772.
Owner: J. R. Hollyhead.
Fleet: 5 coach.
Chassis: 2 Bova. 3 Volvo.
Bodies: 2 Bova. 3 Plaxton.
Ops incl: excursions & tours, private hire, express, continental tours.
Livery: White.

*JOHNSONS (HENLEY) LTD
♿ wc 🛇 Ac R24 ✓ T

LIVERIDGE HILL, HENLEY-IN-ARDEN B95 5QS
Tel: 01564 797000
Fax: 01564 797050
E-mail: info@johnsonscoaches.co.uk
Web site: www.johnsonscoaches.co.uk
Dirs: P G Johnson, J R Johnson **Comm Sec:** Mrs J M Johnson **Ch Eng:** J Lawrence
Traf Man: N Brown
Fleet: 55 - 15 single-deck bus, 37 coach, 3 minicoach.
Chassis: 37 Bova. 6 DAF. 2 Dennis. 3 Mercedes. 5 Optare. 2 Toyota.
Bodies: 37 Bova. 2 Caetano. 2 East Lancs. 3 Mercedes. 5 Optare. 1 Plaxton. 1 UVG. 4 Wright.
Ops incl: local bus services, school contracts, excursions & tours, private hire, continental tours.
Livery: Yellow/Blue/White
Ticket system: Wayfarer Saver
Bodies: 28 Bova. 1 Irizar. 1 Leyland. 2 Mercedes. 8 Plaxton.
Ops incl: school contracts, excursions & tours, private hire, continental tours.
Livery: Yellow/Blue/White.
Ticket System: Setright.

JOSEPHS MINI COACHES
See Staffordshire

*KEN MILLER TRAVEL 🛇
wc ⓣ Ac R24 ✓

10 CHURCHILL ROAD, SHENSTONE WS14 0LP
Tel: 01827 60494
Fax: 01827 60494
Recovery: 07976 303951
E-mail: ken.m.traveluk@amserve.net
Fleetname: Ken Miller Recovery
Prop: Ken Miller
Fleet: 2 single-deck bus, 2 minibus.
Chassis: LDV. Volvo.
Ops incl: school contracts, private hire, express, continental tours.
Livery: Blue/Silver
Ticket system: Wayfarer.

*KINGSNORTON COACHES
wc 🛇 Ac ✓

40 BISHOPS GATE, NORTHFIELD, BIRMINGHAM B31 4AJ
Tel: 0121 550 8519
Fax: 0121 501 6554
Dirs: Richard Egan, Malcolm Stanley
Fleet: 14 - 3 coach, 11 minibus.
Chassis/Bodies: 1 Caetano. 11 LDV. 1 Toyota. 2 Volvo. 2 Van Hool.
Ops incl: school contracts, excursions & tours, private hire, continental tours.

*KINGSWINFORD COACHWAYS
wc 🛇 R24 ✓

HIGH STREET, PENSNETT DY6 8XB
Tel: 01384 401626
Fax: 01384 401580
Recovery: 07831 148222
Dir: C J Wood **Ch Eng:** R J Lamsdale
Ops Man: B A J Probert
Fleet: 9 - 7 coach, 1 midibus, 1 midicoach.
Chassis: 3 Bedford. 4 Volvo.
Ops incl: school contracts, private hire, excursions & tours
Livery: White/Yellow/Green.

LEANDER TRAVEL
See Derbyshire

LUDLOWS OF HALESOWEN LTD wc 🛇 ✓

COOMBS ROAD, HALESOWEN B62 8AA.
Tel: 0121 559 7506.
Fax: 0121 561 4503.
Dirs: Mrs P. C. Ludlow, A. S. Ludlow.
Fleet: 32 - 22 single-deck bus, 7 coach, 2 minibus, 1 minicoach.
Chassis: 8 Dennis 11 Leyland National. 2 Mercedes. 5 Scania. 4 Volvo. 2 Irizar.
Bodies: 2 Duple. 11 Leyland National. 2 Plaxton. 3 Van Hool. 9 Wright.
Ops incl: local bus services, school contracts, excursions & tours, private hire, continental tours.
Livery: Base White and multi-colour.
Ticket System: Wayfarer 3

🛇	Seat belt-fitted vehicles	
R	Recovery service available (not 24 hr)	
R24	24hr recovery service	
✓	Replacement vehicle available	
T	Toilet-drop facilities available	
🚌	Vintage vehicle(s) available	
🚐	Open top vehicle(s)	
Ac	Air conditioning	
♿	Vehicles suitable for disabled	
ⓣ	Coach(es) with galley facilities	
wc	Coach(es) with toilet facilities	

*MCCOLLS OF ARGYLL
Tel: 0121 505 1155
Fax: 0121 505 7367
See Scotland (Argyll & Bute)

*MEADWAY PRIVATE HIRE LTD
MEADWAY COACHES, 28-32 BERKELEY ROAD, HAY MILLS, BIRMINGHAM B25 8NG
Tel: 0121 773 8389
Fax: 0121 693 7171
Fleet: single-deck bus, coach, midicoach, minibus.
Chassis: Bedford. Dennis. Leyland. Mercedes. Transbus. Volvo.
Bodies: Caetano. Leyland. Mercedes. Plaxton. Transbus.
Ops incl: private hire, school contracts.

*NASH COACHES LTD
83 RAGLAN ROAD, SMETHWICK B66 3TT
Tel: 0121 558 0024
Fax: 0121 558 0907
E-mail: nashscoaches@aol.com
Web site: www.nashscoaches.co.uk
Dirs: Ian Powell, Linda Powell, Graham Powell, Walter F Powell
Fleet: 10 - 9 coach, 1 midicoach.
Chassis: 1 Ford. 4 Mercedes. 1 Toyota. 4 Volvo.
Bodies: 1 Caetano. 1 Neoplan. 1 Plaxton. 3 Setra. 4 Van Hool.
Ops incl: excursions & tours, private hire, express, continental tours, school contracts.
Livery: Grey/Red/Blue.

NATIONAL EXPRESS LTD
ENSIGN COURT, 4 VICARAGE ROAD, EDGBASTON, BIRMINGHAM B15 3ES.
Tel: 0121 625 1122.
Fax: 0121 456 1397.
E-mail: reception@nationalexpress.co.uk
Web site: www.nationalexpress.com
Fleetname: National Express.
Ch Exec: D Wormwell
Chassis: Volvo. **Body**: Plaxton.
Ops incl: express.
Livery: White/Blue.
Ticket System: Pre-sale National Express, Wayfarer.

*NEVILLE'S TOURS
4 HARLAND ROAD, SUTTON COLDFIELD B74 4DA
Tel: 0121 308 6942
Prop: Mrs J Neville
Ops incl: excursions & tours, private hire

*NEWBURY TRAVEL
NEWBURY LANE, OLDBURY B69 1HF
Tel: 0121 552 3262
Fax: 0121 552 0230
E-mail: newburytravel@aol.com
Web site: www.newburytravel.co.uk

Man Dir: David Greenhouse **Ch Eng**: Chris Phillips
Fleet: 11 - 5 coach, 3 midicoach, 3 minicoach.
Chassis: 1 Ford Transit. 2 LDV. 3 Mercedes. 5 Volvo.
Bodies: 1 Berkhof. 3 Mercedes. 4 Van Hool.
Ops incl: school contracts, private hire.
Livery: White

NORTH BIRMINGHAM BUSWAYS LTD
38 WOOD LANE, ERDINGTON, BIRMINGHAM B24 9QL
Tel: 0121 377 8554.
Fax: 0121 377 7456.
E-mail: nbb@northbhambusways.co.uk
Web site: www.northbhambusways.co.uk
Chmn: Patrick Lane. **Fin Dir**: Ken Daniels.
Ops Dir: David Wall. **Eng Man**: Les Watts.
Admin Man: Andrew Moore.
Fleet: 29 - 23 double-deck bus. 3 single-deck bus. 1 trainer. 1 recovery vehicle. 1 exhibition.
Chassis: 22 Leyland, 4 Dennis.
Bodies: 8 East Lancs. 2 Alexander. 15 Northern Counties. 1 Reeve Burgess.
Ops incl: local bus services, school contracts, private hire.
Livery: Green/Cream.
Ticket System: Wayfarer.

J P M PARRY
OVEREND ROAD, CRADLEY HEATH B64 7DD
Tel: 01384 569171
Fax: 01384 637753
Ops incl: tram service

PARRYS INTERNATIONAL TOURS LTD
See Staffordshire

PATHFINDER MASONS (FHW) LTD
29 BILSTON LANE, WILLENHALL WV13 2QF.
Tel: 01902 606382.
Fax: 01902 605033.
Dirs: Andrew Winkle, Mrs Anne Arnold, Mrs Jean Winkle
Fleet: 11 coach.
Chassis: 2 Dennis. 5 Ford. 4 Volvo.
Ops incl: excursions & tours, private hire, express, school contracts.

PETE'S TRAVEL
UNITS 4&5, HOWARD STREET INDUSTRIAL ESTATE, HOWARD STREET, WEST BROMWICH B70 0FF
Tel: 0121 505 3245.
Fax: 0121 505 5572.
E-mail: enquiries@petestravel.co.uk
Web site: www.petestravel.co.uk
Fleetname: Pete's Travel, Pete's Tours, Lionspeed, Busy Bus.
Props: Peter Jones, Kevin Jones.
Fleet: 105
Chassis: Dennis, Volvo, Mercedes, Ford Transit, MCW, Dodge.
Bodies: Plaxton, Alexander, Wright, MCW, Carlyle, Mellor.

Ops incl: local bus services, school contracts, private hire.
Livery: Yellow.

*PROSPECT COACHES WEST LTD
81 HIGH STREET, LYE DY9 8NG
Tel: 01384 895436
Fax: 01384 898654
E-mail: sales@prospectcoaches.co.uk
Web site: www.prospectcoaches.co.uk
Man Dir: Geoffrey Watts **Ops Man**: Roslynd Hadley
Fleet: 40 coach.
Chassis: 4 Bedford. 8 DAF. 20 Dennis. 4 Ford. 1 Leyland. 1 Neoplan. 2 Volvo.
Bodies: 2 Caetano. 30 Duple. 1 Neoplan. 7 Plaxton.
Ops incl: school contracts, private hire.
Liveryite.

SECOND CITY TRAVEL
49 ST JOSEPHS ROAD, WARD END, BIRMINGHAM B8.
Tel: 0121 247 7575.
Prop: V. J. Barnes, B. L. Kenning.
Gen Man: M. Richardson.
Fleet: 14 - 12 coach, 2 minibus.
Chassis: Dodge, Leyland.
Ops incl: local bus services, school contracts, excursions & tours, private hire, express, continental tours. **Livery**: Cream.

HARRY SHAW
MILL HOUSE, MILL LANE, BISLEY, COVENTRY CV3 2DU.
Tel: 024 7665 0650
Fax: 024 7663 5681
E-mail: coachhire@harryshaw.co.uk
Web site: www.harryshaw.co.uk
Fleet: includes coach, midicoach, minibus
Chassis: Setra
Bodies: Mercedes. Setra. Van Hool.

*SHEARINGS LTD
BAYTON ROAD, EXHALL CV7 9EJ.
Tel: 024 7664 4633.
Fax: 024 7636 0304.
Gen Man: Carol Carpenter.
See also Shearings Ltd, Greater Manchester.

SHEN CARE VOLUNTARY TRANSPORT
330 GREEN MEADOW ROAD, SELLY OAK, BIRMINGHAM B29 4EE.
Tel/Fax: 0121 476 1816.
Man: J. McKernan.
Fleet: 5 minibus.
Chassis: 1 Ford Transit. 1 Iveco. 3 Leyland.
Services for elderly/less abled.

*SILVERLINE LANDFLIGHT LTD
ARGENT HOUSE, VULCAN ROAD, SOLIHULL B91 2JY
Tel: 0121 711 7799
Fax: 0121 709 0556
E-mail: silverline@landflight.co.uk
Web site: www.landflight.co.uk

Man Dir: Malcolm Breakwell **Co Sec**:
Jim Fell **Bus Dev Dir**: Danny Matthews.
Ops Dir: Richard Knott **Eng Man**:
Roger Nolan **Training Man/Personnel**:
Graham Thompson **Mktg Man**: Ross Furby
Fleet: 13 - 2 single-deck bus, 6 coach,
5 midicoach.
Chassis: 4 MAN. 2 Mercedes. 2 Neoplan.
2 Optare. 1 Scania. 3 Toyota.
Bodies: 3 Caetano. 1 Irizar. 2 Neoplan.
2 Noge. 5 Optare.
Ops incl: private hire
Livery: Silver/Blue

SKYLINERS LTD
See Warwickshire

*T. N. C. COACHES 💺 ✓
257 CHESTER ROAD, CASTLE
BROMWICH B36 0ET.
Tel: 0121 747 5722
Dirs: Neil T Cunningham, K M Cunningham.
Fleet: 5 - 2 coach, 3 minibus.
Chassis: 3 LDV. 1 Leyland. 1 Volvo.
Bodies: include 1 Duple. 1 Park Royal.
Ops incl: school contracts, excursions &
tours, private hire.

TERRY'S COACH HIRE
wc 🍴 💺 A/c ✓
21 PANDORA ROAD, WALSGRAVE,
COVENTRY CV2 2FU
Tel/Fax: 024 7636 2975
E-mail: enquiries@terrys-coaches.co.uk
Web site: www.terrys-coaches.co.uk
Prop: T. C. Hall **Ch Engs**: J. Hall, B Brader
Ops: J. Pring
Fleet: 11 - 1 double-deck bus, 4 single-deck
bus, 5 coach, 1 double-deck coach.
Chassis: 1 Bristol. 1 Dennis. 4 Leyland
National. 3 MAN. 2 Volvo.
Bodies: 4 Leyland National. 2 Noge.
2 Plaxton. 2 Van Hool. 1 Bristol.
Ops incl: excursions & tours, private hire,
continental tours, local bus services, school
contracts.
Livery: Gold with Black/Gold

TIMELINE TRAVEL
🍴 A/c T
40A STATION STREET, WALSALL
WS2 9JT.
Tel: 01922 631590.
Fax: 01922 612040.
E-mail:
shop.walsall@timelinetravel.co.uk
Web site: www.timelinetravel.co.uk
Man Dir: Ian Longworth **Man**: Natalie
Hackett.
Fleet: 15 coach.
Chassis: Iveco. Scania. Volvo.
Bodies: Beulas. Plaxton. Van Hool.
Ops incl: excursions & tours, private hire,
continental tours, school contracts.
Livery: Cream with yellow/red stripes.

*TRAVEL WEST MIDLANDS
1 SOVEREIGN COURT, 8 GRAHAM
STREET, BIRMINGHAM B1 3JR
Tel: 0121 254 7200
Fax: 0121 254 7277
Web site: www.travelwm.co.uk
Ch Exec: Brian Jackson **Fin Dir**: Peter
Coates **Eng Dir**: Jack Henry
Fleet: 1,295 - 974 double-deck bus,
20 articulated bus, 644 single-deck bus,
87 minibus.
Chassis: 21 DAF. 310 Dennis. 51 Leyland.
396 MCW. 261 Mercedes. 88 Optare.
598 Volvo.
Bodies: 414 Alexander. 51 Leyland.
13 Marshall. 396 MCW. 213 Mercedes. 109
Optare. 141 Plaxton. 388 Wright.
Ops incl: local bus services, school
contracts, private hire.
Livery: Red/White/Blue
Ticket System: Wayfarer 3.
Associated companies: Travel Coventry,
Travel Dundee, Travel London

*TRAVEL MIDLAND METRO
♿
METRO CENTRE, POTTERS LANE,
WEDNESBURY WS10 0AR
Tel: 0121 502 2006
Fax: 0121 556 6299
Fleet: 16 articulated tramcars
General Manager: Fred Roberts
Chassis/Bodies: Ansaldo
Ops incl: tram service

*WEST MIDLANDS SPECIAL NEEDS TRANSPORT ♿ 💺
218-220 WINDSOR STREET,
NECHELLS, BIRMINGHAM B7 4NE
Tel: 0121 333 3107
Fax: 0121 333 3345
E-mail: enquiries@ringandride.org
Web site: www.wmsnt.org
Ch Exec: Barry Connor **Ops Man**: Des
Rogers **Co Sec**: John Frater
Fleet: 260 minibus.
Chassis: 80 Mercedes, 10 Renault,
160 Volkswagen. 10 Fiat.
Bodies: 260 other.
Ops incl: local bus services.
Livery: Red/White/Blue
Ticket system: pre-booked

*WICKSONS TRAVEL
wc A/c 💺 T
COPPICE ROAD, BROWNHILLS
WS8 7DG
Tel: 01543 372247
Fax: 01543 374271
Dir: Martin Wickson **Co Sec**: Ms Ann
Wickson **Ch Eng**: Graham Roe
Fleet: 11 - 10 coach, 2 midicoach.
Chassis: 3 DAF. 2 MAN. 2 Mercedes.
6 Volvo
Bodies: 2 Autobus. 2 Caetano. 1 Plaxton.
8 Van Hool.
Ops incl: excursions & tours, private hire,
continental tours, school contracts.
Livery: White/Blue/Orange.

*WINDSOR-GRAY TRAVEL
💺 ✓
186 GRIFFITHS DRIVE,
WOLVERHAMPTON WV11 2JR.
Tel: 01902 722392
Fax: 01902 722339
Owner: Graham Williams
Fleet: 3 - 2 midicoach, 1 minicoach.
Chassis: 1 Bedford. 1 Iveco. 1 Toyota.
Bodies: 1 Plaxton. 2 Caetano.
Ops incl: private hire, school contracts.
Livery: Blue/White/Red

*YARDLEY TRAVEL LTD
wc 🍴 💺
68 BERKELEY ROAD EAST,
HAYMILLS, BIRMINGHAM B25 8MP
Tel: 0121 772 3700.
Fax: 0121 773 8649
Man Dir: R A M Meddings **Dirs**:
R W Meddings, W J A Meddings
Fleet: 11 - 10 coach, 1 minibus
Chassis: 1 Toyota. 10 Volvo.
Bodies: 2 Caetano. 9 Plaxton.
Ops incl: excursions & tours, private hire.
Livery: White/Yellow/Black.

*YOUNGS OF ROMSLEY
wc 🍴 💺 A/c
MALVERN VIEW, DAYHOUSE BANK,
ROMSLEY, HALESOWEN B62 0EU
Tel/Fax: 01562 710717
Prop: R. J. Young
Fleet: 2 - 1 coach, 1 minicoach.
Chassis/Bodies: 2 Mercedes.
Ops incl: excursions & tours, private hire,
continental tours.
Livery: Bronze

*ZAK'S BUS & COACH SERVICES LTD
♿ wc 🍴 💺 A/c R ✓ T
ZAK'S DEPOT, SHADY LANE, GREAT
BARR, BIRMINGHAM B44 9ER
Tel: 0121 360 2362
Fax: 0121 360 2862
Recovery: 07753 960470
E-mail: e-mail@zaksbuses.com
Web site: www.zakscoaches.com
Dir: D M Fazakarley **Co Sec**: C Hart **Gen Man**: M P Lawton
Fleet: 45 - 23 single-deck bus, 9 coach,
1 midicoach, 12 minibus.
Chassis: 1 Bova. 21 Dennis. 1 Iveco. 9 LDV.
1 Leyland. 11 Mercedes. 3 Neoplan.
2 Renault. 1 Setra. 1 Toyota. 1 Volvo.
Bodies: 1 Bova. 1 Caetano. 1 Duple.
1 Marshall. 4 Optare. 21 Plaxton. 1 Setra.
1 Van Hool.
Ops incl: local bus services, school
contracts, excursions & tours, private hire,
express
Livery: White/Gold, White/Blue.
Ticket System: Wayfarer TGX

A/c	Air conditioning
♿	Vehicles suitable for disabled
🍴	Coach(es) with galley facilities
wc	Coach(es) with toilet facilities
💺	Seat belt-fitted vehicles
R	Recovery service available (not 24 hr)
R24	24hr recovery service
✓	Replacement vehicle available
T	Toilet-drop facilities available
🚌	Vintage vehicle(s) available
	Open top vehicle(s)

WEST SUSSEX

ARROW INTERNATIONAL

6 DOONE END, FERRING, WORTHING BN12 5PT.
Tel: 01903 502308
E-mail: arrowcoaches@tinyworld.co.uk
Prop: Linda Gander.
Fleet: 4 - 1 double-deck bus, 3 coach.
Chassis: 1 MCW. 3 Volvo.
Bodies: 3 Jonckheere. 1 MCW.
Ops incl: private hire, continental tours, school contracts.
Livery: Light Blue with dark blue & white flash.

ARUN COACHES/FAWLTY TOURS

1 NORFOLK TERRACE, HORSHAM RH12 1DA.
Tel: 01403 272999.
Fax: 01403 272777.
Prop/Ch Eng: H. Miller.
Fleet: 4 coach.
Chassis: 1 AEC. 1 Bristol. 2 Hestair/Duple.
Bodies: 2 Duple. 1 ECW. 1 Plaxton.
Ops incl: private hire.
Livery: Red/Gold.

J & M BROWN COACHES T/A CRAWLEY LUXURY COACHES

STEPHENSON WAY, THREE BRIDGES RH10 1TN.
Tel: 01293 521002.
Fax: 01293 522450.
E-mail: crawleylux@aol.com
Fleetname: Crawley Luxury Coaches.
Dir: D. L. Brown, G. D. Brown, D. J. Brown.
Ops Man: S. Davidson.
Fleet: 20 coach.
Chassis: 20 Volvo. **Bodies**: 20 Plaxton.
Ops incl: excursions & tours, private hire, school contracts.
Livery: Cream/Green/Grey.

*CHARIOTS OF CRAWLEY

12 FURNACE DRIVE, FURNACE GREEN, CRAWLEY RH10 7SE
Tel/Fax: 01293 513371
Prop: Bert Cullip
Fleet: 1 midicoach.
Chassis: Iveco. **Body**: Indcar.
Ops incl: private hire.

*COMPASS TRAVEL

FARADAY CLOSE, WORTHING BN13 3RB
Tel: 01903 233767
Fax: 01903 820029
E-mail: office@compass-travel.co.uk
Web site: www.compass-travel.co.uk
Man Dir: Chris Chatfield **Ops Man**: M Evans **Eng Man**: M Gallichan
Fleet: 40 - 12 single-deck bus, 5 coach, 16 midibus, 5 midicoach, 1 minibus, 1 minicoach.
Chassis: 12 Dennis. 13 Mercedes. 10 Optare. 5 Volvo.
Bodies: 4 Alexander. 3 Autobus.

3 Jonckheere. 15 Optare. 8 Plaxton. 2 Van Hool. 5 other.
Ops incl: local bus services, school contracts, private hire.
Livery: White/Burgundy.
Ticket System: Almex.

CRAWLEY LUXURY COACHES

See J. & M. Brown Coaches, above

*EMSWORTH & DISTRICT MOTOR SERVICES LTD

See Hampshire

*RICHARDSON TRAVEL LTD

RUSSELL HOUSE, BEPTON ROAD, MIDHURST GU29 9NB
Tel: 01730 813304
Fax: 01730 815985
E-mail: ast@richardsontravel.demon.co.uk
Web site: www.richardson-travel.co.uk
Dir: R W Richardson
Fleet: 13 - 6 double-deck bus. 7 single-deck coach.
Chassis: 1 Dennis. 12 Volvo.
Bodies: 5 Alexander. 1 Caetano. 7 Plaxton.
Ops incl: local bus services, school contracts, excursions & tours, private hire, continental tours.
Livery: Blue.

*ROADMARK TRAVEL LTD

17 OLD MILL SQUARE, STORRINGTON RH20 4NQ
Tel: 01903 740123
Fax: 01903 741125
Man Dir: M W Anderson **Co Sec**: L J Anderson **Dir**: D H Coster.
Fleet: 2 coach
Chassis: 2 Neoplan.
Bodies: 2 Setra.
Ops incl: excursions & tours, private hire, continental tours.
Livery: White/Blue

RONS COACHES LTD

UNIT 13, CHARTWELL ROAD, LANCING BN15 8TU.
Tel: 01903 766655.
Fax: 01903 766622.
Fleetname: King of the Road.
Man Dir: R. Ticehurst. **Dir**: H. Ticehurst.
Fleet: 14 - 1 double-deck bus, 11 coach, 2 minicoach.
Chassis: 4 DAF. 1 Daimler. 4 Dennis. 2 Duple. 2 Mercedes.
Bodies: 2 Berkhof. 3 Duple. 1 Jonckheere. 1 MCW. 4 Plaxton. 2 Reeve Burgess.
Ops incl: excursions & tours, private hire, continental tours, school contracts.
Livery: White/Red/Black.

*RUTHERFORDS

BRAMFIELD HOUSE, CHURCH LANE. EASTERGATE, CHICHESTER PO20 3UZ
Tel/Fax: 01243 543673
Prop: G. R. Bell.
Fleet: 12
Chassis: 7 Leyland. 2 Scania. 1 Toyota. 2 Volvo.
Bodies: 2 Duple. 2 Irizar. 7 Plaxton. 1 Wadham Stringer.
Ops incl: excursions & tours, private hire, school contracts, continental tours.
Livery: White

*SOUTHDOWN PSV

UNITS 3/7, SILVERWOOD, SNOW HILL, SILVERWOOD, COPTHORNE RH10 3EN
Tel: 01342 715222
Fax: 01342 719617
E-mail: southdownpsv@btinternet.co.uk
Web site: www.southdownpsv.co.uk
Man Dir: Steve Swain **Eng Dir**: Simon Stanford **Fin Dir**: Peter Larking **Ops Man**: Paul Llewellyn
Fleet: 12 - 2 double-deck bus, 10 single-deck bus.
Chassis: 11 Leyland. 1 MCW.
Bodies: 1 ECW. 10 Leyland. 1 MCW.
Ops incl: local bus services, school contracts
Livery: White/Blue/Green
Ticket System: Wayfarer

*STAGECOACH SOUTH LTD

BUS STATION, SOUTHGATE, CHICHESTER PO19 8DG
Tel: 01243 536161
Fax: 01243 528743
Man Dir: Andrew Dyer **Eng Dir**: Richard Alexander **Ops Dir**: Philip Medlicott
Fleet: 461 – 127 double-deck bus, 59 single-deck bus, 5 coach, 227 midibus, 49 minibus.
Chassis: 3 Bristol. 186 Dennis. 38 Leyland. 49 Mercedes. 3 Optare. 39 Transbus. 143 Volvo.
Bodies: 308 Alexander. 5 Berkhof. 10 ECW. 11 Jonckheere. 19 Northern Counties. 3 Optare. 74 Plaxton. 1 Roe. 39 Transbus. 1 Brush. 1 Short.
Ops incl: local bus services, school contracts, private hire, express.
Livery: Stagecoach standard
Ticket system: Wayfarer

*SUSSEX COUNTRY TOURS

TERMINAL BUILDING, SHOREHAM AIRPORT BN43 5FF
Tel: 01273 465500
Fax: 01273 453040
E-mail: sxcountry@btclick.com
Dirs: A Wright, K Berry
Fleet: 4 - 3 coach, 1 midicoach
Chassis: 1 Mercedes. 2 Volvo
Bodies: 2 Plaxton. 1 other.

Ops incl: school contracts, private hire.
Livery: White

*W & H MOTORS
wc 🍴 💺 A/c R24 ✔

KELVIN WAY, MANOR ROYAL,
CRAWLEY RH10 2SE
Tel: 01293 510220
Fax: 01293 513263
Recovery: 01293 548111
Web site: www.wandhgroup.co.uk
E-mail: coach@wandhgroup.co.uk
Dir: George Heron
Fleet: 20 - 2 single-deck bus, 12 coach,
3 double-deck coach, 1 minibus,
2 minicoach.
Chassis: 1 Iveco. 1 Leyland. 12 MAN.
2 Toyota.
Bodies: Ayats. Jonckheere. Noge. Van Hool.
Ops incl: local bus services, excursions and tours, private hire, school contracts, continental tours.

WESTRING COACHES 💺
48 MARINE DRIVE WEST, WEST WITTERING PO20 8HH.
Tel: 01243 672411.
Fax: 01243 671366.
E-mail: westring@connectfree.co.uk
Ptnrs: W. J. Buckland, S. A. Buckland.
Fleet: 6 - 1 single-deck bus, 4 coach,
1 midibus, 1 midicoach.
Chassis: 1 Leyland, 1 Optare, 3 Scania.
1 Toyota, 1 Volvo.
Bodies: 1 Caetano. 1 East Lancs.
3 Jonckheere. 1 Optare. 1 Plaxton.
Ops incl: school contracts, excursions & tours, private hire, continental tours.
Livery: Silver with red/pink flash and wolfhound logo.

*WOODS TRAVEL LTD
wc A/c 💺 ✔

PARK ROAD, BOGNOR REGIS PO21 2PX.
Tel: 01243 868080
Fax: 01243 871667
Man Dir: R. Elsmere **Dirs**: T Shaw-Morton,
K Elsmere **Co Sec**: M Elsmere. **Traf Man**:
W. Tregus. **Tours Man**: D. Kirkby-Bott.
Fleet: 14 - 13 coach, 1 midicoach.
Chassis: 13 DAF. 1 Mercedes.
Bodies: 13 Bova. 1 Mercedes.
Ops incl: excursions & tours, private hire, continental tours, school contracts, local bus services.
Livery: Red/White/Blue.

WORTHING COACHES wc
117 GEORGE V AVENUE WEST,
WORTHING EN11 5SA.
Tel: 01903 505805.
Fax: 01903 507285.
Man Dirs: R. D. K. Hart, D. Gander.
Fleet: 7 coach.
Chassis: Volvo.
Bodies: 5 Plaxton. 2 Van Hool.
Ops incl: excursions & tours, private hire, continental tours
Livery: Red/White/Yellow.

YELLOWLINE TOURS LTD
💺

34 TRULEIGH ROAD, UPPER BEEDING BN44 3JR.
Tel: 01903 813428.
Fax: 01243 823840.
Dir: Miss K. Fisher. **Co Sec**: G. Hanton.
Fleet: 1 coach.
Chassis: Leyland. **Body**: Plaxton.
Ops incl: excursions & tours, private hire.
Livery: Yellow/Black/White.

WEST YORKSHIRE, BRADFORD, CALDERDALE

ACRON TRAVEL wc 🍴
102 NEWLAITHES ROAD,
HORSFORTH LS18 4SY.
Tel: 0113 258 8923.
Fax: 0113 250 8204.
Fleetname: Travel Team.
Ptnrs: G. Navey, C. A. Goodmill
Fleet: 8 coach.
Chassis: 3 DAF. 1 MAN. 1 Neoplan.
2 Scania. 1 Volvo.
Bodies: 1 Berkhof. 1 Jonckheere. 2 LAG.
1 Neoplan. 3 Van Hool.
Ops incl: private hire, continental tours.
Livery: White with Blue splash.

ANDERSON'S COACHES
wc 💺 A/c ✔

75 GYPSY LANE, TOWNVILLE,
CASTLEFORD WF10 3PA.
Tel: 01977 552980.
Fax: 01977 557823.
E-mail: info@andersons-coaches.co.uk
Ptnrs: E. Anderson, M. Anderson, P. Anderson.
Fleet: 6 - 4 coach, 1 midibus, 1 minibus.
Chassis: 1 Iveco. 1 Mercedes. 4 Setra.
Bodies: include 4 Setra.
Ops incl: excursions & tours, private hire.

ARRIVA YORKSHIRE LTD
♿ 💺 wc 🍴 A/c T

24 BARNSLEY ROAD, WAKEFIELD WF1 5JX
Tel: 01924 231300
Fax: 01924 200106
Web site: www.arriva.co.uk
Man Dir: Kenneth Clarke **Eng Dir**: Ralph Roberts **Fin Dir**: David Cocker **Ops Dir**: Stuart Bear **Comm Dir**: Phil Booker
Fleet: 434 - 143 double-deck bus,
204 single-deck bus, 7 coach, 80 midibus.
Chassis: 120 DAF. 123 Dennis. 94 Leyland.
14 Optare. 83 Volvo.
Bodies: 163 Alexander. 45 ECW. 10 East Lancs. 18 Ikarus. 46 Leyland. 21 Northern Counties. 58 Optare. 51 Plaxton. 3 Reeve Burgess. 7 Van Hool. 11 Wright.
Ops incl: local bus services, school contract, expresss.
Livery: Blue/Cream
Ticket System: Wayfarer III

*AZTECBIRD LTD
♿ wc 🍴 💺 A/c R T

LOW MILLS, GUISELEY LS20 9LU
Tel: 0113 250 7385
Fax: 0113 250 8204
E-mail: hire@aztecbird.co.uk
Web site: www.aztecbird.co.uk
Gen Man: S J Roby **Ops Man**: A Birch
Ch Eng: G Navey
Fleet: 16 - 7 coach, 4 single-deck bus,
1 double-deck coach, 1 midibus, 3 minibus.
Chassis: 6 DAF. 1 Iveco. 1 MAN.
3 Mercedes. 2 Neoplan. 3 Scania.
Bodies: 1 Beulas. 3 Ikarus. 1 Jonckheere. 1 Mercedes. 2 Neoplan. 3 Optare. 5 Van Hool.
Ops incl: private hire, continental tours, local bus services, excursions & tours
Ticket System: Wayfarer

B & H TOURS wc 🍴 ✔
52 WILSON AVENUE, MIRFIELD WF14 9AT.
Tel/Fax: 01924 497067.
Prop: Barbara Armitage.
Fleet: 1 coach. **Chassis/Body**: Bova.
Ops incl: excursions & tours, private hire, continental tours.
Livery: Cream/Brown.

B & J TRAVEL
3 SANDY LANE, MIDDLESTOWN,
WAKEFIELD WF4 4PW.
Tel: 01924 263334.
Prop: J. S. Bendle.
Fleet: 2 coach.
Chassis: DAF. Volvo.
Bodies: Jonckheere. Plaxton.
Ops incl: school contracts, excursions & tours, private hire.
Livery: Red/White/Blue.

*BLACK PRINCE BUSES LTD
YORK COTTAGE, TEXAS STREET,
MORLEY LS27 0HG

A/c	Air conditioning	
♿	Vehicles suitable for disabled	
🍴	Coach(es) with galley facilities	
wc	Coach(es) with toilet facilities	
💺	Seat belt-fitted vehicles	
R	Recovery service available (not 24 hr)	
R24	24hr recovery service	
✔	Replacement vehicle available	
T	Toilet-drop facilities available	
	Vintage vehicle(s) available	
	Open top vehicle(s)	

West Yorkshire

Tel: 0113 252 6033
Fax: 0113 253 6082
Fleetnames: Black Prince
Man Dir: Brian Crowther **Ch Eng**: David Crowther **Comm Man**: Jack Berry
Fleet: 38 - 24 double-deck bus, 11 single-deck bus, 3 minibus.
Chassis: 1 Leyland. 8 Mercedes. 3 Optare. 26 Scania.
Bodies: 23 Alexander. 3 East Lancs. 1 Leyland. 11 Optare.
Ops incl: local bus services.
Livery: Red/Yellow.
Ticket System: Wayfarer.

BRITANNIA TRAVEL
[wc] [🍴] [●] [🔑]

113 WESTON LANE, OTLEY LS21 2DX.
Tel/Fax: 01943 465591
Prop: A. Broome, Mrs S. Eastwood.
Fleet: 1 coach.
Chassis: Iveco. **Body**: Beulas.
Ops incl: excursions & tours, private hire, continental tours.
Livery: Silver/Red/Blue.

*BROWNS COACHES (SK) LTD
[♿] [wc] [●] [Nc] [🔑]

WHITE APRON STREET, SOUTH KIRKBY WF9 3HQ
Tel: 01977 644777
Fax: 01977 643210
E-mail: browns.sk@speed-mail.co.uk
Web site: www.brownscoaches.com
Fleetname: Browns
Man Dir: Eric Brown **Co Sec**: Mrs J M Brown **Gen Man**: A Griffith **Ch Eng**: D Brown **Traf Man**: S Covell
Fleet: 15 - 5 coach, 5 midicoach, 5 minicoach.
Chassis: 2 Bova. 2 Ford Transit. 1 Iveco. 7 Mercedes. 3 Scania.
Bodies: 2 Bova. 3 Irizar. 3 Transbus. 3 Onyx. 1 Iveco. 3 Advanced.
Ops incl: private hire, school contracts, excursions & tours, continental tours.
Livery: Silver/White.

*CLARKSONS COACHES
[wc] [🍴] [●] [Nc]

52 DONCASTER ROAD, SOUTH ELMSALL, PONTEFRACT WF9 2JN
Tel: 01977 642385
Fax: 01977 640158
E-mail: info@clarksonscoaches.co.uk
Web site: www.clarksonscoaches.co.uk
Chmn: Ken Clarkson **ManDir/Co Sec**: John Hancock **Ops Dir**: Paul Clarkson
Fleet: 7 - 5 coach, 1 minicoach, 1 midicoach.
Chassis: Ford Transit. Mercedes. Neoplan.
Bodies: Mercedes. Neoplan.
Ops incl: excursions & tours, private hire, continental tours.

DALESMAN
[wc] [🍴] [●] [Nc] [🔑]

VICTORIA ROAD, GUISELEY LS20 8DG
Tel: 01943 870228
Fax: 01943 878277
E-mail: dalesman@lineone.net
Fleet: 14 - 8 coach, 3 midicoach, 3 minicoach.
Chassis: 8 DAF. 6 Mercedes.
Bodies: 3 Autobus. 3 Mercedes. 8 Van Hool.
Ops incl: school contracts, excursions & tours, private hire, continental tours.
Livery: White/Blue

DEWHIRST COACHES LTD
[wc] [🍴] [●] [Nc]

THORNCLIFFE ROAD, BRADFORD BD8 7DD
Tel/Fax: 01274 481208
Ops Man: S R Dewhirst
Fleet: 6 - 2 double-deck bus, 4 coach.
Chassis: 1 DAF. 2 MAN. 1 Scania. 2 Volvo.
Bodies: 1 Alexander. 1 East Lancs. 1 Plaxton. 1 Van Hool. 2 EOS.
Ops incl: local bus services, excursions & tours, private hire, continental tours.
Livery: Blue/White

FIRST IN BRADFORD [♿]
BOWLING BACK LANE, BRADFORD BD4 8SP
Tel: 01274 734833
Fax: 01274 736768
E-mail: contact.us@firstgroup.com
Web site: www.firstgroup.com
Man Dir: Jonathan May **Ops Dir**: Khadim Hussain. **Contr Dir**: Brian Wilkinson **Senr Fin Man**: Nicola Marshall
Fleet: includes double-deck bus, single-deck bus, minibus.
Chassis: Leyland. Leyland National. Optare. Volvo.
Bodies: Alexander. Leyland. Leyland National. Optare. Wright.
Ops incl: local bus services, school contacts.
Ticket System: Wayfarer

FIRST IN HALIFAX [♿]
SKIRCOAT ROAD, HALIFAX HX1 2RF.
Tel: 01422 305426
Fax: 01422 346323
Web site: www.firstcalderline.co.uk.
Man Dir: Mick herdman **Ops Dir**: Graham Riley **Comm Dir**: Nigel Winter **Fin Dir**: Christine Haigh, **Eng Dir**: Mark Hargreaves, **Ops Man**: Adrian Arthur.
Fleet: 221 - 85 double-deck bus, 109 single-deck bus, 27 minibus.
Chassis: 2 Bluebird. 60 Dennis. 51 Leyland. 16 MCW. 27 Mercedes. 65 Volvo.
Bodies: Alexander. Bluebird. ECW. MCW. Optare. Plaxton. Roe. Wright.
Ops incl: local bus services, school contracts.
Livery: FirstGroup.
Ticket System: Wayfarer 3.

FIRST IN HUDDERSFIELD
OLD FIELDHOUSE LANE, HUDDERSFIELD HD2 1AG.
Tel: 01484 426313
Fax: 01484 431214
Web site: www.firsthuddersfield.co.uk.
Div Dir: Ian Davies **Man Dir**: Mark Herdman **Comm Dir**: Nigel Winter
Fleet: 160 - 48 double-deck bus. 103 single-deck bus. 9 minibus.
Chassis: 99 Dennis. 17 Leyland. 9 Mercedes. 31 MCW. 4 Scania.
Bodies: MCW. Northern Counties. Plaxton. Roe.
Ops incl: local bus services, school contacts.
Livery: White/Magenta/Blue
Ticket System: Wayfarer.

FIRST IN LEEDS [♿]
KIRKSTALL ROAD, LEEDS LS3 1LH.
Tel: 0113 245 1601
Fax: 0113 242 9721
Web site: www.firstgroup.com www.firstleeds.co.uk
Fleetname: First in Leeds
Div Dir: Ian Davies
Fleet: 487 - 268 double-deck bus, 182 single-deck bus, 15 articulated bus, 22 minibus.
Chassis: 84 Dennis. Ford Transit. 33 MCW. 8 Mercedes. 14 Optare. 65Leyland. 150 Scania. 133 Volvo.
Bodies: Alexander. MCW. Optare. Plaxton. Roe. Wright.
Ops incl: local bus services, school contacts.
Livery: FirstGroup
Ticket System: Wayfarer 3.

GAIN TRAVEL EXPERIENCE LTD
[●] [wc] [🍴] [Nc]

6 FAIR ROAD, WIBSEY, BRADFORD BD6 1QN.
Tel: 01274 603224.
Fax: 01274 678274.
Web site: www.gaintravel.co.uk
E-mail: gaintravel@clara.co.uk
Fleet: 7 - 6 coach, 1 minibus.
Chassis: 6 MAN.
Bodies: 6 Van Hool.
Ops incl: excursions & tours, continental tours, private hire.

STANLEY GATH (COACHES) LTD
[wc] [●] [🍴] [Nc] [R] [🔑] [T]

LEES HALL ROAD, THORNHILL LEES, DEWSBURY WF12 9EQ.
Tel: 01924 466766.
Fax: 01924 458665.
E-mail: info@stanleygath.co.uk
Web site: www.stanleygath.co.uk
Dirs: A. Gath-Bragg, J. R. Bragg. **Gen Man**: P. R. Emerton.
Fleet: 14 - 11 coach. 1 double-deck coach, 1 midicoach, 1 minicoach.
Chassis: 1 DAF. 1 Dennis. 1 LDV. 1 Leyland. 1 Neoplan. 7 Volvo.
Ops incl: excursions & tours, private hire, continental tours, school contracts, express.
Livery: Grey/Cream.

GLENWAY COACHES (HALIFAX)
[●] [wc] [Nc]

LEES HALL ROAD, THORNHILL LEES, DEWSBURY WF12 9EQ.
Tel: 01422 823244.
Fax: 01924 458665.
Dirs: J. R. Bragg, A. Gath-Bragg. **Gen Man**: P. R. Emerton.
Fleet: 4 - 2 single-deck coach, 1 double-deck coach, 1 minicoach.
Chassis: 1 LDV. 1 Neoplan. 2 Volvo.
Ops incl: excursions & tours, private hire, school contracts, express, continental tours.
Livery: Grey/Cream

J D GODSON
3 SANDBED LANE, CROSSGATES,
LEEDS LS15 8JH
Tel: 0113 264 6166.
Fax: 0113 390 9669.
E-mail:
godsonscoaches@hotmail.com
Man Dir: David Godson
Fleet: 8
Chassis: 2 Bova. 3 DAF. 3 Volvo
Bodies: 2 Bova. 1 Caetano. 5 Plaxton.
Ops incl: school contracts, private hire.
Livery: Pink/White/Brown

G. W. GOULDING wc
64 THE RIDGEWAY, KNOTTINGLEY
WF11 0JS.
Tel: 01977 672265, 672059.
Fax: 01977 670276.
Fleetname: B. Goulding.
Prop: G. W. Goulding.
Fleet: 5 - 3 coach, 1 midicoach,
1 minicoach.
Chassis: 1 Bristol. 1 Leyland. 1 Toyota.
2 Volvo.
Bodies: 1 Caetano. 4 Plaxton.
Ops incl: excursions & tours, private hire,
continental tours.
Livery: White with Red/Yellow/Blue stripes.

GRA-CAR COACHES
THE GARAGE, FEATHERSTONE
LANE, FEATHERSTONE WF7 6AN.
Tel: 01977 791950.
Fleet: 2 - 1 single-deck bus, 1 coach.
Chassis: DAF. Leyland.
Ops incl: local bus services, excursions &
tours, private hire.

CENTRAL GARAGE
STANSFIELD ROAD, TODMORDEN
OL14 5DL
Tel/Fax: 01706 813909
Man Dir: D P Guest **Dir:** Mrs A L Guest
Rec Man: A. J. Gledhill.
Fleet: 2 minibus.
Chassis/bodies: 2 Mercedes.
Ops incl: private hire, school contracts,
excursions & tours.

HOWIE'S OF ROBERTTOWN
194 ROBERTTOWN LANE,
ROBERTTOWN, LIVERSEDGE
WF15 7LF
Tel/Fax: 01924 400386.
Props: D. Howie, Susan Howie.
Fleet: 1 coach. **Chassis/Body:** Bova.
Ops incl: excursions & tours, private hire.
Livery: Cream/Purple/Gold.

*ILLINGWORTH COACHES
BELLE VUE GARAGE LTD,
34 PINCHEON STREET, UPPER
WARRENGATE,
WAKEFIELD WF1 4DT
Tel: 01924 373085
Fax: 01924 274110
Dirs: G Illingworth, J Illingworth **Co Sec:**
P Illingworth
Fleet: 3 coach.
Chassis: 3 Scania.
Bodies: 3 Irizar
Ops incl: excursions & tours, private hire,
continental tours.
Livery: White

*INDEPENDENT COACHWAYS LTD
LOW FOLD GARAGE, NEW ROAD
SIDE, HORSFORTH LS28 5TE
Tel: 0113 258 6491
Fax: 0113 259 1125
E-mail:
independentcoachways@yahoo.co.uk
Web site:
www.independentcoachways.co.uk
Dirs: P & C Thomas **Gen Man:** Barry
Rennison **Traf Man:** Stephen Holladay
Eng: Peter Foster
Fleet: 9 - 3 single-deck bus, 6 coach.
Chassis: 3 Scania. 6 Volvo.
Bodies: 9 Plaxton.
Ops incl: private hire, school contracts.
Livery: Blue/Grey.

KEIGHLEY & DISTRICT TRAVEL
CAVENDISH HOUSE, 91-93
CAVENDISH STREET, KEIGHLEY
BD21 3DG
Tel: 01535 603284
Web site:
www.keighleyanddistrict.co.uk
Fleet name: The Zone
Chmn: G R Fearnley
Fleet: 103 - 40 double-deck bus, 63 single-deck bus.
Chassis: Dennis. Volvo.
Bodies: Alexander. Plaxton. Wright.
Ops incl: local bus services, school contracts
Livery: Blue/White, Blue/Red

*J J LONGSTAFF & SONS LTD wc
64 DAISY HILL, DEWSBURY
WF13 1LH
Tel: 01924 463124
Fax: 01924 430345
Fleetname: Longstaff of Mirfield
Dirs: B Longstaff, H Longstaff, S Kaye
Fleet: 6 - 2 single-deck bus, 4 coach.
Chassis: 6 Volvo.
Bodies: 4 Van Hool. 2 Wright.
Ops incl: local bus services, school
contracts, excursions & tours, private hire,
continental tours.
Livery: Blue/Grey/White.
Ticket System: Wayfarer

*A. LYLES & SON
63 COMMONSIDE, BATLEY
WF17 6LA
Tel: 01924 464771
Fax: 01924 469267
Ptnrs: Terence Lyles, Howard Lyles.
Fleet: 7 - 2 single-deck bus, 4 coach.
1 minicoach.
Chassis/Bodies: 3 EOS, 1 Caetano.
2 Optare. 1 Plaxton. 3 Van Hool.
Ops incl: local bus services, school
contracts, excursions & tours, private hire,
continental tours.
Livery: Beige/Brown/Red

*DAVID PALMER COACHES LTD wc
THE TRAVEL OFFICE, WAKEFIELD
ROAD, NORMANTON WF6 2BT
Tel: 01924 895849
Fax: 01924 897750
E-mail:
info@davidpalmercoaches.co.uk
Web site:
www.davidpalmercoaches.co.uk
Dirs: Margaret Palmer, Andrew Palmer, Lisa
Palmer.
Fleet: 9 - 5 coach. 2 midicoach, 1 minibus.
Chassis: 1 DAF. 1 LDV. 4 MAN. 1 Toyota.
Bodies: 1 Caetano. 3 EOS. 1 Mercedes.
1 Noge. 1 Van Hool.
Ops incl: excursions & tours, private hire,
continental tours.
Livery: Silver

PAUL'S TRAVEL
wc R24 T
31 ST JOHN'S ROAD,
HUDDERSFIELD HD1 5DX
Tel: 01484 454040.
Fax: 01484 300900.
Prop: P. Singh.
Fleet: 40 - 2 single-deck bus, 6 coach,
1 midibus, 1 midicoach, 30 minibus.
Chassis: 3 Bova, 2 DAF, 5 Ford Transit.
3 Iveco. 3 LDV. 2 Leyland. 15 Mercedes.
6 Optare. 1 Volvo.
Bodies: 3 Bova. 2 Leyland. 15 Mercedes.
6 Optare. 1 Plaxton.
Ops incl: local bus services, school
contracts, excursions & tours, private hire,
continental tours.

*PULLMAN DINER
wc T
C/O GRANGE STORAGE &
DISTRIBUTION, GRANGE ROAD,
BATLEY WF17 6LW
Tel/Fax: 01924 420777
Web site: www.pullmandiner.co.uk
Prop: Michael Hartey **Ops Man:** Lesley
Price
Fleet: coach
Bodies: Van Hool.
Ops incl: private hire

RED ARROW COACHES LTD
wc R
ASPLEY HOUSE, LINCOLN STREET,
HUDDERSFIELD HD1 6RX.
Tel: 01484 420993.
Fax: 01484 540409.
E-mail: info@redarrowcoaches.co.uk
Web site: www.redarrowcoaches.co.uk
Dirs: Steven R. Moore, Suichwant Singh.

A/c	Air conditioning
♿	Vehicles suitable for disabled
⧫	Coach(es) with galley facilities
wc	Coach(es) with toilet facilities
♥	Seat belt-fitted vehicles
R	Recovery service available (not 24 hr)
R24	24hr recovery service
✓	Replacement vehicle available
T	Toilet-drop facilities available
	Vintage vehicle(s) available
🚌	Open top vehicle(s)

West Yorkshire

Fleet: 10 - 9 coach, 1 midicoach.
Chassis: 1 Ayats. 2 Bova. 2 DAF. 1 Dennis. 2 MAN. 2 Scania.
Bodies: 1 Ayats. 2 Bova. 1 Caetano. 2 Plaxton. 4 Van Hool.
Ops incl: excursions & tours, private hire, continental tours, school contracts.

*JOHN RIGBY TRAVEL

UNIT 3, ADWALTON BUSINESS PARK, 132 WAKEFIELD ROAD, DRIGHLINGTON BD11 1DR
Tel: 0113 285 3366
Fax: 0113 285 3377
E-mail: rigbytrans@travel.tsbusiness.co.uk
Web site: www.johnrigby.co.uk
Owner: John Rigby **Man:** Steve Clayton
Fleet: 8 - 5 coach, 1 midicoach, 2 minibus.
Chassis: 2 DAF. 1 MAN. 1 Mercedes. 1 Toyota. 3 Volvo.
Bodies: 3 Caetano. 2 Plaxton. 2 Van Hool. 1 Crest
Ops incl: private hire, school contracts.

ROLLINSON SAFEWAY LTD

65 HALL LANE, LEEDS LS12 1PQ
Tel: 0113 231 1355
Fax: 0113 231 1344
Man Dir: Paul Rollinson. **Dir:** Peter Rollinson. **Contracts Man:** M. J. Joyce.
Fleet: 72 minibus.
Chassis: 1 Fiat. 3 Ford Transit. 3 Iveco. 20 Mercedes. 45 Renault.
Ops incl: private hire, school contracts.
Livery: Brown/Gold.

*ROPERS COACHES

69 DUCKWORTH LANE, BRADFORD BD9 5EX
Tel: 01274 487973
Fax: 01274 543230
Prop: Stanley Roper, Vera Roper.
Fleet: 1 coach.
Chassis/Body: 1 Bova.
Ops incl: excursions & tours, private hire, continental tours.
Livery: Blue/Silver.

*ROSS TRAVEL

THE GARAGE, ALLISON STREET, FEATHERSTONE WF7 6BB
Tel: 01977 792106
Fax: 01977 690109
Props: Peter Ross, Mary Ross.
Fleet: 17 - 9 single-deck bus, 6 coach, 1 midicoach, 1 minibus.
Chassis: 3 DAF. 1 LDV. 1 MAN. 7 Mercedes. 4 Optare. 1 Scania.
Bodies: 1 Bova. 1 Jonckheere. 1 Leyland. 4 Optare. 5 Plaxton. 1 Setra. 3 Van Hool.
Ops incl: local bus services, excursions & tours, private hire, school contracts, continental tours.
Livery: Red/White.
Ticket System: Wayfarer.

*SHEARINGS LTD

MILL LANE, NORMANTON WF6 1RF
Tel: 01977 603008
Fax: 01977 603114
Ch Exec: D J Slatcher **Fin Dir:** D R Newbold **Gen Man:** Jenny Masters
See also Shearings Ltd, Greater Manchester

PAUL SPENCE COACHES

16 HOPBINE AVENUE, BRADFORD BD5 8ER.
Tel: 01274 392728.
Prop: P. Spence. **Ptnr:** Mrs D. Spence.
Fleet: 3 - 2 coach, 1 minicoach.
Chassis: Ford. MAN. Talbot.
Bodies: Plaxton. MAN. Talbot Express.
Ops incl: excursions & tours, private hire, continental tours, school contracts.

STEEL'S LUXURY COACHES

COACHWAYS, ADDINGHAM, ILKLEY LS29 0PD.
Tel: 01943 830206.
Fax: 01943 831499.
Fleetname: Steels of Addingham
Prop/Gen Man: T. F. Steel.
Co Sec: Mrs J. M. Steel.
Fleet: 12 - 8 coach, 3 midicoach, 1 minicoach.
Chassis: 1 Dennis. 1 MAN. 1 Mercedes. 3 Scania. 5 Volvo. 1 LDV.
Bodies: 2 Berkhof. 2 Irizar. 1 Jonckheere. 6 Plaxton. 1 Van Hool.
Ops incl: excursions & tours, private hire, continental tours, school contracts.
Livery: Red/Black/White.

*E STOTT & SONS LTD

COLNE VALE GARAGE, SAVILE STREET, MILNSBRIDGE, HUDDERSFIELD HD3 4PG
Tel: 01484 460463
Fax: 01484 461463
E-mail: markstott@btconnect.com
Web site: www.stottscoaches.co.uk
Dirs: Mark Stott, Carl Stott, Eric Stott.
Fleet: 25 - 4 single-deck bus, 10 coach, 1 midicoach, 10 minibus.
Chassis: 1 DAF. 5 Leyland. 11 Mercedes. 8 Volvo.
Bodies: 4 Leyland. 1 Optare. 7 Plaxton. 10 Reeve Burgess. 2 Transbus. 1 Van Hool.
Ops incl: local bus services, school contracts, excursions & tours, private hire, continental tours.
Livery: White/Red/Black
Ticket System: Wayfarer.

*STRINGERS PONTEFRACT MOTORWAYS

102 SOUTHGATE, PONTEFRACT WF8 1PN
Tel: 01977 600205
Fax: 01977 704178
E-mail: ms@stringerscoaches.fsnet.co.uk
Ptnrs: Sydney Stringer, Mark Stringer **Sec:** Sonia Stringer **Ch Eng:** Chris Palmer
Trainee Man: Mark E Stringer
Fleet: 9 - 4 coach, 4 midibus, 1 midicoach.
Chassis: 3 Mercedes. 2 Optare. 4 Volvo.
Bodies: 1 Mercedes. 2 Optare. 2 Plaxton. 4 Van Hool.

Ops incl: local bus services, school contracts, excursions & tours, private hire.
Ticket system: Almex

T & S TRAVEL

INDUSTRIAL ESTATE, SOUTH KIRKBY, PONTEFRACT WF9 3NR.
Tel: 01977 644992.
Fax: 01977 608652.
Ptnrs: Mrs L. Stevenson, J. Tebbett.
Fleet: 9 - 4 midicoach, 5 minibus.
Chassis: 2 Ford Transit. 1 Freight Rover. 1 MCW. 3 Mercedes.
Ops incl: local bus services, excursions & tours.

*TETLEYS MOTOR SERVICES

76 GOODMAN STREET, LEEDS LS10 1NY
Tel: 0113 276 2276
Fax: 0113 276 2277
E-mail: iantetley@aol.com
Dir: Ian Tetley **Ch Mechanic:** David Leach
Co Sec: Joan Tetley
Fleet: 15 coach.
Chassis: 3 AEC. 4 Dennis. 8 Volvo.
Bodies: 2 Duple. 10 Plaxton. 3 Van Hool.
Ops incl: private hire, school contracts, express.
Livery: Navy/Sky Blue on white

TWIN VALLEY COACHES

INDUSTRIAL ROAD GARAGE, SOWERBY BRIDGE HX6 2RA.
Tel: 01422 833358.
Props: E. D. and D. M. Pilling.
Fleet: 6 - 2 coach, 2 midicoach, 2 minicoach.
Chassis: 2 Dennis. 2 LDV. 2 Mercedes.
Bodies: 2 Optare. 2 Plaxton.
Ops incl: private hire, excursions and tours, school contracts.
Livery: Green/White.

WAKEFIELD TUTORIAL SCHOOL

COMMERICIAL STREET, MORLEY LS27 8HY.
Tel: 0113 257 6165, 253 4033.
Fleetname: W. T. S. Travel.
Dirs: R. Favell (**Gen Man/Traf Man**), J. A. Crosby. **Sec:** S. Kelson.
Fleet: 1 minicoach.
Chassis: Freight Rover. **Body:** Concept.
Ops incl: excursions & tours, private hire.
Livery: White with Red/Green stripe.

WALLACE ARNOLD COACHES

LOWFIELDS ROAD, LEEDS LS12 6DN.
Tel: 0113 263 6456.
Fax: 0113 231 9670.
Man Dir: S Barber **Sales & Mktg Dir:** Karen Gee
Fleet: 172 - 2 double-deck bus, 170 coach.
Chassis: 2 Leyland. 170 Volvo.
Bodies: 62 Jonckheere. 2 Northern Counties. 102 Plaxton. 6 other.
Ops incl: excursions & tours, private hire,

continental tours.
Livery: Cream/Orange.

R & S WATERSON
[wc] [♿] [✓]

68 HIGHFIELD ROAD,
HEMSWORTH, PONTEFRACT WF9 4EA.
Tel: 01977 610773.
Fax: 01977 613775.
Owner: R. Waterson.
Man: R. Waterson (Jnr).
Tour Op: J. Waterson.
Fleet: 10 - 7 coach, 2 midicoach, 1 minicoach.
Chassis: 1 DAF. 1 Ford. 1 Leyland. 6 Volvo.
Ops incl: excursions & tours, private hire.

*WELSH'S COACHES LTD
[♿] [wc] [A/c]

FIELD LANE, UPTON, PONTEFRACT WF9 1BH
Tel: 01977 643873
Fax: 01977 648143

E-mail: info@welshscoaches.com
Web site: www.welshscoaches.com
Dirs: John Welsh, Judy Welsh
Fleet: 6 - 5 coach, 1 minicoach
Chassis: 1 Mercedes. 5 Setra.
Bodies: 1 Mercedes. 5 Setra.
Ops incl: excursions & tours, private hire, continental tours.
Livery: White/Green/Red.

WORTLEY LINE COACHES
[♿]

115 RING ROAD, LOWER WORTLEY, LEEDS LS12 6AN.
Tel/Fax: 0113 263 8677
Props: Mrs E Rhodes, A R Rhodes
Fleet: 2 midicoach.
Chassis: 1 Renault. 1 Mercedes.
Ops incl: private hire.
Livery: White/Maroon.

*W T S MINICOACHES [♿]

49 PRIESTHORPE ROAD, FARSLEY, LEEDS LS28 5JR

Tel: 0113 257 6165
Web site: www.wyco.ngt/wts
Props: R Favell
Fleet: 2 minicoach.
Chassis: 2 LDV
Body: 2 Onyx.
Ops incl: school contracts, private hire.
Livery: Green/White

THE YORKSHIRE STAG MINIBUS CO
[♿] [A/c] [R24] [✓]

111 BUTTERSHAW LANE, BRADFORD BD6 2DA.
Tel/Fax: 01274 600222
Props: Peter Hillam
Fleet: 7 - 1 single-deck coach, 2 midicoach, 4 minicoach
Chassis: 1 Leyland. 3 Mercedes. 3 LDV
Bodies: 1 Olympus. 1 Autobus. 1 Duple. 2 Onyx. 1 Coachliners.
Ops incl: private hire, school contracts, excursions & tours, continental tours.
Livery: White.

WILTSHIRE

*ANDYBUS AND COACH LTD
[♿] [wc] [🍴] [A/c]

UNIT 6, WHITEWALLS, EASTON GREY, MALMESBURY SN16 0RD
Tel: 01666 510085
Fax: 01666 510157
E-mail: ajcoaches@netcentral.co.uk
Web site: www.andrew-james.co.uk, www.andybus.co.uk
Props: Andrew James
Fleet: 15 - 5 coach, 9 midibus, 1 midicoach
Chassis: 1 Bedford. 2 Bova. 2 Dennis. 1 Ford Transit. 2 Iveco. 1 MAN. 4 Mercedes. 1 Optare. 1 Toyota. 1 Transbus. 1 Volvo.
Bodies: 2 Bova. 1 Caetano. 1 Duple. 1 East Lancs. 2 Mellor. 4 Mercedes. 1 Optare. 6 Plaxton.
Ops incl: local bus services, school contracts, excursions & tours, private hire.
Livery: Cream/Orange/yellow
Ticket System: Wayfarer

APL TRAVEL

PEAR TREE COTTAGE, CRUDWELL SN16 9ES
Tel/Fax: 01666 577774
Prop: A.P. Legg

*AD-RAINS PSV
[♿] [♿] [wc] [A/c] [R]

THE COACH YARD, THE COMMON, BRINKWORTH SN15 5DX
Tel: 01666 510874
Fax: 01666 510815
Recovery: 07831 303295
Fleetname: Ad'rains

Prop: A Griffiths **Ops Man**: C Minchin
Fleet: 8 - 3 coach, 1 midicoach, 3 midibus, 1 minicoach.
Chassis: 1 LDV. 3 Leyland. 3 Mercedes. 1 Volvo.
Bodies: 6 Plaxton. 1 Reeve Burgess. 1 other.
Ops incl: local bus services, school contracts, private hire, excursions & tours.
Livery: White/Blue/Yellow

*BARNES COACHES LTD
[wc] [🍴] [♿] [A/c] [🚌] [✓] [T]

THE SQUARE, ALDBOURNE, MARLBOROUGH SN8 2OU.
Tel: 01672 540330
Fax: 01672 520007
E-mail: travel@barnescoaches.co.uk
Dirs: Lionel Barnes, Terry Barnes.
Fleet: 23 coach
Chassis: 6 Bova. 1 DAF. 15 Volvo.
Bodies: 3 Berkhof. 6 Bova. 2 Plaxton. 11 Van Hool
Ops incl: local bus services, school contracts, excursions & tours, private hire, continental tours.
Livery: Green

*BEELINE (R & R) COACHES LTD
[♿] [R]

BISHOPSTROW ROAD, WARMINSTER BA12 9HQ
Tel: 01985 213503
Fax: 01985 213922
Dirs: M N Hayball, A D Hayball **Gen Man**: N Ennis
Fleet: 30 - 20 coach, 6 midicoach, 4 minibus.

Chassis: 4 Bedford. 12 Mercedes. 14 Volvo.
Bodies: 26 Plaxton. 4 LDV.
Ops incl: local bus services, school contracts, private hire, express
Livery: White
Ticket system: Setright

*BELL'S LUXURY COACHES
[♿] [A/c]

162 CASTLE STREET, SALISBURY SP1 3UA.
Tel: 01722 339422
Fax: 01722 412681
Man: Chris Mills **Ops Man**: S Hursthouse.
Fleet: 8 - 1 midicoach, 2 minicoach, 5 single-deck coach.
Chassis: 1 Dennis. 2 Mercedes. 1 DAF. 3 Volvo. 1 Toyota.
Bodies: 2 Autobus. 1 Caetano. 4 Plaxton. 1 Van Hool. 1 other.
Ops incl: excursions & tours, private hire, school contracts, continental tours.
Livery: Green/Cream.

*BETTER MOTORING SERVICES [♿] [A/c]

104A SWINDON ROAD, STRATTON-ST MARGARET SN3 4PT
Tel: 01793 823747
Fax: 01793 831698
Fleetname: B.M.S. Coaches.
Prop: D G Miles **Eng**: M J Hopkins **Sec**: Mrs M. Mulhern
Fleet: 10 - 8 midicoach, 2 minicoach.
Chassis: 1 Ford. 9 Mercedes.
Bodies: 6 Autobus. 2 Optare. 1 Ford. 1 Onyx.
Ops incl: school contracts, excursions & tours, private hire, continental tours.

A/c	Air conditioning	
♿	Vehicles suitable for disabled	
🍴	Coach(es) with galley facilities	
wc	Coach(es) with toilet facilities	
♿	Seat belt-fitted vehicles	
R	Recovery service available (not 24 hr)	
R24	24hr recovery service	
✓	Replacement vehicle available	
T	Toilet-drop facilities available	
🚌	Vintage vehicle(s) available	
	Open top vehicle(s)	

*C BODMAN & SONS

88 HIGH STREET, WORTON, DEVIZES SN10 5RU
Tel: 01380 722393
Fax: 01380 721969
Ptnrs: R J Bodman, D N Bodman, C J Bodman, K G Heath **Tran Man:** C J Bodman **Ops Man:** G Carter
Fleet: 41 - 21 single-deck bus, 19 coach, 1 minibus.
Chassis: 1 Bedford. 22 Dennis. 1 Iveco. 1 LDV. 3 Leyland. 2 Mercedes. 4 Optare. 6 Volvo.
Bodies: 3 Alexander. 3 Berkhof. 16 Carlyle. 2 Marshall. 1 Mellor. 4 Optare. 9 Plaxton. 2 UVG. 1 Wadham Stringer.
Ops incl: local bus services, school contracts, excursions & tours, private hire.

BUDDENS SKYLARK COACHES LTD

See Hampshire.

*CHANDLERS COACH TRAVEL

158 CHEMICAL ROAD, WEST WILTS TRADING ESTATE, WESTBURY BA13 4JN
Tel: 01373 824500
Fax: 01373 824300
E-mail: info@chandlerscoach.co.uk
Web site: www.chandlerscoach.co.uk
Prop: Margaret L'Anson **Fleet Eng:** Christopher L'Anson
Fleet: 9 coach
Chassis: 1 Bedford. 8 Volvo.
Bodies: 1 Duple. 4 Plaxton. 4 Van Hool.
Ops incl: excursions & tours, private hire, continental tours.
Livery: Old White/Burgundy/Gold

*COACHSTYLE LTD

HORSDOWN GARAGE, NETTLETON, CHIPPENHAM SN14 7LN
Tel/Fax: 01249 782224
Owners: Andrew Jones, Mrs A L Jones
Fleet: 15 - 2 single-deck bus, 13 coach.
Chassis: 4 DAF. 3 Leyland. 1 Scania. 6 Volvo.
Bodies: 3 Berkhof. 1 Caetano. 2 Duple. 3 Jonckheere. 2 Mercedes. 3 Van Hool.
Ops incl: local bus services, school contracts, excursions & tours, private hire, continental tours.

CROSS COUNTRY COACHES

BLACKFORD LANE, CASTLE EATON SN6 6LE
Tel: 01285 810000
Fax: 01285 810142
E-mail: sales@crosscountrycoaches.com
Dir: B. Telford.
Fleet: 12 - 5 double-deck bus, 5 coach, 1 double-deck coach, 1 vintage.
Chassis: 1 Bedford, 5 DAF. 5 Daimler. 1 Setra.
Ops incl: local bus services, excursions & tours, private hire, continental tours, school contracts.

ELLISON'S COACHES

THE GARAGE, HIGH ROAD, ASHTON KEYNES SN6 6NX
Tel: 01285 861224
Fax: 01285 862115
E-mail: sales@ellisonscoaches.co.uk
Web site: www.ellisonscoaches.co.uk
Ptnrs: A. A. Ellison, M. G. Ellison.
Fleet: 18 coach
Chassis: Dennis, Neoplan.
Bodies: Neoplan, Plaxton.
Ops incl: local bus services, excursions & tours, school contracts, private hire, continental tours.
Livery: White/Yellow/Blue/Red

*FARESAVER BUSES

VINCENTS ROAD, BUMPERS FARM INDUSTRIAL ESTATE, CHIPPENHAM SN14 6QA
Tel: 01249 444444
Fax: 01249 448844
E-mail: sales@faresaver.co.uk
Web site: www.faresaver.co.uk
Prop: J V Pickford.
Fleet: 50 - 20 midibus, 20 midicoach, 10 minicoach
Chassis: Mercedes.
Bodies: Alexander. Autobus. Carlyle. Marshall. Mercedes. Plaxton. Wadham Stringer.
Ops incl: local bus services, school contracts, private hire.
Livery: White/Mauve.
Ticket System: Wayfarer 3.

G-LINE MINICOACHES

15 BROAD TOWN ROAD, BROAD TOWN, SWINDON SN4 7RB.
Tel/Fax: 01793 814336.
E-mail: gline@btinternet.com
Chmn: P. McGarry. **Man Dir:** N. McGarry.
Service Dir: J. McGarry.
Tpt Man: N. McGarry.
Fleet: 30 - 4 minicoach, 26 midicoach
Chassis: 4 Ford Transit. 2 Iveco. 10 LDV. 5 Mercedes.
Ops incl: private hire, school contracts.

R. J. HARLEY

119 LONDON ROAD, MARLBOROUGH SN8 1LH.
Tel: 01672 52786.
Fleetname: Harley Travel.
Prop: R. J. Harley.
Gen Man/Traf Man: A. M. Harley.
Fleet: 2 minicoach. **Chassis:** 2 Ford Transit.
Ops incl: local bus services, school contracts, private hire.
Livery: Green/Red.
Ticket System: Setright.

*HATTS COACHES

FOXHAM, CHIPPENHAM SN15 4NB
Tel: 01249 740444
Fax: 01249 740447
E-mail: info@hattstravel.co.uk
Web site: www.hattstravel.co.uk
Man Ptnr: Adrian Hillier **Traf Mans:** Andrew Bridgman, Philip Turner **Ch Eng:** Mike Henderson **Accounts:** Lynn Peglar **Holidays & Off Man:** Marylin Nelson
Fleet: 45 - 25 coach, 2 midibus, 2 midicoach, 8 minibus, 8 minicoach.
Chassis: 1 Ayats. 6 DAF. 1 Dennis. 2 Iveco. 4 MAN. 13 Mercedes. 1 Optare. 4 Renault. 3 Scania. 6 Volvo. 5 other.
Bodies: 4 Autobus. 1 Ayats. 1 Beulas. 2 Berkhof. 4 Irizar. 2 Mellor. 3 Mercedes. 4 Optare. 2 Plaxton. 4 Reeve Burgess. 1 Transbus. 1 UVG. 11 Van Hool. 5 others.
Ops incl: local bus services, excursions & tours, private hire, continental tours, school contracts.
Livery: Lilac
Ticket System: Setright.

ANDREW JAMES QUALITY TRAVEL

FERRIS FARM, OLIVEMEAD LANE, DAUNTSEY SN15 4JF
Tel: 01666 505585
Fax: 01666 504647
E-mail: ajcoach@netcentral.co.uk
Web site: www.andrew-james.co.uk
Fleet: 18 - 12 single-deck bus, 4 coach, 1 midicoach, 1 minicoach.
Chassis: 2 Bova. 1 Dennis. 1 Dodge. 3 Iveco. 1 MAN. 6 Mercedes. 1 Neoplan. 1 Optare. 2 Renault.
Bodies: 2 Bova. 2 Duple. 1 ECW. 1 Neoplan. 3 Optare. 3 Plaxton. 1 Reeve Burgess. 1 Wadham Stringer.
Ops incl: local bus services, school contracts, private hire.
Livery: Yellow/Cream.
Ticket system: Wayfarer

*KINGSTON COACHES

162 CASTLE STREET, SALISBURY SP1 3UA
Tel: 01722 337311
Fax: 01722 412681
Man: C Mills **Ops Man:** S Hursthouse
Fleet: 4 coach.
Chassis: 2 DAF. 1 Dennis. 1 Volvo.
Bodies: 3 Plaxton. 1 Van Hool.
Ops incl: private hire, continental tours, school contracts.
Livery: Red/Cream

*LEVER'S COACHES LTD

162 CASTLE STREET, SALISBURY SP1 3UA
Tel: 01722 417229
Fax: 01722 412681
Man: C Mills **Asst Man:** I Bassindale
Fleet: 6 - 4 coach, 1 midicoach, 1 minibus.
Chassis: 3 DAF. 1 Dennis. 2 Mercedes.
Bodies: 1 Autobus. 1 Plaxton. 3 Van Hool. 1 other.
Ops incl: local bus services, school contracts, excursions & tours, private hire, continental tours.
Livery: Cream/Blue.
Ticket system: Almex

MANSFIELD'S COACHES

27 FINCHDALE, COVINGHAM, SWINDON SN3 5AL.
Tel/Fax: 01793 525375.
Prop: R. E. Mansfield. **Man:** A. Mansfield.
Tran Man: P. Mansfield.

Sec: Mrs M. S. Mansfield.
Fleet: 6.
Chassis: 3 MAN. 2 Mercedes. 1 Toyota.
Ops incl: excursions & tours, private hire, express, school contracts.
Livery: Yellow/Green/Red.
Ticket System: Setright.

*PEWSEY VALE COACHES

HOLLYBUSH LANE, PEWSEY SN9 5BB
Tel/Fax: 01672 562238
Owner: A J Thorne
Fleet: coach, midicoach.
Chassis: Bova. Leyland. Mercedes. Volvo.
Bodies: Bova. Plaxton. Van Hool.
Ops incl: school contracts, excursions & tours, private hire.
Livery: White/Blue/Red

ROBIN'S COACHES

TREDENA, FORD, CHIPPENHAM SN14 8RR
Tel/Fax: 01249 782574
E-mail: info@robinscoaches.co.uk
Web site: robinscoaches.co.uk
Ptnrs: Robin Smith, D. P. Smith.
Fleet: 3 - 2 coach, 1 minibus.
Chassis: 2 Renault. 2 Volvo.
Bodies: 1 Berkhof. 1 Plaxton.
Ops incl: school contracts, excursions & tours, private hire, continental tours.
Livery: White/Blue/Pink

*SEAGER'S COACHES LTD

AUDLEY ROAD, CHIPPENHAM SN14 0EN.
Tel: 01249 654949 **Fax:** 01249 462006
E-mail: seagerscoaches@hotmail.com
Web site: www.seagers-coaches.co.uk
Owner: Jenny Seager **Man:** Tom Woods
Coach Man: Alan Watts
Fleet: 20 - 1 coach, 13 minibus, 2 midicoach (4 welfare).
Chassis: 1 DAF. 10 Ford Transit. 4 Iveco. 2 LDV. 2 Mercedes.
Bodies: Ikarus. 1 Marshall. 1 Mercedes. 3 UVG. 1 Wadham Stringer.
Ops incl: private hire, school contracts.
Livery: White

STAGECOACH WEST

See Gloucestershire

SWINDON VINTAGE OMNIBUS SOCIETY

10 FRASER CLOSE, NYTHE, SWINDON SN3 3RP
Tel: 01793 526001.
Chairm: M. Naughton. **Sec:** D. Nicol. **Treas:** D. Mundy.
Fleet: 1 double-deck bus.
Chassis: 1 Daimler.
Bodies: 1 Weymann.

*TEST VALLEY TRAVEL LTD

BANISTER BARN, NEWTON LANE, WHITEPARISH SP5 2QQ
Tel: 01794 884555
Dirs: J M Norman, Mrs A N Norman
Fleet: 6 - 1 midicoach, 5 minicoach.
Chassis/bodies: 1 Ford. 4 LDV. 1 Toyota. 1 Caetano. Ford/LDV.
Ops incl: private hire, school contracts.
Livery: White with Green/Gold relief.

*THAMESDOWN TRANSPORT LTD

CORPORATION STREET, SWINDON SN1 1DU
Tel: 01793 428400
Fax: 01793 428405
E-mail: j.owen@thamesdown-transport.co.uk
Web site: www.thamesdown-transport.co.uk
Man Dir: John Owen **Eng Dir:** N A Mason
Fin Dir: G W Cooper **Ops Dir:** D G J Burch
Fleet: 112 - 26 double-deck bus, 85 single-deck bus, 1 open-top bus.
Chassis: 1 Daimler. 94 Dennis. 17 Leyland.
Bodies: 9 Alexander. 8 ECW. 7 East Lancs. 3 Northern Counties. 85 Plaxton.
Ops incl: local bus services, school contracts, private hire, express.
Livery: Blue/White/Green (buses), Yellow (school buses).
Ticket System: Wayfarer 3 with MCV.

*TOURIST COACHES LTD

CASTLE STREET, SALISBURY SP1 3UA
Tel: 01722 413136
Fax: 01722 412681
Board Dir: Christopher Moyes, Ian Butcher
Man Dir: Alex Carter **Ops Dir:** Andrew Wickham **Eng Dir:** Geoff Parsons
Fleet: 27 - 21 single-deck bus, 6 midibus
Chassis: 6 DAF. 1 Dennis. 3 LDV. 3 Mercedes. 3 Optare. 1 Toyota. 10 Volvo.
Bodies: 1 Autobus. 1 Caetano. 3 Optare. 12 Plaxton. 1 Reeve Burgess. 5 Van Hool. 4 other.
Ops incl: local bus services, school contracts, excursions & tours, private hire, continental tours.
Livery: Orange/Cream.
Ticket System: Setright.
Associated Companies:
Bells Coaches (**Livery:** Green/Cream)
Levers Coaches (**Livery:** Blue)
Kingston Coaches (**Livery:** Red/Cream)

*VICTORY TOURS

See Dorset.

WORCESTERSHIRE

*ASTONS COACHES

CLERKENLEAP, BROOMHALL, WORCESTER WR5 3HR
Tel: 01905 820201
Fax: 01905 829249
E-mail: info@astons-coaches.co.uk
Web site: www.astons-coaches.co.uk
Man Dir: Richard Conway **Man Dir:** Tony Halford **Tran Man:** Gavin Taylor
Sales & Mktg Man: Amy Wornell
Fleet: 29 - 2 double-deck bus, 1 single-deck bus, 16 coach, 4 midicoach, 5 minibus, 1 minicoach.
Chassis: 2 Dennis. 2 Iveco. 4 LDV. 4 Mercedes. 1 Neoplan. 10 Scania. 6 Volvo.
Bodies: 2 Beulas. 2 East Lancs. 2 Irizar.
1 Jonckheere. 4 LDV. 4 Mercedes. 1 Neoplan. 6 Plaxton. 6 Van Hool. 1 Wright.
Ops incl: local bus services, school contracts, excursions & tours, private hire, express, continental tours.
Livery: White/Purple
Ticket system: ERG TP4000

*BIRMINGHAM & MIDLAND MOTOR OMNIBUS TRUST

See West Midlands

*N N CRESSWELL

WORCESTER ROAD, EVESHAM WR11 4RA
Tel: 01386 48655
Fax: 01386 48656
Props: Mary Cresswell, Sue Cresswell
Ch Eng: William Fairbrother
Fleet: 20 - 15 coach, 2 midicoach, 2 minibus, 1 minicoach.
Chassis: 9 Bedford. 6 Dennis. 5 Mercedes.
Ops incl: local bus services, school contracts, private hire.
Livery: Wessex Blue/White
Ticket System: Wayfarer, Setright.

DUDLEY'S COACHES LTD

POPLAR GARAGE, ALCESTER ROAD, RADFORD WR7 4LS
Tel: 01386 792203
Fax: 01386 793373

Air conditioning	
Vehicles suitable for disabled	
Coach(es) with galley facilities	
Coach(es) with toilet facilities	
Seat belt-fitted vehicles	
Recovery service available (not 24 hr)	
24hr recovery service	
Replacement vehicle available	
Toilet-drop facilities available	
Vintage vehicle(s) available	
Open top vehicle(s)	

Web site: www.dudleys-coaches.co.uk
Dirs: C E Dudley, M E A Dudley **Traf Man:** T P Underwood **Wkshp Man:** B Gallagher.
Fleet: 21 coach.
Chassis: 3 Dennis. 4 Leyland. 14 Volvo.
Bodies: 15 Plaxton. 6 Van Hool.
Ops incl: local bus services, school contracts, excursions & tours, private hire.
Livery: Green/Cream.

FIRST IN WYVERN
HERON LODGE, LONDON ROAD, WORCESTER WR5 2EU.
Tel: 01905 359393.
Fax: 01905 351104.
Man Dir: K. Mills. **Dir Eng:** J. Wright.
Fin Dir: R. Hutchings.
Fleet: 240 - 119 single-deck bus, 7 coach, 114 minibus.
Chassis: 66 Dennis. 60 Leyland. 102 Mercedes. 12 Optare.
Bodies: 53 Leyland. 3 Marshall. 12 Optare. 149 Plaxton. 12 Optare.
Ops incl: local bus services, school contracts.
Livery: White/Magenta/Blue
Ticket System: Wayfarer

*GOLD STAR TRAVEL
COOKSEY LODGE FARM, UPTON WARREN, BROMSGROVE B61 9HD
Tel/Fax: 01527 861685
Prop: Mrs Dorothy Homer.
Fleet: 1 coach.
Chassis/Bodies: 1 Van Hool.
Ops incl: private hire, excursions and tours.
Livery: White/Gold

*HARDINGS COACHES
319 EVESHAM ROAD, CRABBS CROSS, REDDITCH B97 5HL.
Tel: 01527 542590
Fax: 01527 545691
Recovery: 01527 545590
E-mail: john@hardingscoaches.co.uk
Web site: www.hardingscoaches.co.uk
Man Dir: John Dyson
Co Sec: Malcolm Playford
Fleet: 45 - 5 single-deck bus, 36 coach, 4 midicoach.
Chassis: 6 DAF. 6 Leyland. 2 MAN. 8 Mercedes. 18 Scania. 1 Toyota. 4 Volvo.
Bodies: 3 Berkhof. 1 Caetano. 1 East Lancs. 1 Ikarus. 10 Irizar. 5 Mercedes. 1 Optare. 3 Plaxton. 2 Reeve Burgess. 6 Transbus. 12 Van Hool.
Ops incl: local bus services, school contracts, excursions & tours, private hire, continental tours.
Livery: Silver/Grey

*HARRIS EXECUTIVE TRAVEL
58 MEADOW ROAD, CATSHILL, BROMSGROVE B61 0JL
Tel: 01527 872857
Fax: 01527 872708
Jt Man Dirs: J G Harris, S W Harris
Tours Organiser: V A Coles
Fleet Eng: J G Harris
Fleet: 8 - 7 coach, 1 minicoach.
Chassis: 8 Mercedes.
Bodies: 1 Mercedes. 7 Neoplan
Ops incl: excursions & tours, private hire, continental tours.
Livery: White

J B C MALVERNIAN TOURS
NEWTOWN ROAD TRAVEL CENTRE, NEWTOWN ROAD, MALVERN WR14 1PJ.
Tel: 01684 575082.
Fax: 01684 568870.
Fleetname: Jones Bros Coaches
E-mail: info@malverncoaches.co.uk
Web site: www.malverncoaches.co.uk
Props: G. G. & M. A. Crump. **Gen Man:** Michael Yates. **Ch Eng:** A. Jackson.
Fleet: 11 - 10 coach, 1 midicoach.
Chassis: 2 Bova. 1 DAF. 2 Dennis. 2 Leyland. 1 MAN. 1 Toyota. 2 Volvo.
Bodies: 2 Bova. 3 Duple. 3 Plaxton. 1 Van Hool.
Ops incl: local bus services, school contracts, excursions & tours, private hire, continental tours.
Livery: Off-white/Orange.

*KESTREL COACHES
UNITS 1&2, BARRACKS ROAD, SANDY LANE, STOURPORT-ON-SEVERN DY13 9QB
Tel/Fax: 01299 829689
Prop: Michael Wood.
Fleet: 10 - 4 coach, 3 midicoach, 3 minibus.
Chassis: 1 Bedford. 2 Bova. 1 DAF. 1 LDV. 2 Mercedes. 2 Toyota. 1 Citroën.
Bodies: 2 Bova. 3 Caetano. 2 Mercedes. 1 Van Hool. 1 Citroen. 1 other
Ops incl: local bus services, school contracts, private hire.
Livery: White
Ticket System: Almex

*WHITTLE COACH & BUS LTD
FOLEY BUSINESS PARK, STOURPORT ROAD, KIDDERMINSTER DY11 7QL
Tel: 01562 820002
Fax: 01562 820027
Recovery: 01562 82004
E-mail: ron@whittlecoach.co.uk
Chmn: Peter Shipp **Gen Man:** Ron Whittle
Fleet: 49 - 34 coach, 10 single-deck bus, 1 midibus, 2 midicoach, 2 minicoach.
Chassis: 35 Dennis. 1 Freight Rover. 8 Iveco. 2 Mercedes. 3 Optare.
Bodies: 8 Beulas. 1 Mercedes. 2 Northern Counties. 26 Plaxton. 1 Reeve Burgess. 6 UVG. 7 Wadham Stringer.
Ops incl: local bus services, school contracts, excursions & tours, private hire, continental tours.
Livery: White/Blue/Green/Yellow.
Ticket system: Setright/Wayfarer
Now part of EYMS Group Ltd

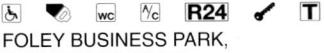

*WOODSTONES COACHES LTD
ARTHUR DRIVE, HOO FARM INDUSTRIAL ESTATE, KIDDERMINSTER DY11 7RA
Tel: 01562 823073
Man Dir: I Meredith **Dir:** R Meredith
Fleet: 6 coach
Chassis: 6 Volvo.
Bodies: 1 Jonckheere. 5 Plaxton.
Ops incl: local bus services, school contracts, excursions & tours, private hire, express, continental tours.
Livery: White/Orange/Yellow/Red.
Ticket system: Setright.

YARRANTON BROS LTD
EARDISTON GARAGE, TENBURY WELLS WR15 8JL.
Tel: 01584 881229.
Dirs: A. L. Yarranton (**Gen Man**), M. L. Yarranton, D. A. Yarranton.
Fleet: 12 - 10 coach, 1 minibus, 1 minicoach.
Chassis: 3 Bedford. 3 Dennis. 3 Mercedes. 2 Volvo.1 Toyota.
Bodies: 2 Berkhof. 2 Caetano. 1 Jonckheere. 2 Mercedes. 4 Plaxton. 1 Duple.
Ops incl: local bus services, school contracts, excursions & tours, private hire, continental tours.
Livery: Green/White/Orange.

Enjoy a range of quality road transport titles from...

Ian Allan PUBLISHING

BRITISH TROLLEYBUSES IN COLOUR
Kevin McCormack
ISBN: 0 7110 3008 1 HB
£14.99

GLORY DAYS: BLACK AND WHITE
Kevin Lane
ISBN: 0 7110 2954 7 HB
£16.99

GLORY DAYS: EASTERN NATIONAL
Richard Delahoy
ISBN: 0 7110 2952 0 HB
£16.99

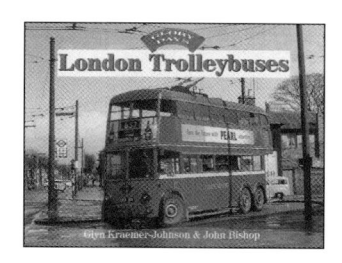

GLORY DAYS: LONDON TROLLEYBUSES
J Bishop & G Kraemer-Johnson
ISBN: 0 7110 2949 0 HB
£16.99

STREETS OF BELFAST
Mark Kennedy
ISBN: 0 7110 2959 8 HB
£14.99

STREETS OF GLASGOW
Alan Millar
ISBN: 0 7110 2994 6 HB
£14.99

Order by post, fax or e-mail:
Ian Allan Publishing Mail Order Dept, 4 Watling Drive,
Hinckley, Leics LE10 3EY
Tel: 01455 2254450 Fax: 01455 233737
e-mail: midlandbooks@compuserve.com OR ORDER ONLINE FROM
www.ianallansuperstore.com

MAIL ORDER P&P
UK - 10% of cost, min £1.50 up to £4.00 max - over £50 POST FREE
Overseas - 15% of cost, min £4.00, 10% for orders over £150

NOW LIVE @ www.ianallanpublishing.com
A brand new website showcasing new Ian Allan Publishing books and magazine updates!

Scottish Operators

ABERDEEN, CITY OF

*BLUEBIRD BUSES LTD

BUS STATION, GUILD STREET, ABERDEEN AB11 6GR
Tel: 01224 591381
Fax: 01224 584202
E-mail: eastscotland@stagecoachbus.com
Web site: www.stagecoachbus.com
Fleetname: Stagecoach Bluebird
Man Dir: Tom Wileman **Dep Man Dir:** Robert Andrew **Ops Dir:** Robert Hall **Eng Dir:** Michael Reid **Ops Man:** Alan Bain **Depot Eng:** Frank Bruce
Fleet: 198 - 36 double-deck bus, 85 single-deck bus, 6 coach, 32 midibus, 39 minibus.
Chassis: 22 Dennis. 31 Leyland. 14 MAN. 39 Mercedes. 92 Volvo.
Bodies: 109 Alexander. 2 Berkhof. 14 Jonckheere. 14 Leyland. 5 Northern Counties. 51 Plaxton. 7 Wright.
Ops incl: local bus services, school contracts, excursions & tours, private hire, express.
Livery: Stagecoach (White/Blue/Orange/Red)
Ticket System: Wayfarer TGX

*FIRST

395 KING STREET, ABERDEEN AB24 5RP
Tel: 01224 650100
Fax: 01224 650140
E-mail: contactus@firstgroup.com
Web site: www.firstgroup.com
Chmn: Martin Gilbert **DepChmn/Ch Exec:** Moir Lockhead
Fleet: 172 - 34 double-deck bus, 107 single-deck bus, 12 coach, 7 articulated bus, 4 open top bus, 2 vintage, 6 minicoach.
Ops incl: local bus services, school contracts, excursions & tours, private hire, express, continental tours.
Livery: Coaches: Silver or White, Buses: Group Magenta Blue/Grey.
Ticket System: Wayfarer 3

*FOUNTAIN EXECUTIVE

HILL OF GOVAL FARM, DYCE AB21 7NX
Tel: 01224 729191
Fax: 01224 729898
Owner: M Ewen
Fleet: 10 - 5 coach, 1 midicoach, 2 minibus, 2 minicoach.
Chassis: 5 Mercedes. 5 Scania.
Bodies: 5 Irizar. 1 Optare. 2 KVC. 2 Concept.
Ops incl: private hire, continental tours.
Livery: Gold.

GRAMPIAN COACHES

395 KING STREET, ABERDEEN AB24 5RP
Tel: 01224 650024
Fax: 01224 650151
E-mail: info@grampian.coaches.co.uk
Web site: www.grampian-coaches.co.uk
Man Dir: George Mair **Ch Eng:** Mike Thomson **Ops Man:** Tom Gordon **Comm Dir:** Joe Mackie **Dir Operations:** Tom McGivern
Fleet: 39 - 1 single-deck bus, 21 coach, 1 open top bus, 13 midibus, 2 midicoach, 6 minicoach.
Chassis: 1 Bluebird. 3 Dennis. 2 Leyland. 13 Mercedes. 5 Scania. 15 Volvo.
Bodies: 4 Alexander. 2 Duple. 4 Irizar. 7 Jonckheere. 1 Leyland. 1 Mercedes. 9 Plaxton. 10 Reeve Burgess. 1 Van Hool.
Ops incl: local bus services, school contracts, excursions & tours, private hire, express, continental tours.
Livery: Silver/White and Blue
Ticket System: Setright

MAIRS COACHES

395 KING STREET, ABERDEEN AB24 5RP.
Tel: 01224 650150.
Fax: 01224 650123.
Man Dir: G. Mair. **Eng Sup:** R. Elrick.
Comm Dir: J. Mackie
Fleet: 26 - 2 double-deck bus, 14 coach, 10 midicoach.
Chassis: 1 DAF. 1 Dennis. 3 Leyland. 8 Mercedes. 3 Renault. 1 Scania. 7 Volvo.
Bodies: 2 Alexander. 2 Duple. 8 Mercedes. 1 Irizar. 6 Plaxton. 2 Van Hool. 3 Dodge.
Ops incl: school contracts, excursions & tours, private hire, express, continental tours.
Livery: Silver/Grey or Maroon/Gold.
Ticket System: Wayfarer/Setright.
Part of FirstGroup.

WHYTES COACH TOURS

SCOTSTOWN ROAD, NEWMACHAR, ABERDEEN AB21 7PP
Tel: 01651 862211
Fax: 01651 862918
E-mail: sales@whytescoachtours.co.uk
Web Site: www.whytescoachtours.co.uk
Ptnrs: Linda A Urquhart, W. J. Whyte, Ian A W Urquhart, Susan Whyte, Steven Whyte.
Fleet: 22 - 14 coach, 4 midicoach, 1 minibus, 3 minicoach.
Chassis: Bova. DAF. Ford Transit. Mercedes. Volvo.
Bodies: Autobus. Beulas. Bova. Caetano. Mellor. Mercedes-Benz. Plaxton. other.
Ops incl: local bus services, school contracts, excursions & tours, private hire, continental tours.
Livery: Two-tone Green.

ABERDEENSHIRE

AMBER TRAVEL

CROSSFIELDS FARMHOUSE, TURRIFF AB53 7QY.
Tel: 01888 563474.
Fax: 01888 563474.
Props: D. Cheyne, S. Cheyne.
Fleet: 5 - 4 coach, 1 midibus.
Chassis: 1 Bedford. 1 Mercedes. 3 Volvo.
Ops incl: school contracts, private hire.
Livery: White/Red/Amber

*CHEYNES COACHES

ALLANDALE, DAVIOT, INVERURIE AB51 0EJ
Tel: 01467 671400
Fax: 01467 671479
E-mail: info@cheynescoaches.co.uk
Web site: www.cheynescoaches.co.uk
Ptnrs: W D Cheyne, R Cheyne, L A Cheyne, M F Cheyne.
Fleet: 12 - 3 single-deck bus, 5 coach, 4 minicoach.
Chassis: 3 Leyland. 4 Mercedes. 5 Volvo.
Bodies: 1 Optare. 3 Plaxton. 5 Van Hool.
Ops incl: local bus services, school contracts, excursions & tours, private hire.
Livery: Silver/Pink/Purple

HAYS COACHES

HALLHILL, COBAIRDY, HUNTLY AB54 7YB
Tel: 01466 740283.
Fax: 01466 740283
Web site: www.hays.co.uk
Ops Man: Karl Fisher **Owners:** C J Hay, S A Hay **Eng:** Brian Milne
Fleet: 15 - 9 coach, 2 midicoach, 4 minibus.
Chassis: 1 Bedford. 1 Ford. 2 Ford Transit. 4 Iveco. 1 Leyland. 2 Mercedes. 3 Volvo.
Bodies: 4 Beulas. 1 Duple. 1 Marshall. 1 Mellor. 2 Mercedes. 3 Plaxton. 1 Van Hool. 2 Mazda.
Ops incl: local bus services, school contracts, excursions & tours, private hire, continental tours.
Livery: Grey/Blue/Red

J W COACHES LTD

DYKEHEAD GARAGE, BLACKHALL, BANCHORY AB31 6PS.
Tel/fax: 01330 823300.
Chmn/Man Dir: J. S. Westaby.
Dir: J. I. Westaby.
Ops Man: A. Anderson.
Fleet: 15 - 5 coach, 6 midibus, 1 midicoach, 3 minibus.
Chassis: 1 Bedford. 6 Freight Rover. 1 Iveco. 4 Leyland. 1 MAN. 2 Mercedes.
Bodies: 5 Carlyle. 3 Duple. 2 Plaxton. 2 Reeve Burgess. 1 Devon. 2 Dormobile.
Ops incl: local bus services, school contracts, excursions & tours, private hire.
Livery: Blue/Turquoise/White.
Ticket System: Setright.

KINEIL COACHES

ANDERSON PLACE, FRASERBURGH AB43 9LG.
Tel: 01346 510200.
Fax: 01346 514774
Man Dir: Ian Neilson
Fleet: 3 double-deck bus, 16 coach, 1 midicoach, 5 minicoach.
Chassis: 1 DAF. 1 Dennis. 1 Freight Rover.

1 Leyland. 5 Mercedes. 16 Volvo.
Bodies: 2 Alexander. 1 Caetano. 2 East Lancs. 1 Jonckheere. 1 Leyland. 4 Mercedes. 2 Plaxton. 1 Reeve Burgess. 11 Van Hool.
Ops incl: local bus services, school contracts, excursions & tours, private hire, continental tours.
Livery: White/Blue/Red.

ALEX MILNE COACHES
THE GARAGE, 4 MAIN STREET, NEW BYTH AB53 7XD
Tel: 01888 544340
Ptnrs: Alex Milne, Brian Milne
Fleet: 12 - 3 coach, 4 minibus, 5 minicoach.
Chassis: 4 Ford Transit. 1 LDV. 5 Mercedes. 3 Volvo.
Bodies: include 3 Plaxton. 3 Van Hool.
Ops incl: local bus services, school contracts, excursions & tours, private hire.
Livery: Blue/White

M W NICOLL'S COACH HIRE
THE BUSINESS PARK, ABERDEEN ROAD, LAURENCEKIRK AB30 1EY
Tel: 01561 377262.
Fax: 01561 378822.
E-mail: malcolm.nicoll@lineone.net
Man Dir: M. W. Nicoll. **Dir:** I. J. Nicoll.
Service Man: A. Gordon.
Gen Man: H. Thomson.
Fleet: 24 - 2 single-deck bus, 6 coach, 3 midibus, 6 midicoach, 2 minibus, 5 minicoach.
Chassis: 1 Bova, 4 Ford Transit, 1 Leyland, 9 Mercedes, 1 Optare, Setra, 2 Toyota, 6 Volvo.
Bodies: 1 Bova, 2 Caetano, 1 Duple, 10 Mercedes, 1 Solo, 6 Van Hool, 4 others.
Ops incl: local bus services, private hire.
Livery: White.
Ticket System: Almex.

*REIDS OF RHYNIE
22 MAIN STREET, RHYNIE, BY HUNTLY AB54 4HB
Tel/Fax: 01464 861212
Recovery: 07831 173681
Owner: Colin Reid.
Fleet: 14 - 4 coach, 2 midibus, 1 midicoach, 7 minibus.
Chassis: 4 Ford Transit. 4 LDV. 3 Mercedes. 4 Volvo.
Bodies: include: 3 Caetano. 2 Mercedes. 1 Van Hool.
Ops incl: local bus services, school contracts, private hire.
Livery: White/Blue/Water Green
Ticket system: Wayfarer 3

SHEARER OF HUNTLY
OLD TOLL ROAD, HUNTLY AB54 6JA.
Tel: 01466 792410.
Fax: 01466 793926.
Props: James W. Shearer, Mrs Irene E. Shearer.
Fleet: 12 - 2 coach, 2 midicoach, 6 minibus,

2 minicoach.
Chassis: 2 Bedford. 5 Ford Transit. 2 LDV. 1 MAN. 2 Mercedes.
Bodies: 2 Plaxton. 2 Reeve Burgess. 2 Riviera. 1 Crystal.
Ops incl: local bus services, school contracts, private hire.
Livery: Burgundy/White.

SIMPSON'S COACHES
21 UNION STREET, ROSEHEARTY, FRASERBURGH AB43 7JP
Tel: 01346 571610.
Fax: 01346 571070.
Web site: www.simpsonscoaches.co.uk
E-mail: info@simpsonscoaches.co.uk
Prop: Ron Simpson.
Fleet: 7 - 5 coach, 2 minicoach.
Chassis: 2 Iveco. 2 Mercedes. 3 Volvo.
Bodies: 2 Beulas. 2 Berkhof. 1 Jonckheere. 1 Mercedes. 1 Reeve Burgess.
Ops incl: excursions & tours, private hire, continental tours.
Livery: White/Blue.

ANGUS

JAMES MEFFAN LTD
PARKEND, KIRRIEMUIR DD8 4PD.
Tel: 01575 572130.
Chmn: F. A. Carter. **Co Sec:** C. Mullen.
Dir/Gen Man: N. Meffan.
Fleet: 20 - 4 coach, 1 midibus, 3 midicoach, 10 minibus, 2 minicoach.
Chassis: 1 Ford Transit. 2 Freight Rover. 4 Leyland. 13 Mercedes.
Bodies: 4 Alexander. 1 Carlyle. 2 Duple. 6 Mercedes. 1 Plaxton. 1 Reeve Burgess. 1 PMT. 1 Scott. 1 Crystal. 1 Mellor. 1 Dormobile.
Ops incl: local bus services, school contracts, private hire.
Livery: Custard and Cream.
Ticket System: Wayfarer Saver.
Part of Traction Group.

*RIDDLER'S COACHES LIMITED
CAIRNIE LOAN, ARBROATH DD11 4DS
Tel: 01241 873464.
Fax: 01241 873504
Dirs: Charles W Riddler, Mrs Gwenda M Riddler.
Fleet: 8 coach.
Chassis: 8 Volvo.
Bodies: 8 Van Hool.
Ops incl: excursions & tours, private hire.

SIDLAW EXECUTIVE TRAVEL (SCOTLAND)
LISHEEN, THE BRAE, AUCHTERHOUSE DD3 0RE.

Tel: 01382 320280.
Fax: 01382 320482.
E-mail: travel@sidlaw.co.uk
Web site: www.sidlaw.co.uk
Man Dir: Bob Costello.
Fleet: 8 - 1 coach, 4 midicoach, 3 minicoach.
Chassis: 1 DAF 1 Ford Transit. 1 Freight Rover. 5 Mercedes.
Ops incl: school contracts, excursions & tours, private hire.
Livery: Silver/Blue.

SMITH & SONS COACHES
See Perth & Kinross.

ARGYLL & BUTE

BOWMAN'S COACHES (MULL) LTD
SCALLACASTLE, CRAIGNURE, ISLE OF MULL PA65 6BA.
Tel: 01680 812313.
Prop: A. Bowman, S. Bowman, I. Bowman, I. Bowman. **Gen Man:** A. Bowman.
Fleet: 12 coach.
Chassis: Bedford. Dennis. Ford. Leyland.
Bodies: Duple. Jonckheere. Plaxton.
Ops incl: local bus services, excursions & tours, private hire.
Livery: Cream/Red.
Ticket System: Setright, Almex.

GARELOCHHEAD COACHES
WOODLEA GARAGE, MAIN ROAD, GARELOCHHEAD PA65 6BA
Tel: 01436 810200.
Fax: 01436 810050.
Prop: Stuart McQueen

HIGHLAND HERITAGE COACH TOURS
DALMALLY HOTEL, DALMALLY, PA33
Fleet: 12 coach.
Chassis: Volvo.
Bodies: Van Hool.
Ops incl: excursions & tours.

HENDERSON HIRING
KINTYRE PLACE, TARBERT PA29 6UL.
Tel: 01880 820220
Fax: 01880 820900.
Prop: D & Mrs E. Henderson.
Fleet: 12 coach.
Chassis: Volvo.
Bodies: Van Hool
Ops incl: excursions & tours.

HIGHLAND ROVER COACHES
BRIDGE OF AWE, TAYNUILT PA35 1H7.
Tel: 01866 822612.
Prop: Angus Douglas.
Fleet: 3 - 2 midicoach, 1 minibus.
Chassis: 3 Mercedes.
Bodies: 1 Autobus. 1 Mercedes. 1 Euro Coach.
Ops incl: local bus services, school

A/c	Air conditioning
♿	Vehicles suitable for disabled
🍴	Coach(es) with galley facilities
WC	Coach(es) with toilet facilities
💺	Seat belt-fitted vehicles
R	Recovery service available (not 24 hr)
R24	24hr recovery service
✦	Replacement vehicle available
T	Toilet-drop facilities available
🚌	Vintage vehicle(s) available
🚐	Open top vehicle(s)

contracts, private hire.
Livery: Brown/Orange/White.
Ticket system: Setright.

*McCOLLS OF ARGYLL

MCCOLLS HOTEL, 1 TOM A MHOID ROAD, WEST BAY, DUNOON PA23 7HN
Tel: 01369 702764
Fax: 01369 703666
E-mail: dw@mccollshotel.co.uk
Web site: www.mccollshotel.co.uk
Dirs: David Wilkinson
Fleet: 8 coach
Chassis: 8 Iveco
Ops incl: excursions & tours, private hire, express

OBAN & DISTRICT BUSES LTD

GLENGALLAN ROAD, OBAN PA34 4HH
Tel: 01631 570500
Fax: 01631 570311
E-mail: enquiries@obanbuses.co.uk
Web site: www.obanbuses.co.uk
Fleetname: Oban & District.
Man Dir: Colin Craig **Dir**: W. G. Craig
Depot Controllers: David Hannah, Donnie McDougal **Workshop Supervisor**: Iain McDonald
Fleet: 23 - 16 single-deck bus, 2 coach, 2 midicoach, 2 minibus, 1 midibus.
Chassis: 4 DAF. 3 Dennis. 2 LDV. 10 Leyland. 2 Mercedes. 1 Optare. 1 Volvo.
Bodies: 10 Alexander. 1 Optare. 5 Plaxton. 4 Wright. 1 Onyx. 2 KL Conversion.
Ops incl: local bus services, school contracts, private hire, express.
Livery: Red/Blue/Honeysuckle
Ticket System: Wayfarer 3
Subsidiary of West Coast Motors

L. F STEWART & SON LTD

DALAYICH, BY TAYNUILT PA35 1HN.
Tel: 01866 833342.
Fax: 01866 833237.
Dirs: R. Maceachen, M. A. Stewart.
Fleet: 4 - 2 coach, 2 minibus.
Chassis: 2 Mercedes. 2 Volvo.
Bodies: 1 Plaxton. 2 Reeve Burgess. 1 Berkhof.
Ops incl: local bus services, school contracts, private hire.
Livery: Red/White/Yellow.

WEST COAST MOTORS

BENMHOR, CAMPBELTOWN PA28 6DN
Tel: 01586 552319.
Fax: 01586 552344
E-mail: e.stacey@westcoastmotors.co.uk
Web site: www.westcoastmotors.co.uk
Chmn/Man Dir: W G Craig **Dir**: C R Craig
Co Sec: J M Craig **Tran Man**: D M Halliday
Fleet Eng: D Martin
Fleet: 45 - 5 single-deck bus, 27 coach, 7 midibus, 2 midicoach, 4 minicoach.
Chassis: Bedford, DAF, Ford Transit, Freight Rover, Mercedes, Optare, Volvo.
Ops incl: local bus services, school contracts, private hire.
Livery: Red/Ivory
Ticket System: Wayfarer.

Scottish Operators

BORDERS

*AUSTIN COACH TRAVEL

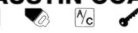

STATION ROAD, EARLSTON TD4 6BZ
Tel: 01896 849360
Fax: 01896 849623
Props: Douglas Austin, Barry Austin.
Fleet: 7 - 6 coach, 1 midicoach.
Chassis: 2 Bova. 4 Mercedes. 1 Volvo.
Bodies: 2 Bova. 1 Plaxton. 4 other.
Ops incl: excursions & tours, private hire, continental tours.
Livery: Pearlescent white

JAMES FRENCH & SON

THE GARAGE, COLDINGHAM, EYEMOUTH TD14 5NS.
Tel/Fax: 01890 771283.
Prop: I. McKcleaver.
Fleet: 12 coach.
Chassis: Volvo.
Bodies: Van Hool.
Ops incl: excursions & tours.

*MUNRO'S OF JEDBURGH LTD

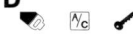

OAKVALE GARAGE, BONGATE, JEDBURGH TD8 6DU
Tel: 01835 862253
Fax: 01835 864297
Dir/Co Sec: Ewan Farish **Dir**: Donald Cameron.
Fleet: 36 - 10 single-deck bus, 8 coach, 13 midibus, 2 midicoach, 3 minibus.
Chassis: 4 DAF. 7 Dennis. 3 LDV. 2 Leyland. 9 Mercedes. 9 Optare. 1 Volvo.
Bodies: 3 Alexander. 1 Duple. 1 Northern Counties. 10 Optare. 9 Plaxton. 2 Transbus. 5 Van Hool. 1 Made to Measure. 3 Jaycas.
Ops incl: local bus services, school contracts, private hire.
Livery: White with red stripe
Ticket System: Wayfarer 2

PERRYMAN SERVICES

WOODBINE GARAGE, BURNMOUTH TD14 5SL.
Tel: 01890 781533.
Fax: 01890 750481.
Man Dir: R. Perryman.

*TELFORDS COACHES LTD

TWEEDEN BRAE, NEWCASTLETON TD9 0TL
Tel: 01387 375677
Recovery: 07711 280475
E-mail: alistair@telfordscoaches.com
Web site: www.telfordscoaches.com
Dir: Alistair S Telford **Ch Eng**: William Johnstone **Ops Man**: Alan Armstrong
Fleet: 13 - 8 coach, 4 midicoach, 1 minibus.
Chassis: 1 Dennis. 1 Dodge. 5 Mercedes. 1 Scania. 5 Volvo.
Bodies: 4 Mercedes-Benz. 8 Plaxton. 1 Van Hool.
Ops incl: local bus services, school contracts, excursions & tours, private hire, continental tours.
Livery: Blue with white vinyls

CLACKMANNANSHIRE

M. LINE INTERNATIONAL COACHES

THE COACH HOUSE, RIVERBANK, ALLOA FK10 1NT.
Tel: 01259 212802.
Fax: 01259 213372.
E-mail: info@m-line.co.uk
Web Site: www.m-line.co.uk.
Ops Man: T. Matchett.
Dir/Fleet Eng: C. W. Christie.
Fleet: 16 - 7 double-deck bus, 5 coach, 4 double-deck coach.
Chassis: 2 Bova. 2 Iveco. 4 Neoplan. 2 Volvo.
Bodies: 6 Alexander. 2 Bova. 4 Neoplan.
Ops incl: local bus services, school contracts, excursions & tours, private hire, continental tours.
Livery: Metallic Rainbow.
Ticket System: Almex.

MACKIE'S COACHES

32 GLASSHOUSE LOAN, ALLOA FK10 1PE.
Tel: 01259 216180.
Fax: 01259 217508.
Prop: J. L. Mackie. **Ch Eng**: J. Miller.
Co Sec: Mrs D. Bartlett. **Traf Sup**: D. Hunter.
Fleet: 18 - 5 single-deck bus, 13 coach.
Chassis: Dennis, Volvo.
Bodies: Jonckheere, Plaxton, Van Hool, Wadham Stringer/UVG.
Ops incl: local bus services, school contracts, excursions & tours, private hire, express, continental tours.
Livery: White/Brown/Beige.
Ticket System: Almex Microfare.

WOODS COACHES

2 GOLF VIEW, TILLICOULTRY FK13 6DH
Tel/Fax: 01259 751753
E-mail: james.woodscoaches@tillicoultry01.fs.net.co.uk
Owner: James Woods **Ops Dir**: John Woods.
Fleet: 11 - 1 coach, 6 midicoach, 4 minicoach.
Chassis: 1 Bova, 1 DAF. 1 Ford Transit, 7 Mercedes, 1 Optare.
Ops incl: school contracts, excursions & tours, private hire, express.
Livery: Silver

DUMFRIES & GALLOWAY

ANDERSON'S COACHES

BLUE BELL HILL, SKIPPERS, LANGHOLM DG13 0LH.
Tel: 01387 380553.
Fax: 01387 380553.
Ptnrs: I. R. Anderson, K. Irving.

Ch Eng: C. Anderson.
Fleet: 6 - 2 single-deck bus, 2 minibus, 2 minicoach.
Chassis: 1 AEC. 3 Ford Transit. 1 Freight Rover. 1 Leyland.
Bodies: 2 Plaxton. 1 Robin Hood. 1 PMT. 1 N/S Transit.
Ops incl: local bus services, school contracts, private hire.
Livery: Red/Orange/Yellow stripe.
Ticket System: Almex.

R. K. ARMSTRONG COACHES wc ♥ A/c ✓

THE PARK, BRIDGE-OF-DEE, CASTLE DOUGLAS DG7 1TR.
Tel: 01556 680250.
Fax: 01556 680409.
E-mail: armstrong@castledouglasprestel.co.uk
Prop: R. K. Armstrong.
Fleet: 9 - 1 single-deck bus, 5 coach, 2 midicoach, 1 minicoach.
Chassis: 2 Scania. 2 Volvo.
Bodies: 4 Mercedes. 1 Neoplan.
Ops incl: local bus services, school contracts, excursions and tours, private hire.

BROWNRIGG'S COACHES

THE GARAGE, THORNHILL DG3 5LZ.
Tel/Fax: 01848 330204.
Prop: W. Brownrigg.

*JAMES GIBSON & SON ♥ wc A/c R24 ✓

16 CHURCH STREET, MOFFAT DG10 9HD
Tel/Recovery: 01683 220200
Fax: 01683 220758
E-mail: enquiries@gibsonscoaches.co.uk
Web site: www.gibsonscoaches.co.uk
Fleetname: Gibsons Coaches
Dirs: J Gibson, Miss M Gibson, Miss J Gibson, J Gibson (jnr)
Fleet: 10
Chassis: 4 Bova. 6 Volvo.
Bodies: 4 Bova. 1 Duple. 5 Van Hool.
Ops incl: school contracts, excursions & tours, private hire, continental tours.
Livery: Red/Maroon

*JAMES KING COACHES ♥ wc A/c ✓

MAIN STREET, KIRKCOWAN, NEWTON STEWART DG8 0HG
Tel: 01671 830284
Fax: 01671 830499
Prop: James King
Fleet: 25 - 2 single-deck bus, 13 coach, 4 midibus, 4 midicoach, 2 minicoach.
Chassis: 1 Bova. 3 Dennis. 9 Mercedes. 2 Optare. 1 Scania. 9 Volvo.
Bodies: 1 Autobus. 1 Bova. 1 Duple. 1 Jonckheere. 1 Optare. 6 Plaxton. 10 Van Hool. 4 other.
Ops incl: local bus services, school contracts, excursions & tours, private hire.

*KIWI LUXURY TRAVEL wc ♥ A/c R

80 QUEEN STREET, NEWTON STEWART DG8 6JL

Tel: 01671 404294
Fax: 01671 403310
E-mail: kiwitravel@btopenworld.com
Web site: www.kiwitravel.co.uk
Ptnr: Ian Allison, Mrs Jan Allison
Fleet: 4 - 3 coach, 1 minibus
Chassis/Bodies: 1 Renault. 1 Plaxton. 2 Van Hool.
Ops incl: local bus services, school contracts, excursions & tours, private hire.

MacEWAN'S COACH SERVICES ♥ wc A/c

JOHNFIELD, AMISFIELD, DUMFRIES DG1 3LS.
Tel: 01387 256533
Fax: 01387 711123
Prop: John MacEwan **Ch Eng**: Peter Maxwell
Fleet: 53 - 16 single-deck bus, 12 coach, 23 midibus, 3 midicoach
Chassis: 1 AEC. 1 Bedford. 1 Bristol. 4 DAF. 3 Dennis. 4 Ford Transit. 1 Iveco. 4 Leyland. 6 MAN. Marshall. 19 Mercedes. 4 Optare. 3 Scania. 3 Volvo.
Bodies: 3 Alexander. 2 Autobus. 1 Duple. 1 ECW. 3 Ikarus. 1 Jonckheere. 6 Marshall. 8 Optare. 12 Plaxton. 1 Reeve Burgess. 2 UVG. 2 Van Hool. 1 Wadham Stringer. 2 Wright. 4 Crystal. 1 DAB. 4 Dormobile.
Ops incl: local bus services, school contracts, excursions & tours, express.
Livery: White/Red/Blue
Ticket system: ERG Transit 400

MCCULLOCH'S COACHES

MAIN ROAD, STONEYKIRK, STRANRAER DG9 9DH.
Tel/Fax: 01776 830236.

DUNDEE CITY

*FISHERS TOURS
wc ♥ A/c ✓ T

16 WEST PORT, DUNDEE DD1 5EP
Tel/Fax: 01382 227290
Recovery: 07974 180771
E-mail: raycosgrove@supanet.com
Web site: www.fisherstours.co.uk
Ptnrs: James Cosgrove, Catherine Cosgrove **Tran Man**: David Kidd
Fleet: 18 - 10 coach, 1 midicoach, 5 single-deck bus, 2 minibus.
Chassis: 4 Iveco. 7 Leyland. 3 Mercedes. 4 Volvo.
Bodies: 1 Beulas. 2 ECW. 1 Marshall. 1 Plaxton. 4 Van Hool. 1 Solara. 2 Touro. 1 Iveco. 3 Derwent. 2 Paramount Express.
Ops incl: school contracts, excursions & tours, private hire, continental tours.
Livery: White/Blue/Turquoise/Yellow.

STRATHTAY SCOTTISH
♿ wc ♥ R ✓ T

SEAGATE BUS STATION, DUNDEE DD1 2HR.
Tel: 01382 228345.
Fax: 01382 202567

Chmn: F. A. Carter. **Man Dir**: C. Mullen
Eng Dir: T. Robertson.
Fleet: 156 - 47 double-deck bus, 54 single-deck bus, 9 coach, 4 midibus, 42 minibus.
Chassis: 4 Daimler. 17 Dennis. 2 Dodge. 1 LDV. 55 Leyland. 35 MCW. 17 Mercedes. 4 Optare. 4 Renault. 17 Volvo.
Bodies: 68 Alexander. 4 Duple. 2 ECW. 18 East Lancs. 19 MCW. 8 Northern Counties. 4 Optare. 8 Plaxton. 11 Reeve Burgess. 5 Wright. 9 Other.
Ops incl: local bus services, school contracts, excursions & tours, private hire.
Livery: Orange/Blue/White.
Ticket System: Wayfarer.

Part of Traction Group.

*TRAVEL DUNDEE (TAYSIDE PUBLIC TRANSPORT CO LTD)
♿ ♥ wc 🚌 🍽 R24 ✓ T

44-48 EAST DOCK STREET, DUNDEE DD1 3JS
Tel: 01382 201121.
Fax: 01382 340010
E-mail: jameslee@traveldundee.co.uk
Web site: www.traveldundee.co.uk
Fleetname: Travel Dundee.
Chmn: Jack Henry **Man Dir**: Jim Lee **Eng Man**: Frank Sheach **Coaching Man**: Helmut Himmerich
Fleet: 131 - 18 double-deck bus, 82 single-deck bus, 20 coach, 6 midicoach, 5 minibus.
Chassis: 8 Dennis. 4 Mercedes. 11 Optare. 8 Scania. 100 Volvo.
Bodies: 18 Alexander. 1 Duple. 3 East Lancs. 11 Optare. 26 Plaxton. 1 Reeve Burgess. 71 Wright. 1 Aitken.
Ops incl: local bus services, school contracts, excursions & tours, private hire.

EAST AYRSHIRE

A1 SERVICE
See Western Buses.

LIDDELL'S COACHES ♿ wc

1 MAUCHLINE ROAD, AUCHINLECK KA18 2BJ.
Tel: 01290 424300/420717.
Fax: 01290 425637.
Prop: J. Liddell. **Ch Eng**: J. Quinn. **Co Sec**: Ms J. Samson. **Ops Man**: Ms M. Milroy.
Fleet: 24 - 8 double-deck bus, 10 coach, 4 midicoach, 2 minibus.
Chassis: 1 Bova. 3 DAF. 2 Dodge. 2 Freight Rover. 10 Leyland. 6 Volvo.
Bodies: 8 Alexander. 1 Bova. 1 Caetano. 3 Duple. 1 ECW. 1 East Lancs. 2 Jonckheere. 4 Paxton. 2 Reeve Burgess. 1 Wright.
Ops incl: local bus services, school contracts, excursions & tours, private hire, express.
Livery: White with Brown/Orange/Lemon stripes.
Ticket System: Setright.

A/c	Air conditioning	✓	Replacement vehicle available
♿	Vehicles suitable for disabled	T	Toilet-drop facilities available
🍽	Coach(es) with galley facilities		Vintage vehicle(s) available
wc	Coach(es) with toilet facilities	🚌	Open top vehicle(s)
♥	Seat belt-fitted vehicles		
R	Recovery service available (not 24 hr)		
R24	24hr recovery service		

*ROWE & TUDHOPE

WEST HILLHEAD, WESTERN ROAD,
KILMARNOCK KA3 1PH
Tel: 01563 525631
Fax: 01563 571489
Recovery: 01563 543386
E-mail: geo.rowe@fsmail.net
Web site: www.roweandtudhope.com
Dir: George Rowe
Fleet: 21 - 2 double-deck bus, 4 single-deck bus, 12 coach, 2 midibus, 1 midicoach.
Chassis: 6 Dennis. 6 Leyland. 3 Mercedes. 6 Volvo.
Bodies: 12 Alexander. 3 Jonckheere. 5 Plaxton.
Ops incl: local bus services, school contracts, exursions & tours, private hire.
Livery: White/Blue multi

EAST LOTHIAN

EVE CARS & COACHES

SPOTT ROAD, DUNBAR EH42 1RR.
Tel: 01368 865500.
Fax: 01368 865400.
Web site: www.eveinfo.co.uk
Ptnrs: Gary Scougall, Vona Scougall.

EAST RENFREWSHIRE

HENRY CRAWFORD COACHES LTD

SHILFORD MILL, NEILSTON G78 3BA.
Tel: 01505 850456.
Fax: 01505 850479.
Dirs: Isobel Crawford, James Crawford, John Crawford.
Fleet: 21 - 1 double-deck bus, 14 coach, 1 midibus, 5 minibus.
Chassis: 1 Ford Transit. 2 Leyland. 1 Mercedes. 1 Scania. 12 Volvo.
Bodies: 1 Alexander. 1 Duple. 1 Jonckheere. 2 Plaxton. 10 Van Hool. 1 Ford Transit. 4 LDV. 1 Onyx.
Ops incl: private hire, express.
Livery: White/two tone Red.
Ticket System: Almex Microfare.

SOUTHERN COACHES (NM) LTD

LOCHLIBO ROAD, BARRHEAD G78 1LF.
Tel: 0141-881 1147.
Fax: 0141-881 1148.
E-mail: reservations@southern-coaches.co.uk.
Web site: southern-coaches.co.uk
Dirs: R. Wallace, D. Wallace, Mary Wallace.
Fleet: 19 - 17 coach, 2 minicoach.
Chassis: 2 DAF. 2 Toyota. 15 Volvo.
Bodies: 2 Caetano. 1 Jonckheere. 8 Plaxton. 8 Van Hool. 1 Ikarus.
Ops incl: school contracts, excursions & tours, private hire, express.
Livery: Cream/Blue/Orange.

EDINBURGH, CITY OF

*AAA COACHES

UNIT 7, RAW CAMPS IND EST, KIRKNEWTON EH27 8DF
Tel: 01506 883000
Fax: 01506 884000
E-mail: aaacoaches@hotmail.com
Web site: www.aaacoaches.co.uk
Man Dir: J T Reenton
Fleet: 15 - 9 single-deck bus, 3 midibus, 3 minibus.
Chassis: 1 Dennis. 3 Ford. 2 Ford Transit. 1 LDV. 3 Mercedes. 2 Scania. 7 Volvo.
Bodies: 5 Jonckheere. 1 Leyland. 3 Mercedes. 2 Plaxton. 2 Sunsundegui. 2 Van Hool.
Ops incl: school contracts, excursions & tours, private hire
Livery: White with Highland scene.

ALLAN'S GROUP
See Midlothian

BROWNS OF EDINBURGH

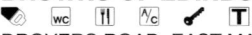

DROVERS ROAD, EAST MAINS INDUSTRIAL ESTATE, BROXBURN EH52 5ND
Tel: 01506 857201
Fax: 01506 859096
E-mail: enquiries@brownscoaches.co.uk.
Web Site: www.brownscoaches.co.uk.
Prop: Ronald Brown
Fleet: 12 single-deck coach.
Chassis: 2 DAF. 3 Scania. 7 Volvo.
Bodies: 2 Berkhof. 3 Irizar. 3 Jonckheere. 4 Van Hool.
Ops incl: excursions & tours, private hire, continental tours.
Livery: White/Blue.

EDINBURGH CASTLE COACHES LTD

117 PITT STREET, LEITH EH6 4DE
Tel: 0131 555 0034.
Fax: 0131 555 2682
E-mail: edincasco@aol.com.
Web site: www.edinburghcastlecoaches.co.uk
Manager: Peter Fyvie.
Fleet: 12 - 8 coach, 2 minibus, 2 midicoach.
Chassis: 1 MAN. 3 Mercedes. 2 Scania. 5 Volvo.
Bodies: 1 Jonckheere. 7 Van Hool. 1 Indcar. 1 Euro Coach.
Ops incl: excursions & tours, private hire, continental tours.

*EDINBURGH TOURS LTD

ANNANDALE STREET, EDINBURGH EH7 4AZ
Tel: 0131 554 4494
Fax: 0131 554 3942
E-mail: sales@edinburghtour.com
Web site: www.edinburghtour.com
Man Dir: N J Renilson   **Fin Dir**: N J Strachan
Ops Dir: W W Campbell   **Eng Dir**: W Devlin
Mktg Dir: I Coupar
Fleet: 19 - 1 double-deck bus, 4 coach, 14 open-top bus
Chassis: 19 Leyland

Bodies: 9 Alexander. 2 East Lancs. 4 Plaxton. 4 Roe.
Ops incl: local bus services, private hire, excursions & tours.
Livery: Green/Cream
Ticket system: Microfare

FAIRWAY TRAVEL

6 BRIARBANK TERRACE, EDINBURGH EH11 1ST.
Tel: 0131 467 6717.
Fax: 0131 467 6717.
E-mail: davy@fairwaytravel.freeserve
Web site: www.fairwaytravel.co.uk
Prop: D. Innes.
Fleet: 4 - 1 coach, 2 midicoach, 1 minibus.
Chassis: 1 DAF. 1 Setra. 2 Toyota.
Bodies: 2 Caetano. 1 Leyland. 1 Setra.
Ops incl: school contracts, excursions & tours, private hire, continental tours.
Livery: Blue and Red on White.

FIRST IN EDINBURGH

CARMUIRS HOUSE, 300 STIRLING ROAD, LARBERT FK5 3NJ
Tel: 01324 602200
Web site: www.firstedinburgh.co.uk
Man Dir: Graeme Torrence
Fleet: 276
Chassis: Dennis. Leyland. MCW. Optare. Scania. Volvo.
Bodies: Alexander. East Lancs. MCW. Optare. Plaxton. Wright.

E & M HORSBURGH
See West Lothian.

*LIBERTON TRAVEL

15-29 ENGINE ROAD, LOANHEAD EH20 9RF
Tel: 0131 440 4400
Fax: 0131 448 0008
E-mail: libertontravel@btconnect.com
Man Dir: Peter McVay
Fleet: 12 - 8 coach, 2 midicoach, 2 midibus.
Chassis: 2 DAF. 4 Dennis. 4 Mercedes. 4 Volvo.
Bodies: 1 Jonckheere. 4 Marcopolo. 4 Mercedes. 3 Van Hool.
Ops incl: school contracts, excursions & tours, private hire.
Livery: White/Purple/Green

*LOTHIAN BUSES

ANNANDALE STREET, EDINBURGH EH7 4AZ
Tel: 0131 554 4494
Fax: 0131 554 3942
E-mail: mail@lothianbuses.co.uk
Web site: www.lothianbuses.co.uk
Man Dir: N J Renilson   **Fin Dir**: N J Strachan
Ops Dir: W W Campbell   **Eng Dir**: W Devlin
Mktg Dir: I Coupar
Fleet: 612 - 479 double-deck bus, 123 single-deck bus, 10 open-top bus.
Chassis: 290 Dennis. 151 Leyland. 171 Volvo.
Bodies: 288 Alexander. 294 Plaxton. 30 Wright.
Ops incl: local bus services.
Livery: Madder/Red/White/Gold
Ticket system: Wayfarer

*MACTOURS LTD
ANNANDALE STREET, EDINBURGH
EH7 4AZ
Tel: 0131 554 4494
Fax: 0131 554 3942
E-mail: sales@edinburghtour.com
Web site: www.edinburghtour.com
Man Dir: N J Renilson **Fin Dir**: N J Strachan
Ops Dir: W W Campbell **Eng Dir**: W Devlin
Mktg Dir: I Coupar
Fleet: 32 - 7 double-deck bus, 1 single-deck bus, 17 open-top bus, 4 midibus, 3 minibus.
Chassis: 20 AEC. 4 Dennis. 5 Leyland. 3 Mercedes.
Bodies: 8 Alexander. 1 ECW. 20 Park Royal. 2 Reading. 1 other.
Ops incl: local bus services, excursions & tours, private hire.
Livery: Red/Cream
Ticket system: Almex Microfare 3

*STANLEY MACKAY COACHES OF EDINBURGH
BUTLERFIELD INDUSTRIAL ESTATE, BONNYRIGG EH19 3JQ
Tel: 01875 822862.
Fax: 01875 822762
E-mail: mackay.coaches@virgin.net.
Web site: www.mackayscoaches.co.uk
Prop: Douglas Mackay.
Fleet: 5 coach.
Chassis/Bodies: includes 4 Setra. 1 Van Hool.
Ops incl: private hire
Livery: Black/Silver

SCOTIA TRAVEL
ROSEBINE GARAGE, 29A MAIN STREET, COALTOWN, GLENROTHES KY7 6HU
Tel: 0131 553 1455/01592 773900
Fax: 01592 775588
Recovery: 01592 773900
E-mail: enquiries@scotiatravel.co.uk
Web site: www.scotiatravel.co.uk
Prop: Alex Henderson
Fleet: 4 - 2 coach. 2 minicoach.
Chassis: 1 Bova. 1 DAF. 2 Mercedes.
Bodies: 1 Bova. 1 Reeve Burgess. 1 Van Hool.
Ops incl: private hire, excursions & tours, continental tours.
Livery: Blue/Gold/White.

SILVER COACH LINES LTD OF EDINBURGH
81 SALAMANDER STREET, EDINBURGH EH6 7JZ
Tel: 0131 554 5413
Fax: 0131 553 3721
E-mail: enquiries@silvercoachlines.com.
Web Site: www.silvercoachlines.com.
Man Dir: Ivan Ford **Ops Dir**: Karl Vanters
Traff Man: John Blair **Co Sec**: Judy Ford
Fleet Eng: Kevin Perves.

Fleet: 15 - 10 coach, 1 midicoach, 4 minicoach.
Chassis: 9 Setra. 4 Toyota. 2 Volvo.
Bodies: 6 Caetano. 9 Setra.
Ops incl: excursions & tours, private hire, continental tours.
Livery: White/Orange/Blue/Silver.

FALKIRK

FIRST SCOTLAND EAST
CARMUIRS HOUSE, 300 STIRLING ROAD, LARBERT FK1 5HP.
Tel: 01324 627175
Fax: 01324 611287.
Prop: FirstGroup plc.
Man Dir: Graeme Torrence **Eng Dir**: W. McCracken. **Fin Dir**: J. Sharkey. **Ops Dir**: T. Roberts.
Fleet: 481 - 176 double-deck bus, 247 single-deck bus, 22 coach, 36 midibus, 54 minibus.
Chassis: 91 Dennis. 91 Leyland. 12 Leyland-DAB. 37 MCW. 45 Mercedes. 23 Optare. 87 Scania. 95 Volvo.
Bodies: Alexander. East Lancs. MCW. Optare. Plaxton. Roe. Wright.
Ops incl: local bus services, school contracts, excursions & tours, private hire, express.
Livery: Cream/Blue or Cream/Green. New vehicles in First Group White/Blue/Magenta.
Ticket System: Wayfarer 3.

P. WOODS MINICOACHES
20 CALDER PLACE, HALLGLEN FK1 2QQ.
Tel: 01324 613085.
Fax: 01324 717976.

FIFE

*FIFE SCOTTISH OMNIBUSES LTD
GUTHRIE HOUSE, GLENFIELD INDUSTRIAL ESTATE, COWDENBEATH KY4 9HT
Tel: 01383 511911
Fax: 01383 516450
Recovery: 01383 511911
E-mail: eastscotland@stagecoachbus.com
Web site: www.stagecoachbus.com
Fleetname: Stagecoach in Fife
Man Dir: Tom Wileman **Dep Man Dir**: Robert Andrew **Ops Dir**: Doug Fleming
Eng Dir: Sandy Brydon
Fleet: 381 - 117 double-deck bus, 110 single-deck bus, 6 coach, 2 open-top bus, 47 midibus, 21 minibus.
Chassis: 29 Dennis. 24 Leyland. 24 MAN. 21 Mercedes. 203 Volvo.
Bodies: 180 Alexander. 2 Berkhof. 9 Leyland. 61 Northern Counties. 49 Plaxton.

Ops incl: local bus services, school contracts, excursions & tours, private hire, express.
Livery: Stagecoach (White/Red/Blue/Orange).
Ticket System: ERG.

KINGDOM COACHES
DEN WALK, METHIL KY8 3JH.
Tel: 01333 26109
Fleet: 3 coach.
Chassis: 2 DAF. 1 Ford.
Bodies: 2 Plaxton. 1 Van Hool.
Ops incl: private hire.
Livery: Yellow/White.

*MOFFAT & WILLIAMSON LTD
MAIN ROAD, GAULDRY, NEWPORT-ON-TAY DD6 8SQ
Tel: 01382 330777
Fax: 01382 330526
Recovery: 01332 330777
E-mail: enquiries@moffat-williamson.co.uk
Web site: www.moffat-williamson.co.uk
Gen Man: J P Williamson
Ops Man: I G Williamson
Fleet: 64 - 9 double-deck bus, 3 single-deck bus, 35 coach, 3 couble-deck bus, 7 midibus, 4 midicoach, 3 minibus.
Chassis: 16 Denris. 1 Iveco. 2 LDV. 8 Leyland. 3 MAN. 6 MCW. 12 Mercedes. 18 Volvo.
Bodies: 3 Alexander. 1 Carlyle. 2 Leyland. 6 MCW. 1 Mercedes. 2 Neoplan. 27 Plaxton. 2 Reeve Burgess. 5 Van Hool. 15 Wadham Stringer.
Ops incl: local bus services, school contracts, private hire, express.
Livery: Brown/Cream/Orange
Ticket System: Wayfarer 3

*RENNIES OF DUNFERMLINE LTD
WELLWOOD, DUNFERMLINE KY12 0PY.
Tel: 01383 620600
Fax: 01383 620624
E-mail: gordon@rennies.co.uk
Web site: www.renniesofdunfermline.co.uk
Chmn: John Rennie **Gen Man**: Gordon Menzies **Tran Man**: Iain Robertson
Co Sec: John Lawrie **Ch Eng**: George Clark
Fleet: 50 - 28 double-deck bus, 15 coach, 1 double-deck coach. 3 midicoach, 3 minibus.
Chassis: 1 Bova. 5 Dennis. 1 Iveco. 1 Irisbus. 20 Leyland. 5 MCW. 5 Mercedes. 1 Scania. 8 Volvo. 3 BMC.
Bodies: 10 Alexander. 1 Beulas. 1 Berkhof. 1 Bova. 6 Caetano. 4 Jonckheere. 10 Leyland. 5 MCW. 3 Mellor. 2 Plaxton. 1 Sunsundegui. 3 Van Hool. 3 Probus.
Ops incl: local bus services, school contracts, excursions & tours, private hire, continental tours.
Livery: Blue/White.
Ticket system: Wayfarer

A/c	Air conditioning
♿	Vehicles suitable for disabled
🍴	Coach(es) with galley facilities
wc	Coach(es) with toilet facilities
♥	Seat belt-fitted vehicles
R	Recovery service available (not 24 hr)
R24	24hr recovery service
✓	Replacement vehicle available
T	Toilet-drop facilities available
	Vintage vehicle(s) available
	Open top vehicle(s)

*ST ANDREWS EXECUTIVE TRAVEL

UNIT 2, TOM STEWART LANE,
ST ANDREWS KY16 8YB
Tel: 01334 470080
Fax: 01334 470081
E-mail: orders@saxtravel.co.uk
Web Site: www.saxtravel.co.uk
Dir: Gordon Donaldson.
Fleet: 7 - 1 coach, 2 minicoach, 4 midicoach.
Chassis: 6 Mercedes. 1 Toyota.
Ops incl: school contracts, excursions & tours, private hire.
Livery: Green/White.

GLASGOW, CITY OF

*ALLANDER COACHES LTD

UNIT 19, CLOBERFIELD ESTATE, MILNGAVIE G62 7LN
Tel: 0141 956 1234
Fax: 0141 956 6669
E-mail: enquiries@allandertravel.co.uk
Web site: www.allandertravel.co.uk
Fleetname: Allander Travel
Man Dir: J F Wilson **Dir:** Mrs E E Wilson
Ch Eng: G S Wilson **Co Sec:** Miss M Brown
Ops Man: G F Wilson
Fleet: 26 - 5 double-deck bus, 4 single-deck bus, 15 coach, 2 midicoach.
Chassis: 4 Bova. 3 Bristol. 4 Dennis. 2 Leyland. 1 Mercedes. 1 Toyota. 11 Volvo.
Bodies: 5 Alexander. 4 Bova. 1 Caetano. 1 Jonckheere. 4 Plaxton. 3 Van Hool. 3 Wadham Stringer. 1 Sitcar.
Ops incl: local bus services, excursions & tours, private hire, school contracts.
Livery: Black/Gold/Orange.
Ticket System: Setright.

*CITY SIGHTSEEING GLASGOW LTD

153 QUEEN STREET, GLASGOW G1 3BJ
Tel: 0141 204 0444
Fax: 0141 248 6582
E-mail: alex@scotguide.com
Web Site: www.scotguide.com
Dirs: A Pringle, Mrs C Pringle.
Fleet: 11 open-top bus.
Chassis/Bodies: 2 Bristol. 9 MCW.
Ops incl: excursions & tours.

*DOIGS OF GLASGOW LTD

TRANSPORT HOUSE, 7 SUMMER STREET, GLASGOW G40 3TB
Tel: 0141 554 5555
Fax: 0141 551 9000
E-mail: andy@doigs.com
Web site: www.doigs.com
Chmn/Man Dir: Andrew Forsyth **Co Sec:** Iain Forsyth **Eng Dir:** William Neil
Fleet: 15 - 1 double-deck bus, 1 single-deck bus, 1 articulated bus, 8 coach, 1 midicoach, 3 minicoach.
Chassis: 1 DAF. 1 Daimler. 1 Dennis. 1 Ford Transit. 1 LDV. 1 Mercedes. 9 Scania.
Bodies: 1 Caetano. 8 Irizar. 1 Marcopolo. 1 Mercedes. 1 Wright. 3 other.
Ops incl: school contracts, excursions & tours, private hire, continental tours.

DUNN'S COACHES
See North Lanarkshire.

FIRST IN GLASGOW

197 VICTORIA ROAD, GLASGOW G42 7AD.
Tel: 0141 423 6600
Fax: 0141 636 3228
Web Site: www.firstgroup.com.
Div Dir: Gary Raven **Fin Dir (West):** Michael Milne **Fin Dir Scotland:** Steve Locker **Eng Dir:** Howie Gray **Dir of Service Delivery:** Larry Stuart **Operations Director, Scotland:** Alex Shearer **PR/Mktg Man:** Nicola Muir.
Fleet: 992 - 396 double-deck bus, 496 single-deck bus, 100 minibus.
Chassis: 126 Dennis. 103 Leyland. 36 MCW. 85 Mercedes. 15 Optare. 130 Scania. 497 Volvo.
Bodies: Alexander. East Lancs. MCW. Optare. Plaxton. Wright.
Ops incl: local bus services.

NEIL MACKELLAIG

11 DUNSYRE PLACE, GLASGOW G23 5EB.
Tel: 0141 946 1895.
Prop: N. Mackellaig.
Fleet: 1 minicoach.
Chassis: Toyota. **Body:** Caetano.
Ops incl: school contracts, private hire.

*JOHN MORROW COACHES

18 ALBION INDUSTRIAL ESTATE, HALLEY STREET, YOKER, GLASGOW G13 4DL
Tel: 0141 951 8888
Fax: 0141 952 6445
Prop: John Morrow.
Fleet: 9 - 7 single-deck bus, 2 midicoach.
Bodies: 1 Leyland. 1 MAN. 5 Mercedes. 2 Toyota.
Chassis: includes 2 Caetano.
Ops incl: local bus services, private hire, school contracts, excursions & tours.
Livery: Brown/Cream
Ticket system: Wayfarer 3

*SCOTTISH CITYLINK COACHES LTD

BUCHANAN BUS STATION, KILLERMONT STREET, GLASGOW G2 3NP
Tel: 0141 332 9644
Fax: 0141 332 4488
E-mail: info@citylink.co.uk.
Web site: www.citylink.co.uk.
Man Dir: Neil Wood **Fin Controller:** Derek may **Ops Man:** Richard Beaton **Mktg man:** Paul Murphy
Ops incl: express.
Livery: Blue/yellow
Ticket system: Wayfarer 3/ATB

SELVEY'S COACHES

HILLCREST HOUSE, 33 HOWIESHILL ROAD, CAMBUSLANG G72 8PW.
Tel: 0141 641 1080.
Fax: 0141 641 2065.
Owner: A. G. Selvey.
Fleet: 8 - 5 coach, 2 midicoach, 1 minicoach.
Chassis: 3 Bedford. 2 Leyland. 1 Mercedes. 2 Volvo.

Bodies: 1 Duple. 1 Jonckheere. 1 Mercedes. 3 Plaxton.
Ops incl: excursions & tours, private hire, school contracts.
Livery: Maroon/Red/Yellow.

HIGHLAND

BEAULY COACH HIRE

THE ROOKERY, WESTER BALBLAIR, BY BEAULY IV4 7BQ
Tel: 01463 782498
E-mail: mhairicormack@aol.com
Props: Mhairi and Gordon Cormack
Fleet: 4 - 1 midibus, 1 minicoach, 2 minibus
Chassis: Mercedes
Ops incl: school contracts

*BLUEBIRD BUSES LTD

6 BURNETT ROAD, LONGMAN INDUSTRIAL ESTATE, INVERNESS IV1 1TF
Tel: 01463 239292
Fax: 01463 712338
Recovery: 01463 239292
E-mail: eastscotland@stagecoachbus.com
Web site: www.stagecoachbus.com
Fleetname: Stagecoach Inverness
Man Dir: Tom Wileman **Dep Man Dir:** Robert Andrew **Ops Dir:** Robert Hall **Eng Dir:** Michael Reid **Ops Man:** Gus Beveridge **Depot Eng:** Iain McKenzie.
Fleet: 48 - 10 double-deck bus, 10 single-deck bus, 25 midibus, 3 minibus.
Chassis: 16 Dennis. 6 Leyland. 3 Mercedes. 9 Transbus. 14 Volvo.
Bodies: 25 Alexander. 4 Northern Counties. 10 Plaxton. 9 Transbus.
Ops incl: local bus services, school contracts, excursions & tours, private hire, express.
Livery: Stagecoach (White/Blue/Orange/Red)
Ticket System: Wayfarer TGX

D&E COACHES

39 HENDERSON DRIVE, INVERNESS IV1 1TR
Tel: 01463 222444
Fax: 01463 226700.
E-mail: decoaches@aol.com
Web Site: www.decoaches.co.uk
Props: D N Mathieson, E Mathieson
Fleet: 12 - 3 coach, 3 midicoach, 6 minibus.
Chassis: 3 Ford Transit. 2 LDV. 4 Mercedes. 3 Volvo.
Bodies: 1 Alexander. 1 Autobus. 2 Plaxton. 1 Reeve Burgess. 3 Van Hool.
Ops incl: local bus services, school contracts, excursions and tours, private hire.
Livery: White with black/red lettering

*DUNCAN MACLENAN

HILL-SIDE, SHIELDAIG, STRATHCARRON IV54 8XN
Tel/Fax: 01520 755239
Prop: Duncan MacLennan
Fleet: 2 - 1 midicoach, 1 minibus.
Chassis/bodies: 1 Ford. 1 Mercedes.
Ops incl: local bus services, school contracts.

*RAPSONS COUCHES LTD

1 SEAFIELD ROAD, INVERNESS
IV1 1TN
Tel: 01463 710555
Fax: 01463 711488
E-mail: info@rapsons.co.uk
Web site: www.rapsons.co.uk
Chairman: Sandy Rapson **Man Dir**: John Lornig **Ops Dir**: Neil MacDonald **Eng Dir**: Russell Henderson **Comm Services Dir**: Alistair Goodall.
Fleet: 233 - 26 double-deck bus, 37 single-deck bus, 118 coach, 2 open-top bus, 50 minibus.
Ops incl: local bus services, school contracts, excursions & tours, private hire, express.
Livery: Blue
Ticket System: Wayfarer 3

SHIEL BUSES

BLAIN GARAGE, ACHARACLE
PH36 4JY.
Tel/Fax: 01967 431272.
E-mail: shiel.buses@virgin.net
Dir: Donnie MacGillivray.
Fleet: 10 - 4 single-deck coach, 6 midibus.
Chassis: 1 Ford Transit. 4 Mercedes. 4 Volvo.
Bodies: 2 Mercedes. 2 Plaxton. 2 Van Hool. 2 Onyx.
Ops incl: local bus services, school contracts, private hire.
Livery: Red/White
Ticket system: Amex

SPA COACHES

KINETTAS, STRATHPEFFER
IV14 9BH.
Tel: 01997 421311.
Fax: 01997 421983.
E-mail: norman@spacoaches.fsnet.co.uk
Prop: N. MacArthur.
Fleet: 28 - 6 double-deck bus, 13 coach, 5 midibus, 2 minibus.
Chassis: 1 DAF. 2 Ford Transit. 5 Mercedes. 14 Volvo.
Bodies: 1 Duple. 7 Alexander. 2 Caetano. 3 Jonckheere. 5 Plaxton. 6 Van Hool. 4 other.
Ops incl: local bus services, school contracts, excursions & tours, private hire, continental tours.
Livery: Orange/White.
Ticket System: Punch Tickets.

*GRAHAM URQUHART TRAVEL LTD

28 MIDMILLS ROAD, INVERNESS
IV23 3NY
Tel: 01463 222292
Fax: 01463 238880
E-mail: graham@urquharttravel.fsnet.co.uk
Dir: John G Urquhart **Sec**: John P Grant

Fleet: 7 - 4 coach, 2 midicoach, 1 minicoach.
Chassis: 1 Ford. 1 Irisbus. 1 MAN. 4 Scania.
Ops incl: excursions & tours, private hire, continental tours.

*WHITE HEATHER TOURS

ALGARVE, BADABRIE, BANAVIE
PH33 7LX
Tel: 01397 772461
Fax: 01397 772255
E-mail: enquiries@whiteheathertravel.com
Web site: www.whiteheathertravel.com
Prop: Adam A MacIntyre
Fleet: 3 midicoach.
Chassis: 1 Mercedes. 1 Toyota.
Bodies: Caetano 2. Crystal 1.
Ops incl: school contracts, excursions & tours, private hire.
Livery: Gold/Green/Red

INVERCLYDE

GILLEN COACHES

UNIT 2, ARDGOWAN INDUSTRIAL ESTATE, PORT GLASGOW PA14 5DG
Tel: 01475 743627
Prop: Michael Gillen.
Web site: www.gillenscoaches.co.uk

GLEN COACHES LTD

6 MACDOUGALL STREET, GREENOCK PA15 2TG.
Tel: 01475 783399.
Fax: 01475 888446.
Owners: W. Wilson, Ms C. Wilson.
Fleet: 10 - 6 coach, 2 midibus, 1 midicoach, 1 minibus.
Chassis: 1 Iveco. 2 Mercedes. 6 Volvo.
Bodies: 1 Beulas. 1 Jonckheere. 2 Plaxton. 5 Van Hool.
Ops incl: local bus services, school contracts, excursions & tours, private hire.
Livery: Blue/White.

MIDLOTHIAN

ALLAN'S GROUP

NEWTONLOAN GARAGE, GOREBRIDGE EH23 4LZ
Tel: 01875 820377.
Fax: 01875 822468
Recovery: 01875 820377
E-mail: allan'scoaches@aol.co.uk
Web Site: www.allan's-group.com
Dir: D W Allan **Ch Eng**: Neil Mitchell **Office Man**: Mrs D Allan
Fleet: 14 - 9 single-deck bus, 5 midicoach.
Chassis: 5 Mercedes. 9 Scania.
Bodies: 5 Sitcar. 9 Van Hool.

Ops incl: school contracts, private hire.
Livery: Blue/Silver.

*WILLIAM HUNTER

OAKFIELD GARAGE, LOANHEAD
EH20 9AE
Tel: 0131 440 0704
Fax: 0131 448 2184
E-mail: sales@hunterscoaches.co.uk
Props: G I Hunter, W R Hunter.
Fleet: 14 - 12 coach, 2 minibus.
Chassis: 3 Toyota. 11 Volvo.
Bodies: 3 Caetano. 11 Van Hool.
Ops incl: school contracts, private hire.
Livery: Brown/Cream

FIRST SCOTLAND EAST

14-16 ESKBANK ROAD, DALKEITH
EH22 1HH.
Tel: 0131 663 1945.
Fax: 0131 660 3989.
Man Dir: Graeme Torrance **Eng Dir**: W. McCracken. **Fin Dir**: J. Sharkey. **Ops Dir**: T. Roberts.
Fleet: 481 - 176 double-deck bus, 247 single-deck bus, 22 coach, 36 minibus.
Chassis: 91 Dennis. 91 Leyland.12 Leyland-DAB. 37 MCW. 45 Mercedes. 23 Optare. 87 Scanic. 95 Volvo.
Bodies: Alexander. East Lancs. MCW. Optare. Plaxton. Roe. Wright.
Ops incl: local bus services, school contracts, excursions & tours, private hire.
Livery: Cream/Yellow and Green, Light Grey/Dark Blue and Magenta.
Ticket System: Wayfarer 3.
See also Edinburgh, Falkirk.

LIBERTON EXECUTIVE TRAVEL

See Edinburgh, City of.

*STANLEY MACKAY COACHES OF EDINBURGH

See Edinburgh, City of

McKENDRY COACHES

100 STRAITON ROAD, LOANHEAD
EH20 9NP.
Tel: 0131 440 1013.
Fax: 0131 448 2160.
E-mail: sales@mckendrycoaches.co.uk
Prop: D. McKendry. **Prtnr**: Ms A. McKendry.
Fleet: 17 - 2 double-deck bus, 1 single-deck bus, 12 coach, 2 minibus.
Chassis: 2 DAF. 1 Leyland. 3 Leyland National. 2 Scania. 6 Volvo.
Bodies: 1 Bova. 1 Caetano. 1 Jonckheere. 1 Van Hool.
Ops incl: excursions & tours, private hire, school contracts.
Livery: Gold/Black/Red.

A/c	Air conditioning
♿	Vehicles suitable for disabled
🍴	Coach(es) with galley facilities
wc	Coach(es) with toilet facilities
💺	Seat belt-fitted vehicles
R	Recovery service available (not 24 hr)
R24	24hr recovery service
✓	Replacement vehicle available
T	Toilet-drop facilities available
🚌	Vintage vehicle(s) available
🚍	Open top vehicle(s)

MORAY

*CENTRAL COACHES
CENTRAL GARAGE, CHURCH ROAD, KEITH AB55 5BR
Tel: 01542 882113
E-mail: watsonsmith@centralcoaches.co.uk
Web site: www.centralcoaches.co.uk
Dirs: William W Smith, Veronica A Smith, William A Smith
Fleet: 10 - 7 coach, 2 minicoach, 1 midicoach.
Chassis: 1 Bova. 4 DAF. 1 Ford. 1 Mercedes. 2 Volvo.
Bodies: 1 Bova. 1 Caetano. 1 Jonckheere. 6 Plaxton. 1 Reeve Burgess.
Ops incl: local bus services, school contracts, private hire.
Livery: White/Red.

KINEIL COACHES
See Aberdeenshire

*MAYNES COACHES
MARCH ROAD INDUSTRIAL ESTATE, BUCKIE AB56 4BU
Tel: 01542 831219
Fax: 01542 833572
Recovery: 01542 835500
E-mail: maynescoaches@talk21.com
Web Site: www.maynes.co.uk
Dir: Gordon Mayne **Ops Man**: David Mayne **Tran Man**: Kevin Mayne **Co Sec**: Sandra Mayne
Fleet: 28 - 21 coach, 5 midicoach, 2 minicoach.
Chassis: 2 Bedford. 3 Bova. 2 DAF. 1 Leyland. 7 Mercedes. 1 Renault. 3 Scania. 2 Toyota. 9 Volvo.
Bodies: 5 Berkhof. 5 Bova. 1 Caetano. 4 Mercedes. 6 Plaxton. 7 Van Hool.
Ops incl: local bus services, school contracts, excursions & tours, private hire, continental tours.
Livery: Blue/White/Gold

NORTH AYRSHIRE

*CLYDE COAST COACHES LTD
55 MONTGOMERIE STREET, ARDROSSAN KA22 8HR
Tel: 01294 605454
Fax: 01294 605460
E-mail: enquiries@clydecoast.com
Web site: www.clydecoast.com
Dirs: Kenneth G McGregor, David H Frazer.
Fleet: 22 - 10 double-deck bus, 2 single-deck bus, 8 coach, 2 minibus.
Chassis: Bova. Leyland. Mercedes. Volvo.
Bodies: Alexander. Bova. ECW. Jonckheere. Mercedes. Van Hool.
Ops incl: excursions & tours, private hire, school contracts.
Livery: Silver Blue metallic

*T & E DOCHERTY
40 BANK STREET, IRVINE KA12 0LP
Tel/Recovery: 01294 278440
Fax: 01294 272510
E-mail: info@coach-hires.co.uk
Web Site: www.coach-hires.co.uk
Owner: Hugh Tait **Gen Man**: Tom Hamilton
Fleet: 31 - 2 double-deck bus, 6 single-deck bus, 11 coach, 4 minicoach, 8 minibus.
Chassis: 7 Bova. 1 Dodge. 2 LDV. 2 Leyland. 10 Mercedes. 2 Optare. 8 Volvo.
Bodies: 2 Alexander. 1 Autobus. 7 Bova. 1 Caetano. 1 East Lancs. 2 LDV. 2 Optare. 6 Plaxton. 1 Reeve Burgess. 2 Van Hool. 6 Wright. 1 Sitcar.
Ops incl: local bus services, school contracts, excursions & tours, private hire, express, continental tours.
Livery: Buses: Blue/Cream. Coaches: Cream/Beige
Ticket System: Wayfarer 3.

*MARBILL COACH SERVICES LTD
HIGH MAINS GARAGE, MAINS ROAD, BEITH KA15 2AP
Tel: 01505 503367
Fax: 01505 504736
E-mail: marbill@btclick.com
Web site: www.marbillcoaches.com
Man Dir: Margaret Whiteman **Eng Dir**: David Barr **Ops Dir**: Connie Barr
Fleet: 66 - 26 double-deck bus, 20 single-deck bus, 18 coach, 2 minicoach.
Chassis: 2 Bova. 34 Leyland. 2 Mercedes. 28 Volvo
Bodies: 26 Alexander. 2 Bova. 25 Plaxton. 12 Van Hool. 1 Beluga.
Ops incl: school contracts, excursions & tours, private hire.

MILLPORT MOTORS LTD
16 BUTE TERRACE, MILLPORT KA28 0BA.
Tel: 01475 530555.
Fleet: 4 single-deck bus.
Chassis: 3 Leyland. 1 Volvo.
Ops incl: local bus services, private hire.
Livery: Blue/Cream.
Ticket System: Almex.

*SHUTTLE BUSES LTD
CALEDONIA HOUSE, LONGFORD AVENUE, KILWINNING KA13 6EX
Tel/Fax: 01294 550757
Man Dir: David Granger
Fleet: 19 - 1 single-deck bus, 3 coach, 9 midibus, 3 midicoach, 3 minibus.
Chassis: 1 AEC. 2 Dennis. 2 Ford Transit. 2 Leyland. 7 Mercedes. 4 Optare. 1 Volvo.
Bodies: 2 Alexander. 1 Autobus. 4 Optare. 7 Plaxton. 1 Reeve Burgess. 3 other.
Ops incl: local bus services, private hire.
Livery: Yellow/White.
Ticket System: Wayfarer 3.

T PATERSON & BROWN LTD
51 HOLMHEAD, KILBIRNIE KA25 6BS.
Tel: 01505 683344.
Fax: 01505 684508
Recovery: 07787 530162
E-mail: patersonscoaches@tiscali.co.uk
Man Dir: Sam Paterson **Tran Man**: Sam Paterson **Eng**: David Paterson **Dir/Sec**: Robert Brown.
Fleet: 7 coach.
Chassis: 4 Bova. 3 Volvo.
Bodies: 4 Bova. 1 Caetano. 1 Plaxton. 1 Van Hool.
Ops incl: excursions & tours, private hire, continental tours, school contracts.
Livery: White with green globes and orange/red/yellow stripe

NORTH LANARKSHIRE

A&C LUXURY COACHES
4 HILLHEAD AVENUE, MOTHERWELL ML1 4AQ.
Tel/Fax: 01698 252652.
Prop: A. Grenfell.
Fleet: 4 - 2 midicoach, 2 minicoach.
Chassis: 1 Leyland. 3 Mercedes.
Bodies: 1 Alexander. 1 Whitacre. 1 MTM. 1 Crystals.
Ops incl: school contracts, private hire.

CANAVAN'S COACHES
CEDAR LODGE, COACH ROAD, KILSYTH G65 0DB.
Tel: 01236 822414.
Prop: M., G., H., & J. Canavan.
Ops incl: local bus services.

DUNN'S COACHES
560 STIRLING ROAD, RIGGEND, AIRDRIE ML6 7SS.
Tel: 01236 722385.
Fax: 01236 722385.
Owner: William G. Dunn. **Eng**: Craig Dunn.
Fleet: 7 - 4 coach, 3 minibus.
Chassis: 1 DAF. 3 Volvo. 1 Leyland. 2 Mercedes.
Bodies: 1 Alexander. 1 Marshall. 4 Plaxton. 1 Van Hool.
Ops incl: local bus services, school contracts, excursions & tours, private hire, express.

ESSBEE COACHES (HIGHLANDS & ISLANDS)
7 HOLLANDHURST ROAD, GARTSHERRIE ML5 2EG
Tel: 01236 423621
Fax: 01236 433677
Man Dir: B. Smith. **Gen Man**: J. Kinnaird.
Ops Man: S. Stewart.
Fleet: 56 - 10 single-deck bus, 19 coach, 2 double-deck coach, 6 midicoach, 19 minibus.
Chassis: 2 DAF. 3 Ford Transit. 13 Leyland. 6 Leyland National. 21 Mercedes. 2 Neoplan. 10 Volvo.
Bodies: 7 Duple. 1 ECW. 1 Jonckheere. 6 Leyland National. 2 Neoplan. 15 Plaxton. 3 Autobus. 2 Crystals.
Ops incl: local bus services, school contracts, excursions & tours, private hire.
Livery: Red/Silver.
Ticket System: Wayfarer.

GOLDEN EAGLE COACHES

MUIRHALL GARAGE, 197 MAIN STREET, SALSBURGH BY SHOTTS ML7 4LS
Tel: 01698 870207
Fax: 01698 870217
E-mail: general@goldeneaglecoaches.freeserve.co.uk
Web site: www.golden-eagle-coaches.co.uk
Ptnrs: Peter Irvine, Robert Irvine, Isabel Irvine.
Fleet: 15 - 5 single-deck bus, 10 coach.
Chassis: 1 Bova. 1 DAF. 6 Leyland. 7 Volvo.
Bodies: 1 Bova. 5 Leyland. 8 Van Hool. 1 other
Ops incl: private hire, excursions & tours, school contracts, .
Livery: White/Maroon/Gold

*HUTCHISON'S COACHES (OVERTOWN) LTD

5 CASTLEHILL ROAD, OVERTOWN, WISHAW ML2 0QS
Tel: 01698 372132
Fax: 01698 376933
Recovery: 01698 372132
E-mail: stewartanderson@hutchisoncoaches.co.uk
Web site: www.hutchisoncoaches.co.uk
Prop: S Anderson, I Anderson, P Anderson
Traf Man: D Gormley.
Fleet: 48 - 27 single-deck bus, 21 coach.
Chassis: 2 DAF. 5 MAN. 9 Optare. 8 Scania. 24 Volvo.
Bodies: 2 Alexander. 1 Berkhof. 1 Duple. 4 Irizar. 2 Northern Counties. 14 Optare. 4 Plaxton. 12 Van Hool. 8 Wright.
Ops incl: local bus services, school contracts, excursions & tours, private hire, continental tours, express.
Livery: Blue/Cream; Silver/Blue/Red
Ticket System: Wayfarer.

IRVINE'S COACHES

LAWMUIR ROAD GARAGE, LAW ML8 5JB.
Tel: 01698 372452
Fax: 01698 376200.
Fleetname: Irvine's of Law.
Prop: Peter Irvine
Fleet: 35 - includes double-deck bus, coach, minicoach.
Chassis: 2 DAF. 4 Dennis. 1 Leyland. 1 MCW. 4 Mercedes. 1 Scania. 4 Volvo.
Livery: Red/Maroon/Cream.
Ticket System: Wayfarer.

LONG'S COACHES LTD

157 MAIN STREET, SALSBURGH BY SHOTTS ML7 4LR.
Tel: 01698 870768.
Fax: 01698 870826.
E-mail: info@longscoaches.co.uk
Web site: www.longscoaches.co.uk
Dir: Peter I. Long.**Co Sec:** Susan Long.
Fleet: 14 - 13 coach, 1 midicoach.
Chassis: 2 Bova. 12 Volvo.
Bodies: 2 Bova. 12 Van Hool.
Ops incl: excursions & tours, private hire, express, continental tours, school contracts.
Livery: Silver/Maroon.
Ticket System: Wayfarer.

*MACPHAILS COACHES

409 HIGH STREET, NEWARTHILL, MOTHERWELL ML1 5SP
Tel: 01698 860249
Fax: 01698 861963
E-mail: macphailscoaches@hotmail.com
Web site: www.macphailscoaches.com
Dirs: Martin MacPhail, Henry MacPhail.
Fleet: 8 coach.
Chassis: 8 Volvo.
Bodies: 1 Plaxton. 7 Van Hool.
Ops incl: excursions & tours, private hire, continental tours.

MCKINDLESS EXPRESS

101 MAIN STREET, BOGSIDE, WISHAW ML2 9PP.
Tel: 01698 356991.
Prop: M. McKindless.
Ops Incl: local bus services, express, school contracts, private hire.
Livery: Cream/Green.

*MCT GROUP TRAVEL LTD

NETHAN STREET DEPOT, MOTHERWELL ML1 3TF
Tel: 01698 253091
Fax: 01698 259208
Web site: www.mctgrouptravel.com
Man Dir: Desmond Heenan **Dir:** Oswald Heenan **Fleet Eng:** Alan Bruce.
Fleet: 14 - 4 coach, 5 midicoach, 5 minicoach.
Chassis: 1 AEC. 2 Dennis. 4 Mercedes. 1 Renault. 6 Toyota.
Bodies: 6 Caetano. 2 Marcopolo. 2 Mercedes. 2 Optare.
Ops incl: excursions & tours, private hire, continental tours.
Livery: Turquoise/Silver

MILLER'S COACHES

22 WOODSIDE DRIVE, CALDERBANK, AIRDRIE ML6 9TN.
Tel: 01236 763671.
Owner: W. Miller. **Tran Man:** T. Miller.
Fleet: 12 - 8 coach, 4 minicoach.
Chassis: 8 Leyland. 4 Mercedes.
Bodies: 2 Alexander. 1 Mellor. 8 Plaxton. 1 Reeve Burgess.
Ops incl: local bus services, school contracts, private hire.
Livery: Black/White/Grey.

SLOCOACH

19 AIRBLES DRIVE, MOTHERWELL ML1 3AS.
Tel: 01698 261490.
Prop: B. Johnston.
Fleet: 4 - 1 midicoach, 1 minibus, 2 minicoach.
Chassis: 1 Ford Transit. 3 Mercedes.
Ops incl: local bus services. school contracts, private hire.

STEPEND COACHES

92 WADDELL AVENUE, GLENMAVIS, AIRDRIE ML6 0NZ.
Tel: 01236 760500.
Prop: S. Chapman.
Ops incl: local bus services.

*TRAMONTANA

CHAPELKNOWE ROAD, CARFIN, MOTHERWELL ML1 5LE.
Tel: 01698 861790.
Fax: 01698 860778
E-mail: wdt@tranta90.freeserve.co.uk
Prop: Douglas Telfer
Fleet: 6 coach
Chassis: 6 Volvo.
Bodies: 2 Caetano. 1 Irizar. 3 Plaxton.
Ops incl: private hire
Livery: White

ORKNEY

ORKNEY COACHES (FORMERLY PEACE'S COACHES)

SCOTTS ROAD, HATSTON INDUSTRIAL ESTATE, KIRKWALL KW15 1JY.
Tel: 01856 870555.
Fax: 01856 877501.
Man Dir: F. Rapson. **Ch Eng:** R. Henderson. **Ch Exec:** A. H. Rapson. **Fin Dir:** J. Lornie.
Ops Dir: A. MacDonald.
Fleet: 44 - 28 coach, 6 midibus, 4 midicoach, 6 minibus.
Chassis: 26 Bedford. 2 Dennis. 4 Ford. 1 MCW. 7 Mercedes. 1 Renault. 2 Toyota. 1 Volvo.
Bodies: 7 Duple. 18 Plaxton. 1 Van Hool. 1 Berkhof. 2 Unicar. 14 Other.
Ops incl: local bus services, school contracts, excursions & tours, private hire.
Subsidiary of Rapsons Coaches.

PERTH & KINROSS

*ABERFELDY MOTOR SERVICES

BURNSIDE GARAGE, ABERFELDY PH15 2DD
Tel: 01887 820433
Fax: 01887 829534

Ac	Air conditioning
	Vehicles suitable for disabled
	Coach(es) with galley facilities
wc	Coach(es) with toilet facilities
♥	Seat belt-fitted vehicles
R	Recovery service available (not 24 hr)
R24	24hr recovery service
✓	Replacement vehicle available
T	Toilet-drop facilities available
	Vintage vehicle(s) available
	Open top vehicle(s)

Web site:
www.aberfeldycoaches.co.uk
Prop: John Stewart **Co Sec:** Lynda Stewart
Fleet: 11 - 8 coach, 1 minibus, 2 minicoach.
Chassis: Bova. Mercedes. Volvo.
Bodies: Alexander. Bova. Plaxton. Van Hool. Onyx.
Ops incl: excursions & tours, private hire, continental tours.
Livery: Silver-Blue/Blue

*BLUEBIRD BUSES LTD

RUTHVENFIELD ROAD,
INVERALMOND, PERTH PH1 3EE
Tel: 01738 629339
Fax: 01738 643264
Recovery: 01738 629339
E-mail:
eastscotland@stagecoachbus.com
robert.robinson@stagecoachbus.com
Web site: www.stagecoachbus.com
Fleetname: Stagecoach in Perth
Man Dir: Tom Wileman **Dep Man Dir:**
Robert Andrew **Ops Dir:** Robert Hall **Eng Dir:** Michael Reid **Ops Man:** Robert Robinson **Depot Eng:** John Dick
Fleet: 69 - 19 double-deck bus, 23 single-deck bus, 1 open-top bus, 3 coach, 16 midibus, 8 minibus.
Chassis: 9 Dennis. 19 Leyland. 9 MAN. 8 Mercedes. 24 Volvo.
Bodies: 59 Alexander. 1 Berkhof. 1 Jonckheere. 3 Plaxton. 3 Wright.
Ops incl: local bus services, school contracts, excursions & tours, private hire, express.
Livery: Stagecoach (White/Blue/Orange/Red).
Ticket System: Wayfarer TGX

*CABER COACHES LTD

CHAPEL STREET GARAGE,
ABERFELDY PH15 2AS
Tel: 01887 870090
Fax: 01887 829352
E-mail: cabercoaches@btinternet.com
Man Dir: Kenneth Carey **Sec:** Alexandre Carey
Fleet: 5 - 1 single-deck bus, 1 coach, 1 midibus, 1 midicoach, 1 minibus, 1 minicoach.
Chassis: 1 LDV. 2 Leyland. 2 Mercedes. 1 Renault.
Bodies: 1 Alexander. 2 Mercedes. 2 Plaxton. 1 Reeve Burgess.
Ops incl: local bus services, school contracts, private hire, excursions & tours.
Livery: White
Ticket system: Almex

*DOCHERTY'S MIDLAND COACHES

PRIORY PARK, AUCHTERARDER
PH3 1AE
Tel: 01764 662218
Fax: 01764 664228
E-mail: docherty.midland@virgin.net.
Web site:
www.dochertysmidlandcoaches.co.uk
Props: Jim & EdithDocherty
Fleet: 20 - 2 single-deck bus, 10 coach, 2 midibus, 4 midicoach, 1 minicoach, 1 vintage.
Chassis: 1 Leyland. 6 Mercedes. 1 Optare. 2 Scania. 10 Volvo.

Bodies: 1 Optare. 7 Plaxton. 8 Van Hool. 2 Wright. 1 Windover. 1 KVC.
Ops incl: local bus services, school contracts, excursions & tours, private hire.
Livery: White/Black/Grey
Ticket System: Wayfarer

*EARNSIDE COACHES

GREENBANK ROAD, GLENFARG
PH2 9NW
Tel: 01577 830360
Fax: 01577 830599
E-mail: earnside@aol.com.
Web site: www.earnside.com
Ptnrs: David Rutherford, Fiona Rutherford
Fleet: 9 - 1 double-deck bus, 7 coach, 1 minibus.
Chassis: 1 DAF. 2 Leyland. 1 Renault. 1 Scania. 4 Volvo.
Bodies: 1 Berkhof. 1 Ikarus. 1 Irizar. 1 Leyland. 4 Plaxton. 1 other.
Ops incl: local bus services, school contracts, excursions & tours, private hire, continental tours.
Livery: Yellow.
Ticket System: Almex.

*HIGHWAYMAN COACHES

STATION ROAD, ERROL PH2 7QB
Tel: 01821 642739
Fax: 01821 642683
E-mail: rng6@tesco.net.
Owner: Robin Gloag
Fleet: 2 double-deck bus, 8 coach, 1 double-deck bus, 2 midicoach.
Chassis: 3 Bova. 2 DAF. 2 Leyland. 4 MAN. 1 Mercedes. 1 Neoplan. 1 Toyota.
Bodies: 3 Bova. 1 Caetano. 2 Leyland. 1 Mercedes. 1 Neoplan. 1 Plaxton. 4 Van Hool.
Ops incl: school contracts, excursions & tours, private hire.
Livery: multicolour

*PEGASUS TRAVEL LTD

28 INVERALMOND ROAD, PERTH
PH1 3TW
Tel/Fax: 01738 444070
E-mail: enquiries@pegasus-travel.co.uk
Web site: www.pegasus-travel.co.uk
Man Dir: Duncan Graham **Co Sec:** Mairi Graham **Ops Man:** Trevor White **Ch Eng:** Guy Batchelor
Fleet: 10 - 7 coach, 3 midicoach.
Chassis: 1 DAF. 3 Mercedes. 6 Volvo.
Bodies: 2 Autobus. 8 Plaxton.
Ops incl: excursions & tours, private hire, school contracts, continental tours.
Livery: White

SMITH & SONS COACHES

THE COACH DEPOT, WOODSIDE,
COUPAR ANGUS PH13 9LW
Tel: 01828 627310
Fax: 01828 628518
E-mail:
www.smithandsonscoaches.com
Prop: I. C. Smith. **Prop/Fleet Eng:** G. Smith.
Office Man: A. Osborne.
Prop/Traf Man: I. F. Smith.
Ops incl: local bus services, school contracts, excursions & tours, private hire,

continental tours.
Livery: White/Orange.
Ticket System: Setright.

*ELIZABETH YULE TRANSPORT

STATION GARAGE, STATION ROAD,
PITLOCHRY PH16 5AN
Tel: 01796 472290
Fax: 01796 474214
E-mail: info.elizabeth-yule@virgin.net
Web site:
www.perthshirecoaches.co.uk
Man: Sandra Bridges
Fleet: 8 - 4 coach, 3 midicoach, 1 minibus.
Chassis: 1 LDV. 3 Mercedes. 4 Volvo.
Ops incl: local bus services, school contracts, private hire.
Livery: White
Ticket System: Almex

RENFREWSHIRE

ALAN ARNOTT

16 TURNHILL CRESCENT, WEST
FREELANDS, ERSKINE PA8 7AX
Fleetname: S & A Coaches, City Sprinter

ARRIVA SCOTLAND WEST

THE GATEHOUSE, PORTERFIELD
ROAD, RENFREW PA4 8JB
Tel: 0141 885 4040
Fax: 0141 885 4088
Web site: www.arriva.co.uk
Man Dir: Ian Craig **Ops Man:** Murray Rogers
Fleet: 184
Chassis: Dennis. Leyland. MCW. Mercedes. Optare. Scania. Volvo.
Bodies: Alexander. Carlyle. East Lancs. MCW. Northern Counties. Optare. Plaxton. Wright. Marshall. Wadham Sringer.
Ops incl: local bus services, school contracts, private hire.
Livery: Aquamarine/Stone.
Ticket System: Wayfarer 3.

JAMES BURNS

24 GLENDOWER WAY, FOX BAR,
PAISLEY PA2 0TH.
Fleetname: Green Line Coaches.

IAN CHESTNUT

36D NORTH ROAD, JOHNSTONE
PA5 8NF.
Fleetname: Reliable Bus.

*CLASSIQUE SUN SALOON LUXURY COACHES

8 UNDERWOOD ROAD, PAISLEY
PA3 1TD
Tel: 0141 889 4050
Fax: 0141 848 7616
Web site: www.classiquetours.co.uk
Prop: David N Dean
Fleet: 8 coach.
Chassis: 1 AEC. 4 Leyland. 3 Volvo.
Bodies: 1 Duple. 4 Plaxton. 2 Harrington. 1 Ramseier+Jenzer.
Ops incl: excursions & tours, private hire, continental tours.
Livery: Various.

FIRST STOP TRAVEL LTD
1 KINGS INCH ROAD, RENFREW.
Tel: 0141 886 1268.
Ops incl: local bus services.

VIOLET GRAHAM COACHES
93 IVANHOE ROAD, FOX BAR,
PAISLEY PA2 0LF.
Tel: 01505 349758.
Fax: 01505 349758.
Owner: V. Rosike.
Fleet: 2 midicoach.
Chassis: 1 Ford Transit. 1 Freight Rover.
Ops incl: school contracts, private hire.

SHETLAND

*R G JAMIESON & SON
MOARFIELD GARAGE, CULLIVOE,
YELL ZE2 9DD
Tel: 01957 744214
Fax: 01957 744270
E-mail: rhjamieson@hotmail.com
Ptnrs: Robert H Jamieson
Fleet: 5 - 2 coach, 2 minibus, 1 minicoach.
Chassis: 1 Dennis. 2 Ford Transit.
1 Marshall. 1 Mercedes.
Bodies: 1 Berkhof. 1 Plaxton. 3 other.
Ops incl: local bus services, school
contracts, excursions & tours, private hire,
continental tours.
Livery: White/Blue (three shades)

*JOHN LEASK & SON
ESPLANADE, LERWICK ZE1 0LL
Tel: 01595 693162
Fax: 01595 693171
E-mail: leasks@zetnet.co.uk
Web site: www.leaskstravel.co.uk
Ptnrs: Peter R Leask, Andrew J N Leask
Fleet: 19 - 4 single-deck bus, 9 coach,
1 midibus, 1 midicoach, 2 minibus.
Chassis: 15 DAF. 1 Dennis. 1 LDV.
2 Mercedes.
Bodies: 6 Ikarus. 9 Plaxton. V Hool.
2 Wright.
Ops incl: local bus services, school
contracts, excursions & tours, private hire.
Livery: Ivory/Blue.
Ticket system: ERG

SHALDER COACHES LTD
LOWER SCORD, SCALLOWAY
ZE1 0UQ.
Tel: 01595 880217.
Fax: 01595 880731.
Dir/Gen Man/Sec: A. Young. **Ch Eng**:
J. Duncan. **Tours Dir**: A. G. S. Morrison.
Fleet: 11 - 5 midibus, 4 midicoach,
2 minicoach.
Chassis: 6 Bedford. 1 Ford Transit. 1 Iveco.
2 MCW. 3 Mercedes. 15 Volvo.
Bodies: 1 Caetano. 9 Duple. 3 Mercedes.
2 MCW. 11 Plaxton. 1 Transit. 4 Pullman.
1 other.

Ops incl: local bus services, school
contracts, excursions & tours, private hire,
continental tours.
Livery: Black/White.
Subsidiary of Rapsons Coaches.

SOUTH AYRSHIRE

*DODDS OF TROON LTD
4 EAST ROAD, AYR KA8 9BA.
Tel: 01292 288100
Fax: 01292 287700
E-mail: info@doddsoftroon.com
Web site: www.doddsoftroon.com
Man Dir: James Dodds **Ops Dir**: Douglas
Dodds **Dir**: Norma Dodds **Eng Man**: John
Gorman
Fleet: 18 - 2 single-deck bus, 14 coach,
2 midicoach.
Chassis: 1 Dennis. 2 Leyland. 4 Scania.
2 Toyota. 9 Volvo.
Bodies: 2 Alexander. 2 Caetano. 3 Irizar.
2 Jonckheere. 3 Plaxton. 6 Van Hool.
Ops incl: school contracts, excursions &
tours, private hire.
Livery: Green/Cream

IBT TRAVEL GROUP
CAIRN HOUSE, 15 SKYE ROAD,
PRESTWICK KA9 2TA
Tel: 01292 477771
Fax: 01292 471770
E-mail: briant@ibtravel.com
Partner: Ian Black
Fleet: 3 coaches
Chassis: Volvo
Bodies: Van Hool
Ops incl: continental tours, private hire
Livery: Blue/Gold flash

KEENAN OF AYR COACH TRAVEL
DARWIN GARAGE, COALHALL, BY
AYR KA6 6ND
Tel: 01292 591252
Fax: 01292 590980
E-mail: mail@keenancoaches.co.uk
Dirs: Tony Keenan, Jamie Keenan **Ch Eng**:
William Gardiner
Fleet: 20 - 3 double-deck bus, 6 single-deck
bus, 9 coach, 2 minibus.
Chassis: 9 Leyland. 2 Mercedes. 9 Volvo.
Ops incl: school contracts, excursions &
tours, private hire.
Livery: Red/Yellow/Orange/White

MILLIGANS COACH TRAVEL LIMITED
LOAN GARAGE, MAUCHLINE
KA5 6AN
Tel: 01290 550365
Fax: 01290 553291
E-mail: milligans1@aol.com
Web Site:
www.milliganscoachtravel.co.uk

Dir: William Milligan **Ops Man**: Alan Cook
Co Sec: Norag Milligan
Fleet: 15 - 11 coach, 1 double-deck coach,
1 midicoach, 1 minibus.
Chassis: 2 DAF. 1 Ford Transit. 1 Leyland.
4 Mercedes. 1 Scania. 6 Volvo.
Bodies: 1 Berkhof. 2 Bova. 1 Duple.
1 Jonckheere. 1 Mercedes. 1 Neoplan.
2 Plaxton. 2 Setra. 3 Van Hool. 1 other.
Ops incl: excursions & tours, private hire,
school contracts.
Livery: Black/Red/Silver

SOUTH LANARKSHIRE

ALFRA COACH HIRE
26 MACHAN ROAD, LARKHALL
ML9 1HG.
Tel: 01698 887581.
Prop: F. Russell.
Fleet: 4 minibus.
Chassis: 2 Ford Transit. 1 Freight Rover.
1 Leyland.
Ops incl: private hire.
Livery: White.

*BEATON COACHES LTD
46 JOHN STREET, BLANTYRE
G72 0JG.
Tel: 01698 822514.
Fax: 01698 710590
Ops Man: J Beaton **Dirs**: R Beaton,
J Beaton (jnr) **Co Sec**: Mrs E Beaton
Ch Eng: I Smith.
Chassis: 2 Bova. 2 DAF. 7 Leyland.
3 Mercedes. 5 Volvo.
Ops incl: school contracts, private hire.

R. & C. S. CRAIG
TOWNFOOT, ROBERTON, BY
BIGGAR ML12 6RS.
Tel: 01899 850655.
Dirs: R. Craig, C. S. Craig.
Traf Man/Ch Eng: J. Harvie.
Gen Man: R. Craig.
Fleet: 3 - 2 minibus, 1 minicoach.
Chassis: Freight Rover.
Ops incl: school contracts, private hire.
Livery: White.

MUIRS COACHES
1 POWELL STREET,
DOUGLAS WATER ML11 9PP.
Tel: 01555 880551.
Fax: 01555 880771.
E-mail: coaches@muirstravel.co.uk
Web site: www.muirstravel.co.uk
Gen Man: G. Muir.
Fleet: 6 - 1 single-deck bus, 1 coach,
1 midicoach, 3 minicoach.
Chassis: 1 Bova. 4 Mercedes. 1 Toyota.
Bodies: 1 Bova. 1 Caetano. 4 Mercedes.
1 Wadham Stringer.
Ops incl: local bus services, school
contracts, excursions & tours, private hire,
continental tours.

A/c	Air conditioning
	Vehicles suitable for disabled
	Coach(es) with galley facilities
wc	Coach(es) with toilet facilities
	Seat belt-fitted vehicles
R	Recovery service available (not 24 hr)
R24	24hr recovery service
	Replacement vehicle available
T	Toilet-drop facilities available
	Vintage vehicle(s) available
	Open top vehicle(s)

PARK'S OF HAMILTON LTD
[wc] [†|] [♿] [A/c] [R24] [✂] [T]

14 BOTHWELL ROAD, HAMILTON ML3 0AY
Tel: 01698 281222
Fax: 01698 303731
Chmn: Douglas Park
Ch Eng: Malcolm Fisher.
Co Sec/Dir: Gerry Donnachie. **Ops Man**: Michael Andrews. **Dir**: Hugh McAteer.
Fleet: 67 - 65 coach, 6 double-deck coach.
Chassis: 2 Neoplan. 60 Volvo. 5 Iveco.
Bodies: 30 Jonckheere. 2 Neoplan. 20 Plaxton. 10 Van Hool. 5 Beulas.
Ops incl: local bus services, school contracts, excursions & tours, private hire, express, continental tours.
Livery: Black
Ticket System: Wayfarer

*SILVER CHOICE COACHES
[wc] [†|] [♿] [A/c] [R24] [✂] [T]

1 MILTON ROAD, COLLEGE MILTON NORTH, EAST KILBRIDE G74 5BU
Tel: 01355 230403.
Fax: 01355 265111
Recovery: 07966 315361
Web site: www.silverchoicetravel.co.uk
E-mail: enquiries@silverchoicetravel.co.uk
Dirs: D W Gardiner, Sandra Gardiner
Fleet: 9 - 6 coach, 3 double-deck coach.
Chassis: 2 Bova. 1 Iveco. 2 Scania. 4 Volvo.
Bodies: 1 Beulas. 2 Bova. 1 Plaxton. 3 Van Hool.
Ops incl: excursions & tours, private hire, express, continental tours.
Livery: Silver

*STAGECOACH WEST SCOTLAND
[♿] [♿] [†|] [🚌] [wc] [🚐] [A/c] [✂] [T]

SANDGATE, AYR KA7 1DD
Tel: 01292 613700
Fax: 01292 613501
Web site: www.stagecoachbus.com
Man Dir: T Wileman **Eng Dir**: S Greer **Ops Dir**: B Chamberlain
Fleet: 431 - 100 double-deck bus, 100 single-deck bus, 42 coach, 16 articulated bus, 3 open-top bus, 105 midibus, 65 minibus.
Chassis: 1 AEC. 78 Dennis. 72 Leyland. 2 Leyland National. 2 MAN. 62 Mercedes. 3 Optare. 3 Scania. 204 Volvo.
Bodies: Alexander. Berkhof. Carlyle. Duple. ECW. East Lancs. Jonckheere. Leyland. Leyland National. Marshall. Mercedes. Northern Counties. Optare. Park Royal. Plaxton. Transbus. Wright.
Ops incl: local bus services, school contracts, private hire, express.
Livery: Stagecoach (White/Blue/Orange/Red)
Ticket System: Wayfarer

*WILLIAM STOKES & SONS LTD
[♿] [wc] [♿] [✂]

22 CARSTAIRS ROAD, CARSTAIRS ML11 8QD
Tel: 01555 870344
Fax: 01555 870183
E-mail: enquiries@stokescoaches.co.uk
Web site: www.stokescoaches.co.uk
Fleet: 29 - 7 single-deck bus, 7 coach, 3 midibus, 2 midicoach

Chassis: Dennis. Leyland. Mercedes. Volvo.
Bodies: Berkhof. Caetano. Ikarus. Marshall. Plaxton. Van Hool.
Ops incl: local bus services, school contracts, excursions & tours, private hire.
Livery: Red/Cream
Ticket System: Almex A90

STONEHOUSE COACHES
48 NEW STREET, STONEHOUSE ML9 3LT.
Tel: 01698 792145.
Prop: N. Collison.
Livery: White/Pink/Navy.

*STUART'S OF CARLUKE
[♿] [†|] [♿] [A/c] [✂]

CASTLEHILL GARAGE, AIRDRIE ROAD, CARLUKE ML8 4UF
Tel: 01555 773533
Fax: 01555 752220
Dir: Stuart Shevill **Ops**: John Hane
Fleet: 49 - 10 double-deck bus, 20 single-deck bus, 15 coach, 2 minibus, 2 minicoach
Chassis: 15 Dennis. 1 Ford Transit. 10 Leyland. 3 Mercedes. 1 Optare. 15 Volvo.
Bodies: Alexander. Caetano. ECW. Jonckheere. Northern Counties. Optare. Plaxton. Reeve Burgess. Van Hool.
Ops incl: local bus services, school contracts, excursions and tours, private hire, express, continental tours.
Livery: Silver/Blue
Ticket system: Wayfarer

*WHITELAWS COACHES
[♿] [wc] [†|] [♿] [A/c] [✂]

LOCHPARK INDUSTRIAL ESTATE, STONEHOUSE ML9 3LR
Tel: 01698 792800
Fax: 01698 793309
E-mail: enquiries@whitelaws.co.uk
Web site: www.whitelaws.co.uk
Ptnrs: George Whitelaw, Sandra Whitelaw, William Whitelaw, George A Whitelaw., Sandra Whitelaw-Ginestri (**Gen Man**), Janet Whitelaw **Ch Eng**: Brian Smart **Tran Man**: William Mclean.
Fleet: 40 - 14 single-deck bus, 12 coach, 11 midibus, 2 midicoach, 1 minibus.
Chassis: 1 DAF. 1 Iveco. 6 Leyland. 3 Mercedes. 29 Volvo.
Bodies: 7 Alexander. 2 Duple. 1 Marshall. 2 Optare. 1 Plaxton. 1 Reeve Burgess. 2 Van Hool. 14 Wright. 10 Sunsundegui.
Ops incl: local bus services, school contracts, excursions & tours, private hire.
Livery: Silver with Red/White/Blue.
Ticket System: Wayfarer 3.

STIRLING

*BILLY DAVIES EXECUTIVE COACHES
[♿] [wc] [†|] [A/c] [R24] [✂]

TRANSPORT HOUSE, PLEAN INDUSTRIAL ESTATE, PLEAN FK7 8BJ
Tel: 01786 816627
Fax: 01786 811433
Web site: www.daviescoaches.com
E-mail: enquiries@daviescoaches.com
Prop: Billy Davies
Fleet: 8 - 5 double-deck bus, 3 coach.
Chassis: 5 MCW. 3 Volvo

Ops incl: local bus services, school contracts, private hire, continental tours.
Livery: Blue (2 shades)
Ticket system: Setright

FITZCHARLES COACHES LTD
[wc] [†|] [♿] [A/c] [✂] [T]

87 NEWHOUSE ROAD, GRANGEMOUTH FK3 8NJ.
Tel: 01324 482093.
Fax: 01324 665411.
E-mail: info@fitzcharles.co.uk
Web site: www.fitzcharles.co.uk
Man Dir: G R Fitzcharles **Dir/Sec**: Mrs O King **Acc Man**: D Fitzcharles **Tran Man**: J Walton **Ch Eng**: M McArther.
Fleet: 16 - 15 coach, 1 minicoach.
Chassis: 2 Ayats. 3 DAF. 2 Leyland. 1 Mercedes. 10 Volvo.
Bodies: 2 Ayats. 5 Caetano. 10 Plaxton. 1 Reeve Burgess.
Ops incl: excursions & tours, private hire, continental tours, school contracts, local bus services.
Livery: Red/Cream.

WEST DUNBARTONSHIRE

D. P. BISHOP
14 LENNOX ROAD, MILTON, DUMBARTON G82 2TL.
Fleetname: DB Travel.

*McCOLL'S COACHES LTD
[♿] [♿] [†|] [wc] [A/c] [R] [✂]

BALLAGAN DEPOT, STIRLING ROAD, BALLOCH G83 8LY
Tel: 01389 754321
Fax: 01389 755354
E-mail: mccolls@btconnect.com
Web site: www.mccolls.org.uk
Man: William McColl **Man Dirs**: Thomas McColl, Janet McColl **Co Sec**: Ann McKinlay **Ops Man**: Liam McColl **Head mechanic**: Eddie McKinley
Fleet: double-deck bus, single-deck bus, coach, minibus.
Chassis: DAF. Dennis. Ford. Ford Transit. Leyland. leyland National. MCW. Mercedes. Volvo. other.
Bodies: Leyland National. MCW. Mercedes. other.
Ops incl: local bus services, school contracts, excursions & tours, private hire.

WEST LOTHIAN

*LES BROWN TRAVEL
[♿] [♿]

9 HARDHILL ROAD, BATHGATE EH48 2BW
Tel: 01506 656129
Fax: 01506 656129
E-mail: les-brown@btconnect.com
Web Site: www.lesbrowntravel.com
Props: Les Brown, Colin Brown
Fleet: 8 - 2 midicoach, 6 minicoach.
Chassis: 5 Ford Transit. 3 Mercedes.
Ops incl: school contracts, excursions & tours, private hire.

*BROWNINGS (WHITBURN) LTD wc ♥
22 LONGRIDGE ROAD, WHITBURN EH47 0DE
Tel: 01501 740234
Fax: 01501 741265
E-mail: george@browningscoaches.fsnet.co.uk
Dir: George Browning
Chassis: Leyland, Volvo.
Bodies: Van Hool.
Ops incl: excursions & tours, private hire, express, school contracts.
Livery: Red/White/Blue.

GLENTANA COACHES LTD ♥
GREENPARK, EDINBURGH ROAD, LINLITHGOW EH49 6AA.
Tel: 01506 670254.
Fax: 01506 846034.
E-mail: glentanacoaches@ic24.net
Web site: www.glentanacoaches.co.uk
Dir: William Ramage **Co Sec**: Alexander Calderwood
Fleet: 6 - 5 minibus, 1 midicoach.
Chassis: 6 Mercedes
Bodies: 5 Mercedes. 1 Optare.
Ops incl: private hire, incl. airport transfer.

*E & M HORSBURGH ♿ ♥
180 UPHALL STATION ROAD, PUMPHERSTON, LIVINGSTON EH53 0PD
Tel: 01506 432251
Fax: 01506 438066
E-mail: horsburgh@btconnect.com
Web site: www.horsburghcoaches.com
Dirs: Eric M Horsburgh, Mark A Horsburgh
Fleet: 59 - 7 double-deck bus, 1 single-deck bus, 2 coach, 23 midibus, 4 midicoach, 22 minibus.
Chassis: 5 Dennis. 11 Ford Transit. 4 LDV. 10 Leyland. 20 Mercedes. 9 Optare.
Bodies: 2 Duple. 11 Ford. 12 Leyland. 16 Mercedes. 9 Optare. 9 Plaxton.
Ops incl: local bus services, school contracts, private hire.
Livery: Golden Yellow/White
Ticket System: Almex

HOUSTOUN TRAVEL ♥ ✔
110 PUMPHERSTON ROAD, UPHALL STATION, LIVINGSTON EH54 5PJ
Tel: 01506 437773.
Fax: 01506 437206.
Prop: Ian Horsburgh.
Fleet: 9 - 1 minibus, 8 minicoach.
Fleet: 1 DAF. 5 Ford Transit. 1 Freight Rover. 2 Mercedes.
Bodies: 1 Carlyle. 1 Leyland. 1 Mercedes. 1 Plaxton. 5 other.
Ops incl: local bus services, school contracts, private hire.

*McKECHNIE OF BATHGATE LIMITED ♥
2 EASTON ROAD, BATHGATE EH48 2QG
Tel: 01506 654337
Fax: 01506 654337
E-mail: pmkcoach@aol.com
Dirs: P McKechnie, Mrs C McKechnie
Fleet: 8 - 4 coach, 2 midicoach, 2 minibus
Chassis/Bodies: 1 Leyland. 3 Volvo. 4 Mercedes
Ops incl: school contracts, private hire.
Livery: White/Turquoise.

*MARTIN'S COACH TRAVEL
wc 🍽 ♥ ✔
1 SUMMERVILLE COURT, UPHALL STATION, LIVINGSTON EH54 5QG.
Tel: 01506 435968.
Fax: 01506 435968.
E-mail: martcoach@aol.com
Prop: Tony Martin
Fleet: 5 coach.
Chassis: 2 Bova. 1 MAN. 2 Volvo.
Bodies: 2 Bova. 3 Van Hool.
Ops incl: excursions & tours, private hire, school contracts.
Livery: White/Green/Orange/Blue

*PRENTICE WESTWOOD
wc 🍽 ♥ R24 ✔ A/c
WESTWOOD, WEST CALDER EH55 8PW
Tel: 01506 871231
Fax: 01506 871734
E-mail: sales@prenticewestwoodcoaches.co.uk
Web site: www.prenticewestwoodcoaches.co.uk
Dirs: Robbie Prentice, David Cowen **Ops Man**: Jock Johnston.
Fleet: 55 - 15 double-deck bus, 33 coach, 4 double-deck bus, 3 midicoach.
Chassis: 4 Bova. 1 DAF. 1 Dennis. 9 Leyland. 4 MCW. 3 Mercedes. 3 Neoplan. 1 Scania. 1 Setra. 28 Volvo.
Bodies: 1 Alexander. 4 Bova. 6 Caetano. 1 Duple. 6 ECW. 1 East Lancs. 1 Ikarus. 5 Jonckheere. 1 Marcopolo. 4 MCW. 3 Neoplan. 2 Northern Counties. 2 Plaxton. 1 Roe. 1 Setra. 11 Van Hool. 2 Wadham Stringer. 1 Sitcar. 2 Scott.
Ops incl: school contracts, private hire, continental tours.
Livery: White/Blue/Red.
Ticket System: Setright, Almex.

WESTERN ISLES

GALSON-STORNOWAY MOTOR SERVICES LTD
wc ♥ R ✔ T
1 LOWER BARVAS, ISLE OF LEWIS
Tel: 01851 840269.
Fax: 01851 840445.
E-mail: galson@sol.co.uk
Web site: www.hebrides.com/galson
Dir: I. Morrison. **Ch Eng**: F. Smith.
Dir/Ops Man: I. Morrison.
Dir/Tran Man: C. Morrison.
Fleet: 14 - 9 coach, 1 midibus, 1 midicoach, 3 minibus.
Chassis: 3 Ford Transit. 6 Leyland. 2 Mercedes. 3 Volvo.
Bodies: 9 Plaxton. 1 Van Hool. 1 Autobus. 3 Ford Transit.
Ops incl: local bus services, school contracts, excursions & tours, private hire.
Livery: Yellow/Cream.
Ticket System: Wayfarer.

*HARRIS COACHES
♿ ♥
SCOTT ROAD, TARBERT, ISLE OF HARRIS HS3 3DL
Tel/Fax: 01859 502441
E-mail: harriscoaches@easynet.co.uk
Ptnr: Norman MacKay
Fleet: 5 - 3 coach, 1 midicoach, 1 minicoach
Chassis: 2 Mercedes. 3 Volvo.
Bodies: 1 Mercedes. 4 Plaxton.
Ops incl: school contracts, excursions & tours, private hire.
Livery: Grey/Red.
Ticket System: Wayfarer.

HEBRIDEAN COACHES
♥ R24 ✔
HOWMORE, SOUTH UIST HS8 5SH
Tel: 01870 620345
Fax: 01870 620301
Ptnrs: D. A. MacDonald, S. MacDonald
Fleet: 8 - 7 coach, 1 midicoach
Chassis: 2 Bedford. 2 Dennis. 2 Ford. 1 Leyland. 1 Mercedes.
Bodies: 1 Alexander. 5 Duple. 1 Plaxton. 1 Crystal Conversions.
Ops incl: local bus services, school contracts, private hire.
Livery: Cream/Green
Ticket System: Almex

KENNEDY COACHES ♥
3 ORINSAY, LOCHS, ISLE OF LEWIS HS2 9RG
Tel: 01851 880375
Prop: M Kennedy
Fleet: 2 - 1 minibus, 1 midibus.
Chassis/Bodies: 1 Ford Transit. 1 Mercedes.
Ops incl: local bus services, private hire

LOCHS MOTOR TRANSPORT LTD
CAMERON TERRACE, LEURBOST, LOCHS, ISLE OF LEWIS HS2 9PE
Tel: 01851 860288.
Fax: 01851 705857.
Dirs: C. MacDonald, R. MacDonald, S. MacDonald, A. MacDonald.
Ch Eng: I. MacKinnon.
Fleet: 20 - 4 single-deck bus, 12 coach, 3 midibus, 1 midicoach.
Chassis: 12 Ford. 1 Freight Rover. 3 Leyland. 4 Mercedes.
Bodies: 5 Alexander. 1 Carlyle. 8 Duple. 2 Marshall. 2 M2M. 3 Plaxton.
Ops incl: local bus services, school contracts, private hire.
Livery: Blue/Cream.

A/c	Air conditioning
♿	Vehicles suitable for disabled
🍽	Coach(es) with galley facilities
wc	Coach(es) with toilet facilities
♥	Seat belt-fitted vehicles
R	Recovery service available (not 24 hr)
R24	24hr recovery service
✔	Replacement vehicle available
T	Toilet-drop facilities available
🚌	Vintage vehicle(s) available
🚍	Open top vehicle(s)

Scottish Operators

Welsh Operators

ANGLESEY

*CARREGLEFN COACHES
CARREGLEFN GARAGE, AMLWCH LL68 0PR
Tel: 01407 710139
Fax: 01407 710217
Prop: Alun Lewis
Fleet: 10 - 1 single-deck bus, 8 coach, 1 minicoach.
Chassis: 2 Bedford. 1 Toyota. 7 Volvo.
Bodies: 4 Caetano. 1 Duple. 5 Plaxton.
Ops incl: local bus services, school contracts, excursions & tours, private hire.
Livery: Blue/Cream

W C GOODSIR
30 TRENWFA ROAD, LANDS END, HOLYHEAD LL65 1LE
Tel: 01407 764340
Livery: White/Black/Yellow/Orange.

ELLIS COACHES
CHURCH STREET, LLANGEFNI LL77 7EB
Tel: 01248 750304
Prop: F. B. Ellis.
Fleet: 14 - 5 double-deck bus, 1 single-deck bus, 8 coach.
Chassis: Bedford. Bristol. Daimler. Ford. Leyland. Volvo.
Bodies: Duple. Plaxton.
Livery: D/D -Yellow/Mushroom/Red, S/D - White/Mauve/Red.

GWYNFOR COACHES
ANEYLFA, 1 GREENFIELD AVENUE, LLANGEFNI LL77 7NU
Tel: 01248 722694
Prop: H. Hughes.

O R JONES & SONS LTD
BUS & COACH DEPOT, LLANFAETHLU LL65 4NW
Tel: 01407 730204
Fax: 01407 730083
Prop: I. W. Jones (**Gen Man**), J. P. Jones.
Ch Eng: D. Williams. **Sec**: M. Cook.
Fleet: 27 - 4 double-deck bus, 10 single-deck bus, 7 coach, 3 midibus, 1 midicoach, 2 minibus.
Chassis: 3 Bedford. 4 Bova. 4 Bristol. 1 DAF. 2 Freight Rover. 10 Leyland National. 3 Mercedes. 2 Scania. 1 Toyota.
Bodies: 2 Alexander. 4 Bova. 1 Caetano. 1 Carlyle. 2 Duple. 1 East Lancs. 4 Leyland National. 3 Northern Counties. 3 Plaxton. 1 Reeve Burgess.
Ops incl: local bus services, school contracts, excursions & tours, private hire, express, continental tours.
Livery: Red/White/Green.

*W E JONES & SON
THE GARAGE, LLANERCHYMEDD LL71 8EB
Tel: 01248 470228
Fax: 01248 852893
Prop: G E Jones
Fleet: 11 - 5 double-deck bus, 2 single-deck bus, 3 coach, 1 minibus.
Chassis: 1 Bedford. 1 Bristol. 1 DAF. 1 Daimler. 1 Dodge. 3 MCW. 1 Mercedes. 1 Volvo.
Bodies: 2 Alexander. 3 MCW. 1 Mercedes. 2 Northern Counties. 1 Plaxton.
Ops incl: school contracts, private hire.
Livery: Red/White

LEWIS-Y-LLAN
MADYN INDUSTRIAL ESTATE, AMLWCH LL68 9DL
Tel: 01407 832181
Fax: 01407 830112
Props: A. H. Lewis, R. M. Lewis.
Fleet: 10 - 2 double-deck bus, 4 coach, 4 midibus.
Chassis: 1 Bedford. 3 Leyland. 3 Mercedes. 2 Volvo. 1 Volkswagen.
Bodies: 1 Alexander. 1 East Lancs. 1 Jonckheere. 1 Leyland. 3 Optare. 3 Plaxton.
Livery: White/Blue.

BLAENAU GWENT

*GARY'S COACHES OF TREDEGAR
42 COMMERCIAL STREET, TREDEGAR NP22 3DJ
Tel: 01495 726400
Fax: 01495 726500
Recovery: 01495 723264
E-mail: sales@garys-coaches.co.uk
Web site: www.garys-coaches.co.uk
Props: Mr & Mrs G A Lane **Ops Man**: D Williams **Ch Eng**: G Cresswell
Fleet: 14 - 12 coach, 1 midicoach, 1 midibus.
Chassis: 1 Bova. 3 Dennis. 2 Leyland. 2 Mercedes. 7 Volvo.
Bodies: 1 Bova. 4 Duple. 2 Mercedes. 5 Plaxton. 2 Van Hool.
Ops incl: excursions & tours, private hire, school contracts, continental tours.
Livery: White/Blue

GRAHAMS COACHES
BRISTOL HOUSE, 1 TILLERY ROAD, ABERTILLERY NP13 1HW
Tel: 01495 212818
Prop: G. T. Davies.
Fleet: 4 coach. **Bodies**: Plaxton.
Ops incl: private hire.
Livery: Cream/Red/Blue.

*HENLEYS BUS SERVICES LTD
HENLEYS COACH GARAGE, VICTOR ROAD, CWMTILLERY NP13 1HU
Tel: 01495 212288
Fax: 01495 320720
Dir: Martin Henley **Head Eng**: Michael Henley **Sec**: Daphne Henley
Fleet: 11 - 6 coach, 4 midibus, 1 minicoach.
Chassis: 4 Leyland. 4 Mercedes. 1 Setra. 2 Volvo.
Bodies: 1 Alexander. 1 Duple. 2 East Lancs. 1 Jonckheere. 1 Leicester. 5 Plaxton. 1 Setra.
Ops incl: local bus services, school contracts, excursions & tours, private hire.
Ticket system: Wayfarer

*STAGECOACH IN SOUTH WALES
See Torfaen

BRIDGEND

*R & D BURROWS LTD
21 CEMETERY ROAD, OGMORE VALE, BRIDGEND CF32 7HR
Tel: 01656 840345
Fax: 01656 841866
Web site: www.burrowscoaches.co.uk
E-mail: burrowscoaches@yahoo.co.uk
Dir: J G Jones
Fleet: 9 - includes 1 double-deck bus
Chassis: 1 DAF. 1 Ford. 3 Leyland. 1 Scania. 1 Setra. 2 Volvo.
Bodies: 1 Alexander. 1 Duple. 3 Plaxton. 1 Setra. 2 Van Hool. 1 Wadham Stringer.
Ops incl: private hire, school contracts.

*G M COACHES
MOUNTAIN VIEW GARAGE, CEFN CRIBWR CF32 0BB
Tel: 01656 740262
Fax: 01656 746040
Owner: Richard G Millington **Man**: Idris Hall
Co Sec: Ann Brain
Eng: Mike Llewellyn
Fleet: 22 - 12 double-deck bus, 1 single-deck bus, 7 coach, 1 double-deck coach, 1 midicoach.
Chassis: 4 Bristol. 10 Leyland. 1 Mercedes. 1 Neoplan. 6 Volvo.
Bodies: 2 Alexander. 3 Berkhof. 4 East Lancs. 3 ECW. 1 Neoplan. 2 Northern Counties. 1 Plaxton. 2 Roe. 3 Van Hool. 1 Robin Hood.
Ops incl: local bus services, school contracts, excursions & tours, private hire.
Livery: Red/Cream.
Ticket System: Setright.

GWYN JONES & SON LTD
wc %c ¶ 🔶 T

WHITE CROFT GARAGE,
BRYNCETHIN CF32 9YR
Tel: 01656 720300, 720182
Fax: 01656 725632
Dirs: John Gwyn Jones, Miriam J. Jones
Fleet: 16 coach.
Chassis: 2 Mercedes. 14 Volvo.
Bodies: 1 Berkhof. 1 Duple. 4 Jonckheere.
2 Mercedes. 2 Plaxton. 6 Van Hool.
Ops incl: excursions & tours, private hire, continental tours, school contracts.
Livery: White/Red/Gold

*PENCOED TRAVEL LTD
wc ¶ 🔶 %c ✔

18 CAER BERLLAN, PENCOED CF35 6RR
Tel: 01656 860200
Fax: 01656 864793
Recovery: 01656 860200
Man Dir: Denise Cook **Ch Eng**: Neil Cook
Co Sec: Andrea Talbot.
Fleet: 10 - 4 double-deck bus, 6 coach.
Chassis: 1 Bristol. 4 DAF. 2 Dennis.
3 Leyland.
Bodies: 1 Berkhof. 1 Jonckheere. 4 Leyland.
1 Plaxton. 3 Van Hool.
Ops incl: private hire, school contracts, continental tours.
Livery: White/Blue

PORTHCAWL OMNIBUS CO LTD wc 🔶

OLD STATION LANE, PORTHCAWL CF36 5TL
Tel: 01656 783269
Fax: 01656 783959
Dirs: J. Williams (**Man Dir**),
Mrs B. N. Williams. **Co Sec**: Mrs P. Phillips.
Man: J. Williams jnr.
Ops Man: G. W. Morgan.
Fleet: 13 - 3 double-deck bus. 1 single-deck bus. 9 coach.
Chassis: 1 Bedford. 3 Daimler. 5 Leyland.
4 Volvo.
Bodies: 1 Duple. 1 Jonckheere. 2 MCW.
1 Northern Counties. 6 Plaxton.
2 Willowbrook.
Ops incl: private hire, school contracts.
Livery: Beige/Maroon or White/Maroon
Ticket System: Almex.

*STAGECOACH IN SOUTH WALES
See Torfaen

CAERPHILLY

CASTELL COACHES LTD
wc ¶ 🔶 %c R24 ✔ T

UNITS 3 & 4 EUROPEAN TERMINAL BUILDING, PANTGLAS INDUSTRIAL ESTATE, BEDWAS CF83 8DR
Tel: 029 2086 1863.
Fax: 029 2086 1864

Recovery: 07967 636659
E-mail: sales@castellcoaches.co.uk
Web site: www.castellcoaches.co.uk
Co Sec: Mrs S Kerslake (**Tel**: 07801 515119)
Dir: C Kerslake. **Ops Man**: B Kerslake (**Tel**: 07801 515117)
Fleet: 21 - 5 double-deck bus, 12 coach, 3 midicoach, 1 minibus.
Chassis: 2 Bova. 4 DAF. 6 Leyland.
4 Mercedes. 7 Volvo.
Bodies: 2 Bova. 1 Duple. 2 Jonckheere. 4 Leyland. 4 Mercedes. 6 Plaxton. 2 Van Hool.
Ops incl: excursions & tours, private hire, continental tours, school contracts.
Livery: White with multicolour

*CROSSKEYS COACH HIRE t/a GLYN WILLIAMS TRAVEL 🔶

PENNAR CROSSING, PONTLLANFAITH NP2 2AW
Tel: 01495 229237
Fax: 01495 222880
E-mail: glynwilliamstravel@vodafone.net
Man Dir: G J Williams **Eng Dir**: T G Williams **Comm Man**: I MacDonald
Fleet: 28 single-deck bus.
Chassis: 22 Dennis. 6 BMC.
Bodies: 16 Caetano. 6 Transbus. 6 BMC.
Ops incl: local bus services.
Livery: Green/White.
Ticket System: Wayfarer TGX

HARRIS COACHES (PENGAM) LTD

BRYN GWYN STREET, FLEUR-DE-LIS NP2 1RZ
Tel: 01443 830455
Fleetname: Shuttle.
Livery: Cream/Maroon/Red

*ISLWYN BOROUGH TRANSPORT LTD
wc ¶ 🔶 %c R T

PENMAEN ROAD DEPOT, PONTLLANFRAITH NP12 2DY
Tel: 01495 235729
Fax: 01495 220871
Web site: www.kingfishertravel.com
Chairmn: D Jones **Man Dir**: Roger Sims
Ops Dir: Graham Mason **Ch Inspector**: Dow Jones
Fleet: 45 - 23 single-deck bus, 16 coach, 3 midibus, 2 midicoach, 1 minibus.
Chassis: 3 DAF. 3 Dennis.1 Ford Transit.
4 Leyland. 1 Leyland National. 12 MAN.
7 Mercedes. 1 Setra. 15 Volvo.
Bodies: 1 Berkhof. 1 Caetano. 9 East Lancs.
9 Jonckheere. 4 Marshall. 10 Optare.
5 Plaxton. 1 Reeve Burgess. 1 Setra. 2 Van Hool. 2 other.
Ops incl: local bus services, school contracts, excursions & tours, private hire, continental tours.
Livery: Blue/White
Ticket System: Wayfarer

*STAGECOACH IN SOUTH WALES
See Torfaen

CARDIFF

CARDIFF BUS R

SLOPER ROAD, LECKWITH, CARDIFF CF- 8TB
Tel: 029 2078 7700
Fax: 029 2078 7742
E-mail: headcffice@cardiffbus.com
Web Site: www.cardiffbus.com
Man Dir: D Brown. **Eng Dir**: D. B. Worsell.
Fleet: 230 - 30 double-deck bus, 100 single-deck bus, 100 midibus.
Chassis: 159 Dennis. 12 Leyland.
20 Optare. 7 Scania. 30 Volvo.
Bodies: 44 Alexander. 12 Leyland.
20 Optare. 154 Transbus/Plaxton.
Ops incl: local bus services.
Livery: Burgess Blue/Cream
Ticket System: ERG

CASTELL COACHES LTD
See Caerphilly

CROESO TOURS 🔶

13 WATERLOO ROAD, PENYLAN, CARDIFF CF23 5AD
Tel: 029 2047 2313
E-mail: jmforster13@hotmail.com
Owner: John M. Forster
Fleet: 3 - 1 midicoach, 1 minibus, 1 minicoach
Chassis: 1 Iveco. 1 LDV. 1 Renault
Ops incl: private hire, school contracts.

GREYHOUND COACHES CO

COACH DEPOT, STATION TERRACE, ELY BRIDGE, CARDIFF CF5 4AA
Tel: 029 2056 ¯467, 2055 2767
Ptnrs: T. James, Florence James.
Fleet: 14 - 13 coach, 1 minibus.
Chassis: 10 Bedford. 1 Ford Transit.
3 Volvo.
Ops incl: local bus services, excursions & tours, private hire
Livery: White/Blue.

PORTHCAWL OMNIBUS CO LTD
See Bridgend.

*STAGECOACH IN SOUTH WALES
See Torfaen

WALTONS COACHES 🔶

31 AVONDALE ROAD, GRANGETOWN CF1 7DT.
Tel: 029 2039 9511.
Dirs: B. J. Walton, Mrs S. F. Walton, R. J. Walton, D. McCarthy.
Fleet: 6 - 4 coach, 2 midicoach.

%c	Air conditioning	
🔶	Vehicles suitable for disabled	
¶	Coach(es) with galley facilities	
wc	Coach(es) with toilet facilities	
🔶	Seat belt-fitted vehicles	
R	Recovery service available (not 24 hr)	
R24	24hr recovery service	
✔	Replacement vehicle available	
T	Toilet-drop facilities available	
🚌	Vintage vehicle(s) available	
🚌	Open top vehicle(s)	

Welsh Operators

Chassis: Bedford. Ford. Mercedes.
Ops incl: private hire, school contracts.
Livery: Blue/White/Red.

WATTS COACHES

OLD POST GARAGE, BONVILSTON CF5 6TT.
Tel/Fax: 01446 781277.
Prop: C. P. Watts. **Tran Man**: J. B. Watts.
Fleet: 23 - 3 double-deck bus, 16 coach, 4 midicoach.
Chassis: 2 Bristol. 2 DAF. 5 Ford. 4 Leyland. 2 MAN. 4 Mercedes. 4 Volvo.
Bodies: 3 Alexander. 3 Caetano. 5 Duple. 1 Optare. 8 Plaxton. 1 Reeve Burgess. 1 Made-to-Measure. 1 Robin Hood.
Ops incl: school contracts, private hire.
Livery: Cream/Red/Gold.

*WHEADONS GROUP TRAVEL LTD

STATION TERRACE, ELY BRIDGE, CARDIFF CF5 4AA
Tel: 029 2057 5333
Fax: 029 2057 5384
E-mail: admin@wheadons-group.co.uk
Web site: www.wheadons-group.co.uk
Prop: Ernest K Wheadon **Ch Eng**: Steve Osling
Fleet: 34 - 20 coach, 10 midicoach, 4 minibus.
Chassis: Ford Transit. Leland. Mercedes. Toyota. Volvo.
Bodies: Autobus. Caetano. Mercedes. Toyota. Van Hool.
Ops incl: private hire, school contracts, excursions & tours, continental tours.

CEREDIGION

*BRODYR JAMES

GLANYRAFON, LLANGEITHO, TREGARON SY25 6TT
Tel: 01974 821255
Fax: 01974 251228
Dirs: D E James, T M G James
Fleet: 16 - 10 coach, 4 midibus, 1 midicoach, 1 minibus.
Chassis: 1 Bedford. 2 Dennis. 1 Ford Transit. 5 Mercedes. 1 Toyota. 6 Volvo.
Bodies: 2 Alexander. 2 Caetano. 1 Jonckheere. 1 Mercedes. 7 Plaxton. 3 Reeve Burgess.
Ops incl: local bus services, school contracts, excursions & tours, private hire.
Livery: White/Red/Gold.
Ticket System: Wayfarer

*R J JONES

44 BRYNCASTELL, BOW STREET, ABERYSTWYTH SY23
Tel: 01970 828073
Prop: R J Jones
Fleet: 3 - 2 coach, 1 minibus.
Chassis: 1 LDV. 1 Leyland. 1 Volvo.
Bodies: 1 Duple, 1 Plaxton, 1 LDV.
Ops incl: school contracts, private hire.
Livery: various (1 Cream, 1 Lilac, 1 White)

LEWIS'S COACHES

BRYNEITHIN, LLANRHYSTUD SY23 5DN.
Tel: 01974 202495.
Owner: M. M. Benjamin.
Fleet: 19 - 16 coach, 3 minibus.
Chassis: 4 Bedford. 4 DAF. 6 Dennis. 3 Ford Transit. 1 Volvo.
Bodies: 10 Duple. 2 Plaxton. 1 UVG. 3 Van Hool.
Ops incl: private hire, school contracts.
Livery: White.

MID WALES TRAVEL

BRYNHYFRYD GARAGE, PENRHYNCOCH, ABERYSTWYTH SY23 3ES
Tel/Fax: 01970 828288
Dirs: Elsie Morgan, Melvyn Evans **Eng**: Heddwyn Morran
Fleet: 16 - 3 single-deck bus, 7 coach, 3 midibus, 1 midicoach, 2 minibus.
Chassis: 2 LDV. 4 Leyland. 4 Mercedes. 6 Volvo
Ops incl: local bus services, school contracts, excursions & tours, private hire.
Livery: White
Ticket System: Setright

*RED KITE COACHES

UNIT 1, GLANDINAS, PENPARCIAU, ABERYSTWYTH SY23
Tel: 01970 624412
Fax: 01970 627927
Prop: G Bryan
Fleet: 1 coach.
Chassis: 1 Mercedes
Ops incl: school contracts, private hire.
Livery: White with blue stripes

*RICHARDS BROS

MOYLGROVE GARAGE, PENTOOD INDUSTRIAL ESTATE, CARDIGAN SA43 3AD
Tel: 01239 613756
Fax: 01239 615193
E-mail: enquiries@richardsbros.co.uk
Web site: www.richardsbros.co.uk
Gen Man: W J M Richards **Ch Eng**: D N Richards **Traf Man**: R M Richards
Ops Man: S M Richards
Fleet: 76 - 24 single-deck bus, 24 coach, 4 minicoach, 3 midicoach, 14 midibus.
Chassis: 15 Bedford. 25 DAF. 10 Dennis. 1 LDV. 1 MAN. 12 Mercedes. 1 Optare. 2 Transbus. 2 Volvo.
Bodies: 7 Alexander. 1 Autobus. 3 Carlyle. 10 Duple. 2 Ikarus. 2 Marshall. 2 Northern Counties. 5 Optare. 18 Plaxton. 2 Reeve Burgess. 2 Transbus. 8 Van Hool. 1 Willowbrook. 3 Wright. 3 Cymric.
Ops incl: local bus services, school contracts, excursions & tours, private hire, continental tours.
Livery: Blue/White/Maroon
Ticket System: Wayfarer

*ROBERTS COACHES

UNIT 4, GLANYRAFON INDUSTRIAL ESTATE, ABERYSTWYTH SY23 3JQ
Tel: 01970 611085
Fax: 01970 626855
Prop: G Roberts

Fleet: 5 coach.
Chassis: 2 DAF. 3 Leyland.
Bodies: Plaxton. Duple.
Ops incl: school contracts, private hire, tours & excursions.
Livery: White or Blue

CARMARTHENSHIRE

*CASTLE GARAGE LTD

BROAD STREET, LLANDOVERY SA20 0AA
Tel: 01550 720335
Man Dir: Derek Jones
Fleet: 12 - 4 midibus, 4 midicoach, 4 minibus.
Chassis: 2 Ford Transit. 2 Freight Rover. 8 Mercedes.
Bodies: Mellor. Mercedes. Optare. Plaxton. Reeve Burgess. Wadham Stringer.
Ops incl: local bus services, school contracts, private hire.

GARETH EVANS COACHES

80 GLYN ROAD, BRYNAMMAN SA18 1SS
Tel: 01269 823127
Fax: 01269 824533
Props: K. Davies, Mrs S. Davies.

FFOSHELIG COACHES

BLAENYCOED ROAD, CARMARTHEN SA33 6EG.
Tel: 01267 281211.
Fax: 01267 281232
Recovery: 07876 027926
E-mail: ffoshelig@aol.com
Owner: Rhodri Evans.
Fleet: 8 - 7 coach, 1 minibus.
Chassis: 1 Leyland. 1 Toyota. 6 Volvo.
Bodies: 1 Caetano. 1 Duple. 1 Jonckheere. 4 Plaxton. 1 Van Hool.
Ops incl: school contracts, excursions & tours, private hire.
Livery: Pale Cream/Brown

GWYN WILLIAMS & SONS LTD

BERLWYN GARAGE, LOWER TUMBLE SA15 5YT
Fleet: 27 - 3 double-deck bus, 8 single-deck bus, 17 coach, 7 minibus
Livery: Two tone Blue/Red.

*JONES INTERNATIONAL

STATION ROAD, LLANDEILO SA19 6NG
Tel: 01558 822985
Fax: 01558 822984
Props: Meirion Jones, Myrddin Jones, Neil Jones **Office Man**: Carole Thompson
Ch Eng: Andrew Vale
Fleet: 7 - 2 single-deck bus, 5 coach.
Chassis: 3 DAF. 3 Leyland. 1 Volvo.
Bodies: 6 Van Hool. 1 Crossley.
Ops incl: excursions & tours, private hire, express, continental tours, school contracts.
Livery: Yellow/Blue

*JONES MOTORS (LOGIN) LTD 🛡 wc A/c R24 ✏ T

LOGIN, WHITLAND SA34 0UX
Tel: 01437 563277
Fax: 01437 563393
E-mail: endaf@joneslogin.co.uk
Web Site: www.joneslogin.co.uk
Fleetname: Jones Login
Man Dirs: Endaf Jones, Arwel Jones **Co Sec**: Ann Jones **Asst Man**: Hannah Jones
Fleet: 24 - 20 coach, 1 midicoach, 2 minibus, 1 minicoach.
Chassis: 1 Bedford. 11 Dennis. 2 LDV. 2 Toyota. 8 Volvo.
Bodies: 2 Caetano. 3 Duple. 1 East Lancs. 16 Plaxton. 2 other.
Ops incl: local bus services, school contracts, excursions & tours, private hire, continental tours.
Livery: Turquoise/Midnight Blue/White
Ticket system: Setright

*LEWIS COACHES WHITLAND 🛡 A/c ✏

THE GARAGE, WHITLAND SA34 0AA
Tel: 01944 240274
Dirs: E Lewis
Fleet: 11 - 8 coach, 1 midibus, 2 minicoach.
Chassis: 1 Bedford. 3 Dennis. 2 LDV. 3 Leyland. 2 Volvo.
Bodies: 1 Berkhof. 1 Duple. 2 Leyland. 1 Optare. 6 Plaxton.
Livery: White with Green/Mink stripes.
Ops incl: local bus services, school contracts, private hire
Livery: White/Green with mink stripes
Ticket System: Wayfarer

*LEWIS-RHYDLEWIS 🛡 wc 🍴 🚌 A/c R ✏ T

PENRHIW-PAL GARAGE, RHYDLEWIS, LLANDYSUL SA44 5QG
Tel: 01239 851386
Prop: T S Lewis
Fleet: 19 - 16 coach, 1 midicoach, 2 minibus.
Chassis: Bedford. Ford Transit. Leyland National. Mercedes. Setra. Volvo.
Bodies: Duple. Plaxton. Setra.
Ops incl: local bus services, school contracts, excursions & tours, private hire, continental tours.
Livery: Cream/Red/Orange/Maroon

*MEYERS COACH HIRE 🛡

CILGWYN, LLANPUMSAINT SA33 6LA
Tel/Fax: 01267 253464
Fleet: 3 - 1 coach, 1 midibus, 1 minibus.
Chassis: 2 Iveco. 1 Leyland.
Bodies: 1 Marshall. 1 Plaxton.
Ops incl: local bus services, school contracts, private hire.
Livery: Grey/White
Ticket System: Setright

MORRIS TRAVEL 🛡 wc A/c ✏ T

ALLTYCNAP ROAD, JOHNSTOWN SA31 3QY
Tel: 01267 235090.
Fax: 01267 238183.
E-mail: sales@morristravel.co.uk
Web site: www.morristravel.co.uk
Man Dir/Chmn: T J Freeman **Ops Dir**: C J Freeman. **Dir/Co Sec**: C M Freeman
Ch Eng: A Jones. **Traf Man**: V Shambrook
Traff Controller: P Davies.
Fleet: 29 - 1 single-deck bus, 19 coach, 1 midibus, 6 minibus, 1 minicoach, 1 midicoach.
Chassis: 4 Bedford. 3 DAF. 1 Ford. 1 Freight Rover. 14 LDV. 2 Mercedes. 1 Optare. 4 Volvo.
Bodies: 1 Berkhof. 1 Duple. 14 Leyland. 1 Ford Transit. 2 Mercedes. 1 Optare. 9 Plaxton.
Ops incl: local bus services, school contracts, private hire.
Livery: Blue/Navy/White.
Ticket System: Wayfarer

TAF VALLEY COACHES

PENRHEOL, WHITLAND SA34 0AG.
Tel: 01994 240908.
Fax: 01994 241264.
Prop: D. C. Edwards.

BRODYR THOMAS BROS

TOWY GARAGE, LLANGADOG SA19 9LU.
Tel: 01550 777438.
Fax: 01550 777807.
Prop: G. Thomas. **Gen Man**: C. Watkin.
Ops incl: local bus services, excursions & tours, private hire.
Livery: Cream/Green.
Ticket System: Setright.

CONWY

ALPINE TRAVEL wc 🍴 A/c 🛡 🚌 🚍 ✏

CENTRAL COACH GARAGE, BUILDER STREET WEST, LLANDUDNO LL30 1HH
Tel: 01492 879133
Fax: 01492 876055
E-mail: chris@alpine-travel.co.uk
Web site: www.alpine-travel.co.uk
Dirs: Bryan Owens, Patricia Owens, Christopher Owens, Christopher Bryan Owens.
Fleet: 84- 46 double-deck bus, 10 single-deck bus, 18 coach, 10 minibus.
Chassis: 5 Bedford. 2 Bova. 40 Bristol. 2 DAF. 2 Dennis. 2 Ford. 3 Leyland. 4 Leyland National. 2 MAN. 10 Mercedes. 10 Volvo.
Bodies: 1 Alexander. 2 Bova. 6 Duple. 40 ECW. 6 East Lancs. 4 Leyland National. 1 Marshall. 1 Noge. 4 Northern Counties. 7 Plaxton. 2 Wadham Stringer, 2 Willowbrook. 8 Robin Hood.
Ops incl: local bus services, school contracts, excursions & tours, private hire, continental tours.
Livery: Green/Cream or White
Ticket System: Setright.

ARRIVA CYMRU LTD ♿ wc 🍴 A/c 🛡 🚌

IMPERIAL BUILDINGS, GLAN-Y-MOR ROAD, LLANDUDNO JUNCTION LL31 9RU
Tel: 01492 592111.
Fax: 01492 592968.
Man Dir: S. Green. **Eng Dir**: M. Evans.
Fin Dir: B. Pegg.
Fleet: 265 - 39 double-deck bus, 129 single-deck bus, 3 coach, 94 midibus.
Chassis: 10 DAF 106 Dennis. 45 Leyland. 94 Mercedes. 2 Scania. 8 Volvo.
Bodies: Alexander, ECW, Northern Counties, Plaxton
Ops incl: local bus services, school contracts, private hire, express.
Livery: Turquoise/Cotswold Stone
Ticket System: Wayfarer III.

GRWP ABERCONWY

MAESDU, LLANDUDNO LL30 1HF.
Tel: 01492 870870.
Fax: 01492 860821.
Fleetname: Great Orme Tours.
Dir: I. Trevette.
Tramway & Coach Man: Rosemary Sutton.
Fleet: 4 midicoach.
Chassis: 3 Bedford. 1 Guy.
Ops incl: local bus services, excursions & tours.
Livery: Blue/Cream.
Ticket System: Amex.

LLEW JONES INTERNATIONAL 🛡 wc 🍴 A/c ✏ T

THE COACHYARD, JOHN STREET, LLANRWST LL26 0DR
Tel: 01492 640320
Fax: 01492 642040
E-mail: enq@llewjones.co.uk
Web site: www.lewjones.co.uk
Owner: Stephen Jones **Ops Man**: Kevin Williams
Fleet: 21 - 12 coach, 1 double-deck coach, 3 midibus, 3 midicoach, 2 minibus.
Chassis: 1 Ayats. 3 DAF. 5 Dennis. 2 LDV. 1 Leyland. 2 MAN. 1 Marshall. 5 Mercedes. 1 Volvo.
Bodies: 1 Ayats. 1 Berkhof. 1 Carlyle. 5 Duple. 1 Jonckheere. 1 Marshall. 1 Noge. 2 Plaxton. 1 Reeve Burgess. 2 Ovi. 2 North Western. 2 LDV. 1 Marcopolo.
Ops incl: local bus services, school contracts, excursions & tours, private hire, continental tours.
Livery: Orange/Brown/White
Ticket system: Almex

ROBERTS MINI COACHES

RHANDIR GARAGE, RHANDIR LL22 8BW.
Tel: 01492 650449.
Prop: W. T. Roberts.

A/c	Air conditioning	✏	Replacement vehicle available
♿	Vehicles suitable for disabled	T	Toilet-drop facilities available
🍴	Coach(es) with galley facilities	🚍	Vintage vehicle(s) available
wc	Coach(es) with toilet facilities	🚌	Open top vehicle(s)
🛡	Seat belt-fitted vehicles		
R	Recovery service available (not 24 hr)		
R24	24hr recovery service		

DENBIGHSHIRE

*BRYN MELYN LTD
ABBEY ROAD, LLANGOLLEN LL20 8SN
Tel: 01978 860701
Web site: www.bryn-melyn.co.uk
Dir: Clive Wilson **Ops Man**: Chris Jones
Fleet: 12 - 4 double-deck bus, 3 single-deck bus, 1 coach, 3 midibus, 1 minibus.
Chassis: 1 Bristol. 3 Dennis. 2 Leyland. 2 MAN. 4 Mercedes.
Bodies: 1 Alexander. 4 East lancs. 2 Leyland. 2 Marshall. 1 Mercedes. 2 Optare.
Ops incl: local bus services, school contracts, private hire
Livery: Yellow/Blue/Red/White
Ticket system: Wayfarer 3

GHA COACHES
MILL GARAGE, BETWS GWERFIL GOCH, CORWEN LL21 9PU
Tel: 01978 753598
Fax: 01978 721441
E-mail: ghacoaches@aol.com
Web site: www.ghacoaches.co.uk
Prop: E. L. Davies, G. Davies, A. Davies.
Livery: Grey/Red/Maroon.

M & H COACHES
8 TREWEN, DENBIGH LL16 3HF.
Tel: 01745 812057.
Prop: Mrs M. Owen.
Livery: Blue/White.

CLWYDIAN TOURS
LLANRHAEADR, DENBIGH LL16 4NT
Tel: 01745 890543.
Fax: 01745 890546.
Prop: David Evans.
Fleet: 15 - 13 single-deck coach, 1 midibus, 1 midicoach.
Chassis: 4 Bedford. 4 Dennis. 2 Ford. 1 Iveco. 1 Leyland. 1 MAN. 1 Toyota. 1 Volvo.
Bodies: 2 Caetano. 5 Duple. 5 Plaxton. 1 Wright. 2 Marcopolo.

VOEL COACHES LTD
DYSERTH LL18 6BP
Tel: 01745 570309.
Fax: 01745 570307.
Man Dir: W M Kerfoot-Davies **Com Man**: Michelle Kerfoot Higginson.
Fleet: 25 - 7 double-deck bus, 4 single-deck bus, 12 coach, 1 minibus, 1 midicoach.
Chassis: Dennis. Mercedes. Scania. Volvo
Bodies: Berkhof. Van Hool.
Ops incl: local bus services, school contracts, excursions & tours, private hire, continental tours.
Livery: Orange.

FLINTSHIRE

EAGLES AND CRAWFORD
53 NEW STREET, MOLD CH7 1NY
Tel: 01352 700217/8
Fax: 01352 750211
E-mail: eaglesandcrawford@supanet.com
Ptnrs: J. F. J. K. & W. P. Eagles.
Fleet: 15 - 6 double-deck bus, 7 coach, 2 minibus.
Chassis: 6 Bristol. 2 Dennis. 1 Freight Rover. 4 Leyland. 1 Mercedes. 1 Toyota. 1 Van Hool.
Bodies: 1 Caetano. 1 Carlyle. 3 Duple. 6 ECW. 1 Mercedes. 1 Optare. 3 Plaxton. 1 Van Hool.
Ops incl: local bus services, excursions & tours, private hire, continental tours.
Livery: White/Blue/Orange.
Ticket System: Almex.

*FOUR GIRLS COACHES
OLD POST OFFICE YARD, CORWEN ROAD, PONTYBODKIN CH7 4TG
Tel: 01352 770438
Fax: 01352 770253
Ptnrs: Carolyn Thomas, Elaine Williams
Fleet: 9 - 7 coach, 1 minibus, 1 minicoach.
Chassis: 1 Bova. 1 DAF. 1 Ford Transit. 5 Volvo.
Bodies: include 1 Caetano
Ops incl: school contracts, excursions & tours, private hire.
Livery: Turquoise/Red/Yellow

JONES MOTOR SERVICES
CHESTER ROAD, FLINT CH6 5DZ.
Tel: 01352 733292.
Fax: 01352 763353.
E-mail: tours@jonescoaches.co.uk
Ptnr: A. Jones.
Fleet: 10 - 9 coach, 1 midicoach.
Chassis: DAF, Iveco, Leyland.
Bodies: Caetano, Duple, Plaxton, Van Hool.
Ops incl: excursions & tours, private hire, express, continental tours, school contracts.
Livery: Blue.

OARE'S COACHES
TY DRAW. BRYNFORD, HOLYWELL CH8 8LP.
Tel: 01352 714868.
Fax: 01352 713339.
Prop: G. A. Oare.
Livery: White/Red/Silver.

P. & O. LLOYD
RHYDWEN GARAGE, BAGILLT CH6 6JJ.
Tel: 01352 710682.
Fax: 01352 710093.
Prop: David Lloyd.
Fleet: 25 - 14 double-deck bus, 2 single-deck bus. 7 coach, 2 midibus.
Chassis: 2 Optare. 16 Leyland. 7 Volvo.
Bodies: 4 MCW. 10 East Lancs. 4 MCW. 2 Plaxton. 5 Van Hool.
Ops incl: local bus services, private hire, school contracts.
Livery: Cream/Red or Cream/Maroon/Gold.
Ticket System: Almex.

PHILLIPS COACHES HOLYWELL LTD
ABBEY BUS GARAGE, COAST ROAD, GREENFIELD CH8 7EP.
Tel/Fax: 01352 711993.
Dir: A. Phillips. **Dir/Co Sec**: L. Williams.
Fleet: 11 - 2 double-deck bus, 1 single-deck bus, 6 coach, 1 midibus, 1 minibus.
Chassis: 6 Bedford. 1 Daimler. 1 Iveco. 1 Leyland. 1 Leyland National. 6 Mercedes.
Bodies: 1 Carlyle. 4 Duple. 1 ECW. 1 Leyland National. 1 MCW. 3 Plaxton.
Ops incl: local bus services, school contracts, private hire.
Livery: Red/Cream.
Ticket System: Wayfarer.

PIED BULL COACHES
53 WOODLANDS CLOSE, MOLD CH7 1UU.
Tel/Fax: 01352 754237.
Prop: R. Williams.
Livery: Blue/White.

TOWNLYNX
CAETIA LLWYD, NORTHOP ROAD, HOLYWELL CH8 8AE.
Tel: 01352 710489.
Prop: S. A. Lee.
Livery: White/Yellow/Blue.

GWYNEDD

*ALPINE TRAVEL (TYWYN)
BEACON GARAGE, TYWYN
Tel: 01492 879133
Fax: 01492 878055
Fleet: 3
Chassis: 1 Leyland. 2 Leyland National.
Bodies: 2 Leyland. 1 Wadham Stringer.
Ops incl: school contracts.
Livery: Dark Green/Cream.

ARVONIA COACHES
THE SQUARE, LLANRUG LL55 4AA.
Tel: 01286 675175.
Fax: 01286 671126.
Prop: R. Morris.
Fleet: 9 - 6 coach, 2 midibus, 1 minibus.
Chassis: 1 Ford Transit. 1 MAN. 1 Mercedes. 1 Volvo. 3 EOS. 2 Van Hool.
Bodies: 2 Alexander. 1 Carlyle. 2 Van Hool. 3 EOS. 1 Noge.
Ops incl: local bus services, excursions & tours, private hire, continental tours.
Livery: White/Orange/Red.
Ticket System: Almex.

CAMBRIAN COAST COACH LINE
RIVERSIDE HOUSE, ABERGYNOLWYN LL36 9YR.
Tel/Fax: 01654 782235.
E-mail: ronbott@talyllyn.freeserve.co.uk.
Prop: Ronald C. Bott.
Fleet: 2 - 1 coach, 1 minicoach, plus 1 taxi.
Chassis: 1 Mercedes. 1 Toyota. 1 Seat.
Ops incl: excursions & tours, private hire.
Livery: Red/Blue.
Ticket System: Setright.

CERBYDAU BERWYN COACHES
BERWYN, TREFOR LL54 5LY
Tel: 01286 660315.
Fax: 01286 660110.
Prop: B. Japheth.
Livery: White/Yellow/Brown.

*CAELLOI MOTORS (T. H. JONES & SON)
[wc] [A/c] [seatbelt] [replacement]

WEST END GARAGE, PWLLHELI LL53 5PH
Tel/Recovery: 01758 612719
Fax: 01758 612335
Props: T H Jones, E B Jones, N Jones, E Jones.
Fleet: 6 - 2 single-deck bus, 6 coach
Chassis: 1 DAF. 1 Mercedes. 5 Volvo. 1 other.
Bodies: 1 Marshall. 1 Neoplan. 1 Plaxton. 4 Van Hool. 1 Wright.
Ops incl: local bus services, excursions & tours, private hire, continental tours, school contracts.
Livery: Multi
Ticket System: Almex

*CLYNNOG & TREFOR
THE GARAGE, TREFOR, CAERNARFON LL54 5HP
Tel: 01286 660208
Fax: 01286 660538
Man Dir: D C Jones **Ch Eng**: E W Griffiths **Co Sec**: I W Williams
Fleet: 38 - 10 double-deck bus, 8 coach, 10 coach, 10 minibus.
Chassis: 1 Bedford. 10 Bristol. 1 Dennis. 1 Iveco. 11 Mercedes. 14 Volvo.
Bodies: 11 Alexander. 7 ECW. 4 Plaxton. 1 Mercedes. 6 Plaxton. 1 Reeve Burgess. 4 Van Hool. 4 other.
Ops incl: local bus services, school contracts, excursions & tours, private hire.
Livery: Red/Cream, White
Ticket system: Wayfarer

*EMMAS COACHES
BAKER STREET GARAGE, DOLGELLAU LL40 1EL
Tel/Fax: 01341 423934
Mobile: 07979 493254
Prop: Barry Thomas
Fleet: 13
Chassis: 1 Bedford. 4 DAF. 2 Leyland. 1 Mercedes. 1 Volvo.
Bodies: 1 Fiat. 1 Ford. 1 Mercedes. 1 Toyota. 1 VW.
Ops incl: local bus service, school contracts, private hire, tours & excursions.
Livery: White/Blue

EXPRESS MOTORS
[wc] [galley] [A/c] [seatbelt] [vintage] [R24] [replacement] [T]

GERALLT, BONTNEWYDD LL54 7UN.
Tel: 01286 881108.
Fax: 01286 882331.
Ptnrs: E. W. Jones & J. A. Jones.
Ch Eng: I. W. Jones. **Ops Man**: K. W. Jones. **Admin Man**: K. Jones.
Fleet: 30 - 8 single-deck bus, 7 single-deck bus, 5 coach, 2 double-deck coach, 5 midibus, 1 midicoach, 2 minicoach.
Chassis: 4 Bristol. 3 DAF. 4 Dennis. 5 Leyland. 2 Leyland National. 2 MAN. 1 MCW. 7 Mercedes. 1 Optare. 1 Volvo.
Bodies: 2 Alexander. 1 Carlyle. 1 Duple. 6 ECW. 2 East Lancs. 1 Jonckheere. 1 Optare. 4 Plaxton. 2 Reeve Burgess. 5 Van Hool. 1 Wadham Stringer. 1 Willowbrook. 3 other.
Ops incl: local bus services, school contracts, excursions & tours, private hire.
Livery: Turquoise, White.
Ticket System: Wayfarer, Setright.

*GRIFFITHS COACHES
[wc] [galley] [seatbelt] [A/c]

3 ELIM COTTAGES, PORTDINORWIC LL56 4JR
Tel: 01248 670530
Fax: 01248 671111
Prop: Hefin Griffiths
Fleet: 10 - 4 double-deck bus, 6 coach.
Chassis/Bodies: 4 Bristol. 1 Berkhof. 5 Jonckheere.
Ops incl: private hire, school contracts.
Livery: Red/Grey/White

*JOHN'S COACHES
NORTH WESTERN ROAD, GLAN-Y-PWLL, BLAENEAU FFESTINIOG LL41 3NN
Tel: 01766 831781
Mobile: 0777 167735
Fax: 01766 831781
Prop: J R Edwards
Fleet: 6
Chassis: 1 Berkhof. 3 DAF. 2 Mercedes.
Bodies: Berkhof. Mercedes. Plaxton.
Ops incl: local bus service, school contracts, private hire.
Livery: White/Red
Ticket System: Wayfarer

KMP (LLANBERIS) LTD
YGLYN INDUSTRIAL ESTATE, LLANBERIS LL55 4HN.
Livery: Blue/Black.

NEFYN COACHES
WEST END GARAGE, ST DAVIDS ROAD, NEFYN LL53 6HE.
Tel: 01758 720904.
Fax: 01758 720331.
Props: B. G. Owen, M. A. Owen, A. G. Owen.
Fleet: 9 - 1 single-deck bus, 4 coach, 4 minicoach.
Chassis: 1 Freight Rover. 1 Leyland. 3 Mercedes. 3 Volvo. 1 Optare.
Bodies: Reeve Burgess, Plaxton.
Ops incl: local bus services, excursions & tours, private hire.
Livery: Multi-colour.

SILVER STAR COACH HOLIDAYS LTD
[disabled] [seatbelt] [wc] [galley] [vintage] [A/c] [replacement] [T]

13 CASTLE SQUARE, CAERNARFON LL55 2NF
Tel: 01286 672333
Fax: 01286 678118
Web site: www.silverstarholidays.com

Man Dir: Elfyn William Thomas **Co Sec**: Helen Jones **Ch Eng**: Barry Thomas **Ops Man**: Eric Wyn Thomas
Fleet: 18 - 5 sing e-deck bus, 9 coach, 4 midibus, 1 vintage.
Chassis: 1 AEC. 1 Bedford. 3 Bristol. 3 Dennis. 1 Leyland. 8 Mercedes. 3 Neoplan. 1 Optare. 2 Setra. 2 Volvo.
Bodies: 1 Alexander. 3 ECW. 3 Neoplan. 1 Optare. 25 Plaxton. 2 Setra. 2 Van Hool. 1 Burlingham.
Ops incl: local bus services, school contracts, excursions & tours, private hire, continental tours.
Livery: Green coaches/Blue buses.
Ticket System: Wayfarer 3

WILLIAMS COACHES (NORTH WALES)
[wc] [A/c] [seatbelt] [R] [replacement]

DEINIOLEN, CAERNARFON LL55 3HH.
Tel/Fax: 01286 870484.
Dirs: I. Williams, E. Williams, H. Williams.
Fleet: 12 - 3 double-deck bus, 1 single-deck bus, 4 coach, 1 double-deck coach, 2 midicoach, 1 minibus.
Chassis: Ford Transit, Leyland, MAN, Mercedes, Optare, Volvo.
Ops incl: school contracts, private hire, continental tours.
Livery: Yellow/White.
Ticket System: Setright, Almex.

MERTHYR TYDFIL

SIXTY SIXTY COACHES
PENTREBACH INDUSTRIAL ESTATE, PENTREBACH CF48 4BE.
Tel: 01685 386060.
Fax: 01685 386161.
E-mail: enquiries@sixsixty.co.uk
Web site: www.sixsixty.co.uk
Prop: G. Handy.
Ops incl: local bus services
Livery: White/Red/Silver.

*STAGECOACH IN SOUTH WALES
See Torfaen

MONMOUTHSHIRE

DUKE'S TRAVEL
See Gloucestershire

*REES MOTOR (TRAVEL)
[wc] [galley] [seatbelt] [A/c]

WAUNLLAPRIA, LLANELLY HILL, ABERGAVENNY NP7 0PW
Tel: 01873 830210
Fax: 01873 832167
Prtnrs: N A Rees, N A Rees, Mrs M E Rees.
Fleet: 10 - 8 coach, 1 double-deck coach, 1 minicoach.

A/c	Air conditioning
[disabled]	Vehicles suitable for disabled
[galley]	Coach(es) with galley facilities
wc	Coach(es) with toilet facilities
[seatbelt]	Seat belt-fitted vehicles
R	Recovery service available (not 24 hr)
R24	24hr recovery service
[replacement]	Replacement vehicle available
T	Toilet-drop facilities available
[vintage]	Vintage vehicle(s) available
[opentop]	Open top vehicle(s)

Welsh Operators

Chassis/Bodies: 1 Bova. 4 Jonckheere. 1 Leyland. 4 Neoplan.
Ops incl: local bus services, school contracts, excursions & tours, private hire, continental tours.

*STAGECOACH IN SOUTH WALES
See Torfaen

NEATH & PORT TALBOT

BLUEBIRD OF NEATH/ PONTARDAWE
9-10 LONDON ROAD, NEATH SA11 1HB.
Tel/Fax: 01639 643849.
Fleetname: Bluebird Coaches (Neath).
Prop: Ian S. Warren. **Ch Eng:** George Warren. **Sec:** Ms Melanie Evans.
Fleet: 21 - 2 double-deck bus, 18 coach, 1 midibus.
Chassis: 2 Bristol. 1 DAF. 1 Mercedes. 17 Volvo.
Bodies: 4 Jonckheere. 1 Mercedes. Leyland. 10 Plaxton. 6 Van Hool.
Ops incl: local bus services, excursions & tours, private hire, continental tours, school contracts.
Livery: White/Blue/Red.

MERLYN'S COACHES (SKEWEN) LTD
THE LODGE, 56 SIDING TERRACE, SKEWEN SA10 6RD.
Tel: 01792 813303.
Fax: 01792 813085.
Props: June John, Andrew Pearce.
Fleet: 14 - 1 single-deck bus, 10 coach, 1 midicoach, 1 minibus, 1 midibus.
Chassis: 4 Leyland. 1 MCW. 1 Renault. 6 Volvo.
Bodies: 1 Caetano. 1 Duple. 7 Plaxton. 4 Van Hool. 1 Cymric.
Ops incl: local bus services, school contracts, excursions & tours, private hire, continental tours.
Livery: White/multi coloured.
Ticket System: Wayfarer.

NELSON & SON (GLYNNEATH) LTD
74A HIGH STREET, GLYNNEATH SA11 5AW.
Tel: 01639 722252.
Fax: 01639 720308.
Fleetname: Nelson's Coaches.
Man Dir: J. L. R. Nelson.
Dir/Co Sec: Mrs J. Nelson.
Fleet: 11 - 10 coach, 1 midicoach.
Chassis: 4 DAF. 1 Ford. 4 Leyland. 1 Mercedes. 1 Volvo.
Bodies: 1 Duple. 1 Jonckheere. 5 Plaxton. 3 Van Hool. 1 Other.
Ops incl: school contracts, excursions & tours, private hire, continental tours.
Livery: White/Red/Orange.

*D J THOMAS COACHES
28 TYNYRHEOL ROAD, BRYNCOCH, NEATH SA10 7EA.
Tel/Fax: 01639 635502
Recovery: 07989 444978
E-mail: mail@djthomascoaches.co.uk
Web site: www.djthomascoaches.co.uk
Dirs: Mrs B Thomas, R Thomas, Mrs A Gibson.
Fleet: 11 - 8 coach, 1 minicoach, 2 minibus.
Chassis: 2 Mercedes. 1 Renault. 8 Volvo.
Bodies: 2 Berkhof. 1 Cymric. 2 Mercedes. 5 Plaxton. 1 Van Hool.
Ops incl: local bus services, excursions & tours, private hire, school contracts.
Livery: White/Red/Yellow/Orange

TONNA LUXURY COACHES LTD
TENNIS VIEW GARAGE, TONNA SA11 3NJ.
Tel: 01639 642727.
Fax: 01639 646052.
Dirs: K. M. Hopkins, Katherine M. Hopkins, A. Hopkins.
Fleet: 20 - 19 coach, 1 minibus.
Chassis: 4 DAF. 2 Leyland. 2 Mercedes. 12 Volvo.
Bodies: 10 Duple. 10 Plaxton.
Ops incl: school contracts, private hire.
Livery: Two-tone Grey/Red.

NEWPORT

*NEWPORT TRANSPORT LTD
160 CORPORATION ROAD, NEWPORT NP19 0WF
Tel: 01633 670563
Fax: 01633 242589
Web site: www.newporttransport.co.uk
E-mail: newporttransport@btconnect.com
Man Dir: T G Roberts **Eng Dir:** J Lyons
Fin Dir: R Macleod **Ops Dir:** R Jones
Fleet: 81 - 14 double-deck bus, 51 single-deck bus, 1 open-top bus, 15 midibus.
Chassis: 17 Dennis. 4 Optare. 60 Scania.
Bodies: 56 Alexander. 4 Optare. 9 Wright. 12 Scania.
Ops incl: local bus services, private hire.
Livery: Green/Cream.
Ticket System: Almex A90 Farespeed

SHAMROCK COACHES
48 HIGH STREET, NEWPORT NP9 1GB
Tel: 01633 251917.
Fax: 01633 256822.
E-mail: shamrockcoaches@btinternet.com
Web site: www.shamrock-travel.co.uk
Man: M. King. **Controller:** R. Cope.
Co Sec: A. Rowe. **Off Man:** C. Ward.
Fleet: 34 - 30 coach, 4 midicoach.
Chassis: 3 Bova. 18 Dennis. 2 MAN. 4 Mercedes. 4 Scania. 3 Volvo.
Bodies: 3 Bova. 8 Duple. 1 Jonckheere.

10 Plaxton.
Ops incl: local bus services, school contracts, excursions & tours, private hire, express, continental tours.
Livery: Yellow/Green.
Ticket System: Wayfarer 3.
See also Shamrock, Rhondda

*STAGECOACH IN SOUTH WALES
See Torfaen

WELSH DRAGON TRAVEL
21 BEAUFORT ROAD, NEWPORT NP19 7ND.
Tel: 01633 761397
E-mail: alan.smith5@ntworld.com
Prop: Alan Barrington Smith.
Fleet: 4 - 1 double-deck bus, 2 coach, 1 open-top bus.
Chassis: 1 Bedford. 1 Bristol. 2 Leyland.
Ops incl: local bus services, school contracts, private hire.
Livery: Red/Cream
Ticket System: Almex

PEMBROKESHIRE

W. H. COLLINS
CUFFERN GARAGE, ROCH, HAVERFORDWEST SA62 6HB.
Tel: 01437 710337.
Fleetname: Collins Coaches.
Prop: P. N. & M. Collins.
Fleet: 18 - 16 minibus, 2 minicoach.
Ops incl: school contracts, private hire.
Livery: Blue/Grey/White.

*EDWARDS BROS
THE GARAGE, BROAD HAVEN ROAD, TIERS CROSS, HAVERFORDWEST SA62 3BZ
Tel: 01437 890230
Fax: 01437 890337
E-mail: edwardsbros@tiscali.co.uk
Web site: www.edwards-tiers-cross.co.uk
Prop: Robert Edwards
Fleet: 17 - 10 coach, 1 midibus, 4 midicoach, 2 minicoach.
Chassis: 1 Bova. 2 Dennis. 2 LDV. 1 Leyland. 5 Mercedes. 6 Volvo.
Bodies: 1 Autobus. 1 Bova. 1 Caetano. 1 LDV. 3 Mercedes. 5 Plaxton. 3 Van Hool. 1 other.
Ops incl: local bus services, school contracts, excursions & tours, private hire.
Livery: Cream/Brown/Yellow or Gold.
Ticket System: Setright

*MIDWAY MOTORS
MIDWAY GARAGE, CRYMYCH SA41 3QU
Tel: 01239 831267
Fax: 01239 831279
E-mail: reesmidway@hotmail.com
Ptnrs: Wyndham Rees, Elan Rees.
Fleet: 15 - 2 single-deck bus, 9 coach, 2 midicoach, 2 minibus.
Chassis: 1 Bova. 4 Dennis. 4 Ford. 1 Ford

Transit. 1 LDV. 1 Optare. 1 Toyota. 2 Volvo.
Bodies: 1 Bova. 2 Caetano. 1 Carlyle.
1 Duple. 1 Mercedes. 1 Optare. 6 Plaxton.
2 Wadham Stringer.
Ops incl: local bus services, school contracts, excursions & tours, private hire, continental tours.
Livery: Silver/Blue
Ticket System: Almex

SILCOX COACHES

WATERLOO GARAGE, PEMBROKE DOCK SA72 4RR.
Tel: 01646 683143.
Fax: 01646 621787.
Chmn: L. W. Silcox **Man Dir**: K. W. Silcox
Co Sec: D. W. Silcox.
Fleet: 76 - 42 single-deck bus, 19 coach, 14 midibus, 1 midicoach.
Chassis: 25 Dennis. 38 Leyland. 1 MAN. 10 Mercedes. 1 Optare. 1 Volvo.
Bodies: 2 Berkhof. 7 Caetano. 5 Duple. 1 East Lancs. 3 Marco Polo. 4 Marshall. 2 Mellor. 1 Optare. 40 Plaxton. 2 UVG. 1 Van Hool. 6 Wadham Stringer. 2 Wright.
Ops incl: local bus services, school contracts, excursions & tours, private hire, continental tours.
Livery: Red/Cream/Blue.

SUMMERDALE COACHES

SUMMERDALE GARAGE, LETTERSTON SA62 5UB.
Tel: 01348 840270.
Props: D. G. Davies, B. J. L. Davies, G. R. Jones.
Livery: Yellow/Blue.

POWYS

*A&E MINIBUSES

PENYBRYN, LLANGYNIEW, LLANFAIR CAEREINION
Tel: 01938 810518
Fleet: 2 - 2 midibus
Chassis/bodies: 1 Mercedes. 1 Ford
Ops incl: school contracts, private hire

*A W COACHES

LLANFAIR CAEREINION
Tel/Fax: 01938 810452
Fleet: 2 - 2 midibus
Dirs: Allen Watkin, Sian Watkin
Fleet: 8 - 4 coaches, 4 minibuses
Chassis: 1 Scania. 3 LDV. 2 Leyland. 1 Mazda. 1 Mercedes.
Bodies: 1 Van Hool. 1 Duple. 1 DAF. 1 Mazda.
Ops incl: school contracts, private hire
Livery: Cream/Orange/Brown

*J ALWYN EVANS

THE OLD STATION YARD GARAGE, TREGARON
Tel: 01974 298546
Fax: 01974 299056

Dirs: J A Evans & Son
Fleet: 14 - 9 coach, 5 minibus
Chassis: 1 DAF. 2 Dennis. 2 Ford. 2 Leyland. 3 Mercedes. 4 Volvo.
Bodies: 2 Duple. 2 Ford. 1 LDV. 3 Mercedes. 6 Plaxton.
Ops incl: school contracts, private hire, excursions & tours
Livery: various

*BEADLES TRAVEL/BRENDAS TRAVEL

10 SHORTBRIDGE ST CORNER, NEWTOWN
ALSO AT: 12 BROAD STREET, WELSHPOOL
Tel: 01686 628925/626933 (Sales Office: 01938 554412)
Props: Harold & Brenda Beadle
Fleet: 12 - 4 coach, 8 midibus.
Chassis: 3 Volvo, 6 Leyland DAF. 1 Mercedes. 1 Ford Transit. 1 Toyota
Bodies: Caetano, Duple, Plaxton, Windsor.
Ops incl: school contracts, excursions & tours, private hire.
Livery: pale & dark Green.

*R N BOWDEN

LOWER GELLI, GOLFA, WELSHPOOL
Tel: 01938 850292
Prop: R N Bowden
Fleet: 2 - 2 midicoach
Chassis/bodies: 2 Mercedes.
Ops incl: school contracts, private hire
Livery: white

ROY BROWNS COACHES

15 HIGH STREET, BUILTH WELLS LD2 3DN
Tel: 01982 552597
Fax: 01982 552286
E-mail: sue@roybrownscoaches.fsnet.co.uk
Web site: www.roybrownscoaches.co.uk
Prop: Nigel W. Brown.
Fleet: 12 - 3 single-deck bus, 1 midibus, 3 midicoach, 5 minibus.
Chassis: 8 Bedford. 3 DAF. 2 Dennis. 1 Ford Transit. 3 Freight Rover. 3 LDV. 2 MAN. 2 MCW. 2 Mercedes. 2 Optare.
Bodies: 4 Caetano. 2 Duple. 3 MCW. 1 Mellor. 2 Optare. 6 Plaxton.
Ops incl: local bus services, school contracts, excursions & tours, private hire, continental tours.
Livery: Maroon/White.
Ticket System: Wayfarer/Setright.

*CELTIC TRAVEL

NEW STREET, LLANIDLOES SY18 6EH
Tel: 01686 412231/412232
E-mail: celtic@irc.ruralwales.org
Props: P. Jones, G. Jones.
Fleet: 20 - 17 coach, 3 minibus.
Chassis: 1 Bedford. 2 DAF. 3 Ford. 3 Leyland. 11 Volvo.

Bodies: Bova, Duple, Ford, Plaxton, Van Hool.
Ops incl: school contracts, excursions & tours, private hire.
Livery: dark/ligh: Grey with green lettering and Welsh Dragon emblem.

*CENTRAL TRAVEL

SMITHFIELD ROAD, NEWTOWN
Tel/Fax: 01686 610224
Props: Richard Bowen
Fleet: 3 - 1 coach, 2 midibus.
Chassis: 1 Bedford. 1 Iveco. 1 Mercedes. 1 Toyota
Bodies: 1 Caetano. 1 Iveco. 1 Mercedes. 1 Plaxton.
Ops incl: school contracts, private hire.
Livery: White with red lettering

*COACHING CONNECTION

14 GREAT OAK STREET, LLANIDLOES SY18 6BN
Tel: 01686 413714
Fax: 01686 411065
Props: David Corfield, Miss Betty Tonks
Fleet: 1 coach
Chassis/Body: Setra
Ops incl: excursions & tours.
Livery: Cream with orange/brown flashes.

*COOKSONS COACHES

HOPE LANE GARAGE, HOPE, WELSHPOOL
Tel: 01938 553465
Prop: Mike Cookson
Fleet: 9 - 5 coach. 4 midibus.
Chassis: 1 Bedford. 2 Volvo. 2 Leyland. 2 Leyland DAF. 2 Ford.
Bodies: Ford, LDV, Plaxton, Van Hool.
Ops incl: school contracts, excursions & tours, private hire.
Livery: Medium Grey with black lettering

*CROSS GATES COACHES

CROSS GATES, LLANDRINDOD WELLS LD1 6RE
Tel: 01597 852000
Fax: 01597 851748
E-mail: peter@ilink.com.uk
Dirs: Peter Knill (**Ops**), Reg Knill **Ch Eng**: Chris Prynne
Fleet: 16 - 11 sing:e-deck bus, 4 coach, 1 midicoach.
Chassis: 3 DAF. 3 Dennis. 1 Mercedes. 2 Optare. 6 Scania. 1 Toyota.
Bodies: 1 Caetano. 2 Carlyle. 1 Irizar. 2 Optare. 4 Plaxton. 5 Van Hool.
Ops incl: local bus services, school contracts, continental tours, private hire.
Livery: Blue/White
Ticket system: Wayfarer

*D G DAVIES

AFON MARTEG GARAGE, PANT-Y-DWR LD6 5NA
Tel: 05978 8232
Prop: D G Davies
Fleet: 2
Chassis: Ford.
Bodies: Duple, Plaxton

- Air conditioning
- Vehicles suitable for disabled
- Coach(es) with galley facilities
- Coach(es) with toilet facilities
- Seat belt-fitted vehicles
- **R** Recovery service available (not 24 hr)
- **R24** 24hr recovery service
- Replacement vehicle available
- **T** Toilet-drop facilities available
- Vintage vehicle(s) available
- Open top vehicle(s)

Ops incl: school contracts, private hire.
Livery: White with red/blue flashing

*DIAL-A-RIDE
THE OLD BREW HOUSE, SEVERN SHOPPING CENTRE, NEWTOWN
Tel: 01686 622566
Fax: 01686 610703
Man/Organiser: Doug Bancroft
Fleet: 7 - 6 midibus, 1 car.
Chassis/Bodies: include 6 Ford Transit
Ops incl: local bus services, private hire.
Livery: White with red lettering

*GEOFF'S MINIBUSES
KERRY, NEWTOWN
Tel: 01686 670381
Fax: 01686 610703
Prop: Geoff Williams
Fleet: 12 midibus.
Chassis/Bodies: 10 Ford Transit. 2 LDV.
Ops incl: school contracts, private hire.
Livery: White with red lettering

*R G GITTINS
THE GARAGE, DOLANOG, WELSHPOOL
Tel: 01938 810439
Prop: R N Bowden
Fleet: 3 - 2 coach, 1 midicoach
Chassis: 1 Bova. 1 DAF. 1 Mercedes.
Bodies: 1 Bova. 1 Caetano. 1 Reeve Burgess.
Ops incl: school contracts, private hire, excursions & tours.
Livery: White - also Orange/Cream/Brown

*GOLD STAR TRAVEL (WALES)
43 LON MAESYCOED, NEWTOWN
Tel/Fax: 01686 628895/0800 597 6868
Dir/Prop: H B Williams
Fleet: 16 - 3 coach, 11 midibus. 2 minibus
Chassis: includes 2 Bedford. 1 DAF. 1 Dennis. 1 Leyland DAF. 2 Ford Transit. 2 Toyota
Bodies: Caetano, Ford, Plaxton.
Ops incl: school contracts, private hire.
Livery: White with gold lettering

*GWYN JONES
THE GARAGE, MEIFOD SY22 6DB.
Tel: 01938 500249
Fax: 01938 500675
E-mail: gwynmeifod@talk21.com
Ptnrs: D G Jones, D J Jones.
Fleet: 7 - 3 coach, 2 minibus, 2 midicoach.
Chassis: 1 Bedford. 1 DAF. 1 Ford Transit. 1 Mercedes. 1 Setra. 2 Toyota.
Bodies: 2 Caetano. 1 Ford Transit.1 Mercedes. 2 Plaxton. 1 Setra.
Ops incl: school contracts, excursions & tours, private hire.
Livery: White with Green/Red stripes.

*HARRY EVANS COACHES
WATERLOO VILLAS, SALOP ROAD, WELSHPOOL
Tel: 01938 553909
Prop: Harry Evans
Fleet: 4 - 2 coach, 1 midibus, 1 minibus.
Chassis: 2 Dennis. 1 LDV. 1 Ford Transit.
Bodies: Duple, Ford, DAF, LDV.
Ops incl: school contracts, private hire.
Livery: Red/Cream

*HERDMAN COACHES
THE OLD STATION GARAGE, THREE COCKS, TALGARTH
Tel/Fax: 01497 847100
Prop: Paul Herdman
Fleet: 10 - 9 coach, 1 midibus.
Chassis: 6 Bedford, 3 DAF. 1 Toyota.
Bodies: Plaxton, Caetano.
Ops incl: school contracts, private hire.
Livery: White/Turquoise

*LAKELINE COACHES
EBRAN-DDU, FELINDRE, KNIGHTON LD7 1YN
Tel: 01547 7662
Dir: J E A Lakelin
Fleet: 4 - 3 coach, 1 minibus.
Chassis: 1 Bedford. 1 DAF. 1 Dennis. 1 Ford.
Bodies: 1 Duple. 1 LDV. 2 Plaxton.
Ops incl: school contracts, private hire
Livery: Pale Blue/Dark Blue

*LEWIS COACHES
THE COACH HOUSE, CEFN COCH ROAD, LLANFAIR CAEREINON
Tel: 01938 810508
Prop: M P Lewis
Fleet: 1 coach
Chassis/bodies: MAN/Caetano
Livery: Cream/orange/Brown
Ops incl: school contracts, private hire

*LLOYDS COACHES/BYSIAU LLOYDS COACHES
ARRIVA GARAGE, STATION ROAD, MACHYNLLETH SY20 8NN
Tel: 01654 702100
Fax: 01974 703900
Mobile: 07712 552953
Dirs: David W LLoyd
Fleet: 7 - 2 coach, 5 bus
Chassis: 3 Leyland. 2 Mercedes. 2 Volvo.
Bodies: Duple. Plaxton.
Ops incl: local bus services, school contracts, private hire.
Livery: Silver/Red/Yellow (coaches), Cream/Orange/Yellow (buses)

*MID WALES TRAVEL (1963) LTD
SMITHFIELD ROAD GARAGE, NEWTOWN
Tel: 01970 828288
Fax: 01970 828940
Props: J S Evans, J M Evans
Fleet: 20 - 10 coach, 2 minibus, 4 midibus.
Chassis: 2 DAF. 3 Ford. 4 Leyland. 5 Mercedes. 6 Volvo.
Bodies: Caetano, Duple, Freight Rover, Plaxton.
Ops incl: local bus service, school contracts, private hire, excursions & continental tours.
Livery: White with dark-blue lettering
Ticket System: Setright
Associated Company: Evans Coaches, Aberystwyth

*OWEN'S MOTORS LTD
TEMESIDE HOUSE, STATION ROAD, KNIGHTON LD7 1DT
Tel: 01547 528303
Fax: 01547 520512
Web site: www.owensmotors.co.uk
Ops Man: D. Owen. **Ch Eng**: T Owen.
Sec/Dir: J Owen
Fleet: 14 - 11 coach, 3 minibus.
Chassis: 3 Dennis. 1 Ford. 2 LDV. 7 Volvo.
Bodies: 2 Duple. 1 Ford Transit. 2 LDV. 8 Plaxton. 1 Van Hool.
Ops incl: local bus services, school contracts, excursions & tours, private hire, continental tours.
Livery: Blue/Grey

*RHIEW VALLEY COACHES
BERRIEW (HENFAES GARAGE), WELSHPOOL
Tel: 01686 640554
Props: D G Haydock
Fleet: 2 coaches.
Chassis: 1 Volvo, 1 DAF
Bodies: 2 Van Hool
Ops incl: school contracts, excursions & tours, private hire.
Livery: Blue/White stripes, Green/Black stripes.

*STAGECOACH IN SOUTH WALES
See Torfaen

*STOCKHAMS COACHES
TIMBERCRAFTS TRADING ESTATE, GILWERN ROAD, CRICKHOWELL NP8 1HW
Tel/Fax: 01873 810343
Prop: Nancy Stockham
Fleet: 8 - 4 coaches, 4 minibuses.
Chassis: 3 Volvo, 1 Leyland. 4 Ford Transit
Bodies: Ford, Plaxton, Van Hool
Ops incl: school contracts, private hire.
Livery: Green/White.

*STRATOS HOLIDAYS/STRATOS TRAVEL LTD
2A SHORTBRIDGE STREET, NEWTOWN SY16
Tel: 01686 629021
Fax: 01686 626092
Prop: Owens Coaches, Four Crosses, Oswestry
Office Man: Colin Jones**Fleet**: 6 - 4 coach, 2 midicoach.
Chassis: 1 Bova. 1 Dennis. 1 Iveco. 1 MAN. 1 Toyota.
Bodies: Bova. Beulas. Caetano. Plaxton. Atlas(Aeta).
Ops incl: excursions & tours, private hire, continental tours.
Livery: Silver/Blue.

TANAT VALLEY COACHES
LLANRHAEDR YM MOCHNANT SY10 0AD
Tel: 01691 780212
Fax: 01691 780634

Recovery: 01691 780212
E-mail: mike@tanat.co.uk
Web site: www.tanatvalley.com
Dirs: R Michael Morris, Peter W Morris
Fleet Eng: Tony Morris **Co Sec**: Sara Morris
Ops Man: Nick Culliford
Fleet: 38 - 9 double-deck bus, 8 single-deck bus, 12 coach, 4 midibus, 1 midicoach, 2 minibus, 2 minicoach.
Chassis: 4 Bedford. 2 Bova. 3 Dennis. 1 Dodge. 2 LDV. 18 Leyland. 1 Leyland National. 2 MCW. 1 Toyota. 4 Volvo.
Bodies: 6 Alexander. 1 Berkhof. 2 Bova. 2 Caetano. 5 Duple. 8 ECW. 6 East Lancs. 1 Leyland National. 2 MCW. 2 Mercedes. 1 Plaxton. 2 Reeve Burgess.
Ops incl: local bus services, school contracts, excursions & tours, private hire, continental tours, express.
Livery: Maroon/Orange/White
Ticket System: Almex

*WEALE'S WHEELS
THE GRADING STATION, LLANDEWI, LLANDRINDOD WELLS LD1
Tel: 01597 851141
Fax: 01597 850007
Prop: M J Weale
Fleet: 10 - 4 coach, 5 midicoach, 1 minibus.
Chassis: 4 Bedford. 1 DAF. 1 Ford. 2 Leyland DAF. 1 Mercedes. 1 Toyota.
Bodies: Caetano, Ford, Plaxton
Ops incl: local bus services, school contracts, private hire.
Livery: Yellow/White

*WILLIAMS COACHES
RICH WAY, THE WATTON, BRECON LD3 7EH
Tel: 01874 622223
Fax: 01874 625218
E-mail: office@williams-coaches.co.uk
Web site: www.williams-coaches.co.uk
Dirs: J L Williams (Snr)**(Chmn)**, D M Williams **(Sec)**, J G Williams J L Williams (Jnr) **Eng**: K Parry **Ops Man**: W Rees
Fleet: 37 - 2 single-deck bus, 19 coach, 3 midibus, 11 minibus, 2 minicoach.
Chassis: 2 Bedford. 1 DAF. 5 Ford Transit. 3 LDV. 2 MAN. 20 Mercedes. 3 Setra. 1 Toyota.
Bodies: 1 Beulas. 3 Bova. 1 Duple. 1 Jonckheere. 2 Leyland. 20 Mercedes. 1 Plaxton. 2 Reeve Burgess. 5 Setra.
Ops incl: local bus services, school contracts, excursions & tours, private hire.
Livery: Orange/Cream.
Ticket system: Setright.

*WILLIAMS MINIBUSES
24 BROOKLAND ROAD, LLANDRINDOD WELLS LD1
Tel: 01597 824577
Dir/Prop: J M Williams
Fleet: 3 minibus
Chassis: 3 Leyland DAF.
Ops incl: local bus service, excursions & tours, private hire.
Livery: White with Blue lettering

RHONDDA, CYNON, TAFF

*BEBB TRAVEL PLC
THE COACH STATIOIN, LLANTWIT FARDRE CF38 2HB
Tel: 01443 215100
Fax: 01443 215134
E-mail: admin@bebbtravel.co.uk
Web site: www.bebbtravel.co.uk
Chmn: N G Bebb **Dir**: David Newman
Fleet Eng: Dave Witte
Fleet: 41 - 20 midibus, 20 coach, 1 midicoach.
Chassis: Mercedes. Volvo.
Bodies: Optare. Sunsundegui. Transbus.
Ops incl: local bus services, school contracts, express
Livery: White/Blue
Ticket System: ERG

EDWARDS COACHES
NEWTOWN INDUSTRIAL ESTATE, LLANTWIT FARDRE CF38 2EE
Tel: 01443 202048.
Fax: 01443 217583.
E-mail: mike@edwardscoaches.co.uk
Web site: www.edwardscoaches.co.uk
Prop: Mike Edwards **Fleet Eng**: Shaun Edwards **Sales Dir**: Jason Edwards
Fleet: 69 - 30 double-deck bus, 35 coach, 1 midicoach, 1 midibus, 2 minicoach.
Chassis: 13 Bova. 6 DAF. Dennis. 2 Ford Transit. 2 Freight Rover. 20 Leyland.1 Mercedes. 1 Toyota. 20 Volvo.
Bodies: 10 Alexander. 13 Bova. 2 Caetano. 4 Duple. 2 Jonckheere. 2 Northern Counties. 10 Plaxton. 2 Van Hool.
Ops incl: local bus services, school contracts, excursions & tours, private hire, continental tours.
Livery: White/Blue
Ticket system: Almex

GLOBE COACHES
BROOKLANDS, FFORCHNEOL ROW, GODREAMAN, ABERDARE CF44 6HD.
Tel: 01685 873622.
Fax: 01685 876526.
Props: W. Jarvis, Mrs M. Jarvis.
Fleet: 15 - 14 coach, 1 midicoach.
Chassis: 4 Bedford. 1 Bova. 2 DAF. 2 Dennis. 2 Leyland. 4 Volvo.
Bodies: 1 Bova. 1 Caetano. 4 Duple. 7 Plaxton. 2 others.
Ops incl: excursions & tours, private hire, school contracts.
Livery: White/Blue.

JONES OF YNYSYBWL
See Shamrock Hoppa.

*MAISEY MINICOACH HIRE
GELYNOG YARD, CASTELLAU ROAD, BEDDAU CF38 2RA
Tel/Fax: 01443 205462
E-mail: info@maiseybus.co.uk
Web site: www.maiseybus.co.uk
Ptnrs: Brian Evans, Graham Evans, Colin Evans.
Fleet: 11 - 2 minibus, 7 minicoach, 2 midibus.
Chassis: 2 Ford Transit. 1 Freight Rover. Iveco. 6 Renault.
Bodies: 7 Cymric. 2 Mellor
Ops incl: school contracts, private hire.
Livery: White/Red

SHAMROCK HOPPA
34 TAFF STREET, PONTYPRIDD
Owner: A. Jones. **Ch Eng**: G. T. Shenwood.
Dev Man: C. Jones. **Traf Man**: G. D. Owen.
Ops Man: R. Williams, R. Cavey.
Fleet: 87 - 5 double-deck bus, 70 single-deck bus, 2 coach, 10 midibus.
Chassis: 1 Bedford. 4 Bristol. 38 Dennis. 2 Iveco. 20 Leyland National. 20 Mercedes.
Bodies: 2 Alexander. 2 Caetano. 20 Leyland National. 20 Mercedes. 13 Northern Counties. 20 Plaxton. 12 Wadham Stringer.
Ops incl: local bus services, school contracts, excursions & tours, private hire, express, continental tours.
Livery: Yellow/Green.
See also Shamrock, Newport.

*STAGECOACH IN SOUTH WALES
See Torfaen.

THOMAS OF RHONDDA
BUS DEPOT, PORTH CF39 0AG.
Tel: 01443 433714.
Fax: 01443 436542.
Man Dir: W.G. Thomas. **Ch Eng**: I. G. Thomas. **Co Sec**: J. E. Thomas.
Fleet: 40 - 20 double-deck bus, 14 single-deck bus, 4 double-deck coach, 2 minibus.
Chassis: 1 Ayats. 3 Bova. 2 Bristol. 3 DAF. 1 Ford. 20 Leyland. 6 Scania. 8 Volvo.

CITY AND COUNTY OF SWANSEA

DIAMOND HOLIDAYS
98 WOODFIELD STREET, MORRISTON SA6 8AS
Tel: 01792 791981
Fax: 01792 781173
E-mail: ryanj@diamondholidays.co.uk
Web site: www.diamondholidays.co.uk
Fin Dir: Chris Roberts.

- Air conditioning
- Vehicles suitable for disabled
- Coach(es) with galley facilities
- Coach(es) with toilet facilities
- Seat belt-fitted vehicles
- R Recovery service available (not 24 hr)
- R24 24hr recovery service
- Replacement vehicle available
- T Toilet-drop facilities available
- Vintage vehicle(s) available
- Open top vehicle(s)

Ops Dir: Peter Jenkins. **Dir**: Sharon Cunningham. **Group Tours Dir**: Eiron Jones. **Tran Man**: Ryan Jones. **Brochure Tours Dir**: Nicky Davies.
Ops incl: excursions & tours, private hire, continental tours.
Livery: Ivory/Maroon/Gold.

FIRST CYMRU BUSES LIMITED

HEOL GWYROSYDD, PENLAN SA5 7BN
Tel: 01792 582233
Fax: 01792 561356
Web Site: www.firstgroup.com
Man Dir: J W Davies **Fin Dir**: Ms A Price
Ops Dir: P Collier **Eng Dir**: P J Davies
Fleet: 333 - 14 double-deck bus, 54 single-deck bus, 191 midibus, 74 minibus.
Chassis: 218 Dennis. 7 Duple. 26 Leyland. 74 Mercedes. 8 Volvo.
Bodies: 18 Alexander. 9 Duple. 7 ECW. 1 East Lancs. 5 Leyland. 6 Marshall. 7 Mellor. 227 Plaxton. 7 Reeve Burgess. 4 Roe. 1 Wadham Stringer. 18 Wright. 1 Cymric. 22 Robin Hood.
Ops incl: local bus services, school contracts, excursions & tours, private hire, express.
Livery: FirstGroup.
Ticket System: Wayfarer III.

HAWKES COACHES LTD

BRIDGE ROAD, WAUNARLWYDD SA5 4SP
Tel: 01792 873336
Fax: 01792 875172
Dirs: R B Hawkes, Mrs J L Hawkes
Fleet: 25 - 2 single-deck bus, 17 coach.
Chassis: 1 DAF. 2 Dennis. 4 Leyland. 10 Volvo.
Bodies: includes 2 Jonckheere.
Ops incl: local bus services, excursions & tours, private hire, school contracts.
Ticket System: Wayfarer

BRIAN ISAAC COACHES LTD

COACH TRAVEL CENTRE, KEMYS WAY, SWANSEA ENTERPRISE PARK SA6 8QF
Tel: 01792 701644
Fax: 01792 310233
E-mail: enquiries@brianisaac.co.uk
Web Site: www.brianisaac.co.uk
Man Dir: Brian Isaac **Tran Man/Co Sec**: Stewart Isaac **Workshop Eng**: David Howells **Tour & Mktg Dir**: Helen Groom
Fleet: 24 - 3 double-deck bus, 14 coach, 5 midibus, 2 minibus.
Chassis: 2 Dennis. 2 LDV. 3 Leyland. 5 Mercedes. 12 Volvo.
Bodies: 1 Berkhof. 2 Duple. 5 Leyland. 5 Optare. 10 Plaxton. 1 Van Hool.
Ops incl: local bus services, school contracts, excursions & tours, private hire, continental tours.
Livery: Blue/Magenta/Gold/White
Ticket System: Wayfarer 3

PULLMAN COACHES LTD

UNIT 41, PENCLAWDD INDUSTRIAL ESTATE, CROFTY SA4 3RT.
Tel: 01792 851430
E-mail: pullmancoaches@aol.com
Web site: www.pullmancoaches.co.uk
Dirs: C. W. Lewis, H. S. Rees.
Fleet: 34 - 8 single-deck bus, 25 coach, 1 minicoach.
Livery: Cream/White/Red/Fawn

*STAGECOACH IN SOUTH WALES

See Torfaen

*TAWE TOURS

57 CAEMAWR ROAD, MORRISTON SA6 7EA
Tel/Fax: 01792 411041
E-mail: b.garnham1@ntlworld.com
Web site: www.tawetours.co.uk
Prop: Bryan Garnham
Fleet: 1 midicoach.
Chassis: 1 Toyota
Ops incl: excursions & tours, private hire.

ARTHUR THOMAS COACHES

91 PONTARDULAIS ROAD, GORSEINON SA4 4FQ.
Props: A. A., J. T., B. E., G. A. Thomas.
Livery: Cream/Red/Blue.

2 TRAVEL GROUP PLC

2 TRAVEL HOUSE, UPPER BANK, PENTRECHWYTH, SWANSEA SA1 7DB
Tel: 01792 483040
Fax: 01792 652422
E-mail: info@2travelgroupplc.co.uk
Web site: www.2travelgroupplc.co.uk
Chmn: Sir Richard Needham **Ch Exec**: Bev Fowles **Ops Dir**: David Fowles **Fin Dir**: Carl Waters **Fl Eng**: Alun Price **Co Sec**: Huw Francis
Fleet: 84 - 23 double-deck bus, 10 single-deck bus, 40 coach, 2 double-deck coach, 1 midicoach, 1 minicoach, 7 minibus.
Chassis: 2 Bristol. 1 DAF. 8 Dennis. 3 Ford. 28 Leyland. 2 MAN. 3 Mercedes. 2 Neoplan. 3 Renault. 1 Toyota. 31 Volvo.
Bodies: 3 Beulas. 1 Bova. 1 Caetano. 6 Duple. 2 ECW. 3 Mercedes. 13 Northern Counties. 27 Plaxton. 24 other.
Ops incl: local bus services, school contracts, private hire, express, continental tours.
Livery: White/Blue/Red
Ticket System: Almex, Wayfarer II

TORFAEN

PHIL ANSLOW TRAVEL GROUP LTD

UNIT 10, PONTNEWYNYDD INDUSTRIAL ESTATE, PONTYPOOL NP4 6YW
Tel: 01495 767888.
Fax: 01495 757771.
E-mail: phil@philanslowtravel.telme.com.
Fleetname: Phil Anslow Travel, Phil Anslow Coaches.
Man Dir: P. Anslow. **Ch Eng**: K. Bick.
Sec: Ms S. J. Anslow.
Bus Op Man: T. Wyburn.
Coach Op Man: Sarah Turton Farr.
Fleet: 55 - 8 single-deck bus, 14 coach, 31 midibus, 2 minibus.
Chassis: 2 Freight Rover. 6 Iveco. 7 Leyland. 4 Leyland National. 25 Mercedes. 11 Volvo.
Bodies: 7 Duple. 1 Jonckheere. 4 Leyland National. 9 Optare. 23 Plaxton. 1 Reeve Burgess. 2 Van Hool. 5 Wadham Stringer. 2 Jaycas. 5 Dormobile.
Ops incl: local bus services, school contracts, excursions & tours, private hire.
Livery: Buses: White/Yellow/Green. Coaches: White.
Ticket System: Wayfarer III.

B'S TRAVEL

13 EAST VIEW, GRIFFITHSTOWN NP4 5DW.
Tel/Fax: 01495 756889.
Ptnrs: J. & Kay Benning.
Fleet: 4 - 2 midicoach, 2 minibus.
Chassis: 2 Mercedes. 1 Mellor. 1 G. M. Coachwork.
Ops incl: private hire, school contracts.
Livery: White with Yellow/Black logo.

*JENSON TRAVEL

UNIT 15, PONTNEWYNDD INDUSTRIAL ESTATE, PONTNEWYNDD, PONTYPOOL NP4 6YW
Tel/Fax: 01495 760539
Props: Gwyn Jenkins, Nicola Jenkins
Fleet: 9 - 3 coach, 3 minibus, 3 midicoach
Chassis: 3 Ford. 3 Mercedes. 3 Volvo.
Bodies: 1 Caetano. 1 Jonckheere. 3 Leyland. 1 Mercedes. 1 Plaxton. 2 Reeve Burgess.
Ops incl: school contracts, excursions & tours, private hire.
Livery: White

*STAGECOACH IN SOUTH WALES

1 ST DAVID'S ROAD, CWMBRAN NP44 1PD
Tel: 01633 838856
Fax: 01633 865299
Web site: www.stagecoachbus.com
Man Dir: John Gould **Com Dir**: Richard Davies **Eng Dir**: David Howe
Fleet: 299 - 19 double-deck bus, 100 single-deck bus, 92 midibus, 88 minibus.
Chassis: 78 Dennis. 14 Leyland. 90 Mercedes. 14 Transbus. 103 Volvo.
Bodies: 154 Alexander. 3 East Lancs. 11 Leyland. 8 Marshall. 21 Northern Counties. 2 Optare. 84 Plaxton. 16 Wright.
Ops incl: local bus services, school contracts, express.
Livery: Stagecoach.
Ticket System: ERG

2 TRAVEL COACHES

2 SOMERSET ROAD, CWMBRAN NP44 1QX
Tel: 01633 872424
Fax: 01633 871010
Web site: www.2travel.com
Ops Dir: David Fowles

VALE OF GLAMORGAN

E S T BUS LTD
LLANDOW INDUSTRIAL ESTATE, COWBRIDGE
Tel: 029 2078 6494
Fax: 029 2078 6493
Dir: C Hookings
Ops incl: local bus services, school contracts
Livery: Maroon/Cream

*HAYWARD TRAVEL (CARDIFF)
2 MURCH CRESCENT, DINAS POWYS CF64 4RF
Tel: 029 2051 5551
Fax: 029 2051 5113
E-mail: info@haywardtravel.co.uk
Web site: www.haywardtravel.co.uk
Ops incl: private hire

*THOMAS OF BARRY
12 PARK CRESCENT, BARRY CF62
Tel/Recovery: 01446 722800
Fax: 01446 722766
E-mail: thomasofbarry@hotmail.com
Web site: www.thomasofbarry.com
Prop: A Jones **Ops Man**: K Jones
Fleet: 71 - 5 double-deck bus, 15 single-deck bus, 30 coach, 2 double-deck coach, 4 open-top bus, 5 midibus, 3 midicoach, 2 minibus, 5 minicoach.
Chassis: 20 Dennis. 2 Irisbus. 2 MAN. 20 Mercedes. 5 Optare. 20 Scania. 2 Volvo.
Bodies: 4 Beulas. 3 Caetano. 5 Duple. 12 Irizar. 6 Leyland. 5 MCW. 9 Mercedes. 15 Plaxton. 2 Sunsundegui. 3 UVG. 6 Van Hool.
Ops incl: local bus services, school contracts, excursions & tours, private hire, express, continental tours.
Livery: White/Maroon.
Ticket System: Wayfarer 3

WREXHAM

*ACTON COACHES
109 HERBERT JENNING AVENUE, ACTON PARK LL12 7YA
Tel/Fax: 01978 352470
Prop: D B Evans.
Fleet: 4 - 3 coach, 1 midibus
Chassis: 1 DAF. 2 Volvo. 1 Mercedes.
Bodies: 1 Plaxton. 1 Caetano. 1 Van Hool. 1 Optare.
Livery: Blue/White
Ops incl: school contracts, private hire

*GEORGE EDWARDS & SON
BERWYN, BWLCHYWYN LL11 5UE.
Tel/Fax: 01978 757281
Props: G F & G Edwards.
Fleet: 7 - includes single-deck bus, coach
Chassis: 1 Bedford. 6 DAF
Bodies: 2 Duple. 1 Optare. 4 Van Hool.
Ops incl: local bus services, school contracts, private hire.
Livery: Red/Ivory/Maroon

*HAYDN'S TOURS & TRAVEL
'BEVERLEY', FIELD HEAD, CHIRK LL14 5PU.
Tel/Fax: 01691 773267
E-mail: christopherwilliams@virgin.net
Ptnrs: M Williams, Chris Williams.
Fleet: 2 coach
Chassis: 1 DAF. 1 Volvo.
Bodies: 1 Duple. 1 Plaxton.
Ops incl: excursions & tours, private hire, school contracts.
Livery: Red/White/Yellow/Orange

*HOWARDS WAY REISEN MINI COACHES
30 GREENFIELDS ESTATE, COEDPOETH, WREXHAM
Tel/Fax: 01978 352470
Prop: W H Howard
Fleet: 2
Chassis/Bodies: 2 Mercedes.
Livery: White with tropical emblem
Ops incl: school contracts, private hire

*JOHN'S TRAVEL
1 BRYN MAELOR, SOUTHSEA LL11 6RD.
Tel/Fax: 01978 753364
Prop: J F H Ithell
Fleet: 4 midibuses
Chassis/bodies: 4 Mercedes
Ops incl: local bus services
Livery: White with red letters

*D. JONES & SON
CLYDFAN, HALL STREET, RHOSLLANERCRUGOG LL14 2LG.
Tel: 01978 842540
Mobile: 07739 206623
Props: D. & G. Jones.
Fleet: 7 - 1 coach, 6 single-deck bus
Fleet: 1 DAF. 4 Dennis. 2 Mercedes.
Bodies: 3 Caetano. 1 Mercedes. 3 Plaxton.
Ops incl: local bus services, school contracts, private hire.
Ops incl: local bus services, private hire
Livery: Blue/Cream.
Ticket system: Wayfarer

*E JONES & SONS
MOUNTAIN VIEW, BANK STREET, PONCIAU LL14 1EN.
Tel: 01978 841613.
Props: J B & G Jones.
Fleet: 7
Livery: Blue/White/Orange.

*PAT'S COACHES
THE BUNGALOW, GAREWEN ROAD, NEW BROUGHTON LL11 1EN
Tel: 01978 720171
Fax: 01978 758459
Props: P C, D K, & J M Davies
Fleet: 14 coach,bus, midibus
Chassis: 3 MAN. 2 Mercedes. 1 Scania. 8 Volvo.
Bodies: 1 Autobus. 2 Berkhof. 2 Jonckheere. 1 Marcopolo. 1 Mercedes. 1 Neoplan. 2 Plaxton. 2 Van Hool.
Ops incl: school contracts, private hire, tours & excursions, continental tours.
Livery: White/Red

*PRICES COACHES
THE HAVEN, BERSHAM ROAD, SOUTHSEA LL11 6TF
Tel/Fax: 01978 756834
Prop: Tecwyn Price
Fleet: 7 - 2 double-deck bus, 4 coach, 1 midibus
Chassis: 2 Leyland. 1 Mercedes. 1 Setra. 3 Volvo.
Bodies: 2 Leyland. 1 Kassbohrer. 1 Mercedes. 2 Plaxton. 1 Van Hool.
Ops incl: school contracts, private hire
Livery: Primrose/Green/Orange

*STRAFFORDS COACHES
UNITS 7/8, FIVE CROSSES INDUSTRIAL ESTATE, MINERA LL11 3RD.
Tel: 01978 756106/752006
Fax: 01978 756106
Props: G A Strafford
Fleet: 12 - 1 double-deck bus, 5 coach, 3 midicoach.
Chassis: 1 Bova. 4 DAF. 1 Iveco. 1 Leyland. 4 Mercedes.
Bodies: 1 Bova. 1 Duple. 1 Iveco. 1 MAN. 4 Mercedes. 1 Plaxton. 2 Van Hool.
Ops incl: school contracts, private hire.
Livery: Cream/Brown/Orange

*T WILLIAMS & SONS
CLARKE STREET BUS GARAGE, PONCIAU LL14 1RT
Tel: 01978 840062.
Prop: J S Williams.
Fleet: 4 coach.
Chassis: 2 Bedford, 1 DAF, 1 Volvo.
Bodies: Duple, Plaxton, Jonckheere.
Ops incl: private hire, school contracts, excursions & tours.
Livery: Blue/Cream.
Ticket System: Setright.

- Air conditioning
- Vehicles suitable for disabled
- Coach(es) with galley facilities
- Coach(es) with toilet facilities
- Seat belt-fitted vehicles
- R Recovery service available (not 24 hr)
- R24 24hr recovery service
- Replacement vehicle available
- T Toilet-drop facilities available
- Vintage vehicle(s) available
- Open top vehicle(s)

CHANNEL ISLANDS

ALDERNEY

RIDUNA BUSES
40C HIGH STREET, ALDERNEY
GY9 3TG
Tel: 01481 823760
Fax: 01481 823030
Prop: A. J. Curtis.
Fleet: 5 - 2 single-deck bus, 2 coach, 1 minibus.
Chassis: 3 Bedford. 1 Freight Rover.
Bodies: 2 Duple. 1 Pennine. 1 Heaver.
Ops incl: local bus services, excursions & tours, private hire.
Livery: Cream/Maroon

GUERNSEY

*ISLAND COACHWAYS LTD
THE TRAMSHEDS, LES BANQUES, ST PETER PORT GY4 6SF
Tel: 01481 720210
Fax: 01481 710109
E-mail: sales@island-coachways.demon.co.uk
Web site: www.island-coachways.demon.co.uk
Man Dir: Mrs Hannah Beacom
Co Sec/Dir: George Boucher

Works Man/Dir: Ben Boucher
Traf Man: John Drillot
Off Man: Mrs Jenny Down
Customer Care Man: Mrs Ann Belben
Fleet: 56 - 38 single-deck bus, 14 coach, 1 midicoach, 3 minibus
Chassis: 1 Cannon. 33 Dennis. 4 Iveco. 9 Leyland. 4 Optare. 4 Renault. 1 Toyota.
Bodies: 1 Caetano. 4 Camo. 33 East Lancs. 3 Elme. 3 Iveco. 2 Leicester. 4 Optare. 6 Wadham Stringer.
Ops incl: local bus services, school contracts, excursions & tours, private hire.
Livery: Bus: Green/Yellow Coach: Cream/Gold
Ticket System: Almex Smartfare.

JERSEY

CONNEX JERSEY
2 CALEDONIA PLACE, WEIGHBRIDGE, ST HELIER JE2 3NG
Tel: 01534 877772
Gen Man: Phillipe Juhles
Fleetname: Connex
Fleet: 33 single-deck buses
Chassis: 33 Dennis
Bodies: 33 Caetano

TANTIVY BLUE COACH TOURS
70/72 LA COLOMBERIE, ST HELIER JE2 4QA
Tel: 01534 706706
Fax: 01534 706705
E-mail: info@jerseycoaches.com
Web site: www.jerseycoaches.com
Man Dir: Mike Cotilard **Ops Dir**: Paul Young
Fleet: 66 - 4 single-deck bus, 60 coach, 2 mdnicoach.
Chassis: 7 Bedford. 3 Cannon. 1 Iveco. 50 Leyland. 2 Optare.
Bodies: 2 Caetano. 6 Carlyle. 7 Duple. 3 Leicester. 2 Optare. 40 Wadham Stringer.
Ops incl: school contracts, excursions & tours, private hire.
Livery: Blue.

WAVERLEY COACHES LTD
UNIT 3, LA COLLETTE, ST HELIER JE2 3NX
Tel: 01534 758360
Fax: 01534 732627
Dir/Gen Man: S. E. Pedersen.
Ch Eng: Peter Evans.
Fleet: 18 - 12 coach, 2 midicoach, 4 minibus.
Chassis: 7 Bedford. 5 Leyland. 2 Mercedes. 1 Renault. 3 VW.
Bodies: 7 Duple. 5 Wadham Stringer. 4 other.
Ops incl: excursions & tours, private hire.
Livery: Yellow/White.

ISLE of MAN

*DOUGLAS CORPORATION TRAMWAY
STRATHALLAN CRESCENT, DOUGLAS IM2 3LD
Tel: 01624 696420
E-mail: pcannon@douglas.org.im
Fleet: tramcars
Ops incl: tram service, private hire.

*ISLE OF MAN TRANSPORT
TRANSPORT HEADQUARTERS, BANKS CIRCUS, DOUGLAS IM1 5PT
Tel: 01624 663366
Fax: 01624 663637
E-mail: info@busandrail.dtl.gov.im
Dir Publ Transp: D R Howard
Fleet:: 109 - 75 double-deck bus, 10 single-deck bus, 24 tram.
Chassis: 33 DAF. 34 Dennis. 18 Leyland.
Bodies: 54 East Lancs. 8 Leyland. 10 Marshall. 10 Northern Counties. 3 Optare.
Ops incl: local bus/tram services, private hirwe
Livery: Red/Cream.
Ticket System: Wayfarer.

*PROTOURS ISLE OF MAN LTD
SUMMERHILL, DOUGLAS IM2 4PF
Tel: 01624 674301
Fax: 01624 675636
Recovery: 01624 674301
Email: toursiom@supanet.com
Chmn: Shaun F Cairns **Dir**: M G Gisbourne, F G Kinnear **Man Dir**: Roy Lightfoot
Traf Man: Dave Bennett
Fleet: 14 - 3 single-deck bus, 5 midicoach, 5 minibus, 1 minicoach.
Chassis: 1 ACE. 12 Bedford. 1 BMC. 1 Bova. 5 DAF. 1 Ford Transit. 4 Iveco. 1 LAG. 3 Leyland. 1 Toyota.
Bodies: 1 Bova. 1 Caetano. 2 Carlyle. 8 Duple. 3 Leicester. 10 Plaxton. 2 Van Hool. 1 Wadham Stringer. 1 BMC. 1 LAG.
Ops incl: local bus services, excursions & tours, private hire, express, continental tours, school contracts.
Livery: White

ISLES OF SCILLY

HERITAGE TOURS
SANTAMANA, 9 RAMS VALLEY,
ST MARY'S TR21 0JX
Tel: 01720 422387
Props: G. Twynham, Mrs P. Twynham.
Fleet: 1 single-deck bus (1948 vehicle).
Chassis: Austin K2. **Body:** Barnard.
Ops incl: excursions & tours, private hire.
Livery: Blue/Cream.

NORTHERN IRELAND

A1 COACH TRAVEL
35 NORBURGH PARK, FOYLE SPRINGS, LONDONDERRY BT48 0RG
Tel/Fax: 028 7130 9323
Prop: J. Bradshaw.
Fleet: 2 midicoach.
Chassis: 1 Mercedes. 1 Renault.
Ops incl: private hire, continental tours, school contracts.

*CHAMBERS COACH HIRE LTD
11 CIRCULAR ROAD, MONEYMORE BT45 7PY
Tel: 028 8674 8152
Fax: 028 8674 8605
E-mail: mail@coachireland.com
Web site: www.coachireland.com
Man Dir: Des Chambers **Dirs**: Mary Chambers, Paul Chambers, Philip Harkness.
Fleet: 46 - 19 coach, 3 double-deck coach, 4 midicoach, 10 midibus, 10 minibus.
Chassis: 3 Iveco. 3 MAN. 23 Mercedes. 17 Scania.
Bodies: 3 Ayats. 17 Irizar. 10 Plaxton. 1 Reeve Burgess. 15 Eurobus.
Ops incl: school contracts, excursions & tours, private hire, express, continental tours.
Livery: Coaches: Yellow with black/silver writing.

DARRAGHS COACHES
22 LISHEEGHAN ROAD, BALLYMONEY BT53 7JY
Tel: 028 2954 0684
Fax: 028 2954 0785
Recovery: 07736 485999
Man: Robert Darragh **Sec**: Kathleen Darragh

*GILES TOURS
63 ABBEYDALE AVENUE, NEWTOWNARDS BT23 8RT
Tel/Fax: 028 9181 1099
E-mail: enquiries@gilestours.co.uk
Fleet: 4 - 3 coach, 1 midicoach.
Chassis/Bodies: includes 1 Mercedes, 3 Van Hool.
Ops incl: excursions & tours, private hire, express, continental tours.

*LAKELAND TOURS
47 MAIN STREET, TEMPO BT94 3LU
Tel: 028 8954 1646
Fax: 028 8954 1424
Recovery: 07779 026597
E-mail: ian@lakelandtours.co.uk
Web site: www.lakelandtours.co.uk
Prop: Ian McCutcheon
Fleet: 5 - 2 coach, 2 midicoach, 1 minicoach.
Chassis: 1 DAF. 2 Leyland. 1 MAN. 1 Mercedes.
Bodies: 1 Mercedes. 1 Noge. 1 Plaxton. 1 Reeve Burgess. 1 Van Hool.
Ops incl: excursions & tours, private hire, school contracts.

*LOGANS EXECUTIVE TRAVEL
58 GALDANAGH ROAD, DUNLOY, BALLYMENA BT44 9DB
Tel: 028 2765 7203
Fax: 028 2765 7559
Web site: www.loganstravel.com
E-mail: coaches@loganstravel.com
Prop: Sean Logan
Fleet: 45 - 23 coach, 15 midicoach, 7 minibus.
Chassis: Mercedes. Volvo.
Ops incl: school contracts, excursions & tours, private hire, continental tours.

LONDONDERRY & LOUGH SWILLY BUS COMPANY LTD
STRAND ROAD, LONDONDERRY BT48 7PY
Fleet: 88 - single-deck bus, coach.
Ops incl: local bus services.

POOTS COACH HIRE LTD
118A PORTADOWN ROAD, TANDRAGEE BT62 2JX
Tel: 028 3884 1504
Fax: 028 3884 1724
Dirs: Jim T Poots, Samuel Poots
Fleet: 6 - 3 coach, 3 midicoach.
Chassis: 1 DAF. 3 Mercedes. 2 Leyland.
Bodies: 3 Plaxton. 3 Reeve Burgess
Ops incl: excursions & tours, private hire, express, school contracts.
Livery: White
Ticket system: Wayfarer

O. ROONEY
4 DANA PLACE, HILLTOWN, NEWRY BT34 5UE
Tel: 028 4063 0825
Fax: 028 4063 8028
Chairperson: Olive Rooney
Co Sec: E. Rooney. **Ops Man**: O. Rooney
Fleet: 10 - 2 double-deck bus, 2 single-deck bus, 4 double-deck coach, 1 midicoach, 1 minibus.
Chassis: 2 Bedford. 1 Bristol. 1 Dennis.
1 Ford. 1 Freight Rover. 4 Leyland.
Bodies: 1 Carlyle. 5 Duple. 3 ECW. 1 Northern Counties.
Ops incl: local bus services, excursions & tours, private hire.
Livery: White with Red/Yellow stripes.

SLOAN TRAVEL
51 KILLOWEN OLD ROAD, ROSTREVOR, NEWRY BT34 3AE
Tel: 028 4173 8459
Fax: 028 4173 9459
Dir/Ch Eng: B. M. Sloan. **Sec**: Ms M. Sloan.
Fleet: 7 - 6 coach, 1 minibus.
Chassis: 4 Bedford. 3 Ford.
Bodies: 2 Duple. 4 Plaxton.
Ops incl: local bus services, school contracts, excursions & tours, private hire, express, continental tours.
Livery: Mixed.

TRANSLINK
CENTRAL STATION, EAST BRIDGE STREET, BELFAST BT1 3PB
Tel: 028 9089 9400
Fax: 028 9089 9401
E-mail: feedback@translink.co.uk
Web site: www.translink.co.uk
Fleetnames: Ulsterbus, Citybus
Chmn: Dr Joan Smyth **Ch Exec**: Keith Moffat **Dir of HR**: Alan Mercer **Dir of Ops**: Philip O'Neil **Fin Dir**: Stephen Armstrong
Mktg Exec: Ciaran Rogan **Head of IT/Projects**: David Laird **Mech Eng Exec**: Malachy McGreedy **Infrastructure Exec**: vacant
Fleet: 1,469 – 20 double-deck bus, 1,274 single-deck bus, 40 coach, 2 double-deck coach, 8 articulated bus, 4 open-top bus, 98 minibus, 23 minicoach.
Chassis: 1 Ayats. 84 Bristol. 10 DAF. 43 Dennis. 819 Leyland.
97 Mercedes. 23 Optare. 5 Renault. 43 Scania. 346 Volvo.
Bodies: 1,023 Alexander. 1 Ayats. 7 Caetano. 4 Duple. 3 ECW. 4 Irizar. 10 Mercedes. 23 Optare. 135 Plaxton. 2 Reeve Burgess. 6 Van Hool. 247 Wright, 6 Other makes.

ULSTERBUS
See Translink

REPUBLIC OF IRELAND

ALLIED COACHES
UNIT 113, GRANGE WAY,
BALDOYLE INDUSTRIAL ESTATE,
BALDOYLE, DUBLIN 13.
Tel: 00 353 1 832 8299, 8300.
Fax: 00 353 1 851 0331.
Prop/Ops Man: J. Nolan.
Ch Eng: J. Hannon. **Sec**: R. Nolan.
Gen Man: J. Healy.
Fleet: 8 - 5 coach, 2 midicoach, 1 minibus.
Chassis: 2 DAF. 1 Leyland. 2 Scania.
Bodies: 2 Jonckheere. Mercedes. 3 Plaxton.
1 Reeve Burgess.
Livery: Black/Red/Cream.

ARAN TOURS LTD
14 LOWER ALBERT ROAD,
SANDYCOVE, Co DUBLIN
Tel: 00 353 1 280 1899
Fax: 00 353 1 280 1799

BARRY'S COACHES LTD
THE GLEN, MAYFIELD, CORK CITY
Tel: 00 353 21 450 5390, 450 1669
(emergencies only)
Fax: 00 353 21 450 9628
Fleet: 15 - 12 coach, 2 minibus,
1 minicoach.
Chassis: 1 AEC. 3 Bedford. 6 Leyland.
2 Mercedes. 2 Volvo.
Bodies: 7 Duple. 1 Jonckheere.
2 Mercedes. 3 Plaxton. 2 Van Hool.
Livery: Blue/White.

BARTON TRANSPORT
STRAFFAN ROAD, MAYNOOTH,
CO KILDARE.
Tel: 00 353 1 628 5688, 628 6338,
628 6026
Fax: 00 353 1 628 6722
E-mail: info@bartons-transport.ie
Web site: www.bartons-transport.ie
Man Dir: P. Barton.
Ch Eng: B. Barton.
Fleet: 35 - 28 coach, 7 minicoach.
Chassis: DAF. Ford. Leyland. Mercedes. Volvo.
Bodies: Plaxton, Van Hool, Moseley. Eurocoach.
Ops incl: express, private hire, excursions & tours
Livery: White/Cream.

RONNIE BRUEN T/A BLUEBIRD COACHES [wc]
72 KILBARRON DRIVE, COOLOCK,
DUBLIN 5.
Tel/Fax: 00 353 1 847 7896.
Dirs: Ronnie Bruen, Keith Bruen.
Fleet: 7 - 3 coach, 2 midicoach, 2 minibus.
Chassis: Ford Transit. Leyland. Mercedes. Volvo.
Bodies: Mercedes. Duple.
Ops incl: private hire, express, school contracts.
Livery: Cream/Red.

BUCKLEY'S TOURS
KILLARNEY, Co KERRY
Tel: 00 353 6431 945
E-mail: buckleys@iol.ie

BURKE BROS (COACHES) LTD [wc]
CLARETUAM, TUAM, Co GALWAY
Tel: 00 353 93 55416
Fax: 00 353 93 55356
Dirs: P .Burke, Ms M. Burke.
Ops Man: P. Steede.
Fleet: 12 - 10 coach, 2 midicoach.
Chassis: Mercedes-Benz, Toyota, Volvo.
Bodies: Caetano, Jonckheere, Plaxton.
Ops incl: local bus services, private hire, continental tours.
Livery: White with Blue/Orange stripes.

*BUS EIREANN
BROADSTONE, DUBLIN 7
Tel: 00 353 1 830 2222
Fax: 00 353 1 830 9377
E-mail: info@buseireann.ie
Web site: www.buseireann.ie
Chmn: John Lynch **Man Dir**: Bill Lilley
Dirs: Treas Honan, Paul Cullen, Anne-Marie Mannix, Gerry Charles, Dick Langford, Katherine Byrne, Jim Hegarty **Ch Op Off**: Tim Hayes **Sec & Fin Man**: Martin Nolan
Ch Eng: Joe Neiland
Fleet: 1,345 - 20 double-deck bus, 789 single-deck bus, 506 coach, 2 open-top bus, 28 minibus.
Chassis: 267 Bombardier/GAC. 163 DAF. 43 Dennis. 3 Iveco. 264 Leyland. 76 Mercedes. 100 Scania. 28 Van Hool. 401Volvo.
Bodies: 46Alexander. 267 Bombardier/GAC. 191 Caetano. 2 CIE. 20 East Lancs. 10 Eurocoach. 31 Hispano. 100 Irizar. 3 Iveco. 15 Leicester. 167 Leyland. 20 Mercedes. 1 Northern Counties. 1 NZMB. 316 Plaxton. 47 Van Hool. 108 Wright.
Ops incl: local bus services, school contracts, excursions & tours, private hire, express.
Livery: White/Red.
Ticket System: Wayfarer.

BUTLERS BUSES
17 BROOKVALE, COBH, Co CORK
Tel/Fax: 00 353 21 811660
E-mail: butlersb@gofree.indigo.ie
Prop: Ian Butler

CAHALANE COACHES
UNIT 6, KILBARRY ENTERPRISE CENTRE, DUBLIN HILL, CORK
Tel: 00 353 21 430 4606
Fax: 00 353 21 430 1200
Fleet: includes 14, 24, 29 and 35-seat coaches

*CALLINAN COACHES LTD
GREGBOY, GLAREGALWAY,
Co GALWAY
Tel: 00 353 91 798324
Fax: 00 353 91 798962
E-mail: info@callinancoaches.ie
Web site: www.callinancoaches.ie
Dir: Thomas Callinan
Fleet: 15 - coach
Chassis: 15 Volvo.
Bodies: 15 Jonckheere.

CARROLL'S COACH HIRE
BALLYMAKENNY ROAD,
DROGHEDA
Tel: 00 353 41 36074.
Props: G. Carroll, P. Caroll (**Man**).
Fleet: 8 coach.
Chassis: Bedford. **Bodies**: Duple.
Ops incl: local bus services, excursions & tours, private hire.
Livery: White.

CLASSIC COACHES
61 HEATHER ROAD, SANDYFORD
INDUSTRIAL ESTATE, FOXROCK,
DUBLIN 18
Tel: 00 353 1 295 2080.
Fax: 00 353 1 295 3982
Fleet: 1 coach

COLLIN'S COACHES
CARRICKAMOSS, Co MONAGHAN
Tel: 00 353 42 9661 631
Fax: 00 353 42 9663 462
E-mail: colcoach@iol.ie

CONWAY COACH AND CHAUFFEUR DRIVE
WILLOW GROVE, REDGATE,
LIMERICK
Tel: 00 353 61 53366
Prop: R. Conway (Gen Man), Val Conway.
Prop/Ch Eng: Patrick Conway. **Prop/Sec**: Audrey Hurley. **Traf Man**: R. Hurley.
Fleet: 11 midicoach.
Livery: White/Red.

COYLES COACHES
GWEEDORE, Co DONEGAL
Tel: 00 353 75 31208.
E-mail: coylescoaches@eircom.net

CRONIN'S COACHES LTD
MALLOW ROAD, CORK
Tel: 00 353 21 430 9090
Fax: 00 353 21 430 5508
Email: cork@croninscoaches.com.
Web Site: www.croninscoaches.com.
Dirs: D. & Joan Cronin. **Ch Eng**: Niall

A/c	Air conditioning
[disabled]	Vehicles suitable for disabled
[galley]	Coach(es) with galley facilities
wc	Coach(es) with toilet facilities
[seat belt]	Seat belt-fitted vehicles
R	Recovery service available (not 24 hr)
R24	24hr recovery service
✓	Replacement vehicle available
T	Toilet-drop facilities available
[vintage]	Vintage vehicle(s) available
[open top]	Open top vehicle(s)

Cronin. **Gen Man**: Nora Cronin.
Fleet: 50 - 47 coach, 3 midicoach.
Chassis: DAF. Leyland. Volvo.
Bodies: Van Hool
Livery: White with red flash.

CROSSON TRUCK & BUS LTD
UNIT 10/12 NEWTOWN INDUSTRIAL ESTATE, COOLOCK, DUBLIN 17
Tel: 00 353 1 848 5811
Fax: 00 353 1 848 5721
Fleetname: Crosson Coaches.
Chmn: S. Crosson. **Man Dir**: A. Kennedy.
Dirs: J. O'Reilly, B. Cullen, S. Crosson.
Fleet: 1 midicoach.
Chassis: Mercedes. **Body**: Euro Coach.
Ops incl: private hire, continental tours.
Livery: White
Main dealer for Mercedes.
Service dealer for Van Hool ZF.

DERO'S COACH TOURS
R24
22 MAIN STREET, KILLARNEY, Co KERRY
Tel: 00 353 64 31251
Fax: 00 353 64 34077
Email: deroscoachtours@eircom.net.
Web site: www.derostours.com
Prop: Ms E. O'Sullivan Quille. **Sales Dir**: Ms C. O'Sullivan, D O'Sullivan.
Fleet: 18 - 12 coach, 4 midicoach, 2 minicoach.
Chassis: 10 DAF. 6 Mercedes. 2 Volvo.
Livery: White with multi red/Silver/Red/Orange.
Relief drivers and guiding agency also.

JIMMY DONNELLY & SON
46 IRISH STREET, ENNISCORTHY, Co WEXFORD.
Tel: 00 353 54 33956
Fleet: 7 - 5 coach, 2 minibus

SEAN DONNELLY
MAIN STREET, GRANARD, Co LONGFORD
Tel: 00 353 43 86540
Fleetname: Pioneer Bus Service
Prop: Sean Donnelly.
Fleet: 20 – 3 single deck bus, 17 coach.
Chassis: Leyland, Leyland National, Scania.
Bodies: Leyland National, Plaxton, Van Hool.

DONOVAN'S COACH HIRE
HEADFORD, KILLARNEY, Co KERRY
Tel: 00 353 64 54041.
Fax: 00 353 64 54041
Props: Joe & Maureen Donovan.
Fleet: 8 - 5 coach, 2 midicoach, 1 minibus.
Chassis: 1 Ford Transit. 3 LDV. 2 Mercedes. 2 Volvo.
Bodies: 2 Jonckheere. 1 Duple. 2 Mercedes. 1 Plaxton.
Ops incl: school contracts, excursions & tours, private hire.

P. DOYLE LTD
ROUNDWOOD, Co WICKLOW
Tel: 00 353 1 281 8119
Fleetname: St Kevins Bus Service.
Prop/Traf Man: P. Doyle.
Gen Man/Ch Eng: J. Doyle.

Sec: John Doyle.
Fleet: 5 single-deck bus.
Chassis: 5 Leyland.
Bodies: 1 Plaxton. 4 others.
Livery: Blue/Cream.
Ticket System: Setright.

*TONY DOYLE COACHES
BALLYORNEY, ENNISKERRY, Co WICKLOW
Tel: 00 353 1 286 7427
Fax: 00 353 1 286 7427
Email: info@tonydoyle.com
Web site: www.tonydoyle.com
Dir: Tony Doyle **Co Sec**: Margaret Doyle
Fleet: 12 - 9 coach, 2 midicoach, 1 minicoach.
Chassis: 3 DAF. 1 Iveco. 4 MAN. 3 Scania.
Bodies: 2 Duple. 3 Irizar. 2 Noge. 1 Plaxton. 3 Indcar.
Ops incl: school contracts, excursions & tours, private hire

DUALWAY COACHES LTD
R24
KEATINGS PARK, RATHCOOLE, Co DUBLIN
Tel: 00 353 1 458 0054
Fax: 00 353 1 458 0808
E-mail: info@dualwaycoaches.com
Web site: www.dualwaycoaches.com
Dirs: Anthony McConn, Mary McConn
Fleet: 42 - 8 double-deck bus, 19 open-top double-deck bus, 2 single-deck bus, 5 coach, 1 midicoach, 7 minibus.

DUBLIN BUS (BUS ATHA CLIATH)
59 UPPER O'CONNELL STREET, DUBLIN 1.
Tel: 00 353 1 872 0000.
Fax: 00 353 1 873 1195.
Email: info@dublinbus.ie
Web site: www.dublinbus.ie
Dirs: Michael Faherty, William McCamley, Susan Spence, David Egan. **Man HR**: Gerry Maguire. **Man Bus Dev**: Paddy Doherty.
Ch Eng: Shane Doyle. **Man Fin & Co Sec**: Katrina Murphy. **Network Serv Man**: Michael Mathews.
Fleet: 1,103 - 774 double-deck bus, 155 single-deck bus, 20 midibus, 20 articulated bus, 134 minibus.
Chassis: 110 DAF, 169 Leyland, 134 Mercedes, 690 Volvo.
Bodies: 887 Alexander, 30 Leicester, 41 Plaxton, 61 Wright, 84 Eurocoach,
Ops incl: local bus services.
Livery: Blue/Cream with orange stripe. City Imp (minibuses): Red/White/Yellow. 'Cityswift' - double- & single-deckers: Grey-Blue-White-Orange.

*DUBLIN MINI COACHES
WASDALE HOUSE, 14 CAMAC PARK, OLD NAAS ROAD, DUBLIN 12
Tel: 00 353 86 1780049
Fax: 00 353 1 696 1001
Email: info.dmc@o2.ie
Web site: www.dublinminicoaches.com
Man Dir: Stephen Millar
Fleet: 8 - 1 midicoach, 7 minicoach.
Chassis: 5 Mercedes. 2 Renault. 1 Toyota.

Bodies: 8 other.
Ops incl: excursions & tours, private hire.
Livery: Turquoise

EIREBUS LTD
CORDUFF ROAD, BLANCHARDSTOWN, DUBLIN 15
Tel: 00 353 1 824 2626
Fax: 00 353 1 824 2267
E-mail: eirebus@iol.ie
Man Dir: Jimmy Kelly **Tran Man**: Derek Graham **Ops Man**: Christine Ryan
Fleet: 49 - 5 single-deck bus, 38 coach, 6 minicoach

ENFIELD COACHES LTD
RATHCORE, ENFIELD, Co MEATH
Tel: 353 (01) 824 2626
Fleet: 3 - 1 coach, 3 minibus

FAHERTY'S COACH HIRE
DRUMONEY, MOYCULLEN, Co GALWAY
Tel: 00 353 91 85228
Fleet: 5 - 4 coach, 1 minicoach

FINEGAN COACH HIRE
29 MAIN STREET, CARRICKMACROSS, Co MONAGHAN
Tel: 00 353 42 61313
Fleet: 7 - 5 coach, 1 midicoach, 1 minibus

EUGENE FINNEGAN (TRANSPORT) LTD
OLD COURT INDUSTRIAL ESTATE, BOGHALL ROAD, BRAY, CO WICKLOW
Tel: 00 353 1 286 0061
Fax: 00 353 1 286 8121
E-mail: finnegan-bray@oceanfree.net
Web site: www.bray.ie
Fleet: 16 - 3 double-deck bus, 2 double-deck coach, 3 coach, 2 midicoach, 2 midibus, 5 minibus.
Ops incl: local bus services.

TOM FOX
MONAGHAN ROAD, ROCKCORRY, Co MONAGHAN
Tel: 00 353 42 42284
Fleet: 2 coach

MARTIN FUREY COACHES LTD
MILLTOWN, DRUMCLIFFE, Co SLIGO
Tel: 00 353 71 63092
Fleet: 5 - 3 coach, 2 minibus

GALVINS COACHES
R24
MAIN STREET, DUNMANWAY, Co CORK
Tel: 00 353 23 45125
Fax: 00 353 23 45407
Dir: R. E. Galvin
Chassis: Ford. Ford Transit. Leyland National. Scania. Volvo.
Bodies: Leyland National. Mercedes. Plaxton. Van Hool. Willowbrook. Duple.
Fleet: single-deck bus, coach, double-deck coach, midibus, midicoach.

*GLYNNS COACH HIRE (ENNIS) LTD

KNOCKADERRY, TULLA ROAD, ENNIS, CO CLARE
Tel: 00 353 65 682 8234
Fax: 00 353 65 684 0678
Recovery: 00 353 8625 97037
Email: info@glynnscoaches.com
Web site: www.glynnscoaches.com
Fleetname: Glynns of Ennis
Chmn: Jackie Cronin. **Sec:** Niamh Cronin.
Fleet: 14 - 5 coach, 4 midicoach, 2 minibus, 3 minicoach.
Chassis: 1 DAF. 1 Iveco. 3 MAN. 5 Mercedes. 1 Setra. 3 Volvo.
Bodies: 1 Ikarus. 3 Indcar. 5 Mercedes. 1 Noge. 2 Plaxton. 1 Setra. 1 Euro.

JAMES GLYNN

GRAIGUE NA SPIDOGUE (POST GRAIGUECULLEN), NURNEY
Tel: 00 353 503 46616
Prop/Gen Man/Traf Man: J. Glynn
Prop/Ch Eng: A. Glynn **Prop/Sec:** Mrs J. Glynn.
Fleet: 4 - 3 single-deck bus, 1 coach.
Livery: Cream/Blue.

GRAYLINE TOURS

THE MALT HOUSE, GRAND CANAL QUAY, DUBLIN 2
Tel: 00 353 1 670 8822
Fax: 00 353 1 670 8731
E-mail: grayline@tlp.ie
Also at DUBLIN TOURIST CENTRE, SUFFOLK, DUBLIN 2
Tel: 00 353 1 605 7705

A. HALPENNY

ASHVILLE, THE SQUARE, BLACKROCK, DUNDALK
Tel: 00 353 42 21608
Fleetname: Violet Bus Service.
Man Dir: John Halpenny
Fleet: 10 - 2 double-deck bus, 2 single-deck bus, 8 coach
Chassis: 10 Volvo.
Bodies: include 1 Sunsundegui
Ops incl: local bus services, private hire, continental tours.
Livery: Red/White/Yellow

HEALY COACHES

CASTLEGAR, GALWAY
Tel: 00 353 91 770066
Fax: 00 353 91 753335
Web site: www.healybus.com
Email: healybus@iol.ie.
Prop: Michael Healy
Fleet: 13 - 2 single-deck bus, 8 coach, 1 open-top bus, 2 midicoach
Chassis: 6 Leyland. 1 MAN. 1 Mercedes. 4 Volvo.
Bodies: 2 Alexander. 1 Duple. 1 ECW. 2 Ikarus. 2 Leyland. 1 Mellor. 1 Noge. 2 Plaxton.

M. HOGAN

LIBERTY STREET, THURLES, Co TIPPERARY
Tel: 00 353 50 421622
Fleetname: Shamrock Bus Service.
Prop/Gen Man: M. Hogan.
Ch Eng: T. Maher. **Sec:** J. Maher.
Fleet: 2 coach.
Livery: Cream/Orange.
Ticket System: Setright.

IRELAND COACHES

COOLQUAY, THE WARD, Co DUBLIN
Tel: 00 353 1 835 2714
Fax: 00 353 1 835 2715
E-mail: irelandcoaches@eircom.net
Fleet: 30 coaches, midicoaches, minicoaches

IRISH COACHES

ULSTER BANK CHAMBERS, 2-4 LOWER O'CONNELL STREET, DUBLIN
Tel: 00 353 1 878 8894/8898
Fax: 00 353 1 878 8916
E-mail: sales@irishcoaches.ie
Web site: www.irishcoaches.ie
Man Dir: Donal Hughes **Assist Man:** Sandra Hutchin **Ops Man:** William Hewitt
Fleet: 9 - 3 coaches, 3 midicoach, 1 minicoach
Chassis: 3 DAF. 3 MAN. 1 Mercedes. 1 Toyota. 2 Volvo
Bodies: include: 1 Caetano. 1 Mercedes. 3 Plaxton. 1 Smit. 2 Indcar.
Ops incl: excursions & tours, private hire

DONAL JOYCE MINIBUS HIRE

GENTIAN HILL HOUSE, KNOCKNACARRA, Co GALWAY
Tel: 00 353 91 521427
Fax: 00 353 91 52 4284
Fleet: 8 -2 minicoaches,8 midibus
Ops incl: excursions & tours, private hire

BERNARD KAVANAGH & SONS LTD

BRIDGE GARAGE, URLINGFORD, Co KILKENNY
Tel: 00 353 56 31189
Fax: 00 353 56 31314
Email: info@bkavcoaches.com.
Web Site: www.bkavcoaches.com.
Joint Man Dirs: Thomas Kavanagh, Patrick Kavanagh
Fleet: 93 - 2 double-deck bus, 1 single-deck bus, 89 coach, 1 double-deck coach.
Chassis: 3 MAN. 2 Mercedes. 40 Scania. 10 Volvo, 4 other.
Bodies: 1 Berkhof. 1 Ikarus. 2 Jonckheere. 1 Mercedes. 2 Plaxton. 2 Setra. 45 Van Hool. 5 other.

J J KAVANAGH & SONS

MAIN STREET, URLINGFORD
Tel: 00 353 56 31106
Fax: 00 353 56 31106
E-mail: info@jjkavanagh.ie
Web site: www.jjkavanagh.ie
Joint Man Dir/Fin Cont: J. J. Kavanagh
Joint Man Dir/Ops Man: Paul Kavanagh
Maintenance Man: Edward Scully
Fleet: 38 - 1 double-deck bus, 36 coach, 1 open-top bus
Chassis: 6 MAN. 25 Setra. 45 Volvo.
Bodies: 15 Caetano. 2 Leyland. 4 Mercedes. 2 Northern Counties. 20 Plaxton. 25 Setra. 7 Van Hool. 1 Wright.
Ops incl: local bus services

M. KAVANAGH

LIMERICK ROAD, TIPPERARY
Tel: 00 353 62 51563
Fax: 00 353 62 51593
E-mail: mattkavanagh3@aol.net
Fleet: 19 - 12 coaches, 5 single-deck bus, 2 minibus.

PIERCE KAVANAGH COACHES

CHURCH VIEW, URLINGFORD, CO KILKENNY
Tel: 00 353 56 31213
Fax: 00 353 56 31599
E-mail: info@kavanaghscoaches.com
Web site: www.kavanaghscoaches.com
Dirs: Pierce Kavanagh, John Kavanagh **Ch Eng:** John Kenny
Co Sec: Jim Bannon
Fleet: 20 - 1 single-deck bus, 18 coach, 1 midicoach.
Chassis: 1 Bova. 1 DAF. 2 Ford. 5 Ford Transit. 4 Leyland. 5 MAN. 1 Mercedes. 3 Scania. 2 Volvo

KEENAN COMMERCIALS LTD

BELLURGAN, DUNDALK, CO LOUTH
Tel: 00 353 42 937 1405
Fax: 00 353 42 937 1893
Fleetname: Anchor Coaches
Man Dir: Seamus Keenan
Fleet: 17 - 8 single-deck bus, 7 coach, 2 minibus.

KENNEALLY'S BUS SERVICE LTD

BLENHEIM, WATERFORD
Tel: 00 353 51 872777
Fax: 00 353 51 872770
Joint Man Dirs: J J Kavanagh, Paul Kavanagh **Tran Man:** Tony Crean
Ops Man: Michael Ryan
Fleet: 27 - 6 double-deck bus, 3 single-deck

Air conditioning	Replacement vehicle available
Vehicles suitable for disabled	Toilet-drop facilities available
Coach(es) with galley facilities	Vintage vehicle(s) available
Coach(es) with toilet facilities	Open top vehicle(s)
Seat belt-fitted vehicles	
Recovery service available (not 24 hr)	
R24 24hr recovery service	

bus, 18 coach
Chassis: 1 AEC. 2 Leyland. 5 MAN. 15 Setra. 30 Volvo.
Bodies: 4 Alexander. 5 Caetano. 4 Northern Counties. 15 Setra. 10 Van Hool. 1 Wright.
Ops incl: local bus services, excursions & tours, private hire, express, continental tours.
Livery: Green/Blue/Red on White
Subsidiary of J J Kavanagh, Urlingford

KENNEDY COACHES
ANNASCAUL, TRALEE, Co KERRY
Tel: 00 353 66 91 57106
Fax: 00 353 66 91 57327
Fleet: 5 - 3 double-deck bus, 3 minibus

K. M. KEOGH
39A WEXFORD ROAD, ARKLOW
Tel: 00 353 40 22560
Fleet: 4 coach

KERRY COACHES LTD
INISFALLEN, 15 MAIN STREET, KILLARNEY, Co KERRY.
Tel: 00 353 64 31945
Fax: 00 353 64 31903
Email: buckleys@iol.ie
Web site: www.kerrycoaches.com
Fleetnames: Buckley Tours, Kerry Tours
Man Dir: M Buckley
Fleet: 19 - 14 coach, 2 midicoach, 3 minibus.

DAVE LONG COACH TRAVEL
CURRAGH, SKIBBEREEN
Tel: 00 353 28 21138
Fleet: 1 coach

LESCLACHA LTD
28 AVONDALE, NEWMARKET-ON-FERGUS
Tel: 00 353 61 71233
Fleetname: Lovetts Coaches
Fleet: 9 - 1 single-deck bus, 6 coach, 1 midibus, 1 minibus.
Chassis: Leyland.

LUAS
RAILWAY PROCUREMENT AGENCY, PARKGATE BUSINESS CENTRE, PARKGATE STREET, DUBLIN 8
Tel: 00 353 1 646 3400
Web site: www.luas.ie
Man, Strategic Planning/PR: Ger Hannon
Fleet: 40 tram
Chassis/bodies: Alstom Citadis
Ops: tram service

P. J. McCONNON
GREENLEE, CLONES ROAD, MONAGHAN
Tel: 00 353 47 82020
Fleet: 4 coaches
Chassis: Volvo
Bodies: Plaxton

JAMES McGEE (BUSES)
BALLINA MAIN ROAD, FALCARRAGH, LETTERKENNY
Tel: 00 353 74 35174
Fleet: 8 minibus.
Chassis: 1 Ford. 3 Toyota.
Ops incl: private hire.
Livery: White

*JOHN McGINLEY COACH TRAVEL
MAGHEERCARTY, GORTAHEEK, LETTERKENNY, Co DONEGAL
Tel: 00 353 7491 35201
Fax: 00 353 7491 35960
E-mail: info@jchhmcginley.com
Web site: www.jchhmcginley.com
Prop: James McGinley
Fleet: 14 - 8 coach, 2 midicoach, 4 minibus.
Chassis: 3 Ford Transit. 2 Mercedes. 8 Volvo.
Ops incl: local bus services, excursions & tours, private hire, express, continental tours.
Livery: Blue/Orange on White

GERALD MANNING
CASTLE ROAD, CROOM, LIMERICK
Tel: 00 353 61 88311
E-mail: gmanning@indigo.ie
Fleet: 13 - 10 coach, 2 minibus, 1 midibus.

ALAN MARTIN COACHES
1 KIRKFIELD COTTAGE, CLONSILLA, DUBLIN 15
Tel: 00 353 1 835 1560
Fax: 00 353 1 835 1816
Dirs: A. Martin, B. C. Martin. **Ch Eng**: M. Reilly. **Traf Man**: M. Clarke.
Fleet: 8 - 6 single-deck bus, 1 double-deck bus, 1 minibus.
Chassis: 6 Ford. 2 Leyland. 4 MAN. 2 Mercedes. 3 Scania. 2 Toyota. 5 Volvo.
Ops incl: local bus services, school contracts, excursions & tours, private hire, express.
Livery: White with two Blue stripes.

MARTIN'S COACHES (CAVAN) LTD
CORRATILLION, CORLOUGH, BELTURBET, Co CAVAN
Tel: 00 353 49 26222
Fax: 00 353 49 23116
E-mail: jimmartin@eircom.net
Dir: James G Martin
Fleet: 16 - 5 coach, 4 midicoach, 7 minibus.
Chassis: 5 DAF. 7 Ford Transit. 3 Mercedes. 1 Toyota.
Bodies: 4 Bova. 2 Caetano. 3 Mercedes.

MD COACH HIRE
25 TARA LAWN, THE DONAHIES, RAHENY, DUBLIN 13
Tel/Fax: 00 353 1 847 9591
Prop: Michael Dunne.

MICHAEL MEERE COACH HIRE
33 CHURCH DRIVE, CLARECASTLE, ENNIS, Co CLARE
Tel: 00 353 65 682 4833
Fax: 00 353 65 684 4544
E-mail: michaelmeere@clarelive.com

MIDLAND BUS CO LTD
LOUGHNASKIN, ATHLONE
Tel: 00 353 90 22427
Dir/Gen Man: N. Henry
Fleet: 14 coach
Chassis: Leyland, Volvo, Mercedes.
Ops incl: local bus services, excursions & tours.

JOE MORONEY
HERMITAGE, ENNIS, Co CLARE.
Tel: 00 353 66 824146
Fax: 00 353 65 686 9480
E-mail: mcoachesennis@eire.com
Fleet: 7 - 1 double-deck coach, 1 coach

MORTON'S COACHES DUBLIN
TAYLORS LANE, BALLYBODEN, DUBLIN 16
Tel: 00 353 1 494 4927
Fax: 00 353 1 494 4694
E-mail: mortonscoaches@clubi.ie, info@circlelinebus.com
Fleet: Circle Line Bus Co
Prop: Paul Morton.
Fleet: 13 - 1 double-deck bus, 3 single-deck bus, 6 coach, 3 double-deck coach
Chassis: 1 Ayats. 6 DAF. 6 Mercedes. 10 Volvo.
Bodies: 1 Ayats. 4 East Lancs. 6 Mercedes. 1 Ovi.
Ops incl: local bus services, school contracts, excursions & tours, private hire, continental tours.
Livery: White

THOMAS MURPHY & SONS
KILBRIDE HOUSE, KILBRIDE LANE, BRAY, Co WICKLOW
Tel: 00 353 1 286 2471
Fleet: 11 - 8 coach, 1 minibus, 2 minicoach.
Chassis: Volvo, Mercedes, Scania.

NAUGHTON COACH TOURS
SHANAGURRANE, SPIDDAL, Co GALWAY
Tel: 00 353 91 553188
Fax: 00 353 91 553302
E-mail: naugtour@iol.i.e
Web site: www.wombat.ie/pages/oneachtain-tours
Dir: Steve Naughton **Dir/Sec**: Maureen Naughton
Fleet: 8 - 5 coach, 1 double-deck bus, 2 midicoach.
Chassis: 1 Daimler. 1 MAN. 3 Mercedes. 1 Toyota. 2 Volvo
Bodies: 1 Caetano. 1 Jonckheere. 1 Leyland. 2 Plaxton.
Ops incl: excursions & tours, private hire

NESTORBUS LTD, GALWAY & DUBLIN
TURLOUGHMORE, ATHENRY, Co GALWAY
Tel: 00 353 91 797144, 00 353 1 832 0094
Fax: 00 353 91 797244
E-mail: busnestor@eircom.net
Web Site: www.busnestor.galway.net
Prop: P. Nestor.
Fleet: 9 - 8 coach, 1 double-deck coach.
Chassis: 8 Mercedes. 1 Setra.
Ops incl: excursions & tours, private hire, express, continental tours.
Livery: Red/Cream

NOLAN COACHES
19 CLONSHAUGH LAWN,
COOLOCK, DUBLIN 17
Tel: 00 353 1 847 3487
Mobile: 0862 592000
Prop: David Nolan
Fleet: 1 coach
Ops incl: school contracts, private hire.

O'CONNELL COACHES
PROTUMNA ROAD, BALLINASLOE
Tel: 00 353 905 43339
Prop: J. O'Connell
Fleet: 5 coach
Chassis: Ford. **Bodies:** Plaxton
Ops incl: private hire.

O'CONNOR AUTOTOURS LTD wc R R24 T
ROSS ROAD, KILLARNEY
Tel: 00 353 64 31052
Fax: 00 353 64 31703
Dir/Gen Man: B. O'Connor.
Ch Eng: R. Downing. **Sec:** C. Enright.
Traf Man: D. Fenton
Fleet: 5 - 1 midibus, 4 minicoach.
Chassis: Leyland. Mercedes. Volvo.
Bodies: Reeve Burgess. Van Hool. Euro.
Ops incl: excursions & tours, private hire.
Livery: Maroon/Yellow.

TOM O'CONNOR
CLOGHANE, TRALEE, Co KERRY
Tel: 00 353 66 713 8140

FEDA O'DONNELL COACHES
RANAFAST, Co DONEGAL
Tel/Fax: 00 353 75 48114
Prop: Pat O'Flaherty.
Fleet: 13 - 9 coach, 2 minibus, 2 minicoach.
Ops incl: express

O'FLAHERTY TRANSPORT LTD
LISDOONVARNA, Co CLARE
Tel/Fax: 00 353 65 74117.
Fleet: 1 midicoach.
Prop: Pat O'Flaherty

*LARRY O'HARA
13 SKIBBEREEN LAWN,
WATERFORD CITY
Tel: 00 353 51 372232
Fax: 00 353 51 357566
E-mail: larryohara@eircom.net
Fleetname: O'Hara Autotours
Props: Larry O'Hara, Helen O'Hara
Fleet: 6 - 2 midicoach, 2 minibus, 2 minicoach.
Chassis/Bodies: 1 Ford Transit. Mercedes.

O'MALLEY COACHES wc
FOILDARRIG, NEWPORT,
Co TIPPERARY
Tel: 00 353 61 378119

Fax: 00 353 61 378002
Owner: E. O'Malley
Fleet: 16 - 2 single-deck bus, 9 coach, 2 midibus, 2 midicoach, 1 minibus.
Ops incl: local bus services, school contracts, excursions & tours, private hire, express.
Livery: Blue/White.

O'S COACHES
LOWER HOUSE GARAGE,
HOSPITAL, Co LIMERICK
Tel: 00 353 61 383 222
Fax: 00 353 61 383 525
E-mail: oscoaches@eircom.net
Prop: Sean F. O'Sullivan **Ch Eng:** Patrick J. Leahy.
Fleet: 12 - 5 double-deck bus, 5 single-deck bus, 2 coach.

O'SULLIVANS COACHES wc
FARRAHY ROAD, KILDORRERY,
MALLOW, Co CORK
Tel: 00 353 22 25185
Fax: 00 353 22 25731
Prop: C O'Sullivan
Fleet: 12 - 9 coach, 3 midicoach.
Chassis: 2 Bedford. 1 Ford Transit. 1 Leyland. 2 Mercedes. 4 Volvo.
Bodies: 1 Duple. 3 Plaxton. 3 Van Hool. 3 Van Conversions.

JACKY POWER TOURS
2 LOWER ROCK STREET, TRALEE,
Co KERRY
Tel: 00 353 66 713 6300
Fax: 00 353 66 712 9444
Fleet: 7 - 5 midicoach, 2 midibus.

JOHN ROSS
97 SLIAGH BREAGH,
PEPPERSTOWN, ARDEE,
Co LOUTH
Tel: 00 353 41 53158
Fleet: 8 - 3 coach, 2 midicoach, 2 minibus, 1 midibus

*ROVER COACHES wc Ac R24 T
LYNN ROAD, MULLINGAR,
Co WESTMEATH
Tel: 00 353 44 40825
Fax: 00 353 44 42280
Recovery: 086 2571645
E-mail: pobrien@pobrien.ie
Man: Patrick O'Brien **Asst Man:** John Farrell **Eng:** Edwin Craig
Fleet: 14 - 7 coach, 3 midibus, 2 midicoach, 2 minicoach.
Chassis: 1 DAF. 2 Ford Transit. 1 MAN. 1 Mercedes. 1 Renault. 5 Volvo.
Bodies: 1 Mercedes. 5 Plaxton. 1 Van Hool.

JOHN RUMLEY
BALLYNOE, TALLOW, Co CORK
Tel: 00 353 58 59148
Fleet: 2 - 1 minicoach, 1 minibus

SEALANDAIR COACHING (IRELAND) LTD
51 MIDDLE ABBEY STREET,
DUBLIN 1
Tel: 00 353 1 873 3411
Fax: 00 353 1 873 2639
E-mail: info@pabtours.com
Web site: www.pabtours.com
Fleetname: PAB Tours
Man Dir: Anthony Kelly
Fleet: 5 coach
Chassis: Leyland
Bodies: Duple

MATT SHANAHAN COACHES
ST MARTINS, LACKEN ROAD,
KILBARRY, WATERFORD
Tel: 00 353 51 74192
Fleet: 2 - single-deck bus

ST KEVINS BUS SERVICE
See P Doyle, above

*SUIRWAY BUS & COACH SERVICES LTD
PASSAGE EAST, Co WATERFORD
Tel: 00 353 51 382209
Fax: 00 353 51 382676
E-mail: suirway@eircom.net
Web site: www.suirway.com
Dir: Brian Lynch
Fleet: 20 - 5 single-deck bus, 15 coach.
Chassis: 1 Leyland. 5 Transbus. 14 Volvo.
Bodies: 1 Duple. 4 Jonckheere. 5 Transbus. 10 Van Hool.
Ops incl: local bus services, excursions & tours, private hire.
Livery: White/Red

TREACY COACHES
ERRIGAL, KILLALA ROAD, BALLINA,
Co MAYO
Tel: 00 353 96 22563
Fax: 00 353 96 70968
E-mail: treacycoaches@eipcom.net
Dirs: A. Treacy (Gen Man). **Sec:** M. Treacy.
Fleet: 8 - 1 minibus, 7 coach.
Ops incl: excursions & tours, private hire, express.
Livery: White/Blue.

Ac	Air conditioning
	Vehicles suitable for disabled
	Coach(es) with galley facilities
wc	Coach(es) with toilet facilities
	Seat belt-fitted vehicles
R	Recovery service available (not 24 hr)
R24	24hr recovery service
	Replacement vehicle available
T	Toilet-drop facilities available
	Vintage vehicle(s) available
	Open top vehicle(s)

SECTION 5

Indices

TRADE INDEX

Several of the traders listed in this index will have more than one entry; only the first is shown here in each case.

A

ABACUS TUBULAR PRODUCTS LTD	29
ABBOT BROWN & SONS LTD	16
AC IS	40
ACTIA UK Ltd	23
AD COACH SALES	12
ADGROUP - ADBUS	30
ADG TRANSPORT CONSULTANTS	43
ADVANCED VEHICLE BUILDERS	11
AFTERMARKET COACH SUPPLIES (UK) LTD	15
AIRCONCO	15
AIR DOOR SERVICES	21
AJP COMMERCIALS	12
AKM TECHSERVICES	43
ALBION AUTOMOTIVE LTD	22
ALEXANDER DENNIS	8
ALLEN & DOUGLAS CORPORATE CLOTHING LTD	41
ALLISON TRANSMISSION	29
ALMEX INFORMATION SYSTEMS	38
ALSTOM TRANSPORT	9
ALTRO TRANSFLOOR	27
AMA LTD	15
AP BORG & BECK / AP LOCKHEED - see Automotive Products	
ARDEE COACH TRIM LTD	34
ARRIVA BUS AND COACH	12
ARVIN MERITOR	17
ASHLEY BANKS LTD	17
ATKINS	45
ATLAS LIGHTING COMPONENTS	31
ATLANTIS INTERNATIONAL	28
ATOS ORIGIN	38
AUSTIN ANALYTICS	43
AUTOMATE WHEEL COVERS	27
AUTOMOTIVE PRODUCTS GROUP LTD	17
AUTOMOTIVE TEXTILE INDUSTRIES LTD	27
AUTOPRO SOFTWARE UK	44
AUTOSOUND LTD	15
AVENTA	44
AVONDALE INTERNATIONAL LTD	12
AVS STEPS	16
AVT SYSTEMS	15
AYATS (GB) LTD	8

B

BABTIE GROUP LTD	45
IAN BALDRY	45
BALFOUR BEATTY RAIL PLANT LTD	40
BANK OF SCOTLAND	47
BARNWELL SERVICES	32
BARRONS CHARTERED ACCOUNTANTS	43
BASE	12
BBA FRICTION LTD	17
BELMONT INTERNATIONAL LTD	47
BEMROSEBOOTH LTD	38
BEST IMPRESSIONS	30
M. BISSELL DISPLAY	38
BLACKPOOL COACH SERVICES	17
BLACKPOOL TRIM SHOPS LTD	35
BLYTHSWOOD MOTORS LTD	12
BMC UK	8
BOMBARDIER TRANSPORTATION	9
CHRIS BORLAND & ASSOCIATES	43
BOTEL LTD	50
BOVA	8
BRADTECH LTD	22
BRECKNELL WILLIS	40
BRIAN NOONE	12
BRIDGE OF WEIR LEATHER CO LTD	41
BRIGADE ELECTRONICS	34
BRIGHT-TECH DEVELOPMENTS	20
BRISTOL BUS & COACH SALES	12
BRISTOL ELECTRIC RAILBUS	40
BRITANNIA ROLL/TICKETMEDIA	38
BRITAX PMG LTD	22
BRITISH BUS PUBLISHING	50
BRITISH BUS SALES	12
BRITTANY FERRIES	46
BROADWATER MOULDINGS LTD	38
DAVID BROWN VEHICLE TRANSMISSIONS LTD	29
BROXWOOD VEHICLE SPECIALISTS	15
BRT BEARINGS LTD	33
COLIN BUCHANAN & PARTNERS	43
BULWARK BUS & COACH ENGINEERING LTD	17
BUS & COACH BUYER	50
BUS & COACH PRESERVATION	50
BUS & COACH PROFESSIONAL	50
BUSES	50
BUS USER	50
BUSS BIZZ	20
BUZZLINES	44

C

SALVADOR CAETANO (UK) LTD	10
CALEDONIAN MACBRAYNE LTD	46
CALOTELS HOTELS	47
CANN PRINT	38
CAPOCO DESIGN	43
CAREYBROOK LTD	45
CARLYLE BUS & COACH LTD	17
CARRIER SUTRAK	15
CENTAUR FUEL MANAGEMENT	28

CHASSIS DEVELOPMENTS	33
CI COACHLINES	50
CIE TOURS INTERNATIONAL	46
CLAN TOOLS & PLANT LTD	34
CLAYTON HEATERS LTD	15
COACH-AID	20
COACH & BUS	47
COACH & BUS WEEK	47
COACH CARPETS	27
COACH DISPLAYS LTD	47
COACH DIRECT	11
COACHFINDER LIMITED	44
COGENT PASSENGER SEATING LTD	35
COLDCARE	15
COLIN BUCHANAN & PARTNERS	43
COMMERCIAL EXHAUSTS	25
CONCEPT COACHCRAFT	11
CONDOR FERRIES	46
CONSERVE UK LTD	15
COOPERS COACH SALES	12
CRAIG TILSLEY & SON LTD	24
CREATIVE MANAGEMENT DEVELOPMENT	51
CRESCENT FACILITIES LTD	25
CREST COACH CONVERSIONS	11
CREWE ENGINES	24
CRONER CCH GROUP LTD	45
CROWN COACHBUILDERS LTD	11
CRYSTALS CONVERSIONS	11
CRYSTALS MIDICOACH SALES	12
CSM LIGHTING	31
CUBIC TRANSPORTATION SYSTEMS LTD	26
CUMMINS UK	25
CUMMINS-ALLISON LTD	18
CYBERLYNE COMMUNICATIONS LTD	15
D	
DAF COMPONENTS LTD	25
DAVID BROWN VEHICLE TRANSMISSIONS LTD	29
R. L. DAVISON & CO LTD	47
DAWSONRENTALS	13
DAYCO — TRANSPORT & TRADE DISTRIBUTION LTD	25
DBG PRODUCTS UK LTD	20
DE LA RUE	38
DEANS POWERED DOORS	21
DECKER MEDIA LTD	43
DFDS TOR LINE	46
DIESEL POWER ENGINEERING	25
DINEX EXHAUSTS LTD	25
DIRECT PARTS LTD	23
DISTINCTIVE SYSTEMS LTD	44
T & E DOCHERTY	44
DRINKMASTER LTD	22
DRIVER HIRE	44
DRURY & DRURY	17
DUDLEYS SCREENWIPERS	42
DUNLOP TYRES	41
DUOFLEX LTD	30
E	
EAST LANCASHIRE COACHBUILDERS LTD	10
EATON LTD	20
EBERSPACHER (UK) LTD	15
KEITH EDMONSON	38
ELITE SEATBELT SPECIALIST LTD	34
ELLIS TRANSPORT SERVICES	45
ELSAN LTD	22
EMINOX LTD	23
ENSIGN BUS & COACH SALES LTD	13
ERENTEK	17
ERF MEDWAY LTD	25
ERRINGTONS OF EVINGTON LTD	13
ESKER BUS & COACH SALES	11
E T M SOFTWARE SERVICES	18
EURO COACH BUILDERS LTD	11
EUROTUNNEL	46
EVOBUS (UK) LTD	13
EXCEL CONVERSIONS	11
EXPO MANAGEMENT LTD	47
EXPRESS COACH REPAIRS LTD	15
F	
R. W. FAULKS FCIT	45
FCAV & CO	16
FIGUREHEAD DATA SYSTEMS	38
FINANCIAL INSPECTION SERVICES LTD	45
FIREMASTER EXTINGUISHER LTD	26
FIRTH FURNISHINGS LTD	27
FIRST CHOICE NAMEPLATES	16
DAVID FISHWICK COACH SALES	13
FJORD LINE	46
FLEETMASTER BUS & COACH LTD	13
FLIGHTS COACH TRAVEL LTD	32
FORD	10
FRANK GUY LTD	11
FTA	48
FTA VEHICLE INSPECTION SERVICE	23
FUMOTO ENGINEERING OF EUROPE	25
FURROWS COMMERCIAL VEHICLES	?3
FWT	43
G	
GABRIEL & CO LTD	29
GARDNER PARTS	29
GHE	17
GKN AXLES LTD	22
GLOBUS BUS & COACH	12
GM COACHWORK	11
IAN GORDON COMMERCIALS	13
GRAMPIAN SOFTWARE LTD	44
GREATDAYS TRAVEL GROUP	47
GREATDAYS, LONDON	47
TONY GREAVES GRAPHICS	43
LEONARD GREEN ASSOCIATES	45

GREIG OF HEREFORD	32
GROUPWAYS LEISURE	51
JOHN GROVES TICKET SYSTEMS	18
FRANK GUY LTD	11

H

HANOVER DISPLAYS LTD	20
HANSAR FINANCE LTD	47
HANTS & DORSET TRIM LTD	17
HAPPICH V&I COMPONENTS LTD	26
THOMAS HARDIE - WIGAN	13
HART BROTHERS	23
HATCHER COMPONENTS LTD	42
HATTS COACHWORKS	17
HAYWARD TRAVEL (CARDIFF)	44
HENRY BOOTH GROUP (see BEMROSE BOOTH)	
HILTECH DEVELOPMENTS LTD	23
J. HIPWELL & SON	42
HISPACOLD	15
HL SMITH TRANSMISSIONS	22
JOHN HOLDSWORTH & CO LTD	41
HOLLOWAY COMMERCIALS	13
B D HOLT	13
HOUSTON RAMM	14

I

IAN ALLAN PRINTING LTD	49
IMAGE & PRINT GROUP	38
IMAGE FIRST	41
IMEXPART LTD	18
IMH BIRMINGHAM LTD	29
IMPERIAL ENGINEERING	18
INDICATORS INTERNATIONAL LTD	20
INDUSTRIAL & COMMERCIAL WINDOW CO LTD	42
INTERFACE FURTEX LTD	41
INOVAS	47
INTERLUBE SYSTEMS LTD	28
INVERTEC	17
IRISBUS (UK) LTD	8
IRISH COMMERCIALS	13
IRISH FERRIES	46
ISLE OF MAN STEAM PACKET COMPANY	46
IVECO	25
ANDY IZATT	45

J

J W GLASS (STEAMY WINDOWS) LTD	42
JANES URBAN TRANSPORT SYSTEMS	50
JAYCAS MINIBUS SALES	11
JBF SERVICES LTD	23
JOHN GROVES TICKET SYSTEMS	18
JOHN BRADSHAW	10
JOHN HOLDSWORTH & CO LTD	41
JONCKHEERE	10
JUBILEE AUTOMOTIVE GROUP	11

K

KAB SEATING LTD	35
KARIVE LTD	30
KEITH EDMONDSON	38
KELLETT (UK) LTD	18
KENT COACHWORKS	17
KERNOW ASSOCIATES	43
KNORR-BREMSE SYSTEMS	18
THOMAS KNOWLES	45
KVC	10

L

LANTERN RECOVERY SPECIALISTS	44
THE LAWTON MOTOR BODY BUILDING CO LTD	17
LDV PLC	10
LEICESTER CARRIAGE BUILDERS	11
LEINSTER VEHICLE DISTRIBUTORS	13
LEISUREWEAR DIRECT	41
LEONARD GREEN ASSOCIATES	45
LEXCEL POWER SYSTEMS PLC	16
LEYLAND PRODUCT DEVELOPMENTS	10
LH GROUP (SERVICES) LTD	22
LHE FINANCE LTD	13
LISTER FURNISHINGS	41
LONDON BUS EXPORT	13
LOOK CCTV	37
LOUGHSHORE AUTOS LTD	13
LUNAR SEATING LTD	35

M

M A C LTD	15
MAJORLIFT HYDRAULIC EQUIPMENT LTD	28
MAJORLINE ENGINEERING LTD	13
MAN TRUCK & BUS UK LTD (MENTOR)	8
MARK TERRILL PSV BADGES	16
MARK TERRILL TICKET MACHINERY	18
MARTYN INDUSTRIALS LTD	17
MASS SPECIAL ENGINEERING LTD	13
MAUN INTERNATIONAL	45
MAUNSELL LTD	45
MCE LTD	24
MCI EXHIBITIONS LTD	47
MCL TRANSPORT CONSULTANTS	44
MCV BUS & COACH	10
McKENNA BROTHERS LTD	21
MELLOR COACHCRAFT	12
MENTOR COACH & BUS	13
MERCEDES-BENZ	8
MET UK LIMITED	21
METRONET REW LTD	36
MID WEST BUS & COACH SALES LTD	13
MINIBUS OPTIONS LTD	12
MINIMISE YOUR RISK	43
MINITRAM SYSTEMS LTD	9
MISTRAL GROUP (UK) PLC	13
MITEC SYSTEMS	44
MOCAP LIMITED	32

MONOWASH (BRUSH REPLACEMENT SERVICE)	41
STEPHEN C MORRIS	43
MOSELEY PCV LTD	10
MOSELEY IN THE SOUTH LTD	13
MOTT MACDONALD	45
MTB EQUIPMENT LTD	34
MULTIPART PSV	16
MVA	43
MYSTERY TRAVELLERS	43

N

MIKE NASH	13
NATIONWIDE CLEANING SYSTEMS	41
NEALINE WINDSCREEN WIPER PRODUCTS	15
NEERMAN & PARTNERS	43
NEOPLAN (MENTOR)	8
NEXT BUS LTD	22
NOGE (MENTOR)	10
NORBURY BLINDS	21
NORFOLKLINE	46
NORTH EAST BUS BREAKERS	13
W. NORTHS (PV) LTD	13
NORTON FOLGATE FG PLC	47
NU-TRACK	17

O

OLYMPUS COACHCRAFT LTD	12
OMNI WHITTINGTON	48
OMNIBUS TRAINING LTD	47
OPTARE COACH SALES	14
OPTARE GROUP	8
OPTARE ROTHERHAM	14
ORVEC INTERNATIONAL	30
OWENS OF OSWESTRY BMC	14

P

P&O IRISH SEA	46
P&O FERRIES	46
PACEL ELECTRONICS	23
PACET MANUFACTURING	15
PARTLINE LTD	15
PARRY PEOPLE MOVERS	9
PASSENGER LIFT SERVICES LTD	31
PASSENGER TRANSPORT CONSULTANCY	43
PERCY LANE PRODUCTS LTD	21
PERKINS GROUP LTD	25
PETERS DOOR SYSTEMS LTD	22
PIAGGIO	11
PINDAR PLC	47
PIONEER WESTON	26
PJ ASSOCIATES	38
PLAXTON LTD	12
PLAXTON COACH SALES	14
PLAXTON PARTS & SERVICE	17
PNEUMAX LTD	33
POWERTRAIN PRODUCTS LTD	22
PRE METRO OPERATIONS	40

PSS - STEERING & HYDRAULICS DIVISION	24
PSV GLASS	42
PSV PRODUCTS	16
PVS MANUFACTURING LTD	12

Q

Q'STRAINT	34
QUALITY ENGINES (QES)	24
QUEENSBRIDGE (PSV) LTD	29

R

HOUSTON RAMM	14
RATCLIFF TAIL LIFTS LTD	31
REGAL COACH SALES LTD	14
RENAULT UK LTD	11
RICHARDS & SHAW TRIM LTD (KUSTOMBILT)	36
RICON UK LTD	31
ROADLEASE	47
ROADLINK INTERNATIONAL LTD	18
ROBERTSON TRANSPORT CONSULTING	43
ROEVILLE COMPUTER SYSTEMS	44
ROHILL BODIES LTD	12
ROUTE ONE	50

S

SAFETEX LTD	34
SALTIRE COMMUNICATIONS	43
SALVADOR CAETANO (UK) LTD	10
SAMMYS GARAGE	44
SC COACHBUILDERS	10
SCAN COIN (UK) LTD	20
SCANIA BUS & COACH (UK) LTD	14
SCANIA	8
SCHADES LTD	38
SEAFRANCE	46
SECURON (AMERSHAM) LTD	34
SERGEANT (P&P) (B&A) LTD	18
SETRA	8
SHADES-TECHNICS	22
SHAWSON SUPPLY LTD	20
SHIRLAW-CATHCART	44
SIEMENS TRAFFIC CONTROLS	40
SIEMENS VDO	37
SILFLEX LTD	20
SKILLPLACE TRAINING	47
SMART CENTRAL COACH	41
SMITH BROS & WEBB	41
SNOWCHAINS EUROPRODUCTS	41
SOMERS VEHICLE LIFTS	28
SOMERBUS	14
SOUTHDOWN PSV	14
SOUTHERN VECTIS PLC	50
SSL	33
STAFFORDSHIRE BUS CENTRE	14
STAGE HOTEL — LEICESTER	47
STANFORD COACHWORKS	12
STATUS	43

STENA LINE	46
STERTIL UK	29
STEPHENSONS OF ESSEX	14
PHIL STOCKFORD GARAGE EQUIPMENT	28
STOKE TRUCK & BUS CENTRE	14
STUART MANUFACTURING CO LTD	38
SUPERFAST FERRIES	46
SUSTRACO	40
SUTRAK: See CARRIER SUTRAK	
SWANSEA CORK FERRIES	46

T

TACHOGRAPH BUREAUX LTD	38
TAGTRONICS LTD	45
TALISMAN	41
TAS PARTNERSHIP	46
TAYLORS COACH SALES	14
TELMA RETARDER LTD	33
TERENCE BARKER TANKS	28
MARK TERRILL PSV BADGES	33
MARK TERRILL TICKET MACHINERY	18
THOMAS AUTOMATICS CO LTD	20
THOMAS HARDIE - WIGAN	13
THOMAS KNOWLES	45
TIFLEX LTD (Treadmaster)	28
TIME TRAVEL (UK) DESIGN & MARKETING	43
TONY GREAVES GRAPHICS	43
TOP GEARS DESTINATIONS	21
TOP LINE TRAVEL OF YORK LTD	44
TOWERGATE CHAPMAN STEVENS	48
TOYOTA	11
TRAMONTANA COACH DISTRIBUTORS	14
TRANMAN SOLUTIONS	45
ALEXANDER DENNIS	8
TRANSFED	47
TRANSIT	50
TRANSPORT DESIGN INTERNATIONAL	24
TRANSPORT STATIONERY SERVICES	49
TRANSPORT TICKET SERVICES	20
TRANSPORTATION MANAGEMENT SOLUTIONS	16
TRAVEL INFOSYSTEMS	45
TRAVEL PATH	51
TRISCAN FUELLING SOLUTIONS	28
TRUCKALIGN	17
TUBE PRODUCTS LTD	36

U

UK COACH & BUS	14
UNITEC PARTS & SERVICE LTD	20
UNITEC REPAIR & SERVICE	18
C. N. UNWIN LTD	31
UWE VERKEN AB	15

V

BOB VALE COACH SALES	16
VAN HOOL	11
VAPOR STONE	24
VARLEY & GULLIVER LTD	31
VARTA AUTOMOTIVE BATTERIES LTD	18
VAUXHALL	13
VDL BUS INTERNATIONAL	9
VDO KIENZLE UK LTD	23
VENTURA	14
VERIFEYE	16
VICTORIA COACH STATION	44
VISECT LTD (TACH:TRAK)	37
V L TEST SYSTEMS LTD	29
VOITH TURBO LTD	29
VOLKSWAGEN COMMERCIAL VEHICLES	11
VOLVO BUS LTD	9
VOLVO COACH CENTRE	14
VOLVO FINANCIAL SERVICES	47
VOLVO INSURANCE SERVICES	48
VOR TRANSMISSIONS LTD	22
VOSA	47
VULTRON INTERNATIONAL LTD	21

W

W. NORTHS (PV) LTD	13
WABCO AUTOMOTIVE UK LTD	18
WACTON COACH SALES & SERVICES	14
WALLMINSTER	30
WARD INTERNATIONAL CONSULTING LTD	37
WAYFARER TRANSIT SYSTEMS LTD	38
WEALDEN PSV LTD	14
WEALDSTONE ENGINEERING	25
WEBASTO PRODUCT LTD	15
WEBB'S	46
WEDLAKE SAINT	48
WESTERN COMMERCIAL	14
WIDNEY UK LTD	34
WHITACRES	12
ALAN WHITE COACH SALES	14
WIGHTLINK FERRIES	46
WIGLEY TREVOR	14
WILSURE INSURANCE BROKERS	48
WILTSHIRE (BRISTOL) LTD	38
WINDOW CLEAN SERVICES	42
WOODBRIDGE FOAM UK LTD	36
WRIGHTBUS LTD	10
WRIGHTSURE INSURANCE SERVICES	48
WS ATKINS see ATKINS	

Z

ZF GREAT BRITAIN LTD	29

OPERATOR INDEX

Operator	Page
1ST CHOICE SCORPIO TRAVEL, *SLOUGH*	73

A

Operator	Page
AAA COACHES, *KIRKNEWTON*	192
A1 COACH TRAVEL, *LONDONDERRY*	216
A1 TRAVEL, *YEOVIL*	157
A1A LTD, *BIRKENHEAD*	139
A2B TRAVEL UK LTD, *PRENTON*	139
A & C LUXURY COACHES, *MOTHERWELL*	196
A & D COACHES, *WORCESTER PARK*	168
A & E MINIBUSES, *LLANFAIR CAEREINION*	209
A & J COACHES OF WASHINGTON CO LTD, *WASHINGTON, TYNE & WEAR*	171
AA, KNIGHTS OF THE ROAD, *GREATER LONDON*	132
A B COACHES LTD, *PAIGNTON*	91
AMK CHAUFFUER DRIVEN, *LIPHOOK*	112
A. P. T. COACHES LTD, *RAYLEIGH*	103
A. R. TRAVEL, *HEMEL HEMPSTEAD*	116
A. W. COACHES, *LLANFAIR CAERINION*	209
ABBEY COACHES, *HIGH WYCOMBE*	77
ABBEY COACHWAYS LTD, *CARLTON, Nr GOOLE*	145
ABBEY TRAVEL LTD, *HITCHIN*	116
G. ABBOTT & SONS, *LEEMING*	146
ABC EUROPEAN TRAVEL, *LEICESTER*	128
ABERFELDY MOTOR SERVICES,	197
ABUS, *BRISTOL*	75
ACE TRAVEL, *BISHOPS STORTFORD*	116
ACE TRAVEL, *BURNTWOOD*	163
ACKLAMS COACHES, *BEVERLEY*	102
ACRON TRAVEL, *HORSFORTH*	179
ACTON COACHES, *WREXHAM*	213
ADAMS TOURS, *BLOXWICH*	173
ADAMSON'S COACHES, *CRAMLINGTON*	150
ADLINGTON TAXIS AND MINICOACHES, *HORWICH*	109
AD-RAINS OF BRINKWORTH	183
AINTREE COACHLINE, *BOOTLE*	139
AIRLINKS — THE AIRPORT COACH CO LTD, *WEST DRAYTON*	132
AIRLYNX LTD, *SOUTHAMPTON*	112
ALAN ARNOTT, *ERSKINE*	198
ALANSWAY COACHES LTD, *NEWTON ABBOT*	91
ALBION COACHES, *WEST BROMWICH*	173
ALDERMASTON COACHES, *ALDERMASTON*	73
ALEC HEAD, *LUTTON, PETERBOROUGH*	149
ALEX MILNE, *NEW BYTH BY TURRIFF*	189
ALEXCARS LTD, *CIRENCESTER*	107
ALFA COACHES LTD, *STOCKTON-ON-TEES*	97
ALFA TRAVEL, *CHORLEY*	124
ALFRA COACH HIRE, *LARKHALL*	199
A-LINE COACHES, *GATESHEAD*	171
ALLAN'S GROUP, *GOREBRIDGE*	195
ALLANDER COACHES LTD, *MILNGAVIE*	194
DOUGLAS C. ALLEN, *SOLE STREET*	120
ALLIED COACHES, BALDOYLE, *DUBLIN*	217
ALLIED COACHLINES LTD, *HAYES*	140
ALMAR TRAVEL, *CHESTER-le-STREET*	97
ALPHA COACH CO, *HULL*	102
ALPHA PERSONALISED TRAVEL LTD, *WATFORD*	116
ALPINE TRAVEL, *LLANDUDNO*	205
ALPINE TRAVEL, *TYWYN*	206
ALTERNATIVE TRAVEL, *SCARBOROUGH*	146
ALTONA COACH SERVICES & TRAVEL CONSULTANT, *GATESHEAD*	171
ALTONIAN COACHES, *ALTON*	112
ALWYN EVANS, *TREGARON*	209
AMBASSADOR COACHES, *SOUTHEND ON SEA*	103
AMBASSADOR TRAVEL (ANGLIA) LTD, *GREAT YARMOUTH*	143
AMBER TRAVEL, *TURRIFF*	188
AMBERLEE UK LTD, *ROCHESETER*	120
AMBERLINE, *WHITLEY BAY*	171
GEOFF AMOS COACHES, *DAVENTRY*	149
AMPORT & DISTRICT COACHES LTD, *ANDOVER*	112
ANDERSON COACHES LTD, *SHEFFIELD*	160
ANDERSON TRAVEL LTD, *LONDON SE1*	133
ANDERSON'S COACHES, *CASTLEFORD*	179
ANDERSON'S COACHES, *LANGHOLM*	190
ANDREW JAMES QUALITY TRAVEL, *CHIPPENHAM*	184
ANDREW'S OF TIDESWELL LTD	88
ANDREWS COACHES, *FOXTON, CAMBRIDGE*	79
ANDYBUS AND COACH, *MALMESBURY*	183
ANGEL MOTORS (EDMONTON) LTD, *TOTTENHAM*	133
ANGELA COACHES LTD, *BURSLEDON*	112
ANGLIAN COACHES LTD, *BECCLES*	166
ANITAS BRITISH & CONTINENTAL TOURS LTD, *STANSTED AIRPORT*	103
PHIL ANSLOW TRAVEL GROUP LTD, *PONTYPOOL*	212
ANTHONYS TRAVEL, *RUNCORN*	81
APL TRAVEL, *CRUDWELL*	183
ARAN TOURS, *SANDYCOVE, Co DUBLIN*	217
ARLEEN COACH HIRE & SERVICES LTD, *PEASEDOWN ST JOHN*	157
ARMCHAIR PASSENGER TRANSPORT LTD, *BRENTFORD*	140
R. K. ARMSTRONG COACHES, *CASTLE DOUGLAS*	191
ARNOLD LIDDELL COACHES, *BRISTOL*	76
ALAN ARNOTT, *ERSKINE*	198
ARON COACHLINES LTD, *HAYES*	141

Operator	Page
ARRIVA COLCHESTER LTD	103
ARRIVA CYMRU LTD, *LLANDUDNO JUNCTION*	205
ARRIVA DERBY LTD	88
ARRIVA GUILDFORD & WEST SURREY, *GUILDFORD*	168
ARRIVA LONDON NORTH EAST	133
ARRIVA LONDON NORTH	133
ARRIVA LONDON SOUTH	133
ARRIVA MIDLANDS, *LEICESTER*	128
ARRIVA MIDLANDS, CANNOCK	163
ARRIVA NORTH EAST LTD, *SUNDERLAND*	171
ARRIVA NORTH WEST, *AINTREE*	139
ARRIVA PASSENGER SERVICES	71
ARRIVA PLC	71
ARRIVA SCOTLAND WEST, *RENFREW*	198
ARRIVA SOUTHEND LTD	103
ARRIVA SOUTHERN COUNTIES, *MAIDSTONE*	120
ARRIVA THE SHIRES LTD, *LUTON*	72
ARRIVA YORKSHIRE, *WAKEFIELD*	179
ARROW INTERNATIONAL, *FERRING*	178
ARROWBROOK COACHES, *CHESTER*	81
ARTHUR THOMAS COACHES, *GORSEINON*	212
ARUN COACHES/FAWLTY TOURS, *HORSHAM*	178
ARVONIA COACHES, *CAERNARFON*	206
ASHALL'S COACHES, *CLAYTON*	109
ASHFORD LUXURY COACHES, *FELTHAM*	141
ASHLEY COACHES PSV, *ROWLANDS GILL*	171
ASHLEY TRAVEL LTD t/a GRANT & McALLIN, *SHEFFIELD*	160
G. ASHTON COACHES, *ST HELENS*	139
ASM COACHES, *WHITSTABLE*	120
ASMAL COACHES, *LEICESTER*	128
J. & F. ASPDEN (BLACKBURN) LTD	124
ASTON BUSES, *KILLAMARSH, SHEFFIELD*	88
ASTONS COACHES, *WORCESTER*	185
ASTONS OF NEWPORT, *SHROPSHIRE*	155
ATHERTON BUS COMPANY, *WESTHOUGHTON*	109
H. ATKINSON & SONS, *NORTHALLERTON*	146
AUSDEN CLARK LTD, *LEICESTER*	128
AUSTIN COACH TRAVEL, *EARLSTON*	190
AUTOCAR BUS & COACH, *TONBRIDGE*	120
AUTODOUBLE LTD, *MILTON KEYNES*	77
AUTOPOINT COACHES, *HAILSHAM*	100
AVALON COACHES (W. H. FOSTER & SON), *GLASTONBURY*	159
AVON COACH & BUS COMPANY, *BIRKENHEAD*	139
AWAY DAYS, *SHANKLIN*	119
AWAYDAYS LTD T/A GEMINI TRAVEL, *IPSWICH*	166
AXE VALE COACHES, *AXBRIDGE*	158
AXE VALLEY MINI TRAVEL, *SEATON*	91
AYREVILLE COACHES, *PLYMOUTH*	91
AZTEC COACH TRAVEL, *BRISTOL*	75
AZTECBIRD LTD, *GUISELEY*	179

B

Operator	Page
B & H TOURS, *MIRFIELD*	179
B & J TRAVEL, *MIDDLESTOWN*	179
B B COACHES LTD, *HALESOWEN*	173
B'S TRAVEL, *PONTYPOOL*	212
BACK-ROADS TOURING CO LTD, *LONDON W5*	133
BAGNALLS COACHES, *SWADLINCOTE*	88
BAILEY'S COACHES LTD, *WATNALL*	151
K T & M BAKER, *LOOE*	84
BAKERS COACHES, *BIDDULPH*	164
BAKERS COACHES, *YEOVIL*	158
BAKERS COMMERCIAL SERVICES, *ENSTONE*	154
BAKERS DOLPHIN COACH TRAVEL, *WESTON-SUPER-MARE*	75, 158
BAKEWELL COACHES, *BAKEWELL*	88
IAN BALDRY, *FELIXSTOWE*	166
BALDRY'S COACHES, *YORK*	146
BAILISS TOURS, *BARTON-IN-THE-BEANS*	128
BANBURYSHIRE ETA LTD, *BANBURY*	154
BANSTEAD COACHES LTD	168
BARCROFT TOURS & EVENTS, *HASTINGS*	100
BARFORDIAN COACHES LTD, *BEDFORD*	72
BARNARD CASTLE COACHES, *RICHMOND*	146
BARNARDS COACHES, *KIRTON LINDSEY*	130
BARNES COACHES LTD, *MARLBOROUGH*	183
BARNSLEY & DISTRICT TRACTION CO	160
BARRATT'S COACHES LTD, *NANTWICH*	81
BARRY'S COACHES LTD, *CORK*	217
BARRY'S COACHES LTD, *WEYMOUTH*	95
BARTON TRANSPORT, *MAYNOOTH*	217
BASFORDS COACHES LTD, *TOWCESTER*	149
BATH BUS COMPANY	158
BATTERSBY SILVER GREY COACHES, *MORECAMBE*	124
BATTERSBY'S COACHES, *WALKDEN*	109
BEACON COACHES, *CHELMSLEY WOOD*	173
BEADLES TRAVEL, *NEWTOWN*	209
K. W. BEARD LTD, *CINDERFORD*	107
BEARWOOD COACHES, *SMETHWICK*	173
BEATONS COACHES LTD, *BLANTYRE*	199
BEAULY COACH HIRE, *WESTER BALBLAIR, BY BEAULY*	194
BEAVIS HOLIDAYS, *BUSSAGE*	107
BEBB TRAVEL, *LLANTWIT FARDRE*	211
BEECHES TRAVEL, *TWICKENHAM*	141
BEECROFT COACHES, *FEWSTON, NR HARROGATE*	146
BEELINE (R&R) COACHES LTD, *WARMINSTER*	183
BEESTONS COACHES LTD	166
BELL'S LUXURY COACHES, *SALISBURY*	183
BEN JOHNSON COACHES, *BRANDESBURTON*	102
B. D. BENNETT, *TAMWORTH*	173
BENNETT'S COACHES, *GLOUCESTER*	107
BENNETT'S TRAVEL, *WARRINGTON*	81
BENNETTS TRAVEL (CRANBERRY) LTD, *GATES HEATH*	164

Operator	Page
BERKELEY COACH AND TRAVEL LTD, *PAULTON, BRISTOL*	75
BERRYS COACHES (TAUNTON) LTD	158
BESSWAY TRAVEL, *WEST HARROW*	141
BEST WAY TRAVEL, *SALTBURN*	97
BETTER MOTORING SERVICES, *STRATTON-ST MARGARET*	183
JAMES BEVAN LTD, *LYDNEY*	108
BEXLEY COACHLINES, *SIDCUP*	120
BIBBY'S OF INGLETON	146
BIG BUS COMPANY, *LONDON SW1W*	133
BILLIES COACHES LTD, *ROTHERHAM*	160
BIRCHWOOD TRAVEL, *WARRINGTON*	81
BIRMINGHAM COACH COMPANY LTD, THE, *WARLEY*	173
BIRMINGHAM INTERNATIONAL COACHES LTD, *TILE CROSS*	174
BIRMINGHAM & MIDLAND MOTOR OMNIBUS TRUST, *WYTHALL*	173
BISHOP COACHES, *LUTON*	72
D. P. BISHOP, *DUMBARTON*	200
BJS TRAVEL, *GREAT WAKERING*	103
BLACK PRINCE BUSES LTD, *MORLEY*	179
BLACKBURN BOROUGH TRANSPORT LTD	125
BLACKPOOL TRANSPORT LTD	125
BLAGDON LIONESS COACHES LTD, *BRISTOL*	75
BLAZEFIELD HOLDINGS	71
BLUE BUS & COACH SERVICES LTD, *BOLTON*	125
BLUE DIAMOND COACHES, *HARLOW*	103
BLUE IRIS COACHES, *NAILSEA*	75
BLUEBIRD BUS & COACH, *MIDDLETON*	109
BLUEBIRD BUSES, *ABERDEEN*	188
BLUEBIRD BUSES, *INVERNESS*	194
BLUEBIRD BUSES, *PERTH*	198
BLUEBIRD COACHES (WEYMOUTH) LTD	95
BLUEBIRD COACHES, *COOLOCK, DUBLIN*	217
BLUEBIRD OF NEATH/PONTARDAWE	208
BLUELINE COACHES, *MAGHULL*	139
BLUE TRIANGLE BUSES, *RAINHAM*	103
BLUEWAYS GUIDELINE COACHES LTD, *LONDON*	133
BLUNSDON'S COACH TRAVEL, *BLADON*	154
BMT (MAYFIELD), *ASTLEY, Nr MANCHESTER*	109
C. BODMAN & SONS, *DEVIZES*	184
A. S. BONE & SONS, *HOOK*	112
A & H BOOTH LTD, *HYDE*	109
BORDACOACH, *RAYLEIGH*	103
BOSTOCK'S COACHES LTD, *CONGLETON*	81
BOTTERILLS, *THORNTON DALE*	146
BOULTONS OF SHROPSHIRE, *CHURCH STRETTON*	155
BOURNEMOUTH TRANSPORT LTD	95
BOW BELLE, *EXETER*	91
L F BOWEN LTD, *TAMWORTH*	164
R N BOWDEN, *WELSHPOOL*	209
ERIC W. BOWERS COACHES LTD, *CHAPEL-EN-LE-FRITH*	88
D K & N BOWMAN, *WREAY, CARLISLE*	86
BOWMAN'S COACHES (MULL) LTD, *CRAIGNURE*	189
BOWYER'S COACHES, *HEREFORD*	115
M. BOYDON & SONS, *WINKHILL*	164
BRADSHAWS TRAVEL, *KNOTT END ON SEA*	125
BRAZIERS MINI COACHES, *BUCKINGHAM*	77
BRENTONS OF BLACKHEATH, *LONDON SE3*	133
BRENTWOOD COACHES	103
BRIAN'S TRAVEL, *SHREWSBURY*	155
BRIAN ISAAC COACHES LTD, *SWANSEA*	212
BRIGHTON & HOVE BUS & COACH CO LTD	100
BRIGHTONIAN COACHES, *BRIGHTON*	100
BRIJAN TOURS, *BISHOPS WALTHAM*	112
BRISTOL ELECTRIC RAILBUS	75
BRITANNIA COACHES, *DOVER*	120
BRITANNIA (PROBUS MANAGEMENT), *TELFORD*	155
BRITANNIA TRAVEL, *OTLEY*	180
BRITTAINS COACHES LTD, *NORTHAMPTON*	149
BRODYR JAMES, *TREGARON*	204
BRODYR THOMAS, *LLANGADOG*	205
BROMYARD OMNIBUS COMPANY, *BROMYARD*	115
A T BROWN, *TELFORD*	155
EDDIE BROWN TOURS LTD, *YORK*	146
EDDIE BROWN TOURS LTD, *NOTTINGHAM*	151
H E BROWN, *CONGLETON*	81
J. & M. BROWN COACHES, *THREE BRIDGES*	178
LES BROWN TRAVEL, *BATHGATE*	200
BROWNINGS (WHITBURN) LTD	201
S H BROWNRIGG LTD, *EGREMONT*	86
BROWNRIGG'S COACHES, *THORNHILL*	191
BROWNS COACHES LTD, *PONTEFRACT*	180
BROWNS COACHES, *ASHFORD*	120
BROWNS LUXURY COACHES, *CARNFORTH*	86
BROWNS COACHES LTD, *DURHAM*	97
BROWNS OF EDINBURGH, *BROXBURN*	192
ROY BROWNS COACHES, *BUILTH WELLS*	209
RONNIE BRUEN, *COOLOCK, DUBLIN*	217
BRYANS OF ENFIELD	133
BRYLAINE TRAVEL, *BOSTON*	130
BRYN MELYN LTD, *LLANGOLLEN*	206
BUCKBY'S COACHES, *ROTHWELL*	149
BUCKLEYS, *DONCASTER*	160
BUCKLEY'S TOURS, *KILLARNEY*	217
BUDDENS COACHES LTD, *ROMSEY*	113
BUFFALO TRAVEL, *FLITWICK*	72
BUGLER COACHES OF BRISTOL	75
R. BULLOCK & CO (TRANSPORT) LTD, *CHEADLE*	109
BURDETTS COACHES LTD, *MOSBOROUGH*	160
BURGHFIELD MINI COACHES LTD, *READING*	73
BURKE BROS (COACHES) LTD, *TUAM, Co GALWAY*	217
BURNHAM PARK COACHES, *PLYMOUTH*	91
BURNLEY & PENDLE	125
JAMES BURNS, *PAISLEY*	198
R & D BURROWS LTD, *OGMORE VALE, BRIDGEND*	202

Operator	Page
BURTONS COACHES LTD, *HAVERHILL*	166
BUS EIREANN, *DUBLIN*	217
TERRY BUSHELL TRAVEL, *BURTON-ON-TRENT*	164
BUTLER BROTHERS, *KIRKBY IN ASHFIELD*	151
BUTLERS BUSES, *COBH, Co CORK*	217
BUTTERS COACHES, *CHILDS ERCALL*	155
BU-VAL, *LITTLEBOROUGH*	109
BUZZLINES, *HYTHE*	120
BYNGS INTERNATIONAL COACHES, *PORTSMOUTH*	112
BYRAN COACHES LTD, *SHEFFIELD*	160
LES BYWATER & SONS LTD, *ROCHDALE*	109

C

Operator	Page
C & G COACH SERVICES, *CHATTERIS*	79
C & M TRAVEL, *AINTREE*	139
C & S COACHES, *HEATHFIELD*	100
C. I. COACHLINES, *CHELMSFORD*	104
C. N. ENTERPRISES (COACH HIRE), *ROMFORD*	104
CABER COACHES, *ABERFELDY*	198
CABIN COACHES, *HAYES*	141
CAELLOI MOTORS, *PWLLHELI*	207
CAHALANE COACHES, *CORK*	217
CALDEW COACHES, *CARLISLE*	86
CALL-A-COACH, *WALTON-ON-THAMES*	168
CALLINAN COACHES, *GLAREGALWAY*	216
CAMBRIAN COAST COACH LINE, *ABERGYNOLWYN*	206
CAMPBELL'S COACHES, *SOUTH SHIELDS*	171
CANAVAN'S COACHES, *KILSYTH*	196
DEN CANEY COACHES LTD, *BIRMINGHAM*	174
CANTABRICA COACHES, *WATFORD*	116
CARADOC COACHES, *CHURCH STRETTON*	155
CARAVELLE COACHES, *EDGWARE*	141
CARDIFF BUS	203
CARDINAL COACHES, *DOVER*	121
CARELINE, *BIRMINGHAM*	174
CARMEL COACHES, *OKEHAMPTON*	92
J. W. CARNELL LTD, *SUTTON BRIDGE*	130
PETER CAROL PRESTIGE COACHING, *WHITCHURCH, BRISTOL*	75
CARR'S COACHES, *SILLOTH*	86
CARREGLEFN COACHES, *AMLWCH*	202
CAROUSEL COACHES, *HIGH WYCOMBE*	77
CARROLL'S COACH HIRE, *DROGHEDA*	217
CARS INTERNATIONAL A. C. T., *ASH*	168
CARSVILLE COACHES, *URMSTON*	109
CASTELL COACHES LTD, *BEDWAS*	203
CASTLE GARAGE LTD, *LLANDOVERY*	204
CASTLEWAYS LTD, *WINCHCOMBE*	108
CATTERALLS COACH OF SOUTHAM, *SOUTHAM*	172
CAVALIER TRAVEL SERVICES, *HOUNSLOW*	133
CAVALIER TRAVEL, *LONG SUTTON*	130
CEDAR COACHES, *BEDFORD*	72
CEDRIC COACHES, *WIVENHOE*	104
CELTIC TRAVEL, *LLANIDLOES*	209
CENTAUR TRAVEL MINICOACHES, *SIDCUP*	133
CENTRAL BUSES, *BIRMINGHAM*	174
CENTRAL COACHES, *KEITH*	196
CENTRAL GARAGE, *TODMORDEN*	181
CENTRAL MINI COACHES, *DOVER*	121
CENTRAL TRAVEL, *NEWTOWN*	209
CENTREBUS, *DUNSTABLE*	72
CENTURION TRAVEL, *MIDSOMER NORTON*	158
CERBYDAU BERWYN COACHES, *TREFOR, PWLLHELI*	206
CHADWELL HEATH COACHES, *ROMFORD*	104
CHALFONT COACHES OF HARROW LTD, *SOUTHALL*	141
CHALFONT LINE LTD, *WEST DRAYTON*	134
CHALKWELL COACH HIRE & TOURS, *SITTINGBOURNE*	121
CHAMBERS COACH HIRE LTD, *MONEYMORE*	216
CHAMBERS COACHES (STEVENAGE) LTD	116
H. C. CHAMBERS & SON LTD, *BURES*	166
CHANDLERS COACH TRAVEL, *WESTBURY*	184
CHAPEL END COACHES, *NUNEATON*	172
CHARIOTS OF CRAWLEY	178
CHARIOTS OF ESSEX LTD, *STANFORD-LE-HOPE*	104
CHARLTON-ON-OTMOOR SERVICES, *OXFORD*	154
CHARTER COACH LTD, *YORK*	146
CHASE COACHES LTD, *CHASETOWN*	164
CHAUFFEURS OF BIRMINGHAM, *EDGBASTON*	174
CHEAM COACHES	168
CHENERY, *DISS*	143
CHENEY COACHES LTD, *BANBURY*	154
CHERRYBRIAR, *LONDON E3*	134
CHESTER CITY TRANSPORT LTD	82
IAN CHESTNUT, *JOHNSTONE*	198
CHEYNE'S COACHES, *INVERURIE*	188
CHILTERN TRAVEL, *HENLOW*	72
CHIVERS COACHES LTD, *WALLINGTON*	168
CITY CIRCLE LTD, *HAYES*	134
CITY SIGHTSEEING GLASGOW LTD, *GLASGOW*	194
CLAPTON COACHES LTD, *RADSTOCK*	158
CLARIBEL COACHES, *TILE CROSS*	174
CLARKES OF LONDON, *LONDON SE26*	134
CLARKSON COACHWAYS, *BARROW IN FURNESS*	86
CLARKSONS COACHES, *SOUTH ELMSALL*	160, 180
CLASSIC COACHES LTD, *ANNFIELD PLAIN*	97
CLASSIC COACHES, *DUBLIN*	217
CLASSIQUE SUN SALOON LUXURY COACHES, *PAISLEY*	198
CLEGG & BROOKING LTD, *STOCKBRIDGE*	113
CLH TRAVEL, *PAIGNTON*	92
CLINTONA MINICOACHES, *BRENTWOOD*	104
CLOWES COACHES, *LONGNOR*	89
CLWYDIAN TOURS, *LLANRHAEADR*	206
CLYDE COAST COACHES LTD, *ARDROSSAN*	196
CLYNNOG & TREFOR MOTORS, *CAERNARFON*	207

Operator	Page
COACH COMPANIONS LTD, *LEOMINSTER*	134
COACH HOUSE TRAVEL, *DORCHESTER*	95
COACHLINERS, *SOUTH SHIELDS*	171
COACH OPTIONS, *MIDDLETON*	125
COACH SERVICES LTD, *THETFORD*	143
COACHING CONNECTION, *LLANIDLOES*	209
COACHMASTER (BRYAN GARRATT), *LEICESTER*	129
COACHSTYLE LTD, *CHIPPENHAM*	184
COACHWAYS, *ROCHDALE*	110
COAST TO COAST PACKHORSE, *KIRKBY STEPHEN*	86
COASTAL & COUNTRY COACHES LTD, *WHITBY*	146
COASTAL COACHES, *NEWICK*	100
COCHRANE'S, *PETERLEE*	97
COFTON COACHES, *REDNAL*	174
COLISEUM COACHES LTD, *WEST END, SOUTHAMPTON*	113
COLLIN PHILLIPSON, *GOOLE*	102, 162
COLLIN'S COACHES, *CARRICKAMOSS, Co MONAGHAN*	217
COLLINS COACHES LTD, *LONDON W7*	134
COLLINS COACHES, *CAMBRIDGE*	79
COLLINS COACHES, *SELBY*	146
W. H. COLLINS, *ROCH*	208
COLRAY COACH HIRE, *BLACKPOOL*	125
COMPASS ROYSTON COACHES, *STOCKTON*	97
COMPASS TRAVEL, *WORTHING*	178
CONFIDENCE BUS/COACH HIRE, *LEICESTER*	129
CONISTON COACHES LTD, *BROMLEY*	134
CONNEX BUS UK LTD, *St HELIER, JERSEY*	214
CONWAY COACH AND CHAUFFEUR DRIVE, *LIMERICK*	217
COOKS COACHES, *WELLINGTON, SOMERSET*	158
COOKS COACHES, *WESTCLIFF-ON-SEA*	104
COOKSONS COACHES, *WELSHPOOL*	209
COOMBS TRAVEL, *WESTON-SUPER-MARE*	158
HENRY COOPER, *ANNITSFORD*	171
COOPERS COACHES, *ROTHWELL*	149
COOPERS COACHES, *WOOLSTON*	113
COOPERS TOURS LTD, *KILLAMARSH*	160
COPELAND TOURS (STOKE-ON-TRENT) LTD, *MEIR*	164
DAVID CORBEL OF LONDON LTD, *EDGWARE*	134
CORPORATE COACHING, *LUTON*	72
COSY COACHES, *KILLAMARSH*	160
COTTRELL'S COACHES, *MITCHELDEAN*	108
COUNTRY HOPPER, *IBSTOCK*	129
COUNTRY LION (NORTHAMPTON) LTD	149
COUNTRYLINER COACH HIRE LTD, *GUILDFORD*	168
COUNTRYSIDE BUS SERVICES, *SCARBOROUGH*	147
COUNTY COACHES, *BRENTWOOD*	104
COUNTY MINI COACHES, *LEICESTER*	129
L. S. COURT LTD, *FILLONGLEY*	172
COURTESY TRAVEL, *SHREWSBURY*	155
COURTLINE: THE OMINI COACH CO, *NUNEATON*	172
COURTNEY COACHES, *BERKSHIRE*	74
COX'S OF BELPER	89
COYLES COACHES, *GWEEDORE, Co DONEGAL*	217
R. & C. S. CRAIG, *ROBERTON*	199
CRAIGGS TRAVEL EUROPEAN, *AMBLE*	150
CRAKERS COACHES, *DEAL*	121
CRAVEN ARMS COACHES, *CRAVEN ARMS*	155
HENRY CRAWFORD COACHES LTD, *NEILSTON*	192
CRAWLEY LUXURY COACHES	178
CRESSWELL'S, *SWADLINCOTE*	89
N N CRESSWELL, *EVESHAM*	185
CRISTAL HIRE COACHES OF SWANWICK	89
CROESO TOURS, *PENYLAN*	203
CRONIN'S COACHES LTD, *CORK*	217
CROPLEY, *FOSDYKE*	130
CROPPER COACHES, *TOTTINGTON*	110
CROSS COUNTRY COACHES, *SWINDON*	184
CROSS COUNTRY HIRE, *POOLE*	95
CROSS GATES COACHES, *LLANDRINDOD WELLS*	209
CROSSKEYS COACHES, *HYTHE, KENT*	121
CROSSKEYS COACH HIRE, *PONTLLANFAITH*	203
CROSSON TRUCK & BUS LTD, *COOLOCK, DUBLIN*	218
CROWN COACHES, *BICKLEY*	134
CROWN COACHES, *LEIGH-ON-SEA*	104
CROYDON TRAMLINK	134
CRUISERS LTD, *REDHILL*	168
CRUSADE TRAVEL, *PENKRIDGE*	164
CRUSADER HOLIDAYS, *CLACTON-ON-SEA*	104
CRYSTALS COACHES LTD, *LONDON SW10*	134
CUCKMERE COACHES, *EASTBOURNE*	100
CUCKMERE COMMUNITY BUS, *POLEGATE*	100
CUMBRIA COACHES, *CARLISLE*	86
CUMFI-LUX COACHES, *HILLINGDON*	141
CUMFY COACHES, *SOUTHPORT*	139
CUNNINGHAM CARRIAGE CO, *CORRINGHAM*	104
CURRIAN TOURS AND COACH HIRE, *ST AUSTELL*	84

D

Operator	Page
D & E COACHES, *INVERNESS*	194
D & G COACH & BUS LTD, *STOKE ON TRENT*	164
D A C COACHES, *GUNNISLAKE*	84
D. C. TRAVEL (DOUGLAS C. ALLEN), *COBHAM, GRAVESEND*	120
D H CARS (DENSTONE), *UTTOXETER*	164
D. R. M. COACHES, *BROMYARD*	115
D.R.M. MINIBUS & COACH TRAVEL, *CHASE TERRACE*	164
D. R. P. MINIBUS TRAVEL, *NEWPORT PAGNELL*	77
D/WAY TRAVEL, *BUNGAY*	143
DAGLISH COACHES, *FRIZINGTON*	86
DAIMLER HIRE, *HALL GREEN*	174

Operator	Page
DALESMAN, GUISELEY	180
DAM EXPRESS, ARDWICK GREEN	110
DAMORY COACHES, BLANDFORD FORUM	95
DANS MINI-BUSES, LONDON E18	134
DARLEY FORD TRAVEL, LISKEARD	84
DARRAGHS COACHES, BALLYMONEY	216
DARTLINE COACHES, EXETER	92
DARWEN COACH SERVICES	125
DAVID PALMER COACHES LTD, NORMANTON	181
BILLY DAVIES EXECUTIVE COACHES, STIRLING	200
D G DAVIES, RHAYADER	209
DAWLISH COACHES LTD	92
ALAN DAWNEY COACH HIRE, SHEPPEY	121
DAWSON'S MINICOACHES, ALFRETON	89
MIKE DE COURCEY TRAVEL LTD, COVENTRY	174
J. K. DEEBLE, LISKEARD	84
DELAINE BUSES LTD, BOURNE	131
DEN CANEY COACHES LTD, BIRMINGHAM	174
DENNIS'S COACHES, DUKINFIELD	110
DERBY COMMUNITY TRANSPORT	89
DEREK HIRCOCKS COACHES, UPWELL, Nr WISBECH	79
DEROS COACH TOURS, KILLARNEY	218
DERWENT COACHES LTD, STANLEY, CO DURHAM	171
DERWENT TRAVEL, AYLESBURY	77
DEWHIRST COACHES, BRADFORD	180
DEWS COACHES, SOMERSHAM	79
DIAL-A-RIDE, NEWTOWN	210
DIAMOND COACHES LTD, MORRISTON	211
DIRECT COACH TOURS, BIRMINGHAM	174
DOBSON'S BUSES LTD, NORTHWICH	82
T. & E. DOCHERTY, IRVINE	196
DOCHERTY'S MIDLAND COACHES, AUCHTERARDER	198
DOCKLANDS MINIBUSES, SILVERTOWN E16	134
DODDS OF TROON LTD, AYR	199
J. DODSWORTH (COACHES) LTD, BOROUGHBRIDGE	147
DOIGS OF GLASGOW LTD	194
JIMMY DONNELLY & SON, ENNISCORTHY, Co WEXFORD	218
SEAN DONNELLY, GRANARD, Co LONGFORD	218
DONOVAN'S COACH HIRE, KILLARNEY	218
DONS COACHES (DUNMOW) LTD, GREAT DUNMOW	104
DORSET QUEEN COACHES, DORCHESTER	96
DOUGLAS CORPORATION TRAMWAY	214
DOWNS MOTORS & OTTER COACHES, OTTERY ST MARY	92
P. DOYLE LTD, ROUNDWOOD, Co WICKLOW	218
TONY DOYLE COACHES, ENNISKERRY, Co WICKLOW	218
K&H DOYLE, RIPLEY	89
TIM DRAPER HOLIDAYS, ALFRETON	89
DRP TRAVEL, MILTON KEYNES	77
DRURY COACHES, GOOLE	102
DUALWAY COACHES & IRISH CITY TOURS, RATHCOOLE, Co DUBLIN	218
DUBLIN BUS	218
DUBLIN MINI COACHES, DUBLIN	218
DUCKWORTH COACHES, GISBURN	125
DUDLEY'S COACHES LTD, WORCESTER	185
DUNCAN MACLENNAN, STRATH-CARRON	194
RAY DUNN COACH TRAVEL, HEDGE END	113
DUNN'S COACHES, AIRDRIE	196
DUNN-LINE, NOTTINGHAM	152
DUNN-LINE (FLIGHTS) LTD, BIRMINGHAM	174
DURHAM CITY COACHES LTD	97

E

Operator	Page
'E' COACHES OF ALFRETON	89
EAGLE COACHES, BRISTOL	75
EAGLE LINE TRAVEL, CHELTENHAM	108
EAGLES & CRAWFORD, MOLD	206
EAGRE, MORTON	131
EALING COMMUNITY TRANSPORT, LONDON W3	134
EARNSIDE COACHES, GLENFARG	198
EASSONS COACHES LTD, ITCHEN	113
EAST LONDON COACHES, ROMFORD	135
EAST TEIGNBRIDGE COMMUNITY TRANSPORT, DAWLISH	92
EAST YORKSHIRE MOTOR SERVICES LTD, HULL	102
EASTBOURNE BUSES LTD	100
A. W. EASTON'S COACHES LTD, STRATTON STRAWLESS	143
EASTONWAYS LTD, RAMSGATE	121
EASTVILLE COACHES LTD, BRISTOL	76
EASTWARD COACHES, IVYBRIDGE	92
EAVESWAY TRAVEL LTD, ASHTON-IN-MAKERFIELD	125
EBLEY COACH SERVICES, NAILSWORTH	108
EDS MINIBUS & COACH HIRE, EAST TILBURY	104
EDINBURGH CASTLE COACHES LTD, LEITH	192
EDINBURGH TOURS, EDINBURGH	192
EDWARDS BROS, TIERS CROSS	208
EDWARDS COACHES, LLANTWIT FARDRE	210
GEORGE EDWARDS & SON, BWLCHYWYN	213
L. J. EDWARDS COACH HIRE, HAILSHAM	100
EIREBUS LTD, DUBLIN	218
ELCOCK REISEN LTD, MADELEY	156
ELITE SERVICES LTD, STOCKPORT	110
ELIZABETH YULE, PITLOCHRY	198
ELLENDERS COACHES, SHEFFIELD	161
ELLIS COACHES, LLANGEFNI	202
P & J ELLIS LTD, LONDON NW10	135
ELLISON'S COACHES, ASHTON KEYNES	184
ELTHAM EXECUTIVE CHARTER, LONDON SE9	135
EMBLINGS COACHES, GUYHIRN	79
EMMERSON COACHES, IMMINGHAM	145
EMMAS COACHES, DOLGELLAU	207

Operator	Page
EMPRESS COACHES LTD, *ST LEONARDS-ON-SEA*	100
EMPRESS MOTORS LTD, *LONDON E2*	135
EMS BUS & COACH, *BIRKENHEAD*	139
EMSWORTH & DISTRICT, *SOUTHBOURNE*	113
ENDEAVOUR COACHES, *BIRMINGHAM*	174
ENFIELD COACHES, *ENFIELD, Co MEATH*	218
ENNIS COACHES, *MATLOCK*	89
ENSIGNBUS COMPANY, *PURFLEET*	104
ENTERPRISE TRAVEL, *DARLINGTON*	98
EPSOM COACHES GROUP	169
ERB SERVICES, *BYKER*	171
ESSBEE COACHES, *COATBRIDGE*	196
E S T BUS LTD, *COWBRIDGE*	213
EUROLINK FOLKESTONE	121
EUROSUN COACHES, *CROMER*	143
EUROTAXIS, *BRISTOL*	76
GARETH EVANS COACHES, *BRYNAMMAN*	204
HARRY EVANS, *WELSHPOOL*	210
EVE CARS & COACHES, *DUNBAR*	192
EXCALIBUR COACHES, *LONDON SE15*	135
EXCALIBUR COACH TRAVEL, *SOUTHMINSTER*	104
EXCEL PASSENGER LOGISTICS LTD, *STANSTED AIRPORT*	105
EXCELSIOR COACHES LTD, *BOURNEMOUTH*	96
EXPERT COACH SERVICES LTD, *GRIMSBY*	145
EXPRESS MOTORS, *BONTNEWYDD, CAERNARFON*	207
EXPRESSLINES LTD, *BEDFORD*	72
EXPRESSWAY COACHES, *ROTHERHAM*	161

F

Operator	Page
FAHERTY'S COACH HIRE, *MOYCULLEN, Co GALWAY*	218
FAIRWAY TRAVEL, *EDINBURGH*	192
FALCON TRAVEL, *SHEPPERTON*	141
FARELINE BUS & COACH SERVICES, *EYE*	167
FARESAVER BUSES, *CHIPPENHAM*	184
FARGO COACHLINES, *BRAINTREE*	105
FARLEIGH COACHES, *ROCHESTER*	121
FARNHAM COACHES	169
FELIX BUS SERVICES LTD, *STANLEY, DERBYS*	89
FENN HOLIDAYS LTD, *MARCH*	79
FERNLEAF COACHES, *MORDEN*	169
FERRERS COACHES LTD, *SOUTH WOODHAM FERRERS*	105
FERRYMAN TRAVEL, *LEYBOURNE*	121
FFOSHELIG COACHES, *CARMARTHEN*	204
DAVID FIELD, *NEWENT*	108
FIFE SCOTTISH OMNIBUSES LTD, *COWDENBEATH*	193
FILER'S COACHES, *PENSFORD, Nr BRISTOL*	76
FILERS TRAVEL, *ILFRACOMBE*	92
FINCHLEY COACHES LTD, *LONDON N11*	135
FINEGAN COACH HIRE, *CARRICKMACROSS, Co MONAGHAN*	218

Operator	Page
EUGENE FINNEGAN (TRANSPORT), *BRAY, Co WICKLOW*	218
FINGLAND'S COACHWAYS LTD, *RUSHOLME*	110
FIRST IN ABERDEEN	188
FIRST IN BERKSHIRE, *BRACKNELL*	74
FIRST IN BRADFORD	180
FIRST BRISTOL, *WESTON-SUPER-MARE*	76
FIRST CHOICE TRAVEL, *PETERBOROUGH*	79
FIRST CYMRU, *SWANSEA*	212
FIRST IN CHESTER & THE WIRRAL	82
FIRST IN DEVON & CORNWALL	84, 92
FIRST IN DORSET, *WEYMOUTH*	96
FIRST EASTERN COUNTIES, *NORWICH*	143
FIRST IN EDINBURGH	192
FIRST IN ESSEX, *CHELMSFORD*	105
FIRST, *GLASGOW*	194
FIRST IN HALIFAX, *HALIFAX*	180
FIRST HAMPSHIRE & DORSET LTD, *SOUTHAMPTON*	113
FIRST IN HUDDERSFIELD	180
FIRST IN LEEDS	180
FIRST LEICESTER	129
FIRST IN LONDON	135
FIRST NORTH WEST, *OLDHAM*	110
FIRST NORTHAMPTON	149
FIRST IN POTTERIES	164
FIRST IN SCOTLAND EAST	193, 195
FIRST SOMERSET & AVON, *WESTON-SUPER-MARE*	158
FIRST IN SOUTH YORKS, *ROTHERHAM*	161
FIRST STOP TRAVEL LTD, *RENFREW*	199
FIRST IN WYVERN, *WORCESTER*	186
FIRST YORK	147
FIRSTGROUP PLC	71
FISHERS TOURS, *DUNDEE*	191
JOHN FISHWICK & SONS, *LEYLAND*	125
FITZCHARLES COACHES LTD, *GRANGEMOUTH*	200
FIVE STAR TRAVEL, *LIVERPOOL*	139
JOHN FLANAGAN COACH TRAVEL, *GRAPPENHALL, WARRINGTON*	82
FLYGHT TRAVEL, *COSHAM*	113
FOCUS COACHES, *PRESTON*	126
FORDS COACHES, *ALTHORNE*	105
FOREST COACHES, *LONDON E6*	135
FORESTDALE COACHES LTD, *CROYDON*	135
FORGET-ME-NOT (TRAVEL) LTD, *IPSWICH*	167
FORMBY COACHWAYS LTD, *T/A FRESHFIELD COACHES*	139
W. H. FOSTER & SON, *GLASTONBURY*	159
FOUNTAIN EXECUTIVE, *ABERDEEN*	188
FOUR GIRLS COACHES, *PONTYBODKIN*	206
FOWLERS TRAVEL, *HOLBEACH DROVE*	131
TOM FOX, *ROCKCORRY, Co MONAGHAN*	218
FRASER EAGLE LTD, *PADIHAM*	126
FREEBIRD, *BURY*	110
FREEBIRD, *TOTTINGTON*	126

FREESTONES COACHES, *BEETLEY*	143
JAMES FRENCH & SON, *EYEMOUTH*	190
FRODINGHAM COACHES, *DRIFFIELD*	102
MARTIN FUREY COACHES LTD, *DRUMCLIFFE, Co SLIGO*	218
L. FURNESS & SONS, *HIGH GREEN*	161

G

G & S TRAVEL, *RAMSGATE*	121
G B COACHES, *MORECAMBE*	126
GHA COACHES, *CORWEN*	206
G. J. TRAVEL LTD, *OTTERSHAW*	169
G. M. COACHES, *CEFN CRIBWR*	202
G. P. D. TRAVEL, *HEYWOOD*	126
GAIN TRAVEL EXPERIENCE LTD, *BRADFORD*	180
GALES COACHES LTD, *HASLEMERE*	169
GALLEON TRAVEL LTD, *HUNSDON*	117
GALLOWAY EUROPEAN, *MENDLESHAM*	167
GALSON-STORNOWAY, *ISLE OF LEWIS*	201
GALVINS COACHES, *DUNMANWAY, Co CORK*	218
GANGE'S COACHES, *COWES*	119
GARDINERS TRAVEL, *SPENNYMOOR*	98
GARELOCHEAD COACHES,	189
GARETH EVANS COACHES, *BRYNAMMAN*	204
GARNETT'S INTERNATIONAL, *BISHOP AUCKLAND*	98
BRYAN GARRATT/COACHMASTER, *LEICESTER*	129
GARRETT COACHES LTD, *NEWTON ABBOT*	92
GARY'S COACHES OF TREDEGAR	202
STANLEY GATH COACHES LTD, *DEWSBURY*	180
GATWICK FLYER, *ROMFORD*	105
GEE-VEE TRAVEL, *BARNSLEY*	161
GEMINI TRAVEL, *MARCHWOOD*	113
GENIAL TRAVEL, *STANWAY*	105
GEOFF'S MINIBUSES, *NEWTOWN*	210
GIBSON'S OF MOFFAT	191
GILES TOURS, *NEWTOWNARDS*	216
GILLEN COACHES, *PORT GLASGOW*	195
R G GITTINS, *WELSHPOOL*	210
GLEN COACHES LTD, *GREENOCK*	195
GLENTANA COACHES LTD, *LINLITHGOW*	201
GLENVALE TRANSPORT, *LIVERPOOL*	140
GLENVIC OF BRISTOL LTD	76
GLENWAY COACHES, *DEWSBURY*	140, 180
GLIDER TRAVEL, *BROWNHILLS*	174
G-LINE MINICOACHES, *SWINDON*	184
GLOBE COACHES, *ABERDARE*	211
GLOVERS COACHES LTD, *ASHBOURNE*	89
GLOWBELLE COACHES LTD, *WEST BROMWICH*	175
GLYN WILLIAMS TRAVEL, *BLACKWOOD*	203
JAMES GLYNN, *NURNEY*	219
GLYNNS COACH HIRE (ENNIS) LTD	219
GO NORTH EAST, *GATESHEAD*	171
GO-AHEAD GROUP	71
J D GODSON, *CROSSGATES*	181
PETER GODWARD COACHES, *SOUTH WOODHAM FERRERS*	105
GOLD STANDARD, THE, *GREENFORD*	135, 141
GOLD STAR COACHES, *TORQUAY*	92
GOLD STAR TRAVEL, *BROMSGROVE*	186
GOLD STAR TRAVEL (WALES), *NEWTOWN*	210
GOLDEN BOY COACHES (JETSIE LTD), *HODDESDON*	117
GOLDEN EAGLE COACHES, *SALSBURGH*	196
GOLDEN GREEN LUXURY TOURS, LONGNOR *BUXTON*	89
GOLDEN PIONEER TRAVEL, *HEREFORD*	115
GOLDENSTAND SOUTHERN LTD, *LONDON, NW10*	135
GOODE COACHES, *NORTHAMPTON*	150
GOODE'S COACHWAYS, *WEDNESBURY*	175
W. C. GOODSIR, *HOLYHEAD*	202
GOODWIN'S COACHES, *BRAINTREE*	105
W. GORDON & SONS, *ROTHERHAM*	161
GOSPEL'S COACHES, *HUCKNALL*	152
G. W. GOULDING, *KNOTTINGLEY*	181
GRA-CAR COACHES, *FEATHERSTONE*	181
GRAHAM URQUHART TRAVEL, *INVERNESS*	195
VIOLET GRAHAM COACHES, *PAISLEY*	199
GRAHAM'S COACHES, *BRISTOL*	76
GRAHAM'S, *KELVEDON*	105
GRAHAMS COACHES, *ABERTILLERY*	202
GRAND HOTEL TOURS, *SANDOWN*	119
GRAMPIAN COACHES, *ABERDEEN*	188
GRAND PRIX COACHES, *BROUGH*	86
GRANGEWOOD TRAVEL, *POTTER HEIGHAM*	143
GRAVES COACHES, *BROXBOURNE*	117
GRAY'S TRAVEL OF COVENTRY	175
GRAYLINE COACHES (HARTWOOD) LTD, *BICESTER*	154
GRAYLINE TOURS, *DUBLIN*	219
GRAYS LUXURY TRAVEL, *HOYLAND COMMON*	161
GRAYSCROFT BUS SERVICES LTD, *MABLETHORPE*	131
A. GREEN (COACHES) LTD, *WALTHAMSTOW*	135
GREEN BUS SERVICE (WARSTONE MOTORS), *GREAT WYRLEY*	164
GREENS COACHES, *THORNEY, PETERBOROUGH*	79
GRETTON'S COACHES, *PETERBOROUGH*	79
GREY DE LUXE COACHES, *HULL*	102
GREYHOUND COACHES CO, *CARDIFF*	203
GREYS OF ELY	79
GRIERSONS COACHES, *STOCKTON-ON-TEES*	98
GRIFFITHS COACHES, *PORTDINORWIC*	207
JEFF GRIFFITHS COACHES, *ST ANNES*	126
GRIMSHAW COACHES, *BURNLEY*	126
GRINDLES COACHES LTD, *CINDERFORD*	108
GROUP TRAVEL, *BODMIN*	84
GROUP TRAVEL, *SHREWSBURY*	156
GROVE COACHES, *HERTFORD*	117
GRWP ABERCONWY, *LLANDUDNO*	205
GUSCOTT'S COACHES LTD, *BEAWORTHY*	92

GWYN JONES, *MEIFOD*	203, 210
GWYN WILLIAMS & SONS LTD, *LOWER TUMBLE*	204
GWYNFOR COACHES, *LLANGEFNI*	202

H

H & M COACHES, *CONSETT*	98
HACKNEY COMMUNITY TRANSPORT, *LONDON*	136
HAGUES COACHES, *ROTHERHAM*	161
HAILSTONE TRAVEL, *BASILDON*	105
PHIL HAINES COACHES, *BOSTON*	131
MIKE HALFORD, *BRIDPORT*	96
A. HALPENNY, BLACKROCK, *DUNDALK*	219
HALTON BOROUGH TRANSPORT LTD, *WIDNES*	82
O. J. HAMBLY & SONS LTD, *LOOE*	84
HAMILTON OF UXBRIDGE	141
HAMPTON COACHES (WESTMINSTER) LTD, *LONDON SE8*	136
R. HANDLEY & SONS LTD, *MIDDLEHAM*	147
HAPPY AL'S COACHES, *BIRKENHEAD*	140
HAPPY DAYS COACHES, *WHITCHURCH*	156
HAPPY DAYS COACHES, *STAFFORD*	165
HAPPY WANDERER TOURS, *LEISTON*	167
HAPPY WANDERER TRAVEL, *BIRMINGHAM*	175
HARDINGS COACHES, *BETCHWORTH*	169
HARDINGS COACHES, *REDDITCH*	175, 186
HARDINGS TOURS LTD, *HUYTON*	140
HARGREAVES COACHES, *HEBDEN, Nr SKIPTON*	147
HARLEQUIN TRAVEL, *IPSWICH*	167
R. J. HARLEY, *MARLBOROUGH*	184
HARPUR'S COACHES, *DERBY*	89
HARRIS COACHES (PENGAM) LTD, *BLACKWOOD*	203
HARRIS COACHES, *GRAYS*	105
HARRIS COACHES, *TARBERT*	201
HARRIS EXECUTIVE TRAVEL, *BROMSGROVE*	186
HARRISON'S TRAVEL, *ALFRETON*	89
D & H HARROD COACHES LTD, *KING'S LYNN*	143
HARROGATE & DISTRICT TRAVEL LTD	147
HARRY EVANS, *WELSHPOOL*	210
HARWOOD COACHES, *WEYBRIDGE*	169
K. G. & R. HATTON, *ST HELENS*	140
HATTS COACHES, *CHIPPENHAM*	184
HAWKES COACHES LTD, *SWANSEA*	212
HAY'S COACHES, *HUNTLY*	188
HAYDN'S TOURS & TRAVEL, *CHIRK*	213
HAYTON'S COACHES, *BURNAGE*	110
HAYWARD TRAVEL (CARDIFF)	213
HEALINGS INTERNATIONAL COACHES, *OLDHAM*	126
HEALY COACHES, *GALWAY*	219
W. L. HEARD & SONS LTD, *BIDEFORD*	92
HEARNS COACHES, *HARROW WEALD*	141
HEATON'S OF SHEFFIELD	161
HEBRIDEAN COACHES, *LOCHBOISDALE*	201
HEDINGHAM & DISTRICT OMNIBUSES LTD, *SIBLE HEDINGHAM*	106
HELLYERS OF FAREHAM	113
HEMMINGS COACHES, *TORRINGTON*	92
HENDERSON HIRING, *TARBERT*	189
HENLEYS BUS SERVICES, *ABERTILLERY*	202
HENRY CRAWFORD COACHES LTD, *NEILSTON*	192
HENSHAWS COACHES, *JACKSDALE*	89, 152
HERBERTS TRAVEL, *SHEFFORD*	72
HERITAGE TOURS, *ST MARY'S, ISLES OF SCILLY*	215
HERDMAN COACHES, *TALGARTH*	210
HERRINGTON COACHES LTD, *FORDINGBRIDGE*	114
HEYFORDIAN TRAVEL LTD, *BICESTER*	154
HIGHLAND HERITAGE COACH TOURS, *DALMALLY*	189
HIGHLAND ROVER COACHES, *TAYNUILT*	189
HIGHWAYMAN COACHES, *PERTH*	198
HILLS OF HERSHAM, *HERSHAM*	169
HILL'S SERVICES, *TORRINGTON*	93
HILLARYS COACHES, *PRUDHOE*	150
DEREK HIRCOCKS COACHES, *UPWELL, Nr WISBECH*	79
JOHN HOBAN TRAVEL LTD, *WORKINGTON*	86
HODDER MOTOR SERVICES LTD, *CLITHEROE*	126
HODGE'S COACHES (SANDHURST) LTD, *SANDHURST*	74
HODGSONS COACHES, *BARNARD CASTLE*	98
HODSON COACHES LTD, *NAVENBY*	131
M. HOGAN, *THURLES, Co TIPPERARY*	219
HOGG EUROPEAN COACHES, *SHEFFIELD*	161
HOLLINSHEAD COACHES LTD, *BIDDULPH*	165
HOLLOWAY COACHES LTD, *SCUNTHORPE*	145
J. R. HOLLYHEAD INTERNATIONAL, *WILLENHALL*	175
G J HOLMES, *CLAY CROSS*	89
HOLMES GROUP TRAVEL, *NEWPORT*	156
HOLMESWOOD COACHES LTD, *ORMSKIRK*	126
HOMEWARD BOUND TRAVEL, *WIMBORNE*	96
HOOKWAYS EDGECUMBES COACHES, *SIDMOUTH*	93
HOOKWAYS GREENSLADES, *EXETER*	93
HOOKWAYS JENNINGS, *BUDE*	84
HOOKWAYS PLEASUREWAYS, *OKEHAMPTON*	93
HOPLEYS BUS & COACH, *TRURO*	84
P. HOPWOOD, *ASKHAM BRYAN, YORK*	147
HORNSBY TRAVEL, *SCUNTHORPE*	145
HORROCKS, *LYDBURY NORTH*	156
E & M HORSBURGH, *PUMPHERSTON*	201
HORSEMAN COACHES LTD, *READING*	74
COLIN HOSKINS MINICOACHES, *STONEHOUSE*	108
JOHN HOUGHTON, *LONDON W5*	136
HOUNSLOW COMMUNITY TRANSPORT	141
HOUNSLOW MINI COACHES, *FELTHAM*	136, 142
HOUSTON'S OF LONDON, *LONDON N15*	136
HOUSTOUN TRAVEL, *LIVINGSTON*	201
HOWARDS WAY, *WREXHAM*	213
HOWIE'S OF ROBERTTOWN, *LIVERSEDGE*	181
HOWLETTS COACHES, *WINSLOW*	77
JIM HUGHES COACHES, *SUNDERLAND*	172
VIC HUGHES & SON LTD, *FELTHAM*	142
HULLEYS OF BASLOW, *BAKEWELL*	89
HULME HALL COACHES LTD, *CHEADLE HULME*	82

HUMBLE'S COACHES, *SHILDON*	98	PAUL JAMES COACHES, *COALVILLE*	129
HUNTS COACHES, *ALFORD*	131	R. G. JAMIESON & SON, *YELL*	199
WILLIAM HUNTER, *LOANHEAD*	195	JANS COACHES, SOHAM, *ELY*	80
HUNTINGDON & DISTRICT	79	JAYLINE TRAVEL, *HORDEN, Co DURHAM*	98
HURST'S COACHES, *WIGAN*	110	JAYCREST LTD, *SITTINGBOURNE*	121
HUTCHISON'S COACHES (OVERTOWN) LTD, *WISHAW*	196	JEFFS COACHES LTD, *TOWCESTER*	150
HUTTON COACH HIRE, *WESTON-SUPER-MARE*	159	JEMS TRAVEL, *STANNINGTON*	161
J. F. HUXLEY, *MALPAS*	82	JENSON TRAVEL, *PONTYPOOL*	212
HYLTON & DAWSON, *GLENFIELD*	129	JOHN MORROW COACHES, *GLASGOW*	194
HYLTONE ENTERPRISES, *HIGH WYCOMBE*	77	JOHN WOODHAMS VINTAGE TOURS, *RYDE IoW*	120
HYTHE & WATERSIDE COACHES, *HYTHE*	114	JOHN'S COACHES, *BLANEAU-FFESTINIOG*	207
		JOHN'S TRAVEL, *WREXHAM*	213
I		BEN JOHNSON, *BRANDESBURTON*	102
IAN BALDRY, *FELIXSTOWE*	166	JOHNSON'S TOURS, *HODTHORPE*	90
IBT TRAVEL GROUP, *PRESTWICK*	199	JOHNSONS (HENLEY) LTD, *HENLEY-IN-ARDEN*	175
ILLINGWORTH COACHES, *WAKEFIELD*	181	D JONES & SON, *RHOSLLANERCRUGOG*	213
IMPACT OF LONDON, *GREENFORD*	136	E JONES & SONS, *PONCIAU*	213
IMPERIAL BUS CO LTD, *RAINHAM*	105	GWYN JONES, *MEIFOD*	203
INDEPENDENT COACHWAYS LTD, *HORSFORTH*	181	JONES EXECUTIVE COACHES LTD, *WALKDEN*	110
INGLEBY'S LUXURY COACHES LTD, *YORK*	147	JONES INTERNATIONAL, *LLANDEILO*	204
INTEGRATED TRANSPORT GROUP LTD, *ANSTON*	161	JONES MOTOR SERVICES, *FLINT*	206
INTERNATIONAL COACH LINES LTD, *THORNTON HEATH*	136	JONES MOTORS (LOGIN) LTD, *WHITLAND*	205
IPSWICH BUSES LTD	167	O. R. JONES & SONS LTD, *LLANFAETHLU*	202
IRELAND COACHES, *Co DUBLIN*	219	P. W. JONES COACHES, *HEREFORD*	115
IRISH COACHES, *DUBLIN*	219	R J JONES, *ABERYSTWYTH*	204
IRVINE'S COACHES, *LAW*	196	T. H. JONES & SON (CAELLOI MOTORS), *PWLLHELI*	207
IRVINGS COACH HIRE LTD, *CARLISLE*	86	W E JONES & SON, *LLANERCHYMEDD*	202
BRIAN ISAAC COACHES LTD, *SWANSEA*	212	JOSEPHS MINI COACHES, *NEWCASTLE-UNDER-LYME*	165
ISLAND COACH SERVICES, *LAKE, IoW*	119	DONAL JOYCE MINIBUS HIRE, *GALWAY*	219
ISLAND COACHWAYS, *ST PETER PORT*	214	JUMBO MINI COACHES, *NOTTINGHAM*	152
ISLE COACHES, *OWSTON FERRY*	161		
ISLE OF MAN TRANSPORT, *DOUGLAS*	214	**K**	
ISLE OF WIGHT COUNCIL, *NEWPORT*	119	K & B TRAVEL, *CLIBURN*	87
ISLEWORTH COACHES	142	K & S COACHES, *MANSFIELD*	152
ISLWYN BOROUGH TRANSPORT LTD, *BLACKWOOD*	203	K. M. MOTORS LTD, *BARNSLEY*	161
IVYBRIDGE & DISTRICT, *IVYBRIDGE*	93	KARDAN TRAVEL, *COWES, IoW*	119
		BERNARD KAVANAGH & SONS LTD, *URLINGFORD*	219
J		J. J. KAVANAGH & SONS, *URLINGFORD*	219
J & C COACHES, *NEWTON AYCLIFFE*	98	M. KAVANAGH, *TIPPERARY*	219
J & D EURO TRAVEL, *HARROW*	142	PIERCE KAVANAGH COACHES, *UPLINGFORD*	219
J & H COACHES, *RYE*	100	KEENAN OF AYR COACH TRAVEL, *COALHALL*	199
J & Y COACHES, *CLITHEROE*	126	KEENAN COMMERCIALS, *DUNDALK, CO LOUTH*	219
J B C MALVERNIAN TOURS, *MALVERN*	186	KEIGHLEY & DISTRICT TRAVEL	181
J C S COACHES, *CORBY*	150	KEL KIR COACHES, *OSWESTRY*	156
J R J COACHES, *CORBY*	150	KENNEALLY'S BUS SERVICE LTD, *WATERFORD*	219
J R TRAVEL, *YORK*	147	KENNEDY COACHES, *LOCHS*	201
J W COACHES LTD, *BANCHORY*	188	KENNEDY COACHES, *TRALEE*	220
JACKSON'S COACHES, *BLACKPOOL*	126	KENT COACH TOURS LTD, *ASHFORD*	122
ANDREW JAMES QUALITY TRAVEL, *CHIPPENHAM*	184	KENT COUNTY COUNCIL, *AYLESFORD*	122
BRODYR JAMES, *TREGARON*	204	KENZIES COACHES LTD, *ROYSTON*	117
JAMES KING COACHES, *NEWTON STEWART*	191	K. M. KEOGH, *ARKLOW*	220
JAMES MEFFAN LTD, *KIRRIEMUIR*	189	KERRY COACHES, *KILLARNEY, Co KERRY*	220
		KESTREL COACHES, *STOURPORT ON SEVERN*	186

Operator Index

KETTLEWELL (RETFORD) LTD	152
R. KIME & CO LTD, *FOLKINGHAM*	131
KINCH BUS LTD, *HEANOR*	129
KINEIL COACHES, *FRASERBURGH*	188
JAMES KING COACHES, *NEWTON STEWART*	191
KINGDOM COACHES, *LEVEN*	193
KINGDOM'S TOURS LTD, *TIVERTON*	93
KINGFISHER COACHES OF YEOVIL LTD	159
KINGFISHER MINICOACHES, *READING*	74
KINGS COACHES, *STANWAY*	106
THE KINGS FERRY, *GILLINGHAM*	122
KINGS LUXURY COACHES, *MIDDLESBROUGH*	147
KINGSNORTON COACHES, *BIRMINGHAM*	175
KINGSLEY COACHES, *BIRTLEY*	172
KINGSMAN INTERNATIONAL TRAVEL, *FAVERSHAM*	122
KINGSMAN SERVICES LTD, *SHEFFIELD*	161
KINGSTON COACHES, *SALISBURY*	184
KINGSWINFORD COACHWAYS, *KINGSWINFORD*	175
KIRBYS COACHES, *RAYLEIGH*	106
KIRKBY LONSDALE COACH HIRE, *CARNFORTH*	126
KIWI LUXURY TRAVEL, *NEWTON STEWART*	191
K M P (LLANBERIS) LTD	207
K N M MINIBUS SERVICES, *OSWESTRY*	156
KONECTBUS, *DEREHAM*	144
K-VALLEY MINI-COACHES, *WOKING*	169

L

LADYBIRD TRAVEL, *WORKINGTON*	87
LADYLINE, *RAWMARSH*	162
LAKELAND COACHES, *HURST GREEN*	127
LAKELAND TOURS, *TEMPO, Co FERMANAGH*	216
LAKELINE COACHES, *KNIGHTON*	156, 210
LAKES SUPERTOURS, *WINDERMERE*	87
LAKESIDE COACHES, *ELLESMERE (SHROPSHIRE)*	156
LAMBS COACHES, *STOCKPORT*	110
LAMBERT'S COACHES (BECCLES) LTD	167
LANCASHIRE UNITED, *BLACKBURN*	127
LANGSTON & TASKER, *BUCKINGHAM*	77
LEANDER COACH TRAVEL, *SWADLINCOTE*	90
JOHN LEASK & SON, *LERWICK*	199
LEE'S COACHES, *LANGLEY MOOR*	98
LEE-ROY COACHES, *BRENTWOOD*	106
LEGAL MINI BUS HIRE, *BLACKWELL, Nr ALFRETON*	90, 152
LENDOR, *MOSSLEY*	110
LEOLINE TRAVEL, *HAMPTON*	142
LEON MOTOR SERVICES LTD, *FINNINGLEY*	162
LEONS COACH TRAVEL, *STAFFORD*	165
LE-RAD COACHES & LIMOUSINES, *WOODLEY Nr STOCKPORT*	82
LESCLACHA LTD, *NEWMARKET-ON-FERGUS*	220
LEVERS COACHES LTD, *SALISBURY*	184
LEWIS COACHES, *WHITLAND*	205
LEWIS-RHYDLEWIS, *LLANDYSUL*	205
LEWIS TRAVEL UK, *LONDON SE1*	136
LEWIS COACHES, *LLANFAIR CAEREINON*	210
LEWIS'S COACHES, *LLANRHYSTUD*	204
LEWIS'S COACHES, *PAILTON*	172
LEWIS-Y-LLAN, *AMLWCH*	202
LIBERTON EXECUTIVE TRAVEL, *EDINBURGH*	192
ARNOLD LIDDELL COACHES, *BRISTOL*	76
LIDDELL'S COACHES, *AUCHINLECK*	191
LINCOLNSHIRE ROAD CAR CO LTD	131
LINK LINE COACHES LTD, *HARLESDEN*	136
LINKFAST LTD T/A S&M COACHES, *BENFLEET*	106
LISKEARD & DISTRICT OMNIBUS, *LAUNCESTON*	84
LITTLE BUS COMPANY, THE, *ELSTREE*	136
LITTLE JIM'S BUSES, *BERKHAMSTED*	117
LITTLE TRANSPORT LTD, *ILKESTON*	90
LIVERPOOL CITY COACHES	142
LLEW JONES INTERNATIONAL, *LLANWRST*	205
P&O LLOYD, *BAGILLT*	206
LLOYDS COACHES, *MACHYNLLETH*	210
LOCHS MOTOR TRANSPORT LTD, *LEWIS*	201
LODGE COACHES, *HIGH EASTER*	106
LOGANS EXECUTIVE TRAVEL, *DUNLOY*	216
LOGANS TOURS, *NORTHFLEET GREEN*	122
LONDON BUSES, *LONDON E8*	136
LONDON CENTRAL, *MITCHAM*	136
LONDON GENERAL, *MITCHAM*	137
LONDON LINK, *GILLINGHAM*	122
LONDONDERRY & LOUGH SWILLY, *LONDONDERRY*	216
LONDON UNITED BUSWAYS LTD, *TWICKENHAM*	142
DAVE LONG COACH TRAVEL, *SKIBBEREEN*	220
LONG'S COACHES LTD, *SALSBURGH*	197
LONGMYND TRAVEL, *SHREWSBURY*	156
J. J. LONGSTAFF & SONS LTD, *DEWSBURY*	181
LONGSTAFF'S COACHES, *MORPETH*	150
LONSDALE COACHES, *CARNFORTH*	127
LOTHIAN BUSES, *EDINBURGH*	192
LUAS, *DUBLIN*	220
LUCKETTS TRAVEL, *FAREHAM*	114
LUDLOWS OF HALESOWEN	175
LUGG VALLEY PRIMROSE TRAVEL, *LEOMINSTER*	115
LUXURY MINI COACH, GREENFORD	137, 142
A. LYLES & SON, *BATLEY*	181

M

M. LINE INTERNATIONAL COACHES, *ALLOA*	190
M & B COACHES & MINIBUSES, *TELFORD*	156
M & E COACHES, *HERSHAM*	169
M & H COACHES, *DENBIGH*	206
M & J TRAVEL, *CRAVEN ARMS*	156
M & M COACH LINES, *HARROW WEALD*	142
M & S MINI-COACHES, *LEOMINSTER*	116
M C H MINIBUSES, *UXBRIDGE*	142
M C T GROUP TRAVEL LTD, *MOTHERWELL*	197
M D COACH HIRE, *DUBLIN*	220
M P MINICOACHES, *TELFORD*	156

Operator	Page
M T P CHARTER COACHES, *LONDON E11*	137
MACTOURS LTD, *EDINBURGH*	193
MacEWAN'S COACH SERVICES, *AMISFIELD*	191
MACKAY COACHES, *BONNYRIGG*	193
NEIL MacKELLAIG, *GLASGOW*	194
MACKIE'S COACHES, *ALLOA*	190
DUNCAN MacLENAN, *STRATH-CARRON*	194
MacPHAILS COACHES, *MOTHERWELL*	197
MacPHERSON COACHES LTD, *SWADLINCOTE*	90, 165
MAGPIE TRAVEL, HIGH *WYCOMBE*	77
MAIRS COACHES, *ABERDEEN*	188
MAISEY, *PONTYPRIDD*	211
GERALD MANNING, CROOM, *LIMERICK*	220
MANOR TRAVEL, *BEEFORD*	102
MANSFIELD'S COACHES, *SWINDON*	184
MARBILL COACH SERVICES LTD, *BEITH*	196
MARCHANTS COACHES LTD, *CHELTENHAM*	108
MARCHWOOD MOTORWAYS LTD, *TOTTON*	114
MARGARET GREEN t/a GREENS COACHES, *THORNEY, PETERBOROUGH*	79
MARPLE MINI COACHES	82, 111
MARSHALLS COACHES, *LEIGHTON BUZZARD*	72
MARSHALLS OF SUTTON-ON-TRENT, *NEWARK*	152
ALAN MARTIN COACHES, *DUBLIN*	220
WALTER MARTIN COACHES, *SHEFFIELD*	162
MARTIN'S OF *TYSOE*	172
MARTIN'S COACH TRAVEL, *LIVINGSTON*	201
MARTINS MINI-COACHES, *LONDON*	137
MARTINS COACHES, *CHAPELTOWN*	162
MARTINS COACHES, *KETTERING*	150
MARTINS SELF DRIVE, *REDFIELD*	76
MARTIN'S COACHES, *CAVAN*	220
MASS TRANSIT, *ANSTON*	162
MASTER TRAVEL, *WELWYN GARDEN CITY*	117
MATTHEWS COACHES, *KINGS LYNN*	144
MAUDES COACHES, *BARNARD CASTLE*	98
MAUN CRUSADER TOURS, *SUTTON-IN-ASHFIELD*	152
MAYFIELD COACHES	162
MAYNE COACHES LTD, *WARRINGTON*	82
MAYNE OF MANCHESTER, *CLAYTON*	111
MAYNES COACHES, *BUCKIE*	196
MAX SERVICES, *LOWESTOFT*	167
ROY McCARTHY COACHES, *MACCLESFIELD*	82
McCOLLS OF ARGYLL, *DUNOON*	176, 190
McCOLLS COACHES, *ALEXANDRIA*	200
P. J. McCONNON, *MONAGHAN*	220
McCULLOCH'S COACHES, *STRANRAER*	191
JAMES McGEE (BUSES), *LETTERKENNY*	220
JOHN McGINLEY COACHES, *LETTERKENNY, Co DONEGAL*	220
McKECHNIE OF BATHGATE LTD	201
McKENDRY COACHES, *LOANHEAD*	195
McKINDLESS EXPRESS, *WISHAW*	197
McLAUGHLIN'S TOURS, *PENWORTHAM*	127
McLEANS COACHES, *WITNEY*	154
MEADWAY PRIVATE HIRE, *BIRMINGHAM*	176
MICHAEL MEERE COACH HIRE, *ENNIS*	220
MEMORY LANE COACHES, *OLD BOLINGBROKE*	131
MEMORY LANE VINTAGE OMNIBUS SERVICES, *MAIDENHEAD*	74
MEREDITHS COACHES, *MALPAS*	82
MERLYN'S COACHES (SKEWEN) LTD	208
MERVYN'S COACHES, *MICHELDEVER*	114
MESSENGER COACHES, *ASPATRIA*	87
METRO COACHES, *STOCKTON-ON-TEES*	147
METROBUS LTD, *ORPINGTON*	137
METROLINE, *HARROW*	137
METROLINK, *MANCHESTER*	111
MEYERS COACHES, *LLANPUMSAINT*	205
MID DEVON COACHES, *CREDITON*	93
MIDLAND BUS CO LTD, *ATHLONE*	220
MID WALES TRAVEL, *NEWTOWN*	210
MID WALES TRAVEL, *PENRHYNCOCH*	204
MIDWAY MOTORS, *CRYMYCH*	208
MIKES COACHES, *BASILDON*	106
MIL-KEN TRAVEL LTD, *LITTLEPORT*	80
MIL-KEN TRAVEL LTD, *NEWMARKET*	167
KEN MILLER TRAVEL, *SHENSTONE*	175
MILLER'S COACHES, *AIRDRIE*	197
MILLIGANS COACH TRAVEL, *MAUCHLINE*	199
MILLMAN COACHES, *GRIMSBY*	145
MILLMAN'S OF *WARRINGTON*	83
MILLPORT MOTORS LTD	196
ALEX MILNE, *NEW BYTH*	189
MINIBUS & COACH HIRE, *EARL STONHAM*	167
MINIBUS SERVICES, *WATFORD*	117
MINI-BUS SHUTTLE SERVICE, *LONDON SW1*	137
MINSTERLEY MOTORS, *SHREWSBURY*	156
MK METRO LTD, *MILTON KEYNES*	77
MITCHAM BELLE, *MITCHAM*	137
MOFFAT & WILLIAMSON LTD, *GAULDRY*	193
MOOR TO SEA, *NEWTON ABBOT*	93
MOORE'S COACHES LTD, *HOLMES CHAPEL*	83
MOORLAND BUSES, *WESTON COYNEY*	165
J. R. MORLEY & SONS LTD, *WHITTLESEY*	80
JOE MORONEY, *ENNIS*	220
MORRIS TRAVEL, *CARMARTHEN*	205
JOHN MORROW COACHES, *GLASGOW*	194
MORTON'S COACH, *DUBLIN*	220
MOSLEYS TOURS, *DEWSBURY*	162
MOTTS COACHES (AYLESBURY) LTD, *STOKE MANDEVILLE*	77
MOUNTAIN GOAT LTD, *WINDERMERE*	87
MOUNTS BAY COACHES, *PENZANCE*	84
C. W. MOXON LTD, *OLDCOTES*	152
MUIRS COACHES, *DOUGLAS WATER*	199
MULLEYS MOTORWAYS LTD, *IXWORTH*	167
LEN MUNDEN & SON LTD, *BRISTOL*	76
MUNRO'S OF JEDBURGH	190
THOMAS MURPHY & SONS, *BRAY, Co WICKLOW*	220

Operator	Page
GAVIN MURRAY & ELLISONS COACHES, *ST HELENS*	140
MYKANN COACH HIRE, *SWADLINCOTE*	90
MYTTON TRAVEL, *MINSTERLEY*	156

N

Operator	Page
NASH COACHES LTD, *SMETHWICK*	176
NATIONAL EXPRESS GROUP PLC	71
NATIONAL EXPRESS LTD, *EDGBASTON*	176
NAUGHTON COACH TOURS, *SPIDDAL*	220
N. C. B. MOTORS LTD, *WEM*	157
NEALS TRAVEL LTD, *ISLEHAM, ELY*	80
NEFYN COACHES, *NEFYN, PWLLHELI*	207
NEIL MACKELLAIG, *GLASGOW*	194
NELSON & SON (GLYNNEATH) LTD, *NEATH*	208
W. H. NELSON (COACHES) LTD, *WICKFORD*	106
NESBIT BROS LTD, *MELTON MOWBRAY*	129
NESTORBUS LTD, *GALWAY & DUBLIN*	220
NEVILLE'S TOURS, *SUTTON COLDFIELD*	176
NEW BHARAT COACHES LTD, *SOUTHALL*	137
NEW ENTERPRISE COACHES, *TONBRIDGE*	122
NEWBOURNE COACHES, *LEIGHTON BUZZARD*	137
NEWBURY COACHES, *LEDBURY*	116
NEWBURY TRAVEL, *OLDBURY*	176
NEWPORT TRANSPORT LTD	208
M. W. NICOLL'S COACH HIRE, *LAUREiNCEKIRK*	189
NIDDRIE COACHES, *MIDDLEWICH*	83
NIELSEN TRAVEL SERVICES, *SHEFFIELD*	162
NIGEL JACKSON TRAVEL, *QUENIBOROUGH*	129
NOLAN COACHES, *COOLOCK, DUBLIN*	221
NORFOLK GREEN, *KINGS LYNN*	144
NORTH BIRMINGHAM BUSWAYS LTD, *ERDINGTON*	176
NORTH SOMERSET COACHES, *NAILSEA*	76
NORTHERN BLUE, *BURNLEY*	127
NORTON MINI TRAVEL, *STOCKTON-ON-TEES*	98
NOTTINGHAM CITY TRANSPORT LTD	152
NOTTINGHAM EXPRESS TRANSIT	152
NOTTS & DERBY TRACTION CO LTD, *HEANOR*	90
NU-VENTURE COACHES LTD, *AYLESFORD*	122

O

Operator	Page
OTS MINIBUS & COACH HIRE, *CONSTANTINE*	84
O'CONNELL COACHES, *BALLINASLOE*	221
O'CONNOR AUTOTOURS LTD, *KILLARNEY*	221
TOM O'CONNOR, *TRALEE*	221
FEDA O'DONNELL, *DONEGAL*	221
O'FLAHERTY TRANSPORT, *LISDOONVARNA*	221
LARRY O'HARA, *WATERFORD*	221
O'MALLEY COACHES, *NEWPORT, Co TIPPERARY*	221
O'S COACHES, *HOSPITAL, Co LIMERICK*	221
O'SULLIVANS COACHES, *MALLOW, Co CORK*	221
OARE'S COACHES, *HOLYWELL*	206
OBAN & DISTRICT BUSES LTD	190
OCEAN COACHES, *PORTSLADE*	100
DAVID OGDEN COACHES, *ST HELENS*	140
OLYMPIA TRAVEL, *HINDLEY*	127
OLYMPIAN COACHES LTD, *HARLOW*	106
THE ORIGINAL LONDON TOUR, *WANDSWORTH*	137
ORKNEY COACHES, *KIRKWALL*	197
OWEN'S COACHES LTD, *YATELEY*	114
OWEN'S MOTORS LTD, *KNIGHTON*	210
OWENS OF OSWESTRY LTD	157
OXFORD BUS COMPANY	154

P

Operator	Page
P&M COACHES, *WICKFORD*	106
DAVID PALMER COACHES LTD, *NORMANTON*	181
PARAGON TRAVEL, *UTTOXETER*	165
PARAMOUNT MINI-COACHES, *PLYMOUTH*	93
PARK'S OF HAMILTON	200
PARKERS COACHES, *SWADLINCOTE*	90
PARKSIDE TRAVEL, *BROXBOURNE*	117
J P M PARRY, *CRADLEY HEATH*	176
PARRYS INTERNATIONAL TOURS LTD, *CHESLYN HAY*	165
PASSENGER TRANSPORT LOGISTICS LTD, *MILTON KEYNES*	78
PAT'S COACHES, *NEW BROUGHTON*	213
T PATERSON & BROWN LTD, *KILBIRNIE*	196
PATHFINDER MASONS, *WILLENHALL*	176
PATRON TRAVEL, *FLINTHAM*	153
PAUL'S TRAVEL, *HUDDERSFIELD*	181
PAVILION COACHES, *HOVE*	101
D. A. PAYNE COACH HIRE, *ST NEOTS*	80
PAYNES COACHES & CAR HIRE LTD, *BUCKINGHAM*	78
PC COACHES OF LINCOLN	132
PEARCES PRIVATE HIRE, *WALLINGFORD*	154
PEARSON COACHES, *HULL*	102
PEELINGS COACHES, *KING'S LYNN*	144
PEGASUS COACHWAYS LTD, *RETFORD*	153
PEGASUS TRAVEL, *PERTH*	198
PEMICO TRAVEL, *BERMONDSEY*	138
PENCOED TRAVEL LTD, *BRIDGEND*	203
PENMERE MINIBUS SERVICES, *FALMOUTH*	85
PENNINE MOTOR SERVICES, *GARGRAVE*	147
PENINSULA DRIVERS, *IVYBRIDGE*	93
PERRY'S COACHES, *MALTON*	147
PERRYMAN SERVICES, *BURNMOUTH*	190
PETE'S TRAVEL (LIONSPEED LTD), *WEST BROMWICH*	176
PETER CAROL PRESTIGE COACHING, *WHITCHURCH, BRISTOL*	75
PETERBOROUGH TRAVEL CONSULTANTS *PETERBOROUGH*	80
PETE'S TRAVEL, *WEST BROMWICH*	176
PEWSEY VALE COACHES, *PEWSEY*	185
PHIL ANSLOW TRAVEL GROUP LTD, *PONTYPOOL*	212
PHILLIPS COACHES HOLYWELL LTD, *GREENFIELD*	206

PHILLIPS COACHES, *SOUTH WOODHAM FERRERS*	106	READING & WOKINGHAM COACHES, *WOKINGHAM*	74
COLLIN PHILLIPSON MINICOACHES, *OUSEFLEET*	162	READING HERITAGE TRAVEL, *READING*	74
PICKERING COACHES, *SOUTH GODSTONE*	169	READING TRANSPORT LTD	74
PIED BULL COACHES, *MOLD*	206	REAYS COACHES LTD, *WIGTON*	87
JOHN PIKE COACHES, *ANDOVER*	114	RED ARROW COACHES LTD, *HUDDERSFIELD*	181
PLANET TRAVEL, *EARITH*	80	RED KITE COMMERCIAL SERVICES *LEIGHTON BUZZARD*	72
PLANTS LUXURY TRAVEL, *CHEADLE, STAFFS*	165	RED ROSE TRAVEL LTD, *AYLESBURY*	78
PLASTOWS COACHES, *WHEATLEY*	154	REDROUTE BUSES, *NORTHFLEET*	122
DAVID PLATT COACHES & MINITRAVEL OF LEES *OLDHAM*	111	REDBY TRAVEL LTD, *SUNDERLAND*	172
PLYMOUTH CITYBUS LTD	93	REDFERN COACHES (MANSFIELD) LTD	153
POOTS COACH HIRE, *TANDRAGEE*	216	RED KITE COACHES, *ABERYSTWYTH*	73
PORTHCAWL OMNIBUS CO LTD	203	REDLINE COACHES, *LEYLAND*	127
JOHN POWELL TRAVEL, *HELLABY*	162	REDWING COACHES, *LONDON* SE24	138
POWELLS COACHES, *CREDITON*	93	REDWOOD TRAVEL, *MAYFORD*	169
POWELLS COACHES, *SHERBORNE*	96	REDWOODS TRAVEL, *CULLOMPTON*	94
JACKY POWER TOURS, *TRALEE*	221	REES MOTOR (TRAVEL), *LLANELLY HILL, ABERGAVENNY*	207
POYNTERS COACHES, *ASHFORD, KENT*	122	REEVES COACH HOLIDAYS, *CHORLEY*	127
PREMIER TRAVEL SERVICES, *CAMBRIDGE*	80	REG'S COACHES LTD, *HERTFORD*	117
PREMIER TRAVEL, *BRISTOL*	76	REGAL BUSWAYS, *CHELMSFORD*	106
PRENTICE WESTWOOD, *WEST CALDER*	201	REGENT COACHES, *WHITSTABLE*	123
PRESTIGE PEOPLE CARRIERS, *CREWE*	83	REIDS OF RHYNIE, *RHYNIE, BY HUNTLY*	189
PRESTON BUS LTD	127	RELIANCE LUXURY COACHES, *BENFLEET*	106
PRESTWOOD TRAVEL, *GREAT MISSENDEN*	78	RELIANCE MOTOR SERVICES, *SUTTON-ON-FOREST*	148
PRICES COACHES, *SOUTHSEA, WALES*	213	RELIANCE TRAVEL, *GRAVESEND*	123
PRIMROSE COACHES OF CORNWALL, *HAYLE*	85	RELIANCE TRAVEL, *GREAT GONERBY*	132
PRINCESS SUMMERBEE COACHES, *WEST END, SOUTHAMPTON*	114	RELIANT COACHES LTD, *HEATHER*	129
PRIORY MOTOR COACH CO LTD, *NORTH SHIELDS*	172	RENNIES OF DUNFERMLINE LTD	193
F PROCTER & SON LTD, *FENTON*	165	RENOWN COACHES, *BEXHILL ON SEA*	101
PROCTERS COACHES (NORTH YORKSHIRE), *LEEMING BAR*	148	REXQUOTE HERITAGE COACHES, *BISHOPS LYDEARD*	159
PROSPECT COACHES (WEST) LTD, *STOURBRIDGE*	176	REYNOLDS COACHES OF CAISTER, *GREAT YARMOUTH*	144
PROTOURS (ISLE OF MAN), *DOUGLAS*	214	REYNOLDS DIPLOMAT COACHES, *WATFORD*	117
PROVENCE PRIVATE HIRE, *ST ALBANS*	117	RHIEW VALLEY COACHES, *WELSHPOOL*	210
PULFREYS COACHES, *GRANTHAM*	132	RICHARDS BROS, *MOYLGROVE*	204
PULLMAN COACHES LTD, *SWANSEA*	212	RICHARDSON COACHES, *HARTLEPOOL*	99
PULLMAN DINER, *KNOTTINGLEY*	181	RICHARDSON TRAVEL LTD, *MIDHURST*	178
		RICHMOND'S COACHES, *BARLEY*	118
R		RIDDLER'S COACHES, *ARBROATH*	189
R & B COACHES, *LUDLOW*	157	RIDLERS, *DULVERTON*	159
BEELINE (R. & R.) COACHES LTD, *WARMINSTER*	183	RIDUNA BUSES, *ALDERNEY*	214
R. D. H. SERVICES, *PLUMPTON*	101	JOHN RIGBY TRAVEL, *DRIGHLINGTON*	182
R J COACHES, *CORBY*	150	RIGBY'S, KIRKHAM'S, GRIMSHAW'S *ALTHAM*	127
R. K. F. TRAVEL, *STROOD*	122	RINGWOOD COACHES, *STAVELEY*	90
RADLEY COACH TRAVEL, *BRIGG*	145	RIVERSIDE COACHES, *TELFORD*	157
RADMORES COACHES, *PLYMPTON*	94	ROADLINER PASSENGER TRANSPORT	96
RAINHAM COACH CO, THE, *GILLINGHAM*	122	ROADLINER TRAVEL, *CREWE*	83
RAMBLER COACHES, *HASTINGS*	101	ROADMARK TRAVEL LTD, *STORRINGTON*	178
RAMON TRAVEL, *BOSCOMBE*	96	ROBERTS COACHES, *ABERYSTWYTH*	204
RANGER TRAVEL, *SOUTH CROYDON*	169	ROBERTS COACHES, *HUGGLESCOTE*	129
RAPSONS GROUP, *INVERNESS*	195	ROBERTS MINI COACHES, *RHANDIR*	205
RAYS COACHES, *PLYMOUTH*	94	ROBERTS TOURS	99
RB TRAVEL, *PYTCHLEY*	150	ROBIN HOOD TRAVEL LTD, *RUDYARD*	165

Operator	Page
ROBIN'S COACHES, *CHIPPENHAM*	185
ROBINSON KIMBOLTON, *KIMBOLTON*	80
ROBINSONS HOLIDAYS, *GREAT HARWOOD*	127
ROBINSONS COACHES, *APPLEBY*	87
ROBINSONS COACHES, *STUKLEY*	78
RODGER'S COACHES, *CORBY*	150
ROEVILLE TOURS LTD, *ADWICK-LE-STREET*	162
ROLLINSON SAFEWAY LTD, *LEEDS*	182
ROLYN TRAVEL, *BEDFORD*	73
ROMDRIVE, *MELTON MOWBRAY*	130
RONDO TRAVEL, *HARROGATE*	148
RONS COACHES LTD, *LANCING*	178
RONSWAY, *LEIGHTON BUZZARD*	118
O. ROONEY, *HILLTOWN*	216
ROPERS COACHES, *BRADFORD*	182
ROSELYN COACHES, *PAR*	85
JOHN ROSS, *ARDEE, Co LOUTH*	221
ROSS TRAVEL, *FEATHERSTONE*	181
ROSSENDALE TRANSPORT LTD, *RAWTENSTALL*	128
ROUNDABOUT BUSES, *SIDCUP*	123
ROVER COACHES, *MULLINGAR*	221
ROVER EUROPEAN TRAVEL, *HORSLEY, STROUD*	108
ROWE & TUDHOPE COACHES, *KILMARNOCK*	192
ROWELL COACHES, *LOW PRUDHOE*	151
ROY BROWNS COACHES, *BUILTH WELLS*	209
ROYLES TRAVEL, *SHEFFIELD*	162
ROY PHILLIPS, *SLEAFORD*	132
JOHN RUMLEY, *TALLOW, Co CORK*	221
RUTHERFORDS TRAVEL, *EASTERGATE*	178
S	
S&M COACHES, *BENFLEET*	106
SAFEGUARD COACHES, *GUILDFORD*	170
SAFFORDS COACHES LTD, *SANDY*	73
SALOPIA COACHES LTD, *WEM*	157
SANDERS COACHES, *HOLT*	144
SANDGROUNDER, *SOUTHPORT*	128
SARGEANTS BROS LTD, *KINGTON*	116
SCARBOROUGH & DISTRICT	148
SCARLET BAND, *WEST CORNFORTH*	99
SCHOFIELD TRAVEL LTD, *LOUGHBOROUGH*	130
SCOTIA TRAVEL, *GLENROTHES*	193
SCOTLAND & BATES, *APPLEDORE*	123
SCOTTISH CITYLINK COACHES LTD, *GLASGOW*	194
SEAVIEW SERVICES, *SANDOWN*	120
SEA VIEW COACHES (POOLE) LTD	96
SEAGER'S COACHES LTD, *CHIPPENHAM*	185
SEALANDAIR COACHING (IRELAND) *DUBLIN*	221
SEARLE'S AUTO SERVICES, *THORNHAUGH, Nr PETERBOROUGH*	80
SEATH COACHES, *EAST STUDDAL, Nr DOVER*	123
SECOND CITY TRAVEL, *BIRMINGHAM*	176
SELVEY'S COACHES, *CAMBUSLANG*	194
SELWYNS TRAVEL, *MANCHESTER AIRPORT*	111
SELWYNS TRAVEL, *RUNCORN*	83
H. SEMMENCE & CO LTD, *WYMONDHAM*	144
SERENE TRAVEL, *BEDLINGTON*	151
SEWARDS COACHES, *AXMINSTER*	94
SHAFTESBURY & DISTRICT MOTOR SERVICES	96
SHALDER COACHES LTD, *STROMNESS*	199
SHAMROCK COACHES, *NEWPORT*	208
SHAMROCK HOPPA, *PONTYPRIDD*	211
MATT SHANAHAN COACHES, *WATERFORD*	221
HARRY SHAW, *COVENTRY*	176
SHAWS OF MAXEY, *PETERBOROUGH*	80
SHEARER OF HUNTLY	189
SHEARINGS LTD, *EXHALL*	176
SHEARINGS LTD, *NORMANTON*	182
SHEARINGS LTD, *WARRINGTON*	83
SHEARINGS LTD, *WIGAN*	111
SHEN CARE VOLUNTARY TRANSPORT, *SELLY OAK*	176
SHERBURN VILLAGE COACHES	99
SHERWOOD TRAVEL, *IMMINGHAM*	145
SHIEL BUSES, *ACHARACLE*	195
SHIRE COACHES, *ST ALBANS*	118
SHIRE TRAVEL INTERNATIONAL, *HEDNESFORD*	165
SHOREY'S TRAVEL & TRANSPORT, *MAULDEN*	73
B. R. SHREEVE & SONS LTD, *LOWESTOFT*	168
SHROPSHIRE COUNTY COUNCIL, *SHREWSBURY*	157
SHUTTLE BUSES LTD, *KILWINNING*	196
SIDLAW EXECUTIVE TRAVEL, *AUCHTERHOUSE*	189
SIESTA INTERNATIONAL, *MIDDLESBROUGH*	148
SILCOX COACHES, *PEMBROKE DOCK*	209
SILVER CHOICE TRAVEL LTD, *EAST KILBRIDE*	200
SILVER COACH LINES, *EDINBURGH*	193
SILVER STAR COACH HOLIDAYS LTD, *CAERNARFON*	207
SILVERDALE LONDON LTD, *LONDON NW10*	138
SILVERDALE TOURS (NOTTINGHAM) LTD, *NOTTINGHAM*	153
SILVERLINE TRAVEL, *BIGGLESWADE*	73
SILVERLINE LANDFLIGHT, *SOLIHULL*	176
SILVERWING SPECIALISED TOURS, *HULL*	102
WILLIAM SIM & SON, *BOOT*	87
SIMMONDS COACHES LTD, *LETCHWORTH*	118
SIMONDS COACH & TRAVEL, *BOTESDALE*	144
SIMPSON'S COACHES, *ROSEHEARTY*	189
SIXTY SIXTY COACHES, *PENTREBACH*	207
D. W. SKELTON, *BRIDGWATER*	159
SKILLS MOTOR COACHES, *BULWELL*	153
SKINNERS OF OXTED	170
SKYLINERS LTD, *NUNEATON*	172
SLACKS TRAVEL, *MATLOCK*	90
SLEAFORDIAN COACHES, *SLEAFORD*	132
H. & A. SLEEP, *BERE ALSTON*	94
SLEIGHTS COACHES, *SWINTON*	162
SLOAN TRAVEL, *ROSTREVOR*	216
SLOCOACH, *MOTHERWELL*	197
SMITH & SONS COACHES, *COUPAR ANGUS*	198
JOHN SMITH & SONS, *THIRSK*	148

Operator	Page
SMITH'S COACHES (BE & GW SMITH), SHEPTON MALLET	159
SMITH-BUNTINGFORD	118
SMITHS COACHES (MARPLE) LTD	83, 111
SMITHS COACHES, CORBY GLEN, Nr GRANTHAM	132
SMITHS COACHES, LISKEARD	85
SMITHS CONTINENTAL TRAVEL, BRENZETT	123
G. A. SMITHS COACHES LTD, TRING	118
SMITHS MOTORS (LEDBURY) LTD	116
SNOWDON COACHES, EASINGTON	99
SOLENT BLUE LINE, SOUTHAMPTON	114
SOLENT COACHES, RINGWOOD	114
SOLID ENTERTAINMENTS, GRIMSBY	145
SOMERBUS, BRISTOL	76
SOUL BROS LTD, OLNEY	78
SOUTH DORSET COACHES LTD, SWANAGE	96
SOUTH GLOUCESTERSHIRE BUS & COACH COMPANY, PATCHWAY, BRISTOL	76
SOUTH LANCS TRAVEL, ATHERTON	111
SOUTH MIMMS TRAVEL LTD	118
SOUTH WEST COACHES LTD, WINCANTON	159
SOUTHDOWN PSV, COPTHORNE	178
SOUTHERN COACHES (NM) LTD, BARRHEAD	192
SOUTHERN VECTIS PLC	71
SOUTHERN VECTIS, NEWPORT, IoW	120
SOUTHGATE COACHES LTD, LONDON N11	138
SOUTHLANDS TRAVEL LTD, SWANLEY	123
SOUTHNOR COACHES, DARTFORD	123
SOVEREIGN BUS & COACH CO LTD, STEVENAGE	118
SOVEREIGN COACHES, LYME REGIS	96
SPA COACHES, STRATHPEFFER	195
PAUL SPENCE COACHES, BRADFORD	182
SPENCERS COACHES, NEWARK	153
SPOT HIRE TRAVEL, BEARSTED	123
SPRATTS COACHES LTD, WRENINGHAM	144
SQUIRRELL'S COACHES, HITCHAM	168
ST ANDREWS EXECUTIVE TRAVEL	194
ST KEVINS BUS SERVICE (P. DOYLE), ROUNDWOOD, Co WICKLOW	221
STAGECOACH IN CAMBRIDGE, CAMBRIDGE	80
STAGECOACH EAST, NORTHAMPTON	150
STAGECOACH IN DARLINGTON	99
STAGECOACH DEVON, EXETER	94
STAGE COACH IN EAST KENT & HASTINGS	123
STAGECOACH IN HASTINGS, ST LEONARDS ON SEA	101
STAGECOACH EAST MIDLANDS, CHESTERFIELD	90
STAGECOACH GROUP	71
STAGECOACH IN HAMPSHIRE, BASINGSTOKE	114
STAGECOACH HANTS & SURREY, ALDERSHOT	114
STAGECOACH HARTLEPOOL	99
STAGECOACH KINGSTON-UPON-HULL	102
STAGECOACH LONDON, ILFORD	138
STAGECOACH MANCHESTER, ARDWICK	111
STAGECOACH NORTH EAST, SUNDERLAND	172
STAGECOACH NORTH WEST, CARLISLE	87
STAGECOACH IN OXFORDSHIRE	154
STAGECOACH SOUTH, CHICHESTER	178
STAGECOACH IN SOUTH WALES, CWMBRAN	212
STAGECOACH IN WARWICKSHIRE, RUGBY	172
STAGECOACH SUPERTRAM	162
STAGECOACH WEST, GLOUCESTER	108
STAGECOACH WEST SCOTLAND, AYR	200
F. W. STAINTON & SON LTD, KENDAL	87
STALLION COACHES, CHELMSFORD	106
STAN'S COACHES, MALDON	106
STANLEY MACKAY COACHES OF EDINBURGH BONNYRIGG	193
STANLEY TAXIS & MINICOACHES	99
STANSTED TRANSIT, STANSTED	118
STANWAYS COACHES, KIDSGROVE	166
STARLINE BAND SERVICES, CLEVEDON	159
STEEL'S LUXURY COACHES, ILKLEY	182
STEPEND COACHES, GLENMAVIS	197
STEPHENSONS OF EASINGWOLD	148
STEPHENSONS OF ESSEX LTD, ROCHFORD	106
STEVE'S OF AMBLESIDE LTD	87
L. F. STEWART & SON LTD, DALAYICH, BY TAYNUILT	190
STEVE STOCKDALE COACHES, SELBY	148
STODDARDS LTD, CHEADLE, STAFFS	166
STOKE BUS SERVICES, PAIGNTON	94
STOCKHAMS COACHES, CRICKHOWELL	210
WILLIAM STOKES & SONS LTD, CARSTAIRS	200
STONEHOUSE COACHES	200
STONES COACHES OF BATH	159
E STOTT & SONS, MILNSBRIDGE	182
STOTT'S TOURS (OLDHAM) LTD	111
STRAFFORD'S COACHES, MINERA	213
STRATHTAY SCOTTISH, DUNDEE	191
STRATOS TRAVEL LTD, NEWTOWN, POWYS	210
STREAMLINE (MAIDSTONE) LTD	124
STREETS COACHWAYS LTD, BARNSTAPLE	94
STRINGERS PONTEFRACT MOTORWAYS	182
STUARTS OF CARLUKE	200
STUDIO WORKSHOPS LTD, IVER HEATH	78
SUIRWAY BUS & COACH SERVICES LTD, PASSAGE EAST, Co WATERFORD	221
SULLIVAN BUSES, POTTERS BAR	118
SUMMERDALE COACHES, LETTERSTON	209
SUMMERFIELD COACHES LTD, SOUTHAMPTON	115
SUNBEAM COACHES LTD, NORWICH	144
SUNBURY COACHES, SHEPPERTON	142
SUNRAY TRAVEL, EPSOM	170
SUN-SET COACHES, PENZANCE	85
SUPERTRAVEL MINICOACHES, SPEKE	140
SURELINE COACHES, WOKING	170
SUSSEX COUNTRY TOURS, SHOREHAM	178
SUSSEX PIONEER COACHES, BRIGHTON	101
SUTTON COMMUNITY TRANSPORT	170
SWALLOW COACH CO LTD, RAINHAM, ESSEX	107
SWANBROOK BUS, CHELTENHAM	108

Operator Index

Operator	Page
SWEYNE COACHES, *GOOLE*	103
SWIFTS HAPPY DAYS TRAVEL, *DONCASTER*	162
SWIFTSURE TRAVEL (BURTON UPON TRENT) LTD	166
SWINDON VINTAGE OMNIBUS, *SWINDON*	185
G. E. SYKES & SON, *APPLETON ROEBUCK*	148

T

Operator	Page
T & S TRAVEL, *PONTEFRACT*	182
T LINE TRAVEL, *MELTON MOWBRAY*	130
TF MINI COACHES, *BARKING*	107
T M TRAVEL, *STAVELEY*	91
T N C COACHES, *CASTLE BROMWICH*	177
TAF VALLEY COACHES, *WHITLAND*	205
F. T. TAGG COACHES, *SUTTON-IN-ASHFIELD*	153
TALLY HO! COACHES, *KINGSBRIDGE*	94
TANAT VALLEY COACHES, *LLANRHAEDR YM, OSWESTRY*	210
TANGNEY TOURS, *BOROUGH GREEN*	124
TANTIVY BLUE COACH TOURS, *ST HELIER, JERSEY*	214
TAPPINS COACHES, *DIDCOT*	155
TARGET TRAVEL GROUP LTD, *CRAMLINGTON*	151
TATES COACHES, *MARKYATE*	118
TAVISTOCK COMMUNITY TRANSPORT, *GREENLANDS*	85
TAW & TORRIDGE COACHES LTD incorporating LOVERINGS COACHES, *MERTON*	94
TAWE TOURS, *MORRISTON*	212
TAYLORS OF SUTTON SCOTNEY LTD	115
TELFORD'S COACHES, *NEWCASTLETON*	190
TELLINGS GOLDEN MILLER BUSES LTD, *TWICKENHAM*	170
TELLINGS GOLDEN MILLER COACHES LTD, *TWICKENHAM*	170
TERRY'S COACH HIRE, *COVENTRY*	177
TERRY'S COACHES, *HEMEL HEMPSTEAD*	118
TEST VALLEY TRAVEL, *WHITEPARISH*	185
TETLEYS MOTOR SERVICES, *HUNSLET*	182
THAMESDOWN TRANSPORT LTD, *SWINDON*	185
ARTHUR THOMAS COACHES, *GORSEINON*	212
THOMAS BROS, *LLANGADOG*	205
D J THOMAS COACHES OF NEATH	208
EDWARD THOMAS & SON, *WEST EWELL*	170
THOMAS OF BARRY	213
THOMAS OF RHONDDA, *PORTH*	211
THOMAS PATERSON & BROWN LTD, *KILBIRNIE*	196
THOMPSON TRAVEL, *ROTHERHAM*	162
THOMPSON'S, *FRAMLINGHAM*	168
THOMSETT'S COACHES, *DEAL*	124
THORNES INDEPENDENT LTD, *HEMINGBROUGH*	148
F. E. THORPE & SONS LTD, *LONDON W10*	138
THREE STAR (LUTON) LTD	73
TILLEY'S COACHES, *BUDE*	85
TIMELINE TRAVEL, *BOLTON*	111
TIMELINE TRAVEL, *WALSALL*	177
TIM'S TRAVEL, *SHEERNESS*	124
E. TITTERINGTON & SON, *BLENCOW*	88
TOMORROWS TRANSPORT, *ENFIELD*	138
TONNA LUXURY COACHES LTD, *NEATH*	208
TOP COACHES, *TIMSBURY*	159
TOP LINE TRAVEL, *YORK*	148
TOTNES & DARTMOUTH RING & RIDE, *TOTNES*	94
TOURIST COACHES LTD, *SALISBURY*	185
TOURMASTER COACHES LTD, *PETERBOROUGH*	132
TOWER COACHES, *WIGTON*	88
TOWLERS COACHES, *WISBECH*	81
TOWN & COUNTRY COACHES, *NEWTON ABBOT*	94
TOWN & COUNTRY MOTOR SERVICES LTD, *HURWORTH MOOR, Nr DARLINGTON*	99
TOWN & COUNTRY TRAVEL, *CRAVEN ARMS*	157
TOWN & COUNTRY TRAVEL, *PURFLEET*	107
TOWNLYNX, *HOLYWELL*	206
TRACKS VEHICLE SERVICES, *ROMNEY MARSH*	124
TRACTION GROUP	72
TRAMONTANA, *MOTHERWELL*	197
TRANS-CONTINENTAL COACHES, *CLEVEDON*	159
TRANSIT EXPRESS TRAVEL, *LENTON*	153
TRANSLINC LTD, *LINCOLN*	132
TRANSLINK, *BELFAST*	216
TRATHENS TRAVEL SERVICES, *PLYMOUTH*	94
2 TRAVEL COACHES, *CWMBRAN*	212
2 TRAVEL GROUP, *SWANSEA*	212
TRAVEL DUNDEE	191
TRAVEL LONDON, *LONDON SE5*	138
TRAVEL MIDLAND METRO, *WEDNESBURY*	177
TRAVEL RITE EAST KENT, *EYTHORNE*	124
TRAVEL WEST MIDLANDS, *BIRMINGHAM*	177
TRAVEL WRIGHT, *NEWARK-ON-TRENT*	153
TRAVELGREEN COACHES, *DONCASTER*	163
TRAVELINE, *MINEHEAD*	160
TRAVELLERS CHOICE, THE, *CARNFORTH*	128
TRAVELLERS CHOICE, THE, *BARROW IN FURNESS*	88
TRAVEL PATH, *GRANTHAM*	132
TRAVELSURE, *SEAHOUSES*	151
TRAVEL-WRIGHT, *MOUNTSORREL*	130
TREACY COACHES, *BALLINA, Co MAYO*	221
TRELEY MOTORS, *PENZANCE*	85
TRENT BARTON, *HEANOR*	91
TRINGWOOD TRAVEL, *WALTON ON THAMES*	170
TRUEMAN TRAVEL	115
TRURONIAN LTD, *TRURO*	85
TRUSTLINE SERVICES LTD, *HUNSDON*	119
TUERS MOTORS LTD, *PENRITH*	88
TURNERS TOURS, *CHULMLEIGH*	94
TURNERS COACHWAYS (BRISTOL) LTD, *BRISTOL*	76
TW COACHES LTD, *SOUTH MOLTON*	95
T W H TRAVEL, *LONDON SE15*	138
TWIN VALLEY DEN-ROY COACHES, *SOWERBY BRIDGE*	182
TYNE VALLEY COACHES LTD, *HEXHAM*	151
TYNEDALE GROUP TRAVEL, *HALTWISTLE*	151
TYRER TOURS LTD, *NELSON*	128

U

ULSTERBUS, *BELFAST*	216
UNICORN COACHES LTD, *HATFIELD*	119
UNITY COACHES, *RETFORD*	153
UNIVERSITYBUS LTD, *HATFIELD*	119
GRAHAM URQUHART TRAVEL, *INVERNESS*	195

V

VALES COACHES (MANCHESTER) LTD	112
VENTURE TRANSPORT (HENDON) (1965) LTD, *HARROW*	142
VICEROY OF ESSEX LTD, *SAFFRON WALDEN*	107
VICTORY TOURS, *HANDLEY, Nr SALISBURY*	96
VIKING COACHES, *HEYWOOD*	112
VIKING MINICOACHES, *BROADSTAIRS*	124
VIKING TOURS & TRAVEL, *SWADLINCOTE*	91
VILLAGER MINIBUS, *SHARNBROOK*	73
VINCE COACHES, *BURGHCLERE, Nr NEWBURY*	74
VISCOUNT CENTRAL COACHES, *BURNELY*	128
VISION TRAVEL, *WATERLOOVILLE*	115
VISTA COACHWAYS, *YATTON*	160
VOEL COACHES LTD, *DYSERTH*	206

W

W & H MOTORS, *CRAWLEY*	179
W M TRAVEL, *WISBECH*	81
W T S MINICOACHES, *FARSLEY*	183
WAINFLEET MOTOR SERVICES LTD, *NUNEATON*	173
WAKEFIELD TUTORIAL SCHOOL, *MORLEY*	182
WALDEN TRAVEL LTD, *SAFFRON WALDEN*	107
WALLACE ARNOLD COACHES LTD, *TORQUAY*	95
WALLACE ARNOLD COACHES, *LEEDS*	182
WALLIS COACHWAYS, *BILSTHORPE, Nr NEWARK*	153
WALTONS COACHES, *GRANGETOWN, CARDIFF*	203
WARREN'S COACHES (KENT & SUSSEX) LTD *TICEHURST*	101
WARREN'S COACHES (TENTERDEN) LTD	124
WARRINGTON BOROUGH TRANSPORT LTD	83
WARRINGTON COACHES, *ILAM*	91
WARSTONE MOTORS LTD, *GREAT WYRLEY*	165
WATERHOUSE TOURS LTD, *POLEGATE*	101
WATERSIDE TOURS, *HYTHE*	114
R. & S. WATERSON, *HEMSWORTH*	183
PAUL WATSON TRAVEL, *DARLINGTON*	99
WATTS COACHES, *BONVILSTON, Nr CARDIFF*	204
WAVERLEY COACHES LTD, *ST HELIER, JERSEY*	214
WEALE'S WHEELS, *LLANDRINDOD WELLS*	211
WEARDALE MOTOR SERVICES LTD *STANHOPE*	99
WEAVAWAY TRAVEL, *NEWBURY*	74
WEBB'S *PETERBOROUGH*	81
WEBBER BUS, *BRIDGWATER*	160
WELLGLADE LTD	72
WELSH DRAGON TRAVEL, *NEWPORT, MONMOUTHSHIRE*	208
WELSH'S COACHES, *PONTEFRACT*	183
WEST COAST MOTORS, *CAMPBELTOWN*	190
WEST MIDLANDS SPECIAL NEEDS TRANSPORT *BIRMINGHAM*	177
WESTBUS UK LTD, *HOUNSLOW*	138
WESTERHAM COACHES, *OXTED*	170
WESTERN GREYHOUND, *NEWQUAY*	85
WESTRINGS COACHES, *WEST WITTERING*	179
WEST'S COACHES LTD, *WOODFORD GREEN*	107
WESTWAY COACH SERVICES, *LONDON SW20*	138
WHEADONS GROUP TRAVEL, *CARDIFF*	204
WHEAL BRITON COACHES, *TRURO*	85
WHIPPET COACHES LTD, *FENSTANTON*	81
WHITE BUS SERVICES, *WINDSOR*	74
WHITE HEATHER TOURS, *FORT WILLIAM*	195
WHITEGATE TRAVEL, *NORTHWICH*	83
WHITELAWS COACHES, *STONEHOUSE*	200
WHITTLE COACH, BUS & HOLIDAYS, *KIDDERMINSTER*	186
WHYTES COACH TOURS, *NEWMACHAR*	188
WICKSONS TRAVEL, *BROWNHILLS*	177
WIDE HORIZON LUXURY TRAVEL, *HINCKLEY*	130
WILBYS COACHES, *BROUGHTON*	145
ALBERT WILDE COACHES, *HEAGE*	91
WILFREDA BEEHIVE, *ADWICK-LE-STREET*	163
WILKINSONS TRAVEL, *ROTHERHAM*	163
F R WILLETTS & CO, *PILLOWELL Nr LYDNEY*	108
WILLIAMS COACHES (NORTH WALES), *DEINIOLEN*	207
T WILLIAMS & SONS, *WREXHAM*	213
WILLIAMS COACHES, *BRECON*	211
WILLIAMS MINIBUSES, *LLANDRINDOD WELLS*	211
F. T. WILLIAMS TRAVEL, *CAMBORNE*	85
GLYN WILLIAMS TRAVEL, *BLACKWOOD*	203
GWYN WILLIAMS & SONS LTD, *LOWER TUMBLE*	204
T. WILLIAMS & SONS, *PONCIAU*	213
WILLIAMSONS OF *ROTHERHAM*	163
WILLS MINI COACHES, *KINGSBRIDGE*	95
WILSON'S COACHES, *ROSSINGTON*	163
WILTAX, *ADDLESTONE*	170
WILTS & DORSET BUS COMPANY LTD, *POOLE*	97
WINDSOR-GRAY TRAVEL, *WEDNESFIELD*	177
WINDSORIAN COACHES LTD, *WINDSOR*	74
WINGATES TOURS, *MELLING*	140
WINGS LUXURY TRAVEL LTD, *HAYES*	139
WINN BROS, *NORTHALLERTON*	148
PAUL S. WINSON COACHES LTD, *LOUGHBOROUGH*	130
WINTS COACHES, *BUTTERTON, Nr LEEK*	166
WISE COACHES LTD, *HAILSHAM*	101
WISTONIAN COACHES, *SELBY*	148
MAL WITTS EXECUTIVE TRAVEL, *GLOUCESTER*	109
WOLD TRAVEL, *DRIFFIELD*	103
WOOD BROTHERS TRAVEL LTD, *BUCKFASTLEIGH*	95
WOODS COACHES LTD, *LEICESTER*	130
WOODS COACHES, *TILLICOULTRY*	190
P. WOODS MINICOACHES, *HALLGLEN*	193

Operator	Page
WOODS TRAVEL LTD, *BOGNOR REGIS*	179
WOODSTONES COACHES LTD, *KIDDERMINSTER*	186
WOODWARD'S COACHES LTD, *GLOSSOP*	91
WOOTTENS, *CHESHAM*	78
J.P.A. WORTH, *BUXTON*	166
WORTHEN TRAVEL, *LITTLE MINSTERLEY*	157
WORTHING COACHES	179
WORTHS MOTOR SERVICES LTD, *ENSTONE*	155
WORTLEY LINE COACHES, *LEEDS*	183
WRAYS OF HARROGATE	149
WRIGHT BROS (COACHES) LTD, *NENTHEAD*	88
LEN WRIGHT BAND SERVICES LTD, *WATFORD*	119
WRIGLEY'S COACHES, *IRLAM*	112

Y

Operator	Page
YARDLEY TRAVEL LTD, *BIRMINGHAM*	177
YARRANTON BROS LTD, *TENBURY WELLS*	186
YELLOW BUSES, *BOURNEMOUTH*	97
YELLOW ROSE COACHES, *CARNFORTH*	128
YELLOWLINE TOURS LTD, *UPPER BEEDING*	179
YEOMANS CANYON TRAVEL LTD, *HEREFORD*	116
YESTERYEAR MOTOR SERVICES, *DISEWORTH, DERBY*	91
YORKS COACHES, *COGENHOE*	150
YORKSHIRE COASTLINER LTD, *MALTON*	149
YORKSHIRE STAG MINIBUS CO THE, *BRADFORD*	183
YORKSHIRE TERRIER, *SHEFFIELD*	163
YORKSHIRE TRACTION CO, *BARNSLEY*	163
YOUNGS OF ROMSLEY, *HALESOWEN*	177
YULE, *PITLOCHRY*	198

Z

Operator	Page
Z & S COACHES, *AYLESBURY*	78
Z CARS OF BRISTOL, *BEDMINSTER*	76
ZAK'S BUS & COACH SERVICES, *GREAT BARR*	177